SCHOOL OF
ORIENTAL AND AFRICAN STUDIES

POLITICAL AND SOCIAL CHANGE IN MODERN EGYPT

POLITICAL AND SOCIAL CHANGE IN MODERN EGYPT

HISTORICAL STUDIES FROM THE OTTOMAN CONQUEST TO THE UNITED ARAB REPUBLIC

EDITED BY
P. M. HOLT
Professor of Arab History
School of Oriental and African Studies
University of London

LONDON
OXFORD UNIVERSITY PRESS
NEW YORK TORONTO
1968

Oxford University Press, Ely House, London W. 1
GLASGOW NEW YORK TORONTO MELBOURNE WELLINGTON
CAPE TOWN SALISBURY IBADAN NAIROBI LUSAKA ADDIS ABABA
BOMBAY CALCUTTA MADRAS KARACHI LAHORE DACCA
KUALA LUMPUR HONG KONG TOKYO

PRINTED IN GREAT BRITAIN

CONTENTS

CONTRIBUTORS

HASAN ADALI: Chief Archivist, Başbakanlık Arşivi, Istanbul.

ŞINASI ALTUNDAĞ: Professor of History, University of Ankara.

J. N. D. ANDERSON: Professor of Oriental Laws in the University of London; Director of the Institute of Advanced Legal Studies.

GABRIEL BAER: Associate Professor of the History of Islamic Countries, Institute of Asian and African Studies, The Hebrew University, Jerusalem.

ABDEL HAMID EL-BATRIK: Professor of Modern History, College for Women, Ain Shams University.

H. S. DEIGHTON: Fellow of Pembroke College, Oxford.

ARTHUR GOLDSCHMIDT, JR.: Assistant Professor of History, The Pennsylvania State University.

P. M. HOLT: Professor of Arab History in the University of London.

ELIE KEDOURIE: Professor of Politics in the University of London.

JACOB M. LANDAU: Senior Lecturer on the Political Systems of the Middle East, School of Economics and Social Sciences, The Hebrew University, Jerusalem.

AFAF LOUTFI EL SAYED: Assistant Professor of History, The American University in Cairo.

AHMED ABDEL-RAHIM MUSTAFA: Associate Professor of Modern History, Ain Shams University.

PATRICK O'BRIEN: Lecturer in Economics with reference to the Near and Middle East, School of Oriental and African Studies, University of London.

ANDRÉ RAYMOND: Directeur-Adjoint de l'Institut Français d'Études Arabes de Damas.

STANFORD J. SHAW: Associate Professor of Ottoman History and of Turkish, Harvard University.

GAMAL EL-DIN EL-SHAYYAL: Professor of Islamic History and Dean of the Faculty of Arts, Alexandria University.

NADA TOMICHE: Scientific Director of *Cahiers de l'Orient contemporain*, Institut d'Études Islamiques de l'Université de Paris.

P. J. VATIKIOTIS: Professor of Politics with reference to the Near and Middle East in the University of London.

MAHMUD ZAYID: Associate Professor of Arab History, The American University of Beirut.

LIST OF PLATES AND FIGURES

Plates 1 to 3 are kindly supplied by Mr. Hasan Adalı, Figure 1 by M. André Raymond, and Figure 2 by Mr. P. K. O'Brien.

ABBREVIATIONS

BIFAO	*Bulletin de l'Institut Français d'Archéologie Orientale du Caire.*
B.M.	British Museum, London.
BSOAS	*Bulletin of the School of Oriental and African Studies*, London.
EI^1, EI^2	*The Encyclopaedia of Islam*, 1st edn. (Leiden, 1913–38); 2nd edn. (Leiden, 1960–).
GAL, *S*	C. Brockelmann, *Geschichte der arabischen Literatur* and *Supplementband.*
Al-Jabartī, *ʿAjāʾib*	ʿAbd al-Raḥmān b. Ḥasan al-Jabartī, *ʿAjāʾib al-āthār fiʾl-tarājim waʾl-akhbār*. References are to the Būlāq edition of 1297/1879–80.
JAOS	*Journal of the American Oriental Society.*
JESHO	*Journal of Economic and Social History of the Orient.*
JRAS	*Journal of the Royal Asiatic Society.*
P.R.O.	Public Record Office, London.
WI	*Die Welt des Islams.*
WZKM	*Wiener Zeitschrift für die Kunde des Morgenlandes.*
ZDMG	*Zeitschrift der Deutschen Morgenländischen Gesellschaft.*

NOTE ON TRANSLITERATION

DISTINCT systems of transliteration have been employed for Arabic and Turkish terms respectively. The system for Arabic is given below: for Turkish the accepted system of orthography has been used. Some anomalies are inevitable. Personal names of Arabic origin (e.g. Selim, Mehmed) are given in the Turkish form when they refer to sultans, grand *vezirs*, or other officials who are important in a general Ottoman, rather than an Egyptian, context. The names of figures prominent in Egyptian history, whatever their ethnic origins, are given in their Arabic forms. Similarly, specifically Ottoman titles of office (e.g. *defterdar*) are given in the Turkish form, while others (e.g. *qāḍī*, *kāshif*) are given in the Arabic form. A few words which have become naturalized are used in their conventional English forms (e.g. pasha, fellah—but *fallāḥīn*), as are the names of large and well-known towns and other localities.

SYSTEM OF TRANSLITERATION FROM ARABIC

ء	ʾ	ط	ṭ
ب	b	ظ	ẓ
ت	t	ع	ʿ
ث	th	غ	gh
ج	j (occasionally g)	ف	f
ح	ḥ	ق	q
خ	kh	ك	k
د	d	ل	l
ذ	dh	م	m
ر	r	ن	n
ز	z	ه	h
س	s	و	w
ش	sh	ى	y
ص	ṣ		
ض	ḍ	ة	-a (in the construct state -at)

INTRODUCTION

THE essays printed in this volume represent, in revised form, papers contributed to a Conference on the Modern History of Egypt, held in April 1965 at the School of Oriental and African Studies in the University of London. The participants in the Conference included, besides the authors of these essays, Professor Jacques Berque (Paris) and Dr. Nadav Safran (Harvard), who wished to make their own arrangements for publication. The Conference was financed by a generous allocation made by the Director (Professor C. H. Philips) from the research and development funds of the School. As the initiator of the Conference, I wish to record my gratitude to him for making its holding possible, for his advice and encouragement, and for his address to the opening session. I am deeply obliged to Mr. Albert Hourani (St. Antony's College, Oxford), and to Professors Bernard Lewis and Edith T. Penrose (both of the School of Oriental and African Studies) for taking the chair at sessions of the Conference. My thanks are also due to members of the administrative and clerical staff of the School for the work they undertook in connexion with the Conference, and especially to the Assistant Secretary (Mr. M. Gatehouse), upon whom fell the principal burden of its organization. Finally, the cost of production of this volume has been met by the School, and I have much pleasure in making due acknowledgement of its subvention for this purpose.

The Conference was in a sense the successor of one held in 1958, upon which it was largely modelled. The 1958 Conference was concerned with an extensive survey of the historiography of the Middle East:[1] the 1965 Conference sought, in a more limited field, not only to examine the source-materials available to the historians, but also to produce a progress-report on types of research which are currently proceeding. Through the discussion and ultimate publication of papers, it was hoped to make a positive contribution to the understanding of the modern history of Egypt, and also (perhaps an equally valuable service at this stage) to indicate sources that have been insufficiently exploited, and aspects and problems which have been inadequately studied.

The papers published in this volume are divided into three groups. The first comprises seven studies in source-materials. The principal Arabic sources for the history of Egypt from the Ottoman conquest to the French occupation are reviewed by the present writer who draws attention to the need for a critical investigation of these materials, which are almost entirely unpublished

[1] See Bernard Lewis and P. M. Holt, *Historians of the Middle East* (London, 1962). Historical Writing on the Peoples of Asia, iv.

(pp. 3–12). Professor Baer's account of ʿAlī Mubārak's great topographical encyclopedia, *al-Khiṭaṭ al-jadīda*, investigates its sources and demonstrates its utility to the student of nineteenth-century Egypt (pp. 13–27). Arabic sources alone are, however, insufficient for the understanding of many aspects of modern Egyptian history: the Turkish materials are indispensable for a study in depth of administrative and political developments. The wide range of these sources, represented both by archives and chronicles, in Cairo as well as Istanbul, is surveyed by Professor Shaw (pp. 28–48). His paper is supplemented by two more specialized studies: one by Professor Altundağ on archival materials concerning the nineteenth century (pp. 49–51), the other by Mr. Adalı dealing with the light thrown by the Yıldız archives on Egyptian history in the time of Sultan Abdülhamid II (pp. 52–58). The increasing involvement of Britain in Egypt during the nineteenth century produced an abundance of source-materials in English: the writings of travellers and residents, the papers and letters of statesmen and officials, and the archives of the British government. These in all their variety are considered in Mr. Deighton's essay (pp. 59–67). The voluminous collection of papers left by Joseph Hekekyan, an Armenian engineer who served the nineteenth-century rulers of Egypt, is described against the background of their author's life by Dr. Mustafa (pp. 68–75).

The second group of papers consists of four studies on the period from 1517 to 1798. In the first, the present writer attempts to trace the main lines of political change between the Ottoman conquest and the coming of Bonaparte (pp. 79–90). Professor Shaw's paper describes administrative and fiscal developments during the same period (pp. 91–103). To a very large extent, Egypt was (and still is) dominated politically by Cairo, and M. Raymond's essay in topographical history establishes significant links between the urban structure of Cairo and the popular revolts of the eighteenth century (pp. 104–16). Finally, Professor Shayyal constructs a picture of intellectual and social conditions in the same century, using mainly materials drawn from the chronicle of al-Jabartī (pp. 117–32).

It is significant of the present state of research that the last group of papers, comprising studies in the history of the nineteenth and twentieth centuries, should be by far the largest and most diversified of the three. Five of the papers are surveys covering long periods of years. The first of these is a comprehensive examination by Professor Baer of social change between the beginning of the nineteenth century and the outbreak of the First World War (pp. 135–61). The economic background of change is investigated over a rather longer period by Mr. O'Brien, who furthermore indicates the unevenness of the data on which such an investigation must necessarily be based (pp. 162–95). Dr. Landau contributes a specialized study of a minority: the Jews of Egypt, whose changing position in Egyptian society since the nineteenth century he demonstrates (pp. 196–208). The influence of the West appears in Professor Anderson's paper as the dominant influence in legal reform from the mid-nineteenth to the mid-twentieth century (pp. 209–30). But 'the West' itself needs analysis: it is an artificial term, comprehending an infinite range of individual influences upon, and reactions to, Egypt. This variety, as exemplified from English writings, is the subject of Mr. Deighton's paper (pp. 231–48).

The remaining eight papers are specialized contributions covering shorter chronological periods. Again, it is significant of the present condition of our studies that they are mainly concerned with the years before 1848 and after 1882. Two of them deal with aspects of the social structure in the early nineteenth century: that by Dr. Tomiche on the social hierarchy in the time of Muḥammad 'Alī (pp. 249–63); and that by Dr. Loutfi El Sayed, which demonstrates the rise and decline of the '*ulamā*' as a political force (pp. 264–80). Aspects of Muḥammad 'Alī's policy are the subjects of the next two papers. Professor Batrik traces the extension and collapse of his power in the Yemen (pp. 281–90) while Dr. Mustafa investigates the dismantling of the elaborate system of monopolies, which had been the basis of his economic autonomy (pp. 291–307). We then pass on to three papers dealing with aspects of the political ferment under British domination. Mr. Goldschmidt and Dr. Zayid examine the origins and development of two important political organizations: the Nationalist Party founded by Muṣṭafā Kāmil (pp. 308–33), and the Liberal Constitutionalist Party, linked ultimately with Muṣṭafā Kāmil's opponents (pp. 334–46). One phase of the complex political struggle, both between the Egyptian politicians and the occupying power, and among the Egyptians themselves, forms the subject of Professor Kedourie's paper on the genesis of the constitution of 1923 (pp. 347–61). The volume ends with a study of the contemporary political situation by Professor Vatikiotis (pp. 362–87).

Since the papers were circulated to the participants in advance of the Conference, the actual sessions were devoted to discussion. It would clearly not be feasible to offer here a full transcription of extempore and wide-ranging comment and clarification, much of which was concerned with matters of detail. Nevertheless, it was clear that there were some matters of general and pre-eminent importance for all working on the history of modern Egypt.

The first was the actual scope of the subject under discussion. There has been, perhaps, a tacit and empirical decision by students of Egyptian history that the modern period begins about the opening of the nineteenth century, with the French expedition in 1798, or the acquisition of power by Muḥammad 'Alī in 1805. There are, indeed, cogent reasons for adopting this starting-point. At the level of political events, Bonaparte's expedition was the first large-scale and effective European attack on the Arab provinces of the Ottoman Empire, and was to initiate a century and a half of growing political domination. The accession of Muḥammad 'Alī in Cairo was the first step in the resumption of dominance by the sultan's viceroy after nearly two centuries during which power had been detained by the garrison-officers and the beys. More than that, it led to the establishment of an hereditary viceroyalty and a dynastic rule which was formally terminated only in 1953. In a broader context, with the nineteenth century began that process of administrative, social, and cultural westernization which has made the Egypt of today so different from the Egypt of ʿAlī Bey or ʿAbd al-Raḥmān al-Jabartī.

All this is undoubtedly true, but there is a danger of neglecting the underlying continuity of Egyptian history. The French occupation was a startling phenomenon, and one ominous of the future, but in itself it did not achieve any lasting changes. Muḥammad ʿAlī was, in a well-known phrase, 'the founder of modern Egypt'; he was also the last and most successful of the local despots who achieved autonomy during the long Ottoman decline. Even the process of westernization, which up to a generation ago seemed capable of description and explanation in simple terms of reception or rejection, human progress and historical inevitability, now reveals itself as most complex. The history of the last sixteen decades is not self-contained and self-explanatory. We cannot understand the eddies of the current of history, and the structure of the new society (or even ascribe meaning to the adjective) without a fuller understanding of the protean traditional society of Egypt, and the vicissitudes of its politics in the sixteenth, seventeenth, and eighteenth centuries.

Periodization is necessarily somewhat artificial, and, of course, the Ottoman conquest of 1517 did not mark a complete breach in historical continuity: indeed, as I have suggested elsewhere,[1] the conquest could with some exaggeration be regarded as an incident in Mamluk factional struggles. Nevertheless, Egypt from being the metropolitan territory of an empire, in which Arabic was the language of government and culture, was degraded to a peripheral province of a much more extensive polity, in which Turkish had the dominant role in administration, and an important one in culture. The events of 1517 were formative of important conditions within which later political and social factors were to work.

Just as there is a danger of being bemused into ascribing to the nineteenth and early twentieth centuries an historical unity and coherence which is the artificial result of a limited selection of source-materials and an arbitrary formulation of questions, so there is a danger, for the same reasons, of over-emphasizing the individuality of Egyptian history. The simplicity of the geography of Egypt, the natural restrictions placed by nature on contact with neighbouring countries, create a presumption that here we have an isolated people, whose history can be studied in isolation. While there is an element of truth in the insistence on the individuality of modern Egyptian history, it cannot, at least down to 1882, be understood apart from the general history of the Ottoman Empire. Thus, relaxation of Ottoman control in

[1] See below, 'The pattern of Egyptian political history from 1517 to 1798', at p. 80.

seventeenth- and eighteenth-century Egypt, and the passing of power to men of local origin or domicile, was not a unique development, but a phenomenon which may *mutatis mutandis* be exemplified elsewhere in both the Arab and the Turkish provinces. Even when, under Muḥammad ʿAlī and his successors, the Egyptian government acquired a very high degree of autonomy from the sultanate, historical processes such as administrative centralization, or the reception of Western legal concepts, ran closely parallel courses in Cairo and Istanbul, and some measure of cross-fertilization is probable. Institutional and personal links between the suzerain and the tributary government, which subsisted until 1914, would certainly repay investigation.

A second matter which arose in the discussion on these papers was the significance and validity of some of the categories and concepts employed. It is clear, for example, that certain terms require further analysis and definition. What, for example, is the precise meaning of 'the Mamluks' in the context of the military *élite* of Ottoman Egypt? Even the beylicate, which is commonly thought of as an exclusively Mamluk preserve, included (as late as the eighteenth century) freeborn Muslims and Jewish converts. When we pass to the regimental officers of the Seven Corps of the garrison, the situation is no less confused, since they included masters and members of Mamluk households, as well as others who were immigrants, and some whose status is obscure. Until an exhaustive investigation of the data provided by al-Jabartī *and his predecessors* has been carried out, we can make only tentative statements about the military *élite* of Ottoman Egypt, and we should speak of 'the Mamluks' in this period always with great caution. Apart from this example, there has been, perhaps, a tendency to create over-rigid categories, and to ascribe action to 'the beylicate' or 'the *ʿulamāʾ*' instead of analysing individual motives.

A similar problem arises in the use of terms and concepts borrowed from European history. 'Feudalism' is perhaps no longer a serious menace: it has been qualified almost out of existence, and retains a precise (if unhistorical) meaning only in the journalist's or the politician's vocabulary of pejoratives. But there are other terms, particularly perhaps connected with economic history, such as 'bourgeoisie', 'agrarian revolution', and 'industrialization', which are necessary but must be defined in their local context, if they are not to generate false notions of the nature of historical development in Egypt. A more insidiously dangerous term, at least to a British or American student, is 'party', since it is clear that in composition, organization, objectives, and political functions the Egyptian parties from the time of ʿUrābī down to that of al-Naḥḥās were very different from those of Britain or the United States during the same period.

A fourth matter which engaged the attention of the Conference was the nature of the historical process in modern Egypt. The comment was made, for example, that there has sometimes been too great a tendency to attribute developments to the qualities of rulers. Much writing on nineteenth-century Egyptian history has been couched in these personal terms; and indeed this seems to be an inevitable stage in the transition from traditional chronicling to a more sophisticated and interpretative historiography. The best safeguard would seem to be the acquisition of a wider field of comparison, both in knowledge of the more advanced historiography of other regions, and in awareness of developments parallel to those in Egypt throughout the Near East and even beyond.

Another concept which is still dominant in contemporary views of the historical process in Egypt is that of the central importance of foreign domination. In its extreme form, this presents modern Egyptian history as determined by a series of violent and catastrophic changes induced from outside—the Ottoman conquest, the French occupation, the rule of Muḥammad ʿAlī and his dynasty, the British occupation. While clearly containing some measure of truth, this view, reflecting as it does political sentiments, hampers historical investigation by assuming discontinuity and by over-emphasizing a single political factor. The Ottomans, the French, the ruling house, and the British were not acting at will upon an Egyptian community which reacted only to their stimuli; to some extent the alien masters were themselves patient of indigenous developments which they had not instigated and which they did not direct. Here again, a comparative approach is helpful. For example, the political organizations of the later nineteenth and early twentieth century are commonly (and to some extent rightly) characterized as 'nationalist' and seen as combating the alien dominations of the Turco-Circassian ruling *élite* and the British. But, when their leadership and tactics are examined in detail, they can no longer be regarded as unequivocally nationalist; they fall into the wider category of subversive, younger-generation movements, represented elsewhere in the Near East by their contemporaries, the Young Ottomans and the Young Turks.

A radical view, which aroused much controversy in the Conference, was that of the primacy of politics in Egypt, as in Near Eastern society generally. In this view the basic and permanent factor was that of military rule under successive régimes through many centuries. Between the ruling military *élite* and the mass of the community was a schism, which the westernization of the governmental machine had only deepened. Seen from this standpoint social developments were largely irrelevant to political history; they had no autonomy of origin, and could make little impression on the rulers.

This doctrine usefully draws our attention to two phenomena of modern Egyptian history which merit detailed and critical examination. The first is the persistence of autocratic régimes based on military power as the norm of government. Nevertheless, to speak of 'military rule' without further distinction as the sole, or at least the most important, historical factor, is not really sufficient. At every stage, the structure of the military organization, and the relations subsisting between it and the ruler, must be examined. There is not much in common among the military foundations of the autocracies of ʿAlī Bey, Muḥammad ʿAlī Pasha, and Lord Cromer. In consequence, ʿAlī Bey, depending as he did upon an association of Mamluk household factions, exerted and was subject to political pressures very different from those known to Muḥammad ʿAlī, with his new-model conscript army, or Cromer, supported by the British occupation forces. Each of these autocratic military régimes stood in a different relation to a changing Egyptian society.

The second phenomenon to which this doctrine draws our attention is the use of social change to justify or even to legitimize a régime. Down to the nineteenth century, it is probably true to say that independent or autonomous governments in Egypt (as elsewhere in the Muslim lands) based their *theoretical* claims to authority on religious or historical grounds. The rulers, that is to say, claimed to act by delegation from the caliph (as did the Sunnī dynasties to 1517), by divine right of descent from the Prophet (as did the Fatimids), by right of a quasi-messianic function in the restoration of Islam (as was asserted on behalf of Selim I), or by right of succession to the former Mamluk sultans (as was at least implied by Riḍwān Bey in the seventeenth, and ʿAlī Bey in the eighteenth, century).

With the impact of the West on Egypt, new forms of justification were adduced. Bonaparte's proclamation on his landing in Egypt appropriately combines the old and the new themes. Besides asserting that 'The French are the true Mussulmen', who 'have at all times been the true and sincere friends of the Ottoman Emperors, and the enemies of their enemies', his manifesto offers, not merely the ending of tyranny (a traditional Islamic promise), but a career open to talent: 'the Supreme Being, who is just and merciful towards all mankind, wills that in future none of the inhabitants of Egypt shall be prevented from attaining to the first employments and the highest honours.'[1] This foreshadows the watchwords of social reform and progress which (with their synonyms and currently popular variations) have been employed to justify régimes from the time of Muḥammad ʿAlī onwards. This use of the concept of social reform as a political device does not, of course, mean that it is no more than an empty slogan, nor does it exclude the possibility that social change, instituted by a ruling *élite* for its own purposes, may in course of time reciprocally and very profoundly affect the ruling *élite* itself. The frustated ʿUrābī revolution, and the successful Army Revolution of 1952 are instances of this development: their significance is not fully explained by classifying them simply as the emergence of new military régimes.

It will be clear from the foregoing remarks, and from a study of the essays in this volume, that we are still pioneers in the study of modern Egyptian

[1] *Copies of original letters from the army of General Bonaparte in Egypt* . . . (London, 1798), [i], p. 236. Cf. al-Jabartī, *ʿAjā'ib*, vol. iii, p. 5.

history. Important bodies of source-material remain incompletely known, considerable periods of time are as yet inadequately explored, concepts derived from obsolete or unhistorical thinking inhibit our approach to more than one aspect of our subject. Nevertheless, as compared with the situation even ten years ago, much has been accomplished, and these essays indicate the directions in which progress is being made. All of us who participated in the Conference hope that the outcome of our research and discussion will help to advance knowledge in this field.

P. M. HOLT

School of Oriental and African Studies
London

January 1966

PART ONE

STUDIES IN SOURCE-MATERIALS

Ottoman Egypt (1517–1798): An Account of Arabic Historical Sources

P. M. HOLT

HISTORICAL writing in Arabic on Ottoman Egypt during the period from the conquest to the French occupation is reasonably copious and varied in kind. It has not yet been adequately evaluated, and its full exploitation is still far in the future. Very little of the material has been published, nor has much work been done on the manuscript sources. The consequence of this is that writers on the period have depended excessively on the few published works, especially on the chronicle of al-Jabartī, and on the writings of French scholars, especially those who were associated with Bonaparte's expedition to Egypt. This in turn has led to a certain distortion of the history of the first two centuries of Ottoman rule, owing to the retrojection of conditions and institutions of the later eighteenth century.

The historical writing which will be surveyed in this paper was produced in Egypt by persons who were domiciled in, or native to, that country. A certain amount of information may also be obtained from alien Arabic sources.[1] The Egyptian material is mostly in the form of chronicles, the framework of which, however, is not necessarily strictly annalistic. There are two grave limitations on the scope of this material. First, there is an almost complete absence of contemporary writing for about seventy years from the termination of Ibn Iyās's chronicle in 928/1522, and this period is only thinly covered by later writers. This lack of contemporary chronicles, and the sparseness of the data provided by sources of the eleventh/seventeenth century, suggest that this 'dark age' was, in fact, a time in which there were few dramatic political occurrences. Nevertheless it was an important period of institutional transition, and our ignorance of developments in the middle and later tenth/sixteenth century seriously affects our understanding of events in the following period.

The second limitation of scope of the Egyptian material persists throughout the whole of the period here surveyed. The data provided refer almost

[1] Among the alien Arabic sources may be noted (i) the biographical dictionaries of al-Ghazzī, al-Muḥibbī, and al-Murādī; (ii) Quṭb al-Dīn Muḥammad b. Aḥmad al-Makkī, *al-Barq al-yamānī*, for information on the Mamluk and Ottoman exploits in the Yemen, and sidelights on Egypt in the early Ottoman period; (iii) Aḥmad b. Zaynī Daḥlān, *Khilāṣat al-kalām fī umarā' al-balad al-Ḥarām*, for relations between Ottoman Egypt and the *amīrs* of Mecca. The Syrian and Lebanese sources for the intervention in Syrian affairs of *Bulut kapan* 'Alī Bey and Muḥammad Bey Abu'l-Dhahab are fully indicated by Dr. Abdul-Karim Rafeq in *The Province of Damascus 1723–1783* (Beirut, 1966).

exclusively to Cairo, and particularly to the governing and military *élite* of the city. While it is no doubt true that the capital dominated the political life of Egypt, and the military grandees dominated the capital, there were, even in the political sphere, developments outside Cairo of which we obtain only infrequent and inadequate glimpses from the chroniclers. It is, for example, clear that for nearly three centuries after the Ottoman conquest, Upper Egypt played a political role of immense importance: over long stretches of time it was a virtually autonomous region, under tribal or beylical rulers; alternatively, it was a territory of refuge for members of factions defeated in the capital. This we can trace from the chroniclers, but only in episodic fashion. Another grave deficiency is the lack of data on the tribes. Here again it is clear that the nomads and semi-nomads of the desert fringe had an important and complex influence on Egyptian political history, but it is impossible to study their significance in detail, by regions and periods. Since our information even on political events is so limited and one-sided, it goes without saying that the chroniclers alone are inadequate sources for reconstructing the social and economic history of Ottoman Egypt.

The following survey gives a brief account of various sources in chronological order. It is not exhaustive, but includes all the works with which I am personally acquainted.[1]

A. WRITINGS OF THE EARLY OTTOMAN PERIOD IN EGYPT

1. Al-Ishbīlī, *al-Durr al-muṣān*

This short work, which was completed on 10 Ṣafar 923/4 March 1517 (i.e. while Selim I was still in Egypt) is an Arabic literary *fethname.*[2] Written in a mixture of *saj'* and verse, it is full of encomia of Selim, who is presented as the successor of the Patriarchal Caliphs, and as a quasi-messianic figure engaged in holy war against the Safavids and Mamluks. The historical events reviewed are the Chaldirān campaign and its sequel, the overthrow of 'Alā' al-Dawla, and in much greater detail the operations against the Circassian Mamluk sultanate. As a record of events, the work should be regarded with caution, but it throws an interesting light on the propaganda used to justify Selim's warfare against other Muslim sovereigns.

2. Ibn Iyās, *Badā'i' al-zuhūr*

The author's eyewitness account of the collapse of the Circassian Mamluk sultanate, and the establishment of Ottoman rule in Egypt, forms the last portion only of a long and detailed chronicle. It is the sole reliable first-hand account in Arabic of developments from the appearance of the Ottoman threat

[1] Shortened forms of the authors' names and the titles of the works are given in the text. For further particulars, see the Bibliographical Appendix.

[2] See the article 'Fatḥnāme' (G. L. Lewis) in *EI*², vol. ii, pp. 839–40.

to the events immediately following the death of the viceroy, Khā'ir Bey (Muḥarram 922/February 1516–Ḥijja 928/November 1522).

3. Ibn Zunbul, *Ta'rīkh ghazwat al-sulṭān Salīm khān ma' al-sulṭān al-Ghawrī*

Although this work appears to supplement that of Ibn Iyās in providing a history of the Ottoman conquest and early Ottoman period, it must be used with very great caution. Dating in its present form from the middle years of the tenth/sixteenth century,[1] it is a collection of heroic prose sagas rather than a sober narrative.[2] The campaign of Selim against al-Ghawrī forms only the first part of the work, and is contained in the first sixteen of the 155 folios of the Bodleian manuscript. The core of this romance of chivalry (for such it is), is constituted by an account of the valiant life and death of Ṭūmān Bāy, who is depicted as a kind of Circassian Roland, a doomed hero encountering overwhelming odds. This saga of Ṭūmān Bāy occupies nearly a hundred folios. It is characterized by literary devices and legendary features. Ṭūmān Bāy and his faithful followers stand in contrast to the traitors to their race, Khā'ir Bey, Jānbardī al-Ghazālī, the *kāshif* Jānim al-Sayfī, and to the treacherous Arab chief, Ḥasan b. Mar'ī. Sultan Selim is a somewhat colourless figure, the tool of Khā'ir Bey. Numerous speeches by the leading figures give an impression that the narrator is possessed of inside knowledge, not to say omniscience, but these should be regarded as purely literary devices, incidental to the unfolding of the plot.

Ibn Zunbul further gives in detail three episodes from the reign of Sultan Süleyman—the revolts respectively of Jānbardī al-Ghazālī, of the *Kāshifs* Jānim and Īnāl, and of Aḥmad Pasha al-Khā'in. These are perhaps of greater authenticity than the earlier parts of the work: the accounts of Jānbardī and Aḥmad al-Khā'in can be tested against independent sources, while part of the information concerning the revolt of the latter is reported in the first person from a named participant.

The central theme of Ibn Zunbul's romance is the decline and fall of the Circassians in Egypt. He does not seek to elucidate historical causation: it is sufficient that God willed the end of the Circassian sultanate and the Ottoman triumph. Nevertheless he harks back repeatedly, and resentfully, to the

[1] It is not easy to fix the original *terminus ad quem* of the work. The Bodleian manuscript has brief notices of the two viceroyalties of Sulaymān Pasha, which were interrupted by his expedition to India. Sulaymān Pasha was finally recalled from Egypt on 10 Muḥarram 945/8 June 1538 (Hammer). The manuscript then lists as viceroys a certain Muḥammad Pasha, a relative of the sultan, and 'Alī Pasha al-Ṭawāshī, a pious man, who died in office. It is impossible to bring this sequence into agreement with the established list of viceroys. The only viceroy who died in office about this time was Sulaymān Pasha's successor, Da'ūd Pasha (d. 956/1549, Hammer). His successor was Semiz 'Alī Pasha (recalled 961/1554, Hammer), but 'Alī Pasha the Eunuch (al-Ṭawāshī, al-Khādim) was viceroy in 966–7/1559–60 (Hammer).

[2] The rapid development of legends around a dramatic event has been documented for a more recent period of Egyptian history by Dr. Pierre Cachia in his paper, 'Narrative folk-ballads of modern Egypt', presented at the Second Congress of Arabic and Islamic Studies, Cambridge, August 1964.

Ottoman use of artillery and firearms. It was these unfair weapons which, under God, brought about the destruction of the Circassian chivalry.

B. WRITINGS OF THE ELEVENTH/SEVENTEENTH AND TWELFTH/EIGHTEENTH CENTURIES

4. Al-Isḥāqī, *Akhbār al-uwal*

This work has acquired an unmerited importance through publication: it is by no means in the same category as the other published chronicles, of Ibn Iyās and al-Jabartī. It is a jejune compendium of Islamic and Egyptian history in ten chapters. Of these, only the tenth, amounting to under an eighth of the whole work, deals with events in Ottoman Egypt, but an account of the actual conquest appears in the previous chapter under the notice of Sultan Selim I. The tenth chapter deals in succession with the viceroys from Khā'ir Bey to Ibrāhīm Pasha, who was recalled in Ramaḍān 1032/July 1623. The practice of using the periods of office of viceroys as units of chronology, in preference to writing annals in the strict sense, was widely followed by later historians of Ottoman Egypt.

5. *The Continuation of al-Isḥāqī*

A manuscript in the Bibliothèque Nationale (MS. arabe 1854), which lacks both a title and the name of the author, is a recension and continuation of the ninth and tenth chapters of al-Isḥāqī's *Akhbār al-uwal.* Within the period covered by the original, there is some additional material, notably accounts of the revolts of Jānim and Īnāl (fols. 52a–57a), and of Khā'in Aḥmad Pasha (fols. 58a–63a), which are taken from Ibn Zunbul. The material taken from *Akhbār al-uwal* has been reorganized, so that the notice of each Ottoman sultan (from Chapter 9 of *Akhbār*) is followed directly by the notices of the viceroys who governed Egypt in his reign (from Chapter 10). The chronicle is continued down to 1084/1673. Since al-Isḥāqī died in 1060/1650, his authorship of at least the final portion of the *Continuation* is excluded.

6. Marʿī b. Yūsuf, *Nuzhat al-nāẓirīn*

A minor chronicle of little worth, which goes down to the viceroyalty of Bayram Pasha (appointed 1035/1626).

7. Al-Ghamrī, *Dhakhīrat al-iʿlām*

Another minor chronicle, written in atrocious verse and therefore presumably intended for entertainment rather than for edification. It goes down to 1040/1630.

8. Ibn Abi'l-Surūr

There are two versions of Ibn Abi'l-Surūr's chronicle of Ottoman Egypt, forming part of two distinct works:

(*a*) *al-Rawḍa al-zahiyya.* The second part of this work (50 out of 76 folios in the Bodleian MS. Pocock. 80) gives an account of the rulers of Egypt from antediluvian times. Of this, the final portion (fols. 57–76) covers the Ottoman period to the viceroyalty of Khalīl Pasha, which began in Rabīʿ I 1041/October 1631.[1]

(*b*) *al-Kawākib al-sāʾira.* This is a general work on Egypt in twenty chapters. The British Museum manuscript consists of 132 folios. The third chapter deals with the rulers of Egypt from antediluvian times, the last portion (fols. 13b–69a) covering the Ottoman period down to Muḥammad Pasha (1062/1651–2). The text appears to be identical with that of *al-Rawḍa al-zahiyya* as far as 1041/1631.

In both versions Ibn Abi'l-Surūr's chronicle, which follows the usual pattern of division into viceroyalties, is a source of primary importance for the events of the first half of the seventeenth century. The longer version is particularly valuable for the information it gives about the career of Riḍwān Bey al-Faqārī.

9. Anon., *Qahr al-wujūh*

This pseudo-historical genealogical work purports to trace the descent of Riḍwān Bey al-Faqārī (d. 1066/1656) from the Circassian Mamluk sultan, Barsbāy, and, further, to demonstrate the origin of the Circassians from a clan of Quraysh. The work is chiefly valuable for the insight it affords into Mamluk aims in the mid eleventh/eighteenth century.[2]

10. Al-Ṣāliḥī, *Waqʿat al-ṣanājiq*

Two chapters of historical narrative are inserted in a framework of religious texts and pious reflections: in the Paris manuscript the historical portion occupies 42 out of 96 folios. The second chapter of the work (fols. 12a–45a) deals with the great revolt of the Faqārī beys in 1071/1660, which led to the almost complete annihilation of this faction. The third chapter (fols. 45a–53b) deals with the earlier revolt of Muḥammad Bey al-Faqārī in Upper Egypt (1069/1658). Both accounts are minutely detailed, forming a diary of the events they describe.

11. Anon., *Zubdat ikhtiṣār*

This is a chronicle of Ottoman Egypt, constructed on the usual pattern of viceroyalties. The unique manuscript, in the British Museum, consists of forty-one folios. The detailed account of events begins (fol. 6a) with the

[1] Thus the Bodleian MS. Pocock. 80. The Bodleian MS. Bruce 35 resumes the list of governors down to Ṣafar 1061/January 1651, but this appendix is a mere list of names and dates, probably added by another hand.

[2] See further, P. M. Holt, 'The exalted lineage of Riḍwān Bey: some observations on a seventeenth-century Mamluk genealogy', *BSOAS*, vol. xxii. 2 (1959), pp. 221–30.

middle decades of the eleventh/seventeenth century, and goes down to 1111/1699, with an additional entry for 1113/1701–2. The author has clearly used *Waqʿat al-ṣanājiq* for his account of the troubles of 1069/1658 and 1071/1660, since his narrative follows this closely, although his phraseology is more colloquial than that of al-Ṣāliḥī. The later part of the work is so full as to be almost a diary. It is a most valuable source for the last decades of the seventeenth century.

12. Anon., *Paris Fragment*

This work, of which neither the title nor the author's name has survived, consists of seventy-eight folios containing parts of two chapters. The first, of which the beginning is lacking, is a history of the Ottoman sultans, starting (in the present state of the manuscript) about the middle of the fifteenth century. At its close (fol. 25b) Ahmed III is spoken of as the reigning sultan, and the last event to be mentioned is the war with Russia in Qaʿda 1123/July 1711. The second chapter (denoted Chapter 4 in the manuscript) deals with the viceroys of Egypt in the Ottoman period, the extant portion ending with the events of Qaʿda 1120/February 1709: thus about three *hijrī* years are lacking. The later part of this chapter is very full. It both supplements and continues *Zubdat ikhtiṣār*, but the details of the narrative and the phraseology show it to be an independent source.

13. Aḥmad Çelebi, *Awdaḥ al-ishārāt*

This work, extant in a unique manuscript in Yale, deals with the viceroys of Egypt from Khā'ir Bey to the departure of Bakīr Pasha in Jumādā II 1150/September 1737. For the period covered also by the *Paris Fragment*, there is a fairly close resemblance in subject-matter (but not in phraseology) between the two chronicles.[1]

14. The Damurdāshī Group of Chronicles[2]

This group of chronicles may be distinguished from those surveyed above by the following characteristics:

(i) The language in which they are written is very colloquial, while the earlier chronicles at least attempt to present a literary style.

(ii) The framework of viceroyalties is no longer carefully preserved: these chronicles are constructed episodically around the exploits of the military grandees of the Faqāriyya and Qāsimiyya.

(iii) After an introduction describing the Faqārī and Qāsimī factions, all these chronicles begin with the opening of the twelfth *hijrī* century.

[1] For a comparison of some passages in the two chronicles, see P. M. Holt, 'The career of Küçük Muḥammad (1676–94)', *BSOAS*, vol. xxvi. 2 (1963), pp. 270–1.

[2] See further, P. M. Holt, 'Al-Jabartī's introduction to the history of Ottoman Egypt', *BSOAS* vol. xxv. 1 (1962), pp. 41–45.

Although the chronicles of this group exhibit a marked family resemblance, they also show considerable variations of phraseology, suggesting that they are different narrators' versions of a common theme, rather than recensions of a written original. Like the work of Ibn Zunbul, these chronicles contain many reported speeches, conveying an impression of inside knowledge, but again this is, probably, a literary device. There is probably a saga element in these chronicles, and the data they appear to provide should be used with caution.

Three versions are distinguishable in the manuscripts known to me:

(*a*) Al-Qīnalī, *Majmūʿ laṭīf*. This is a large fragment, which in its present form goes down to 1152/1739.

(*b*) Anon., *Kitāb* (*Majmūʿ*) *al-durra al-munṣāna*. In its complete form (in the Bodleian manuscript), this version goes down to 1168/1754–5. There is a large fragment in the Cambridge manuscript.

(*c*) Al-Damurdāshī, *al-Durra al-muṣāna*. This version goes down to 1169/1756, and shows marked differences from the anonymous version.

15. Anon., *History of the Year 1191*

This is a work of the same type as the Damurdāshī Group. Written in colloquial Arabic, it deals with the exploits of the grandees.

C. WRITINGS OF THE EARLY THIRTEENTH/NINETEENTH CENTURY

16. Al-Sharqāwī, *Tuḥfat al-nāẓirīn*[1]

This work was composed at the request of the retinue of the grand vezir, Yūsuf Pasha, whom the author met at Bilbays in Ramaḍān 1214/January–February 1800. It is a very thin compendium of Egyptian history, and is practically worthless.

17. Al-Khashshāb[2]

Two short historical works may be attributed to this writer:

(*a*) *Tadhkira*. This is a brief chronicle of Ottoman Egypt in the eighteenth century, down to the beginning of the French occupation, contained in twenty-six folios.

(*b*) *Khulāṣat mā yurād*. Although the author is not named, a note in French (fol. 1a) states that the manuscript is an autograph of the archivist of the Divan of Cairo in 1216 (i.e. 1801–2). Al-Khashshāb held under Menou a post which might be so described. The work, in thirty folios, is a biography of

[1] See Gamal El-Din El-Shayyal, *A history of Egyptian historiography in the nineteenth century* (Alexandria, 1962), pp. 12–14.

[2] See El-Shayyal, op. cit., pp. 14–15; David Ayalon, 'The historian al-Jabartī and his background', *BSOAS*, vol. xxiii. 2 (1960), pp. 241–3.

Murād Bey, and appears to be the only work of this type in the period here surveyed.

18. Al-Jabartī, *'Ajā'ib al-āthār*

Of al-Jabartī's monumental work, the first two volumes, dealing with events from 1100/1688–9 to the eve of the French invasion in 1213/1798, fall within the period surveyed in this paper. The principal problems relating to the composition of the work have been discussed in detail by Professor Ayalon, and the remarks which follow should be read in connexion with his studies.[1]

The first volume, which ends with 1189/1775–6, presents particular difficulties. It should be regarded as an historical introduction to the main body of the work. Al-Jabartī himself draws attention to the year 1190 as that from which he kept a regular record of events. His own account of his sources for the first volume is neither full nor explicit. He speaks of the neglect and dispersal of Egyptian historical manuscripts, culminating in the action of the French, who 'took what they found to their country'[2] thereby giving us a *terminus a quo* for the composition of this volume. He refers, rather contemptuously, to writings by common soldiers, and, with rather more respect, to the chronicle of Aḥmad Çelebi, which, he says, like the other works, ended in 1150. Owing to the absence of chronicles after that date, he had recourse to informants, official registers, and funerary inscriptions. From 1170 to 1190, he was himself a witness of events—he was born in 1167/1753.

Al-Jabartī's use of four identifiable sources can be established for this first volume.[3] These are:

(i) The chronicle of al-Isḥāqī, and probably its continuation;
(ii) The chronicle represented by the *Paris Fragment*;
(iii) A chronicle or chronicles of the Damurdāshī Group;
(iv) On his own admission, Aḥmad Çelebi.

He also includes some folk-tales of a legendary nature. From this it follows that the first volume is of uneven value. Down to the middle of the eighteenth century, he combines (although he does not fully synthesize) sources of varying quality. Only from 1170/1756–7 onwards, after the end of the Damurdāshī Group, does his chronicle acquire independent evidential value: before that date, recourse should be had to the older sources.

[1] Ayalon, 'The historian al-Jabartī and his background', *BSOAS*, vol. xxiii. 2 (1960), pp. 217–49; Al-Djabartī, *EI*², pp. 355–7.

[2] Jabartī, *'Ajā'ib*, vol. i, p. 6.

[3] See further, P. M. Holt, 'Al-Jabartī's introduction to the history of Ottoman Egypt', *BSOAS*, vol. xxv. 1 (1962), pp. 38–51, and also 'The career of Küçük Muḥammad (1676–94)', *BSOAS*, vol. xxvi. 2 (1963), pp. 269–72.

BIBLIOGRAPHICAL APPENDIX

1. ʿAlī b. Muḥammad al-Lakhmī al-Ishbīlī al-Maghribī al-Dimashqī, *al-Durr al-muṣān fī sīrat al-muẓaffar Salīm khān*, ed. Hans Ernst (Cairo, 1962). *GAL, S*, vol. iii, p. 1303.

2. Muḥammad b. Aḥmad b. Iyās, *Badāʾiʿ al-zuhūr fī waqāʾiʿ al-duhūr*, ed. Muḥammad Muṣṭafā, vol. v (2nd edn., Cairo, 1380/1961). *GAL*, vol. ii, p. 295; *S*, vol. ii, p. 405.

Partial translation by W. H. Salmon, *An account of the Ottoman conquest of Egypt in the year* A.H. *922* (A.D. *1516*) (London, 1921). Full translation by Gaston Wiet, *Journal d'un bourgeois du Caire*, Tome ii (Paris, 1960). The latter translation is made from a better text, and is preferable in itself.

3. Aḥmad b. Zunbul al-Rammāl al-Maḥāllī, *Taʾrīkh ghazwat al-sulṭān Salīm khān maʿ al-sulṭān al-Ghawrī*. Bodleian Library, Oxford; MS. Bruce 21. *GAL*, vol. ii, pp. 43, 298; *S*, vol. ii, p. 409.

4. Muḥammad b. ʿAbd al-Muʿṭī al-Isḥāqī al-Manūfī, *Kitāb akhbār al-uwal fī man taṣarrafa fī Miṣr min arbāb al-duwal* (Cairo, 1311). *GAL*, vol. ii, p. 296; *S*, vol. ii, p. 407.

5. [*The continuation of al-Isḥāqī.*] Author's name and title lacking. Bibliothèque Nationale, Paris; MS. arabe 1854. At fol. 110b (within the portion derived from al-Isḥāqī), the author's name is given as Muḥammad b. Isḥāq: this, of course, gives no clue as to the continuator.

This was perhaps the first Arabic chronicle of Ottoman Egypt to be translated into a European language: it was almost certainly the source of the 'Abrégé chronologique de l'histoire de la Maison Ottomane et du gouvernement de l'Égypte', in M. Digeon, *Nouveaux contes turcs et arabes* (Paris, 1781).

6. Marʿī b. Yūsuf al-Ḥanbalī al-Maqdisī, *Nuzhat al-nāẓirīn fī taʾrīkh man waliya Miṣr min al-khulafāʾ waʾl-salāṭīn*. Bodleian, MS. D'Orville 544. The portion dealing with the viceroys of Ottoman Egypt also appears as the continuation of Ibn Zunbul in the British Museum, London; MS. Or. 3031. *GAL*, vol. ii, p. 369; *S*, vol. ii, p. 496.

7. Ahmad b. Saʿd al-Dīn al-Ghamrī, *Dhakhīrat al-iʿlām: Taʾrīkh umarāʾ Miṣr fiʾl-Islām*. British Museum, MS. Or. 6377. *GAL*, vol. ii, p. 297; *S*, vol. ii, p. 408.

8. Shams al-Dīn Muḥammad b. Abiʾl-Surūr al-Bakrī al-Ṣiddīqī:

(*a*) *al-Rawḍa al-zahiyya fī / wulāt Miṣr waʾl-Qāhira*. Bodleian, MS. Pocock. 80. / *akhbār Miṣr waʾl-Qāhira al-muʿizziyya*. Bodleian, MS. Bruce 35.

(*b*) *al-Kawākib al-sāʾira fī akhbār Miṣr waʾl-Qāhira*. British Museum, MS. Add. 9973. *GAL*, vol. ii, p. 297; *S*, vol. ii, p. 408.

Al-Kawākib was described in detail by Silvestre de Sacy in *Notices et extraits des manuscrits de la Bibliothèque du Roi*, vol. i (1788), pp. 165–280. The portion of the third chapter dealing with the Ottoman period is translated in full.

9. Anon., *Qahr al-wujūh al-ʿābisa bi-dhikr nasab / umarāʾ al-Jarākisa waʾttiṣālihi bi-Quraysh*. Rylands Library, Manchester; MS. Arabic 791, fols. 236–66. / *al-Jarākisa min Quraysh*. British Museum, MS. Or. 3030 *GAL, S*, vol. ii, p. 406. A printed version, which I have not seen, is mentioned.

10. Ibrāhīm b. Abī Bakr al-Ṣāliḥī al-Ḥanbalī, *Tarājim al-ṣawāʾiq fī waqʿat al-ṣanājiq*. Bibliothèque Nationale, MS. arabe 1853. *GAL*, vol. ii, p. 299; *S*, vol. ii, p. 410.

11. Anon., *Zubdat ikhtiṣār ta'rikh mulūk Miṣr al-maḥrūsa.* British Museum, MS. Add. 9972.

12. [*Paris Fragment.*] Author's name and title lacking. Bibliothèque Nationale, MS. arabe 1855.

13. Aḥmad Çelebi b. ʿAbd al-Ghanī al-Ḥanafī al-Miṣrī, *Awdaḥ al-ishārāt fī man tawallā Miṣr al-Qāhira min al-wuzarā' wa'l-bāshāt.* Yale University Library; Landberg MS. no. 3.

14. (*a*) Muṣṭafā b. Ibrāhīm al-Maddāḥ al-Qīnalī, *Majmūʿ laṭif.* Nationalbibliothek, Vienna; MS. Hist. Osm. 38. *GAL*, vol. ii, p. 299; *S*, vol. ii, p. 410.
(*b*) Anon., *Kitāb* (*Majmūʿ*) *al-durra al-munṣāna fī waqāīʿ* (*sic*) *al-kināna.* Bodleian, MS. Bruce 43; University Library Cambridge; MS. Add. 2787. *GAL, S*, vol. ii, p. 411 (the Cambridge manuscript only).
(*c*) Aḥmad al-Damurdāshī, *kâhya* of ʿAzeban, *al-Durra al-muṣāna fī akhbār al-kināna*, British Museum, MS. Or. 1073–4. *GAL*, vol. ii, p. 300.

15. [*History of the year 1191.*] Anon., no title. Bibliothèque Nationale, MS. arabe 1856. The first line after the *basmala* is a species of title, and reads: *Fī ta'rīkh ʿām 1191 mā waqaʿa fi'l-kināna min dawlat Muḥammad Bayk. GAL, S*, vol. ii, p. 411.

16. ʿAbdallāh b. Ḥijāzī al-Sharqāwī, *Tuḥfat al-nāẓirīn fī man waliya Miṣr min al-wulāt wa'l-salātīn.* Printed in the margin of 4. Al-Isḥāqī, *Akhbār al-uwal* (Cairo, 1311). *GAL*, vol. ii, p. 479; *S*, vol. ii, p. 729.

17. Ismāʿīl b. Saʿd al-Khashshāb:
(*a*) *Tadhkira li-ahl al-baṣā'ir wa'l-abṣār maʿ wajh al-ikhtiṣār.* Bibliothèque Nationale, MS. arabe 1958. This brief chronicle of Ottoman Egypt in the twelfth *hijrī* century forms the basis of Delaporte, 'Abrégé chronologique de l'histoire des Mamlouks d'Égypte', *Description de l'Égypte, État moderne*, vol. II. i, pp. 165 ff. *GAL, S*, vol. ii, p. 720.
(*b*) *Khulāṣat mā yurād min akhbār al-amīr Murād*, Bibliothèque Nationale, MS. arabe 1859. The completion of the manuscript is dated in the colophon 18 Muḥarram 1216/31 May 1801.

18. ʿAbd al-Raḥmān b. Ḥasan al-Jabartī, *ʿAjā'ib al-āthār fi'l-tarājim wa'l-akhbār* (Būlāq, 1297). *GAL*, vol. ii, p. 480; *S*, vol. ii, p. 730.

ʿAlī Mubārak's *Khiṭaṭ* as a Source for the History of Modern Egypt

GABRIEL BAER

ʿALĪ PASHA MUBĀRAK'S *al-Khiṭaṭ al-tawfīqiyya al-jadīda* (Būlāq, 1304–5/1886–9) has been the subject of a number of reviews by orientalists and of special chapters in some books on Mubārak by Arab authors.[1] Most of these have stressed the parts of this work that deal with ancient and medieval Egypt. The reviewers certainly were right in saying that Mubārak's account of the history and topography of ancient and medieval Egypt was no more than a compilation based on medieval Arab authors and European orientalists of the nineteenth century.[2] Thus the Egyptologist and the historian of medieval Islam will not find much interesting material in this work. In the nineteenth century, when it was published, it was perhaps of use to educated Egyptians who preferred to become acquainted with Egypt's heritage through the Arabic work of a Muslim, but today it no longer fulfils even this purpose. However, according to Mubārak's words in his preface, he wrote this work also for another important purpose: like the medieval Arab authors, especially al-Maqrīzī, who wrote the history and described the geography of Egypt in their time, he wanted to give an account of contemporary Egypt as a record for later generations. The result was not only an enormous opus of more than one and a half million words, but also a unique and outstanding product of modern Arabic literature. Before trying to answer the question whether this work is of use to the historians of modern Egypt, we shall first survey the sources on which the parts dealing with modern Egypt are based, and the way in which Mubārak presents his material.

I. MUBĀRAK'S SOURCES

1. *Official documents*

Prior to the publication of Mubārak's *Khiṭaṭ*, Régny, Amici, and Dor had already published their statistical yearbooks, and in 1884 the government had

[1] K. Vollers in *ZDMG*, vol. xlvii (1893), pp. 720 ff.; idem in *EI*[1] and *EI*[2]; C. Brockelmann, *GAL*, vol. ii, p. 634, *S*, vol. ii, p. 733; I. Goldziher in *WZKM*, vol. iv, 1890, pp. 347 ff. The first Arabic book on Mubārak was Muḥammad Pasha Durrī, *Taʾrīkh ḥayāt al-maghfūr lahu ʿAlī Mubārak Bāshā* (Cairo, 1311/1894), based on Mubārak's autobiography in his *Khiṭaṭ*. The best modern Arabic work is Maḥmūd al-Sharqāwī and ʿAbdallāh al-Mishadd, *ʿAlī Mubārak, ḥayātuhu wa-daʿwatuhu wa-āthāruhu* (Cairo, 1962), including on pp. 102 ff. a complete list of Mubārak's works. See also Muḥammad Aḥmad Khalafallāh, *ʿAlī Mubārak wa-āthāruhu* (Cairo, 1957), and Saʿīd Zāyid, *ʿAlī Mubārak wa-aʿmāluhu* (Cairo, 1957). Many

[*footnotes 1 and 2 continued overleaf*

issued the results of the 1882 census.[1] Moreover, there can be no doubt that Mubārak had access to additional unpublished statistical material—in the course of his career he had been responsible for the ministries or departments of *waqf*, education, public works, and railways. It cannot be said that he has systematically used this material. Here and there he mentions the *dafātir al-taʿdād* (census registers) as a source for the administrative divisions of Egypt (xiv. 140; xvii. 61) or the spelling of place-names (xv. 17; xvii. 59); he quotes *kitāb al-iḥṣāʾāt al-miṣriyya li-sanat 1872* (probably Régny's yearbook) for the number of foreigners in Egypt and their geographical distribution (vii. 65), and he uses Régny's statistics, without mentioning the source, for his figures on the movement of ships and goods and the members of guilds in Alexandria (vii. 74–75, 79–84).[2] Similarly, he gives population figures for Cairo according to the 'censuses' of 1872 and 1882 (i. 98).[3] However, Mubārak does not say from what source he derived his figures on the population of other towns and villages. Population figures are given mainly for Sharqiyya province, very few for places in Minūfiyya, Gharbiyya, and Buḥayra, and none at all for Upper Egypt. There can be no doubt that for this purpose he did not use the 1882 census, in which detailed figures on every town and village in Egypt are tabulated. To judge by the ratio of Mubārak's figures to those of the census, the former probably relate to the middle 1870s.[4] Indeed, this seems to be the time at which most of Mubārak's *Khiṭaṭ* was written.[5]

A second type of official documents used by Mubārak are title-deeds and the cadastral survey. Although he does not explicitly say so, his detailed figures on the *zimām* (registered area) of many villages obviously derive from the cadaster. Only on one occasion he mentions as a source the *taʾrīkh al-masāḥa li-sanat 1228*, i.e. Muḥammad ʿAlī's cadastral survey (xiv. 116). Apparently he is on much firmer ground when he speaks about urban real estate. Urban title-deeds (*ḥujaj amlāk*) are used for locating buildings and

other Arabic histories and collections of biographies include sections on Mubārak; most of them are also based on his autobiography. Since all these reviews and books include a general description of the *Khiṭaṭ*, we have refrained from repeating these details here.

[2] Even the classics are often quoted from modern French works—see vol. xvii, p. 28.

---

[1] E. de Régny, *Statistique de l'Egypte* (Alexandria, 1870–3); F. Amici, *Essai de statistique générale de l'Egypte* (Cairo, 1879); E. Dor, *Statistique des écoles civiles* (Cairo, 1875); Ministère de l'Intérieur, *Recensement général de l'Egypte 1882* (Cairo, 1884).

[2] Régny (1870), pp. 69–72. There are, however, some differences between Mubārak's and Régny's lists.

[3] To the best of the present writer's knowledge, no census whatever was taken in 1872. Mubārak's figures apparently are based on Régny (1873), p. 20 whose data were calculated according to official records of population movement.

[4] We have arrived at this conclusion by calculating the ratio of Régny's figures for the early 1870s and Amici's for the late 1870s to those of the census (both Régny and Amici give only totals for provinces).

[5] See, for instance, xviii. 34: *al-ān yaʿnī sanat iḥdā wa-tisʿīn wa-miʾatayn wa-alf*, i.e. 1874; x. 21, and xii. 105: *al-ān aʿnī sanat 1293* (1876). However, in the parts on Cairo and on the Nilometer later data have been used: for instance, the 1882 census (see above); see also iii. 124, where events that occurred in 1880 are related, and xviii. 109–10 (data for the years 1887–8).

institutions which no longer existed in Mubārak's time (e.g. ii. 82), and on the basis of the *dafātir al-dā'ira al-baladiyya* (municipal records) he prepared a list of buildings in Cairo according to their different types, their use, and the number of their owners (i. 94). However, Mubārak's most important source of this kind are *waqfiyyāt*, *waqf* documents to which he had access as Minister of Waqfs. In no other modern Arabic work known to the present writer have *waqf* documents been used as extensively as in the *Khiṭaṭ*. They serve Mubārak in various ways: to locate buildings, streets, and institutions (ii. 36; iii. 65; etc.), to discover facts about prices and currencies in the eighteenth century (xx. 150 f.), and even as a source for the history of the Bakrī family (iii. 121). Moreover, Mubārak publishes in full (or almost in full) seven *waqfiyyāt* from the nineteenth century and thirteen from the eighteenth century, in addition to thirty-two older ones. This is doubtless first-rate material for the economic, social, and cultural history of Egypt.

Mubārak also had recourse to the archives of the Wafā'ī order of *sharīfs* (*dafātir al-sādāt al-wafā'iyya*). But unfortunately these documents are used only in the part dealing with currencies and prices (xx. 151 ff.) and not as a source for the history of the order and the family: in the chapter on the Sādāt (v. 138 f.) they are not mentioned and the narrative is based on other sources.

2. *Personal observation*

Both Goldziher and Brockelmann[1] affirm that most of Mubārak's demographic, topographic, economic, and anthropological data are based on personal observations made in the course of his many official tours through the country. Others claim that Mubārak obtained most of his facts from engineers and officials of the Ministry of Public Works.[2] It seems to us that, although he benefited from the knowledge of many assistants, his personal experience certainly served as a most important source for writing the *Khiṭaṭ*.

The principal part of his work based on personal experience is his extensive autobiography (about 17,000 words, ix. 37–61). It includes most interesting personal observations on the condition of the rural population in Muḥammad 'Alī's day, education in Egypt throughout the century, the educational missions to Europe, literary activity in Egypt, engineering works and communications, *waqf*, the army, the higher bureaucracy of Egypt, the '*ulamā*', etc.

In many cases Mubārak explicitly states that a specific fact came to his knowledge through personal observation. These include the description of mosques and mausoleums (ii. 25, 62, 199), the location of schools (ii. 7, 46), the development of railway stations (vii. 90), questions connected with a slaughterhouse (i. 104), etc. In many other cases he does not definitely say so,

1 *GAL*, 1st edn., vol. ii, p. 482.

2 Cf. Vollers in *EI*²; 'Abd al-Raḥmān al-Rāfi'ī, *'Aṣr Ismā'īl* (2nd edn., Cairo, 1948), vol. i, p. 240; Khalafallāh, p. 154.

but since they also concern *waqf*, public works, railways, education, and the army, he must have come across these matters in the course of his official career. Almost all the personal observations made on matters that were not connected with his career concern buildings he saw or people he met in Cairo or Alexandria, but not in provincial towns or villages.

3. *Oral evidence*

Mubārak frequently relates what he was told by his contemporaries. Many of them supplied him with their biographies: officials (viii. 18, 22; x. 98), the manager of a *waqf* (x. 40), *'ulamā'* (viii. 73, 74; ix. 2, 86, 87; xi. 9; xii. 118; xiv. 141; xv. 11), army officers (vii. 85; xi. 86), engineers (ix. 7; xii. 143), interpreters and writers (xi. 68; xvii. 62), physicians (xi. 88; xiv. 125), and even a sailor (xiv. 100). Many biographies of *'ulamā'* were supplied by their sons, most of them students or teachers at the Azhar (iv. 41; viii. 27, 29; ix. 33; xi. 14; xii. 19; xiv. 96, 140; xv. 40). In some cases Mubārak made special inquiries to obtain a biography (iv. 38).[1]

Obviously Mubārak tried to continue the famous tradition of Arabic biographical literature, and particularly to collect biographies of the *'ulamā'* of his time, completing thereby the collections of his predecessors (al-Sakhāwī, al-Sha'rānī, al-Jabartī, and others) whom he frequently quotes. But it is also evident that *'ulamā'* were in a better position than anybody else to supply him with information on the subjects in which he was interested. According to his own evidence, *'ulamā'* were the source for his account of a *mawlid* (xiii. 50), of the history of the Bakrī family (iii. 121), etc. Similarly, in reply to his inquiry Coptic priests supplied him with information about their community, churches, convents, etc. (vi. 72).

However, Mubārak's oral sources include not only *'ulamā'*. He received information about the exploration of the Suez area from Gastinel Bey[2] (xii. 76), and about the Eastern desert from somebody who had toured the area in order to find marble (x. 21–24). A detailed description of the *ḥajj* was supplied by a person who for fourteen years had served as *kātib al-ṣurra*[3] (ix. 22). In some cases Mubārak just quotes 'a reliable source' (ii. 112; xi. 84; xii. 63).[4]

In addition, Mubārak used to ask the inhabitants of a town-quarter or a village about many things that interested him (vi. 25). He asked a native of a village who had become an Azharī (viii. 30), an official of the Public Works Department born in a neighbouring village (xiii. 41), or the head of the most important family of the village and the owner of its land (xii. 96–97). Such

[1] Sharqāwī and Mishadd, p. 110, belittle the importance of these biographies. The reason seems to be the above-mentioned controversy about Mubārak's original contribution (see references in preceding note).

[2] A teacher of chemistry in Egyptian military schools.

[3] The clerk responsible for the money paid by Egypt to the Ḥijāz on the occasion of the *ḥajj*.

[4] *Balaghanī mimman athiq, akhbaranī man athiqu bihi, akhbara bihi thiqātuhum*, etc.

witnesses and others supplied him with information about wells and pools (ix. 19), the local saint and his tomb (xiv. 99), local customs (xv. 73), etc. At one place his local witness gave him an interesting and detailed account of a *mawlid* (xii. 96–97). In another case Mubārak states that his witness supplied him with the general description of the village related in the *Khiṭaṭ*. Scores of similar descriptions are scattered throughout this work without their sources being mentioned; probably a great part of them is based on information supplied by the natives of the villages.

4. *Written Arabic sources*

The eighteenth and nineteenth centuries are not very rich in Arabic historical and geographical literature on Egypt. Nevertheless, Mubārak could have used more Arabic works on these subjects than he did. He does not mention Niqūlā Turk's history of the French occupation (published in Paris in 1839), Iskandar Abkārius's history of Ibrāhīm Pasha (published in Cairo six years before the publication of the *Khiṭaṭ*), Muḥammad Amīn Fikrī's geography,[1] al-Sharqāwī's history,[2] or Salīm al-Naqqāsh's book.[3]

Admittedly, all these books are much inferior to the outstanding work of that period, al-Jabartī's history, which is frequently mentioned and quoted by Mubārak. If a village or a town had been mentioned by al-Jabartī, Mubārak in his section on that village or town generally quotes from al-Jabartī the whole passage on the event connected with the place. Thus a large number of passages from al-Jabartī are scattered all over the *Khiṭaṭ*, among them scores of biographies, especially of *'ulamā'*.

Another book by an Arabic author of the nineteenth century is al-Tūnisī's travels[4] quoted by Mubārak for the description of the desert routes between the Nile, the Oases, and the Sudan, including a detailed description of the Oases (and a biography of al-Tūnisī) (xvii. 33). Besides al-Jabartī and al-Tūnisī, the only modern Arabic author mentioned by Mubārak is Buṭrus

[1] Muḥammad Amīn Fikrī, *Jughrāfiyyat Miṣr* (Cairo, 1296/1879). The reason was perhaps that Fikrī himself had extensively used the manuscript of the *Khiṭaṭ* for his book. See his introduction, p. *jīm*. However, in the second volume there is a long biography of Fikrī (ii. 46 ff.), and his help is acknowledged by Mubārak in his *'Alam al-dīn* (Alexandria, 1299/1882), pp. 7–8.

[2] 'Abdallāh al-Sharqāwī, *Tuḥfat al-nāẓirīn fī man walā Miṣr min al-wulāt wa'l-salāṭīn* (Cairo, 1281/1864–5). This is a remarkable omission because Mubārak has a biography of al-Sharqāwī including a long list of his works (xiii. 63 f.). The biography is based on al-Jabartī. On al-Sharqāwī's history see D. Ayalon, 'The historian al-Jabartī and his background', *BSOAS*, vol. xxiii. 2 (1960), pp. 248–9, and sources quoted there.

[3] Salīm al-Naqqāsh, *Miṣr li'l-Miṣriyyīn* (Alexandria, 1884). This omission may be explained either by the fact that by 1884 the manuscript of the *Khiṭaṭ* was already more or less completed, or by Mubārak's aversion to anything connected with the 'Urābī movement (see below).

[4] *Tashḥīdh al-adhhān bi-sīrat bilād al-'arab wa'l-sūdān: Voyage au Darfour . . . par le Cheykh Mohammed ibn-Omar el-tounsy, autographié et publié par Mr. Perron* (Paris, 1850); (cf. *GAL*, *S*, vol. ii, pp. 748–9).

al-Bustānī, from whose encyclopedia he quotes almost exclusively biographies of medieval Arab savants.

Finally, there is no trace in Mubārak's *Khiṭaṭ* to show that he used the Arabic press of Egypt, which by his time had already developed to a considerable degree.

5. *Works in European languages*

Among the European sources used by Mubārak for his account of modern Egypt the *Description de l'Égypte* occupies the first place. It is called by him *Khiṭaṭ al-faransāwiyya* or *Kutub al-faransāwiyya* or *Kitāb al-jamʿiyya al-faransāwiyya al-khāṣṣ bi-khiṭaṭ Miṣr.*[1] It is very frequently quoted for matters concerning both ancient Egypt and Egypt at the time of the French occupation. Mubārak uses the *Description* for information on the topography and economic conditions of Egyptian towns and villages at the time of the French occupation (for instance, xi. 60; xii. 98, 102; xv. 70, 94; xvi. 52; etc.), on population figures and administration at that time (i. 98; xii. 47), on mosques, hospitals, and convents (i. 96–97; ii. 104; xii. 54), on the Nilometer (xviii. 34, 93), and on various other topographical and historical questions. With the exception of one or two of these quotations, no numbers of volume and page are given.

The works of European officials who served the Muḥammad ʿAlī family are used by Mubārak rather sporadically, and surprisingly enough, more often than not in connexion with matters which are not their principal concern. Dr. Clot-Bey, for instance, who established the medical school at the time of Muḥammad ʿAlī and laid the foundations of a health service in Egypt, wrote a book about the plague in Egypt[2] which is not quoted by Mubārak. He uses Clot's *Aperçu général*[3] for various subjects: not for its detailed sections on health and hospitals, but for the digging of the Maḥmūdiyya canal (vii. 50), Muḥammad ʿAlī's navy (vii. 52–54), figures on Egypt's religious and ethnic communities (vii. 54, without mentioning that they are taken from Clot), Muḥammad ʿAlī's army (vii. 55–57), Suez (xii. 75), and industry at the time of Muḥammad ʿAlī (xv. 91). It is interesting to note that most of this material is concentrated in the seventh volume of the *Khiṭaṭ* dealing with Alexandria. The book of Linant de Bellefonds,[4] who was Director of Public Works in Egypt at the time of Muḥammad ʿAlī and who made the first plans for the Delta barrage, is mentioned by Mubārak only in connexion with various

[1] European books in general are designated *kutub al-Faranj* (see below).

[2] A. -B. Clot-Bey, *De la peste observée en Égypte* (Paris, 1840). For publications of Clot in Arabic see Yūsuf Sarkīs, *Muʿjam al-maṭbūʿāt al-ʿarabiyya waʾl-muʿarraba* (Cairo, 1928), p. 1567. None of these is quoted in the *Khiṭaṭ*.

[3] A. -B. Clot-Bey, *Aperçu général sur l'Égypte* (Paris, 1840), 2 vols. The author's name is rendered *Qūlūṭ*, although in the section on Cairo we find *Shāriʿ Klūt* (iii. 112). The book is called *taʾrīkhuhu li-Miṣr* (vii. 52).

[4] M. A. Linant de Bellefonds, *Mémoires sur les principaux travaux d'utilité publique exécutés en Égypte depuis la plus haute antiquité jusqu'à nos jours* (Paris, 1872–3).

topographic questions (xiv. 74; xvii. 27, 28, 65) but not with regard to public works and irrigation.

However, two other European officials are quoted on matters with which they were concerned in Egypt. One is Hamont, the manager of Muḥammad 'Alī's private estates. His book[1] is mentioned exclusively in connexion with horse-breeding and sheep-raising (xii. 120; xv. 30), but then Hamont was not an admirer of Muḥammad 'Alī and his book is full of severe accusations against him. It was therefore no suitable material to be quoted by Mubārak who was a loyal servant of the Muḥammad 'Alī family. The second is Cailliaud who was employed by Muḥammad 'Alī to explore the Eastern Desert and search for emeralds. Mubārak translates his account of this expedition (xiii. 21).[2]

Like the quotations from European officials, Mubārak's use of books written by European consuls and travellers seems to have been rather occasional. Beginning with the eighteenth century, the first is de Maillet, the French consul in Egypt during the years 1692–1708. His book[3] is also mentioned in connexion with the emeralds question (xiii. 23), but the same author seems to be meant when instead of *Māyyh* we find *Māny* (vii. 39, 40, 42), *Māby* (vii. 44, 48), or *Māly* (vii. 38), since all these passages deal with Alexandria at the beginning of the eighteenth century (on misprints of foreign names see below). The emeralds question is also the subject of a quotation from Bruce,[4] one of the two British travellers mentioned by Mubārak (he probably used the French translation of his book).[5] The letters of Savary[6] who toured Egypt in the years 1776–7 are cited only in connexion with two subjects, the description of Rosetta (xi. 75; xv. 4) and the monasteries near Suez (xii. 76). But even more astonishing is the scanty use made of the famous travels by Volney[7] (spelled *Wūlny* or *Fūlny* or *Wlyn* or *Flyn*). The curious thing is that Mubārak twice quotes medieval Arabic authors according to Volney (vii. 16; xiii. 10), and twice questions of Egyptology (vii. 33; xvi. 9), but he does not mention

[1] P. N. Hamont, *L'Égypte sous Méhémet-Ali* (Paris, 1843). On its background see J. M. Carré, *Voyageurs et écrivains français en Égypte* (Cairo, 1956), vol. i, pp. 293–4.

[2] F. Cailliaud, *Voyage à l'Oasis de Thèbes et dans les déserts situés à l'Orient et à l'Occident de la Thébaïde fait pendant les années 1815–1818.* Rédigé et publié par M. Jomard . . . contenant: . . . *3° Des recherches sur les oasis, sur les mines d'émeraude, et sur l'ancienne route du commerce entre le Nil et la Mer Rouge* (Paris, 1822–4), 2 vols. Cf. Carré, vol. i, pp. 225–8. The author's name is spelled by Mubārak *Kābū*, but this seems to be a misprint of *Kāyū*.

[3] *Description de l'Égypte . . ., composé sur les mémoires de M. de Maillet par l'Abbé Le Mascrier* (Paris, 1735). Cf. Carré, vol. i, pp. 56–63.

[4] James Bruce, *Travels to discover the source of the Nile, in the years 1768, 1769, 1770, 1771, 1772 and 1773* (London, 1790), 5 vols.

[5] James Bruce, *Voyage en Nubie et en Abyssinie* (Paris, 1790–2), 5 vols. Thomas Shaw's travels, which had also been translated into French, are quoted once, in connexion with the Nilometer (xviii. 92).

[6] C. E. Savary, *Lettres sur l'Égypte* (Paris, 1785–6), 3 vols. Cf. Carré, vol. i, pp. 80–104.

[7] C. F. C. Volney, *Voyage en Syrie et en Égypte, pendant les années 1783, 1784 et 1785* (Paris, 1787). This is the original form of the title, which is usually cited as *Voyage en Égypte et en Syrie.*

him at all in connexion with the conditions of Egypt at the end of the eighteenth century, except for the Nilometer (xviii. 92–93).

The first European traveller of the nineteenth century mentioned by Mubārak appears in the *Khiṭaṭ* as *al-dukdū Ra'jūs* or *al-dūk dū Rājūs*. This is no other than Maréchal Auguste Marmont, duc de Raguse, who in 1843 travelled in eastern Europe, south Russia, Turkey, and Egypt.[1] He is quoted on springs and monasteries near Suez (xii. 70, 75), the battle of Shubrākhīt in 1798 (xii. 119), the artillery school at Ṭurā (xiii. 32), and the natron concession (xiii. 34). The next is Ampère, son of the famous physicist, who travelled in Egypt in 1844–5 (not in 1830, as stated in Mubārak).[2] In the *Khiṭaṭ* we find the translation of part of his description of Alexandria (vii. 30). *Jrky al-Firinsāwī* seems to be Gisquet (cf. vii. 39: *Kitāb Jsky*), who travelled in Egypt a few months prior to Ampère, and whose book[3] is also mentioned in the part of the *Khiṭaṭ* dealing with Alexandria (vii. 37). That Mubārak quotes the superficial account by H. Bernard of the campaign of Muḥammad ʿAlī against the Wahhābīs (xii. 81), may be explained by the fact that he found it in Arabic translation.[4]

In addition to these European authors who are mentioned by name, Mubārak frequently uses travel accounts without naming their author. He just says that a specific information is taken from *baʿḍ al-sayyāḥīn*, *baʿḍ man sāḥa fī Miṣr*, *baʿḍ al-faransāwiyya fī siyāḥatihi*, or *baʿḍ man sāfara fī tilka al-jihāt fī waqtinā hādhā* (viii. 100; xiv. 121; xvi. 20; xvii. 30, 39, 55, etc.). Moreover he sometimes just says that his information is derived from a European source—*baʿḍ kutub al-Ifranj* (for instance, xvii. 7, 38, etc.). Similarly, his biographies of some orientalists and travellers are taken from what he calls *qāmūs al-Ifranj* or *al-qāmūs al-ifranjī* or *qāmūs jūghrāfiyyat al-ifranjī* [*sic*][5] (x. 52; xi. 68, 75; xii. 38; etc.).

Finally, Mubārak apparently had access to some journals in European languages. He mentions two of them: the Egyptian *Moniteur*[6] (xiv. 133) and the *Journal Asiatique* (xii. 40, 83). However, neither is used for information on modern Egypt.

6. *Summary*

To sum up: the European sources used by Mubārak are all French works, either written by French authors or translated into French. Yet from the vast literature on modern Egypt written in French, Mubārak made a very

[1] *Voyage du Maréchal duc de Raguse* (Paris, 1837–9), 5 vols. Cf. Carré, vol. i, pp. 279–84.

[2] J. J. Ampère, *Voyage en Égypte et en Nubie* (Paris, 1868). First published in *Revue des deux Mondes* (1846–9). Cf. Carré, vol. ii, pp. 49 ff.

[3] J. H. Gisquet, *L'Égypte, les Turcs et les Arabes* (Paris, 1848). Cf. Carré, vol. i, pp. 295 f.

[4] ʿAbdallāh Abu'l-Suʿūd, *Ta'rīkh al-diyār al-miṣriyya fī ʿahd al-dawla al-Muḥammadiyya al-ʿAliyya, ta'līf Barnār wa-tarjamat Abu'l-Suʿūd* (Cairo, 1292/1875). French original: H. Bernard, *Notices géographiques et historiques sur l'Égypte* (Paris, 1867), Part iii.

[5] Probably P. Larousse, *Le grand dictionnaire universel du xixe siècle* (1865–76).

[6] First published in 1874; from 1885—official publication.

small selection; some of the most important are not on his list. Moreover, he uses the sources in a rather capricious way: generally each is quoted on one subject only, not always the principal contribution of the author to the knowledge of modern Egypt. He never mentions the title of the works he cites, let alone the number of the page on which the quoted passage is found.

But even Arabic written sources, official and non-official, published and unpublished, are used by Mubārak in a rather irregular manner. They do not, therefore, make a significant contribution to the importance of the *Khiṭaṭ* as a source for modern Egyptian history. This statement must be qualified by two important exceptions: urban title-deeds and *waqf* documents.

As against this, much of the information which is based on oral evidence and on his own personal experience makes a substantial contribution to our knowledge of nineteenth-century Egypt, although the way he presents this material is in many cases unsatisfactory.

II. PRESENTATION OF MATERIAL

1. *Arrangement*

In the arrangement of the vast material contained in the *Khiṭaṭ*, Mubārak does not deviate from the tradition of medieval Arabic works of a similar kind. He deals with each Egyptian town or village in alphabetical order—with the exception of Cairo (i–vi) and Alexandria (vii). All the information on a specific place available to Mubārak, its topography, economic conditions, ancient, medieval, and modern history, the biographies of prominent people born in the place, etc., is presented under one heading—the name of the place. Mubārak must have worked with the aid of an enormous card index or an equivalent apparatus. He did not try, however, to arrange his material according to subjects—with the exception of some parts of the volumes dealing with Cairo and the last three volumes, dealing respectively with the Nile, the canals, and coins and currencies. In general the result is a compilation pieced together from heterogeneous items. Only in a few cases does he critically compare different accounts of the same event, or different sets of data.

The arrangement of the material according to towns and villages made it difficult for Mubārak to deal with general subjects which are not connected with a particular place. Many of these subjects, especially in the field of political history, are just omitted; others are dealt with incidentally, where a slight connexion with a particular place could be established. Thus Mubārak gives an account of Muḥammad 'Alī's army, the conquest and exploration of the Sudan, and various other subjects, in the volume dedicated to Alexandria (mostly according to Clot, as we have seen). The discussion of many places includes the biography of persons who had almost no connexion at all with these places: they are just mentioned incidentally (x. 17–21, 37, etc.).

For instance, Mubārak tells us that the inhabitants of Nazlat Sīdī ʿĪsā (Minyā province) falsely claim that Maʿrūf al-Karkhī, a *Ṣūfī* of the eighth century, is buried in a tomb near this village. This does not deter him, however, from taking the opportunity not only to relate the biography of that *Ṣūfī* but also to describe Karkh, a quarter of Baghdād, and even Baghdād itself (xii. 37). A few pages further on he says that a certain al-Sinjārī was not connected with a place in Egypt called Sinjār in medieval times but with Sinjār in the Iraqi–Syrian Jazīra; nevertheless—*lā baʾsa bi-sawq tarjamatihi* . . . (xiii. 56).

Thus much interesting information is scattered throughout the volumes of the *Khiṭaṭ*, but it is often impossible to guess where to find it. The *Khiṭaṭ* has of course no index, a shortcoming of which Jurjī Zaydān already complained.[1] True, there are very detailed tables of contents at the beginning of each of the twenty volumes. They include not only the names of the towns and villages which are described in the volume, but also the biographies and other subjects dealt with in connexion with the description of this or that town. But it is not always easy to use these tables, and they certainly do not compensate for the lack of an index. Moreover, they are not even complete. To give only one example out of many: the table of contents of the ninth volume does not include the interesting description of the great *mawlid* annually held in Upper Egypt, to be found on pages 61–62 of that volume.

2. *Accuracy*

Unfortunately, accuracy is not one of the merits of Mubārak's *Khiṭaṭ*. Many of the errors obviously are misprints. As we have seen, it only rarely happens that a foreign name is printed in the same transliteration wherever it is mentioned, and many of these names are not easily recognizable. But the distortion of foreign names is by no means the only type of misprints, as stated by Goldziher.[2] If in fact there would have been a *maʿmal zujāj* (glass factory) in Bīr Shams (Minūfiyya) in the nineteenth century, this would have been very important for the industrial development of Egypt (x. 25); unfortunately it was certainly only a *maʿmal dajāj* (a building for the hatching of fowls' eggs by artificial heat) like those that existed in many Egyptian villages at that time.[3] The discrepancy between Régny's and Mubārak's figures on members of Alexandria's guilds may also be the result of misprints.[4] Similarly, some errors in topographic and geographic data may be explained by misprints: *fī al-shimāl al-qiblī* (xiv. 97) certainly is a printing error, and so

[1] Jurjī Zaydān, *Taʾrīkh ādāb al-lugha al-ʿarabiyya* (2nd edn., Cairo, 1937), vol. iv, p. 252. This certainly is one reason why only few authors have used the *Khiṭaṭ*. The preparation of such an index would be an important service to the study of modern Egypt.

[2] 'Störende Druckfehler kommen nur in den häufigen fremden Eigennamen vor' (*WZKM*, *supra*).

[3] Cf. x. 4–7, and *passim*. Also E. W. Lane, *An account of the manners and customs of the modern Egyptians* (Everyman edn.), pp. 317–19.

[4] See n. 2, p. 14.

probably is *Snūr* instead of *Sīnrū* (viii. 26) or *al-Mndīsha* instead of *al-Mūshiyya* (xvii. 31).

However, there are many topographical and geographical errors which definitely cannot be explained as misprints. The most frequent are wrong bearings of a place in relation to other places. We have noted more than forty errors of this kind. It is improbable that they resulted from the use of wrong maps: Mubārak certainly had access to the map of his colleague Maḥmūd al-Falakī published in 1872–3,[1] and to the map of Jacotin which was published together with the *Description de l'Égypte.*[2] The examination of these maps shows that they were not the source of Mubārak's errors. The *Khiṭaṭ* is not provided with a map.

But there are also topographical errors of various other kinds. In some cases Mubārak locates a village on the wrong side of the Nile (e.g. Dandara—xi. 60); sometimes he confuses two different villages which have similar names (e.g. Minyat Ḥabīb al-Gharbiyya and Minyat Ḥabīb al-Sharqiyya, xvi. 61); in some cases he gives a wrong name (e.g. Banī Mazār instead of Banī Ṣāliḥ, vii. 15; Khārija instead of Dākhila, xv. 70; Baḥr Rashīd instead of Baḥr Dimyāṭ, xvi. 60, etc.). There are even villages which are altogether wrongly located, or about which a number of wrong data are given (e.g. Shabās al-Shuhadā, xii. 115; Maḥallat Diyāy, xv. 29, etc.).

Many of the statements about distances between two places are wrong. The distance between Burdayn and Shubrā al-Nakhla is not 1,500 metres (ix. 15) but at least nine kilometres; between Bulqīna and Dār al-Baqar al-Qibliyya not two (ix. 80) but six kilometres; between al-Kawm al-Akhḍar and Abī Ḥummuṣ not five (xv. 12) but approximately seventeen kilometres, between al-Manāja and Ṣān al-Ḥajar not four (xv. 74) but about twenty kilometres, etc., etc. But in most cases he states distances in terms of time and the time one needs to travel from one place to another depends of course upon the vehicle one uses.

Finally, there is at least one grave error concerning the number of inhabitants of a town. Mubārak writes that al-Maḥalla al-Kubrā has about 50,000 inhabitants and is the greatest town of Lower Egypt except Alexandria (xv. 18). This cannot have been correct. According to the 1882 census al-Maḥalla al-Kubrā had 27,823 inhabitants, and even in the more accurate 1897 census no more than 31,100 were counted. Both censuses showed that both Ṭanṭā and Damietta were larger than al-Maḥalla al-Kubrā, and in 1897, it was also surpassed by Manṣūra, Damanhūr, and Port Said. Similarly, Mubārak claims that the town of Rashīd (Rosetta) continuously grew and developed (xi. 75). In fact, the construction of the Maḥmūdiyya canal and the development of

[1] Maḥmūd Bey al-Falakī, *Khariṭat al-wajh al-baḥrī li'l-aqālīm al-Miṣriyya* (published by A. Kauffmann, Cairo. Lithogr. F. A. Brockhaus, Leipzig, 1289/1872–3).

[2] Jacotin, *Carte topographique de l'Égypte et de plusieurs parties des pays limitrophes, levée pendant l'expédition de l'armée française* (Paris, 1821).

Alexandria caused the decline of Rosetta throughout the nineteenth century; from the middle of the century onwards even the absolute number of its inhabitants continuously declined.

3. *Critical approach and prejudices*

Referring to information on ancient times in the *Khiṭaṭ*, Goldziher pointed out as a remarkable fact that Mubārak sometimes expressed critical thoughts about texts and their contents.[1] The same may be said with regard to some of the information on modern Egypt. For instance, comparing data on mortality at the time of the French occupation with those of the second half of the nineteenth century, Mubārak remarks that, since they show a rise in the mortality rate, they cannot be correct, because the improvement of health conditions certainly brought about a decline in the rate of mortality (i. 98–99). However, his critical approach is considerably limited by certain social and political prejudices.

Mubārak accepts without hesitation the genealogies of his contemporaries who supplied him with their biographies. Many of them claimed of course that they were descended from Arab tribes, holy shaykhs, or the family of the Prophet (e.g. iv. 41; ix. 7; x. 98; xi. 68; xiv. 96; etc.). Mubārak's criterion for the truth of information about people often is their social status. For instance, he does not believe a story told by al-Jabartī which disparages the Bakrī family, because 'it is inconsistent with the honour of this highly respected house' (iii. 113). Moreover, he relates as an undisputed fact that whenever a member of this family is nearing death, there appears on his heel a scar like that caused by the bite of a serpent. The reason is that their ancestor, Abū Bakr, was bitten by a serpent in a cave. In 1297/1880 ʿAlī al-Bakrī died, and a few days before his death the scar had appeared (iii. 124). As against this, he condemns many superstitions and beliefs in supernatural forces current among the lower classes (e.g. ii. 75, 113).[2]

An equally important limit of Mubārak's critical approach is his prejudice in favour of the Muḥammad ʿAlī family. He glorifies without reservation Egypt's rulers of the nineteenth century (e.g. vii. 55, 57, 60, 65; x. 80, 82, 83, etc.). There is no ground for Sharqāwī's and Mishadd's assertion that the praise was modified by criticism:[3] in the passage adduced by Sharqāwī and

[1] *WZKM*, *supra*, p. 349. However, in each of these cases one should examine whether or not Mubārak copied the criticism from the European works which he used as sources for the classics. See above, n. 2, p. 13, and below, n. 2, p. 24.

[2] Mubārak also criticizes many popular customs (e.g. iv. 112, 119; xi. 15; etc.). However, the criticism of some customs connected with the *mawlid al-Badawī* at Ṭanṭā (xv. 29) mentioned by Goldziher (*supra*, 351) is not an opinion originally expressed by Mubārak but is quoted by him, together with the whole passage, from his source. Cf. ʿAbd al-Wahhāb al-Shaʿrānī, *al-Ṭabaqāt al-kubrā* (Cairo, n.d., Maṭbaʿat Ṣabīḥ wa'awlāduhu), vol. ii, pp. 120–1.

[3] Sharqāwī and Mishadd, p. 205. Sharqāwī and Mishadd (89) claim that in his *ʿAlam al-dīn* Mubārak is more critical, but even there we find no more than moralizing which may be understood as indirect criticism of the rulers. It is interesting to note that Sharqāwī and

Mishadd (xviii. 138) Mubārak only states that the expenses on the celebration of the opening of the Suez Canal amounted to about one-sixth of Egypt's annual revenues, but his account of the celebration leaves no doubt that he did not disapprove of this fact, or for that matter, of Ismāʿīl's wastefulness. The following is an interesting illustration of Mubārak's loyalty to the Muḥammad ʿAlī family. In connexion with the town of Banhā, Mubārak quotes from al-Jabartī a long paragraph about Shaykh ʿAbdullāh al-Banhāwī (ix. 89). He omits, however, from al-Jabartī's account the passages in which al-Jabartī describes the corruption of the ruling class during the early years of Muḥammad ʿAlī's rule.[1]

Mubārak does not laud all the rulers of Egypt in the nineteenth century with equal fervour, but he seems to distribute his praises according to subjective criteria. To judge by the *Khiṭaṭ*, it was ʿAbbās who continued Muḥammad ʿAlī's work of developing and modernizing Egypt, and afterwards Ismāʿīl, while Saʿīd is not mentioned at all in this connexion (vii. 60–65). The obvious reason for this view of modern Egyptian history is the fact that Mubārak was in ʿAbbās's favour, while he fell into disgrace at the time of Saʿīd.

Similarly, opponents of the Muḥammad ʿAlī family are punished by the omission of their biography from the *Khiṭaṭ*. Sharqāwī and Mishadd have dealt in detail with the omission of ʿUmar Makram's biography,[2] and we find a similar attitude towards all those who had any connexion with the ʿUrābī revolt.[3] Neither Hirriyya near Zaqāzīq, the native village of ʿUrābī, nor Maḥallat Naṣr, the village in which Muḥammad ʿAbduh was born, are mentioned in the *Khiṭaṭ*, and there are no biographies of ʿUrābī, Muḥammad ʿAbduh, ʿAbdallāh Nadīm, or other prominent persons connected in some way or other with the revolt.

III. THE SUBJECT-MATTER OF THE *KHIṬAṬ*

Paradoxical as it may sound, the principal importance of Mubārak's *Khiṭaṭ* is not its contribution to the historical geography and topography of Egypt. The main reason for this is its lack of accuracy and the numerous mistakes dealt with above. Moreover, it should be pointed out that while in 1882 there were in Egypt 3,651 towns and villages (3,692 in 1897) and about 8,600 smaller places (more than 14,000 in 1897), Mubārak discusses only 1,155 of them.[4]

Mishadd justify Mubārak's unreserved loyalty to the Muḥammad ʿAlī family by the benefits he received from its ruling members.

1 Cf. Jabartī, *ʿAjāʾib*, vol. iv, p. 64.

2 Sharqāwī and Mishadd, pp. 149–51.

3 On the relation between Mubārak and ʿUrābī's group see ibid., pp. 191 ff. See also his own account, ix. 55–58. For Mubārak's general political, religious, and cultural attitudes his other works are more important than the *Khiṭaṭ*.

4 In this count we have included villages discussed in detail by Mubārak under the heading of another place, but not villages mentioned by name only on which no details are given.

This is by no means a negligible number, but one should not forget that the majority of Egyptian villages are not included in this geographical encyclopedia.

The study of Egypt's political history benefits even less from Mubārak's *Khiṭaṭ* than the study of geography and topography. Although the detailed enumeration of administrative institutions and the description of local government in every town and village is quite useful, little other political information is included in the *Khiṭaṭ* which may not be found elsewhere. Here and there Mubārak relates events connected with the Muḥammad 'Alī family, but his original contribution is rather small. Generally he contents himself with copying al-Jabartī's account of events connected with a specific place. As we have seen, the arrangement of his material according to towns and villages made it difficult for him to include in his work much of Egypt's political history.

There is much material on economic history in the *Khiṭaṭ*, though not to an equal extent on its different subdivisions. Except for coins and currencies, few financial questions are dealt with by Mubārak. As against this, the work is rich in information on agriculture, land-tenure and landownership, rural trade, the specific crafts of many of Egypt's villages, towns, and districts, and the general economic development of various towns. Commerce, transport, and communications are also treated of in detail, but while there is copious information on internal commerce and trade routes one finds comparatively little on maritime transport and foreign trade.

The *Khiṭaṭ* supplies essential information on the social structure of the Egyptian village and the Egyptian town in the nineteenth century. Subjects dealt with are, for instance, the various kinds of dwellings, the division into quarters and the social character of the different quarters of specific towns and villages, the split of the rural population into two factions, the foundations of new villages, rural and urban institutions (the *maḍyafa*, the *sūq*, etc.), and the urban guilds. In addition, many towns and villages are described in detail, and comparison with their present structure may yield interesting results for the study of their social development.

Of major importance is Mubārak's material on the various social groups and classes in nineteenth-century Egypt. We find in the *Khiṭaṭ* unique information on Egypt's tribes and the process of their settlement, on rural families and notables, on merchants, officials, army officers, physicians, engineers, and particularly *'ulamā'*. A great part of this information is included in biographies and autobiographies which shed light on the origin and social background of members of these groups, their position in society, and their rise or decline.

Other aspects of social life frequently dealt with by Mubārak are religious and ethnic communities (Copts, foreigners, etc.), the position and status of women, health conditions, and particularly education, one of the main fields of his official activity. In connexion with education (and some of the biographies) we also find interesting information on cultural and literary development, and Mubārak even reproduces a number of poems written by his contemporaries, but in this respect the *Khiṭaṭ* certainly is no more than a minor source of secondary importance. On the other hand, the descriptions of marriage and funeral rites, food and dress, reception of guests, and various other customs, serve as a substantial addition to Lane's work and the *Description de l'Égypte.*

It would seem to us, however, that the pre-eminent importance of the *Khiṭaṭ* consists in the abundant and interesting information on various aspects of religious life in Egypt in the nineteenth century. From *waqf* documents and Mubārak's personal experience as Minister of Waqfs we receive a clear picture of the situation and problems of this institution at that time. A most illuminating section on the Azhar includes, among other things, descriptions of social life at this institution, material conditions of the students, relations between different groups of students, etc. Furthermore, there is much information on other religious institutions in Egyptian towns and villages, such as religious courts, mosques, and convents. However, Mubārak's treatment of popular religion is at least as illuminating as that of orthodox Islam. He describes hundreds of saints' tombs in towns and villages, their history and the beliefs and customs connected with them, the religious and social position of the *sharīfs*, the various *Ṣūfī* orders and their shaykhs, scores of *mawlids* and the customs and rites connected with each of them, as well as changes that occurred in their celebration. Goldziher was certainly right when, in the first review of the *Khiṭaṭ* ever published, he decidedly stressed this aspect of Mubārak's work.

To sum up: the importance of Mubārak's *Khiṭaṭ* is in the field of social history.[1] It goes without saying that in this field too Mubārak's shortcomings have to be taken into account; but there can be no doubt that his work is an indispensable and unique source for the study of the social history of Egypt in the nineteenth century.

[1] There can be no doubt that social anthropologists could use this work to a much larger extent than they have done up till now. For instance, in a recently published bibliography specializing in social anthropology (L. H. Coult, Jr., *An annotated bibliography of the Egyptian fellah* (Florida, University of Miami Press, 1958), Mubārak's *Khiṭaṭ* is mentioned (no. 102, p. 31), but the compilers of the bibliography were content with reading a sample. In the subject index the *Khiṭaṭ* appears under the headings: historical background, topography, settlement patterns, marriage ceremonies, and death, burial, and funeral (in contrast with other references no numbers of pages are given). But the *Khiṭaṭ* is not indexed under building construction, dress, agricultural methods, landownership, crafts and rural industries, administration, inter-village quarrel, religion, education, *mawlids*, and many other subjects on which there is important material in Mubārak's work.

Turkish Source-materials for Egyptian History

STANFORD J. SHAW

I. INTRODUCTION

THE era of Ottoman rule in Egypt, from the conquest by Sultan Selim I in 1517 until Muḥammad 'Alī's rise to power, has largely been ignored as a subject of serious research by students of Egyptian history. The Egyptians themselves prefer to deprecate it as a time of barren stagnation to be avoided and, if possible, entirely forgotten as quickly as possible. Western historians have been repelled by the relative scarcity and extreme difficulty of the sources available for the period, in contrast to those for the régimes before and after. Since Ottoman Egypt was ruled almost entirely by foreigners whose official language was Ottoman Turkish, the surviving documents are mostly in that language rather than Arabic, with the sole exception of those emanating from the courts of justice, and few historians interested in modern Egypt possess the linguistic and palaeographic skills required to make use of them. So they have either avoided the subject entirely or relied on the few Arabic sources which have survived to the exclusion of the Turkish ones. To disregard the Arabic sources would be foolish, but to accept their statements uncritically without consulting the Turkish ones is a proceeding no longer acceptable for reputable scholarly study in this field.[1] It is the object of this paper to enumerate and describe the principal Turkish sources available for the study of Egypt from 1517 in the hope that it will encourage their use in future studies of the subject.

[1] The principal studies of value on Ottoman Egypt to 1798 published by Egyptians are: Maḥmūd al-Sharqāwī, *Miṣr fi'l-qarn al-thāmin 'ashar* (Cairo, 1955–6); Muḥammad Tawfīq and Ḥasan 'Uthmān, 'Ta'rīkh Miṣr fi'l-'Ahd al-'Uthmānī', *Kitāb al-majmal fi'l-ta'rīkh al-Miṣrī* (Cairo, 1942), pp. 231–84; Tawfiq al-Ṭawīl, *al-Taṣawwuf fī Miṣr ibbān al-'aṣr al-'Uthmānī* (Cairo, 1938); Muḥammad Anīs, *Madrasat al-ta'rīkh al-Miṣrī fi'l-'aṣr al-'Uthmānī* (Cairo, 1962); Muḥammad Rif'at Ramaḍān, *'Alī Bey al-Kabīr* (Cairo, 1950); and Shafiq Ghorbal, 'Miṣr 'inda mafraq al-ṭuruq', *Majallat Kulliyat al-Adab, al-Jāmi'a al-Miṣriyya*, vol. iv (1936), pp. 1–71. See also references in S. J. Shaw, 'The Ottoman Archives as a Source for Egyptian History', *JAOS*, vol. lxxxiii (1963), pp. 447–52. While the studies mentioned are of interest and value, they are entirely dependent on Arabic sources, with the exception only of Tawfīq and Ramaḍān, who made considerable use of the Turkish archival sources. It is unfortunate that Tawfīq's works on the Janissary corps in Ottoman Egypt and on Ottoman palaeography and diplomatics have never been published.

II. ARCHIVAL SOURCES

The official records of Ottoman rule in Egypt are found principally in six archives:

1. *Dār al-Maḥfūẓāt* archives, the Citadel, Cairo.[1]
2. Abdin Palace archives, Cairo.[2]
3. *Sharī'a* court archives (*al-Maḥkama li'l-Aḥwāl al-Shakhṣiyya*), Sharia Nur al-Zalam, Hilmiyya, Cairo.[3]
4. *Başbakanlık Arşivi.* Archives of the Prime Minister's Office, Defterdarlık, Istanbul.[4]
5. *Topkapı Sarayı Arşivi.* Archives of the Palace of the Sultan, Istanbul.[5]
6. *Hariciye Arşivi.* Archives of the Turkish Ministry of Foreign Affairs. Defterdarlik Building, Istanbul.

Physically, the Ottoman administrative records can be placed in two broad classifications—registers (sing: *defter*) and individual documents (*evrak*) of all kinds.[6] However, for the purposes of research, a much more meaningful distinction is that among orders and reports, financial records, and judicial materials.

1. *Political and administrative orders and reports*

Orders and decrees issued by the Ottoman Imperial Council on all matters of interest to it, including Egypt, are found in its general *Mühimme* registers, which are preserved at the *Başbakanlık Arşivi* in Istanbul, in 263 volumes from 1553 to 1906. The materials in each register, and the registers themselves, are arranged in chronological order; indexes are available only for the first 68 volumes of the series, for 1553 to 1590. Materials concerning Egypt after that time can be found only by reading through all the registers, of which there are 43 additional volumes for the years up to 1707.[7] While the series

[1] Described in S. J. Shaw, 'Cairo's Archives and the History of Ottoman Egypt', *Report on current research, Spring, 1956* (Middle East Institute, Washington, 1956), pp. 59–72; idem, 'al-Wathā'iq al-Miṣriyya fi'l-'ahd al-'Uthmānī', *Majallat Ma'had al-Makhṭuṭāt al-'Arabiyya*, vol. ii (1956), pp. 1–16; Muḥammad Aḥmad Ḥusayn, *al-Wathā'iq al-ta'rīkhiyya* (Cairo, 1945), pp. 93–94.

[2] Jean Deny, *Sommaire des Archives turques du Caire* (Cairo, 1930).

[3] S. J. Shaw, 'Cairo's archives', pp. 66–67; Deny, *Sommaire*, pp. 214–17.

[4] Mithat Sertoğlu, *Muhteva bakımından Başvekâlet Arşivi* (Ankara, 1955); S. J. Shaw, 'Archival Sources for Ottoman History: The Archives of Turkey', *JAOS*, vol. lxxx (1960), pp. 1–12; B. Lewis, 'The Ottoman archives as a source for the history of the Arab lands', *JRAS*, 1951, pp. 139–55; idem, 'Başvekalet Arşivi', *EI²*, vol. i, pp. 1089–91.

[5] The index to this collection was partially published by Tahsin Öz, *Arşiv kılavuzu* (Istanbul, 1940); the rest of the catalogue is available in manuscript form at the archives. See also Shaw, ibid., pp. 6–7.

[6] Deny, *Sommaire*, pp. 143–57; J. Reychman and A. Zajączkowski, 'Diplomatic: iv. Ottoman Empire', *EI²*, vol. ii, pp. 313–16.

[7] Sertoğlu, pp. 16–23, lists the years covered by each volume of the *Mühimme* series; they are also discussed in Uriel Heyd, *Ottoman documents on Palestine, 1552–1615* (Oxford, 1960), and Gliša Elezović, *Iz Carigradskih Turskih Arhiva Mühimme Defteri* (Belgrade, 1950).

continues to the nineteenth century, the orders and decrees concerning Egypt and Arabia after that time were set down in a separate series of registers called *Mühimme-i Mısır* (Egyptian affairs), of which fourteen volumes survive for the years 1119/1707 to 1330/1911, while a fifteenth volume, called *Mühimme-i Mısır Mektumî* (Secret Egyptian affairs), covers 1256/1840 to 1333/1914.[1] Individual copies of the orders, as well as their preliminary drafts, and reports from Ottoman officials concerning conditions in Egypt are found in a number of document collections at the same archives.[2] In the Ali Emiri collection, they must be sought out among documents concerning all aspects of Ottoman affairs which are catalogued only according to the reign of the sultan from whose time they emanate. In the Ibn ül-Emin and Cevdet collections, the latter covering mainly the eighteenth and early nineteenth centuries, they can be found by consulting catalogues arranged according to general subject, with Egypt appearing most frequently in the *Askeri* (military), *Maliye* (financial affairs), and *Eyalat-ı mümtaze* (special provinces) volumes. The bulk of Ottoman documents concerning Egypt during the nineteenth century are found in the *Hatt-ı Hümayun* and *Irade* collections. The former, which covers the years from 1792 to 1839, includes all sorts of orders and reports, not just the 'Imperial Rescripts' that its name implies. It is of particular value for documents on the French expedition to Egypt, the rise of Muḥammad ʿAlī and his relations with the Porte, and the rise of the Wahhābīs in Arabia and Egypt's military actions against them. Catalogues are available only in the Latin script, each item being summarized in detail, and the documents are arranged, for the most part, by specific subject. Most of the archival documents concerning the Empire after 1839 have been arranged in chronological order in the *Irade* document collection, for which catalogues covering each year are available in Arabic script. However, while researchers on most subjects, in the absence of an index, must read through almost a hundred catalogues to find materials, students of Egypt have been particularly blessed. All materials concerning it have been removed from the regular collection and catalogued separately in chronological order under the name *Mesail-i Mısriye* (Egyptian problems). This collection has a great deal of material not only on Ottoman–Egyptian relations, but also internal Egyptian affairs and the penetration of European merchants and capitalists into both countries. Other special *Irade* collections of the same type which are of particular importance to students of Egyptian and Arab history are: *Mesail-i Trablus Garp* (problems of Tripoli of Libya); *Hicaz ve askeri demiryolları müdiriyeti* (directorship of the Ḥijāz and military railroads); and *Harici mesail-i siyasiye* (foreign political problems), including British activities in al-ʿAqaba and Kuwait, those

[1] S. J. Shaw, *The financial and administrative organization and development of Ottoman Egypt, 1517–1798* (Princeton, N.J., 1962), pp. xix–xx, hereafter referred to as Shaw, *Financial organization*; Sertoğlu, p. 24.

[2] The documents collections are described in Sertoğlu, pp. 68–72, and Shaw, 'Archival Sources', pp. 4–6.

of France in Tunisia and Algeria, and problems involved in the construction and operation of the Suez Canal and Britain's occupation of Egypt.

It should be noted that whereas the other document collections cited contain only individual documents, most of the materials in the *Irade* collection are arranged in dossiers, with all documents leading to specific orders retained together.

Finally, the archives surviving from Abdülhamid II's Yıldız Palace, also in the possession of the *Başbakanlık Arşivi*, include a rich collection of papers concerning Egypt during his reign (1876–1909), but these are available only on a limited basis at present.[1]

The *Topkapı Saray* archives possess numerous documents and registers concerning Egypt, ranging from the letters exchanged between Selim I and the Mamluk rulers and governors before the Ottoman invasion to reports concerning the French expedition to Egypt and Muḥammad ʿAlī's rise to power. They are particularly rich in reports from the Ottoman governors and treasury officials concerning the political and military activities of the Mamluk factions and confederations in Cairo during the eighteenth century and concerning Ottoman financial and administrative interests in Egypt. All the materials in these archives are arranged in an alphabetical index, of which the first part (covering subjects beginning with the letters A through H) has been published by Tahsin Öz, former director of the museum. The remainder of this catalogue is available in manuscript form at the Palace. At the present time, a committee directed by the distinguished Turkish historian, Ismail Hakki Uzunçarşılı, is preparing a new and more detailed catalogue of these materials, but until the fruits of its work are ready, the old catalogue remains available and usable.

Some of the more important items in the collection[2] are:

1. Ottoman conquest of Egypt: E6341; E6344; E7649; E3670; E5962; E6362; D10588; E5469; E8358; E6072; E5594; E5483; E5850; E9654; E5596; E5808; E6196; E11355; E5807; E5464; E12282.
2. Ottoman Egypt in the sixteenth and seventeenth centuries: E3396; E11919.
3. Egypt's contributions in cash and kind to the Porte: D1859; E8711; D2889; E9914; D7694; E9953; E4581; E4830; E5608; E230; E4219; E5199; E1095; E11395; E370; E11511; E6177.
4. Reports on Egypt under ʿAlī Bey al-Kabīr: E2229; E2283; E5272; E5252; E1648; E3217; E3374; E840; E2103; D4641; D5909.
5. Expedition of Gazi Hasan Pasha to Egypt: E1951.
6. Reports on Egypt under Murād Bey and Ibrāhīm Bey: E1653; E9757; E4273; E1070; D2866; E5657.
7. The French expedition to Egypt: E6696; E4173; E4193; E2926; E9036;

[1] Sertoğlu, pp. 74–78.

[2] The prefix D indicates *Defter*; E indicates *Evrak*: see above, p. 29.

E2007; E3954; E5725; E1427; E4754; E5019; E3979; E2559; E6989; E5164; E1173; E297.

8. Egyptian tax-farms: E3913; E5285; D638; D958; D169; D656; D4193; E3218; E2665; E10811; E4340.
9. Revenues and expenditures of the Treasury of Cairo: D10085; D9893; D6730; D3083; D8794; D3082; D3084; D9051; D4106; D9650; D569; D8103; D8047; D8058; D8038; D479; D10618; D5908; D3086; D9191; D8577; D3491; D2849; D4944; D4091; D4193.
10. Ottoman *waqfs* in Egypt: D3887; D5698; D5599; D1943; D1364; D1858; D1859B; D1839; D6656; E4787; E2519; E10598; E7450; E794; E10812.
11. The mint of Cairo: E169; E8711; E10265.

The Ottoman Ministry of Foreign Affairs (*Hariciye Vekâleti*) was organized out of the *Reisülküttab*'s office as a separate department only in 1836, and most of its materials concern the years after that time. During the nineteenth century, the official language of this department was French, and the catalogues and most of the documents are written in that language. Dossiers of special interest to students of Egypt are nos. 1005 (report on taxation in Egypt, 1813); 813 (health problems in Egypt, 1839–43); 1114 (Muḥammad ʿAlī's expedition to Arabia); 611 (military and political events during the French Expedition to Egypt); 614 (revolt of Muḥammad ʿAlī in 1832–3); 616 (the Egyptian army and navy); reports on Egyptian political and economic affairs are arranged according to date in the following cartons: 18 (1859–78); 272 (1879–82); 273 (1883–5); 274 (1886–95); 275 (1896–1907); 276 (1908–22); 1345 (1841–83); 1347 (1850–83). Ottoman Turkish documents concerning Egypt before 1800 are collected in cartons nos. 1489 and 894. Materials concerning the Ottoman commissioners sent to Egypt in 1882 and 1913 are in carton no. 258. Similar materials are available in these archives for western, central, and eastern Arabia, Lebanon, Palestine, Syria, Tunisia, and Tripoli.

The Citadel archives in Cairo, which possess most of the Ottoman administrative materials concerning Egypt before 1807, have no registers of Ottoman orders and decrees. The most important collection of this kind in Egypt is that of the Council of State, called *Sijillāt al-Dīwān al-ʿālī*, held at the Sharīʿa court archives.[1] There are twenty-one registers in all, covering the years from 1054/1644 until 1914. They include copies of the important Ottoman *fermans* received from Istanbul; records of Council decisions in civil and criminal cases appealed from lower courts; Council decrees to the people of Egypt; orders appointing judges to the provincial courts; and the annual proclamations certifying that the Nile had reached its peak and that the financial and

[1] These registers are described in Deny, *Sommaire*, pp. 215–16; in my inventory of the Cairo archives, 'Cairo's Archives' I said (p. 67) that these registers were 'no longer located' at the Sharīʿa Archives: however, subsequently when civil administrators replaced the shaykhs in charge of these archives in January 1956, the registers were discovered concealed in a closet at the Archives, and they were then made available to me.

agricultural year had begun. While the orders received from Istanbul are in Turkish, most of the materials originating in Egypt are recorded in Arabic.

The Citadel archives possess 729 catalogued Ottoman *fermans* and 10,543 orders of the governor and the Imperial Council, in addition to innumerable uncatalogued documents of various kinds. The *Sharīʿa* court archives have approximately fifty *fermans* dated from 1765 to 1870, concerned mainly with titles to *waqf* properties and appointments to judicial positions.

With the rapid development of modern state machinery in Egypt under Muḥammad ʿAlī and his successors, the government lost the severely financial and military character imposed by the Ottomans and expanded its functions to include all those normally undertaken by a modern state. As the scope and activities of the central government widened, it was inevitable that councils based on function should evolve and that these should gradually develop into modern government departments, a process similar to that occurring in Turkey at the same time.[1] But while the language of administration gradually became Arabic, especially under Muḥammad ʿAlī's successors, the bulk of the records of government were kept in Turkish until late in the nineteenth century, and these are preserved principally in the Abdin archives in Cairo, with records of lesser importance also kept at the Citadel.

The nineteenth-century Turkish archives in Cairo originally were divided between the Abdin palace and the Citadel and inventoried in Deny's *Sommaire des archives turques*. Deny listed eighty-one registers of letters and telegrams to and from the Ottoman officials and Egyptian representatives in Istanbul between 1807 and 1914 (pp. 231–44, 249–55), approximately 45,000 documents of the same kind stored in 100 cartons (pp. 255–84), in addition to almost 2,000 registers and 100,000 documents, mostly written in Turkish, concerning internal administrative and political matters of various kinds. These include registers and documents emanating from the following principal councils and departments:

		Deny ref.
1. *Meclis-i Mülkiye*, or Assembly of Civil Affairs	1245/1829–1254/1839	pp. 108, 377–9
2. *Kâhya Divanı*, or Council of the lieutenant of the governor, who also acted as governor of Cairo	1220/1805–1292/1876	pp. 116, 381–6
3. *Divan-ı Mülki-i Mısır*, or Council of Civil Affairs, successor to the Ottoman Imperial Council of the Citadel, in charge of internal affairs except for financial ones.	1226/1811–1271/1855	pp. 111–15, 387–92
4. The Treasury (*al-Khazīna*) and Financial Council (*Maliye Divanı*).	1220/1805–1308/1890	pp. 393–414

[1] Deny, *Sommaire*, pp. 90–143.

		Deny ref.
5. Ministry of the Interior (called *Dīwān al-Dākhiliyya* and later *Niẓārat al-Dākhiliyya*)	1226/1811–1303/1886	pp. 415–28
6. Privy Council (*al-Majlis al-Khuṣūṣī*)	1265/1848–1291/1875	pp. 429–31, 120
7. Council of Justice (*Jam'iyyat al-Ḥaqqāniyya*)	1258/1842–1265/1849	pp. 121–2, 433–4
8. Council of Education (*Dīwān al-Madāris*)	1250/1834–1291/1875	pp. 435–7
9. Supreme Judicial Council (*Majlis al-Aḥkām*)	1265/1848–1293/1877	pp. 123, 439–41
10. Police of Cairo (*Zabtiye-i Mısır*)	1260/1844–1286/1870	pp. 124, 443–5
11. Municipality of Alexandria (*Muhafaza-ı Iskenderiye*)	1222/1807–1300/1883	pp. 125, 447–50
12. Council of War (*Dīwān al-Jihādiyya*)	1243/1827–1306/1888	pp. 125, 451–7
13. Council of Public Works (*Dīwān al-Abniyā' wa'l-Ashghāl al-'Umūmiyya*)	1242/1826–1283/1867	pp. 125, 459
14. Council of Commerce (*Dīwān al-Tijāra wa'l-Mabyū'āt*)	1234/1818–1272/1856	pp. 125, 461–2
15. Imperial Arsenal of Būlāq (*Tarsānat Būlāq*)	1243/1827–1271/1855	p. 463
16. Provincial Inspection (*Taftīsh 'Umūm al-aqālīm*)	1222/1807–1290/1873	pp. 479–85
17. Council of Domains and Concessions (*Dīwān Shāfālik wa-'uhad Saniyya*)	1236/1820–1270/1854	pp. 497–513
18. Chamber of Notables (*Majlis Shūrā'l-Nuwwāb*)	1283/1867–1295/1878	pp. 515–17

However, the vicissitudes which engulfed the Abdin Palace following the fall of the dynasty have left the collection in a state requiring entirely new inventories and catalogues, and the Egyptian Archival Commission is now undertaking this work.

Finally, many Ottoman documents can be found outside the official archives, in libraries and private collections throughout the world. Some are included in manuscript volumes catalogues only as *munsha'āt*, document collections, and considerable time is needed to locate them, the originals of which, in many cases, cannot be found elsewhere. The most important of these is the *Kanunname-i Mısır*, a collection of basic laws decreed in Egypt in the year 931/1524–5 and collected as a kind of 'constitution', or at least a legal reference collection, for later administrators. Neither the *Kanunname* as a whole nor its individual constituent laws are found in the archives, but manuscripts of it are found in a number of libraries.[1] The Ottoman land code issued for Egypt in 1553 is preserved only in a manuscript in the Bibliothèque Nationale (Paris), Ancien Fonds Turc. 114 (40 fols.), edited and translated by Stanford J. Shaw as 'The land law of Ottoman Egypt (960/1553): A contribution to the study of landholding in the early years of Ottoman rule in Egypt', *Der Islam*, vol. xxxviii (1962), pp. 106–37. In the same library, Suppl. Turc. 74 contains twenty-five decrees from Sultan Mahmud I to Rāghib Muḥammad Pasha in Cairo in 1161/1748 concerning military salaries and wages, the assignment of tax-farms, and dispatch of the *irsaliye* to Istanbul. Suppl. Turc. 82, entitled *Munsha'at-ı Mustafa Efendi*, compiled by the scribe of the Egyptian treasury in charge of assigning *muqāṭa'as* to tax-farmers, is a collection of letters to and from the principal Ottoman officials in that country during the early seventeenth century. (118 fols. dated 23 Rajab 1023/29 August 1614.) Suppl. Turc. 830 is a discussion of legal problems involved in tax collection and landholding in Egypt, written in 1019/1610 by Mehmed b. Yusuf, *kadıasker* of Anatolia. Suppl. Turc. 805 is a collection of letters compiled by Katibizade Çelebi, the bulk of which are letters between the grand vezir and governor of Egypt, and between the latter and officials in the Holy Cities from 1070/1659 to 1074/1664. Add. MS. 7846 in the British Museum contains Turkish documents on landholding, taxation, and prices in Ottoman Egypt during the seventeenth century.

In the National Library in Vienna, A.F. 239 (424), entitled *Munsha'āt Ibrāhīm Bey al-Daftardār* (Flügel, i. 280–1), by the director of the Ottoman Treasury in Cairo, includes administrative and financial papers from the archives concerning the seventeenth century (101 fols.). In Cairo, MSS. *Ta'rīkh Turkī* 574 to 579 in the *Dār al-Kutub* contain numerous Turkish documents concerning landholding, taxes, and *waqfs*; *Ta'rīkh 'Arabī* 2784 *Ta'rīkh Ṭal'at* 2075 and *Ta'rīkh 'Arabī* 2807 have *fermans* concerning the seventeenth and eighteenth centuries. *Ta'rīkh Taymūr* 2052 contains Arabic and Turkish letters sent to Syria by 'Alī Bey al-Kabīr and French and Arabic proclamations issued by the French during the expedition. Muṣṭafā Fāḍil Pasha MSS. 107 and 8742, entitled *Majmū'at al-farmānāt wa'l-khuṭūṭ al-hūmāyūnī*, contain numerous Ottoman decrees concerning Egypt in the eighteenth century. *Ta'rīkh Taymūr* 2656, *Majmū'at mukātabāt*

[1] The oldest and most complete of these is in the *Topkapı Sarayı* Museum Library, Emanet Hazine MS. 2063 (80 fols.): other copies are in the Bibliothèque Nationale (Paris), Ancien Fonds Turc. MS. 82 (53 fols.); Aya Sofia Library (Istanbul), MS. K. 4871, fols. 118–57; Millet Library (Istanbul), Hekimoglu Ali Paşa MS. 558, fols. 33b–71a; and Süleymaniye Library (Istanbul), Esad Efendi MS. 1827/1 (40 fols.). The latter, an incomplete copy, was published by Ö. L. Barkan in *XV ve XVI inci asırlarda Osmanlı imparatorluğunda ziraî ekonominin hukukî ve malî esasları* (Istanbul, 1943), 354–87. There is an eighteenth-century French translation of the code, published in J. M. Digeon. *Nouveaux contes turcs et arabes* (Paris 1781), vol. ii, also MS. as N.G.F. 1919 in the Bibliothèque Nationale dated 1778, but a modern edition and translation of this basic code is badly needed.

rasmiyya min Muḥammad ʿAlī Pāshā waʾl-kushshāf wa-ghayrihim contains Turkish and Arabic letters and orders concerning internal administrative and political affairs under Muḥammad ʿAlī. *Taʾrīkh Taymūr* 2417 contains Arabic and Turkish letters to and from Muḥammad ʿAlī, ʿAbbās Pasha, Saʿīd Pasha, and Mūrād Bey in the early years of the nineteenth century.

In Istanbul the Municipal Library (*Belediye Kütüphanesi*) has a number of important collections of this kind. Cevdet Yazmaları O. 48 (110 fols.) contains letters to and from Ottoman governors in the seventeenth century. Cevdet Yazmaları K. 69 contains letters exchanged between Gazi Hasan Pasha and the Egyptian *Mashāyikh al-Balad* during the former's expedition to Egypt in 1785. Belediye Yazmaları B. 24 is a 112-folio manuscript of a memorial (*lâyiha*) given to the sultan concerning the activities of the Egyptian khedives in about 1885. Belediye Yazmaları O. 83 is a register of the *waqfs* inherited by the Ottomans from Mamluk times and of their fate in the first decade of Ottoman rule.[1] Belediye Yazmaları K. 356 is a description of the Egyptian financial system in 1830 together with proposals for its reform (70 fols.). Istanbul Archaeological Museum MS. 386 contains copies of thirteen Ottoman *fermans* sent to Egypt between 1840 and 1887. Istanbul University Library T.Y. 6715 has copies of fifty Ottoman *fermans* sent to Egypt and Syria in 1832 and 1833. The Ruşen Eşref archives collection at the *Topkapı Saray* possesses eleven official reports sent to Istanbul by Gazi Hasan Pasha during his expedition to Egypt, together with a number of Ottoman orders to him (item nos. 26, 34, 67, 78–83).

2. *Financial records*

The main object of Ottoman rule in Egypt was financial—to assure the maximum exploitation of its urban and rural wealth and the diversion of as much as possible of the resulting revenues to the Imperial Treasury through taxes and other means; and at the same time to fulfil the Treasury's obligations for salaries and other expenditures of various kinds in Egypt, the Holy Cities, and the Porte. All matters not in some way concerned with the acquisition, protection, and disposal of the sultan's revenues were considered to be outside the scope of his government. For this reason, most of the orders and decrees referred to in the preceding section were in some way connected with the financial function, especially those concerning the centuries before Muḥammad ʿAlī. And by far the bulk of materials contained in the archives are concerned with the Treasury revenues and expenditures.

(*a*) *Cadastral registers*

While it was a normal Ottoman practice to make periodic cadastral surveys of the lands subject to taxation, this was not done in Egypt. In the early years

[1] The Bayezid General Library has the autograph copies of the first three volumes of al-Jabartī's chronicle, in the Ahmed Cevdet division of the Veliuddin collection, MSS. no. 79 (vol. i, 642 pp.), no. 80 (vol. ii, 466 pp.) and no. 81 (vol. iii, 456 pp.).

of Ottoman rule, the older Mamluk registers were used as the basis of the tax system until a newer Ottoman survey, completed only in 1608, was ready for use. Once introduced, the latter was retained virtually without change until the new cadaster compiled by the French in 1799 and 1800, and that of Muḥammad ʿAlī, drawn up between 1813 and 1815.[1] I have been unable to locate the registers of the Mamluk and Ottoman cadastral surveys either in Cairo or Istanbul, but the Citadel archives do possess a few severely damaged registers of this type which may prove to have been part of one or the other.[2] The two modern surveys are available in virtually complete form in the Citadel and Abdin archives, respectively. In addition, the surveys and reports compiled as part of the French cadastral survey have been preserved in the *Archives de la Guerre* of the French *Ministère de la Guerre*, located in the Château de Vincennes in Paris. These reports provide an exhaustive description of Egypt's economic and social situation before and during the French Expedition, but aside from the articles published shortly thereafter in the *Description de l'Égypte* and *Mémoires sur l'Égypte* by the scholars and geographers who accompanied Bonaparte, they have been exploited hardly at all.[3]

(*b*) *Budgets*

The Ottoman Empire did not compile or use budgets of revenues and expenditures drawn up in advance of the financial year until the nineteenth century. The only sort of budgetary control was a tendency to tie certain expenditures to specific fixed revenues. However, in Egypt there were account summaries (*ijmāl*) compiled at the close of each year, and including the main items of revenue and expenditure and the surplus left for delivery to the Porte as the annual tribute, called *irsaliye hazine*.[4] In addition, a few *ijmāl* registers were drawn up by special reform commissions sent to Egypt periodically to restore the balance of revenues over expenditures so that the Porte would continue to receive its regular annual revenues. Unfortunately, however, only a very few accounts covering all items of revenue and expenditure have survived:

Financial year	Archives	Register number
1004/1595–6	BBA (*Başbakanlık Arşivi*)	Maliyeden müdevvere 1999
1005/1596–7	BBA	Maliyeden müdevvere 5671
1009/1600–1	BBA	Maliyeden müdevvere 5672

[1] Shaw, *Financial organization*, pp. 16–19, 67; idem, 'The Land Law of Ottoman Egypt', *Der Islam*, vol. xxxviii (1962), pp. 106–37.

[2] Idem, 'Cairo's archives', p. 64.

[3] A general inventory of these archives is provided in Marc-André Fabre, *Inventaire des archives conservées au service historique de l'état-major de l'armée. Château de Vincennes: Archives modernes* (Paris, 1954), pp. 36–40.

[4] Ö. L. Barkan, 'Daftar-i Khāḳānī', *EI*[2], vol. ii, pp. 81–83.

Financial year	Archives	Register number
1010/1601–2	BBA	Maliyeden müdevvere 5672
1011/1602–3	BBA	Maliyeden müdevvere 5672
1020/1611–12	BBA	Maliyeden müdevvere 5162
1023/1614–15	BBA	Maliyeden müdevvere 5658
1024/1615–16	BBA	Tapu 726
1025/1616–17	BBA	Tapu 734
1041/1631–2	TKS (*Topkapı Sarayı*)	D. 2849
1058/1648–9	TKS	D. 4944
1082/1671–2	BBA	Kepeci 2302
1083/1672–3	BBA	Maliyeden müdevvere 1489
1094/1683–4	Dār al-Maḥfūẓāt, Cairo	2106
1107/1695–6	BBA	Ibn ül-Emin, Maliye 4122
1180/1766–7	BBA	Cevdet, Maliye 1245
1201/1787–8	BBA	Ali Emiri, I Abdülhamid 10161
	TKS	E. 1095
1208/1793–4	TKS	E. 5637
1212/1797–8	M. R. X. Estève, 'Mémoire sur les finances de l'Égypte', *Description de l'Égypte*, 1st edn., *État Moderne*, vol. i, pp. 299–398: 2nd edn., vol. xii, pp. 41–248.	

In addition the archives possess more general statements of the total annual revenue and expenditure which were sent to Istanbul each year along with the *irsaliye* shipments.[1] Modern budgetary procedures were inaugurated only under Muḥammad ʿAlī, and the regular annual budgets which were compiled hereafter are preserved in full in the Turkish section of the Citadel archives.

(*c*) *Departmental accounts*

It should be noted that the Cairo archives possesses only one complete account of the Treasury budget in Ottoman times, that for the year 1094/1683–4, so it must be assumed that these were compiled primarily for dispatch to Istanbul along with the *hazine*. The bulk of the Citadel financial records consists of the annual registers of certain Treasury departments, each of which was in charge of specific revenues and expenditures:

1. *Land taxes*. Within the Treasury, assignment of the urban and rural tax-farms, collection of their taxes from the *multazims*, and distribution of the revenues to provide for the specified Treasury expenditures were handled by a number of different departments. Each of these kept its own account books, which were summarized in quarterly and annual registers of *muqāṭaʿa* revenues from all sources compiled by the *Ruzname* department of the Treasury.[2] These registers contain the accounts of each *muqāṭaʿa*, the villages

[1] Listed in Shaw, *Financial organization*, pp. 400–1.
[2] Ibid., pp. 343–6, 355–62.

included in each, the tax-farmers holding *iltizāms* to share in its land taxes, and the total taxes which they owed and paid to the Treasury each year. The Citadel archives have approximately 1,500 of these registers, called *Dafātir iltizāmāt al-wilāyāt al-qibliyya wa'l-baḥriyya*, covering the years from 1069/1658 to 1223/1808. There is a separate series of approximately 1,000 registers under the same title running from 1223 to 1270/1853, in which the gradual disappearance of the tax-farm system and rise of a centralized tax-gathering organization and private land ownership can be traced. The series entitled *Dafātir uṣūl wilāyāt* comprises 170 registers, running from 1237/1821 to the end of the nineteenth century, containing the records of the centralized tax-gathering organization built up in place of the tax-farm system. These registers give much more detailed accounts of the individual taxes paid by each village than do the tax-farm registers, which are principally records of what the tax-farmers paid the Treasury, not what they were paid by the cultivators.[1] The tax-farmers' records themselves, for the Ottoman period at least, have largely disappeared, although miscellaneous bits and pieces can be found among the various document collections in Cairo.

2. *Taxes on urban sources of wealth.* All the urban sources of wealth belonging to the Treasury, such as market taxes, customs duties, and the like were also organized in *muqāṭa'a* units, but these were assigned also as fiefs (*timar*) or directly to salaried agents (*emins*), as well as tax-farms. Regardless of the manner in which their administration was assigned, the Treasury revenues from them were recorded in common registers classified as *Dafātir iltizāmāt al-jamārik wa-iltizāmāt ḍarā'ib mutafarriqa*, of which approximately two hundred have been found running from 1123/1711 to 1245/1829. These registers list the sources of revenue included in each *muqāṭa'a*, their holders, the total taxes owed for each, the portion of these taxes allowed to be deducted locally to meet local expenses (*mukhrijāt*), and the amounts actually sent to the Treasury each year. There are almost no records of the customs duties and taxes actually levied on trade, commerce, and industry by the holders of these *muqāṭa'as*.[2]

3. *Other sources of revenue.* The most important Treasury revenues collected directly from individuals were the *kuşufiye-i kebir* taxes levied on high administrative officials and the *jizye* poll-taxes on non-Muslims. However, while information concerning these revenues can be pieced together from various sources, no regular series of registers has as yet been uncovered for either of them.

4. *Salary registers.* The bulk of Treasury expenditure went to the salaries and wages paid to the officials in the Ottoman hierarchy of government and to the officers and soldiers of the military corps. These are recorded in a series of approximately 1,800 registers held by the Citadel archives, covering the

[1] Idem, 'Cairo's archives', pp. 62–63; Deny, *Sommaire*, pp. 182–4, 199–207.

[2] Shaw, *Financial organization*, pp. 101–33, 362–90; idem, 'Cairo's archives', pp. 62–63.

years from 1083/1672 to 1307/1889 under the title *Dafātir jarāya wa-ʿalīq*, and giving the name and rank of each official and soldier together with the salary and rations to which he was entitled by virtue of his rank and position. These registers are invaluable in indicating the organization and state of the various military corps and administrative groups as well as the extent to which the various positions were held by persons sent from Istanbul and by local men representing the Mamluk parties. The pensions (sing. *waẓīfa*) paid to retired soldiers are included in the corps' salary registers; those paid to persons of religious occupation and intent are indicated in a series of approximately one hundred registers called *Defter-i murattabat*, running from 1092/1681 to 1256/1840.[1]

5. *Other expenditures*. The Treasury's miscellaneous expenditures in Egypt for the maintenance of irrigation systems, roads, and the like and to provide for the costs of maintaining forts, bribing Arab tribes, and taking other measures to maintain security were deducted as *mukhrijāt* from the land-tax collections, and are itemized as such in the *muqāṭaʿa* registers mentioned before. Separate registers itemize the pensions, wages, and expenditures for food and other supplies sent to the Holy Cities, but these have not been fully arranged and catalogued. Finally, the expenditures for provisions and supplies sent to Istanbul are itemized in the general account books and *irsaliye* registers, but no separate accounts have been found to the present time.

6. *Financial orders and reports*. Important financial materials are included in the general political and administrative order registers and document collections previously mentioned. However, in addition to these there are special financial collections which can be consulted for this purpose. For the years preceding 1800, the Kâmil Kepeci and *Maliyeden müdevvere* collections at the *Başbakanlık Arşivi* contain numerous order registers of the Imperial Treasury of Istanbul, and these include considerable material on financial affairs in Egypt.[2]

In Cairo there are no registers of orders and decrees devoted specifically to financial matters before the nineteenth century. However, there are 26,559 financial documents of various kinds catalogued in seven registers emanating from the *Ruzname* department of the Treasury, principally from the seventeenth to the mid-nineteenth centuries.[3] The Abdin archives possess approximately 260 registers of orders concerning the Treasury (*Hazine*) and Financial Council (*Maliye Divanı*) during the nineteenth century, in addition to approximately 15,000 catalogued financial documents of various kinds.[4] It should be noted that most of the financial documents for the nineteenth century are among those in the *Ruzname* collection at the Citadel, rather than at Abdin.

[1] Shaw, *Financial organization*, pp. 184–224, 391–8; idem, 'Cairo's archives', p. 63.

[2] Sertoğlu, pp. 62–67, 72–74, 83; Shaw, 'Archival sources', pp. 3–4.

[3] Deny, *Sommaire*, pp. 190–213, 533–48.

[4] Ibid., pp. 393–414.

3. *Judicial materials*

The most important, but by far least exploited, archival materials concerning Egypt's economic and social life as well as its religious affairs, are those found in its *Sharī'a* courts, in particular the central court archives at the *Maḥkama li'l-Aḥwāl al-Shakhṣiyya* in Cairo. Most of the court registers are arranged chronologically in fifteen separate series, running from the sixteenth to the nineteenth centuries. Three series cover matters dealt with by the central court (*Maḥkamat al-Bāb al-'Ālī*), one concerning general matters, one concerning inheritance and property settlements for members of the military corps (*al-Qisma al-'Askariyya*), and the third (*al-Qisma al-'Arabiyya*) registering the same matters for civilians. The remaining thirteen series comprise the records of the various local courts in Cairo and vicinity.[1]

4. *Published archival materials*

Only a very small number of official Ottoman documents concerning Egypt have been published. Selim I's correspondence with the Mamluk rulers and officials as well as documents recording his successful invasion of Egypt are included in Ahmed Feridun, *Munsha'āt al-Salāṭīn* (Istanbul 1274/1857–8). Many of the *fermans* in the Cairo archives were published and translated by the grand rabbi of Cairo, Haïm Nahoum (Ḥayyim Naḥūm), in *Recueil de firmans impériaux ottomans adressés aux valis et aux khédives d'Égypte, 1006 H.–1322 H. (1597 J.C.–1904 J.C.)* (Cairo, 1934). Most of the figures contained in the financial registers are reproduced in tabular form and analysed in S. J. Shaw, *The financial and administrative organization and development of Ottoman Egypt, 1517–1798* (Princeton, N.J., 1962).

In the nineteenth century the official Egyptian government newspaper, *al-Waqā'i 'al-Miṣriyya*, was published primarily in Turkish from its inception in 1828 until the middle of the century, and it contains most of the important orders and decrees issued by the Egyptian rulers during that time. The first attempt to publish the Turkish correspondence of Muḥammad 'Alī was compiled by the secretary of Muḥammad 'Alī's Imperial Council, Mustafa Hayret Efendi al-Siwasi, *Insha-ı Hayret Efendi: Riyaz-ı küteba ve hiyaz-ı üdeba* (Būlāq, 1241/1825). The collection includes 594 letters and orders divided by subject into (*a*) letters to and from the Ottoman court and harem (*b*) correspondence with the grand vezir and *şeyhülislam* in Istanbul (*c*) letters to Ottoman governors, in particular those of Crete, Tunis, and Algiers (*d*) letters to judges and religious personages in Egypt, and (*e*) letters to Egyptian officials and agents in Istanbul. A similar collection, but mainly of *résumés* rather than entire documents, was published by G. Talamas Bey, *Recueil de la correspondance de Mohamed Aly, Khédive d'Égypte* (Cairo, 1913), but its publication was forbidden at the last minute and only a few copies

[1] Shaw, 'Cairo's archives', pp. 66–67.

survive. Finally, Shawqī ʿAṭāllāh al-Jamāl, an Egyptian scholar, recently has published documents translated from Turkish as well as Arabic ones concerning Egypt's role in the Red Sea during the nineteenth century, as *al-Wathā'iq al-ta'rīkhiyya li-siyāsat Miṣr fi'l-Baḥr al-Aḥmar, 1863–1879* (Cairo, Egyptian Society of Historical Studies, 1959). It should be noted that Asad Rustum's two collections, *Materials for a corpus of Arabic documents relating to the history of Syria under Mehemet Ali Pasha* (Beirut, 1930–4) and *Les campagnes d'Ibrahim Pacha en Syrie et en Asie Mineure 1831–1840* (Heliopolis, n.d.), published under subsidy by the late dynasty, ignore entirely the Turkish documents available on the subject in the Cairo archives, and are highly selective even among the Arabic ones, so they should be used with caution.

Enver Ziya Karal has published Turkish orders and decrees concerning Egypt in his two collections on the reign of Sultan Selīm III (1789–1807), *Selim III' ün hatt-ı hümayunları* (Ankara, 1942) and *Selim III' ün hatt-ı hümayunları—Nizam-i cedit—1789–1807* (Ankara, 1946). The earlier volume contains a number of Turkish documents on Bonaparte's invasion of Egypt (pp. 47–87), and the struggles among the Egyptian Mamluk beys after the departure of the British and French troops (pp. 140–52); the latter includes numerous sections on Egypt in Selim III's various internal reform documents. A large number of important Ottoman documents concerning Muḥammad ʿAlī's rise to power and rule in Egypt have been published in the following works: Ali Fuat, 'Mısır valisi Meḥmed Ali Pāṣa', *Türk Tarih Encümeni Mecmuası*, no. 19/96, pp. 64–128; Kâmil Pasha, *Tarih-i siyasi-i devlet-i aliye-i Osmaniye* (Istanbul, 1327/1325); *Majmūʿat al-farmānāt al-shāhāniyya al-ṣādira ilā wulāt Miṣr wa-khudaywīhā* (Cairo, 1933); and Şinasi Altundağ, *Kavalalı Mehmet Ali Paşa isyanı—Mısır meselesi, 1831–1841*, I. Kısım (Ankara, 1945). Turkish materials concerning Ottoman-Egyptian relations during the early Tanzimat period are published in Reşat Kaynar, *Mustafa Reşit Paşa ve Tanzimat* (Ankara, 1954), while documents concerning these relations between 1885 and 1915 are in the memoirs of Said Pasha, *Said Paşanın hâtirâtı* (Istanbul, 1328), and in an official Ottoman Red Book on the Egyptian question published at the start of the First World War, Hariciye Nezareti, *Mısır meselesi* (Istanbul, 1334). Documents concerning Ottoman-Egyptian relations before and during the First World War are included, in full or part, in Yusuf Hikmet Bayur, *Türk inkılâbı tarihi* (3 vols. in 7, Istanbul, 1940–57).

5. *Availability and use of the archival materials*

The Ottoman archives in Istanbul are now freely available to scholars wishing to use them to study any aspect of Ottoman history up to 1914. The *Başbakanlık* and *Hariciye* archives are open to foreigners who apply to the respective ministries through the intermediary of their embassies, while the *Topkapı Saray* archives and library, as well as other libraries in Istanbul, can be used on application to their directors. In all three archives, most of the historic materials for the years up to 1800 have been catalogued, although in the *Topkapı Saray*, a commission is now in the process of making a new and more detailed catalogue. The *Hariciye* and *Topkapı Saray* materials can easily be located in subject indexes available in the students' rooms. However, the *Başbakanlık* materials are catalogued only by reign of sultan or general subject, and considerable time is required to read through the hundreds of catalogues in order to find all relevant materials.

In Egypt the situation is somewhat different. In the Citadel, all the financial registers have been arranged together by date, regardless of their departments of origin. However, while many of the more important orders and other documents were registered in several catalogues over the years (Deny, pp. 187–213), a tendency of the successive directors to apply new numbering systems to them has left the older catalogues of little use. In addition to this, the vast majority of the documents are not at all catalogued or available, and little work is being done to remedy this. The nineteenth-century materials at the Abdin palace were carefully catalogued and inventoried in the 1920s and 1930s (see Deny, pp. 3–33, 231–574), but unfortunately over the years the renumbering of old materials and acquisition of new collections, along with the general difficulties suffered by the archives during the Revolution have left the collection badly in need of new catalogues. Under the enlightened direction of the Archives Commission these are now being compiled, and it is to be hoped that it will not be too long before they will be available for public use.

The greatest difficulties facing most scholars wishing to make use of the Ottoman archival materials result less from any unavailability than they do from the unusual difficulty of their language and script. Even for those knowing Ottoman Turkish, its complex and specialized administrative language requires special training. Moreover, the *divani* and *siyaqat* scripts in which most of the materials are written were known only to a few, even in Ottoman times. Some studies have been made of Ottoman palaeography, epigraphy, and diplomatics, but these are of little assistance to persons beginning their work in the archives. In addition, there are no reference works indicating the meanings of the numerous special symbols and marks used by the Ottoman scribes, and while some historical dictionaries of technical terms are available, considerably more work needs to be done in this field before the research scholar will be able to use such materials with full confidence.

III. OTHER TURKISH SOURCES

Administrative and financial records, however important they are as authoritative indications of the structure of Ottoman government and society, are still only the bones of history, the bare outlines written by and for persons fully educated in the Ottoman system and lacking the stimulus or desire to explain it. Much of the real meat of Ottoman history in Egypt is provided by the orders and reports already indicated and also by various official and unofficial chronicles and descriptions which have been produced over the centuries.

1. *Chronicles.* All the Ottoman chronicles devoted considerable attention to events and conditions in Egypt, from Hoca Saduddin's *Tāj al-tawārīkh* (Istanbul, 1863), and Lûtfi Pasha's *Tevarih-i al-i Osman* (Istanbul, 1925), which contain material on Selim I's conquest, up to and including the work of Ahmed Lûtfi, who chronicled much of the nineteenth century.[1] Since their accounts were often based on personal as well as official reports from Ottoman officials and others returning from Cairo, they often provide important information not found elsewhere.

In addition to the general chronicles there also are a number of important Ottoman works devoted more or less specifically to Egypt.[2] The conquest itself is described in a number of *Selimnames*, by Kalkandelenli Sücudi,[3] Amasyalı Keshfı Mehmed Çelebi (d. 931/1524),[4] Celalzade Nişancı Koca Mustafa Çelebi (d. 975/1567),[5] Süheyli Efendi,[6] and Sa'dī b. 'Abd al-Muta-'ālī.[7] Works specifically devoted to Selim's defeats of the Mamluks and occupation of the country are: the anonymous *Fethname-i diyar-ı Arab*,[8] *Tarih-i feth-i Mısır* by Shiri Ali, son of one of Selim's leading ministers,[9] *Tuḥfat al-ghuzāt*, written in the seventeenth century by Ahmed Hamdi,[10] and *Feth-i Mısır tarihi*, by Yūsuf b. Meḥmed Milevi, written in 1127/1715.[11]

[1] For a list of the principal Ottoman historians and the years covered by their works, see S. J. Shaw, 'The Ottoman view of the Balkans', *The Balkans in transition*, ed. C. and B. Jelavich (Berkeley, California, 1963), pp. 76–77. More complete discussions of the Ottoman historians can be found in Franz Babinger, *Die Geschichtsschreiber der Osmanen und ihre Werke* (Leipzig, 1927), Bursalı Mehmed Tahir, *Osmanlı müellifleri* (Istanbul, 1915–28), and *Istanbul kütüphaneleri tarih-cografya yazmaları katalogları* (T. C. Maarif Vekilliği, Istanbul, 1943–4).

[2] See also H. Jansky, 'Beiträge zur osmanischen Geschichtsschreibung über Ägypten', *Der Islam*, vol. xxi (1933), pp. 269–78.

[3] MSS. copies in: Istanbul, Topkapı Saray, Revan 1284/1; Vienna, Nationalbibliothek H.O. 30 (Flügel, ii. 215); Paris, Bibliothèque Nationale, Suppl. Turc. 1166 (Blochet, ii. 186).

[4] MSS. copies: Istanbul, Süleymaniye Library, Esad Efendi 2147; Vienna, National-bibliothek, H.O. 31 (Flügel, ii. 211); see *Osmanlı müellifleri*, vol. iii, p. 122; Babinger, p. 50.

[5] MSS. copies: Istanbul, Topkapı Saray, Revan 1274, Bağdad Köşk 196, and Hazine 1415 (Fehmi Edhem Karatay, *Topkapı sarayı müzesi kütüphanesi Türkce yazmaları katalogu* (Istanbul, 1961), vol. i, pp. 208–9); London, British Museum, Add. 7848 (Rieu, 50–51). See also *Osmanlı müellifleri*, vol. iii, p. 57; Babinger, p. 103.

[6] MS. copy: Paris, Bibliothèque Nationale, Suppl. Turc. 812 (Blochet, ii. 68).

[7] MSS. copies: Istanbul, Topkapı Saray, Revan 1277; Hazine 1424; Paris, Bibliothèque Nationale, Paris, Ancien Fonds Turc. 74 (Blochet, i. 28); see Babinger, pp. 60–61.

[8] MS. in Istanbul, Nuruosmaniye Library, 4087.

[9] MS. in Istanbul, Topkapı Saray, Emanet hazinesi 1433/2, fols. 218b–267b. Despite the title, the book also includes information on Selim's life, his struggles with his father and campaigns in Anatolia before moving against Egypt.

[10] MS. in Bursa, Orhan Gazi Library 1022, fols. 52a–91b on Egypt.

[11] MS. in London, British Museum, Or. 3211 (Rieu, 59–60). This is a translation of the Arabic work of Aḥmad b. Zunbul, with considerable additions to show the Ottoman side of the campaign. The Arabic original was published in Cairo in 1861–2.

Even more important for students of Ottoman Egypt's political and administrative history are a series of Turkish chronicles compiled in Egypt by officials, usually but not always at the request of the Ottoman governors of the time.

The first and, in many ways, most important of these is ʿAbd al-Ṣamad b. Sayyid ʿAlī b. Da'ūd al-Diyārbakrī, *Dhikr al-khulafā' wa'l-mulūk al-Miṣriyya*, covering the years from 901/1495 and 948/1542.[1] The author was a member of the Ottoman religious class, came to Egypt with Selim I, and remained in the country after that time, serving several times as *qāḍī* of Damietta, and also as adviser of Da'ūd Pasha, governor between 1538 and 1549. It was at the instigation of the latter that he translated into Turkish the history of Egypt by Ḥasan b. Ṭūlūn, covering the years to 904/1498, and then added his own observations for the years up to and including the first half of his master's reign, to 947/1541. The author's continuation provides an extremely detailed account of Egypt immediately before, during, and after the conquest. It more than supplements Ibn Iyās's Arabic chronicle for the same period, and continues for an additional twenty-seven years beyond the conclusion of the latter. Since the author spent a considerable time in Damietta, he provides useful detailed information on the Ottoman campaigns in the Delta against the unconquered bedouin and mamluk bands as well as efforts to restore the lands to cultivation, confiscate the Mamluk fiefs, and establish a regular system of administering the land taxes of the country. His stay in Cairo is reflected in the information provided about the revolt against Ottoman rule led by Aḥmad Pasha in 1524–5, while his judicial interests are manifest in materials concerning matters of jurisprudence and landholding rights.

Meḥmed b. Yūsuf al-Khallāq, *Tarih-i Mısır-ı Kahire* chronicles the years from 923/1517 to 1128/1716.[2] The work is devoted primarily to military and political events, and is especially good on the conflicts among the various Mamluk factions and between them and the Ottoman governors after 1680. ʿAbd al-Karīm b. ʿAbd al-Raḥmān, *Tarih-i Mısır*[3] also starts in 1517 and goes to 1094/1682, with a short introduction on Egypt since the Arab conquest. While it is basically also a political history, since the author was Arabic secretary in the Cairo treasury from 1699 to 1705, he includes considerably

[1] MSS. copies: Istanbul, Millet Library, Tarih 596; London, British Museum, Add. 7846 (Rieu, pp. 66–67); Cairo, *Dār al-Kutub*, *Ta'rīkh Turkī* 190 (*Fihrist*, 238); Gotha, *Geschichte* 156 (Pertsch, p. 128). See Babinger, pp. 58–59; Shaw, 'The Ottoman archives as a source for Egyptian history', *JAOS*, vol. lxxxiii (1963), pp. 448–9.

[2] MSS. copies: Vienna, Nationalbibliothek, H.O. 37 (Flügel, ii. 161–2); Paris, Bibliothèque Nationale, Suppl. Turc. 512 (Blochet, i. 378–9); Istanbul University Library, T.Y. 628; Saint Petersburg, Oriental Institute, MS. 58 (Rosen, 30). See also Babinger, pp. 244–5; Brockelman, *GAL*, vol. ii, p. 298.

[3] MSS. copies: Istanbul, Süleymaniye Library, Hacı Mahmud Efendi 4877; Istanbul, Millet Library, Hekimoglu Ali Paşa 705; London, British Museum, Add. MS. 7878 (Rieu, 69–70); Paris, Bibliothèque Nationale, Suppl. Turc. 1098 (Blochet, ii. 162–3). See also Babinger, p. 243; *Osmanlı müellifleri*, vol. iii, p. 182.

more financial and economic history than did Meḥmed b. Yūsuf. Maḥmūd b. ʿAbdallāh b. Meḥmed al-Baghdādī, *Tarih-i Mısır*[1] provides an abridgement and translation of the Arabic *Ḥusn al-muḥāḍara* of al-Suyūṭī as far as the Ottoman conquest, and then continues it to 1090/1679. Approximately half the work concerns Ottoman Egypt, and while the political chronicle is little more than a list of rulers, there is useful information on Cairo's civil and military organization as well as descriptions of its mosques, *madrasas*, and other monuments of interest. Abdullah Çelebi Ridwan Paşazade, *Tarih-i Mısır* is a history of Egypt from earliest times to 1058/1648.[2] The last half of the work includes a description of the country in Ottoman times and of the Ottoman campaigns to occupy the country, but its political history is not as detailed and valuable as that given in the previous works cited.

There also are a number of Turkish works describing specific events or periods. The *Tarih-i Mısır* by Yusuf Efendi, scribe of the Circassian corps, describes events between 1629 and 1631, and is particularly good on the struggles among the military corps and the beginning of the rebirth of Mamluk power in Egypt.[3] *Vekayi-i Ali Paşa*, by Kelami, describes the efforts of Silāḥdār ʿAlī Pasha to quell Mamluk misrule and oppression in 1601–2.[4] *Tevarih-i salatin-i al-i Osman* by Katib Ali Efendi,[5] scribe in the Ottoman palace for thirty years in the mid-seventeenth century, and subsequently secretary to the governor of Egypt between 1644 and 1646, describes events in Egypt during that time. Muṣṭafā b. Aḥmad ʿAlīzāde (d. 1008/1599) in *Ḥālāt al-Qāhira min al-ʿādāt al-zāhira*[6] describes events which he witnessed in Egypt in 1567–9, when he served there as secretary to Lala Muṣṭafā Pasha, commander of the expedition to the Yemen at that time, and again in 1595–7, when he served as director (*defterdar*) of the Treasury of Egypt. In addition, he provides a useful description of Egypt's treasury and its tax system. *Al-Rawḍa al-zahiyya fī taʾrīkh al-umarāʾ al-Miṣriyya al-ʿUthmāniyya* by Meḥmed b. Meḥmed Kātibzāde al-Miṣrī, describes events in Egypt between

[1] MSS. copies: London, British Museum, Add. 7861 (Rieu, 69): Vienna Nationalbibliothek, Mxt. 691 (Flügel, ii. 145); Paris, Bibliothèque Nationale, Suppl. Turc. 173 (Blochet, i. 247); Cairo, *Dār al-Kutub, Taʾrīkh Turkī* 33 (*Fihrist*, 175).

[2] MSS. copies: London, British Museum, Or. 1132 (Rieu, 68), Add. 24956 (Rieu, 69); Vienna, Nationalbibliothek, H.O. 6 (Flügel, ii. 90–91); Paris, Bibliothèque Nationale, Suppl. Turc. 1041 (Blochet, ii. 143), Suppl. Turc. 1043 (Blochet, ii. 143–4); Gotha, MS. 157 (Pertsch, 129–30); Cairo, *Dār al-Kutub, Taʾrīkh Turkī* 17 (*Fihrist*, 175); *Taʾrīkh Turkī* 8 (*Fihrist*, 175); Istanbul University, T.Y. 1505, T.Y. 6038; Topkapı Saray, Revan 1141 (Karatay, i. 196), Revan 1412 (Karatay, i. 197), Revan 1413, Revan 1428; Istanbul, Süleymaniye Library, Hamidiye 900, Murad Molla 1416, Fatih 4363; Istanbul, Archaeological Museum 1338; Ankara University, Dil ve Tarih-Cografya Fakültesi Library, Mustafa Con MS. 1/44895, Ismail Saib Sencer MS. 2239; Bursa, Burhanuddin Library, MS. 9391. See also Babinger, pp. 176–7; *Osmanlı müellifleri*, vol. iii, pp. 103–4.

[3] Süleymaniye Library, Esad Efendi MS. 2148 (55 fols.).

[4] Süleymaniye Library, Halet Efendi MS. 612 (148 fols.).

[5] Ankara University, Dil ve Tarih-Cografya Fakültesi Library, Muzaffer Ozak 1050 (82 fols.).

[6] Istanbul, Süleymaniye Library, Mehmediye 5427; Usküdar, Selim Aga MS. 757; Cairo, *Dār al-Kutub, Taʾrīkh Turkī* 146 (*Fihrist*, 197). See Babinger, p. 133.

1704 and 1719, and concentrates in particular on the struggles among the Mamluk parties and confederations.[1] *Ta'rīkh al-Waqā'i'* by al-Amīr Ahmed Bey, gives an account of events in Egypt between November 1786 and August 1787.[2] *Ta'rīkh al-waqā'i'*, by Mehmed Şefik Efendi, describes events in Cairo from December 1698 to October 1700.[3]

The Ottoman role in the campaigns against the French Expedition to Egypt (1798–1801) is described in the following works: Hasan Izzet, *Ziyaname*,[4] Mehmed Emin Karahanzade, *Mısır seferi hakkında tarihçe*,[5] which concern the campaigns of grand vezir Gürcü Yusuf Ziya Pasha, and *Gazavat-ı Hüseyn Paşa*,[6] concerning the naval campaign led by Küçük Hüseyn Pasha, grand admiral of the Ottoman fleet.

2. *Descriptions*. No more valuable sources can be found than those describing Ottoman Egypt written by contemporary travellers and residents, but these, like personal archives, are singularly lacking, in Turkish as well as in Arabic. By far the most important material of this kind which is available is the travel report of Evliya Çelebi (1614–83), *Seyahatname* (Istanbul, 1898–1938), of which volume x (1938) is devoted almost entirely to Egypt as it appeared at the time of his visit, at the close of the seventeenth century. While there are doubts as to the reliability of much of his information concerning south-eastern Europe in the earlier volumes, all the material concerning Egypt has been checked against archival and other sources and found accurate. His detailed descriptions of the cities, markets, and public buildings are unmatched in any other work concerning the Ottoman period, as are his statements concerning the governmental and judicial administration in the country. It should be noted, however, that the published edition is defective—words, numbers, and often entire sentences were omitted or misread by the editors, and it is imperative for researchers to make use of one of the manuscript copies of this work, if at all possible.[7]

The only other Turkish-language description of any value is a short but extremely interesting account compiled by Cezzar Ahmed Pasha under the

[1] Cairo, *Dār al-Kutub, Ta'rīkh Turkī* 152 (*Fihrist*, 90) Istanbul, Topkapı Saray, Ruşen Eşref MS. 2.

[2] Vatican, Turco 60 (Rossi, 45–47).

[3] Cairo, *Dār al-Kutub, Ta'rīkh Turkī* 75 (*Fihrist*, 177), 68 fols.

[4] MSS. copies: Istanbul University Library, T.Y. 6115; Istanbul, Millet Library, Ali Emiri Tarih 413; Paris, Bibliothèque Nationale, Suppl. Turc. 1027 (Blochet, ii. 136).

[5] Istanbul University Library, T.Y. 6114 (26 fols.). See *Osmanlı müellifleri*, vol. iii, p. 49; Babinger, p. 333 n.

[6] Cairo, *Dār al-Kutub, Ta'rīkh Turkī* 195 (*Fihrist*, 212).

[7] The oldest and best copy of vol. x is found in the Bağdad Köşk collection of the Topkapı Saray Library, Istanbul, MS. 303 (copy date 1155/1742–3), another excellent copy is in the Yıldız collection of the Istanbul University Library, T.Y. 5973 (457 fols., Neskh). For detailed studies of his life and personality, see Dr. Meşkure Eren, *Evliya Çelebi Seyahatnamesi birinci cildinin kaynakları üzerinde bir araştırma* (Istanbul, 1960); Cavit Baysun, 'Evliya Çelebi', *Islam Ansiklopedisi*, vol. iv, pp. 400–12; J. von Hammer, *Narrative of Travels in Europe, Asia and Africa in the Seventeenth Century by Evliyá Efendí* (London, 1834–50).

name *Nizamname-i Mısır* (ed. and tr. Stanford J. Shaw as *Ottoman Egypt in the Eighteenth Century* (Cambridge, Mass., 1962)). Originally an Egyptian Mamluk, Cezzar had broken with his master ʿAlī Bey al-Kabīr and fled from the country to Syria, where he joined the Ottoman service. In 1785, while serving as governor of Syria, he compiled the report in response to a request by the Imperial Divan for information concerning that country preparatory to the expedition led by Gazi Hasan Pasha to end the virtual rebellion of the Mamluk leaders of the time, Murād Bey and Ibrāhīm Bey. Although much of the report is merely a formal description of the country, its real value comes in the insights it gives into Egypt's social system, people, and military organization.[1]

[1] The author and date are not mentioned in the manuscript. While some of the historical events referred to in the report concern Egypt and Syria in the 1770s, the fact that it was *submitted* in 1785 and written by Cezzar Pasha are clearly documented in the official chronicle of Ahmed Vasif, Istanbul Archaeological Museum, MS. 355, fols. 210a–13b, summarized also in Cevdet (*Tertib-i cedid*), vol. iii, pp. 246–7.

Ottoman Archival Materials on Nineteenth-century Egyptian History

ŞINASI ALTUNDAĞ

GENERALLY speaking, the archival materials in Turkey can be found in four places:

1. The archive of the Prime Minister's Office (*Başbakanlık Arşivi*),
2. The archive of the Topkapı Palace (*Topkapı Sarayı Arşivi*),
3. The archive of the Ministry of Foreign Affairs (*Hariciye Arşivi*),
4. The *Qāḍīs'* Registers (*Şer'iyye Sicilleri*), which were provincial archives and which were under the administration of the *qāḍīs*.

1. The archive of the Prime Minister's Office contains the most important collections, from the point of view of both the significance of its materials as well as their variety and abundance:

(*a*) *Mısır Mühimme Defterleri* (the registers of important affairs of Egypt). Especially the *defters* numbered 11, 12, 13, 14, 15 are directly connected with our subject. *Defter* 12, for example, contains a document of instructions to Muḥammad 'Alī Pasha, which may be summarized as follows:

> Order to Muḥammad 'Alī Pasha, who was appointed governor of Egypt, following his appointment as the governor of Jedda. . . . The disturbances in Egypt have been troubling the people there and the peace and security have been lost. We know of your capacity and industry and also we are informed that all the Egyptian religious scholars and the relatives of the Prophet (*sādāt*) are grateful to you. Therefore we leave Egypt in your charge. Hold the country under discipline; protect the poor; support the two holy cities (Mecca and Medina); make sure that the pilgrims and the merchants travel in peace and safety. As we have given you this post, which will attract the envy of even the vezirs, so that you could open the road to Yanbu' and send soldiers and arms to the holy cities, do not even sleep, but work day and night for this purpose.

The document is dated in the first part of Rabī' I 1220/May–June 1805: cf. Cevdet, *Tarih*, vol. viii, p. 26.

(*b*) *Irade Defterleri* (the registers of the imperial orders). These are two registers, the first one dealing with the second phase of the Egyptian problem (1839–81); that is, the retreat of Ibrāhīm Pasha from Syria, the character and the latest situation of the Egyptian problem, the decisions taken concerning this, etc. It also contains correspondence on the amount of tax collected in Egypt, etc. The second register deals especially with the Suez Canal. To these documents one can add other *irade defterleri* documents.

(*c*) *Hatt-ı hümayunlar* (the imperial rescripts). A great part of these were kept in special boxes, classified according to subject-matter. At present they are classified in a different way, being given serial numbers together with a brief summary of each. The desired document can be found from the 'special register' by looking at the number of the boxes. The following boxes must especially be considered in connexion with our subject:

Box no.	The name of the subject
69	*Vahhabî meselesi* (The Wahhābī problem)
70–73	*Mısır'ın evvelki vak'ası* (the first Egyptian occurrence)
74, 75	*Mısır'ın vak'a-i ahiresi* (the last Egyptian occurrence)
76	*Akka hakkında* (Document on Acre)
78	*Selim Paşa* (*Şam*) (Selim Pasha, governor of Damascus)
156–8	*Mora vuku'atı* (the Greek revolt in Morea)
215	*Tahmisçi vak'ası* (Tahmisçi's revolt against the Sublime Porte)
220	*Jezayir ve Mısır* (Algiers and Egypt)
223	*Mısır'a dair* (Documents on Egypt, No. 50 007–50 758)
231	*Vahhabîler* (the Wahhābīs)

Apart from these, the archive contains some special classes made at various times and in these many documents can also be found in connexion with our subject. For instance, the classes of Ibn ül-Emin Mahmud Kemal, Kâmil Kepeci, and Ali Emiri. The archive also contains special registers concerning the finances of Egypt.

2. Topkapı Palace Archive: the documents here have been classified according to the alphabetic order of subject-matter. At the present we are in possession of two pamphlets prepared in accordance with this rule of classification and published under the name of *Topkapı sarayi müzesi arşivi klavuzu*. The first of these pamphlets, published in 1938, includes the letters A, B, C, and also contains photographic reproductions of fourteen documents (see, e.g., Amedî Efendi No. E—Evraq—4143). The second stops with the letter H. The Topkapı Palace Archive documents are, however, being studied anew and are undergoing a reclassification in our day.

3. Foreign (*Hariciye*) Archive: the great majority of the documents here are in French. Some of the important ones among them were, however, translated into Turkish. It is possible that other such Turkish versions may also exist in the Prime Ministry Archive and the Topkapı Palace Archive. Among the folders the one numbered 614 is important. It contains such important documents as letters from the king of England and British ministers brought back by Namık Pasha who was sent as special envoy to London.[1]

[1] See Şinasi Altundağ, *Kavalalı Mehmet Ali Paşa isyanı, Mısır-meselesı* (*1831–41*), I. Kısım (Ankara, 1945), p. 10; idem, 'Mehmet Ali isyanında yardım için Namık paşa'nın Ingitereye gõnderilmesi', *Tarih Vesikaları Dergisi*, nos. 12, 14; idem, 'Kavalalı Mehmet Ali Paşa

4. The *Qāḍīs*' Registers, which were recorded by the *qāḍīs*, were tantamount to provincial archives of the Ottoman Empire. As the Islamic religion was in reality religion plus state, not only the application and control of religious laws and precepts but also those of the laws and regulations based upon local traditions and usages (a form of law which underwent great development in the Ottoman Empire), were entrusted to the *qāḍī*. Thus, in the Ottoman Empire, the *qāḍī* was both the executive officer and supervisor of all the regulations related to administrative, financial, political, and cultural institutions. He was entrusted with the enactment and registration of all orders issuing from the capital. The *qāḍī* was therefore charged with the setting up and upkeep of the Ottoman provincial archives. In addition to daily local incidents and court cases, all orders sent from the capital, including pacts (capitulations), laws, and new regulations, were recorded in the *qāḍīs*' registers. The majority of these registers were written in Turkish, documents concerning religious matters such as *waqf* and *'itq* being in Arabic.

These *Qāḍīs*' Registers also contain many documents concerning our present subject. See, e.g. Mevlana Museum, Konya, Register No. 72, p. 103; No. 74, p. 66, 229, and also Kastamonu Museum, Tahmisçi Revolt. As these latter have been well classified it is very easy to consult them.[1]

isyanında Namık Paşa'nın yardım talep et. üzere 1832 senesinda memuriyet-i mahsusa ile Londra'ya gönderilmesi', *Belleten*, nos. 23–24.

[1] Compare Uzunçarşılı, *Tahmisçioglu vak'ası*, and S. Altundağ, *Kavalalı Mehmet Ali Paşa isyanı, Mısır-meselesi (1831–41)*, I. Kısım (Ankara, 1945), pp. 18–30.

Documents pertaining to the Egyptian Question in the Yıldız Collection of the *Başbakanlık Arşivi*, Istanbul

HASAN ADALI

THE *Başbakanlık Arşivi* in Istanbul contains some of the most important source material of Egyptian history in recent centuries.[1] The relevant documents run into hundreds of thousands. Neglect of this material has resulted in some serious gaps in recent writing on Ottoman Egypt. The material in the Turkish archives is not as well known to Western scholars as it should be.[2] Recently, however, Western scholars have begun to visit and use our archives, and some works based entirely on this material have been published.[3] The *Başbakanlık Arşivi* contains materials which are important not only for Turkey, but also for the territories that were under Ottoman rule.[4] The oldest materials in the archives are almost as old as the Empire; but the documents survive in bulk only from the fifteenth century. In all, the archives contain perhaps more than fifty million items. I wish here to discuss a body of material which has not yet been used. These are the materials relating to Egypt in the Yıldız Archives, the contents of which are still being classified.

The Yıldız Palace was the symbol of a régime.[5] It was the personal residence of the sultans, but it was also the nerve-centre of their government. It contained groups responsible for dealing with the various branches of government; these groups, comprising administration, economics, military affairs, finance, education, religion, and foreign affairs, were placed under trusted servants. Everything depended on the person of the sultan. Abdülhamid II (1876–1909) was by nature extraordinarily suspicious. He demanded information on every conceivable topic, and often decided even the most trivial issues in person. The civil and military authorities in the provinces would frequently refer important problems directly to the Palace; foreign embassies would

[1] In this matter, see Mithat Sertoglu, *Muhteva bakımından Başvekalet Arşivi* (Ankara, 1955).

[2] Bernard Lewis, 'The Ottoman Archives as a source for the history of the Arab lands', *JRAS*, 1951, pp. 139–55. Idem, *Notes and documents from the Turkish Archives* (Jerusalem, Israel, 1952).

[3] S. J. Shaw, *Financial organization* (Princeton, N.J., 1962).

[4] Bernard Lewis, 'The Ottoman archives, a source for European history', *Report on Current Research, Spring 1956* (Washington, 1956), pp. 17–25; also in *Archives*, vol. iv (1960), pp. 226–30.

[5] For Yıldız Palace, see Fuat Ezgü, *Yıldız Sarayı Tarihçesi* (Istanbul, 1962).

enter into direct negotiations. Official negotiations would take place between embassies and the Yıldız Palace, and the official government, i.e. the Sublime Porte, would only be informed afterwards.[1]

The documents accumulated in this thirty-three-year period of Abdülhamid II's autocracy now constitute the *Yıldız Tasnifi* in the *Başbakanlık Arşivi*. There is, however, one serious loss. Abdülhamid also preserved with great care the unofficial reports (*jurnaller*) submitted to him. Classification of these reports began after the reactionary *coup d'état* of April 1909, but this was later abandoned, and many of the documents were destroyed for political reasons. Others passed into private hands, and some of these have been published.[2] Only a small number of these reports are now to be found among the Yıldız papers. The main body of the Yıldız material was classified under forty main headings by a committee set up by order of the Cabinet. Documents regarded as important were separated; the rest were mixed up; and the original grouping was destroyed. Today the whole process has been reversed, and the collection has been reconstituted as it was in the Yıldız Palace. Thus the archives can at last be made available to scholars.

Under Abdülhamid II the Egyptian Question was of great concern to the Ottoman government. Egypt was not entirely separated from the Empire either before or after 1882. The British occupied Egypt, but did not touch Ottoman sovereignty; they merely announced that they would stay in the country as long as they felt it necessary. There are thus many documents relating to Egypt in the Yıldız archive. Abdülhamid was in the habit of grouping documents according to the questions with which they dealt; thus when a question came up again, he could easily inform himself of its antecedents. This habit arose from his determination to be fully aware of all that was going on. The Egyptian Question was one such subject. The relevant documents were systematically assembled in the Egyptian dossier. Some were even collected in bound volumes; e.g. the register relating to Egypt and the Ḥijāz,[3] the four volumes of copies of the minutes of the Council of Ministers relating to the Egyptian Question up to 1889,[4] the register of summaries of *irades* relating to the Egyptian Question from 1839 to 1892,[5] and the minutes of the Special Council.[6] In addition to these there are certain groups of documents in the Yıldız collection of special importance for Egypt; e.g. the correspondence concerning the Egyptian Question in the years 1881–1907 in folder 132, documents from the khedive signed by Tawfīq Pasha and ʿAbbās Ḥilmī Pasha along with some unsigned documents in folder 133,

[1] Osman Nuri, *Abdülhamid-i sani ve devri saltanatı* (Istanbul, 1327), vol. ii, p. 591. E. Z. Karal, *Osmanlı Tarihi* (Ankara, 1962), vol. viii, pp. 89–120.

[2] On the destruction of the Journals, see Asaf Tugay Ibret, *Saray dedikodulari ve II. Abdülhamid'e verilen jurnaller* (Istanbul, 1963).

[3] *Başbakanlık Arşivi, Yıldız*, no. 967 (group 36).

[4] *Yıldız*, no. 2475 (group 36).

[5] *Yıldız*, no. 2476 (group 36).

[6] *Yıldız*, no. 2475 (group 36).

documents written from Yıldız Palace to the khedive in folder 134, documents from the Palace to the commissioner extraordinary, Gazi Ahmet Muhtar Pasha in folder 135, and various signed documents relating to the Egyptian Question in folder 138.[1]

The proper study of these materials, which consist of thousands of pieces, will be a very long task. They cover foreign affairs, economic problems, and some more specific issues, such as the ʿUrābī Pasha Question and the Suez Canal. Taken as a whole, the materials show that the connexion between Egypt and the Ottoman Empire was closer and more regular than has been thought. This is true even after the British occupation. To clarify this point I shall discuss some selected documents.

The first is a telegram sent by the Khedive Ismāʿīl to Abdülhamid on 23 June 1879. The British and French consuls-general in Cairo had delivered an ultimatum requiring Ismāʿīl's abdication in favour of his son.[2] In this telegram, the khedive requested Ottoman protection on the grounds that Egypt was a part of the Ottoman Empire. He himself was merely an official in the sultan's administration; the action of the foreign consuls was an infringement of the rights of the Ottoman state, and it was contrary to the law of nations.[3] However, the Ottoman government complied with the wishes of the British and French, and removed the khedive from office.[4]

My second example is the ʿUrābī Pasha Question. The activities of ʿUrābī Pasha and his nationalist confederates were among the most important phenomena leading up to the British occupation. The combined intervention of France and Britain under the Khedive Tawfīq Pasha had created a strong feeling against the foreigners. ʿUrābī Pasha and his confederates wanted the deposition of the khedive because of his pro-British policy. With a little support from the Ottoman side, this current took shape as a national movement. The idea was to replace Tawfīq Pasha by Ḥalīm Pasha.[5] Tawfīq Pasha knew that the Ottoman government was sympathetic towards Ḥalīm Pasha, and did not, therefore, request Ottoman aid against the local patriots. Instead, he followed the advice of the British and French consuls-general, and announced that he was going to establish a constitutional government in Egypt.

Abdülhamid took up the idea of using the struggle between the khedive and the patriots to bring about the replacement of Tawfīq Pasha by Ḥalīm Pasha. He began to investigate Egyptian affairs. The captain who had collected the letter of the patriotic politician, Maḥmūd Sāmī al-Bārūdī from the journalist Hikmet Efendi, and brought it to Istanbul, was interviewed by

[1] *Yıldız*, no. 424 (*Mısır işleri gurubu*): documents concerning the Egyptian Question.

[2] *Yıldız*, no. 1167 (*Mısır işleri gurubu*): Ismāʿīl Pasha's telegram. See Plate 1.

[3] *Yıldız*, no. 1209 (*Mısır işleri gurubu*): folder of documents relating to the removal of Ismāʿīl Pasha.

[4] Ibid.

[5] *Yıldız*, no. 1401 (group 31, Prince Ḥalīm Pasha's documents).

the Council of Ministers.[1] The Mālikī *mufti* of Egypt, Muḥammad ʿAlīsh, sent a telegram to Abdülhamid about Egyptian affairs and the unpopularity of Tawfīq Pasha.[2] Instructions were sent to Dervish Pasha, who had been sent to Egypt in connexion with this situation.[3] There are a number of documents which illustrate the close relationship between ʿUrābī Pasha, his supporters, and the Ottoman government. Some of them are the reports from Said Efendi, who had been sent to Egypt secretly to sound the views of ʿUrābī Pasha and his group.[4] The communications sent by ʿUrābī Pasha himself and by his friend, Maḥmūd Sāmī al-Bārūdī Pasha, deserve special mention. In a signed and sealed letter of 1 August 1882, written in Turkish, ʿUrābī Pasha complains of the influence of the foreign powers and asserts the dependence of Egypt on the caliphate. Egypt must not be allowed to fall into foreign hands. The supporters of the caliphate in Egypt (ʿUrābī Pasha and his group) would fight to the last. They placed great reliance on the Ottoman government. They had a full understanding with the administration in Egypt. Anti-Ottoman publications in Egypt should not be taken seriously; they were paid for by foreign funds and did not reflect the Muslim view.[5] At the end of the letter, ʿUrābī Pasha promised to give further detailed information the next week. This shows that he was in regular correspondence with the Ottoman government. Others of his letters are extant. A letter of 25 May 1882 gives a similar account of the Egyptian situation at great length.[6] According to ʿUrābī Pasha all the trouble in Egypt arose from the maladministration of Tawfīq Pasha. The incompetent khedive had put all his affairs in the hands of the British consul-general. British ambitions to invade Egypt derived from this situation: they were able to do whatever they wished by manipulating the khedive. Their object was to reduce Egypt to a dependency like India. Patriots had either been imprisoned or executed. The Egyptian people had made him their leader to save them from this danger. He would fight to secure this, as well as preserving their status as Ottoman subjects. The khedive had suborned some of the troops against them, but all his policies had failed, for no one was prepared to accept his acting as a British puppet. Nevertheless the British consul-general was still the dominating force in Egyptian affairs. They were therefore afraid that the khedive might withdraw from the Ottoman Empire. The rumour that European lives were in danger was a lie: they were safe. He was fighting for Islamic unity, and was prepared to sacrifice his life: this was shown by what he had already done. This was the whole truth. Tawfīq Pasha was not just incompetent, he was

[1] *Yıldız*, no. 1208 (*Mısır işleri gurubu*): folder of documents concerning the question of ʿUrābī Pasha.

[2] Ibid.

[3] *Yıldız*, no. 1740 (*Mısır işleri gurubu*).

[4] *Yıldız*, no. 1208: Said Esad Efendi's representation.

[5] *Yıldız*, no. 1208: ʿUrābī Pasha's letters. See Plate 2.

[6] *Yıldız*, no. 1208: ʿUrābī Pasha's representation.

wicked. Everybody there was waiting for an *irade* deposing him and appointing Ḥalīm Pasha. Since these letters were written by a very important figure, in a critical period of Egyptian history, they deserve some attention. I may add that there are many more documents concerning ʿUrābī Pasha in the archives.[1] Here I will mention only the letters of his supporter, Maḥmūd Sāmī al-Bārūdī Pasha.[2]

After the British occupation of Egypt, a treaty was signed between the Ottomans and the British government on 24 October 1885. This treaty consisted of seven articles and specified that each government should send a high commissioner to Egypt. Britain thereby acquired the right to share the government of Egypt with the Ottoman government.[3] Gazi Ahmet Muhtar Pasha was sent as the Ottoman high commissioner, and the same terms were repeated in the instructions he received from the Council of Ministers on 21 December 1885. These instructions were as follows:

First, the Ottoman high commissioner was to attempt to find a peaceful solution to the Sudan Question; to hold discussions with the khedive concerning the restoration of law and order; to inform the British high commissioner of the progress of these discussions, and to co-operate with him in determining joint measures accordingly.

Second, the Sudanese revolt was essentially a revolt against the British army. The Sudanese would submit if they received assurances that the British would leave Egypt. According to the treaty signed by the Ottoman Empire and Britain, the British army was to leave Egypt after the restoration of law and order through the offices of the Ottoman high commissioner, and the execution of administrative reforms. It was the duty of the Ottoman high commissioner to explain to the high-ranking and most prominent Sudanese that they had to obey the khedive, who was the representative of the sultan.

Third, the two high commissioners and the khedive were to put the Egyptian army in order. The army was to consist of 18,000 men. If the Sudan did not quieten down, the two high commissioners and the khedive were to agree on measures to send this army to the Aswān area, to reinforce the military occupation of the area, and to communicate these decisions to Istanbul.

Fourth, the two high commissioners and the khedive were to investigate all aspects of Egyptian administration and to take necessary measures by *ferman*.

Fifth, the Ottoman government recognized obligations contracted by the khedive provided they did not clash with the privileges awarded by *ferman*.

Sixth, the high commissioners were to report to their governments when they were satisfied that Egypt and the border areas were being competently administered. Since the evacuation of British troops from Egypt depended on this, the greatest attention was to be paid to the execution of measures that

[1] *Yıldız*, no. 1639 (*Mısır işleri gurubu*): ʿUrābī Pasha's letters.
[2] *Yıldız*, no. 1208: Maḥmūd Sāmī al-Bārūdī Pasha's letter.
[3] *Yıldız*, no. 316 (*Mısır işleri gurubu*).

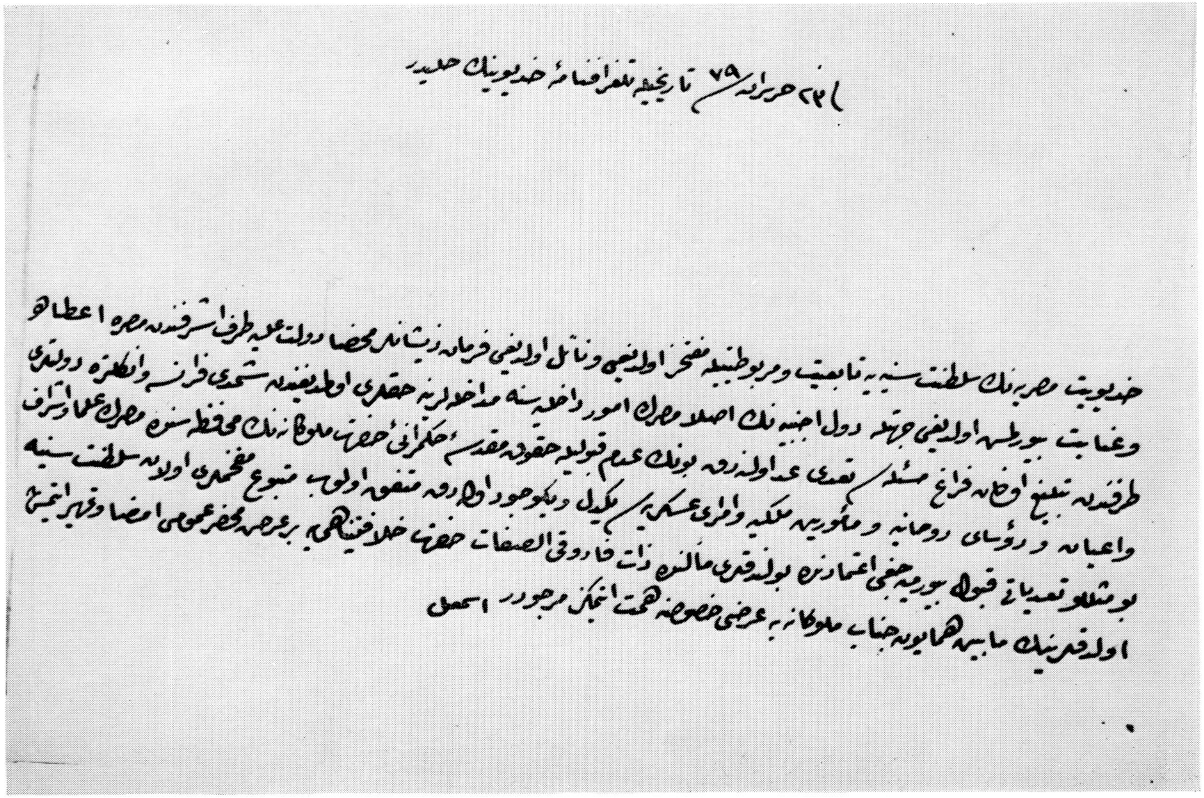

PLATE I. Ismāʿīl Pasha's telegram (*Yıldız* No. 1167)

PLATE 2. ʿUrābī Pasha's letter (*Yıldız* No. 1208)

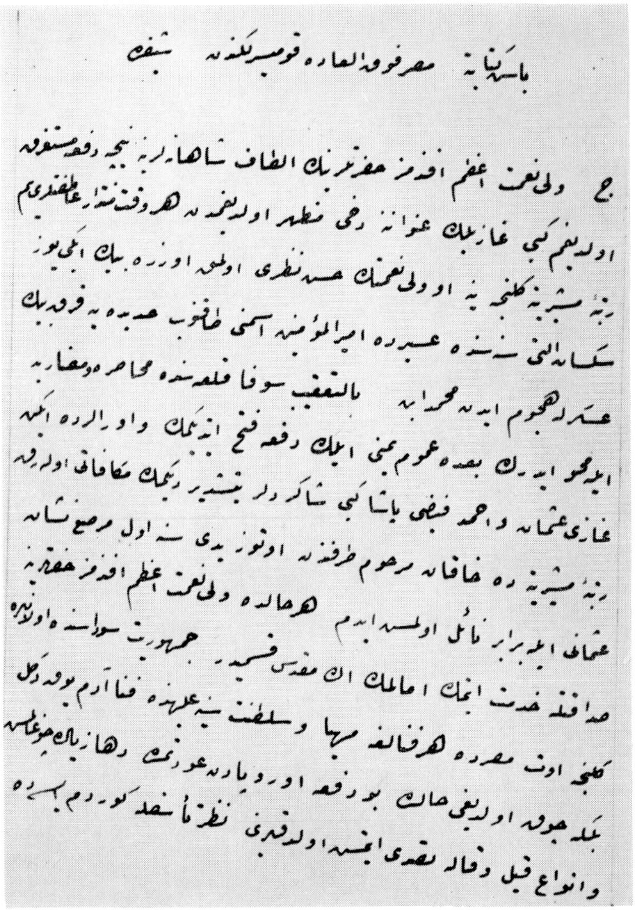

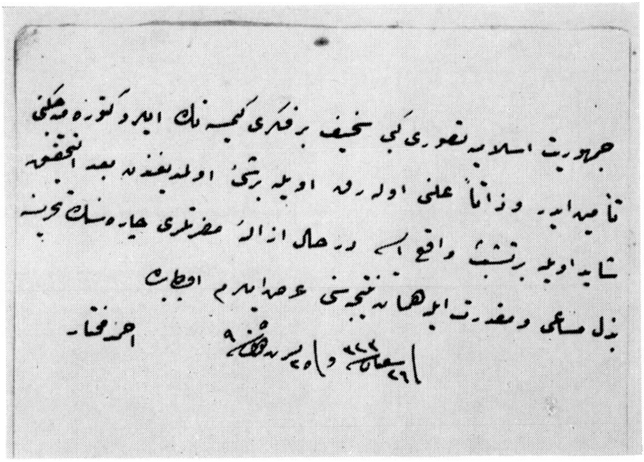

PLATE 3. Telegram from Muhtar Pasha (*Yıldız* No. 2041)

would secure the rapid and effective re-establishment of order and good administration.

Seventh, Sir Henry Drummond Wolff had demanded the inclusion in the treaty of three paragraphs which were later removed from the text. These concerned the drafting of Ottoman troops and officers to Egypt to reform the Egyptian army and put down the negro slave trade. The Ottoman high commissioner was not to enter into any discussion of the restoration of these provisions.[1]

As appears from these instructions, Ottoman sovereignty over Egypt was preserved. The khedive could only act within the framework of the privileges granted by *ferman.* The British occupation was to be temporary, and British troops were to be withdrawn when law and order had been re-established. However, the British did not in fact leave Egypt, and Ottoman attempts to secure this by diplomatic means were a failure.[2] In a report of 15 May 1891 the grand vezir Kâmil Pasha remarked that he would be indebted to anyone who could negotiate a treaty providing for the evacuation of the British from Egypt. This shows the impotence of the Ottoman government in the face of this situation.[3]

In spite of this, Ahmet Muhtar Pasha continued his work in Egypt with a large staff.[4] This is shown by the reports he sent on Egyptian affairs. Besides the normal political reports which he sent,[5] we find reports relating to such subjects as the character and activities of the new khedive, ʿAbbās Ḥilmī Pasha.[6] The size of the Egyptian army,[7] Egyptian finances,[8] the administration of wages,[9] foreign loans,[10] the import of jute,[11] and so on. One of these reports is of particular interest. The Ottoman government had complained to Ahmet Muhtar Pasha about his failure to report republican activities in Egypt. In reply[12] he sent a telegram in cipher dated 25 January 1905. After first protesting his loyalty, he stated that Egypt was full of enemies of the sultanate who were ready to engage in every kind of wickedness; he regretted that their number seemed to have increased during his visit to Europe; but he insisted that no one would advance such a disgraceful idea as the establishment of an Islamic republic, at least in public. He would make inquiries, and should such a plan come to light, he would do all in his power to deal with it.

1 *Yıldız*, no. 2550 (*Mısır işleri gurubu*). Instructions to Gazi Ahmet Muhtar Pasha.
2 *Yıldız*, no. 1782 (*Mısır işleri gurubu*).
3 *Yıldız*, no. 1784, 1783 (*Mısır işleri gurubu*).
4 *Yıldız*, no. 2113 (Group 31, Kâmil Pasha's documents).
5 *Yıldız*, no. 2537 (Group 31, Muhtar Pasha's documents).
6 *Yıldız*, no. 2161 (Group 31, Muhtar Pasha's documents).
7 *Yıldız*, no. 2180 (Group 31, Muhtar Pasha's documents).
8 *Yıldız*, no. 2185 (Group 31, Muhtar Pasha's documents).
9 *Yıldız*, no. 2182 (Group 31, Muhtar Pasha's documents).
10 *Yıldız*, no. 2156 (Group 31, Muhtar Pasha's documents).
11 *Yıldız*, no. 2142 (Group 31, Muhtar Pasha's documents).
12 *Yıldız*, no. 2041 (Group 31, Muhtar Pasha's documents). Telegram from Muhtar Pasha. See Plate 3.

In this short paper I have tried to suggest the importance of the material in the *Başbakanlık Arşivi* by discussing a few of the documents it contains. In my opinion, the study of Egyptian history in the modern period cannot dispense with these materials. As Turkish archivists, we shall be only too glad to welcome those wishing to make use of this material, and we shall do all in our power to help them.

Some English Sources for the Study of Modern Egyptian History

H. S. DEIGHTON

IF the extant manuscript descriptions of early modern Egypt in England are remarkable for anything at all it is their relative paucity. 'If it rayned gold [at Alexandria]', wrote an official of the Levant Company in the seventeenth century, 'wee should not think it worth the while to go and fetch it'.[1] And, for all that there was an unbroken line of English consuls at Cairo from the appointment of Miles Fleetwood in 1698 until 1757,[2] English accounts of Egypt remain in very short supply until the end of the eighteenth century.

Serious political interest in Egypt began in the 1780s. Before that there were few travellers, and only one of any consequence, whose manuscripts are in the British Museum. The Reverend Richard Pococke, a great traveller in the early part of his life and best known for his published accounts of the British Isles, visited Egypt in 1737 and subsequently published an account of his eastern travels of which Dr. Samuel Johnson thought but poorly.[3] There is a manuscript account of this journey[4] but Pococke wrote from ancient texts rather than from observation, and what there was of observation concerned only antiquities and speculation upon them. English only in point of location are a *Relazione dello stato presente dell'Egitto* in German and Italian of Johann Michael Wansleben from 1668,[5] and the *Descrizione del suo viaggio fatto nell'Egitto* in 1744 of Giuseppe Luigi Assemani.[6] For good measure, although necessarily of limited appeal, it might be added that there is a collection of the papers of the celebrated Romany scholar, C. G. Leland. This includes a manuscript diary of a visit to Egypt, between November 1872 and February 1873, written, after the first few days, in the Romany language.[7]

1 Alfred C. Wood, *A history of the Levant Company* (London, 1935), p. 125.

2 Ibid., pp. 165–7.

3 *Boswell's life of Johnson*, ed. G. Birkbeck Hill (Oxford, 1887), vol. ii, p. 346.

4 Add. MS. 22995.

5 Add. MSS. 8779, 8780.

6 Add. MS. 8781.

7 Add. MSS. 27168–37174. As might be expected, there are in the British Museum a number of documents in French bearing on the history of Egypt. For example—Add. MS. 10599 is a Turkish copy with an official French translation of the treaty concluded between Muḥammad 'Alī Pasha and Vice-Admiral Sir Edward Codrington in August 1828; Add. MSS. 9845, 17324, 22932, 23003 f. 3 (letter of Bonaparte to his brother Joseph complaining of the infidelities of Josephine), and Add. MS. 37076 (Nelson Papers—letters intercepted by ships of the Royal Navy during the French occupation of Egypt). Add. MSS. 34197–9 is a journal of travels in the Eastern Mediterranean during the years 1828–38 by Adolphe de Riguet, Comte de Caraman, of which vol. i (Add. MS. 34198) contains a long summary of impressions of Egypt.

There are some remains of the autograph journals made during his travels, of William George Browne, author of *Travels in Africa, Egypt and Syria, 1792–1798* (London, 1806),[1] and some manuscripts of J. L. Burckhardt, the author of *Travels in Nubia*,[2] relating to Egypt, Arabia, and the Bedouin in the years 1814–17. Unpublished travel journals for a slightly later period are those of R. R. Master, in the years 1818–19, with original drawings[3] and the diary of Henry Westcar, during 1823–9.[4]

The magnet of antiquities was responsible for the most considerable collections of manuscripts of travel to Egypt which are to be found in the British Museum. During the 1820s a small but distinguished band of Englishmen, attracted principally by the dramatic unfolding of the life of the pharaonic world, had gone to live and study in Egypt. Two of them, John Gardner Wilkinson,[5] and James Burton[6] (later Haliburton), have their place in the history of Egyptology. Another was Edward William Lane, the author of *Modern Egyptians*.[7] The British Museum has five collections of papers deriving from members of this small colony. James Burton (1788–1862) is represented by his *Collectanea Egyptiaca*, which was presented to the Museum in 1864.[8] He spent nearly twenty years in Egypt, working as a geologist for Muḥammad ʿAlī and travelling with Lane. Most of his papers are concerned with antiquities and contain a good many drawings and plans, but there are diaries of the period covered by his stay in Egypt, and other papers, including some relating to an approach made by Jeremy Bentham to Muḥammad ʿAlī with a view to the English philosopher becoming the tutor, in England, of ʿAbbās.[9] Robert Hay, of Linplum (1799–1863) was another leading Egyptologist of the time, whose papers[10] include a diary covering although not completely, the years 1824–30. The Lane papers[11] include many manuscripts and drawings relating to antiquities, the latter chiefly made with the *camera lucida*, but there is also contemporary matter and a manuscript account of the political rise and the reign of Muḥammad ʿAlī to the year 1828, largely dependent upon the work of the Arabic historian al-Jabartī, and a long paper

[1] Add. MS. 6132.

[2] 2nd edition, London, 1822, Add. MSS. 30239–40.

[3] Add. MS. 51313. Journal of a tour of Egypt, Palestine, and Greece, 1818–19, transcribed by his son in 1884.

[4] Add. MS. 52283. Copy made in 1950 from the original in the German Archaeological Institute in Cairo. This document has a good deal about Upper Egypt and an index of names.

[5] Sir John Gardner Wilkinson (1797–1875), F.R.S., 1833. Lived in Egypt 1821–33.

[6] James Burton (1788–1862), who resumed his father's name of Haliburton in 1838, was in Egypt in 1820–39, worked as a geologist for Muḥammad ʿAlī, published *Excerpta hieroglyphica*, 1822–8, and travelled with E. W. Lane.

[7] *An account of the manners and customs of the modern Egyptians* (1st edn., London, 1836; many reprints).

[8] Add. MSS. 25613–75.

[9] Add. MS. 25663, f. 139. Jeremy Bentham to Mehemet Ali—'Chef de l'Egypte—28 Apr. 1828.

[10] Add. MS. 31054.

[11] Add. MSS. 34080–8.

entitled 'Speculation on the Situation and Resources of Egypt' which includes the observation that 'France in possession of Egypt would possess the Master Key to all the trading Nations of the Earth'. There are letters of Egyptologists to Robert Hay, especially for the years 1832–3,[1] with some interesting political comment and speculation, notably by John Gardner Wilkinson.[2] The journals of J. Hyde[3] cover an antiquarian expedition in the years 1818–21 and include extracts from letters with some matter of contemporary interest. The Hekekyan Papers in the British Museum are separately treated in this volume by Dr. Mustafa.[4]

Official documents begin with the awakening of interest in the political life and economic possibilities of Egypt, which occurred in Britain and in British India, during the last decades of the eighteenth century. Most of them are housed in the Public Record Office and are catalogued under 'Turkey'.[5] There are exceptions to this, notably[6] a collection of consular documents covering intermittently the period from the appointment of consul-general Baldwin in 1785 until 1818. But from 1817 (with a minor exception in 1818) Egypt reported through Constantinople and correspondence is listed under 'Turkey'. Other sources for this early period are in the India Office Library.[7] These may be supplemented from the Hardwick Papers in the British Museum[8] which contain correspondence from Sir Robert Ainslie (?1730–1812), ambassador to Constantinople, 1776–92. These letters cover a period from 1776 to 1787, with a gap between August 1778 and September 1783. There are further papers relating to the Red Sea route and Egypt and its neighbourhood in the British Museum.[9] These include records of the travels, in the early nineteenth century, of George, Viscount Valentia, and contain papers of Henry Salt (1780–1827), who was for a while Valentia's secretary, and subsequently, from 1818 to 1827, British consul-general in Egypt. Salt was closely associated with the British Egyptological visitors of the 1820s and died a Fellow of the Royal

[1] Add. MS. 38094. Robert Hay, of Linplum (1799–1863), was in Egypt from 1826 to 1836. He published *Illustrations of Cairo* in 1840.

[2] Robert Hay himself left an incomplete diary of his stay in Egypt which covers in part, the years 1824–1826–1827 and 1830. Add. MS. 31054.

[3] Add. MSS. 42102–3.

[4] For Add. MSS. 37448–71, see Ahmed Abdel-Rahim Mustafa, 'The Hekekyan Papers', pp. 68–75.

[5] Principally F.O. 78; but there is much material elsewhere in the Foreign Office archives at the Public Record Office, e.g. F.O. 198. This material is clearly indicated in the printed catalogue. There is material, too, in the records of the Service Departments. Military records, which should be approached by way of the admirable, printed 'Alphabetical Guide to War Office and Military Records', contain e.g. W.O. 6/183/280, 'Surrender of Arabi' and W.O. 1/345/309 'Egypt before the French Invasion'. See also—Admiralty, 50/276 in connexion with the bombardment of Alexandria.

[6] P.R.O., F.O. 24/126.

[7] The Factory Records of the India Office were used by H. L. Hoskins in *British routes to India* (London, 1928).

[8] Notably Add. MS. 35574.

[9] See especially Add. MSS. 19289; 19290; 19291; 19292; 19338; 19339–49; and 19418–27.

Society.[1] There is matter on the conflict about the projected Red Sea route in the Charles James Fox Papers[2] and in the Warren Hastings Papers.[3]

For the period of the great war with France, 1792–1815, the extensive materials in the Public Record Office which are to be found under the categories 'Admiralty' and 'War and Colonial Office', as well as under 'Foreign Office', may be supplemented with materials in the British Museum—notably, the Hudson Lowe, Nelson, Bunbury, Wellesley, Windham, and Liverpool Papers, and the letters of Sir Alexander Ball. These sources have been extensively and effectively used by the late Shafiq Ghorbal, in *The beginnings of the Egyptian question and the rise of Mehemet Ali* (London, 1928), and more recently by Piers Mackesy, *The war in the Mediterranean, 1803–1810* (London, 1957). Their treatment was systematic and seems to make more detailed reference unnecessary.

An introduction to the sources of the period, during Palmerston's first term at the Foreign Office, when the traditional British attitude to Egypt was being formulated, and for the period of crisis at the end of that decade, may be found in publications which are easily available—in particular, Sir Charles Webster, *The foreign policy of Lord Palmerston, 1830–1841* (London, 1951) and F. S. Rodkey, 'The Efforts of Briggs and Company to Guide British Policy in the Levant, 1821–1841'.[4] Master source of information to those, notably at Holland House, who were opposed to Palmerston on this issue, was Sir Robert Wilson, whose extensive papers contain material which includes a 'Sketch of the Turco-Egyptian Question' written in September 1839.[5]

British official sources are still very full for the period between the end of that crisis and the outbreak of the Crimean War, and they may be supplemented by reference to private papers in the Aberdeen Papers, and the Palmerston Papers, both in the British Museum. Into the Anglo-French alliance of the Crimean War period, the news that Ferdinand de Lesseps had secured a *ferman*, authorizing him to dig the Suez Canal, projected a divisive element which greatly heightened the importance of Egyptian affairs in the eyes of British officials.[6] Official documents relating to the diplomatic struggle over the Canal project are many and they were sometimes collected for convenience.[7] Private letters illustrating the issue of the Suez Canal as it affected

[1] Henry Salt (1780–1827) went on a mission to Abyssinia for the British Government, 1809–11, and was the discoverer of the inscriptions at Abu Simbel.

[2] Add. MS. 47563.

[3] See especially Add. MSS. 29201 and 29210.

[4] In *Journal of Modern History*, vol. v (1933), pp. 324 ff.

[5] The Sir Robert Wilson (1777–1849) Papers are Add. MSS. 30095–148. The 'Sketch' referred to is in Add. MS. 30132, f. 204.

[6] For an account of its effect on the British Cabinet and of Palmerston's almost single-handed, and entirely decisive, resistance to the project, see the Duke of Argyll, *Autobiography and memoirs* (London, 1906), vol. i, p. 568.

[7] See for example F.O. 198/27 (kept at Ashridge), a volume of 'Confidential Print', dated 19 Dec. 1865, and covering and analysing correspondence respecting the Suez Canal project between 1859 and 1865.

the relations of England and France, are in the Papers of Lord Cowley (1804–84), British ambassador at Paris, 1852–67. These are in the Public Record Office. There is some useful matter for the period to the end of the Crimean War in the Stratford Papers in the Public Record Office, and for the period following it, in the Palmerston Papers in the British Museum, and in the Clarendon Papers in the Bodleian Library at Oxford.[1] Lord Clarendon's correspondence with his Cabinet colleagues and with British officials in Egypt, are especially useful. During his last term at the Foreign Office, which saw the opening of the Suez Canal in 1869 and, in the same year, a good deal of Anglo-French anxiety and mutual suspicion arising from the dispute between the Porte and khedive, Egypt played a considerable part in his correspondence, especially in his private correspondence with the prime minister, Gladstone, which is found in the Clarendon Papers. They were concerned among other things, to 'purge' Great Britain 'of the recollection of that incomprehensible aversion to the Suez Canal'.[2]

The period of greatest British interest in Egypt began with the purchase of the khedive's Suez Canal shares at the end of 1875. Official material for this episode, as for other Suez Canal affairs, is found in the special Suez Canal volumes in the Public Record Office into which matter relating to the Suez Canal, and taken from all files, was collected together each year.[3] The purchase was preceded by an international dispute about the measurement of merchant tonnage to be used as a basis for charging dues for passage through the canal. This dispute, which began in 1872, led to the sitting of an International Tonnage Commission in Constantinople and to a crisis in Egypt, early in 1874, when the attempt to implement the recommendations of the Commission was resisted by Lesseps.[4] An official précis of the documents relating to this issue covering the period from its emergence in 1872 until the time of its writing (20 February 1874), is found in one of the Suez Canal volumes.[5] The story of the purchase proper, may be said to have begun with a telegram dated 15 November 1875, drafted in the hand of Lord Derby, at that time foreign secretary, and sent to the British consul-general in Egypt in connexion with a story that the khedive might sell his interest in the Suez Canal to a combination of French capitalists. This is covered in volumes in the same series.[6]

Much less detailed, but more revealing of motives and of the slow emergence of policy, are the private papers of some of the ministers most closely involved. Notable among these are the Disraeli Papers.[7] Once the crucial step—of

[1] Lord Clarendon was foreign secretary from 1853 to 1858, from 1865 to 1866, and from 1868 to his death in 1870.

[2] Gladstone to Clarendon, 29 Sept. 1869.

[3] It was listed under Turkey, i.e. F.O. 78.

[4] For the events of this, see three articles published simultaneously in *The Times* for 7 May 1874.

[5] F.O. 78/2368.

[6] e.g. F.O. 78/2432.

[7] At Hughenden Manor, High Wycombe, Bucks. These contain, among other things,

purchase—had been taken, there were widely different views as to what should follow in an always divided Cabinet. The 'forward' view was expressed by the colonial secretary, Lord Carnarvon,[1] and the sort of pressures in this sense to which ministers were subject, might be illustrated from the private letters of Sir Bartle Frere, a senior Indian civil servant, to Lord Salisbury, then secretary of state at the India Office.[2] A principal proponent in the Cabinet of the more cautious view was the chancellor of the exchequer, Sir Stafford Northcote. Expression of his doubts may be found in the Iddesleigh Papers in the British Museum—Sir Stafford was created Earl of Iddesleigh in 1885. Egyptian affairs had already at that time, for Great Britain, a strong financial content and there is much matter relating to Egypt during the years immediately after the purchase, in these papers. Public reaction to the purchase was enthusiastic, but the private concern of some public figures, both about this enthusiasm and about possible implications for British policy, was expressed not only in the Iddesleigh Papers but in those of the opposition leaders, Gladstone and Granville.[3]

When Egypt again commanded the urgent attention of the British government, in the aftermath of the Treaty of Berlin, Lord Salisbury had become foreign secretary, and for the episode of the deposition of the Khedive Ismāʿīl and the establishment of the Dual Control, the Salisbury Papers are the principal private source. They contain correspondence with his Cabinet colleagues, with British officials (in both the British and the Egyptian services) in Egypt, and, especially valuable, with Lord Lyons, the British ambassador in Paris.

The crisis which led to the occupation in 1882, occurred after the Liberals had returned to power two years earlier. The Gladstone–Granville correspondence therefore assumes an additional importance and the Granville Papers contain private correspondence with officials in Egypt with Cabinet colleagues and others and with Lord Lyons, in Paris. A continuous narrative of opinions and events, compiled as it were from just outside the door of the Cabinet Room, may be derived from the diaries of Sir Edward Hamilton, one of Gladstone's private secretaries, which are to be found in the Hamilton Papers in the British Museum.[4] There are letters

a collection of Suez Canal papers (Box 75), including an outline of the Suez Canal issue from 1872 to July 1875; an incomplete draft of the story of the Cave Mission, and other relevant documents—and other matter elsewhere in this collection.

[1] See the Carnarvon Papers in the Public Record Office—P.R.O. 30/6.

[2] In the Salisbury Papers, at Christ Church, Oxford.

[3] See the Gladstone Papers in the British Museum and the Granville Papers in the Public Record Office—P.R.O. 30/29. The correspondence between Gladstone and Lord Granville has been edited by Miss Agatha Ramm in two volumes covering the period 1868 to 1876, and published by the Royal Historical Society in 1952, and in the two volumes of *The political correspondence of Mr. Gladstone and Lord Granville, 1876–1886* (Oxford, 1962).

[4] These Papers should be used with a certain caution for reasons which have been set out in R. R. James, *Rosebery, A biography of Archibald Philip, fifth Earl of Rosebery* (London, 1963), p. 513.

relating to the resignation of John Bright in the Bright Papers, in the British Museum.

Two very different views as to what ought to be British policy towards Egypt were at that time being actively and influentially canvassed. Their most important protagonists were Wilfred Scawen Blunt on the one hand, and on the other, Sir Charles Dilke, then under-secretary of state at the Foreign Office, with his political collaborator, Joseph Chamberlain. Some of Blunt's correspondence at that time is to be found in the Gladstone Papers, the Hamilton Papers, and in John Morley's Papers (also in the British Museum). It is unfortunate that Blunt's own papers are not yet available, although the time-limit set upon them in his will has long expired.[1] There seems no reason to doubt that they would constitute a valuable source if they were to be made accessible. Blunt was highly emotional and not always accurate, but what he says is always worth investigation and surprisingly often stands up to it. Dilke was, by reason of his office, in close contact with events in Egypt and no less valuably, with private individuals, among them Gambetta, in France. His papers have been very heavily edited, usually by excision with a pair of scissors.[2]

The Marquis of Dufferin and Ava was British ambassador at Constantinople from 1881 until he became viceroy of India in 1884, and from Cairo (1882–3) advised on the reconstruction of Egyptian administration after Tel-el-Kebir. There is matter in his papers.[3] Sir Edward Vincent (later Viscount D'Abernon) was financial adviser to the Egyptian government 1883–9: the D'Abernon Papers in the British Museum contain several volumes of incomplete diaries for the period of his close connexion with Egypt, and some drafts for a projected book on the country, which seems to have been composed about the year 1887. They contain marginalia in the hand of Sir Evelyn Baring (Lord Cromer). Cromer's continuous association with Egypt began with his appointment as British agent and consul-general in 1883, although he had worked in Cairo in lesser roles with a short break from 1877 to 1880. The bulk of the Cromer Papers are in the Public Record Office and there are valuable private letters to and from him in the Granville Papers and in the Salisbury Papers.

Materials for the study of the first great crisis in the triangular relationship Great Britain–Egypt–the Sudan, are extensive, and have been extensively used.

From June 1885 to the end of the century, the most important continuous

[1] They are in the FitzWilliam Museum, Cambridge, which is the holder of Blunt's copyrights. They were not made available even to his grandson, Lord Lytton, for the preparation of the Earl of Lytton, *Wilfrid Scawen Blunt. A memoir by his grandson* (London, 1961).

[2] Anyone intending to use them should read the comments of R. R. James, op. cit., pp. 514–15, and of his latest biographer Roy Jenkins, *Sir Charles Dilke. A Victorian tragedy* (London, 1958).

[3] In private hands.

private source for material on Anglo-Egyptian relations is the Salisbury Papers. These include many letters from Sir Henry Drummond Wolff, who conducted a special mission to Constantinople in order to negotiate with Turkey on the future of Egypt in 1885, was British commissioner charged with the reorganization of Egyptian administration 1885–6, and who negotiated the second Convention with Turkey (May 1887), which proved abortive owing to the opposition of France and Russia. The Cromer and Salisbury Papers are essential for the study of the reconquest of the Sudan, as are (though to a lesser extent) the Kitchener Papers, in the Public Record Office.

The Milner Papers[1] contain letters for the period of Milner's employment by the Egyptian government, and for some time after it—among them are letters of this period from Cromer, Eldon Gorst, Reginald Wingate, and others. There is matter in the Joseph Chamberlain Papers,[2] the Rosebery Papers,[3] and in the Harcourt Papers.[4] Official papers in the Public Record Office are now available until after the declaration of the protectorate of 1914 and they may be substantially supplemented by reference to the private papers of a number of public men of the time. Available papers for the study of British foreign policy during the years 1895–1906 have recently been worked over very thoroughly by Dr. J. A. S. Grenville and by Mr. George Monger.[5] Students of Anglo-Egyptian history in these years, would be well advised to start from their lists of 'manuscripts consulted'. Mr. Monger's comments on private papers[6] are especially useful. Among them it seems worth while to single out the Asquith Papers,[7] although these contain little matter bearing directly upon Egypt. The series of 'Cabinet letters', that is reports upon Cabinet deliberations made by the prime minister to the king, makes it possible to see the dates upon which Egyptian affairs were considered by the Cabinet during the prime ministership of Asquith. Other papers which would repay examination are those of (Sir) Austen Chamberlain,[8] of the two foreign secretaries, Lord Lansdowne (Conservative) and Sir Edward Grey (Liberal), and of Lord Carnock (Sir Arthur Nicholson), who spent some years in the British embassy in Constantinople in the late nineteenth century and was subsequently (1910–16) permanent under-secretary of state for foreign affairs. There is a note about each of these collections of papers in Mr. Monger's bibliography.

Finally, and quite essential for the study of British policy towards Egypt during the period from the occupation to the protectorate, are the 122

[1] At New College, Oxford

[2] In the Birmingham University Library.

[3] Still in private hands; but used by R. R. James in his life of Lord Rosebery.

[4] At Stanton Harcourt, Oxfordshire.

[5] See J. A. S. Grenville, *Lord Salisbury and foreign policy. The close of the nineteenth century* (London, 1964) and George Monger, *The end of isolation. British Foreign Policy, 1900–1907* (London, 1963).

[6] Op. cit., pp. 333–7.

[7] In the Bodleian Library at Oxford.

[8] Housed, alongside those of his father, in Birmingham University Library.

volumes of photographs of documents comprising Cabinet papers for the years 1880–1914 and minutes and memoranda of the Committee of Imperial Defence down to 1914, which this year (1965) became available in the Public Record Office. Simultaneously the Stationery Office published lists under each heading, setting out the documents of which photographs appear in these volumes.[1]

More or less simultaneously with the outbreak of the First World War in 1914 and the proclamation of the Protectorate, the 'fifty year rule' becomes operative and the official papers are not yet available. Equally, and not surprisingly, the supply of private papers begins to dry up. Of these, for the period from the proclamation of the Protectorate, two collections are most important. The Wingate Papers are the papers of Sir Reginald Wingate, for seventeen years governor-general of the Anglo-Egyptian Sudan and for three years British high commissioner in Egypt. 'This huge collection', as Miss Elizabeth Monroe calls it,[2] is in the School of Oriental Studies at Durham University. An appropriate starting point for its use would be Sir Reginald Wingate's *Life* by his son.[3] Another considerable collection available for students of the period immediately after the end of the First World War, is the Milner Papers. These are rich in letters, memoranda, and reports relating to the Milner Mission and the subsequent negotiations, and include personal diaries for the years 1919–22. These diaries usually contain one short page of entries for each day. They are for the most part devoted, apart from a good deal of comment about the weather, to entries which show how Lord Milner spent the day and who he met, and only sometimes contain reference to topics discussed. But they are useful, like the 'Cabinet letters' in the Asquith Papers, for establishing the chronology of events, discussions, and decisions.

Some indication of some of the documents which may be expected eventually to become available for this later period may be gathered from the published work of the late Lord Wavell, on Lord Allenby,[4] who used the Allenby Papers and was given access by the Foreign Office to the official documents of the period,[5] and the first Lord Lloyd, who appears to have enjoyed comparable facilities for his books on Egypt during the period 1908–34.[6]

[1] *List of Cabinet papers, 1880–1914*, H.M. Stationery Office, 10*s*., and *List of papers of Committee of Imperial Defence to 1910*, also H.M. Stationery Office, 3*s*.6*d*.

[2] In her book—*Britain's moment in the Middle East* (London, 1963), p. 229.

[3] Sir Ronald Wingate, *Wingate of the Sudan* (London, 1955).

[4] Field-Marshal Viscount Wavell, *Allenby in Egypt* (London, 1944); revised edn. in *Allenby, soldier and statesman* (London, 1946).

[5] Op. cit. (1944), p. 7.

[6] Lord Lloyd, *Egypt since Cromer*, vol. i (London, 1933), and vol. ii (London, 1934).

The Hekekyan Papers

AHMED ABDEL-RAHIM MUSTAFA

THE Hekekyan Papers (British Museum, Add. MSS. 37448–71), which were first referred to by Heyworth-Dunne in his book *Introduction to the history of education in modern Egypt* (London, 1939), have not yet been properly evaluated. For they shed new light on the conditions of Egypt during a period which, up till now, has not yet attracted the proper attention of historians, viz. Egypt from 1840 to 1863. They, moreover, contain the autobiography of the writer and his personal impressions during the years (1818–30) he passed in England. From this point of view Hekekyan can be compared with such persons as Rifāʿa al-Ṭahṭāwī, who wrote his reminiscences of the period he passed in Paris, and Fāris al-Shidyāq, who registered his impressions of England at a later period. The Hekekyan Papers, also, contain invaluable information and drawings related to the excavations carried out in Egypt under the auspices of the British Royal Society.

Joseph Hekekyan Bey was born at Istanbul (*c.* 1807) in a Roman Catholic Armenian family. From the time of his childhood his father[1] had a vague hope of sending his son to England to acquire his education; and the opportunity was provided after the father went to Egypt and became a translator in Muḥammad ʿAlī's service. In 1817 Muḥammad ʿAlī decided to send a large number of the sons of his officials to study in Paris; and Hekekyan's father asked the *vali* to send his son, who was residing with his mother at Istanbul, to England. The request was complied with. When Hekekyan arrived at Dover he knew no language but Turkish;[2] and was full of the excitement felt by an Oriental youth at the first encounter with Europe. His tutor in England was Samuel Briggs, a former British consul-general in Egypt. Stonyhurst College was chosen for him because of his Catholic faith. Till 1824 he continued studying English, together with the curriculum of the day: Latin, French, etc. After finishing his course he received instructions from Boghos Bey, the Egyptian secretary for Commerce and Foreign Affairs (11 December 1824), conveying the order of the *vali* to devote his attention to the theory and practice of textile machinery, and the construction of roads, bridges, canals, and embankments.[3] He accordingly entered into these special pursuits at the beginning of May 1825. Before his return to Egypt it was

[1] Referred to in the Hekekyan Papers as being *Michirdiz* and *Megrdieh Aga*.

[2] MS. 37463, fol. 566. Although Hekekyan himself, in his autobiography, admits that before leaving Istanbul, he had some knowledge of Armenian and French. (MS. 37448, fol. 163.)

[3] MS. 37463, fols. 317–19.

judged advisable that he should visit the cotton factories of Glasgow to see the methods employed in spinning and weaving in Scotland as well as in Manchester.[1] During his residence in Manchester and Glasgow he was indefatigable in collecting useful information on the subject of the cotton manufacture.

In the autumn of 1831 Hekekyan returned to Egypt. He had entirely forgotten his mother tongue; and Muḥammad 'Alī gave him an interpreter to assist him in his duties, in the pursuance of which he suffered not a little from the deeply rooted notions which he had acquired in that land of industry.[2] He was made chief overseer in the cotton mills of al-Ḥawd al-Marṣūd, Khurunfish, Būlāq, and Mabyaḍa; and had twenty students allotted to him from the Qaṣr al-'Aynī College, to be taught the rudiments of geometry, arithmetic, and machinery with the aid of an interpreter paid by the government. In 1834 the School of Engineering was inaugurated at Būlāq; and in 1835 the School of Engineers at al-Qanāṭir al-Khayriyya, which contained thirty students,[3] was joined to it, together with the School of Mines at Old Cairo.[4] Hekekyan was appointed director of the new School of Engineering;[5] and became ex-officio member of the Board of Education which was inaugurated in 1836.[6] In the late thirties he was appointed director of the School of Operations. He was, moreover, one of the founders of the *Société Égyptienne* which came into being in 1835, having as one of its objects to render services to the foreign travellers passing through Egypt. It also had a library which could furnish a centre for their meetings. Hekekyan was more than once director of the *Société*, which collected a large number of books and had a special interest in publications dealing with the East: its history, geography, religions, and habits. It even aspired, in due course, to publish books related to its special interests.[7] Between 1844 and 1850 he headed three expeditions to search for coal in different parts of the Egyptian deserts and mountains. In 1849, during the reign of 'Abbās Ḥilmī I, he was appointed president of the Board of Health. But a chronic ophthalmia com-

1 MS. 37462, fol. 650.

2 Ibid., fol. 50.

3 Aḥmad 'Izzat 'Abd al-Karīm, *Ta'rīkh al-ta'līm fī 'aṣr Muḥammad 'Alī* (Cairo, 1938), pp. 360–1. Cf. Muḥammad Fu'ād Shukrī, *Binā' dawla: Miṣr Muḥammad 'Alī* (Cairo, 1948), p. 645, where he estimates the number of students at the school as being 225.

4 Aḥmad 'Izzat 'Abd al-Karīm, op. cit., loc. cit.

5 Muḥammad 'Alī once wrote to Mukhtār Bey, the director of the Board of Schools concerning the curriculum of the School of Engineering, as follows: 'Education should not be superficial. I did not send Hekekyan to be a lord in Europe; but to come back and to teach such students as are useful to the nation and to the country. It is your duty to direct him to teach them seriously and enthusiastically; otherwise he will be severely punished with the stick.' Quoted in Aḥmad 'Izzat 'Abd al-Karīm, op. cit., p. 425.

6 Hekekyan directed the attention of the Pasha to the education of girls: Muḥammad Fu'ād Shukrī, op. cit., p. 666.

7 Jamāl al-Dīn al-Shayyāl, *Ta'rīkh al-tarjama wa 'l-ḥaraka al-thaqāfiyya fī 'asr Muḥammad 'Alī* (Cairo, 1951), pp. 64–65. The *Société* subsequently declined and its valuable books are now in the Dār al-Kutub of Cairo, in compliance with the will of its last members: Hekekyan, Thurborn, and Kiani Bey.

pelled him to retire from service in 1851, although in March of the same year he received verbal orders from ʿAbbās to execute in the name of his government certain specific researches in the Nile valley for the Royal Society of London.[1] In April of the same year he sought some sort of English protection to shelter him from the 'possible violence and caprice of reckless despotism', since 'several individuals of both sexes are known to have disappeared suddenly, nobody knowing their fate'. This sad state of things, coupled with his family connexions with Artin Bey,[2] who was the butt of the *vali*'s disfavour, made him pass anxious hours, and compelled him to apply for English protection.[3]

His fears, however, were not justified; and he continued his excavations together with Mr. Leonard Horner of the British Royal Society till the end of 1856, when he completed his final reports and expedition of samples, surveys, and drawings. Apart from that, Hekekyan was occupied from 1854 to the close of 1861 with his own researches which he embodied within the compass of an ordinary volume. Encouraged by several scientific men with whom he had from time to time conversed on the subject, he wished to get his book published in England. He requested the *vali* of Egypt, Muḥammad Saʿīd Pasha, to help him to meet the charges for the preparation for the press, and the printing of, two hundred copies of the memoir.[4] Saʿīd agreed, and paid £500;[5] and the book was published in London in 1863 for private circulation, under the title of *A treatise on the chronology of Siriadic monuments*.

At the time Hekekyan published the book nothing definite is known about his social standing; since he describes himself as being 'Hekekyan Bey of Constantinople—formerly in the Egyptian service'. His private papers, journals, correspondence, notes, and sketches, etc. (1829–74), mostly in English, were later presented to the British Museum by his son Tito Hekekyan Pasha, who was a prominent Armenian of Alexandria.[6]

The Hekekyan Papers fall into twenty-four volumes, which are classified as follows:[7]

Vol. I (MS. 37448): Rough notes and sketches, 25 April–8 May 1829; and (fol. 26) Journal in England, July 1829–January 1830. Followed (fol. 162b) by an autobiography, written on the voyage to Egypt, July–September 1830: and Journal of the voyage, and (fol. 296) notebook journals in Egypt, 29 August 1840–23 August 1841.

Vol. II (MS. 37449): Journals continued; October 1841–8 April 1844 (fols. 2b–316); 9–16 April, 1844 (reversing the volume); 3 May 1844–11 October 1844 (fols. 323–

[1] MS. 37463, fols. 317–19.

[2] Hekekyan was married to Artin's sister.

[3] MS. 37452, fol. 48; from Hekekyan to Briggs, dated 29 Apr. 1851.

[4] MS. 37463, fols. 178–9 (Memorandum, dated 21 July 1862).

[5] Ibid., fols. 182–3, 188–9.

[6] ʿUmar Ṭūsūn, *al-Biʿthāt al-ʿilmiyya fī ʿahd Muḥammad ʿAlī thumma fī ʿahday ʿAbbās al-awwal wa-Saʿīd* (Cairo, 1934), p. 107.

[7] See the catalogue of the Additional Manuscripts at the British Museum.

494b); followed by some field notebooks, 22 Shawwāl–5 Dhu 'l-Qa'da 1257/6–20 December 1841 (fol. 504) and 12 March–30 April 1844 (fol. 527).

Vol. III (MS. 37450): Journals continued, 18 Shawwāl 1260–13 Muḥarram 1267/ 31 October 1844–16 November 1850.

Vol. IV (MS. 37451): Journals: 6 February–14 April 1846.

Vol. V (MS. 37452): Journals continued, combined with records of archaeological and geological excavations, viz.:

(*a*) Journal: 22 February–16 August 1851 (fol. 1);
(*b*) Journal of excavations: 10 May–4 June 1853; in German kept by Baron d'Erben, acting as assistant to Hekekyan Bey (fol. 106);
(*c*) Remarks on Egyptian desert and topography in general (fol. 174);
(*d*) Detailed description of excavations in 1852 and 1854 (fol. 198);
(*e*) Journal of excavations: 15 April–26 July 1854 (fol. 34b).

Vol. VI (MS. 37453): Journals continued, viz. Journal of excavations, supplementary to the proceedings, etc.

Vol. VII (MS. 37454): Field notebooks and sketch-books.

Vol. VIII (MS. 37455): General account of excavations in 1852–4.

Vol. IX (MS. 37456): Journals, 1862, viz.:

(*a*) Journal of travel up the Nile in February 1862;
(*b*) Sketch-book of the same journey;
(*c*) Journal of a visit to England, 16 May–22 October 1862.

Vol. X (MS. 37457): Sketches of antiquities excavated, etc. 1854, followed by tables of Nile-levels, etc.

Vol. XI (MS. 37458): Drawings (some in colours), plans, and tables of Egyptian antiquities and excavations.

Vol. XII (MS. 37459): Correspondence of Hekekyan Bey with Leonard Horner and others on the subject of his excavations; 1851–64.

Vol. XIII (MS. 37460): Letter-book on the same subject; 1851–4.

Vols. XIV–XVI (MSS. 37461–3): General correspondence in Western languages (1821–74).

Vol. XVII (MS. 37464): Tables of levels, borings, and other geological data—in Arabic; 1851–4.

Vol. XVIII (MS. 37464): Miscellaneous official correspondence and papers, in Turkish and Arabic; 1836–68. These include correspondence relating to the Turco-Egyptian conflict (1838–9), and others exchanged with Hekekyan in his capacity as director of the School of Engineering.

Vol. XIX (MS. 37466): Miscellaneous state-papers and reports relating to Egyptian affairs; *c.* 1838–49, etc., chiefly in French—including:

(*a*) Capitulations governing the relations of Turkey with France and other states.
(*b*) Regulations of the French Ministry of War for a school: 'École d'application du corps royal d'état-major'; 24 November 1828.

(*c*) Report on minerals, etc., in the Sudan; viz.:
   (i) by Rosseger; Resserres (al-Ruṣayriṣ, on the Blue Nile): 20 February 1838;
   (ii) Boreani, on auriferous sands in Dar Berta;
   (iii) d'Arnaud, on gold-washing apparatus, magazines, . . ., etc., 21–22 May 1839.

(*d*) Report to the *vali* by Jules Poulain 'sur la filature et le tissage du coton', marked 'de la part d'Artin Bey pour l'instruction de M. Hekekyan Bey' (*c.* 1843).

(*e*) Note statistiche relative alla provincia Dahahlie [Daqahliyya] . . . 1845–6, in Italian.

(*f*) Report by Hekekyan Bey on the education of young Egyptian officers in Paris; 21 March 1849. Preceded by other papers on the same subject.

(*g*) Report by F. Cléry to Artin Bey, minister of Foreign Affairs, on means of transit in Egypt.

(*h*) Traduction du discours qu'a eu lieu entre S. Ex. L'Émir Bechir el-Chehabé et les Druzes de la Montagne de Liban.

Vols. XX–XXII (MSS. 37467–9): Notebooks, written probably *c.* 1868–72, fair-copied, numbered I–X of chronological data and remarks.

Vols. XXIII–XXIV (MSS. 37470–1): Three treatises or drafts of a treatise on 'Geo-chronology' or a system of Egyptian and biblical chronology based on theoretical relation of the Egyptian cubit to the secular variations of surface-level in Egypt.

In order to evaluate the data contained in the Hekekyan Papers, and to acquire a proper estimate of their value as to the history of modern Egypt, it is essential to examine the nature of the man himself: his ideas, outlook, and activities.

Hekekyan was an engineer who had the opportunity of access into the harem, and who had wide circles of acquaintances both in Egypt and Europe, especially in England. He went on various missions to different parts of Egypt, and was thus fully acquainted with the social life in the desert, the countryside, and towns. He took part in official discussions, and his official occupations, together with his education, gave him a deep insight into the condition of Egypt and the international fluctuations of his time. His knowledge of many languages (among others, English, French, German, Armenian, Turkish, Italian, Arabic, and Persian), together with his personal experiences, more than deepened his thoughts and enriched his remarks. It also made of him a cosmopolitan figure, who, although a man of applied science, had literary taste,[1] and thought in the terms of humanity at large.

Hekekyan had passed in England twelve years, during which he witnessed

[1] In 1841 he wrote: 'A Persian Dervich comes every night to my "mandara" and passes an hour or two with me in reading, commenting and conversing in Persian. I have ordered a Shah Namé and some history in prose. I study the Old Testament in German—collating it with an English edition which assists me in the translations.' (MS. 37449, fol. 5.)

the development of the industrial revolution and the establishment of the principles of free trade and liberalism. He thus maintained that 'education and free commerce would bring people to their senses' and help them to govern themselves—a point of view he later expressed in a council presided over by 'Abbās I and attended by Nubar and others.[1] He advocated the institution of public establishments, where the poor and the rich, the plebeian and noble—and even the king's sons—should receive one and the same education and enjoy equal privileges with the meanest. These establishments, in his view, should be under the peculiar care of the government and be supported (maintenance, education, and clothing) from taxes levied on all the nation.[2] Postulating the cosmopolitan visions of the Physiocrats, he dreamt of one world connected together by communications and trade for the benefit of the whole human race:

> Agriculture and manufacture are the chief materials of Commerce. We transport the produce of one part of the earth to another, where they [*sic*] are converted into these forms in which they are sent back and are of use, either as tending to the supply of our urgent wants, or the gratification of our luxury. All nations should form one family and should mutually assist each other; when they come to be thus blended with one another, that grand object of nature will be consummated, to which every improvement that is effected in the various parts of the earth invariably tend [*sic*].[3]

He even advocated an international system of education, whereby, 'moral education would be one in all places; no new system would be admitted without the knowledge of mankind'.[3] The conditions of the East, at that time, were not prepared for such progressive ideas; and Hekekyan, though impressed by what he considered to be the enlightened despotism of Muḥammad 'Alī, was critical of Eastern rule:

> Usurpers in the East seldom enjoy the hereditary possession of their territories, because their children are brought up with less care than even the children of ancient families enjoying the sovereign dignity.[4]

Again:

> In oriental diplomacy there is more of *acting* and stage-deception than in European diplomacy. Nothing is more feasible and better calculated to take with ambassadors mostly, than to pull a man to pieces and driving him away with ignominy except thereby the better to impose upon and attain an object proposed. The history of the East abounds in such examples from the time of Cyrus downwards. The only difficulty in the way of a man's playing his part well and comfortably is the uncertainty in which he may be in the sincerity of the chief agent. Mutual suspicions cannot be overcome—and a disavowal is a matter of course as in the cabinets of Europe.[5]

[1] MS. 37452, fol. 19.
[2] MS. 37448, fol. 37.
[3] Ibid., fol. 57.
[4] Ibid., fol. 58.
[5] MS. 37452, fol. 38; dated 26 Mar. 1851.

This outlook naturally tended to cause Hekekyan to condemn 'the tyranny' exercised by the village shaykhs or headmen over the small cultivators in their villages,[1] with the result that the *fallāḥīn* abandoned their cultivation and preferred to enter the service of the bedouin, or hid in towns where they entered service or similar work. It also turned him against 'despotism', especially that of ʿAbbās I, under whose reign Hekekyan at times felt so insecure as to ask for British protection, as has been explained. This estimate of the autocracy then prevalent in Egypt was confirmed by the man in the street. Asked by Hekekyan about his opinion of ʿAbbās, a donkey-driver said that he [ʿAbbās] was idle and cruel towards the poor:

putting them to hard labour in the deserts and paying them nominally nothing. . . . He said that many of his countrymen died daily in the works of the Pasha's palaces. He had the good sense to think that His Highness should have laid out money rather in improving 'Massr' [Cairo] than to build in deserts. He said that if the levies were abolished, the Viceroy would be pardoned his manifold sins—it was unjust and cruel to deprive parents of the services of an only son for whom they would willingly pay a thousand piastres rather than lose their aide [*sic*] in agricultural labours.[2]

The social remarks contained in the Hekekyan Papers are thus of great value in depicting the social and political conditions of Egypt in his time. They draw their colourfulness and realistic touch from the fact that Hekekyan himself had had the opportunity of journeying in different parts of the country and contacting different categories of its population. Speaking of the Nubians, he records that:[3]

They have preserved the characteristics distinguishing them without any perceptible change for thousands of years. Their type of features and physical conformation represented in sculptures adorning Egyptian and Nubian monuments dating more than forty centuries before our time, may be said to have been faithful representations of the people as they now exist. . . . They are hospitable, industrious and lovers of peace and order. They are fond of literature, and manifest by their acts their conviction that their children should be early instructed in reading and writing. Though they have peculiar dialects, Arabic is the learned language among them. . . . These Nubians are the Savoyards of Africa.

He had contacts with the bedouins that enabled him to give us the following description of their conditions under ʿAbbās I:

Abbas Pasha favours them designedly, and shuts his eyes at their acts of depredation and extortion over the Fellahs. Ameer Tahawy is well known to have stolen a fine horse belonging to a rich Shek in the Behéréh, which he rides without the least fear. The Shek has petitioned the governor but without effect. The Kelaats[4] which are continually getting issued out to the chiefs of the wild tribes are a proof that the

[1] MS. 37449, fols. 91–92; dated 28 Jan. 1843.
[2] MS. 37452, fol. 26; dated 6 Mar. 1851.
[3] MS. 37468, fols. 40–42.
[4] i.e. robes of honour.

present viceroy places much value on winning the affections of the Bedoweens. But the sharp Bedoweens know well to what to attribute such signs of friendship, and are emboldened by that weakness, to recommence their ancient trade of plundering. The fellah sheks on the other hand will commence their highway robberies. Shek Abbassa of the Behera can summon around twelve thousand muskets to his service. These sheks are the nobility of the country. They would not give their daughters in marriage to the Turks—not even to the Sultan, nor to the first house in Europe. They claim the right of robbery within the limits of their territories. In better times they levied tolls.[1]

As Hekekyan had witnessed a certain kind of social transformation as to the relationship between the Muslims and non-Muslims in Egypt, he noticed that the Muslim feeling against Christians had lost its wonted bitterness. Another feeling replaced it, more intense in its action; 'that of jealousy and fear and hatred of Europeans and of those sects which are supposed to sympathise with Europeans'.[2]

In his estimate of personalities Hekekyan resorted to the analytical approach, which gives weight to the social and psychological factors inherent in the portrait he paints. Thus he describes ʿAbbās I as being 'a young man, though possessed of qualities which by cultivation might be of use to him and to the country—yet from the bad education he has had, and from the ignorant, selfish men he is surrounded by, he is become a downright tyrant and a madman'.[3]

Again, he gives us the following estimate of Boghos Bey, who had served Muḥammad ʿAlī more than thirty years:

Boghos Bey was an excellent man in private—and no-one had better qualities than him [*sic*] in his official capacity—it being recollected that he had to serve a tyrant. He may be ranked amongst the greatest of Eastern ministers because he continued in the good graces of a tyrant and a tyrannical court for so many years. The secret of his policy was to do nothing of his own opinion—to risk nothing in that way—and never to give his opinion in a private way to the Pasha—in public never to contradict him.[4]

Added to all this the Hekekyan Papers include drawings and maps, as well as social information on the dwellings of different sections of the population of Egypt, their dresses and habits. Last of all, it must not be forgotten that Hekekyan was the first public servant in the Egyptian administration in the nineteenth century who kept his diaries and preserved his correspondence. This, added to the fact that he wrote most of his reminiscences in English, must be a result of his residence in England.[5]

[1] MS. 37452, fol. 17; dated 2 Mar. 1851.
[2] MS. 37450, fol. 335.
[3] Ibid., fol. 334.
[4] MS. 37449, fol. 235; dated Rajab 1259.
[5] Hekekyan's autobiography, written in 1829 and included in MS. 37448, demonstrates the inaccuracy of Ibrahim Abu-Lughod's statement (*The Arab rediscovery of Europe* (Princeton, N.J., 1963), p. 69) that Rifāʿa al-Ṭahṭāwī was the only student, sent by Muḥammad ʿAlī to Europe, who recorded his years of residence abroad.

PART TWO

STUDIES IN THE HISTORY OF THE EARLY MODERN PERIOD (1517–1798)

The Pattern of Egyptian Political History from 1517 to 1798

P. M. HOLT

THE political history of Egypt during the two hundred and eighty years from the conquest by Selim I to the conquest by Napoleon Bonaparte conforms to a general pattern observable throughout the Arab provinces of the Ottoman Empire. Four main phases may be discerned in the period: first, a phase of acquisition, including not only the initial military conquest, but the subsequent suppression of related revolts, and the assimilation (partial in the case of Egypt) of the conquered territory to the general Ottoman provincial system; secondly, a phase of quiescence, the heyday of classical Ottoman administration; thirdly, a phase of internal conflict, marking the breakdown of the classical administrative system; and, fourthly, the emergence of locally based autonomous rule, restoring to a limited extent the lost political stability.

Such a course of events can be traced in the Fertile Crescent provinces. In Egypt the pattern is modified by a local factor of outstanding importance: the survival of the Circassian *élite*, which had been the military basis of the Mamluk sultanate before the Ottoman conquest, and the continuation of the system of Mamluk recruitment. This meant that Egypt was provided with a quasi-indigenous group imbued with traditions of military and political authority: hence, to some extent, the character of the local autonomy which finally emerged was predetermined.

This paper will consist of an examination of the four phases into which the period is divided. Up to the present no detailed and comprehensive study of the political history of Egypt under Ottoman rule has been made. Accepted accounts of this period have tended to rely heavily on the work of the savants who accompanied Bonaparte to Egypt, and on the chronicle of al-Jabartī. These sources, while valuable and authoritative for the late eighteenth century, throw little light on the first two hundred years of Ottoman rule.[1]

[1] Some aspects of this topic are examined in greater detail in my articles; 'The exalted lineage of Riḍwān Bey: some observations on a seventeenth-century Mamluk genealogy', *BSOAS*, vol. xxii. 2 (1959), pp. 221–30; 'The beylicate in Ottoman Egypt during the seventeenth century', *BSOAS*, vol. xxiv. 2 (1961), pp. 214–48; 'Al-Jabartī's introduction to the history of Ottoman Egypt', *BSOAS*, vol. xxv. 1 (1962), pp. 38–51; and 'The career of Küçük Muḥammad (1676–94)', *BSOAS*, vol. xxvi. 2 (1963), pp. 269–87. A more extended survey of the period is contained in my book, *Egypt and the Fertile Crescent 1516–1922* (London, 1966). The Arabic sources on which my account is chiefly based are surveyed in the companion paper, 'Ottoman Egypt (1517–1798): an account of Arabic historical sources', pp. 3–12.

The phase of acquisition: 1517–25

The Ottoman conquest of Egypt in 1517 was the consequence, by no means inevitable, of Selim's campaign against Qānṣawh al-Ghawrī in northern Syria in the previous year. The campaign appears, at its outset, to have had a limited military objective: the elimination of the threat which the Mamluks offered to the Ottoman flank during Selim's hostilities against Shah Ismāʿīl. This objective was attained by the defeat of al-Ghawrī at Marj Dābiq, and the Ottoman occupation of Aleppo. The Mamluk forces were routed, their power in Syria was disintegrating, the death of the old sultan, and the disarray of the ruling *élite*, had taken the strength out of the Mamluk–Safavid alliance. With the occupation of Damascus, and the amputation of Syria from the Mamluk sultanate, Selim might well have felt that his aims were achieved.

That he went on to undertake the hazardous crossing of the Sinai Desert, and to attack the entrenched power of the Mamluk sultanate in Cairo itself, is not explicable on strictly military grounds. In making his decision to advance into Egypt, Selim appears to have been influenced by Khā'ir Bey, the former Mamluk governor of Aleppo, who had gone over to the Ottomans at Marj Dābiq. Selim was, in fact, confronted by a situation endemic in Mamluk politics: the division of the ruling *élite* into rival factions, each seeking the means of securing its own supremacy. In consequence of Selim's victory in Syria the factions polarized into a resistance group, centring around the new sultan, Ṭūmān Bāy, and a collaborationist group, headed by Khā'ir Bey, which was prepared to turn Selim's intervention to its own profit. Between the two reconciliation was impossible: hence the reckless bravado with which Ṭūmān Bāy and his retinue rejected Selim's attempts to negotiate; hence also the ferocious insistence of Khā'ir Bey that the defeated sultan should be hanged at the Zuwayla Gate.

From this it follows that the campaign of 1516–17 cannot be regarded as a simple clash between Ottomans and Mamluks, in which Selim sought the total defeat of his opponents. By allying himself with one Mamluk faction against the other, Selim committed himself to the maintenance of Mamluk recruitment and the Mamluk *élite* as such: not surprisingly he appears in later chronicles as a heroic figure, the patron and protector of Mamluk chivalry. Although the Mamluks hostile to the Ottomans were proscribed, this was only a temporary measure. When Selim withdrew from Egypt and Khā'ir Bey ruled as viceroy in the Citadel of Cairo, the fugitives emerged from hiding, and were restored to favour under the new régime.

Inalcık has observed, although with special reference to the fourteenth and fifteenth centuries, that

> It appears that in the Ottoman conquests there were two distinct stages that were applied almost systematically. The Ottomans first sought to establish some sort of

suzerainty over the neighbouring states. They then sought direct control over these countries by the elimination of the native dynasties.[1]

This was substantially the policy which was followed in regard to Egypt. Although the Mamluk sultanate ceased to exist, Khā'ir Bey as viceroy retained something of the status of the defunct sovereigns. His residence was in the Citadel, and he kept up some of the old royal observances, such as the reception of the four chief judges at the beginning of each month. Moreover, although in theory he held his viceroyalty by an annual tenure, he died in office in 1522, having outlived Selim by two years.

His death was followed by a disturbed period, corresponding to the second stage of Ottoman conquest according to Inalcık's scheme. Two significant events occurred: an Ottoman was appointed as viceroy; and a revolt broke out, headed by two high Mamluk officials, the *kāshifs* Jānim al-Sayfī and Īnāl. This was suppressed by a force composed entirely of Ottoman troops from the garrison of Egypt. Shortly afterwards, in 1523–4, Mamluk resentment flared out in a last insurrection. At its head was the viceroy Aḥmad Pasha. The rebels were overcome by a loyalist junta in Cairo, and in the following year (1525) the Ottoman grand vezir, Ibrahim Pasha, paid a brief visit to Egypt to set affairs in order. This event may be taken as closing the phase of acquisition, since it resulted in the promulgation of the *Kanunname* of Egypt—the edict which codified accepted administrative practice.

The phase of quiescence: 1525–86

During the sixty years which followed the promulgation of the *Kanunname*, Egypt has little recorded history. Ottoman authority was strengthened in the fringes of the territory. About the middle of the sixteenth century Lower Nubia, lying between the First and Third Cataracts, was annexed, and an Ottoman province was created on the Red Sea coast in the Suakin–Massawa region. Both these achievements were accomplished by a Circassian Mamluk, Özdemir Pasha, whose earlier career had been in Egypt and the Yemen. The Mamluk sultanate had established a foothold in the Yemen during its last years, and its dominion had been inherited by the Ottomans. Both Mamluks and Ottomans were appointed as governors, and Egypt continued to be the base from which the sultan's authority over the Yemen was asserted.

The effective control of Upper Egypt had been a problem to governments seated in Cairo throughout the Middle Ages. In the fifteenth century a fraction of Hawwāra (an arabized Berber tribe), which had been settled in Upper Egypt by Barqūq, became dominant in the area.[2] Their position was recognized by Selim, at the Ottoman conquest, and their ruling clan, Banū 'Umar, governed Upper Egypt, which was not listed in the *Kanunname* among the

[1] Halil Inalcik, 'Ottoman methods of conquest', *Studia Islamica*, vol. ii (1954), at p. 103.

[2] For the history of Hawwāra in Egypt, see the article, 'Hawwwāra', in *EI*².

districts administered by *kāshifs*. On various occasions there were clashes between Ottoman viceroys and these 'princes of Upper Egypt' (*umarā' al-Ṣa'īd*). In 1576 Banū 'Umar were deprived of their powers, and Upper Egypt was placed under the direct rule of an appointed governor.

The phase of internal conflict: 1586–1711

A manifest decline in the strength and quality of administrative control in the later years of the sixteenth century was a phenomenon common to all parts of the Ottoman Empire; and is to be explained, at least in part, by the damage done by prolonged inflation to the salaries of the officials and soldiery. In Egypt the Ottoman decline inaugurated a long period of political instability, which was only mitigated by the emergence of the beylicate as the *de facto* ruling group in Egypt. The phase of internal conflict was interrupted by two periods of remission; one in the earlier, and one in the later part of the seventeenth century, during which the Ottoman viceroys temporarily re-asserted their authority, and suppressed local tendencies to disorder and autonomy. The second of the periods, it may be noted, coincided very closely with the Indian summer of the Köprülü grand vezirate. When it ended the movement towards autonomy reappeared.

The early symptoms of the Ottoman decline in Egypt were a series of sporadic revolts against the viceroys. The first of these, in 994/1586, was provoked by an investigation into a deficiency in the revenue sent from Egypt to the sultan. An insurrection of the troops took place, and the viceroy was brought down from the Citadel. This was the first occasion on which the local troops had ventured to remove the sultan's representative from office. Another revolt was made against his successor, in 997/1589, during which the viceroy was attacked and his quarters pillaged. In spite of the mediation of the chief judge and other notables, the viceroy was forced to capitulate to their demands. The revolts recurred and increased in severity. In 1006/1598 the rural soldiery assembled and marched on Cairo. The viceroy fell into their hands, but managed to escape to the Citadel. Three years later, in 1009/1601, another viceroy provoked an insurrection over the administration of the government grain-stores, and was forced to yield to the mutineers' demands. Then in 1013/1605 rebel troops intercepted a viceroy outside Cairo, killed him, and displayed his head on the Zuwayla Gate.

This sequence of revolts came to a head under a strong viceroy, Mehmed (Muḥammad) Pasha, who held office from 1016/1607 to 1020/1611. He began with a rigorous investigation into the fatal insurrection of 1013/1605, and went on to suppress an illegal levy (*ṭulba*) made by the troops serving in the sub-provinces of Egypt. These rural troops belonged to the cavalry corps (*sipahis*),[1]

[1] For further information on the *sipahis*, see S. J. Shaw, *The financial and administrative organization and development of Ottoman Egypt, 1517–1798* (Princeton, N.J., 1962), pp. 196–7.

particularly to that recruited from Mamluks, and hence known as the *Çerakise* (Circassians). Their financial emoluments were poor, and, as mentioned above, they had already played a prominent part in at least one revolt.

The viceroy's action brought about a very menacing revolt of the *sipahis*, who assembled under oath at the shrine of Aḥmad al-Badawī at Ṭanṭā. Thence they marched on Cairo. Their insurrection took on a separatist complexion, since they appointed a sultan and ministers. The mutineers found themselves faced by a motley but impressive force at al-Khānqa, and their resistance crumbled. Some were executed, others exiled to the Yemen. The chronicler, Ibn Abi'l-Surūr, speaks of this bloodless victory as being 'in truth the second conquest of Egypt during the sacred Ottoman government', and there is an element of truth in this exaggeration. It was a triumph of the Ottoman administration over opponents who were mostly Circassian Mamluks, and had attempted to set up an independent sultanate. To the quiet and law-abiding folk of Egypt the strong rule of Mehmed Pasha, henceforward known as *Kul kıran* (breaker of the Mamluks), seemed to presage the return of good governance under the Ottoman sultan.

The real threat to the sultan's control of Egypt did not come from the separatist ambitions of Mamluk troopers, but from the beys, who at this time were still following a policy of collaboration with the Ottoman administration. The beylicate was an order of high-ranking military functionaries who stood in a particularly close relationship to the viceroy, but who were not included in the cadre of officers of the seven corps of the Ottoman garrison. The beylicate in Egypt was different in nature from the beylicate in the older Ottoman provinces, and may well have been a survival of the high amirate which had existed under the Mamluk sultans. Although it appears to have been a Mamluk institution by origin, its membership was not confined exclusively to Mamluks. The beys were, however, predominantly Circassian, and increasingly so during the eighteenth century.

The beylicate is important because, during the seventeenth century (and perhaps before), its members acquired a prescriptive right to certain great offices of state: that of commander of the Pilgrimage (*amīr al-Ḥajj*), treasurer (*defterdar*), and acting viceroy (*qā'im maqām*). They were, furthermore, appointed as governors of Upper Egypt, as well as to military governorships in other sub-provinces. As this latter practice became increasingly common the *kāshifs* who had been the administrative heads of the sub-provinces at the time of the *Kanunname*, declined in status and became subordinates of the beys. That the beys were primarily military functionaries is demonstrated by the fact that they were put in command of the annual tribute-convoy to Istanbul, and were appointed as *serdars* of forces required for military action either within Egypt, or elsewhere in the Ottoman Empire. Officers of the corps were apparently not appointed to these special commands. The ultimate emergence of the beylicate as the real ruling institution in Egypt may, from the political aspect, be ascribed to these two factors: its close association with the traditional Mamluk ruling *élite*; and its original lack of particularized functions, which preserved it from the obsolescence which overtook the specifically Ottoman institutions in Egypt, and rendered it flexible and adaptable in changing circumstances.

The viceroyalty of *Kul kıran* Mehmed Pasha proved to be an episode, not the starting point of a genuine revival of Ottoman administration in Egypt. The next trial of strength came in 1032/1623, when the soldiery refused to accept a new viceroy, and reinstated the one who had been recalled. What is significant on this occasion is that the beys, who had hitherto been supporters of legitimate authority, joined with the troops to refuse recognition to the viceroy-designate. A few years later, apparently for the first time, they took the initiative, and offered collective resistance to a viceroy who had procured the assassination of one of their number in 1040/1631. When the viceroy refused to give the grandees (i.e. the beys and the corps officers) satisfaction for this deed, they invested a bey as acting viceroy, and sent reports, drafted in Turkish and Arabic, to Istanbul. The sultan's government confirmed the action of the grandees, who thereby established a precedent, which in the next century became a prescriptive right, to suspend an obnoxious viceroy, and transfer his powers temporarily to one of their own number.

For about thirty years after this event the beys dominated the political scene in Egypt. Their ascendancy was precarious because they were not united amongst themselves, and their inveterate factionalism exposed them to the intrigues of the transient viceroys, who lacked the military power to confront them openly. The factions of the grandees were both deeply divided and permanent, since the beylicate was largely monopolized by two rival households. One of these, the Faqāriyya, was Circassian and Mamluk in its ethnic composition and structure.[1] The other, the Qāsimiyya, certainly contained some members who were Bosniaks, but, whatever its origins, it became assimilated to a Mamluk household in its structure. Neither the Faqāriyya nor the Qāsimiyya can be traced back beyond the date we have now reached, although a legend, related by al-Jabartī, ascribes to the two households eponymous founders in the time of Selim I. The names of the two households were extended to wider groupings because of the links which were established between them and older factions among the indigenous population of Egypt. These older factions were known as Niṣf Saʿd and Niṣf Ḥarām, and became identified with the Faqāriyya and Qāsimiyya respectively.

During most of this first ascendancy of the beylicate the Faqāriyya had the upper hand. Their household and faction were headed by a remarkable Circassian, Riḍwān Bey al-Faqārī who held the position of commander of the Pilgrimage almost without a break from 1040/1631 until his death in 1066/1656. Riḍwān's power and influence inevitably made him the target of attacks,

[1] See further my article, 'Dhu'l-Faḳāriyya', in *EI*², vol. ii, p. 233.

from both the Ottoman authorities and his factional rivals, but he survived or evaded all attempts to destroy him. There is some reason to think that, early in his career, he contemplated exploiting his position as commander of the Pilgrimage to found a revived Mamluk sultanate in Egypt. Such at least would seem to be the significance of a curious genealogy, written in 1041/1632, which purports to trace Riḍwān's ancestry back to the Mamluk sultan, Barsbāy, and indeed further, to Quraysh of Mecca! But this project was conceived at the time when power was vigorously assumed by Murad IV, and nothing came of it.

When Riḍwān died he left a powerful household and faction. Attempts by the viceroys and the Qāsimiyya to oust them from the two important posts of commander of the Pilgrimage and governor of Upper Egypt were at first unsuccessful. In 1071/1660 they imprudently played into the hands of the viceroy, who was acting in concert with Aḥmad Bey the Bosniak, the leader of the Qāsimiyya. The Faqāriyya were proscribed and, after a military operation, their leading beys were dispersed and destroyed. They were not completely extirpated, and the household of Ḥasan Bey, a *mamlūk* of Riḍwān Bey, was to play an important part in the politics of the next generation. For the time being, however, they were eclipsed by the Qāsimiyya. Nevertheless, Aḥmad Bey was not allowed to acquire a position of predominance like that of Riḍwān. In 1072/1662 the viceroy procured his assassination. The beylicate, divided into factions and deprived of leadership, did not react to this as it had done to the similar assassination in 1040/1631. For about thirty years the beys sank back into obscurity.

The ascendancy of the beylicate is a peculiarly Egyptian phenomenon. Elsewhere in the Arab provinces the decline of the classical Ottoman administration is accompanied by a rise in the political importance of the garrison Janissaries (*Mustaḥfiẓān*) and allied forces, and conflicts between them and other elements of the allied forces and the population. This phenomenon appeared, with local variations, in Baghdād, Damascus, and Aleppo. In Cairo the Janissaries did not play an important role until the later years of the eleventh/seventeenth century.[1] From 1087/1676 to 1106/1694 an important political figure was an obscure junior officer of the Janissaries named Küçük Mehmed (Muḥammad). Building up his power by intrigue and gang-leadership, he made himself on several occasions the boss of the Janissaries, ousting his opponents and overthrowing his regimental superiors the high officers of the corps. During his last period of power, from 1103/1692 to 1106/1694, he showed some of the qualities of a popular leader, and his assassination in the latter year was at least partly brought about by grain-speculators, whose operations he had obstructed.

Küçük Mehmed's authority was transient. The importance of his career lies rather in the fact that through him the Faqāriyya re-emerged on the

[1] For the Janissaries of Egypt, see Shaw, *Financial organization*, pp. 189–91.

political scene and renewed their conflict with the Qāsimiyya, which was to plague Egypt for forty years. The Faqāriyya were at this time led by Ibrāhīm Bey al-Faqārī, and were allied to another household, the Qāzdughliyya, which was not, however, represented in the beylicate. The Qāzdughliyya household was founded by a regular officer of the Ottoman garrison-corps, and until the middle of the eighteenth century none of its members became beys. Ibrāhīm Bey al-Faqārī sought to acquire the *ri'āsa*, or supremacy among the military grandees. To do this he needed control of the Janissaries, many of whose officers were Qāsimī partisans. Through collusion with Küçük Mehmed he was able, in 1103/1692, to oust the Qāsimiyya, and restore the ascendancy of the Faqāriyya, until he died of plague in 1107/1695.

The twenty years which followed the *coup d'état* of Ibrāhīm Bey and Küçük Mehmed in 1103/1692 are a period of complex and unstable political groupings. Broadly speaking, there were two great schisms in the ruling and military groups: between the Faqāriyya and the Qāsimiyya among the grandees; and between the Janissaries and the other six corps, headed by Azeban.[1] Temporary fragmentations of the major factions, and opportunist alliances of individuals and groups, which crossed factional divisions, complicate the picture. The result was a recurrent and anarchic struggle for power, in which the viceroys were for the most part impotent onlookers, necessary only as the legitimating authority for the acts of the dominant group.

Matters came to a head in the Great Insurrection of 1123/1711, when the various animosities and rivalries which had long existed resolved themselves, and two major parties emerged.[2] The occasion of the dispute was another Janissary boss, Afranj Aḥmad, who had acquired power in much the same way as Küçük Mehmed. Afranj Aḥmad's opponents obtained the support of the Azeban, and fighting broke out between them and the Janissaries. The Qāsimiyya supported the Azeban, while part of the Faqāriyya assisted Afranj Aḥmad and the Janissaries. In a battle of the Mamluk factions outside Cairo one of the Qāsimī leaders was killed, and henceforward the rivalry between Qāsimiyya and Faqāriyya turned into a relentless vendetta, each faction striving to wipe out the other. The Great Insurrection ended with the triumph of the Qāsimiyya, the flight of their leading Faqārī opponents, and the death of Afranj Aḥmad. This was the last time that a Janissary boss played a significant part in Egyptian politics. The ascendancy passed to the military grandees.

The ascendancy of the grandees: 1711–98

Although the substance of political power in Egypt passed conclusively into the hands of the military grandees in the early twelfth/eighteenth century, they maintained in being the old framework of administration, and paid

[1] For this rival infantry corps to the Janissaries, see Shaw, *Financial organization*, pp. 191–2.

[2] This has been examined in detail by André Raymond, 'Une "Révolution" au Caire sous les Mamelouks. La Crise de 1123/1711', *Annales islamologiques*, vi (Cairo, 1965), 95–120.

outward deference to the commands of the sultan, communicated through his viceroy. Accepting this nominal Ottoman sovereignty, they contended among themselves for the supremacy (*riʾāsa*), which had earlier been the objective of Ibrāhīm Bey al-Faqārī. *Riʾāsa* was not a constitutional concept: it was a primacy among peers recognized by the grandees. It could be held by one grandee alone, or by two or more in coalition. There were no rules for its transfer or devolution, and its lapse was followed by a struggle of factions and individuals.

On the morrow of the Great Insurrection the beys and the high officers of the seven corps of the garrison were of equal importance. The fact was that by the early twelfth/eighteenth century the whole of the military *élite* of Egypt had been assimilated to the Mamluk system of organization and patronage. This is demonstrated by the three great households of grandees—the Faqāriyya of Circassian Mamluk origin; the Qāsimiyya with its Bosniak element, but already assimilated to the Mamluk pattern by the mid-eleventh/seventeenth century; and the Qāzdughliyya, founded by Turkish (*Rūmī*) officers of the corps, but becoming indistinguishable from a Mamluk household during the twelfth/eighteenth century. The schism between the Qāsimiyya and the Faqāriyya (with their Qāzdughlī allies) was a distinction of far greater political importance than the formal differences of function between the beys and the officers of the corps. Nevertheless, as the century went on, the beylicate came to overshadow the high-ranking officers in the corps in prestige and power. It is significant that, whereas down to and including Ibrāhīm Kâhya al-Qāzdughlī (d. 1168/1754) none of the Qāzdughliyya had entered the beylicate, ten of Ibrāhīm's own *mamlūks* became beys.

This concentration of power in the beylicate, rather than among the military grandees as a whole, is reflected in the appearance of a special term to signify the holder of the *riʾāsa*. The title *shaykh al-balad* has been noted by Stanford J. Shaw as having been first applied in the Ottoman archives to Muḥammad Bey Charkas, in the third decade of the eighteenth century; (see n. 2, p. 100). It is first applied by al-Jabartī to Ḥusayn Bey al-Ṣābūnjī, who held the position in, or shortly after, 1170/1756–7.[1] The title of *shaykh al-balad* was apparently never applied to an officer of the corps who held the *riʾāsa*. As a matter of fact, after the death of Ibrāhīm Kâhya and his partner in the *riʾāsa*, Riḍwān Kâhya, which followed soon after, no officer of the corps was ever a contender for the supremacy.

Although the grandees held in effect supreme power in Egypt from 1123/1711 until the arrival of Bonaparte in 1213/1798, the effectiveness of their rule was diminished by the factional struggles which had characterized Mamluk society since the Middle Ages. Immediately after the Great Insur-

[1] Three other terms appear to have been used at this time as synonymous for *shaykh al-balad*. They are *amīr Miṣr* (first used of Ismāʿīl Bey b. Īwāẓ; d. 1136/1723–4), *kabīr al-balad* and *kabīr al-qawm*.

rection the Qāsimiyya were in the ascendancy, although this faction split into rival groups. Their mutual hostility offered an opportunity to the Faqāriyya, who finally broke the power of the Qāsimiyya in 1142/1730. Although fragments of the Qāsimiyya remained in being, they had lost for ever the supremacy in Egypt. The instability of the early twelfth/eighteenth century permitted a revival of Hawwāra power in Upper Egypt. The tribal chief, Shaykh Humām, belonged to Niṣf Ḥarām, and was an ally of the Qāsimiyya. After the debacle of 1142/1730 Qāsimī refugees took service under Humām, and were assimilated to his tribesmen.

The ascendancy of the Faqāriyya was followed by the inevitable fragmentation of the victorious faction into rival groups. A first struggle eliminated the one Faqārī leader who did not belong to the Qāzdughliyya. This left the supremacy in the hands of Ibrāhīm Kâhya al-Qāzdughlī, who established a duumvirate with another officer of the corps, Riḍwān Kâhya al-Julfī—the head of a small Mamluk household. The duumvirate lasted for about seven years, and after the death of Ibrāhīm Kâhya (1168/1754), as we have seen, a struggle for power began among the members of his Mamluk household.

The ultimate victor in this struggle was a certain ʿAlī Bey, usually entitled 'the Great', but known in his own time by the nicknames of *Bulut kapan*, 'the Cloud-catcher', or *Jinn* 'the Demon'. ʿAlī was a young *mamlūk* of Ibrāhīm Kâhya's household, and was raised to the beylicate after his master's death. In 1173/1760, through an alliance with the head of the Qāzdughliyya household, he obtained recognition by the grandees as *shaykh al-balad*, and forthwith launched himself on a meteoric career which made him almost an independent ruler.[1] He pursued his opponents with a ruthlessness which shocked observers, and betrayed his benefactors and associates with a callous opportunism. He packed the beylicate with his own *mamlūks* and clients. His closest colleagues were two beys of his own creation, Ismāʿīl, another former *mamlūk* of Ibrāhīm Kâhya, and one of his own household, Muḥammad, who was distinguished by the nickname of *Abu'l-Dhahab*, 'The Father of Gold'. ʿAlī's career met with setbacks, but gradually all opposition in Egypt was overcome. The power of Hawwāra was broken, and Shaykh Humām, the paramount tribal chief of Upper Egypt, died miserably in 1183/1769.

With Egypt apparently secure, ʿAlī Bey began to expand his power outside its borders. The Ḥijāz, which had been a dependency of the Mamluk sultanate, remained in close relations with Cairo in the Ottoman period, and in 1184/1770–1 ʿAlī was delegated by the sultan to intervene in a dynastic conflict between two Hashimite claimants to the amirate of Mecca. Abu'l-Dhahab was sent with an expeditionary force which installed the protégé of

[1] This account of the rise of ʿAlī Bey is based upon the narratives in Jabartī, *ʿAjāʾib*, vol. 1, pp. 206–8, 250–3, 380. The chronology and sequence of events have been criticized by Stanford J. Shaw: see n. 1, p. 101 and his article 'The Ottoman archives as a source for Egyptian history', *JAOS*, vol. lxxxiii (1963), at pp. 451–2.

the sultan and of ʿAlī Bey. In the following year ʿAlī's armies invaded Syria, but Abu'l-Dhahab, having taken Damascus, was prevailed upon to retire. He and his former master engaged in a struggle for the supremacy and in 1186/1772 ʿAlī fled from Egypt. He joined forces with Shaykh Ẓāhir al-ʿUmar of Galilee, another potentate whose loyalty to the sultan was suspect. Some months later ʿAlī attempted to return to Cairo, but his small force was intercepted by Abu'l-Dhahab on the edge of the Delta and ʿAlī received wounds from which he died (Ṣafar 1187/May 1773).

ʿAlī Bey, we are told by al-Jabartī, 'used to read books of anecdotes and histories and biographies of the Egyptian kings', and like Riḍwān Bey before him, he dreamt of a restored Circassian sultanate. In some respects his career foreshadows that of Muḥammad ʿAlī Pasha, but his attempt to make himself independent of the Ottomans was premature. Muḥammad ʿAlī Pasha had two advantages which were denied to ʿAlī Bey. He was not a Mamluk and was able to use, in the vital early years of his rule, a military force which was independent of Mamluk rivalries and factionalism. Furthermore, the way had been prepared for him by the French invasion and the subsequent Anglo-Ottoman occupation of Egypt, which had debilitated his Mamluk opponents.

ʿAlī Bey revived the long dormant tradition of Mamluk resistance to Ottoman suzerainty. Abu'l-Dhahab, his successor as *shaykh al-balad*, resumed the more usual policy of concealing effective autonomy under ostensible collaboration with the sultan's government. His rule was, however, cut short by his death in 1189/1776, when on campaign against the rebel Shaykh Ẓāhir al-ʿUmar. His death was followed by another period of struggle among the Qāzdughliyya for the *riʾāsa*, the chief competitors being Ismāʿīl Bey and two *mamlūks* of Abu'l-Dhahab, Ibrāhīm Bey and Murād Bey. These two succeeded in establishing a duumvirate; Ibrāhīm Bey, the elder colleague, being *shaykh al-balad*, and Murād commander of the Pilgrimage. Their partnership was by no means always harmonious.

In the year 1200/1786 the Ottoman government made a determined attempt to break the power of Ibrāhīm and Murād, and to re-establish control over Egypt. An expeditionary force was dispatched under the command of the admiral Gazi Hasan Pasha. The news of Hasan Pasha's landing at Alexandria threw the Mamluk grandees into confusion, but ultimately they determined on resistance. Meanwhile, Hasan Pasha was distributing propagandist proclamations in Arabic, and promising a reduction in taxes and the restoration of the *Kanunname* of Süleyman. The opening stages of the ensuing campaign resembled the events of 1798. Murād led a force down the Rosetta branch of the Nile, and was defeated by the Ottomans. Ibrāhīm fled from Cairo and was joined by Murād in the south.

Hasan Pasha and the Ottoman viceroy assumed power in Cairo, and a series of reforms was promulgated. These were intended not only to weaken the duumvirs and their supporters, but to emphasize the Islamic character of the restored Ottoman régime. So far the expedition had succeeded without difficulty, but at this point a military deadlock developed, with Hasan Pasha holding Cairo and the Delta, but unable to dislodge the duumvirs from Upper Egypt. Terms were offered by Hasan Pasha, and refused by Ibrāhīm and Murād. Meanwhile, a collaborationist group had formed around Ismāʿīl Bey, who was appointed *shaykh al-balad* by the Ottomans. By the end of the winter of 1201/1787 Hasan Pasha's forces had occupied the Nile valley as far as Aswān, and the duumvirs had withdrawn into Nubia. But this ground could not be permanently held by the Ottomans, and Hasan Pasha's services were required elsewhere, since war was about to break out between the Empire and Russia. Before he left, in Dhu'l-Ḥijja 1201/October 1787, he tried to secure the political gains which had accrued from his occupation of Egypt. Ismāʿīl Bey, he hoped, would be able to maintain his position, and was provided with armaments and 500 Ottoman troops. Ibrāhīm and Murād were to remain in Upper Egypt, and not to enter Cairo. Hardly had Hasan Pasha left Egypt before his settlement was upset. Ismāʿīl was ousted, and the duumvirs re-established their rule.

The restored government of Ibrāhīm and Murād continued until the arrival of Bonaparte and the French in July 1798. The expedition of Hasan Pasha failed to produce any lasting results, and probably did not seriously weaken the Mamluk grandees. Nevertheless, it had some interesting features. It was an early experiment in the policy of destroying local autonomies which was to be pursued vigorously by Sultan Mahmud II in the following century. It demonstrated the appeal to Islamic sentiment to win support for the Ottoman sultanate. Finally, the continued resistance of the duumvirs in Upper Egypt was an example of a difficulty which had long beset the powers controlling Cairo, and one which was to be overcome finally only by Muḥammad ʿAlī Pasha.

Landholding and Land-tax Revenues in Ottoman Egypt

STANFORD J. SHAW

LANDHOLDING in Egypt went through three relatively distinct stages in the almost three centuries of Ottoman dominion from the conquest by Sultan Selim I in 1517 to the arrival of the French expedition in 1798. These stages were directly and intimately connected with the strength of Ottoman rule and the ability of the sultan's officials in Egypt to maintain their master's suzerainty and laws against the interests and desires of the locally based Mamluk factions, parties, and confederations.

The half-century following the conquest was, in many ways, the period of greatest Ottoman strength in Egypt. Although continued resistance by bedouin tribes and former Mamluk soldiers and administrators limited the scope of the sultan's authority, this resistance was steadily beaten back by large numbers of troops sent from Istanbul, and within the expanding area of direct Ottoman authority these troops enforced the sultan's writ more completely than ever was the case in later centuries. During this period the bases of Ottoman institutions in Egypt were formulated and established, with the practices of previous local régimes largely preserved, although covered with an Ottoman veneer, as was the case elsewhere in the Empire.[1]

All the sources of wealth in the Empire, urban and rural alike, were considered to be the property of the sultan, part of his imperial possessions, to be exploited for his benefit and that of the ruling class which he supported and maintained. The older Mamluk *iqṭāʿs* were retained as the basic units in which these imperial possessions were organized and assigned to agents for the purpose of administering and exploiting their revenues, although as time passed the term *muqāṭaʿa* was more and more applied to them.[2] But while

[1] S. J. Shaw, *The financial and administrative organization and development of Ottoman Egypt, 1517–1798* (Princeton, N.J., 1962), pp. 12–14 (hereafter referred to as Shaw, *Financial organization*): idem, 'The Ottoman archives as a source for Egyptian history' (hereafter referred to as 'Ottoman archives'), *JAOS*, vol. lxxxiii (1963), pp. 447–52; ʿAbd al-Ṣamad b. Sayyid ʿAlī, *Dhikr al-khulafāʾ waʾl-mulūk al-Miṣriyya* (Millet Library, Istanbul, Ali Emiri Tarih, MS. 596), fols. 428*b*–433b.

[2] The assignment of *muqāṭaʿas* as *timars*, *iltizāms*, and *emanets* in Ottoman Egypt during the eighteenth century, described in my *Financial organization*, p. 27, and denied by P. M. Holt in *BSOAS*, vol. xxvi. 1 (1963), pp. 185–6, is fully attested in the hundreds of *muqāṭaʿa* registers held by the Ottoman archives in Cairo, listed in Shaw, ibid., pp. 352–62; see also idem, 'Ottoman archives', p. 448; I. H. Uzunçarşılı, *Osmanlı devletinin merkez ve bahriye teşkilâtı* (Ankara, 1948), pp. 383–4; Mehmed Zeki Pakalın, *Osmanlı tarih deyimleri ve terimleri sözlüğü* (1946–57), vol. ii, pp. 578–9; H. A. R. Gibb and Harold Bowen, *Islamic society and the West*, vol. i, part 2 (London, 1957), p. 21 n.

the units of organization survived, the feudal system by which the Mamluks had held them was entirely abandoned. Fiefs were a characteristic part of the Ottoman system until the sixteenth century, but they were almost entirely eliminated in Ottoman Egypt, with the exception only of a few urban market taxes in the major ports, which were assigned as fiefs to the naval commanders of the Ottoman ships based there.[1] The reasons for this must remain subject to conjecture until more detailed studies are made of landholding in the Ottoman Empire as a whole. Initial findings indicate that the conquest of Egypt coincided with a general Ottoman move towards introducing other landholding systems in addition to feudalism. There were various reasons for this. The central Ottoman government was becoming increasingly efficient and able to administer sources of revenue directly, without the intermediary of fief holders. At the same time the feudal cavalry corps which formerly had constituted the bulk of the Ottoman army were becoming less important as a result of the introduction of gunpowder and fire-arms and the creation of the Janissaries and other salaried infantry and artillery corps in order to exploit them. The creation of these corps and the expansion of the Ottoman bureaucracy to meet the needs of an expanding and ever more complicated Empire forced the Treasury to seek considerably increased cash revenues so that it could pay their salaries, while under the feudal system most of the land revenues went to the fief-holders in return for their military and administrative service.[2] Moreover, Egypt was intended to provide an important part of the grain requirements of the rest of the Empire, and the administration of its lands by means of fiefs would only divert most of this grain from the government treasuries to those of the fief-holders. Finally, it seems that Selim's effort to end the fief system in Egypt was connected with his desire to destroy the financial power of the surviving Mamluks and, at the same time, to prevent his officials and soldiers from building up local power which, in such a distant and wealthy land, would make it possible to ignore the wishes and interests of the central government.[3] Persons dependent on regular salaries distributed by the Treasury were far more subject to government control than were those possessing independent revenues such as fiefs.

But regardless of the exact motives, we do know that the early Ottoman governors in Egypt followed a conscious policy of eliminating the feudal Mamluk *iqṭāʿs* found at the time of the conquest, even going so far as to confiscate those *iqṭāʿs* which previously had been made into private property

[1] Shaw, *Financial organization*, pp. 134–7.

[2] Uzunçarşılı, *Osmanlı tarihi*, vol. ii, pp. 543–66, 571–4; idem, *Kapukulu ocakları* (Ankara, 1943), vol. i, 144–705; Halil Inalcık, 'Osmanlı Imparatorluğunun kuruluş ve inkişafı devrinde Türkiye'nin iktisadî vaziyeti üzerinde bir tetkik münasebetiyle', *Belleten*, vol. xv (1951), pp. 629–40, and especially pp. 651–61, 676–84. The gradual replacement of many fiefs by tax farms has not yet been fully studied, but is apparent by examination of the cadastral and tax registers found in the *Başbakanlık Arşivi* in Istanbul, in particular in the Kâmil Kepeci and *Maliyeden müdevvere* collections.

[3] Shaw, *Financial organization*, pp. 41–43; ʿAbd al-Ṣamad, fols. 336b, 164b, 398b.

or turned over to *waqfs*. Mamluks who acknowledged the sultan's authority and entered his service were provided with the same sort of salaries as were the regular members of the Ottoman ruling class which they now were joining.[1]

Confiscating fiefs was relatively easy. But in addition to its military function feudalism also was a means of administration—of assuring that the lands would be watered, cultivated, and defended and that taxes would be levied and collected, and the early Ottoman governors found it extremely difficult to devise a satisfactory substitute to accomplish these tasks. Direct administration by salaried officials, characteristic of modern governments, was very appealing to them. But in an age of poor communications and relatively weak central governments, it was impossible to secure efficiency and honesty from officials unless they were given some sort of financial interest in their undertakings. At first the Treasury did try to administer the landed *muqāṭaʿas* in *emanet*—directly through its own salaried agents, the *emins*. These were the closest Ottoman equivalents to modern bureaucrats; they were paid salaries, and they were supposed to send all their tax collections to the Treasury, profiting from them in no way, at least legally.[2] Each of the *emins* was given one or more of the *muqāṭaʿas* to administer, while the tasks of local security formerly undertaken by the Mamluk fief-holders were cared for by the provincial governors and local military garrisons. But this system soon proved to be unworkable. Since the *emins*' salaries did not depend on the amounts of their collections, they lacked the stimulus to be thorough and efficient, and sought extra-legal revenues in various ways. Moreover, the Treasury was unable to find sufficient men to occupy these posts. Former Mamluks were excluded because of fears they would be disloyal and might use their positions to raise another revolt like that led by Aḥmad Pasha in 1524 and 1525; nor were Ottoman soldiers appointed because of the urgent need for their military talents.[3] Only Ottomans sent especially from elsewhere in the Empire and a few Copts and Jews were appointed as *emins*, and even the latter, for the

[1] Shaw, ibid., pp. 41–50; idem, 'The land law of Ottoman Egypt (960–1553): A contribution to the study of landholding in the early years of Ottoman rule in Egypt', *Der Islam*, vol. xxxviii (1962), pp. 106–37.

[2] Shaw, *Financial organization*, pp. 26, 31, 64; Uzunçarşılı, *Merkez teşkilâtı*, pp. 332 n., 378; Pakalın, vol. i, pp. 524–6; Halil Sahillioğlu, 'Bir mültezim zinem defterine göre XV. yüzyıl sonunda Osmanlı Darphane mukataaları', *Istanbul Üniversitesi Iktisat Fakültesi Mecmuası*, vol. xxiii (1962–3), pp. 145–218 and especially 147–8; Fahri Dalsar, *Bursa'da ipekçilik* (Istanbul, 1960), pp. 250–2; Abdurrahman Vefik Bey, *Tekalif kavaidi* (Istanbul, 1328), vol. i, pp. 176–84; Gibb and Bowen, vol. i. 2, p. 21 n.

[3] It should be noted that this Mamluk revolt was not quickly suppressed in 1524, as suggested by P. M. Holt in *BSOAS*, vol. xxvi (1963), p. 186. Although its leader Aḥmad Pasha was killed within a short time, his followers continued to resist, and gained control of much of the countryside. Only with the arrival of large numbers of Ottoman troops commanded by the grand vezir Ibrahim Pasha was the revolt finally crushed and the Ottoman governors given sufficient power to establish their laws and institutions in the country. See Shaw, 'Ottoman Archives', pp. 448–9.

most part, refused when possible on the grounds that the salaries were insufficient compensation for the work involved. As a result, the Treasury was compelled to give numerous *muqāṭaʿas* to each *emin*. Since the *emins* could not, therefore, care for all their holdings personally, they had to administer them through agents, called *ʿāmils*; and despite numerous official admonitions, the *ʿāmils* were drawn from the only ready source of manpower, the former Mamluk officers and soldiers. To entice them, the positions were given as tax-farms (*iltizām*). The *ʿāmils* acted as tax-farmers (sing. *multazim*), paying fixed annual sums to the *emins* and keeping the balance of the tax collections as profits for themselves. Under the motivation of individual profit the *ʿāmils* became extremely exacting and energetic collectors, in the process seeing to the restoration of large tracts of lands which had fallen out of cultivation in the years of anarchy which accompanied and followed the Ottoman conquest. So it was not long before they were making far more money than were their superiors and were able to force the Treasury to accept their tax-farms as a *fait accompli*, as the regular means by which the rural *muqāṭaʿas* were to be administered.[1]

As was to be the case on numerous occasions throughout the history of Ottoman Egypt, as in fact was the case elsewhere in the Empire, the Ottoman rulers skilfully adjusted to a situation which they could not control or change and fitted it into their own system in order to secure the same ends by different means. The main object of Ottoman rule in Egypt was to secure the maximum exploitation of its sources of revenue for the benefit of the Imperial Treasury. *Emanets* had not accomplished the job. Tax-farms were accepted because they accomplished the tasks of administration and tax collection far more successfully and because there was no other choice. While, as we shall see, the *multazims* absorbed an increasing portion of the tax collections for themselves, they did provide the Treasury with sufficient revenues to meet its obligations as well as with sufficient grain to feed Istanbul and Anatolia, and this, in the end, was the important thing. The *emins* rapidly receded into the regular Treasury bureaucracy and became no more than officials and scribes in charge of assigning the tax-farms and collecting their taxes.[2] It is important to note that the Egyptian tax-farmers evolved not out of the *emins*, who originally held the *muqāṭaʿas*, but the *ʿāmils*, their subordinates, and that the tax-farms were introduced not as the result of conscious government policy but as the result of necessity. This process went on throughout the first half of the seventeenth century, and was both cause and manifestation of the process by which Mamluk houses were formed and rose to political power. For all practical purposes it was complete by 1671, the

[1] Shaw, *Financial organization*, pp. 31–34; *Mühimme defteri* (hereafter referred to as *Müh.*), vol. vi, 221: 474; vol. xxii, 184: 354; vol. xxiii, 11: 75; vol. xxxvii, 275: 326; Dalsar, *Ipekçilik*, pp. 251–2; Vefik, *Tekalif*, pp. 238–9.

[2] Shaw, *Financial organization*, pp. 345–8.

last year in which officials sent from the Porte held effective power in the major administrative positions of the Ottoman hierarchy in Egypt.[1]

So the classical form of landholding in Ottoman Egypt was the tax-farm. Some lands were assigned to objects entirely outside the imperial possessions, in perpetuity to *waqfs*,[2] temporarily as *kushūfiyya* plots set aside to provide the *khāṣṣ* revenues of the governor and other high officials,[3] and as *waṣiyya* holdings in each village for the individual profit of their tax-farmers.[4] In these cases the sultan relinquished the right of his Treasury to exploit the lands involved, so their holders did not have to pay it any part of the taxes collected from the cultivators. But these lands were only a very small part of the total, and even here the holders often secured their administration by assigning them as private tax-farms, often to the same tax-farmers who exploited the neighbouring Treasury lands.

With the *muqāṭa'as*, the Treasury retained the substance of the land as the agent of the sultan and assigned it temporarily to tax-farmers. The latter did not acquire any property rights. They secured only the temporary use and the right to share in its tax revenues in return for their function as administrators. And they had to share even this limited title with the peasant cultivators, who had their own legal rights in return for cultivating the land and paying its taxes.

Each tax-farm was assigned to the highest bidder at an auction (*muzāyada*) held by the Treasury whenever there were vacancies. The purchase price, called *badal al-iltizām*, formed part of the personal revenues of the sultan rather than those of the Treasury, and so reflected his continued suzerainty and ultimate ownership of the usufruct of the land. Legally the auction was supposed to be consummated only if the bidding pushed the sale price to or above the 'value price' (*değer baha*) an ill-defined concept which varied according to the value of the holding, but which was supposed to equal eight times the average annual profit earned by the previous tax-farmer. In fact, the Treasury had no official knowledge of these profits, since the tax-farmers carefully concealed them in order to avoid increased impositions on their holdings. So, in the end, it was assumed that these profits were one-eighth

[1] Shaw, ibid., p. 6; idem, 'Ottoman archives', p. 448. The names and ranks of the holders of positions in the 'Ottoman hierarchy' of government in Egypt are given in the salary registers held by the Ottoman archives in Cairo, listed in Shaw, *Financial organization*, pp. 391–7 and described in my 'Cairo's Archives and the History of Ottoman Egypt', *Report on research, Spring, 1956* (Middle East Institute, Washington, 1956), pp. 59–72, and in particular p. 63. Compare Holt, *BSOAS*, vol. xxvi. 1 (1963), p. 186.

[2] Shaw, *Financial organization*, pp. 41–45, 269–70. *Rizqas* in many ways were like *waqfs*, but instead of being beneficiaries of land-tax revenues as such, they were fixed annual rents established on landed and non-landed *muqāṭa'as* for purposes similar to those of *waqfs*, as well as to supplement military salaries. See Shaw, 'Land law', pp. 106–18; Gibb and Bowen, vol. i. 1, pp. 173, 177. Compare Helen Anne B. Rivlin, *The agricultural policy of Muḥammad 'Alī in Egypt* (Cambridge, Mass., 1961), pp. 32–35.

[3] Shaw, *Financial organization*, pp. 40, 318.

[4] Ibid., pp. 22, 57–58.

of whatever the purchase price was, and no auction was ever voided on the grounds that this price was not reached.[1] As a result, the sultan's revenue from this source was considerably less than was originally intended.

It should be noted that while each *muqāṭaʿa* usually consisted of a principal village and the smaller towns and cultivated areas in its vicinity, it was rare for such a unit to be held by a single tax-farmer, especially after the middle of the seventeenth century. Each farm customarily was shared in partnership by five to ten tax-farmers, each of whom also held similar fractional shares in numerous other *muqāṭaʿas*. Such partners were mutually responsible for each others' tax obligations, but only in respect to those arising from the farm which they held together. *Multazims* were partners irrespective of differences in rank, age, military corps, and residence, and their mutual rights and obligations did not depend on or vary according to these factors. While members of the military corps and Mamluk parties held many of the tax-farms, many also were held by merchants, scribes, religious men, bedouin chiefs, members of the Ottoman imperial family, high officials of the Porte, and retired Ottoman soldiers and officers living both in Egypt and Istanbul.[2] During the eighteenth century they were concentrated more and more in the hands of the chiefs of the great Mamluk houses and their slaves, wives, and children.[3] If the tax-farmers failed to carry out their obligations, if they voluntarily gave up their holdings or died (with or without legal heirs), their holdings were supposed to be declared vacant (*maḥlūl*) and seized (*hazine-mande*) for the Treasury so that they could be sold at auction once again.

The total taxes levied on the cultivators was known as *al-māl al-ḥurr* or 'pure tax'. That portion delivered to the Treasury was the *māl al-kharāj* or *māl mīrī*. Tax moneys retained in the provinces and villages for local purposes were called the *mukhrijāt*, or 'deductions', while the collections retained by the tax farmers for themselves was their 'profit', or *fāʾiż*. In principle the basic land tax was originally set in the sixteenth century at the average rate of four or five *paras* per feddan cultivated, and the current state of cultivation and consequent taxes owed by the lands in each *muqāṭaʿa* were written into the great cadastral survey compiled during the last half of that century.[4] In later times this rate and the taxes which it represented were known as *al-māl*

[1] Shaw, *Financial organization*, pp. 35–36; Evliya Çelebi, *Seyahatname*, vol. x (Istanbul, 1938), p. 134; Jabartī, vol. ii, p. 151; *Müh. Mısır*, vol. i, 67a: 296; vol. iv, 36b: 164.

[2] The holders' names and occupations are listed in the *muqāṭaʿa* registers held by the Ottoman archives in Cairo, listed in Shaw, *Financial organization*, pp. 352–62, and described in idem, 'Cairo's Archives', pp. 62–63. See also J. Deny, *Sommaire des archives turques du Caire* (Cairo, 1930), pp. 176–7.

[3] Shaw, *Financial organization*, p. 53; idem, *Ottoman Egypt in the age of the French Revolution* (Cambridge, Mass., 1964), p. 50; *Müh. Mısır*, vol. iv, 21b: 90; vol. vii, 74: 152.

[4] Shaw, *Financial organization*, pp. 64–66, 95–97, 16–19; idem, 'Land law', pp. 107–8; idem, *French Revolution*, p. 149; Gibb and Bowen, vol. i. 2, p. 40. Although the sixteenth-century cadaster is mentioned in the chronicles and other sources, I have not been able to find its registers in the archives.

al-qadīm, or 'old tax'. If lands in individual *muqāṭa'as* were known to have changed in fertility and cultivation, their taxes could be individually increased (*ziyāda*) or decreased (*tanzīl*) by order of the governor. In addition, general increases in the rate of taxation above that established in *al-māl al-qadīm*, independent of any change in fertility or cultivation, were also made under the term *muḍāf*. If lands were not fully cultivated owing to shortage in the Nile flow or other natural disasters, the governor could declare them dry (*sharāqi*) and their taxes lowered or remitted for the year or years involved.[1]

But over the years this system fell badly out of adjustment. No further general cadastral survey was made until the French occupation at the end of the eighteenth century.[2] While some changes in cultivation and taxes were entered into the old registers, for the most part newly cultivated lands were entirely ignored and untaxed, and the tax demands sent by the Treasury to each *muqāṭa'a* on the books were exactly the same in the eighteenth century as they were two hundred years before, although considerable changes had occurred in their fertility and cultivation. Only efforts of the tax-farmers and local officials to adjust the taxes on individual lands within each *muqāṭa'a* counteracted the full effects of this situation.

During the sixteenth century, *al-māl al-ḥurr* and *māl al-kharāj* were virtually identical since all cultivated lands were taxed; the bulk of collected taxes went to the Treasury, and only a very small percentage was diverted to administrative and local expenditures. However, during the centuries of Ottoman rule the Treasury's share of the total land-taxes collected became less and less. A major stimulus to this was the tremendous debasement of Ottoman currency in Egypt during this time. The silver *para*, which was legally fixed at 1·28 grams of silver weight and 100 per cent. purity in the sixteenth century fell to 0·689 grams and 70 per cent. in 1698 and 0·225 grams and 30 per cent. in 1798.[3] The gold sequin fell from a purity of 99·6 per cent. and weight of 3·448 grams in 1595 (equal to 300 *paras*) to 2·592 grams and 69·8 per cent. at the end of the eighteenth century. The *fındıklı* gold coin, first minted in 1703 with a legal weight of 3·510 grams and purity of 96·8 per cent. fell to 3·448 grams and 75 per cent. by the end of the century.[4] In response to this and the consequent inflation of prices it was inevitable that the tax rate per feddan should be increased, and it was by *muḍāfs* totalling 5,000 *paras* added

[1] Shaw, *Financial organization*, pp. 65–68; Rivlin, pp. 28, 128, 129; Gibb and Bowen, vol. i. 2, p. 60.

[2] Shaw, *French Revolution*, pp. 122–5; Rivlin, pp. 54–56; Jabartī, vol. iv, pp. 203–4, 207–9; E. Driault, *Mohamed Aly et Napoléon, 1807–1814* (Cairo, 1925), pp. 241–2; 'Abd al-Raḥmān al-Rāfi'ī, *Ta'rīkh al-ḥaraka al-qawmiyya wa-taṭawwur niẓām al-ḥukm fī Miṣr* (Cairo, 1955), vol. i, pp. 109–14. The registers of this cadaster are found at the Dār al-Maḥfūẓāt archives at the Citadel in Cairo.

[3] Shaw, *French Revolution*, p. 168; Samuel-Bernard, 'Mémoire sur les monnoies d'Égypte', *Description de l'Égypte*, 2nd edn., vol. xvi, p. 463; *Müh. Mısır*, vol. vi, 86a; *Müh.*, vol. cviii, 349.

[4] Shaw, *French Revolution*, p. 169; Samuel-Bernard, op. cit., pp. 446–51.

to every 25,000 *paras* of *al-māl al-qadīm*, increasing the average tax per feddan to about seven *paras* at the end of the eighteenth century. The total Treasury revenues from the land tax increased from 44,478,312 *paras* in 1596 to 75,212,389 *paras* in 1798, an increase of about 60 per cent. over the original amount.[1] This increase would not seem unfair in view of the concurrent debasement of currency. But in fact the total of *al-māl al-ḥurr* increased from about fifty million *paras* annually at the end of the sixteenth century to 411,800,052 *paras* in 1798, an increase of about 800 per cent.; and of the latter figure only 21 per cent. went to the Treasury, and 12 per cent. to the provincial governors and local village officials, while the remaining 67 per cent. was left in the hands of the tax-farmers and their agents. Most of this was accomplished through manipulation of the *mukhrijāt* charges levied on the cultivators as costs of collection by military and civil agents of the provincial governors and tax-farmers. Over the years, a definite process was followed in increasing these taxes. Once such a charge was legalized by usage, the governors appropriated them as part of their own revenues, so new extra-legal taxes had to be imposed, and they in turn were legalized in time. Since the provincial governors were usually called *kāshif*, those *mukhrijāt* charges which went for their benefit were subsequently called *kushūfiyya*; those which were collected primarily for the benefit of the tax-farmers and their agents were known as *barrānī* charges, and these rapidly became just as important elements in their incomes as were their legal *fā'iż* profits. Thus, by such means, the Mamluks allowed the Treasury to receive only the portion of the land-tax increase which was directly related to the debasement of the currency. While the tremendous increase in taxes came mainly in the *kushūfiyya* and *barrānī* charges as well as in cultivated lands not taxed by the Treasury, these went almost entirely to the Mamluks and their houses.[2]

What was the position of the tax-farmers in relation to the cultivators? This also varied according to the relative strength of the Ottoman officials and Mamluk houses. The *multazims* usually were not able or willing to administer their varied holdings personally, so they acted through agents, their military subordinates appointed as *qā'immaqāms* to each village and their business managers, the *ṣarrāfs*, who were assigned to supervise all their holdings in individual districts and provinces. In villages where the *muqāṭa'as* were shared by several tax-farmers, administration for all was usually carried out by the agents of the one with the largest interest. So there was added another level of officials who had to be supported in some way by the cultivators. And this was not all. The tax-farmers' agents were only in charge of supervising cultivation and taxation operations. They were not ordinarily supposed to have direct contact with the cultivators. This was done by the village chiefs and other local officials, who also were supported by special taxes levied on the

[1] Shaw, *Financial organization*, pp. 68–74.
[2] Ibid., pp. 91–97.

lands as part of the ***mukhrijāt***. It was only when these officials and the peasants they directed failed in their duties, so that the lands were not cultivated and the taxes not paid on time and in full, that the tax-farmers or their agents were entitled to take direct action to secure the revenues guaranteed them by virtue of their *muqāṭaʿas*.[1]

The peasant's right to his plot of land was officially known as his *athar*. So long as he cultivated the land and delivered his taxes on time he could not be deprived of it. But he was not attached to it, and could legally give it up if he wished at any time. He could leave it to heirs, and even hire other peasants to work it and so fulfil his obligation if he was unable to labour for one reason or another. The peasants were protected from oppression and exaction by Ottoman law, enforced in the courts, at least so long as the Ottoman régime was strong enough to enforce it.[2]

During the first century of Ottoman rule in Egypt the Ottoman hierarchy of government had the military power to enforce its laws, drive the bedouin bands out of the settled areas, and restore the devastated lands to cultivation. Since thousands of peasants had fled from the lands and many of them had been killed, they were in relatively short supply. So the governors, *emins*, tax-farmers, and military officers seeking to restore the lands had to compete with each other to secure peasants to accomplish this, and they did so by promising not only to observe the peasants' rights but to expand them. Taxes were lowered or remitted entirely for certain periods of time on lands newly restored to cultivation. Forced labour was abolished, and peasants were paid for voluntary labour on public works and the private *waṣiyya* plots belonging to the tax-farmers. Cultivators were allowed to buy and sell *athars* and to build up their own small estates so long as they continued to cultivate their lands and pay their taxes. And tax-farmers who violated peasant rights in any way were severely punished, often by direct military action as well as by process of law.[3]

But beginning in the late seventeenth century, these conditions changed radically. The decline of Ottoman military power in Egypt had two important results: on one hand, the military garrisons were no longer able to maintain security in the lands. Bedouins again began to raid the settled areas, and village disputes over irrigation waters abounded. In addition to this the Ottoman officials were no longer able to control the Mamluks and their houses. The

[1] Ibid., pp. 52–56; Rivlin, pp. 22–24; Michel-Ange Lancret, 'Mémoire sur le système d'imposition territoriale et sur l'administration des provinces de l'Égypte', *Description de l'Egypte* (1st edn., Paris, 1809), vol. i, pp. 236, 240–1, 246, 257; Gibb and Bowen, vol. i. 2, pp. 260–1.

[2] Shaw, *Financial organization*, pp. 20–21; Rivlin, pp. 23–24; Gibb and Bowen, vol. i. 1, p. 260; Lancret, pp. 235–6, 244–5, 257–8.

[3] Shaw, *Financial organization*, p. 21; Silvestre de Sacy, 'Mémoire sur la nature et les révolutions du droit du propriété territoriale en Égypte, depuis la conquête de ce pays par les Musulmans, jusqu'à l'expédition des Français', *Bibliothèque des Arabisants Français*, ed. G. Foucard, Prémière Série, *Silvestre de Sacy* (Cairo, 1923), vol. ii, p. 36.

Mamluk *mashāyikh al-balad* became the real rulers of the country in place of the Ottoman governors.[1] This coincided with a time of greatly increased population, in Egypt, as elsewhere in the Mediterranean area, during the late sixteenth and early seventeenth centuries. With more peasants now available than there was land for them to cultivate, it was not difficult for the tax-farmers to treat the men as they wished and to substitute compliant cultivators for those who tried to assert their rights. The *multazims* now burdened the cultivators with numerous extra levies, cheated them by varying the units of measure by which their cash and kind payments were measured, and forced them to assume large debts with usurious rates of interest from which few were able to escape. Peasants were deprived of the right to buy and sell *athars*, and heirs were required to pay large sums before they were allowed to assume their rights. They were subjected to forced labour without pay, and often were compelled to hand over their sons to fulfil the *multazims*' military obligations to the Ottoman army. With the Ottoman government powerless to protect them, the peasants were deprived of the fruits of their labour except for the bare minimum needed for them to survive, and they fell into deeper and deeper misery and subjection. As they responded to these conditions by fleeing from the lands, those of their fellows who remained had to bear even greater burdens. Only the local judges and village authorities provided some sort of protection by mediating with the Mamluks, but this was of limited value indeed. Small wonder that famine and depopulation were characteristics of Ottoman Egypt by the time the French came upon the scene.[2]

For all practical purposes the Mamluk leaders gained permanent possession of their followers' *muqāṭaʿas* during the eighteenth century. Whenever a vacancy occurred they named the new holders from among members of their own party and paid the transfer fees to the Treasury. In order to observe the legal forms this was accomplished by withdrawing the vacated tax-farms from the auctions and instead awarding them directly to the Mamluk nominees in a process known as *musalehe*, or 'settlement'. The auction price was replaced by a fee called *bedel-i musalehe* or *ḥulwān*, set at three times the assumed annual profit of the holding concerned. By this process the Mamluk houses built up large estates of *muqāṭaʿas*. When one house defeated another, and killed or scattered its members, the properties of the defeated were transferred to the victorious party in return for the *ḥulwān* payments to the Treasury.[3]

[1] Shaw, *Financial organization*, pp. 22–25; idem, *French Revolution*, pp. 60–61; Gibb and Bowen, vol. i. 1, pp. 260–1.

[2] Shaw, *Financial organization*, pp. 72–73, 80–94. The first Mamluk *Shaykh al-balad* was Çerkes Mehmed Bey (Muḥammad Bey Charkas), who held power between 1720 and 1726 (*Müh. Mısır*, vol. iii, 121b), not Ibrāhīm Katkhudā, as stated in my *Financial organization*, p. 6, and not his second successor Ḥusayn Bey al-Ṣābūnjī, as stated by Jabartī, vol. i, p. 206 and repeated by Holt (*BSOAS*, vol. xxvi, p. 187).

[3] Shaw, *Financial organization*, pp. 35–38, 165, 168, 313; Rivlin, pp. 22, 39; Gibb and Bowen, vol. i. 1, p. 260.

It should be noted that these conditions applied principally to Lower Egypt. In Middle and Upper Egypt, where bedouin tribes predominated increasingly in the eighteenth century, lands were usually held communally and assigned to individual cultivators annually as soon as the extent of the Nile flood became apparent. In these places the *athars* belonged not to individual peasants but to the tribes and villages as wholes, and the individual peasants' plots changed annually according to the extent of the Nile flood. The tax-farmers and government officials dealt not with individual villages, but with the tribal chiefs, who themselves administered the lands and controlled the peasants according to tribal customs rather than those prevailing in the areas of direct Ottoman control. Here also payments were made mainly in kind, and taxes were assessed not according to the number of feddans cultivated, at an established rate per feddan (called *faddāna*), but according to the number of bushels harvested (called *kelale*). On the whole, the bedouin areas remained far more stable and better administered in the late seventeenth and early eighteenth century, while the lands to the north fell into increasing anarchy. However, during the independent rule of ʿAlī Bey al-Kabīr between 1758 and 1773,[1] his military expeditions almost completely destroyed the power of the bedouin tribes. In the remaining years of the century the grain-producing lands of Upper Egypt fell under the regular Ottoman *muqaṭaʿa* system, with the same regulations and conditions as those imposed elsewhere.[2]

One might ask, with justice, why such a situation was accepted by both the Ottomans and the Mamluks. Why did the Ottoman government agree to Mamluk control of the administrative machinery of government, and Mamluk diversion of the bulk of the land-tax revenues for their own profit? And why did the Mamluks continue to pay taxes and *ḥulwān* fees to a government which lacked any real military power to enforce its suzerainty? As far as the Ottomans were concerned they really had no other choice, and were compelled to make the best of a bad situation. Suppression of the Mamluks required a military expedition which could not be spared from the increasingly dangerous fronts in Europe and the East. The fate of Gazi Hasan Pasha's expedition to Egypt for this purpose is a case in point. In addition, the Ottoman governors were able to keep the Mamluk houses and confederations relatively equal and play them off against each other, so that none was completely dominant, and all were willing to recognize Ottoman suzerainty, pay the required taxes and *ḥulwān* fees, and perform their duties in return for the benefits which Ottoman legal support brought. These taxes and payments were essentially confiscations of the properties of dead and defeated Mamluks who were no longer able to resist, and were thus a return to the Treasury

1 ʿAlī Bey first came to power in 1758 (see *Müh. Mısır*, vol. vii, 193: 413; H. Dehérain, *L'Égypte turque* (Paris, 1931), p. 123), not in 1760 as stated by Holt (*BSOAS*, vol. xxvi. 1 (1963), p. 187) or in 1763 as I stated in my *Financial organization*, p. 7.

2 Shaw, *Ottoman Egypt in the eighteenth century* (Cambridge, Mass., 1962), pp. 26–28; idem, *Financial organization*, pp. 24–25; Rivlin, p. 25.

of the revenues previously secured in various illegal ways. So long as they provided the Treasury with the equivalent of the revenues it used to receive by means of the regular administrative and financial system, the Porte was content to leave the latter in the hands of the Mamluks.[1]

The only adjustment which was made in the legal façade was the acceptance of a new kind of *muqāṭaʿa*, the *malikâne*, which in Ottoman Egypt was defined as an inheritable tax-farm, in fact virtual private property, whose owner still owed taxes, but who could buy and sell it and leave it in inheritance so long as the *ḥulwān* fees were paid in return.[2] This was the final step of the long process we have described. The transformation of the *muqāṭaʿas* from *emanets* into *iltizāms* and then *malikânes*, and the diversion of most of the land-tax revenues from the Treasury to the Mamluk houses were both causes and manifestations of the Mamluk rise to power. But the survival of Ottoman suzerainty, despite everything, and the continued Mamluk payment of large sums to the Treasury, showed to a large extent the success of the Ottoman efforts to mould the new situation to their own advantage.

It can be argued with a good deal of justice that the tax-farm system was ideal for Ottoman Egypt, given the conditions of the time. It assured the Treasury of a continued flow of revenues with a minimum of administrative cost to itself. It gave the tax-farmers a permanent and continued interest in the fertility of the land, so that they would not over-exploit it and drive the peasants away. It subjected the cultivators to regular taxes, and protected them against arbitrary illegal impositions. But this was the case only so long as the Porte was able to maintain its political and military hegemony, and so make the system operate as it was supposed to. Once the Mamluks gained control this was no longer the case. One might assume that if a single Mamluk house or confederation had been able to seize complete power and eliminate its rivals, it would have assumed the same position as that held previously by the Ottomans. It would have had the same interest in preserving fertility and cultivation in order to assure a regular and permanent flow of revenues. But once a situation arose in which a number of equally balanced Mamluk parties, confederations, and factions fought for power, each group had to subordinate such long-range considerations to the more immediate needs of survival. So collections on the estates of each Mamluk house became little more than large-scale raiding expeditions at harvest time, with the Mamluks often carrying off as much as they could find regardless of formal tax assessments and collections. It was only when ʿAlī Bey al-Kabīr, and later Murād Bey and Ibrāhīm Bey, established some sort of hegemony among the Mamluks that these conditions were at least partially remedied.[3] But their régimes were

[1] Shaw, *Financial organization*, pp. 313–15.

[2] Ibid., pp. 30, 39. On the *malikâne* elsewhere in the Ottoman Empire, see Gibb and Bowen, vol. i. 2, pp. 22–23, 46; Uzunçarşılı, *Merkez teşkilâtı*, pp. 203, 347; Pakalın, vol. ii, pp. 395–7; *Raşid tarihi*, vol. iv, pp. 167–77.

[3] Shaw, *Financial organization*, pp. 24–25, 90–97; Rivlin, pp. 3–4.

relatively limited in time, and the end-result was the depopulation, famine, and devastation which characterized the country in the last years of the eighteenth century. While the new situation was therefore beneficial to the Mamluks and Ottoman Treasury, Egypt as a whole suffered terribly in the years preceding the French expedition.

Quartiers et mouvements populaires au Caire au XVIIIème siècle

ANDRÉ RAYMOND

Les historiens égyptiens du XVIIème et du XVIIIème siècle accordent la plus grande part de leur attention aux faits politiques dans lesquels la caste dominante des mamelouks joue le rôle principal: de la société proprement égyptienne n'apparaissent guère que les *ʿulamā'* et les bourgeois du commerce et de l'artisanat. Les masses populaires, petits artisans et compagnons des corporations professionnelles, prolétariat aux occupations mal définies de la ville, sont laissées comme en dehors de l'histoire; elles n'y font irruption qu'à l'occasion de brèves crises où se révèle la profondeur de mouvements sur lesquels on ne possède par ailleurs que peu de renseignements. C'est à une étude de la géographie des quartiers populaires au Caire et des mouvements qui y prirent naissance au XVIIIème siècle que seront consacrées les considérations qui vont suivre.

Il est plus aisé de « déduire » la carte même des quartiers populaires au Caire par une approche « négative » (en définissant les zones qui les excluent: quartiers de grand activité économique du centre, quartiers bourgeois et aristocratiques), que de la tracer à partir des maigres informations directes données par les chroniques et la *Description de l'Égypte.* Au centre de la vieille ville fatimide de Qāhira (qui occupait le quart nord-est de l'agglomération ottomane) se pressaient la plupart des centres d'activité économique et commerciale de la ville, le long de la Qaṣaba qui joignait Bāb al-Futūḥ à Bāb Zuwayla, et des rues adjacentes: on trouvait à l'intérieur de Qāhira 141 des 205 *wakālas* que localise la *Description de l'Égypte,* et 12 *khāns* sur 13, ainsi que la plupart des métiers de luxe et des artisanats très différenciés. L'activité économique atteignait là un tel degré de concentration que les zones d'habitation étaient rejetées vers la périphérie de Qāhira: il s'agissait d'ailleurs souvent de quartiers de résidence bourgeoise, comme celui de Sabʿ Qāʿāt, ou comme les environs d'al-Azhar (où habitaient de préférence les *ʿulamā'*), les négociants et les cheikhs construisant par ailleurs volontiers, un peu plus loin, près du Khalīj et autour de l'Ezbekiyeh, des demeures cossues. La caste dominante des mamelouks (beys, *kāshifs* et officiers des milices), résidait hors de Qāhira, dans quelques quartiers privilégiés et assez exclusifs: autour de la Birkat al-Fīl, le long des rives du Khalīj al-Miṣrī, dans la région de jardins de la « rive gauche » du Khalīj, avec une prédilection de plus en plus marquée, vers la fin du XVIIIème siècle, pour l'Ezbekiyeh.[1]

[1] Voir notre article, «Quartiers de résidence aristocratique au Caire au XVIIIème siècle», dans *JESHO*, vol. vi. 1 (1963), pp. 58–103.

Les Quartiers Populaires au Caire

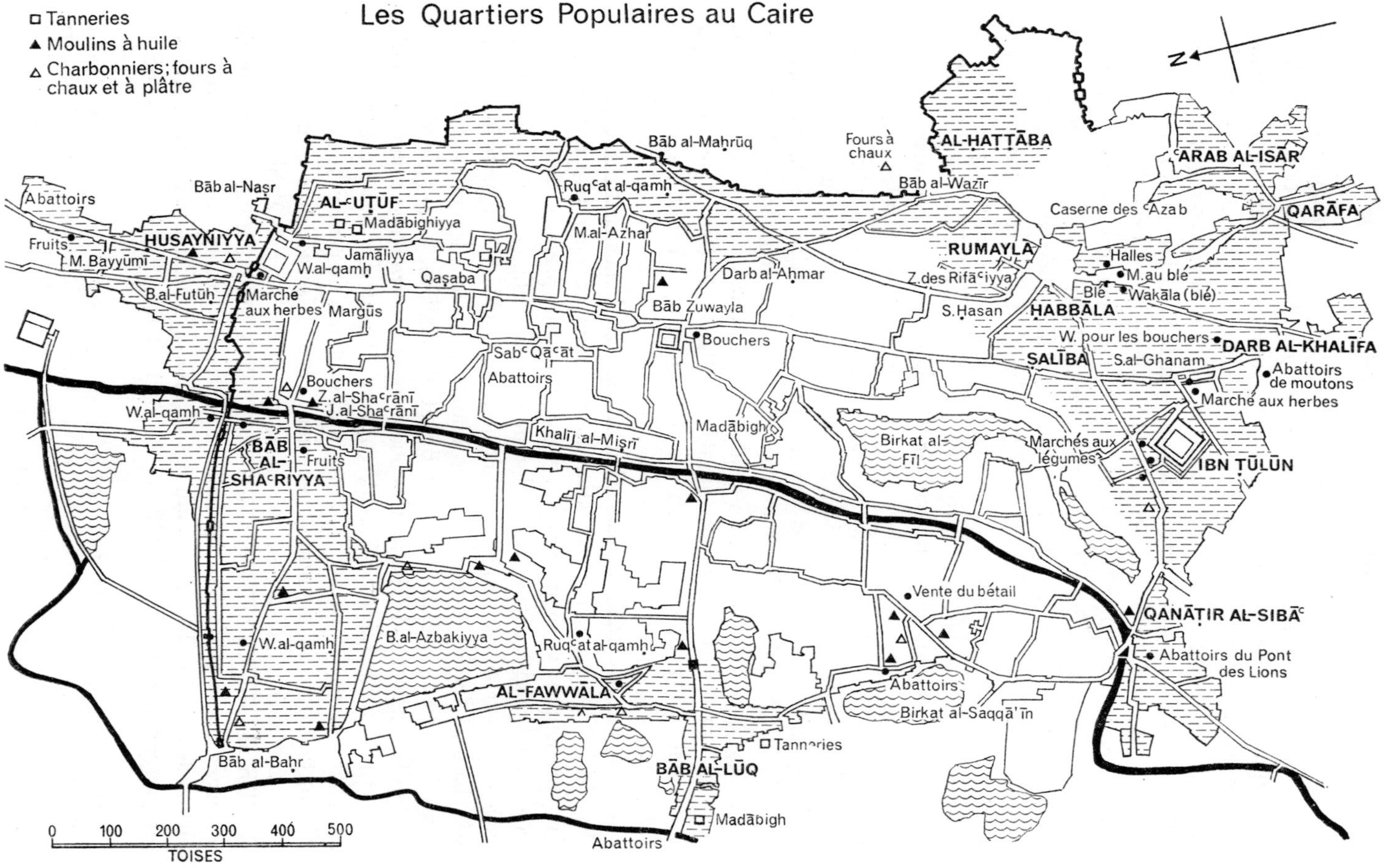

Les régions de peuplement populaire au XVIIIème siècle occupaient les vides de la carte dont nous venons de tracer les grandes lignes. C'est bien là en effet que se trouvaient tous les quartiers dont les noms reviennent sous la plume des chroniqueurs, quand il est question de mouvements populaires au Caire. C'étaient, à l'intérieur même de Qāhira, entre les régions d'intense activité économique du centre et les murs de la ville, les zones périphériques du nord (en particulier le quartier de al-ʿUṭūf) et de l'est (de l'angle nord-est de l'enceinte à la porte de Bāb al-Wazīr); les quartiers qui entouraient la Citadelle (en particulier al-Ḥaṭṭāba, au nord, et ʿArab al-Isār, au sud); puis toute la zone sud de la ville (Rumayla, Ḥabbāla, Bāb al-Qarāfa, Darb al-Khalīfa, Ṣalība, Ibn Ṭūlūn et Qanāṭir al-Sibāʿ; à l'ouest le quartier excentrique de Bāb al-Lūq et de Fawwāla, et le quartier situé à proximité de l'Ezbekiyeh entre Bāb al-Shaʿriyya et Bāb al-Baḥr; enfin au nord de Qāhira, le quartier extérieur de al-Ḥusayniyya. Une description de ces quartiers, pour être historiquement exacte, devrait prendre en considération les changements survenus dans certains secteurs: par exemple la conquête des anciennes tanneries (*madābigh*), au sud-ouest de Bāb Zuwayla, par une population aisée, après leur transfert dans la région de Bāb al-Lūq; ou en sens contraire, près de la Citadelle, le déclin des quartiers qu'abandonnait de plus en plus l'aristocratie. C'est à un tableau semblable que conduisent le recensement et le report sur la carte des termes qui dans le plan de la *Description de l'Égypte* indiquent un peuplement pauvre: « masures », « cahutes », « ruines » (*kharāba*), « hoch » (*ḥawsh*).[1]

Cet habitat populaire correspondait, sur le plan de la structure économique du Caire, aux lieux d'implantation de certaines activités peu différenciées (en particulier alimentaires) ou gênantes. Au premier type ressortissaient les grandes corporations des métiers de l'alimentation qui s'étaient développées dans ces zones périphériques de la ville. Tout particulièrement les abattoirs (et les corporations de bouchers qui en dépendaient) installés à al-Ḥusayniyya, à Bāb al-Lūq, à Birkat al-Saqqā'īn, à Qanāṭir al-Sibāʿ et à Ibn Ṭūlūn/Darb al-Khalīfa (les abattoirs qui se trouvaient dans le centre de Qāhira, dans Ḥārat al-Yahūd, correspondaient aux besoins d'un autre quartier pauvre, le quartier juif, que nous excluons de cette étude comme les divers quartiers de minorités). Venaient ensuite les activités rattachées au commerce des grains, à l'est de Jamāliyya, autour de Bāb al-Shaʿriyya, près de Bāb al-Lūq, et tout particulièrement dans les environs immédiats de Rumayla où se trouvaient les halles et entrepôts principaux du Caire. Ou encore les métiers liés à la vente des légumes (toute une série de marchés, *khuḍāriyya*, autour d'Ibn Ṭūlūn et de Darb al-Khalīfa, et à Bāb al-Futūḥ)

[1] Dans l'acception du mot «hoch» tel qu'il est défini par la *Description*: «de grandes cours ou enceintes pleines de cahutes de quatre pieds de haut, où logent une foule de pauvres gens, entassés pêle-mêle avec leurs bestiaux» (*État moderne*, vol. ii. 2, p. 696). Voir aussi Aḥmad Amīn, *Qāmūs al-ʿādāt* (Le Caire, 1953), p. 184.

et des fruits (à al-Ḥusayniyya et près de Bāb al-Shaʿriyya). Parmi les activités gênantes qui excluaient le voisinage d'un habitat « riche », certaines étaient liées aux précédentes, comme les tanneries: les principales avaient été transférées de Bāb Zuwayla à Bāb al-Lūq, d'autres se trouvaient dans le voisinage de al-ʿUṭūf. Également implantées dans les quartiers populaires périphériques étaient les huileries (nombreuses entre Bāb al-Shaʿriyya et Bāb al-Baḥr, et près de Birkat al-Saqqā'īn), les charbonneries, les fours à chaux et à plâtre.

La prédominance, dans ces quartiers, d'activités liées aux produits alimentaires de base (en particulièrement aux grains) rendait leur population particulièrement sensible aux fluctuations de la conjoncture économique (disettes, cherté des prix). Par leur position en marge de la ville (al-Ḥusayniyya et Bāb al-Lūq constituaient en réalité de véritables faubourgs) les quartiers populaires étaient des zones de contact et de passage: al-Ḥusayniyya s'étirait le long de la route du pèlerinage; Bāb al-Shaʿriyya et Bāb al-Lūq se trouvaient sur les voies qui conduisaient à Būlāq; le quartier sud menait vers le Vieux Caire, et d'autre part Rumayla et Darb al-Khalīfa étaient un lieu de passage pour le pèlerinage vers le Qarāfa.[1] Les brassages et les échanges qui s'y opéraient peuvent rendre en partie compte de la tension sociale et de l'activité religieuse dont ils étaient le théâtre. Ces caractéristiques expliquent aussi le grand développement pris, dans ces quartiers, par les activités de « distraction » plus ou moins licites. Les centres de divertissement les plus célèbres étaient Bāb al-Lūq, connu comme tel dès l'époque de Maqrīzī et, à l'époque ottomane, Rumayla. Les débits de boisson et les maisons de tolérance de Bāb al-Lūq étaient signalés par la plupart des voyageurs: Evliya Çelebi estimait à 800 le nombre des prostituées qui y exerçaient leur activité et consacrait un long développement à ces corporations. Les mauvais lieux de Ḥusayniyya, où les voyageurs trouvaient tous les plaisirs qui sont habituellement associés aux routes de pèlerinage, n'étaient pas moins réputés. Plusieurs fois fermés du cours du XVIIIème siècle (notamment par ʿAlī ağa en 1703 et par ʿAbdallāh pacha vers 1730) ces lieux de plaisir survécurent aux tentatives faites pour imposer au Caire le respect des bonnes mœurs.

Chacun de ces quartiers populaires tirait sa physionomie propre de la conjonction qui s'y opérait entre organisations de métiers (corporations) et organisations religieuses (confréries), une conjonction qui en période de crise pouvait être singulièrement explosive.

L'originalité et le dynamisme de Ḥusayniyya paraissent avoir essentiellement reposé, au XVIIIème siècle, sur les rapports entre la corporation des bouchers et la confrérie des Bayyūmiyya. La présence d'abattoirs à l'extrémité nord du quartier entraînait l'installation, à proximité, d'un grand nombre de bouchers. D'après Evliya Çelebi il y avait 2200 *jazzārīn* dans l'ensemble du

[1] Voir les remarques de L. Massignon dans son article, «La Cité des Morts au Caire», *BIFAO*, 1958, pp. 25–79.

Caire, répartis en trois corporations, dont 200 pour la seule corporation des abattoirs de Bāb al-Futūḥ.[1] La liste des corporations de 1801 mentionne effectivement une corporation de « bouchers de moutons » dans le quartier de Ḥusayniyya (corporation n° 41).[2] Les bouchers qui sont en général des gens de forte complexion physique et de caractère résolu, avaient au Caire de puissantes traditions corporatives: dans les mouvements qui se produisirent dans Ḥusayniyya vers la fin du XVIIIème siècle, ils fournirent des « leaders » populaires, et leur *ṭā'ifa* fut le noyau autour duquel se développa l'agitation. Al-Jabartī nous a conservé le nom de trois bouchers dont deux au moins furent liés au quartier et y exercèrent une grande influence sur la population: le *mu'allim* Dar' dont la fille épousa le cheikh Ḥasan al-Kafrāwī (mort en 1787/8) (celui-ci dut sans doute en partie à ces liens de famille le prestige qu'il acquit dans le quartier dont il fut, un temps, le représentant et le défenseur); Aḥmad Sālim al-Jazzār, qui était également le cheikh des Bayyūmiyya, et pour qui le quartier se souleva par deux fois en 1786 et 1790. Et il nous paraît probable que Ibn Sham'a, cheikh des bouchers et un des chefs populaires lors des événements de 1805, dans lesquels Ḥusayniyya joua un rôle très actif, était également lié au quartier.[3] Le deuxième principe sur lequel se fondait la vie du quartier au XVIIIème siècle, était d'essence religieuse: il s'agissait de la confrérie des Bayyūmiyya dont l'activité était liée à Ḥusayniyya, depuis sa fondation, d'ailleurs très récente. 'Alī al-Bayyūmī, qui avait d'abord adhéré à la *ṭarīqa* des Khalwatiyya puis à celle des Aḥmadiyya, était devenu, dans le quartier de Ḥusayniyya où il s'était installé, le centre d'un véritable culte, qui avait été le point de départ de la formation d'une nouvelle confrérie. Après sa mort (il avait vécu de 1696–7 à 1769–70) la mosquée qui porta son nom et son tombeau connurent une grande activité religieuse, qui se traduisait en particulier par un *mawlid* extrêmement fréquenté. La nouvelle *ṭarīqa* se développa naturellement parmi les bouchers de Ḥusayniyya comme en témoignent les fonctions qu'y détenait Aḥmad Sālim al-Jazzār; son emprise sur le quartier se manifesta au cours des incidents auxquels le cheikh fut mêlé. On peut supposer également que les Khalwatiyya (auxquels 'Alī al-Bayyūmī avait appartenu) jouèrent un rôle actif dans la vie spirituelle du quartier: le sayyid 'Alī ibn Mūsā, personnage influent de l'ordre (et professeur au Mashhad al-Ḥusaynī) fut un notable de Ḥusayniyya, et après sa mort (en 1772–3) son frère Badr al-Dīn fut le « leader » du quartier (dont il dirigea le mouvement en 1798).[4]

Nous trouvons dans le quartier voisin de Bāb al-Sha'riyya, souvent cité lui aussi à l'occasion de mouvements populaires, un même faisceau d'influences corporatives et mystiques, mais les liaisons n'apparaissent pas avec

[1] Evliya Çelebi, *Seyahatname*, vol. x, p. 366.

[2] Voir notre article «Une liste des corporations de métiers au Caire en 1801», *Arabica*, 1957, pp. 150 à 163.

[3] Jabartī, *'Ajā'ib*, vol. ii, pp. 103, 165, 189; vol. iii, p. 336.

[4] Ibid., vol. i, p. 371.

autant de netteté que dans Ḥusayniyya. Les métiers dominants étaient ici ceux des marchands de fruits et des marchands de grains (la liste de 1801 mentionne une corporation des « transporteurs de grains de la place de Bāb al-Shaʿriyya », n° 73). On peut supposer que la confrérie des Shaʿrāwiyya jouait un rôle important dans le quartier au centre duquel s'élevaient le mausolée de ʿAbd al-Wahhāb al-Shaʿrānī et la mosquée qui portait son nom. L'influence des Bakriyya, dont le cheikh avait sa résidence près de l'Ezbekiyeh, était également particulièrement sensible dans le quartier qui s'étendait entre Bāb al-Shaʿriyya, la Birkat et Bāb al-Baḥr.

Le quartier sud, des alentours de la Citadelle au Khalīj, avait perdu ses habitants aisés et il avait été submergé par une population pauvre et agitée dont les bastions étaient le Darb al-Khalīfa et les alentours de Ibn Ṭūlūn. Les habitations y étaient particulièrement misérables et les négociants francs assuraient que le « fanatisme » y était plus marqué qu'ailleurs. En 1800 les habitants de Bāb al-Qarāfa et de ʿArab al-Isār se qualifiaient eux-mêmes de « pauvres gens » (*Innanā nās fuqarāʾ l-ḥāl*).[1] Les principales activités de ce quartier étaient le commerce des grains (il y avait à Rumayla une corporation des « transporteurs de grains »: n° 48) et celui des légumes (autour d'Ibn Ṭūlūn), auxquels s'ajoutaient les abattoirs (corporation des « bouchers de moutons du quartier Khalīfa »: n° 51). La cherté et le manque des grains furent dans les dernières années du XVIIème siècle et les premières du XVIIIème la cause d'émeutes répétées à Rumayla. Un siècle plus tard, en 1805, un personnage du quartier, Ḥajjāj al-Khuḍarī al-Rumaylātī, chef de la corporation des marchands de légumes, conduisit les gens du quartier au combat et contribua à l'avènement de Muḥammad ʿAlī. Ce quartier était par ailleurs le théâtre d'une intense activité religieuse, dont le centre principal était la confrérie des Rifāʿiyya. Le *maqām* du cheikh Sīdī Aḥmad al-Rifāʿī se trouvait face à Sulṭān Ḥasan (à l'emplacement actuel de la mosquée al-Rifāʿī). Son *mawlid* était très réputé: Aḥmad Çelebi raconte qu'en rajab 1140 (février 1728) l'affluence fut si grande et si tumultueuse que dix-sept personnes moururent piétinées dans la bousculade.[2] Sayyida Zaynab, à Qanāṭir al-Sibāʿ, était un autre centre d'activité religieuse. La vigueur du sentiment religieux de la population de ces quartiers s'exprima également dans le succès (jugé de mauvais aloi par les esprits orthodoxes) qu'y remportèrent des saints hommes, comme le cheikh al-Shīmī, dont la réputation déplaça les foules à Rumayla en 1698, et qui y connut une fin tragique.[3]

L'organisation des quartiers populaires reposait, comme dans toute la ville, sur la division en *ḥārāt* (dont il y avait une soixantaine au Caire), « enceintes de maisons plus ou moins étendues, et ordinairement closes par des portes

[1] Archives de la Guerre (Vincennes), B6, 43, avril 1800.

[2] Aḥmad Çelebi b. ʿAbd al-Ghanī, *K. awdaḥ al-ishārāt* (Yale University Library: Landberg MS. no. 3), f. 206a.

[3] Aḥmad al-Damurdāshī, *al-Durra al-muṣāna* (B.M. MS. Or. 1073–4), vol. i, pp. 103–4.

qui sont fermées la nuit »,[1] avec leur réseau hiérarchisé de rues, de l'artère centrale (*darb*) qui donnait souvent son nom au quartier, aux ruelles (sing. *'aṭfa*) et aux impasses. Mais cette organisation paraît avoir été particulièrement forte et vivante dans les quartiers populaires. Dans les *ḥārāt* tendaient à se rassembler les gens de même métier, ou les individus de même origine ethnique et de même religion. A l'abri de ses murs et de ses portes, gardées par des *bawwābīn*, le *ḥāra* constituait un groupe homogène et vivait d'une existence propre. Il était placé sous l'autorité d'un *shaykh al-ḥāra*, secondé par un *naqīb*.[2] Cette organisation ressemblait beaucoup à celle des corporations de métiers (les quartiers étaient d'ailleurs considérés par le pouvoir comme des *ṭawā'if* comme les autres) à laquelle elle était superposée, sans cependant qu'il y eût de conflit entre elles: la base du quartier était souvent une corporation de métier; d'autre part autant qu'au *shaykh al-ḥāra*, qui paraît avoir eu surtout des pouvoirs administratifs et de police, l'influence dans le quartier appartenait à des notables des corporations ou des confréries dominantes. C'est naturellement dans les *ḥārāt* populaires, là où la densité de population était forte, et puissantes les structures professionnelles et religieuses, que la solidarité de quartier devait trouver sa forme la plus complète et la plus vigoureuse.

L'esprit de corps du quartier s'exprimait normalement par des manifestations collectives auxquelles sa population (et en particulier la jeunesse) participait en cortèges colorés et bruyants, avec accompagnement de tambours et de flûtes (*al-ṭubūl wa'l-zumūr*) derrière des porteurs de torches (*mashā'il*) et de drapeaux (*bayāriq*): ces oriflammes étaient peut-être des emblêmes distinctifs du quartier, mais c'étaient sans doute le plus souvent les bannières de la principale confrérie. Ces cortèges s'organisaient à l'occasion d'un mariage (*zaffa*), d'une circoncision, de la fête d'un saint local, ou d'une célébration de caractère plus général, comme le *mawlid* du Prophète. À cette occasion des rassemblements formés dans les différents quartiers du Caire se réunissaient à la nuit tombée pour une procession qui parcourait ensuite la ville, en visitant les mosquées sur son chemin. Les quartiers se rassemblaient d'une manière moins pacifique pour se défendre contre les agressions dont la collectivité ou un individu étaient les victimes: les chroniques nous donnent maints exemples de ces réactions d'autodéfense. Fréquemment aussi l'agressivité latente des quartiers et les rivalités qui existaient traditionnellement entre quartiers voisins donnaient naissance à des batailles rangées, opposant les quartiers les uns aux autres: Aḥmad Çelebi raconte par exemple comment en 1148/1736 les gens de Ḥusayniyya se prirent de querelle avec les habitants de Būlāq, et en vinrent aux mains avec eux dans le quartier de

[1] *Description de l'Égypte, État moderne* (Paris, 1809–12), vol. ii. 2, p. 661.

[2] L'existence d'un *shaykh mashāyikh al-ḥārāt* n'est pas attestée avant 1803 (Jabartī, *'Ajā'ib*, vol. iii, p. 240). Dans un document de 1800 (Archives de la Guerre, B6, 45, 26 mai), relatif au quartier de Ḥanafī il est également question d'un «Cheikh des cheikhs» sans que soient précisées ses attributions.

l'Ashrafiyya;[1] et 'Alī pacha Mubārak rapporte les bagarres, presque rituelles, qui opposaient, hors du Caire, dans le *khalā'* voisin, les gens des quartiers de Ḥusayniyya, de Ḥaṭṭāba et de 'Uṭūf, jusqu'en plein cœur du dix-neuvième siècle.[2]

Les autorités envisagèrent parfois d'utiliser à leur profit les forces populaires des quartiers. L'histoire du Caire aux XVIIème et XVIIIème siècles fournit plusieurs exemples de tentative de mobilisation de ces « milices » populaires: envoi par le pacha, en 1613, contre les *'askers* révoltés, de la *ṭā'ifa* du *ḥārat al Fawwālā*,[3] ou encore levée par Ismā'īl bey, en 1777, des gens des quartiers (*ahl al-ḥārāt wa 'l-'uṣab*).[4] Mais dans l'ensemble, les gouvernants paraissent plutôt avoir considéré avec suspicion et appréhension ces forces difficiles à contrôler. Les chroniqueurs (qui appartenaient à la « bourgeoisie » égyptienne) réagissaient de la même façon quand ils décrivaient les explosions de violence collective qui partaient des « bas-quartiers » de la ville. Les noms mêmes qu'ils donnaient aux troupes des quartiers populaires et des faubourgs avaient des acceptions invariablement péjoratives, qui en disaient long sur la crainte et le dégoût qu'elles inspiraient aux bien-pensants: *al-'uṣab* (les « bandes »),[5] *al-shuṭṭār* (les « voyous »),[6] *al-zu'ar* (les « vauriens »),[7] *al-ghawghā'* (la « populace »),[8] *al-awbāsh* (la « pègre »),[9] *al-ḥarāfīsh* (la « canaille »).[10] Beaucoup de ces mots étaient associés depuis un lointain passé avec la *futuwwa* et ils en gardaient une « aura » de mystère et de menace.[11] Ces troupes étaient en effet le dernier avatar de la *futuwwa* qui se survivait par la projection, sur le plan du quartier, de la conjonction des liens de métier et des aspirations mystiques qui l'avaient caractérisée dans sa dernière phase.[12] Cette conjonction qui s'opérait dans les cérémonies d'initiation, plus ou moins secrètes, aux confréries et aux corporations, n'apparaissait au grand jour qu'à l'occasion des mouvements qui se développaient fugitivement dans les quartiers populaires: aussi est-il très difficile de savoir quelles en étaient les modalités précises, de même qu'il est très difficile de dire comment étaient exactement organisées ces « bandes » de quartiers qui jouèrent de toute

[1] Aḥmad Çelebi, *K. awdaḥ al-ishārāt*, f. 252a.
[2] 'Alī Mubārak, *al-Khiṭaṭ al-jadīda* (Būlāq, 1306), vol. ii, p. 84.
[3] Muḥammad b. 'Abd al-Mu'ṭī al-Isḥāqī, *K. akhbār al-uwal* (Le Caire, 1296), p. 256.
[4] Jabartī, *'Ajā'ib*, vol. ii, p. 13.
[5] Ibid., p. 13; vol. iii, pp. 331, 335; vol. iv, p. 91.
[6] Muḥammad b. Aḥmad b. Iyās, *Badā'i' al-Zuhūr*, vol. v (Istanbul, 1932), p. 117; Aḥmad b. Zunbul al-Rammāl (MS. B.N. 1838), f. 124b; Jabartī, *'Ajā'ib*, vol. iii, p. 28.
[7] Ibn Iyās, *Badā'i'*, vol. iv (Istanbul, 1931), pp. 17, 96, 232; vol. v, pp. 117, 137, 150, 153; Ibn Zunbul, fol. 124b; Jabartī, *'Ajā'ib*, vol. iii, pp. 25, 93.
[8] Ibid., vol. i, p. 317; vol. iii, pp. 25, 297, 335 (*al-ghawghā' min al-'āmma*).
[9] Ibid., pp. 13, 91, 93, 240; vol. iv, pp. 108, 190 (employé à propos des *ṭuruq* populaires que condamne le chroniqueur).
[10] Ibid., vol. iii, pp. 93, 99.
[11] A propos de Ṭanṭā, en 1768, al-Jabartī emploie un autre mot également lié à la *futuwwa*, celui de *'ayyārūn* (les «errants»).
[12] Voir les indications précieuses données par Aḥmad Amīn, *al-Sa'laka wa 'l-futuwwa* (Le Caire, 1952), pp. 89–95.

évidence un rôle si important dans la mobilisation des masses populaires aux XVIIème et XVIIIème siècles.

Du fait des lacunes, déjà signalées, dans notre information en ce qui concerne les mouvements populaires, il est souvent malaisé d'établir les faits eux-mêmes avec précision: à plus forte raison l'interprétation qu'on peut en donner est-elle largement hypothétique. Avec cette réserve, il nous paraît possible de distinguer, des dernières années du XVIIème siècle au début du XVIIIème, deux phases dans l'histoire des mouvements populaires au Caire: pendant la première, ils paraissent liés à la conjoncture économique; durant la seconde, ils semblent plutôt dépendre de la conjoncture politique.

Pendant la soixantaine d'années qui s'écoulèrent de 1675 à 1735, les mouvements populaires au Caire furent des réactions immédiates aux difficultés monétaires et alimentaires que connaissait alors l'Égypte. Les troubles monétaires étaient dus essentiellement aux manipulations de la monnaie la plus couramment utilisée par la population, le *para* d'argent (*medin, niṣf fiḍḍa*). Le taux de change en *paras* des principales monnaies d'or et d'argent pendant cette période donne une image de cette dépréciation:

	Monnaies d'or		Monnaies d'argent	
	Sharīfī bunduqī	Sharīfī muḥammadī	Riyāl	Kalb
1674	95	85	42	40
1697	120	95	64	48
1700	132	102	66	52
1703	200	150	130	80
1723	190	—	100	75

Le *para* qui, à l'origine pesait 1,28 g, était supposé peser 0,689 g (et contenir 70% d'argent pur) en 1698; en 1703 il ne pesait plus que 0,518 g.[1] La circulation de quantités considérables de pièces rognées (*maqāṣīṣ*) jetait la confusion dans les échanges et causait une grande gêne à la population, du fait de la hausse des prix qui en résultait.

Le deuxième élément de la crise était l'extraordinaire amplitude des variations dans les prix des principaux produits alimentaires, en particulier du blé, en période de mauvaise récolte. Alors que le prix de l'*ardab* de blé était en moyenne de 30 *niṣf* les bonnes années, on enregistra les prix suivants au moment des principales périodes de disette:

1677–8	180
1689	120

[1] Voir S. J. Shaw, *Ottoman Egypt in the age of the French Revolution* (Harvard, 1964), pp. 167 et suivants.

1694	180 (270 en 1695, et 600 en 1696)
1705–6	240
1714	120 (et 214 en 1718)
1722	180
1736	100

Le rapprochement de ces chiffres fait apparaître une périodicité approximativement décennale pour les pointes les plus accentuées. C'est à la même périodicité qu'obéissent les principaux mouvements populaires relevés par les chroniqueurs.

Les premières de ces émeutes de la faim eurent lieu en ṣafar 1089/avril 1678, jumādā 1098/mai 1687 et muḥarram 1107/septembre 1695: elles eurent pour cadre Rumayla et se déroulèrent suivant un scénario à peu près invariable. Dans une période de rareté et de cherté extrêmes des grains, les « sujets » (*ra'iyya*) se rassemblaient en bas de la Citadelle pour protester et réclamer des mesures appropriées; la manifestation donnait lieu à des désordres au cours desquels on brisait, à Rumayla, la porte des entrepôts aux grains (*ḥawāṣil, ruq'a*) qui étaient ensuite pillés ainsi que les boutiques voisines; les violences prenaient fin par une répression sévère (il y eut 13 morts en 1678) ou par un effort plus ou moins efficace pour taxer les denrées et pour approvisionner les marchés. Que Rumayla ait été le théâtre de ces divers mouvements s'explique, d'une part par la proximité du centre politique du pays où l'on portait tout naturellement les doléances, d'autre part par l'existence en cet endroit des principaux marchés en grains, et enfin par la présence dans cette région du Caire d'une population pauvre que les difficultés économiques affectaient particulièrement (les *ṣighār al-Rumayla*, les « petites gens » de Rumayla, dont parle le chroniqueur en 1695).[1]

Après que l'année 1705 se fut passée sans crise, en dépit de la grande cherté que connut alors l'Égypte, les mouvements populaires reprirent ensuite, suivant le même rythme décennal. En muḥarram 1128/décembre 1715, les troubles eurent pour cause une tentative du pacha pour édicter un tarif des monnaies, frapper un nouveau *para* et interdire l'utilisation des pièces rognées: il y eut une véritable émeute au Caire; les souqs furent fermés et les manifestants montèrent à la Citadelle où ils obtinrent un édit de taxation des prix: mais il fallut cependant un mois pour que les marchés reprennent leur activité normale. Les troubles de 1722, 1723 et 1724 furent exceptionnellement graves: ils eurent pour cause directe la cherté des grains qui devait d'ailleurs persister de 1721 à 1728. Il y eut d'abord, vers dhu'l-qa'da 1134/août–septembre 1722, lorsqu'une crue médiocre eut fait monter le prix de *l'ardab* de blé à 180 *niṣf fiḍḍa*, une émeute au cours de laquelle les *ra'iyya* lapidèrent les beys qui se rendaient à la réunion du *Divan*. Puis, en dhu'l-ḥijja 1135/septembre 1723, un mouvement à Rumayla et enfin, en rabī' I

[1] *K. tarājim al-ṣawā'iq fī wāqi'at al-ṣanajiq* (MS., Le Caire, Dār al-Kutub), t. 2269, p. 890.

1137/novembre 1724, un soulèvement et des incidents sanglants près de la Citadelle. Le dernier mouvement de cette série se produisit en dhu'l-ḥijja 1145/juin 1733; le haut prix des denrées, combiné avec le désordre monétaire, provoqua un nouveau soulèvement des *ra'iyya*; toute la ville fut fermée, et l'apparition des manifestants à Rumayla décida les beys à édicter des mesures d'urgence, afin d'éviter que le mouvement ne tourne à l'émeute.

Pendant plusieurs décades, nos textes cessent alors de mentionner des mouvements populaires graves, silence que l'on ne peut expliquer par la seule insuffisance de nos sources.[1] La cause de ce retour au calme doit sans doute être cherchée dans la stabilité que connut apparemment l'Égypte entre 1735 et 1770. Les remarques de Jabartī sur la tranquillité du pays, sur l'abondance des denrées et leur bas prix sous le gouvernement de Ibrāhīm et Riḍwān katkhudā, jusqu'en 1755, puis à l'époque de 'Alī bey, sont corroborées par ce que nous savons de l'évolution des prix et des monnaies à cette époque: il ne paraît pas y avoir eu de montées en flèche des prix comparables à celles qui s'étaient si souvent produites pendant le demi-siècle précédent, en dehors de la période de hausse de 1743–5. Par ailleurs la dévalorisation du *para* se ralentit quelque peu: en 1736 le *funduqlī* d'or valait 146 *niṣf*; en 1764 il en valait 160, ce qui indiquait une dépréciation modérée pendant cette période de trente ans; pendant le même laps de temps le *riyāl* passait de 78 à 85 *paras* ce qui confirme cette tendance. Toutefois cette accalmie ne devait pas durer: après 1770 et 1780 on voit réapparaître les signes de trouble économique qui accompagnent une nouvelle période de désordres et d'anarchie. La décadence de la monnaie reprit à un rythme précipité: le *bunduqī* passa de 160 *paras* en 1769 à 220 en 1789 et à 340 en 1798. Le poids légal du *para* qui était de 0,570 g (avec 60% d'argent) vers le milieu du siècle, tomba à 0,354 g avant 1789 (50% d'argent) et à 0,302 g (avec 37% d'argent) avant l'arrivée des Français,[2] ce qui représentait une dévalorisation des 2/3. D'autre part, à partir de 1780, les périodes de cherté et de disette devinrent à nouveau plus fréquentes: en 1783 le blé atteignit le prix de 10 *riyāl* l'*ardab*; 1785 fut encore une année de cherté; puis, après une periode de baisse en 1787, le prix de l'*ardab* monta à 9 *riyāl* 1/2 en 1789, 6 en 1791, 18 en 1792, et ne descendit pratiquement plus au dessous de 200 *niṣf fiḍḍa* jusqu'en 1798.

A ces conditions économiques fâcheuses, qui étaient de nature à créer dans les milieux populaires un état d'inquiétude et d'agitation, s'ajoutèrent les effets du régime mamelouk qui se caractérisa à la même époque par une recrudescence de violences et d'exactions, cependant que les cadres

[1] Encore que cette insuffisance des sources entre 1750 et 1770 pose effectivement de graves problèmes: la chronique de Aḥmad Çelebi s'interrompt en 1737, et celle de Qīnalī en 1739. La chronique de Damurdāshī ne dépasse pas 1755–6. On ne dispose plus alors que de la chronique de Jabartī qui ne devient vraiment complète que vers 1770, lorsque l'auteur aborde des événements dont il a été le témoin.

[2] Shaw, *Ottoman Egypt*, p. 168.

politiques et sociaux traditionnels se décomposaient à partir de ʿAlī bey. Les brutalités, devenues habituelles, les exigences fiscales, de plus en plus oppressives, fournirent à partir de 1780 des occasions pour des désordres qui n'étaient plus, comme un siècle plus tôt, une simple réaction à des « stimuli » économiques: les mouvements populaires constituaient une forme de protestation élémentaire contre l'oppression. Ils s'approfondirent et prirent un caractère véritablement politique à partir de 1798; cette évolution, déjà sensible au moment des événements de 1786, était le résultat d'un part d'une certaine « prise de conscience » par les masses, et par leurs « leaders », et d'autre part de l'action de représentants de la bourgeoisie égyptienne qui prirent la tête des mouvements populaires et les orientèrent en vue de la réalisation de leurs objectifs propres.

Le conflit de 1777 entre al-Azhar et les beys avait encore les caractères des mouvements traditionnels des *ʿulamāʾ* et des étudiants de la mosquée-université, encore que le concours « d'un nombre considérable de gens sans aveu »[1] en eût singulièrement accentué la gravité. En 1786 le mécontentement latent contre le système de spoliations instauré par Murād bey et Ibrāhīm bey se cristallisa dans des incidents qui mirent en mouvement certains quartiers populaires du Caire: en jumādā I 1200/mars 1786, les violences d'un bey mouradite à l'encontre du boucher Aḥmad Sālim qui, ainsi que nous l'avons déjà dit, était également cheikh des Bayyūmiyya, provoquèrent un mouvement de révolte dans le quartier de Ḥusayniyya, et les beys durent négocier avec le chef occasionnel du mouvement, le cheikh al-Dardīr. Peu après, au mois de shawwāl/juillet–août 1786, c'était à l'Ezbekiyeh que la foule s'ameutait, après un attentat dont un maraîcher avait été victime de la part d'un mamelouk. L'intervention de la Porte dans les affaires égyptiennes, et l'arrivée du Capitan Pacha firent espérer à la population du Caire la fin de l'injustice; aussi répondit-elle avec un certain enthousiasme à l'appel du pacha Muḥammad en août 1786: cette réaction justifiait les craintes d'Ibrāhīm bey touchant la possibilité d'un soulèvement des *raʿiyya* et prouvait en tout cas leur réceptivité à la propagande ottomane dirigée contre les mamelouks. Les espoirs que l'on plaçait dans l'action de Ḥasan pacha furent finalement déçus et son expédition fut un échec politique; cependant les mouvements populaires se poursuivirent. En muḥarram 1202/octobre 1787, les corporations professionnelles s'insurgèrent contre un projet d'emprunt de Ismāʿīl bey. En rajab 1202/avril–mai 1788, le quartier de Bāb al-Shaʿriyya se souleva à la suite de l'exécution sommaire de l'un de ses habitants. Deux ans plus tard, en muḥarram 1205/octobre 1790 Ḥusayniyya se dressa à nouveau derrière les Bayyūmiyya pour défendre Aḥmad Sālim al-Jazzār, et les émirs durent composer avec les émeutiers.

C'est l'occupation française qui devait donner une ampleur nouvelle à ces mouvements locaux et les transformer en un combat à double caractère,

[1] Archives Nationales (Paris), C. C. Caire, B1, 336, 17 juin 1777.

religieux et national, dans lequel les Français affrontaient outre les troupes ottomanes et les débris du régime mamelouk, les forces populaires du Caire. Dans les deux grandes révoltes du Caire (octobre 1798 et mars–avril 1800) les quartiers populaires de Ḥusayniyya, de al-ʿUṭūf, de Bāb al-Lūq, du Qarāfa, de ʿArab al-Isār fournirent des troupes, la direction du mouvement étant assurée par des membres de la « bourgeoisie » égyptienne, *ʿulamāʾ* ou grands commerçants (ʿUmar Makram, Aḥmad al-Maḥrūqī, Aḥmad Muḥarram). En 1798 comme en 1800 c'est dans Ḥusayniyya que les passions atteignirent leur comble, ce quartier étant dans chacune de ces occasions le dernier à mettre bas les armes. La participation des quartiers populaires aux événements qui aboutirent à l'avènement de Muḥammad ʿAlī en 1805 fut tout aussi importante: mais cette fois, à côté des chefs « traditionnels », dont le plus représentatif était ʿUmar Makram, des « leaders » populaires jouèrent un rôle actif dans la direction du mouvement, tels Ḥajjāj, le cheikh des marchands de légumes de Rumayla, ou Ibn Shamʿa, le cheikh des bouchers; ils figuraient l'un et l'autre dans le cortège de la victoire qui alla le lundi 10 rabīʿ II 1220/ 8 juillet 1805 accueillir le *kapıcı* porteur de la nomination de Muḥammad ʿAlī comme pacha du Caire. Avec eux, et avec les *ʿulamāʾ*, dont l'action avait été déterminante tout au long de la crise, défilèrent ce jour-là les gens des quartiers dont l'appui avait contribué au succès militaire de Muḥammad ʿAlī et lui avait donné comme la sanction d'un assentiment populaire: Bāb al-Shaʿriyya, al-Ḥusayniyya, al-ʿUṭūf, al-Khalīfa, al-Qarāfa, Rumayla, al-Ḥaṭṭāba, al-Ḥabbāla. Pour la première fois depuis des siècles, à la faveur de l'ébranlement produit par l'expédition française et de la décomposition du régime mamelouk, les masses populaires faisaient l'histoire au Caire, au lieu de la subir.

Cet épisode étonnant de l'histoire de l'Égypte devait cependant être bref: l'alliance qui s'était nouée entre les éléments populaires et la bourgeoisie égyptienne, et qui avait été pour Muḥammad ʿAlī un marchepied vers le pouvoir, ne survécut pas à la victoire. Leur aspiration à la stabilité politique satisfaite, les *ʿulamāʾ* ne désiraient plus que le retour à la « normale », ce qui était conforme aux vœux de Muḥammad ʿAlī. Bon gré mal gré les *raʿiyya* durent se résigner à désarmer; leurs chefs, ʿUmar Makram et Ḥajjāj, furent progressivement neutralisés et éliminés. La chappe pesante de l'autorité de Muḥammad ʿAlī tomba sur l'Égypte, et les masses populaires du Caire retournèrent à leur obscurité séculaire.

Some Aspects of Intellectual and Social Life in Eighteenth-century Egypt

GAMAL EL-DIN EL-SHAYYAL

I. THE DECLINE OF INTELLECTUAL LIFE IN EGYPT: SIXTEENTH TO EIGHTEENTH CENTURY

WITH the conquest of Egypt by the Ottomans, Istanbul became the centre of gravity of the Muslim world. This fact may explain the regrettable deterioration of the intellectual life in Egypt during the Ottoman period which lasted for three centuries. As Istanbul was now the seat of the sultan and capital of the Muslim empire, it also became the centre of cultural life. It was not strange therefore that energetic activity in compiling books was widespread among the Ottoman *'ulamā'* since Turkish became the official language of the state. Apart from this fact, Sultan Selim I took with him on leaving Egypt for Turkey a great number of Egyptian *'ulamā'* and artisans, as well as most of the rare and unique Arabic manuscripts.

The isolation imposed on Egypt during the Ottoman period was largely responsible for the decline of cultural and economic life. The supreme power in Egypt was divided among three authorities: the Ottoman pasha, the *Dīwān*, and the Mamluks, but it was soon greatly concentrated in the hands of the Mamluk beys. This phenomenon was very obvious during the eighteenth century when the Ottoman Empire began to decline and found itself engaged in continuous wars with Russia and Austria. The Mamluk beys were very much occupied with their own interests and rivalries. Their ruthless policy of plundering people, and confiscating their properties, harassed the Egyptians to a great extent. Thus the only course left for the Egyptians was to complain to the *'ulamā'*, who, in their turn asked the *amīrs* to put an end to all this injustice. In this way the *'ulamā'* were able to assume the national leadership based ultimately on the *Sharī'a* which was the law of the state.

Al-Azhar mosque was by far the greatest institute all over Egypt for higher studies from which the *'ulamā'* graduated, a task which was shared by a good number of other *madrasas* and college-mosques. Undoubtedly al-Azhar mosque was the most important and famous institute because of the many rich *waqfs* (endowments) for its students and teachers. The number of its professors in the Ottoman period amounted to sixty or seventy. The main bulk of students at al-Azhar came from Cairo and other Egyptian cities, while others belonged to various other Muslim countries.

There were in Egypt about twenty towns which had schools for higher studies, each town had from one to seven *madrasas*. The principal teachers in all these schools were usually graduates of al-Azhar, but in their turn students of these schools supplied al-Azhar with many of its prominent scholars. Strangely enough not one of the head shaykhs of al-Azhar in the eighteenth century was of Cairene origin. The most active of these provincial schools were at Alexandria, Damietta, Rosetta, Manṣūra, al-Maḥalla, Dasūq, and Ṭanṭā in Lower Egypt, and in Qūs, Qinā, and Ṭahṭā in Upper Egypt.

Students then still adhered to the old tradition of travelling in search of knowledge. Examples are frequent in the two histories of al-Jabartī and al-Murādī. In order to achieve this purpose students usually travelled to Damietta, Alexandria, Ṭanṭā, Ṭahṭā in Egypt, and to Damascus, Jerusalem, Mecca, and Medina in the neighbouring countries. Only a few went to Istanbul, where they practised teaching at some of its schools.

The range of studies in those college-mosques and religious schools was relatively narrow, as most attention was paid to Arabic linguistics—including rhetoric and prosody—jurisprudence, theology, logic, and elementary mathematics. The system of education in these institutes had many interesting features. According to Lane-Poole, 'The constitution of the Azhar University is ideally perfect. The poorest youth who comes to it will be immediately welcomed, and will be taught all that the professors know. He will receive the highest education that a Moslem can receive, by Moslem methods, without being called upon to pay a single piastre.'[1] Yet Gibb and Bowen say that 'there was much to offset against this ideal picture. A proportion of the students may have been enrolled in al-Azhar or other *madrasas* simply for the sake of the free distribution of food enjoyed by the pupils. But while in theory a *madrasa* education was open to all seekers after knowledge, the *Şeyḫly* profession was, in practice, almost exclusively hereditary.'[2] In addition to this some of the teachers were nominated to teach in more than one school, or to hold more than one post, which left them with very little time to do their work efficiently.

The most serious ground of criticism, however, is the limitation in both subjects and outlook. The teachers did not write any original books. They repeated the old text-books which their predecessors had written. It is clear from the biographies of the eminent *'ulamā'* and shaykhs of the age that some of them wrote quite a great number of books and pamphlets. However, none of these works were of great value or added anything new to our knowledge. All they did was to write commentaries on old texts, or annotate such commentaries. In fact, this age can be called the age of commentaries.

[1] S. Lane-Poole, *Social life in Egypt*, p. 84; cited in H. A. R. Gibb and H. Bowen, *Islamic society and the West*, vol. i, part 2 (London, 1957), p. 159.

[2] Ibid.

The scientific situation in eighteenth-century Egypt can be fairly estimated through the examination of the works of the *'ulamā'* and thinkers. As a result of losing its political independence the Arab world lived in complete isolation. Its relations with western Europe had been entirely severed. People were living in the darkness of the Middle Ages. The situation became worse because of the setback caused by the increase of the number of mystics (or Ṣūfīs). Sufism became a kind of a form of hallucination, and people believed greatly in the occult sciences and superstitions. Lunatics were taken for saints, imbeciles for respected shaykhs. Shaykhs who wrote treatises on such subjects were highly estimated by the common people and even by the *élite* and the educated.

The deterioration of medicine, theoretically and practically, may be considered an aspect of the decline of culture and learning in Egypt during the eighteenth century. At the beginning of the seventeenth century there still survived some of the medical knowledge which had flourished in the Muslim world. Yet this knowledge was greatly influenced by magic and astrology. The medical craft was, like other crafts, largely hereditary. 'It is not uncommon', Gibb and Bowen say, 'to find a *Ḳâḍî* or *'Âlim* as the head of the corporation of physicians, and other men of religion practising medicine.'[1]

In his contribution to the *Description de l'Égypte* entitled 'Notice sur les médicamens usuels des Égyptiens' the French writer Rouyer cited useful information in connexion with medicine in Egypt towards the end of the eighteenth century. Pharmaceutical science had deteriorated. *Bīmāristāns* were used as ordinary hospitals and at the same time as lunatic asylums. It was then that a caste of surgeon-barbers appeared who practised medicine and surgery. By the end of the eighteenth century there appeared in Cairo a number of European physicians and pharmacies. Rouyer mentions that there were in Cairo three pharmacies, two of which were run by some Venetians and the third by a Greek. Most of their clients were Europeans and Christian Syrians, beside some Egyptians, Moslems, and Copts. In addition to this fact two European medical books were translated into Arabic and Turkish.

Other studies, known to the Arabs as 'philosophical sciences' or 'sciences of the ancients' (*'ulūm al-awā'il*), such as philosophy, astronomy, and mathematics, deteriorated in the same way as medicine. There are many proofs of this decline in the writings of European travellers such as Volney and Savary. In describing the scientific and industrial situation in eighteenth-century Egypt, Volney said that ignorance was widely spread all over the country and among all classes of people, as in the whole of the Ottoman Empire. It left profound traces on literature, science, fine arts, and even on small crafts. One could hardly find a watchmaker in Cairo, and if found he would most probably have been a European. On the other hand goldsmiths were many in Cairo: they were more numerous than in Aleppo for example. In spite of

[1] Op. cit., p. 162.

ignorance there were skilled weavers of silk and golden textiles. Volney concludes by saying that it was due to al-Azhar that Egypt was the centre of studies for the Muslim Orient.

Al-Jabartī, the historian of eighteenth-century Egypt, described faithfully and plainly the decline of learning in his time. He related that the Ottoman governor, Aḥmad Pasha (1162–3/1749–50), was a learned man and fond of mathematics. On his arrival in Cairo and settlement in the Citadel he declared his desire to meet the great *ʿulamā*ʾ of al-Azhar, in order to discuss with them some mathematical problems. At their first meeting the *ʿulamā*ʾ could not give an answer to the problems, but they named one who had mastered this subject. This was Shaykh Ḥasan al-Jabartī, the historian's father. Al-Jabartī says that Shaykh ʿAbdallāh al-Shubrāwī (shaykh of al-Azhar) used to say to his father (Shaykh Ḥasan) whenever he met him: 'May God save you as you have saved our faces before the pasha; if you had not been found we should have been considered by the pasha as asses.'

The literary studies and productions of this century show as a whole the same characteristic degeneration. This decline is sometimes accounted for by an excessive concentration upon scholastic, religious, and mystic works. This is, however, no more than part of the truth. In fact scholastic productions, though plentiful, were of small originality. 'But little else could be expected', as Gibb and Bowen say, 'for the cultivation of profane literature depended largely upon the encouragement of patrons, and the subjection of the Arabic provinces to Ottoman control deprived them of this support except to a limited extent.'[1] The two authors continue,

> the main causes of the literary decline are rather to be looked for in the conditions of its existence: and more especially in the absence of fruitful contact with the outside world. Lacking any healthy stimulus or criticism from without, it was suffering from a kind of introversion and living on its own past. Its links even with the contemporary literature in Turkish and Persian were of the slightest, except possibly in Aleppo. A second cause of weakness was the narrowness of the literary circle, with the inevitable consequence of artificial standards, which put a premium upon style and discouraged invention and originality.

We may add that the sort of life the literary men lived during that age was mainly responsible for the weakness of their production. The economic situation deteriorated, and poverty prevailed. Thus literary men had fewer aspects of civilization to inspire them and as a result they neglected the meaning, and only cared for embellishing the style. They did their best to write different kinds of poems such as those poems which could be read from right to left as well as from left to right. They also wrote a lot of puzzle poems denoting the date of the death of a great man or of the building of a monument, and so forth.

[1] Op. cit., p. 163.

The signs of this decline in the cultural movement were also evident in historical writings which, after continuing without a break from the time of Ibn ʿAbd al-Ḥakam, came to a virtual stop, that is unless we consider as history the writings of a mystic like al-Shaʿrānī, who wrote biographies of Ṣūfīs in his book *al-Ṭabaqāt al-kubrā*.

It is true that Ottoman Egypt had a number of historians, but they can hardly be compared with their predecessors, the historians of the fifteenth century. To illustrate this fact, we give here some examples of the few Egyptian historians who lived in the Ottoman period. Muḥammad b. Abi'l-Surūr al-Bakrī al-Ṣiddīqī lived in the eleventh/seventeenth century and died in 1087/1676–7. He wrote three historical works which are still in manuscript: *al-Rawḍa al-ma'nūsa fī akhbār Miṣr al-maḥrūsa*, a history of the governors and judges of Ottoman Egypt to the year 1054/1644–5; *ʿUyūn al-akhbār wa-nuzhat al-abṣār*, a short history of Egypt and the different dynasties which ruled it till the end of the Mamluk period; and *al-Minaḥ al-raḥmāniyya fi'l-dawla al-ʿuthmāniyya*, a history of the Ottoman sultans to the year 1029/1619–20. Muḥammad b. ʿAbd al-Muʿṭī al-Isḥāqī al-Manūfī lived in the eleventh/seventeenth century. We know from his biography by al-Muḥibbī that he was a good judge, a learned man, and a historian. He studied in his native city and also in Cairo, but he died in Manūf in 1060/1650. He wrote much poetry and a historical work entitled *Laṭā'if akhbār al-uwal fī man taṣarrafa fī Miṣr min arbāb al-duwal*, which contains a preface, ten chapters, and a conclusion. It is a history of Egypt from the Arab conquest to the beginning of the eleventh/seventeenth century. The book was published many times in Cairo in the years 1276/1859–60, 1296/1878–9, and 1300/1882–3. Marʿī al-Ḥanbalī, a historian of the tenth/sixteenth century, wrote a work entitled *Durar al-fawā'id al-munaẓẓama fī akhbār al-Ḥajj wa-ṭarīq Makka al-muʿaẓẓama*. It gives a full description of the pilgrimage-route and its different stations, as well as biographies of the caliphs, the *Ṣaḥāba*, the princes, and the notable personalities of different nationalities who performed the pilgrimage to Mecca. Only the first volume of this book is extant and it is still in manuscript form.

In conclusion we may add that the Egyptians were pioneers in writing biographical dictionaries of notable men who lived in one century. The historian Ibn Ḥajar wrote the biographies of the eighth/fourteenth century in his book *al-Durar al-kāmina fī aʿyān al-mi'a al-thāmina*. He was followed by his pupil al-Sakhāwī who wrote the biographies of the notable men of the ninth/fifteenth century in his book *al-Ḍaw' al-lāmiʿ fī aʿyān al-qarn al-tāsiʿ*. This kind of historical writing ceased in Egypt by the beginning of the Ottoman period and was transferred to the hands of Syrian historians. An Egyptian historian, Aḥmad Taymūr, tried to write the biographies of the thirteenth *Hijrī* century but he finished only a small part of it which was published after his death in Cairo (1940) under the title of *Tarājim aʿyān al-qarn al-thālith ʿashar*.

II. BEGINNINGS OF THE REFORM MOVEMENT IN EGYPT IN THE LATE EIGHTEENTH CENTURY

As a result of these developments, a spirit of stagnation imposed itself on the thoughts of the Muslim world. Moreover, the power of compiling books diminished, and gradually ceased. Cries for reform stopped, except in a few cases when the *'ulamā'* stepped forward to defend the interests of the nation. However, this stagnation gradually came to an end during the eighteenth century when there appeared in Egypt, and Syria too, sparks of reform reflected in three forms. First, the bold and noble attitude of the *'ulamā'* aiming at curbing injustice and restraining oppressive *amīrs* and governors. In the meantime they did their best to defend the rights and interests of the natives. Secondly, the attempts of some persons and groups to attack the so-called saints and dervishes, and to abolish innovations and superstitions. These reformers tried to eradicate the abuses that stained Islam. Thus they called for the destruction of the tombs and shrines, and denied strongly that the dead were able to fulfil any message, or that they were sacred. Thirdly, the appearance of a number of *'ulamā'* and thinkers who might be considered as the pioneers of a new cultural renaissance. We shall discuss in detail each of these symptoms according to their importance.

1. *The leadership of the* 'ulamā'

During the Ottoman period Egypt was governed by three powers: the Turkish pasha, his garrison officers, and Mamluk *amīrs*. These masters did not care at all for the people's rights, which were entirely neglected. Their authority would have been absolutely limitless but for the spiritual leadership of the *'ulamā'*, who were looked upon as defenders of the Faith and transmitters of the Qur'ān. The *amīrs* and the military caste feared nothing more than the dynamic influence of this spiritual and religious leadership. On the other hand it may be noticed that there was no connexion between the masses and their rulers. The latter were entirely alien: in feelings, race, and tongue, while the *'ulamā'* were of the same stock, brought up in the country and sharing the feelings of the people. Moreover they acquainted themselves deeply with Islam and comprehended that it is a religion based on equality and justice, opposing despotism and above all holding the ruler responsible for his subjects. Islam, too, obliged the governor, any governor, to follow the right path of justice and fairness. Thus the *'ulamā'* were regarded by the rulers and people as the symbol of the *Shar'*, the holy law, which should be strictly adhered to by the rulers of Muslim states. It was recognized by rulers and subjects alike, that the *'ulamā'* had, during the Ottoman period, a sort of unquestionable leadership.

When harassed by their rulers, the people used to complain to the *'ulamā'* who, in their turn, gave advice which sometimes was severe and sometimes mild. Rulers always listened to the *'ulamā'*, and responded to their mediation. Examples of this are many. In 1114/1702 it happened that vendors were harassed because of counterfeit currency. They gathered together, entered al-Azhar mosque, complained to the *'ulamā'*, and compelled them to accompany them to the *Dīwān*. The pasha held a meeting which was attended by the *amīrs*, the Turkish judge, the *ağas*, the chief of the *Ashrāf*, and the eminent *'ulamā'*. The meeting resulted in a satisfactory decision which preserved the rights of the people.

On another occasion, in 1148/1735, the Ottoman sultan gave orders that a certain expenditure for the good and welfare of the people was to be abolished. Members of the *Dīwān* held a meeting to hear the declaration of the sultan's decree. The Ottoman judge commented that the sultan's orders should be obeyed and not opposed. No sooner had he uttered these words than an Egyptian *'ālim* called Sulaymān al-Manṣūrī, said to him publicly:

> O chief of Islam, these allowances were issued by the representative of the sultan whose acts have the same force as those of the sultan himself. These were the traditions followed by previous rulers, and those expenditures were dedicated by charitable ends—mosques and water fountains. They should therefore not be stopped, as that would mean abolishing charities and suspending the rites of Islam. No true Muslim who has a full and sincere belief in God and His Prophet would dare to sustain that. Thus the present order of the sultan should be opposed, as it is against law, and no one can agree with the master in a matter of contradicting the *Sharī'a*.

The shaykh's opposition was effective and succeeded in revoking the order.

The motive of such a shaykh was to apply the ideals of duty and justice represented by Islam. Thus the rulers of the age always took into consideration the importance of the *'ulamā'*'s authority which depended on Islamic law and the people's support. For this reason, too, most of the rulers respected the *'ulamā'* and used to ask them their advice; a fact which is reflected in the biography of Shaykh Muḥammad b. Sālim al-Hifnī, related by al-Jabartī, who describes him as the most influential man in Egypt, without whose consideration no state question could be settled.

Of the same category was Shaykh 'Alī al-Ṣa'īdī who was a contemporary of 'Alī Bey al-Kabīr and Muḥammad Bey Abu'l-Dhahab, the two *amīrs* who first attempted to gain independence. They respected him so much that they used to kiss his hands and never failed to fulfil his demands. Shaykh 'Alī used to write down memoranda of people's petitions, and go with them to Abu'l-Dhahab, who never let him down. So that he might not hesitate, Shaykh 'Alī would say to him: 'Never regret anything unjustifiable you miss in this world. Our world is not eternal and death is our final destination. On the day of resurrection God will blame us for not advising you, therefore I have advised you and fulfilled my duty.' And for fear that the *amīr* might not apply justice, the shaykh would face him exclaiming: 'Protect yourself from

Hell-fire', then he would take the *amīr*'s hand in his and say: 'I fear that fire may burn this hand.'

Near the end of the eighteenth century, during the reign of the two tyrants, Murād and Ibrāhīm, a quarrel arose between an ordinary poor man and one of the Mamluk *amīrs*. On being condemned by the judge, the *amīr* was exasperated, and refused to obey the order of the court. But the *'ulamā'* who considered themselves protectors of the *Sharī'a*, insisted that it should be respected. A fearful demonstration headed by Shaykh al-Dardīr and supported by the masses, passed through the streets of Cairo, shops were closed, and serious results were expected. Some wise *amīrs* fearing that anarchy would be widespread, induced the tyrannical ruler to act according to the law. He accepted verbally, but the *'ulamā'* had no faith in him and insisted that his acceptance should be written down. Thus they set down a charter in which the *amīrs* declared that orders of the court had to be carried out.

Shortly afterwards the *wālī* (chief of police) of Cairo resorted to the use of force in collecting government dues from a butcher in al-Ḥusayniyya quarter, and tried to arrest him illegally. The inhabitants of al-Ḥusayniyya revolted and appealed to Shaykh al-'Arūsī, who supported their cause before the *amīrs* and asked them to adhere to the law. Not only did he succeed in making them obey him, but they also dismissed the *wālī* and appointed a new one, who went straight to al-Azhar and propitiated the *'ulamā'*.

In 1209/1795 the inhabitants of Bilbays complained to Shaykh al-Sharqāwī against the severe measures taken by their governor. Being a native of the province of Sharqiyya, and having suffered too from this governor, the shaykh approached Murād and Ibrāhīm with the intention of stopping this injustice. But the two obstinate rulers did not respond to his request. On seeing that he was let down, he urged the people to revolt. They responded willingly and anarchy spread all over Cairo, a matter which might have had due consequences. The pasha, as al-Jabartī says, left the Citadel for Ibrāhīm's residence, where the *amīrs* were gathered and sent word asking the *'ulamā'* to come to him. The Shaykhs al-Sādāt, al-Sharqāwī, al-Bakrī, and al-Amīr attended and discussed the problem among themselves. The decision was taken that the *amīrs* should repent and accept the *'ulamā'*'s terms, and the matter was settled peacefully on conditions. The *amīrs* were to follow the right path and prevent their followers from oppressing the people. As the judge was present he wrote down a charter containing those conditions and it was signed by the pasha as well as by Murād and Ibrāhīm. The revolt ended and the shaykhs returned to their homes surrounded by cheering crowds.

2. *The struggle against innovations and superstitions*

The second symptom was represented by the voices raised in Egypt in the eighteenth century to abolish the innovations spread by the mystics and dervishes. In fact, Egypt in particular and the other Arab lands in general were transformed during the Ottoman period into a big *khānqāh*. Various mystic orders spread all over the Arab countries. It is of interest that all these orders grew either in the eastern parts or in the western parts of the Muslim world, but none in Egypt itself, and thus no Egyptian was the head of any order. They penetrated, though, into Egypt where they were welcomed by its inhabitants, flourished amongst them, and consequently were ramified. As a consequence of widespread ignorance and abject poverty, most of the Egyptians, the peasants and artisans in particular, attached themselves closely to these orders. The reason for this was that they tried to find in spiritual orders and the promised other world with its many favours, a compensation for their present poverty and the injustice of their rulers.

We notice also that fundamental differences existed between the Ṣūfīs and the *faqihs* before and during the Ottoman period. The way leading to knowledge, in the *faqīh*'s opinion, was the *Sharīʿa*, the study of the Qur'ān, traditions, and jurisprudence. With the Ṣūfīs this way was through intuition, devotion, and the extreme love of God. A few Ṣūfīs only, such as Ibn ʿAtā'allāh al-Sikandarī of the thirteenth century and ʿAbd al-Wahhāb al-Shaʿarānī of the sixteenth century, mastered both *fiqh* and mysticism.

Pure mysticism, as a retreat for the soul and spirit, is not perilous to society. Some mystic orders, such as the Shādhiliyya were against passivity, and insisted upon their members making an effort to obtain a livelihood. When every lunatic and imbecile pretended to be a saint, when Ṣūfīs exaggerated the value of their so-called miracles, mysticism became a source of peril in the Ottoman period. To add fuel to the fire the mystics wrote treatises menacing people who slackened in their belief in Ṣūfīs and their miracles, whether alive or dead, a matter which differed entirely from the true and simple precepts of Islam. Therefore it was not strange to hear now and then voices raised against these innovations clothed in the mantle of religion and mysticism. This criticism and this resistance was sometimes violent and took, at other times, the shape of theoretical arguments. In both cases it was led by governors and soldiers, or by *ʿulamā'*, faqīhs, preachers, and poets.[1]

Bonaparte also reacted with some severity when he was struck by the folly of the lunatics. In 1215/1800 he asked the *ʿulamā'* their opinion concerning those mendicants who wandered in the markets uncovering their genitals and crying. They pretended holiness, yet they never prayed or fasted as other Muslims do. He asked the *ʿulamā'* whether Islam prohibited or allowed these deeds. The *ʿulamā'* answered that these deeds were strictly forbidden by both religion and tradition. Thus Bonaparte thanked them and gave his orders to the police to arrest them; those who were really insane were confined to the asylum, and those who were not mentally deficient were sent into exile if they refused to obey orders.

[1] For two illustrative examples, see Appendix I.

The most important manifestations of the struggle between the *faqīhs* and the Ṣūfīs were *fatwās* and treatises compiled by the contemporary *ʿulamāʾ* criticizing the mystics and disparaging them. A specimen of the *fatwās* is the one issued by al-Shaykh ʿAlī al-Ṣaʿīdī in 1197/1782–3 as an answer to the question raised about the way of *dhikr* followed by the Muṭawwiʿa order. The followers of this order used flags, drums, and long rosaries. They also made use of singers. The young men amongst them used to wear pantaloons and wind blankets round their heads while sitting behind those who performed the *dhikr*. One of the treatises was that written by the Hanafite Shaykh Muḥammad Ṣafī al-Dīn in 1105/1693–4 and called 'The Burning Thunderbolt' (*al-Ṣāʿiqa al-muḥriqa*) in which he fiercely attacked mysticism and its followers, especially those who mixed games and dancing with their religious rites, and used to turn in the circles of *dhikr* moving their hands backward and forward and shaking their heads up and down, right and left imitating the Christians in their game called 'The running of the cock' (*rakḍ al-dīk*).

Poetry also was a third party in attacking those persons pretending to be holy saints. Frequently poetry was the voice which expressed the conditions of a society and political events. There lived in eighteenth-century Egypt a good poet called Ḥasan al-Badrī al-Ḥijāzī. Al-Jabartī, in his history, transcribed many of al-Ḥijāzī's poems, which reflected clearly and ironically the political and social life of Egypt at that time. He frequently attacked those ignorant pretenders and false mystics.[1]

In all these attempts the attack took a negative form. Al-Jabartī, however, mentioned only one positive attempt which aimed at abolishing innovations. The leader of this movement was a *Rūmī* (a Turk) who used to deliver sermons in al-Mu'ayyad mosque in Cairo. One evening in Ramaḍān 1123/ October–November 1711, after finishing his religious advice, he started criticizing the practices of the people of Cairo in the holy shrines, such as lighting candles and lamps over the Ṣūfīs' tombs, and kissing the thresholds. He commented that this deed was pure impiety which should be stopped, and it was the duty of those responsible to abolish it. He also denied al-Shaʿrānī's assertion in *al-Ṭabaqāt*, that some Ṣūfīs had seen the heavenly book, and even that prophets had seen it. Also he declared that domes erected over the saints' tombs and *tekkes* should be razed to the ground and not built any more. The last innovation he mentioned was the crowding of the dervishes at the Zuwayla gate during the nights of Ramaḍān. What was said by this preacher was something entirely new and bold, especially at that time. He preceded the well-known reformer, Muḥammad b. ʿAbd al-Wahhāb, by thirty-three years. He tried to do what Ibn ʿAbd al-Wahhāb wanted to do afterwards, to stop evil not only by words but also by force.

[1] For two specimens of his verse in translation, see Appendix II.

Those who were attending his speech in al-Mu'ayyad mosque responded to his call. After the *tarāwīḥ* prayer the preacher left the mosque followed by his attendants, with arms and clubs in their hands. They gathered at the Zuwayla gate, pulled down all the rags hanging on the gate while they shouted 'Where are the "saints" (*awliyā'*)?' Thus the thrones of the shaykhs and saints began to totter. The matter was no more a *fatwā* issued or a poem recited, but became a club ready to break the head and a weapon ready to kill. Therefore the mob, infatuated by their Ṣūfīs hurried to the *'ulamā'* of al-Azhar requesting them to issue their opinion about this preacher and his sayings.

It may sound strange that those same *'ulamā'* attacked the preacher's call and eradicated it. But in fact it does not appear strange to me, because not all the *'ulamā'* of al-Azhar were against mysticism, for some of them took part in both *Sharī'a* and *taṣawwuf*. The majority of them, too, were orators, *imāms*, preachers, or teachers in college mosques. They received good salaries from the *waqfs* of these mosques and institutes. They also had a share in the gifts and alms offered to the saints' tombs. And after all those *'ulamā'* were state officials for whom it was difficult to respond to this development or to support it.

Two Azhar shaykhs, Aḥmad al-Nafarāwī and Aḥmad al-Khalīfī by name, issued a *fatwā* against the preacher's opinion, and asked the governor to reprove him. The people conveyed this verdict to the preacher. After reading it he became angry and said to his followers. 'If the *'ulamā'* have given that decision contradicting me, let them face me in the law-court and argue it out with me.' Going on he asked them: 'Would you back me up and support justice?' They answered at once: 'We are with you and will never let you down.' Then he left his chair and went through the Cairo streets followed by a demonstration of about a thousand of his disciples.

When the judge saw so many people in front of his house he became very frightened and asked them what they wanted. They replied: 'We wish you to call the two shaykhs who issued the verdict in order to question them.' The judge said: 'Send away this gathering, and I will call the two shaykhs and will listen to the debate.' Not obeying his demand they surrounded the judge, asking him to give his opinion about the verdict. The judge, afraid of the demonstrators criticized the verdict and described it as invalid. They were not satisfied with that verbal criticism, so they asked him to write it down. As the judge was not sincere in what he said, he soon found a pretext, saying, 'There is no time now and the witnesses have gone. We may as well postpone the matter till tomorrow.' The demonstrators became very angry. They attacked the interpreter (as the judge was Turkish and could not understand Arabic) and struck him. The judge seized the opportunity and fled with his harem. But the people did not leave the acting judge before they obtained from him a written document, justifying the preacher's opinion and annulling the two shaykhs' verdict. Yet this step did not put an end to the revolt. Some days later, as people went to al-Mu'ayyad mosque to attend their preacher's lessons, they did not find him, and a rumour was spread that the judge had prevented him from preaching.

One of the preacher's disciples said: 'O people, let him who would support justice follow me.' The speaker was followed by multitudes with whom he went to the judge. On seeing them all the people in court were terrified, the eyewitnesses fled and there remained only the judge. They entered and asked him about their shaykh, but he answered that he knew nothing about his whereabouts. On hearing that they said to him: 'Come with us to the *Dīwān* and let us speak to the pasha about this matter. We will ask him to bring our opponents who sanctioned the killing of our shaykh, and we will dispute with them. If they are proved right, they will be set free, otherwise we will kill them.' The judge went despite himself, while the demonstrators walked in front and behind him until they reached the *Dīwān*.

When asked by the pasha about the reason for his untimely arrival the judge answered him: 'Look at these people who are crowding the *Dīwān* and the courtyard they have brought me.' Then he told him the story. Afraid of the crowds and their anger, and apprehending misfortune if he should oppose them, the pasha issued orders to his men to bring the two shaykhs in order to dispute with the preacher. The people dispersed, and brought their preacher and seated him on his chair in the mosque. He agreed that they should make the two shaykhs go with him to the judge, before whom they would discuss the matter.

But as the pasha was not serious in his talk with them, he sent, after they left him, a message to the two Mamluk *amīrs*, Ibrāhīm Bey and Qayṭās Bey, informing them of what had happened, and describing the impolite behaviour of the mob. He declared that their aim was to stir up sedition, and to humble him and the judge. He ended his letter by warning the two beys that he, as well as the judge, would leave the country for good if they failed to put an end to that disturbance. The Mamluk *amīrs* ordered the preacher to be sent into exile, and his followers to disperse. Orders were also issued to the *aġa* to mount his mule and arrest whoever he might find; then he was to enter al-Mu'ayyad mosque, and drive away those who dwelt in it.

That is how Egypt witnessed the first reform movement in the eighteenth century. Unfortunately it lasted only for a few days and ended unsuccessfully. The reason for this failure was the fact that Egyptian society was not yet ready to accept such a movement. It is regrettable that al-Jabartī does not give the name of the preacher. Where had he grown up and studied? Who were his tutors? What sort of study had he obtained? By whom was he influenced? Was he inspired, like Ibn ʿAbd al-Wahhāb, by Ibn Taymiyya, or was his movement a natural reaction against the innovations and jugglery he used to see in Cairo and other Egyptian cities? All these are questions which still need answers.

3. *Spontaneous cultural reform*

Towards the close of the eighteenth century we detect the first sign of a spontaneous cultural revival. It was an internal movement which emerged from within Egypt, independently of any outside influence, from either the east or the west. It was started by a group of Egyptian writers who appeared on the cultural scene and who were unequalled during the three preceding centuries either in their number or in the amount of material they produced. Shaykh Ḥasan al-Jabartī excelled in the mathematical and astronomical studies. In the field of literature there were such men as Shaykh Muḥammad al-Shubrāwī, Shaykh Ḥasan al-ʿAṭṭār (who occupied, at one time the post of shaykh of al-Azhar), and Shaykh Ismāʿīl al-Khashshāb. In the field of linguistics and theological studies there were Sayyid Muḥammad Murtaḍā al-Zabīdī, and in history there was Shaykh ʿAbd al-Raḥmān al-Jabartī.

It is most likely that this awakening would have taken the form of a national revival which would bring back to life the old glories and the legacy of the past. But this spontaneous awakening was interrupted by the advent of the French expedition. This was accompanied by a number of scientists and men of learning who brought in their train many features of a culture completely different from anything which the Egyptians had known. A number of Egyptian *ʿulamāʾ* contacted those scientists, visited the institute which they founded in Cairo, frequented the library, and admired the press they brought with them. They were overwhelmed with what they saw and started to compare their own culture with that which the French brought with them.

After that many developments took place in Egypt. The French evacuated the country: some internal disturbances took place, Muḥammad ʿAlī became vali of Egypt, and a new régime was introduced. The new governor realized from the start that Egypt had to copy from the West if its aim was a true revival, and if it was not to be left behind on the road to progress. New schools were opened, students were sent on educational missions to Europe, and in these circumstances the movement of writing came to a standstill, while a movement of translation began which lasted throughout the reign of Muḥammad ʿAlī.

APPENDIX I

(*a*) *Shaykh ʿAlī al-Bakrī*

ʿAlī al-Bakrī was an example of a lunatic in whom people had unquestioning faith. In his biography, given in the obituaries of the year 1207/1792–3, al-Jabartī says that ʿAlī al-Bakrī was insane, and that he usually roamed about the streets of Cairo, bare-headed and shamefully naked. Sometimes he was seen bare-footed with only a shirt on his back and a coarse cap on his head, muttering incoherently, and followed by the children and the mob. People were divided into two groups: some repudiated him and others believed in him. But the majority inclined to him and believed in his holiness.

A certain brother of his was so crafty that he tried to take advantage of the credulity of the people. He therefore prevented ʿAlī from wandering in the streets, he detained him in his residence, clothed him, and pretended that he was a holy man. People visited him in his house, and listened carefully to his ravings, which they interpreted according to their whims. Votive offerings and charitable gifts were sent to him by all sorts of people, eminent persons as well as wives of *amīrs*. His brother became very rich, and Shaykh ʿAlī himself became very fat and looked like a huge beast as a result of the large quantities of food he used to consume.

Moreover Shaykh ʿAlī was accompanied in his perambulations by an insane woman. People rapidly believed in her holiness and spread the rumour that the shaykh had bewitched her and that she, too, had become a saint. Afterwards she used to go with him in male dress, followed by multitudes of people and little children. Some of them undressed themselves, and tried to imitate the two shaykhs in their gambolling. It was said that these people were bewitched and influenced by Shaykh ʿAlī. The woman shaykh used sometimes to ascend a high step and utter obscenities and people gathered round her in crowds, kissing her hand, and asking for her blessing. The followers of both increased in such a way that whenever they passed through a street there arose a terrific clamour, followed by confusion, in the midst of which shops were robbed.

Once this parade passed by the house of a soldier called Jaʿfar Kāshif. He arrested Shaykh ʿAlī and took him, the woman, and the crowd of mad followers into his house, after driving away the rest of the mob. He gave the shaykh something to eat and beat the woman and the others very severely and finally sent the woman to the asylum.

Yet people kept believing in the holiness of both the shaykh and the woman even after their death. On the death of ʿAlī al-Bakrī his brother built a shrine over his tomb and appointed Qur'ān reciters and singers to recite poems praising his deeds and virtues. While visiting his tomb the shaykh's followers used to cry, wipe their faces against the tomb window and steps, and ladle up the air round it and put it in their pockets and sleeves. The woman remained in the asylum for some time, after which she was released. She became a female shaykh in her own right, enjoying the belief of people and women in particular. After her death they used to celebrate her birthday and send vows and offerings to her tomb.

(*b*) *The sacred goat*

A servant of the shrine of Sayyida Nafīsa in Cairo got a goat and pretended that the Sayyida had committed the goat to his charge. He spread the rumour that the goat could perform miracles. Very soon the story of the goat became well known to everybody in Cairo. The people believed wholeheartedly in the goat, and sent it many gifts of pistachio nuts, almonds, sugar, and rosewater. Women presented it with necklaces, bracelets, and golden ornaments. Many people, foremost among whom were the wives of the *amīrs* and eminent ladies flocked in groups to visit the goat and receive its blessing.

When the rumour reached ʿAbd al-Raḥmān Katkhudā, he sent for the man and his she-goat, pretending that he, with the women of his household, would like to obtain the blessing of the goat. The guardian, with the goat in his arms, went to the *amīr*'s house in a parade, with drums and pipers in front of him, and flags around him. When he reached his destination the *amīr* welcomed him and led the she-goat to his harem. Then he ordered it to be slaughtered and fed his guests including the guardian with its meat.

When the visit was over the guardian asked the *amīr* to give him back his goat, but the *amīr* told him that he had already eaten it. He reproached him severely and gave orders that the shaykh should be taken back to his house in a parade. This parade was quite different from the previous one. The skin of the goat was put over the shaykh's turban, drums and pipers around him, and the masses mocked him till he arrived at his house.

APPENDIX II

Specimens of the satirical verse of Ḥasan al-Ḥijāzī

(*a*) Would that we were dead before seeing, as now we do, every crazy idiot become a lodestar, whom the people invoke in times of distress, and even take to be a god in place of the Almighty. Thus they have forgotten God, and declare that only such a man can mitigate the ills of men. When he is dead, they make a shrine of his tomb, and travel to it on pilgrimage from every place. Some kiss his grave, some kiss the threshold of the shrine, and some kiss the floor. So indeed do the pagans to their idols, in propitiation. But the learned and the scholars of the Holy Qur'ān are all much hated and much tortured. They are accused of immorality and perjury, of tyrannizing and oppressing the people, of pillage and plunder. All this is indeed the result of their inner blindness, the darkness of their souls. Woe to a man whose heart God has made insensible. I, Ḥasan al-Ḥijāzī, say that it is evil to break the laws of the *Sharīʿa*. Beware, O beware of doing the deeds of the ignorant people—even if they be the deeds of a teacher using books. Such a teacher makes of his knowledge a trap used for his worldly ends. Thus he is equal in sin to a dog—nay, even a dog is better than he, for the dog faces no punishment on the Day of Judgement.

(*b*) Beware of those who carry beads and lean on staves, who dress in sackcloth and use a jug and a bucket and roam everywhere, glorifying God. In particular, beware of those hairy Satanic shaykhs. The devilry in them outnumbers their hairs: nay, indeed, it cannot be counted. Their trickery is as boundless as the sea: in comparison to their tricks, even the sea would be only a drop. Satan himself is but one of their followers, and turns to them for help and guidance. He calls to them, saying, 'Teach me of your knowledge, for I cannot do without your trickery. You lead, and I will follow, for none is like you in my society or my circle.' In full-throated ease, they call, 'O honest, noble men. O Shāfiʿī, chief of all the mystics. O Rāfiʿī, O Rifāʿī. O people of eminence. O Sīdī Aḥmad. O masters of the universe, help us to carry the burden.' It is money they want and nothing else. But truly, in my opinion, they are in wickedness the greatest on earth.

BIBLIOGRAPHY

Clot-Bey, A. -B., *Aperçu général sur l'Égypte* (2 vols., Paris, 1840): Arabic trans., Muḥammad Mas'ūd (tr.), *Lamḥa 'āmma ilā Miṣr* (Cairo, n.d.).

Combe, Etienne, 'L'Égypte Ottomane' in *Précis de l'histoire d'Égypte*, vol. iii (Cairo, 1933), pp. 1–128.

Dehérain, Henri, 'L'Égypte Turque' in G. Hanotaux (ed.), *Histoire de la nation égyptienne*, vol. v (Paris, 1931).

Ghorbal, Shafik, *The beginnings of the Egyptian question and the rise of Mehemet Ali* (London, 1928).

Gibb, H. A. R., and Bowen, Harold, *Islamic society and the West*, vol. i, parts 1 and 2 (London, 1950, 1957).

Heyworth-Dunne, J., *An introduction to the history of education in modern Egypt* (London, [1939]).

al-Jabartī, 'Abd al-Raḥmān b. Ḥasan, *'Ajā'ib al-āthār fi'l-tarājim wa'l-akhbār* (4 vols., Būlāq, 1297).

Lane, E. W., *An account of the manners and customs of the modern Egyptians* (1st edn., 2 vols., London, 1836; many reprints): Arabic trans., 'Adlī Ṭāhir Nūr (tr.), *'Ādāt wa-akhlāq al-Miṣriyyīn al-muḥdathīn* (Cairo, 1950).

Lane-Poole, S., *Social life in Egypt* (London, n.d.).

al-Muḥibbī, Muḥammad Amīn b. Faḍlallāh, *Khulāṣat al-athar fī a'yān al-qarn al-ḥādī 'ashar* (4 vols., Cairo, 1284).

al-Murādī, Muḥammad Khalīl b. 'Alī, *Silk al-durar fi a'yān al-qarn al-thānī 'ashar* (Cairo, 1291).

Rouyer, 'Notice sur les Médicamens usuels des Égyptiens' in *Description de l'Égypte, État moderne*, vol. i, pp. 1217–32.

Savary, C. E., *Lettres sur l'Égypte* (3 vols., Paris, 1785–6): English trans., *Letters on Egypt* (2 vols., London, 1787).

El-Shayyal, Gamal El-Din, *Ta'rīkh al-tarjama fī Miṣr fī 'ahd al-ḥamla al-frinsiyya* (Cairo, 1951).

—— *Ta'rīkh al-tarjama wa'l-ḥaraka al-thaqafiyya fī 'aṣr Muḥammad 'Alī* (Cairo, 1952).

—— *Rifā'a al-Ṭahṭāwī* (Cairo, 1958).

—— *al-Ḥarakāt al-iṣlāḥiyya wa-marākiz al-thaqāfa fi'l-sharq al-islāmī al-ḥadīth* (Publications of the Institute of Higher Arabic Studies, Cairo, 1957–8).

—— *A history of Egyptian historiography in the nineteenth century* (Publications of the Faculty of Arts, Alexandria University; Alexandria, 1962).

al-Ṭawīl, Tawfīq, *Ta'rīkh al-taṣawwuf fī Miṣr ibbān al-'ahd al-'uthmānī* (Cairo, 1946).

Volney [Constantin-François Chassebeuf], *Voyage en Égypte et en Syrie* (1st edn., 2 vols., Paris, 1787; ed. Jean Gaulmier, Paris and The Hague, 1959).

PART THREE

STUDIES IN THE HISTORY OF THE NINETEENTH AND TWENTIETH CENTURIES

Social Change in Egypt: 1800–1914

GABRIEL BAER

Continuity and change

In a recently published book on the intellectual evolution of modern Egypt the author devotes one chapter to the political, economic, and social transformation between the years 1804 and 1882. Summing up, he arrives at the following conclusions: 'The cumulative effect of the developments that we have described amounted to nothing less than a complete transformation of the basic character of the life and organization of Egyptian society.'[1] This statement surely requires a number of qualifications. So does the opposite view that, except for some superficial borrowing from the French, Egyptian society did not change at all under Muḥammad ʿAlī, ʿAbbās, Saʿīd, and Ismāʿīl.[2] Social change in nineteenth-century Egypt was a complex process which needs to be investigated in detail.

Evidently the traditional structure of the family and the status of women did not undergo any change at all. At the beginning of the twentieth century the extended family was still prevalent in Egypt as a unit of property-owning as well as of dwelling, uniting as it did the father of the family, his wife or wives, his unmarried daughters and sons, and his married sons with their wives and children in a single house or in apartments closely grouped or attached to one another. The father of the family owned all the family possessions and controlled the family labour-force and its income. Parents arranged the marriages of their sons and daughters, who generally were not allowed to make their own decisions in this matter.[3] ('Clan' endogamy, and particularly cousin-marriage, was the rule.) The family was divided into seniors and juniors, and the distinction between those of greater or less consideration was based on relative age.[4] Similarly, the family was strictly divided into two worlds—of men and women.

Although the forerunners of a feminist movement had appeared as early as the end of the nineteenth century, their aims were as yet very modest and their influence on actual life was not felt until much later. At the beginning

[1] N. Safran, *Egypt in search of political community* (Cambridge, Mass., 1961), p. 38.

[2] See, for instance, Earl of Cromer, *Modern Egypt* (London, 1908), vol. ii, ch. 34.

[3] Cf. F. Schwally, *Beiträge zur Kenntnis des Lebens der mohammedanischen Städter, Fellachen und Beduinen im heutigen Ägypten* (Heidelberg, 1912), pp. 5, 9–10, 15–16.

[4] Cf. E. F. Tugay, *Three Centuries, family chronicles of Turkey and Egypt* (London, 1963), p. 233. Mrs. Tugay's description relates to Turco-Egyptian families of the upper class at the beginning of the twentieth century, but it certainly is valid for other classes too, and even for a later period. See, for instance, H. Ammar, *Growing up in an Egyptian village* (London, 1954), pp. 52–53.

of the twentieth century male and female society were no less segregated from one another than at the beginning of the nineteenth. Urban women did not unveil or emerge from their seclusion before the First World War,[1] while in some regions fellah women had not worn a veil even a century earlier.[2] But where peasant women used to veil in the nineteenth century, they continued to do so in the twentieth (for instance, women of well-to-do fellah families in certain parts of Upper Egypt).[3] The wife was supposed to be submissive, obedient, devoted, and respectful to her husband. He could easily divorce her, and urban husbands frequently used this right. According to authors who wrote at the end of the nineteenth and the beginning of the twentieth century, polygamy was relatively common not only among wealthy families but also among the lower classes.[4] None of the legal reforms relating to the status of Muslim women had been introduced before the First World War.

Moreover, not marriage and divorce only continued to be regulated by traditional religious law, but also all other matters of 'personal status', such as adoption, guardianship, heritages, wills, and *waqf*. This, however, was not the only field in which religion retained its social function. By the end of the nineteenth century the Ṣūfī *ṭarīqas* had not yet been superseded as the principal form of organization of the population of Egypt by any kind of secular association; the secret societies at the end of the century were restricted to very small groups. The *ṭarīqas* constituted the framework of social gathering and played an important role at public festivals, which served as the main expression of social consciousness of the masses. Almost all these festivals had a religious content, and the most significant of them were the hundreds of *mawlids* (*mūlids*), small ones in almost every Egyptian village and larger ones in provincial towns and the capital. These *mawlids* had not lost their vitality during the whole period with which we are dealing, nor had the veneration of the 'shaykhs' in whose honour the *mawlids* were held.[5] Thus religion, particularly popular religion, was a social factor in which very little

[1] Schwally, pp. 8–9.

[2] U. J. Seetzen, *Reisen . . .*, vol. iii (Berlin, 1854), p. 265 (written 1807–8); J. A. St. John, *Egypt and Nubia* (London, 1845), pp. 97, 186–7, 190, 283–4, 335, 415, 425–6; 'Alī Pasha Mubārak, *al-Khiṭaṭ al-tawfīqiyya al-jadīda* (Cairo–Būlāq, 1886–9), vol. xii, p. 134; vol. xiv, p.68.

[3] Mubārak, vol. viii, pp. 28, 51, 105; vol. ix, p. 88; vol. xi, p. 64; vol. xiii, p. 69; W. S. Blackman, *The fellahin of Upper Egypt* (London, 1927), pp. 37–38; A. Boktor, *School and society in the valley of the Nile* (Cairo, 1936), p. 63.

[4] Schwally, pp. 16–17, 20, 34; A. von Fircks, 'Stand, Bewegung und wirtschaftlicher Zustand des ägyptischen Volkes 1894', *Zeitschrift des königlichen preussischen statistischen Bureaus*, vol. xxxv (1895), p. 154. It is interesting to note that about the middle of the nineteenth century some observers had the opposite impression. Cf. Bayle St. John, *Village life in Egypt* (London, 1852), vol. i, p. 55; N. W. Senior, *Conversations and journals in Egypt and Malta* (London, 1882), vol. i, p. 165 (written in 1855). A possible reason for a rise in the proportion of polygamous families in the course of the second half of the century is the abolition of slavery.

[5] For the beginning of the twentieth century see, for instance, Sayyid Quṭb, *Ṭifl min al-qarya* (Cairo, 1945), pp. 77 ff. For the 1870s and 1880s hundreds of examples are given by Mubārak, *passim.*

change, if any, occurred during the nineteenth century. The same may be said of course about a large variety of customs, such as marriage and funeral rites, which were not always directly connected with religion.

If such institutions as the family, the status of women, and the social function of religion did not undergo any change during the nineteenth century, one can hardly speak about 'a complete transformation of the basic character . . . of the Egyptian society'. That they did not change is certainly connected with the fact that during that period Egypt was not transformed from an agrarian into an industrial society. Moreover, after the failure of Muḥammad ʿAlī's industrial experiment,[1] no serious industrial development took place in Egypt for decades. Some of Muḥammad ʿAlī's factories were liquidated by ʿAbbās and Saʿīd, and others were sold by Saʿīd or given in *iltizām* to private individuals. These, however, made little headway, since they had to pay a large variety of burdensome taxes.[2] Ismāʿīl tried to revive industrial initiative by privately taking over government enterprises and by sending missions abroad to acquire new factories. A few were bought (a paper factory, for instance), but production turned out to be uneconomic. Therefore a whole group of factories was liquidated in 1875 and the buildings turned into barracks.[3] Only two branches continued to flourish: the sugar industry, run by the government, and cotton gins, established mainly by foreigners. In general, however, foreign capital was interested in public utility companies (water, gas, and railways) rather than in industry. As to local Egyptian capitalists, in addition to the taxes which discriminated against them, important factors deterred them from investing in industry. Industrial investment involved a great risk, because of the small market and the competition of European products, compared with the large gains of investment in agricultural land, made possible through the vast expansion of agricultural production at the time. The British occupation changed this situation only in so far as most of the oppressive taxes were abolished, but Cromer opposed industrial development, arguing that without introducing protective customs duties such development would be impossible, and that, if he did introduce protective customs, he would be acting against his free-trade convictions, while Egypt would lose her income from customs on European merchandise.[4]

[1] For analyses of Muḥammad ʿAlī's failure see A. E. Crouchley, *The economic development of modern Egypt* (London, 1938), pp. 72–76; M. Fahmy, *La révolution de l'industrie en Égypte . . . (1800–1850)*, (Leiden, 1954), pp. 98 ff.; H. A. B. Rivlin, *The agricultural policy of Muḥammad ʿAlī in Egypt* (Cambridge, Mass., 1961), pp. 198–200.

[2] See, for instance, Amīn Sāmī, *Taqwīm al-nīl* (Cairo, 1936), Pt. III, vol. i, pp. 149–50; vol. ii, pp. 901–2; Nubar to Stanton, No. 347, Cairo, 12 Apr. 1871, P.R.O., F.O. 141/75, Pt. 2; Barr to Stanton, Alexandria, 24 Feb. 1875, F.O. 141/92; A. von Kremer, *Aegypten* (Leipzig, 1863), vol. ii, p. 35.

[3] Sāmī, Pt. III, vol. ii, pp. 499, 598–9, 793, 862, 964–6; vol. iii, pp. 1105, 1253.

[4] Cromer to Bergne, Cairo, 2 May 1901 (Private), F.O. 633/8 (Cromer Papers), 319–21. For the absence of an Egyptian entrepreneur class see also C. Issawi, *Egypt in revolution* (London, 1963), pp. 29–30.

As a result, his economic policy was extremely unfavourable to industrial development.

All this does not mean, however, that during the nineteenth century no changes occurred in the socio-economic structure of Egypt. Although no industry emerged, Egypt underwent a considerable economic development, which has been aptly summarized as follows: '. . . the subsistence economy under which the country had lived for centuries was replaced by an export-oriented economy, the bulk of Egypt's available reserves of land, water, and underemployed labour were brought into use and its total output and exports increased several times, with a consequent rise in real per-capita income and in the level of living.'[1] In addition, during that time Egypt almost suddenly came into close contact with the West which culminated in foreign intervention in Egyptian affairs and in the British occupation of Egypt. The rulers of Egypt attempted to introduce an efficient and modern system of government and tried to achieve independence of the Ottoman Empire. All this had some far-reaching social consequences.

Bedouin settlement and changes in rural society

To begin with, during the nineteenth century Egypt largely solved its problem of nomadic tribes, which cannot be said about any other country of the Middle East.[2] Although at the beginning of the century nomads apparently did not constitute more than about 5–6 per cent. of the population,[3] their political and social influence on the settled population bore no proportion to their numbers. This state of affairs rapidly changed with Muḥammad ʿAlī's accession. To crush the power of the bedouins Muḥammad ʿAlī used various means: he kept hostages in the capital, recruited tribes as irregulars for his wars, requisitioned their horses, and from 1833 on, he appointed bedouin shaykhs as governors of districts.[4] Furthermore, in order to solve the problem once and for all and to induce the tribes to settle on the land, he and his successors granted the shaykhs large tracts of land as their private property.[5]

Muḥammad ʿAlī's policy seems to have been crowned with success. The Hanādī section of the Western Desert nomads was transferred to Sharqiyya province and settled there;[6] the Fawā'id branch of the Libyan Barāghīth,

[1] C. Issawi, *Egypt in revolution*, pp. 18 ff.

[2] For detailed treatment of this subject see G. Baer, 'Some aspects of bedouin sedentarization in 19th century Egypt', *WI*, N.S., vol. v, no. 1–2, pp. 84–98.

[3] See F. Mengin, *Histoire de l'Égypte sous le gouvernement de Mohammed-Aly* (Paris, 1823), vol. ii, pp. 307–17, 616 (bedouin infantry and cavalry together being calculated at about one third of the bedouin population); *Campbell Report*, F.O. 78/408B.

[4] Mengin, vol. i, p. 397; vol. ii, p. 300; A. von Prokesch, *Erinnerungen aus Aegypten und Kleinasien* (Vienna, 1830), vol. ii, pp. 237–8; A. -B. Clot-Bey, *Aperçu général sur l'Égypte* (Paris 1840), vol. ii, p. 121; Mubārak, vol. xiv, p. 38.

[5] For details of the development of bedouin landed property see G. Baer, *A history of landownership in modern Egypt 1800–1950* (London, 1962), pp. 56–60.

[6] G. W. Murray, *Sons of Ishmael* (London, 1935), pp. 294–6; A. M. Ammar, *The people of Sharqiya* (Cairo, 1944), vol. i, pp. 39–40.

who had come to Egypt together with the Hanādī during the turbulent period of the eighteenth century and raided Giza province as late as February 1813, settled in the nineteenth century in the provinces of Fayyūm, Banī Suwayf, and Minyā:[1] the powerful Hawwāra, the rulers of Upper Egypt in the eighteenth century, were finally crushed by Muḥammad ʿAlī's son Ibrāhīm in 1813, and by the beginning of the twentieth century they were 'lost in the fellahs';[2] and the Ḥabā'iba, who dominated the Delta in the eighteenth century, are no longer mentioned by writers of the late nineteenth and the twentieth centuries. An illuminating example of sedentarization is given by the assimilation of the Ahl al-ʿĀ'idh in Sharqiyya province at the beginning of the nineteenth century. When Muḥammad ʿAlī came to power they were, in Mubārak's words, *fī khushūnat al-ʿArab*, i.e. 'coarse nomads', 'and they had many feuds with other bedouin tribes and none of the obligations of fellahs, and they frequently raided neighbouring people and villages'. By building roads Muḥammad ʿAlī forced them into submission 'and they were given the choice between exemption from treatment as fellahs along with expropriation of their lands and date palms, like other nomads who inhabit hills and live in crude tents, and treatment as fellahs along with permission to keep their property. They chose the fellahs' way of life and were considered as Egyptian fellahs and treated like them in all matters, such as taxes, digging of canals, etc.' From then on, and during the nineteenth century, many of the more important ʿĀ'idh shaykhs founded new villages and settled there with their families and attendants.[3] According to the population censuses of 1897 and 1907, the proportion of nomads in the total population of Egypt had shrunk to less than one per cent. and even their absolute number was smaller than a century before.

Settlement on the land, of course, did not change overnight the old habits and social values of the tribes. Many of them continued to consider agricultural work as disgraceful and let the land to fellahs, a practice which was prohibited again and again by decrees issued in 1837, 1846, and 1851, until they gave it up during the second half of the century.[4] Many went on dwelling in tents even after settlement, and some of them kept tents together with fixed houses.[5] But considerable social change did take place nevertheless. One of its aspects was the growing importance of formal religion among the tribes that settled down: they established Qur'ān schools, provided their guest-houses with mosques, and hired *imāms* for religious instruction and the performance of prayers.[6] However, the most important consequence of bedouin settlement was the break-up of tribal unity. Part of the tribes moved

[1] Jabartī, *ʿAjā'ib*, vol. iv, p. 174; Mubārak, vol. xvii, p. 33; Murray, pp. 289–90.
[2] Jabartī, *ʿAjā'ib*, vol. iv, p. 185; Murray, p. 297.
[3] Mubārak, vol. xiv, pp. 3, 5.
[4] Cf. Y. Artin-Bey, *La propriété foncière en Égypte* (Cairo, 1883), pp. 261–4.
[5] Schwally, p. 32; Mubārak, vol. xvii, p. 21.
[6] Ibid., vol. ix, p. 38; vol xv, p. 44; vol. xvii, pp. 20–25.

to towns, where the shaykhs became government officials, acquired large mansions, and intermarried with the ruling class,[1] while the 'rank and file' of the tribes became part of the lower classes: most of the first railway-workers in Egypt were bedouins.[2] The development of cash crops and the rising prices of agricultural products were a powerful incentive for the shaykhs to acquire large tracts of land and they emerged as big landowners, while the members of the tribes were 'lost among the fellahs'. The growing wealth of the shaykhs led to the establishment of luxurious households, and they became alienated from the tribesmen, a process which was bound to create friction between them and their former fellow tribesmen, and there were even cases of revolts against the shaykhs.[3]

A similar process of social differentiation took place among the settled rural population. At the end of the eighteenth century the rulers of the Egyptian countryside were the *multazims* or tax-farmers, a great part of whom were town-dwellers; the rural population proper was divided into a small layer of wealthy families of village notables[4] and the mass of the fellahs, who did not own the land they tilled, and among whom no significant differences seem to have existed. During the nineteenth century a profound change in the social structure of rural Egypt was brought about through the replacement of the traditional subsistence economy by the growing of cash crops; by the transformation of the land from state property into the full private property of individual citizens;[5] and finally, by the gradual introduction of a modern westernized system of administration.

The *multazims* were liquidated by Muḥammad ʿAlī and in the course of the nineteenth century other urban groups emerged as big landowners (see below). The socio-economic position of the families of village notables underwent great fluctuations until they reached the apogee of their wealth and power under Ismāʿīl; afterwards both their wealth and their power declined, mainly as a result of the restriction of their fiscal and political authority under the British occupation, and most of those who remained wealthy moved to towns.[6] The landed property of many of these formerly prosperous families gradually split up through inheritance. This was one of the factors which caused the emergence of a completely new rural class in Egypt—that of owners of medium-sized landed property. At the end of the nineteenth century these medium-sized properties of between five and fifty feddans (approximately acres) covered about 35 per cent. of the privately owned landed property.[7]

[1] Mubārak, vol. xiv, pp. 3–5; vol. xvii, p. 33; Ammar, *The people of Sharqiya*, p. 43, n. 2; cf. *al-Ahrām*, 21 Jan. 1954.

[2] Mubārak, vol. vii, p. 91.

[3] Ibid., vol. xiv, p. 3.

[4] On the ups and downs of this group, from the end of the eighteenth century until 1950, see G. Baer, 'The village shaykh in modern Egypt', in U. Heyd (ed.), *Studies in Islamic history and civilization* (Jerusalem, 1961), pp. 121–53. On the socio-economic position of this group at the end of the eighteenth century see pp. 138–9.

[5] See Baer, *Landownership*, pp. 1–12.

[6] Idem, 'Village shaykh', pp. 141–4, 148–50.

[7] Idem, *Landownership*, pp. 25–26.

Similarly, the fellahs split into owners of small plots and landless tenants and labourers. This too was the corollary of the development of private ownership of land and of a market economy. In the course of the nineteenth century part of the land gradually was registered in the name of the fellahs who tilled it, but for a variety of reasons many of them lost it again. The burden of taxation often forced cultivators to abandon their land and forfeit ownership rights, and in many cases land was confiscated on the non-payment of taxes. Another burden that turned many small landowners into landless peasants was the corvée (chiefly for public works connected with flood prevention and irrigation) and the levying of men for the army. In addition, in the second half of the century, fellah indebtedness became an acute problem. During the nineteenth century there was a gradual transition from payment of taxes in kind to cash payments, and fellahs began to borrow from money-lenders. This was facilitated by the introduction of modern laws of mortgage with the establishment of the Mixed Courts in 1875. From then on it became possible for creditors to foreclose on land for the non-payment of a debt. Recurring slumps, droughts, floods, and cattle-plagues aggravated the plight of fellahs, many of whom lost their land to their creditors.[1] At the end of the century there were in Egypt less than a million landowners who, together with their families, cannot have amounted to more than six million persons. Since the total population numbered about ten million of whom at least eight million lived in villages, by that time between one and two million peasants must have been landless.

While stimulating social differentiation among Egypt's rural classes, the emergence of a market economy also widened the gulf between Upper and Lower Egypt. The greater proximity of Lower Egyptian villages to the mercantile and cultural centres of the country brought with it greater economic opportunities as well as a faster cultural development. According to Mubārak, in the 1870s or 1880s most Azhar students from Lower Egypt knew the Qur'ān by heart before coming to the Azhar university, while students from Upper Egypt did not, and the latter were much poorer than their fellow students from the Delta.[2] Visiting Egypt in 1883, Mr. Villiers Stuart observed a sharp distinction between 'the thriving population of the Delta and the poverty-stricken population of the south'.[3] At the end of the century this differentiation led to a considerable migration from Upper Egypt to the Delta (and consequently to the occasional deterioration of security in Lower Egypt).[4] Between the population censuses of 1897 and 1907 the population

[1] Ibid., pp. 28–38.

[2] Mubārak, vol. iv, pp. 28–29.

[3] *Reports by Mr. Villiers Stuart, M.P., respecting reorganization in Egypt*, Egypt No. 7 (1883), C.-3554, pp. 8–9, 16.

[4] Cf. *Majmū'at al-awāmir al-'alīyya wa'l-dakrītāt*, vol. x (Cairo–Būlāq, 1888), pp. 499–502; *Report on the administration, finances, and condition of Egypt and the progress of reforms*, Egypt No. 3 (1892), C.-6589, pp. 27–28; Sayyid Quṭb, pp. 165 f.

of Lower Egyptian provinces (the city and desert governorates excepted) grew by 18·7 per cent., while that of the four Upper Egyptian provinces grew only by 12·3 per cent.

The development of a market economy and of private ownership of land, as well as the growth of social differentiation among the village population, effected yet another important change in Egypt's rural society—the dissolution of the village community. Until the middle of the nineteenth century, village lands in Upper Egypt and in some areas of Middle Egypt were periodically redistributed among the villagers, and in Lower Egypt the village shaykh used to reallocate land whenever fellahs failed to pay their share of the taxes. The village was collectively responsible for the payment of a fixed tax-quota imposed on it, and for the supply of labour for public works.[1] In the 1850s the practice of periodically redistributing village land in Upper and Middle Egypt was discontinued, and Saʿīd's land-law of 5 August 1858 considerably extended the individual fellah's property rights to the land he held. At about the same time Saʿīd abolished collective village responsibility for tax payment, and introduced individual tax assessments. The remaining function of the village community as a corporate body was abolished in the 1880s, when the corvée (and later the obligation to turn out for fighting locusts and floods) became the individual duty of every villager.[2]

Guilds, town quarters, and religious communities

The dissolution of the village community was only one aspect of a more comprehensive process. There were other corporate bodies which had formed the traditional structure of Egyptian society, and which disintegrated in the course of the nineteenth century. Perhaps the most important of these bodies were the urban guilds.[3]

It has been the assumption of most writers who touched on this subject that the creation of a large-scale industry by Muḥammad ʿAlī was responsible for the guilds' decline or even for their disappearance.[4] The obvious proof of the fallacy of this theory is the fact that until the 1880s a ramified system of guilds existed in Cairo and in many other towns in Egypt, comprising almost the whole indigenous gainfully occupied population. Throughout the century the shaykhs of the guilds controlled and supervised the guild members' activities and ensured that the instructions of the government were carried out; they were made responsible for the misdemeanours of their guilds' members; they supplied labour and services to the government and private employers; and they arbitrated in disputes among the members of the

[1] See G. Baer, 'The dissolution of the Egyptian village community', *WI*, N.S., vol. vi, no. 1–2 (1959), pp. 56–64.

[2] Ibid., pp. 64–68 and sources quoted there.

[3] See G. Baer, *Egyptian guilds in modern times* (Jerusalem, 1964).

[4] For detailed discussion of this theory and of the question why the guilds survived until the end of the nineteenth century see ibid., ch. v.

guilds. Until the last quarter of the century the shaykhs were responsible for the payment of taxes by the guild members, and collected these taxes, while their advice was sought with regard to the assessment of the taxes to be paid by the guilds; until 1880 they fixed maximum wages for guild members; and until the late 1860s they assisted the authorities in fixing prices of comestibles. It was the function of the guilds to restrict the number of people exercising a specific trade, and in many occupations the guilds kept a monopoly of their trades until the last decade of the nineteenth century.[1]

The interest of the government in maintaining the guild system was not the only reason for its long survival. Not less important was the fact that the guilds did not disintegrate as a result of class struggle among the various strata of its members. There was no rigid system of apprenticeship, no clear-cut distinction between apprentice and journeyman, and it was relatively easy for an apprentice or a journeyman to become a master. No associations of journeymen emerged in Egypt, and no sharp economic or social differentiation developed between the guilds' masters and the shaykhs, whose economic and social position did not rise much above that of other members of the guilds. With one or two exceptions, shaykhs did not become contractors, and no such transformation occurred in artisan guilds. This was mainly due to the fact that, after the failure of Muḥammad ʿAlī's industrial experiment, no serious industrial development took place in Egypt for decades. Therefore, the emergence of new kinds of economic organization capable of superseding the traditional guilds was delayed for a long time. Indigenous merchants did not form chambers of commerce and industry before the second decade of the twentieth century. The first labour trade union was established in 1899, and by 1911 there were no more than eleven unions, some of them with exclusively foreign membership.

The final decline and disappearance of the guilds was mainly the result of the influx of European goods and of Europeans settling in Egypt. This happened during the second half of the nineteenth century. By the end of the century many branches of Egypt's local crafts had succumbed to European competition.[2] Merchant guilds were equally hit by a complete change of Egypt's commercial system. On the one hand the traditional organization of the *sūq* gradually dissolved, retail trade spreading all over the town and foreigners infiltrating into branches which previously had been monopolized

[1] For details and documentation see ibid., ch. iv.

[2] See, for instance, Kremer, vol. ii, pp. 35, 166; H. de Vaujany, *Alexandrie et la Basse-Égypte* (Paris, 1885), p. 140; A. Métin, *La transformation de l'Égypte* (Paris, 1903), pp. 247, 292; A. Wright and H. A. Cartwright, *Twentieth century impressions of Egypt* (London, 1909), p. 230; *Commercial reports*, 1881, vol. xc, p. 29; al-Ḥukūma al-miṣriyya, *Taqrīr lajnat al-tijāra wa'l-ṣināʿa* (Cairo, 1919), pp. 133–4; W. V. Shearer, 'Report on the weaving industry of Assiout', and N. L. Ablett, 'Notes on the industries of Assiut', *L'Égypte contemporaine*, vol. i (1910), pp. 185, 333. An interesting and detailed account of the changes in clothing habits all over the country, involving the replacement of indigenous manufacture by import of foreign goods, is found in Mubārak, vol. ix, p. 88.

by Egyptian merchants. Thus the control of the guild shaykhs was made impossible. On the other hand foreign trade was completely transformed: in the past it had dealt mainly in Sudanese, Arabian, and Oriental goods, Cairo being one of the most important centres of this trade and Egyptian, Syrian, and Turkish merchants being engaged in it. During the nineteenth century the export of cotton to Europe and the import of European industrial goods into Egypt became the main business of foreign trade, while Greeks and other Europeans became the principal importers and exporters. Moreover, like the artisans, Egyptian merchants suffered from a large variety of oppressive taxes and duties, from which foreign merchants were exempted by the Capitulations.[1]

The heaviest blow, however, was dealt to the guilds towards the end of the century, when Europeans began to disregard the shaykhs of the guilds as suppliers of labour.[2] This was made possible by the growth of Egyptian towns, especially during the last quarter of the century (see below). The influx of people into towns considerably increased the number of those who were not members of guilds and thus made it difficult for the guilds to maintain their monopolies.

Finally, towards the end of the nineteenth century, Egyptian administration was reorganized, and became more efficient. Thus the state could do without the link of the guilds, and step by step their administrative, fiscal, and economic functions shrank until they lost most of them. About the middle of the century, changes in the system of taxation deprived the shaykhs of the function of distributing among the members of the guilds a fixed tax-quota imposed on the guild as a whole. Saʿīd officially abolished the monopolies of the guilds (1854–6), but did not succeed in carrying out his decrees in this respect. No further changes in the guilds' functions were introduced during the rule of Ismāʿīl (1863–79). But in the 1880s and the 1890s the government published a series of decrees providing for professional permits to be issued by official authority, not by the guild shaykhs. Another group of decrees fixed wages for a number of public services, thereby curtailing the shaykhs' function in this matter. In 1881 the shaykhs were relieved of the task to collect the taxes, and by 1892 all taxes on the guilds, and thereby the remaining fiscal functions of the shaykhs, had been abolished. Monopolistic practices of specific guilds were prohibited during the years 1887–90, and in 1890 the complete freedom of all trades was announced. The last of the more important functions of the guild shaykhs, that of supplying labour, disappeared during the first decade of the twentieth century.[3] By that time, however, not many of the guilds survived, and after the First World War the guilds no longer performed any function in the public life of Egypt.

[1] Cf. *Commercial reports*, 1873, vol. lxiv, p. 231; 1880, vol. lxxiii, p. 559; 1889, vol. lxxix, p. 23; 1892, vol. lxxxii, p. 24; West to Stanton, no. 35, Suez, 13 July 1870, F.O. 141/72; de Vaujany, p. 139; Fircks, pp. 166, 198.

[2] Métin, p. 292.

[3] For details and documentation see Baer, *Egyptian guilds*, chs. iv and v.

While the Egyptian government ceased to appoint shaykhs of guilds before the First World War, every town-quarter was headed by a shaykh (*shaykh al-ḥāra*) even much later. In the course of the nineteenth century the fiscal functions and police duties of these shaykhs were transferred to government departments; on the other hand they were assigned a large number of new administrative functions, of many of which they were deprived again at the beginning of this century. Still some functions remained in their hands, such as making reports of births and deaths.[1] But the town-quarter had lost its significance as a social unit.

The gates by which Cairo's quarters were separated from each other had been demolished already by Bonaparte.[2] However, after the French occupation apparently they were re-established: some later sources state that they were still closed,[3] others that this practice had ceased;[4] in some distant towns, such as Asyūṭ, it seems to have persisted much longer.[5] In the past each quarter had its gang of youths organized after the pattern of the medieval *futuwwa* associations, and there were frequent fights between the gangs of the different quarters. During the nineteenth century the vigour of these feuds seems to have diminished, although apparently they did not completely disappear, as claimed by Mubārak.[6] One reason for the weakening of solidarity among the inhabitants of a specific quarter was the fact that each of these quarters, once inhabited by people of similar social status, became in the course of time much more heterogeneous: Mubārak tells us about two quarters of Cairo in which only high officials and notables had lived in the past, and which about the middle of the century had become socially mixed.[7]

Even people belonging to different religious communities began to mix and live together in the same quarter. During the first half of the nineteenth century strict segregation seems to have been the rule, and members of each community inhabited separate quarters.[8] But as early as 1858 the British consul in Cairo wrote: 'Formerly the Christians were assembled in particular quarters, with a certain amount of organisation for defence: they are now to a considerable extent scattered, and the protection which they have so long

[1] Law no. 23 of 11 Aug. 1912, *Journal officiel*, no. 96, 1912. For parallel developments of the functions of the village shaykh see Baer, 'Village shaykh', *passim*.

[2] Cf. *Histoire scientifique et militaire de l'expédition française en Égypte* (Paris, 1830–6), vol. iv, p. 97.

[3] See, for instance, Bayle St. John, vol. i, p. 129; Mubārak, vol. i, p. 78.

[4] Cf. Dr. Stacquez, *L'Égypte, la Basse Nubie et le Sinai* (Liège, 1865), p. 65. Aḥmad Amīn, *Ḥayātī* (Cairo, n.d.), p. 33.

[5] Stacquez, p. 135; G. Charmes, *Cinq mois au Caire* (Paris, 1880), p. 227.

[6] Mubārak, vol. ii, p. 84; Aḥmad Amīn, *Qāmūs al-ʿādāt wa'l-taqālīd wa'l-taʿābīr al-miṣriyya* (Cairo, 1953), pp. 304–5; Amīn, *Ḥayātī*, pp. 39–40. See also J. Berque, *Les Arabes d'hier à demain* (Paris, 1960), pp. 18, 225–6, according to whom the social importance of the town-quarter in Damascus seems to have been much more persistent.

[7] Mubārak, vol. ii, p. 28; vol. iii, p. 54.

[8] Cf. J. Bowring, *Report on Egypt and Candia* (London, 1840), p. 8; E. W. Lane, *Cairo fifty years ago* (London, 1896), pp. 60–69.

enjoyed has led to the abandonment of all organisation . . . even in the quarters which are still exclusively Christian.'[1] Nevertheless, at the end of the nineteenth and the beginning of the twentieth century there still were quarters almost exclusively inhabited by Muslims, such as Khalīfa and Sayyida Zaynab in Cairo or Mīnat al-Baṣal in Alexandria: in 1897 there were 56 *shiyākhāt* (sub-quarters) in Cairo, out of 195, in each of which lived less than 10 Copts, and in Alexandria 34 out of 108. In smaller towns religious segregation was even more persistent. The overwhelming majority of Copts lived in mixed villages, not in villages inhabited exclusively by Copts: in 1897 and 1907 there were only twelve villages with less than ten Muslims. But usually Copts and Muslims lived in separate parts of the village.[2] In this respect, as in others, we find that the religious community retained much of its social significance throughout the nineteenth century. Generally speaking, all persons engaged in a specific urban occupation belonged to one community; where the trade was practised by people of more than one community they usually formed separate guilds.[3] As late as the beginning of the twentieth century 97–98 per cent. of all *ṣarrāfs* (tax-collectors) were Copts.[4] By that time a new class of educated Muslims had emerged which attempted to enter many of the occupations formerly monopolized by the Copts, especially certain branches of government employment. This, however, created a sharp antagonism between the two communities culminating in the rival congresses of Copts and Muslims held in 1911.[5]

But even if the religious community kept its vitality as a social unit, the economic position, social status, and political power of the heads and officials of the religious institutions declined considerably during the nineteenth century. Like the village community, the religious community ceased under Saʿīd to constitute a corporate body for administrative purposes, and in January 1855 the *jizya*, the special tax on non-Muslim communities, was abolished.[6] This deprived the religious functionaries of minority communities of important administrative functions. The Coptic clergy was further weakened by permanent intrigues and quarrels, as well as by growing Protestant and Catholic missionary activity. In 1874 the members of the community founded a secular council, *al-Majlis al-millī al-ʿāmm li'l-Aqbāṭ al-Urthūdhuks*. One of its explicit purposes was to take over the Coptic *waqfs* from the clergy. An official regulation of 14 May 1883 vested the management of all Coptic *khayrī waqfs* in this council. From then on the power of the

[1] Walne to Green, Cairo, 5 July 1858, encl. in Green to Malmesbury, no. 104, Alexandria, 7 July 1858, F.O. 78/1402.

[2] Cf. Mubārak, vol. ix, p. 87; vol. xii, p. 3; vol. xiv, p. 68; etc.

[3] Cf. ibid., vol. i, pp. 99–100; vol. iii, p. 34; vol. vii, p. 74; vol. ix, pp. 85, 87, 92; vol. x, p. 52; vol. xi, p. 14; vol. xii, pp. 44, 95, 104, 148; vol. xiv, p. 121; etc.

[4] See K. Mikhail, *Copts and Moslems under British control* (London, 1911), p. 44, n. 1.

[5] Ibid., *passim*.

[6] Sāmī, Pt. III, vol. i, p. 106.

Coptic patriarch, the clergy, and the monks was severely undermined by secular organizations.[1]

The Muslim *'ulamā'* did not fare much better. At the end of the eighteenth and the beginning of the nineteenth century the *'ulamā'* were among the chief *multazims* in Egypt. Like the Mamluk *amīrs* they built luxurious palaces, surrounded themselves with servants and hangers-on, employed officials, and took enormous interest in their property and wealth. Under Bonaparte they had attained a position of great political importance.[2] But this golden age for the *'ulamā'* did not last longer than it took Muḥammad 'Alī to consolidate his rule. After he had overcome their opposition and confiscated their *iltizāms* and *rizaq aḥbāsiyya* a precipitate decline in their position took place.[3] In 1831 the *muftī* of Manṣūra complained that the *'ulamā'* had become poor people, and in 1863 von Kremer wrote that they had completely lost their former influence and importance, and that many of the *'ulamā'* originated from the peasant population.[4] A few years later another author said: '. . . all that he (the *qāḍī*) has saved from the ruins of his former splendour is a certain moral influence among his religious brethren, an influence that is daily declining'.[5]

The decline of the Turkish element

Another important group whose position in Egyptian society declined during the nineteenth century was the 'Turks', later called 'Turco-Egyptians'. These were people from all over the non-Arab countries under Ottoman rule whose common characteristic was that they spoke Turkish. There were Turkish students at the Azhar university, Turkish dervish convents in Cairo, and Turkish merchants—concentrated in the part of Cairo's market called Khān al-Khalīlī. But the importance of the Turkish element derived from the fact that during the first quarter of the century all officials above the rank of *shaykh al-balad* (village headman) were 'Turks'[6] (the fiscal tasks were performed by Copts). Similarly, all army officers of higher rank and most junior officers and N.C.O.'s were Turks, even long after fellahs had been recruited by Muḥammad 'Alī as soldiers for the first time in the history of Islamic

[1] See S. H. Leeder, *Modern sons of the Pharaos* (London, n.d. [1918?]), pp. 255–64; Baer, *Landownership*, pp. 178–81.

[2] Ibid., pp. 60–61; Mubārak, vol. iv, pp. 31 ff.; vol. xiii, pp. 63–64; vol. xiv, pp. 93–94; vol. xv, pp. 7, 27–28; vol. xvii, pp. 10–12.

[3] Rifā'a al-Ṭahṭāwī's father was forced to emigrate from his town. See ibid., vol. xiii, p. 53.

[4] Michaud et Poujoulat, *Correspondance d'Orient* (Paris, 1834), vol. vii, p. 12 (Apr. 1831); Kremer, vol. ii, pp. 94–95. The peasant origin of many of Egypt's *'ulamā'* in the nineteenth century is illustrated by Mubārak's numerous biographies.

[5] C. B. Klunzinger, *Upper Egypt; its people and its products* (London, 1878), p. 74. On the miserable economic position of the *'ulamā'* at the beginning of the twentieth century see J. Dorpffer, 'Les revenus de l'Université d'El Azhar', *La Revue Égyptienne*, 20 May 1912, pp. 33–42.

[6] E. W. Lane, *The manners and customs of the modern Egyptians* (Everyman edn.), p. 129.

Egypt. Since the ruling dynasty was also 'Turkish', the whole ruling class of Egypt was an oligarchy speaking a foreign language.[1] Through grants of large tracts of land they became the most important land-owners in nineteenth-century Egypt.[2] Their gradual and partial replacement by Arabic-speaking Egyptians was one of the most significant social changes of the nineteenth century.

The early attempts of Muḥammad ʿAlī to replace the Turks in the lower ranks of the administration with Egyptian village and bedouin shaykhs has been often described.[3] The experiment was not entirely successful, and in any case the post of *mudīr* (governor of a province) was retained by Turks.[4] In 1840 Muḥammad ʿAlī tried for the first time to replace Turkish officers in the fleet with 'Arab' (Egyptian) ones.[5]

Saʿīd resumed the experiment on a larger scale. He ordered that one-third of all officials acting as *nāẓir qism* and one quarter of those acting as *ḥākim khuṭṭ* be replaced by Egyptians (*abnā' al-ʿArab*).[6] In June 1858 he appointed an Egyptian *nāẓir qism* to the office of *mudīr* of Giza province.[7] Addressing himself to the village shaykhs, Saʿīd reminded them that his father's experiment had failed because of their incompetence, threatened them with severe punishment if they did not succeed, and appealed to their pride by making them responsible, in case of failure, for perpetuating the rule of *abnā' al-Turk*.[8] Towards the end of Saʿīd's day 'the majority of Turkish employés were dismissed service'.[9]

Simultaneously Saʿīd tried to create an Egyptian officer-class in the army. For this purpose (among others) he recruited the sons of village shaykhs, who had been exempt from army service till then.[10] One of those recruited was Aḥmad ʿUrābī, who by 1860 had reached the rank of colonel (*qā'im maqām*).[11] Although Saʿīd tried to instil Arab-Egyptian national feeling into

[1] According to numerous estimates throughout the century their number did not exceed 20,000, including of course merchants, etc.

[2] Cf. Baer, *Landownership*, pp. 39–49.

[3] See, for instance, ibid., p. 50; idem, 'Bedouin sedentarization', p. 87; idem, 'Village shaykh', pp. 145–6; and a detailed account in Rivlin, pp. 109–11.

[4] According to a list sent by Consul Murray to Palmerston on 28 May 1847, at that time all the pashas of Egypt were non-Egyptians. See F.O. 141/13 and 78/707. For the time of ʿAbbās see Bayle St. John, vol. i, pp. 64–65, and for the early years of Saʿīd's rule—Senior, vol. i, pp. 251–2 (written Jan. 1856).

[5] Larking to Palmerston, no. 18, Alexandria, 6 Oct. 1840, F.O. 78/414.

[6] Sāmī, Pt. III, vol. i, pp. 189, 192–3 (Oct. 1856); Harris to Bruce Luxor, 19 Dec. 1856, F.O. 141/30 and 78/1222. (*Qism* was a district, *khuṭṭ* a sub-district).

[7] Sāmī, Pt. III, vol. i, p. 283.

[8] Ibid., pp. 185–6. This is an extremely interesting and remarkable document.

[9] Hekekyan Papers, vol. xvi, B.M. Add. MS. 37463, ff. 121–3 (written on 10 Apr. 1861). Cf. Colquhoun to Russell, Alexandria, 11 Nov. 1861, F.O. 78/1591. Colquhouns' explanation of this development was Saʿīd's desire to weaken his dependence on the Porte.

[10] Kremer, vol. i, p. 256; Senior, vol. i, pp. 261, 293.

[11] Aḥmad ʿUrābī, *Kashf al-sitar ʿan sirr al-asrār fi'l-nahḍa al-miṣriyya*, etc. (Cairo, n.d.), vol. i, pp. 12–13. Cf. W. S. Blunt, *Secret history of the English occupation of Egypt* (New York, 1922), pp. 99–100, 367.

the recruits, many shirked the service or deserted their units, and in 1861 Sa'īd dismissed most of the newly created army.[1]

Ismā'īl continued Sa'īd's policy, but apparently the result was only a partial replacement of Turkish *mudīrs* by Egyptians.[2] By the end of the 1870s, however, the lower ranks of the administration had been completely Egyptianized. The same was the case in the army,[3] but there the Turks and Circassians succeeded in retaining their monopoly of commanding positions. This was one of the grievances which led to the 'Urābī revolt.

As a result of this revolt and the British occupation the Egyptian army was disbanded. The new army consisted of Egyptians under British command, the Turks and Circassians having lost their controlling position. Similarly, the higher posts of the civil administration were filled with Britons and other Europeans. As a result of the loss of their political power, the Turks also gradually lost their position as the largest landowners: except for some of the *waqfs* they had founded in the nineteenth century, few of their large estates survived. The only exception was the Muḥammad 'Alī family.[4] It not only continued to own a considerable proportion of Egyptian land, but it also retained its Turkish character. All the members of this family spoke Turkish and many of them never learnt to speak Arabic well; Fārūq was the first ruler of the Muḥammad 'Alī family at whose court Arabic was spoken.[5]

Most of the other 'Turkish' families had in the mean time lost their Turkish character. The supply of new 'Turkish blood' gradually ceased, and as early as Muḥammad 'Alī's time many Turks left Egypt.[6] Many of those who remained married Egyptian women and the children spoke Arabic.[7] In the 1820s a visitor to Cairo still wrote: 'The first thing that astonishes a stranger in Cairo is the squalid wretchedness of the Arabs, and the external splendour of the Turks.'[8] Only twenty years later Hekekyan remarked that the dress of the Turks had been adopted by a great number of the Arab inhabitants of Egypt and that there was a gradual approach to equality.[9] Towards the end of the century the character of the remaining Turco-Egyptians grew more Egyptian from year to year.[10]

[1] 'Urābī, p. 16. Sāmī, Pt. III, vol. i, pp. 380–1; Colquhoun to Russell, ibid.

[2] See lists of *mudīrs* at the beginning of every year in Sāmī, Pt. III, vol. iii, *passim*. Conflicting views have been expressed by J. C. McCoan, *Egypt as it is* (London, n.d. [1877]), p. 115; Klunzinger, pp. 66–67; and D. Mackenzie Wallace, *Egypt and the Egyptian question* (London, 1883), pp. 147–8, 152.

[3] For the biographies of a large number of officials and army officers of fellah origin see Mubārak, *passim*.

[4] Cf. Baer, *Landownership*, pp. 131–8. See also Th. Neumann, *Das moderne Ägypten* (Leipzig, 1893), p. 40.

[5] Tugay, pp. 57, 162, 241.

[6] Bowring, p. 9; Senior, vol. i, pp. 252–3; vol. ii, pp. 66, 128.

[7] Kremer, vol. i, p. 67.

[8] R. R. Madden, *Travels in Turkey, Egypt, Nubia, and Palestine in 1824, 1825, 1826, and 1827* (London, 1829), vol. i, p. 307.

[9] Hekekyan Papers, vol. iii, B.M. Add. MS. 37450, f. 100 (written 23 Oct. 1845).

[10] Cf. Cromer, *Modern Egypt*, vol. ii, pp. 169–70.

No wonder, therefore, that in the course of the nineteenth century Arabic gradually replaced Turkish as the language used in government offices. As early as 1840 Bowring wrote that the use of Arabic for official purposes was growing.[1] In 1858 Saʿīd issued an order to the effect that official correspondence be conducted in Arabic, but that the change should be gradual where Turkish officials were concerned.[2] In 1869 Ismāʿīl renewed this order and even dismissed the Turkish dragomans, but a few months later he was compelled to allow the use of Turkish in the army.[3] By the end of the century, however, Arabic had completely replaced Turkish in official use.

The abolition of slavery

Traditional Egyptian society comprised yet another essential element which disappeared during the nineteenth century, namely slavery. The Mamluks, who virtually ruled Ottoman Egypt, had been defeated by Muḥammad ʿAlī, and during the nineteenth century only a few rich Egyptians owned white male slaves.[4] Female Circassians, however, as well as black slaves, both male and female, served a large variety of purposes throughout the century. Circassian females were mostly kept in the harems of wealthy Turks, but Egyptians too preferred them to black concubines, whenever they could afford to buy them.[5] The concubines of middle-class Egyptians generally were Abyssinians (Galla), while male and female negro slaves were used for domestic service.[6] Black eunuchs were kept only by the Muḥammad ʿAlī family and the upper class of Turks,[7] but other domestic slaves were owned by almost all layers of Egyptian society: bedouins, fellahs, village notables, shop-keepers, merchants, craftsmen, religious functionaries, physicians, and all ranks of officials and army officers.[8] Christians and Jews also kept slaves, and so did even foreigners residing in Egypt.[9]

[1] Bowring, p. 9.

[2] Sāmī, Pt. III, vol. i, pp. 283–5.

[3] H. Stephen, *Das heutige Aegypten* (Leipzig, 1872), p. 201; R. Buchta, 'Die Aegypter', *Das Ausland* (1882), 847; Sāmī, Pt. III, vol. ii, p. 849.

[4] According to Lane, *Manners and customs*, pp. 136–7, the owners were mainly Turks; but see Mubārak, vol. xvii. p. 4, for an Egyptian physician, Ibrāhīm al-Nabrāwī, who owned 'many *mamālīk*'. At the time of his death ʿAbbās owned about 500 Mamluks—see Bruce to Clarendon, Cairo, 2 Aug. 1854, F.O. 78/1036. In any case, among the 8,092 slaves manumitted between Aug. 1877 and Nov. 1882 there were only 22 white male slaves. See *Further correspondence respecting reorganization in Egypt*, Egypt No. 6 (1883), C.-3529, p. 91.

[5] Lane, op. cit., p. 190; Tugay, pp. 178–9, 184, 191–3, and *passim*; for amusing results of the acquisition of Circassian concubines by prosperous fellahs during the cotton boom of the 1860s see Mackenzie Wallace, pp. 269 ff.

[6] Lane, op. cit., pp. 190–1, 136.

[7] Ibid., p. 137; Bruce to Clarendon, Cairo, 17 Jan. 1855, F.O. 84/974; Tugay, p. 191.

[8] Mubārak, vol. viii, p. 82; vol. ix, p. 39; vol. xiv, p. 38; vol. xvii, pp. 4, 23; Calvert to Reade, Alexandria, 2 July 1867, F.O. 141/62; Rogers to Stanton, Mansura, 12 May 1873, and West to Vivian, Suez, 5 Aug. 1873, F.O. 141/82; Borg to Vivian, Cairo, 1 July 1878, F.O. 141/120; and see in particular 'List of slaves freed by Thos. F. Reade', in *Memorandum by Consul Reade on slave trade in Egypt*, London, 13 Aug. 1868, F.O. 84/1290.

[9] See 'List of slaves', ibid.; Gilbert to Palmerston, Alexandria, 7 Nov. 1848, F.O. 84/737;

Domestic slavery was by no means the only form of slavery in nineteenth-century Egypt. Contrary to the prevalent assumption, agricultural slavery was not uncommon. In 1840 Bowring wrote that the attempts made by European landowners in Asyūṭ to employ slaves for field labour (the peasants had been recruited for military service) had failed: the cost was much higher than that of fellah labour.[1] However, on the large farms of the Muḥammad ʿAlī family, especially on Ismāʿīl's sugar plantations in Upper Egypt, slaves were employed as agricultural labourers.[2] Moreover, between Isnā and Kurūskū in Upper Egypt not only large proprietors but also fellahs used slaves for work on their farms throughout the century.[3] As late as 1884 nine-tenths of the men who worked the water pumps in Isnā province were slaves.[4] Most of the slaves manumitted in 1885 and 1886 by the official Bureaux established for this purpose were agricultural slaves from Isnā province.[5] In Lower Egypt the use of slaves for farm-work was only the temporary result of extraordinary prosperity of the peasants coinciding with shortage of labour. Thus the profits derived from the cotton boom during the time of the American Civil War were invested by part of the Delta peasantry in the purchase of slaves to be employed on their farms and on newly acquired land; but even as late as 1873 it was said that 'most of the slaves sold at [the *mawlid* of] Tanta are for land labour; the principal purchasers are farmers'.[6] At that time fellahs also used to evade the corvée by sending their slaves as substitutes.[7] It may be added that in Suez slaves were employed for work in coastal sailing vessels.[8]

Until the British occupation the rulers of Egypt persistently tried to use slaves as soldiers. Muḥammad ʿAlī's not so successful attempts to acquire slaves in the Sudan for his army have been frequently described, and we need not go into details. In Saʿīd's time slaves were taken mainly for his Sudanese units, even after he had prohibited the slave-trade, and also for his bodyguard.[9] But even Ismāʿīl continued to enlist slaves for his troops, and

Vivian to Derby, Alexandria, 30 June 1877, F.O. 84/1472; Pezzoni to Nesselrode, Alexandria, 24 May 1828, in R. Cattaui, *Le règne de Mohammad Aly d'après les archives russes en Égypte*, vol. i (Cairo, 1931), pp. 230–6; Senior, vol. i, p. 207; Lane, *Manners and customs*, p. 104; Mubārak, vol. xiv, p. 53.

[1] Bowring, pp. 16, 89.

[2] Hekekyan Papers, vol. iii, f. 224 (written in Jan. 1847); Rogers to Clarendon, Cairo, 24 Nov. 1869, F.O. 84/1305.

[3] For the 1840s see, for instance, Hekekyan Papers, vol. ii, B.M. Add. MS. 37449, ff. 469–70.

[4] *Further correspondence respecting the finances and conditions of Egypt*, Egypt No. 4 (1889), C.-5718, p. 44; cf. Della Sala to Riaz, Cairo, 12 Sept. 1880, F.O. 141/140.

[5] *Correspondence respecting slavery in Egypt*, Africa No. 4 (1887), C.-4994, pp. 9–12.

[6] Rogers to Vivian, Cairo, 3 Sept. 1873, F.O. 141/82; *Confidential memorandum on slave dealing in Alexandria* (signed Ali Hassan), Alexandria, 2 and 6 June 1873, F.O. 141/84 (also 84/1371).

[7] Reade to Stanley, Alexandria, 9 Aug. 1867, F.O. 141/63.

[8] West to Vivian, Suez, 28 July 1873, F.O. 141/82.

[9] *Memorandum by Mr. Petherick*, Dec. 1860, and *Report of Dr. J. Natterer . . . dated 5 Apr. 1860*, encl. in Colquhoun to Russell, Alexandria, 29 May 1860, F.O. 84/1120;

in the 1870s many of the slaves who tried to achieve their freedom through the British consulates were sent by the authorities to the army.[1] Since the government needed slaves for this purpose, distant provinces were required to pay their taxes in slaves. Such a system of taxation was practised mainly during the rule of Muḥammad ʿAlī, but some cases were reported even in the 1860s and 1870s; the provinces concerned were the Sīwa Oasis, Upper Egypt, Nubia, and the Sudan.[2] In the early 1840s, scarcity of money caused the government to pay salaries in slaves—salaries not only of troops in the Sudan, but also of individuals in Egypt.[3]

It is definitely impossible to establish the exact number of slaves in Egypt at any time in the nineteenth century. About 1840 they were estimated at between 20,000 and 30,000.[4] At that time the yearly import seems to have amounted to about 10,000–12,000, but during the 1840s and 1850s it declined to about 5,000 or even less.[5] According to a census taken some time in the 1850s the number of slaves in Cairo was 11,481.[6] During the early 1860s the import of slaves grew tremendously as a result of the boom: it was estimated at 10,000–15,000 yearly;[7] but at the end of the decade it declined again, and during the 1870s it did not amount to more than a few hundreds every year.[8] About 20,000 slaves were manumitted by the official Bureaux between 1877 and 1889,[9] but many others were directly freed by their masters. The number of slave-dealers in Cairo declined from 78 in 1879 to 32 in 1882, and by the late 1880s the professional slave-trade had vanished.[10] Although Egyptians still

Colquhoun to Russell, Alexandria, 1 July 1863, F.O. 84/1204; Petherick to Colquhoun, Cairo, 17 Mar. 1865, F.O. 141/57.

[1] Vivian to Derby, Cairo, 8 Dec. 1876, F.O. 84/1450; Reade to Stanley, Alexandria, 9 Aug. 1867, F.O. 141/63; Rogers to Stanton, Cairo, 23 Apr. 1872, F.O. 141/78, Pt. 2; Harding to Stanton, Mansura, 30 May 1873; Consular Agent at Mansura to Vivian, 23 June and 22 July 1873, F.O. 141/82; *Statement by Saîd el Soudani*, encl. in Borg to Governor of Cairo, 18 Apr. 1878, F.O. 141/119; etc.

[2] Barnett to Aberdeen, Alexandria, 17 Apr. 1842, F.O. 84/426 (also 78/502); Campbell to Palmerston, Cairo, 15 Mar. 1839, F.O. 78/373; *Memorandum by Mr. Petherick*, ibid., Vivian to Derby, ibid. (1876).

[3] Muḥammad ʿAlī to governor-general of the Sudan, encl. in Barnett to Aberdeen, Alexandria, 12 Mar. 1842, F.O. 84/426; Hekekyan Papers, vol. ii, f. 125 (written in 1843).

[4] Cf. Bowring, p. 10 (18,500); *Campbell Report* (22,000); F. Mengin, *Histoire sommaire de l'Égypte sous le gouvernement de Mohammed-Aly* (Paris, 1839), pp. 157–9 (27,500).

[5] Kremer, vol. ii, p. 86; *Memorandum on the slave trade . . . by Mr. Coulthard*, encl. in Colquhoun to Russell, Alexandria, 8 June 1860, F.O. 84/1120.

[6] M. J. Colucci Bey, 'Quelques notes sur le cholera qui sévit au Caire en 1850 et 1855', *Mémoires . . . présentés . . . à l'Institut Égyptien*, vol. i (Paris, 1862), p. 607.

[7] Stanton to Clarendon, Alexandria, 9 May 1866, F.O. 84/1260; Reade to Stanley, Alexandria, 9 Aug. 1867, F.O. 141/63.

[8] Borg to Vivian, Cairo, 23 Aug. 1878, F.O. 141/121.

[9] *Further correspondence respecting reorganization in Egypt*, Egypt No. 6 (1883), C.-3529, p. 91; *Further correspondence respecting the finances and condition of Egypt*, Egypt No. 4 (1889), C.-5718, p. 44.

[10] Ibid., pp. 40–44; Borg to Lascelles, Cairo, 8 Sept. 1879; F.O. 141/129; *Correspondence respecting slavery in Egypt*, Africa No. 4 (1887), C.-4994, p. 7; H. Steckner, *Beim Fellah und Khedive* (Halle a.S., 1892), pp. 45, 177–8.

owned domestic slaves in the 1890s (and some Turkish families still kept Circassian females),[1] in the twentieth century slavery in Egypt no longer constituted a problem.

There can be no doubt that official measures taken against the slave-trade were one of the most important causes for the final disappearance of slavery in Egypt. The story of these measures has never been told in full, but it cannot be told here.[2] To a large extent they were the result of foreign initiative and pressure, especially British. They consisted of a number of official edicts prohibiting the traffic in slaves; two Anglo-Egyptian conventions for the suppression of slavery and the slave-trade, concluded in 1877 and 1895 respectively; the appointment of foreigners, mainly British, as governors in the Sudan and commanders of special naval missions in the Red Sea with the explicit purpose of suppressing the slave-trade; the active intervention of British consuls in Egypt in order to secure the freedom of slaves; and, from 1877 on, the establishment of official Bureaux, and later a special service, for the manumission of slaves. In the 1890s persons trading in slaves were effectively prosecuted and some measures were also taken to provide for manumitted slaves.

However, were it not for the internal development of Egyptian society, the administrative measures against slavery could never have succeeded. This is borne out by the tremendous obstacles the campaign against slavery encountered and by its ineffectiveness for a long time. Even at a later stage of the campaign, when the khedive sincerely tried to enforce the prohibition, it had to be implemented by officials who themselves owned and purchased slaves, received bribes for disregarding the evasion of the law (sometimes in the form of a proportion of the illegally sold slaves), or even traded in slaves themselves and supplied them to influential and rich persons.[3] In the Sudan, Baker, and later Gordon, did not lack energy to enforce the prohibition of the trade, but neither had at his disposal an administrative machine strong enough to rule the country against the powerful organization of slave-trading interests.[4] Moreover, the slave-traders had deep roots in Egyptian society. This fact is well illustrated by the case of a caravan caught near Asyūṭ in the spring of 1880.[5] It was established that strong personal and commercial connexions existed between the slave-dealers, the head of Asyūṭ's merchant guild, and the influential merchants and notables of the town.

[1] Newmann, p. 40; Fircks, p. 144; G. Legrain, *Fellahs de Karnak* (Paris, 1902), p. 334; Tugay, pp. 28, 155.

[2] For a summary of measures taken in the Sudan see P. M. Holt, *A modern history of the Sudan* (London, 1961), pp. 64 ff. See also J. Scott, 'L'abolition de l'esclavage en Égypte', *Revue de l'Islam* (Paris), vol. iv, 1901, which is particularly useful for later developments.

[3] Reade to Stanley, Alexandria, 9 Aug. 1867, F.O. 141/63; Borg to Vivian, Cairo, 1 July 1878, F.O. 141/120; Borg to Lascelles, ibid., Cookson to Malet, Alexandria, 17 May 1880, F.O. 141/138; Della Sala to Riaz, Cairo, 12 Sept. 1880, F.O. 141/140.

[4] Cf. Holt, pp. 64–70.

[5] F.O. 141/138, 139, 140, *passim*.

The abolition of slavery also involved a conflict between Islam and Islamic law on the one hand, and Western concepts and modern innovations on the other. Many Muslims considered the attempts to do away with slavery an encroachment on Qur'anic law and tradition. This led to very tangible consequences: the *qāḍīs* refused to perform marriages of female slaves who had not been formally freed by their masters and completely disregarded official certificates.[1] The result was that many of the freed female slaves became prostitutes.

But even with regard to male slaves, the question arose what to do with them after manumission. In the 1860s it often happened that slaves freed by the authorities and left alone were soon restored to their former state of slavery.[2] Sometimes they joined gangs of robbers.[3] It was very difficult for them to find work:[4] before the 1880s no free labour market had developed in Egypt. Labour was supplied by guilds, each of which monopolized its specific craft or trade, and there were few opportunities for outsiders.

Most of these impediments to the abolition of slavery vanished during the last two decades of the nineteenth century. The Mahdist revolution cut off the principal source of supply, and after the reconquest of the Sudan an effective administration was established capable of suppressing such vestiges of the trade as still existed.[5] But Egyptian society had changed too. A small but important section of Egyptians had changed their attitudes towards slavery as a result of their cultural contact with Europe, and when in 1896 the revised Anglo-Egyptian convention was discussed in the Legislative Council it did not meet with any opposition. However, the most important change was the gradual emergence of a free labour market. Free labour became available and former slave-owners began to see that it was much cheaper and far less troublesome than slave-labour.[6] This was not only the result of the abolition of monopolies (see above), but also of the urbanization which took place in the 1880s and 1890s.

Urbanization and the new urban society

During three-quarters of the nineteenth century the process of urbanization in Egypt did not reach significant proportions. From the 1820s to the 1840s the ten largest towns of Egypt at that time seem to have grown at about the same rate as the rural population, and between 1846 and 1882 at a somewhat smaller rate (by about 46 per cent., as against more than 50 per cent. for the

[1] Cf. Borg to Vivian, Cairo, 15 Aug. 1878, F.O. 141/121; Borg to Lascelles, ibid., Della Sala to Malet, Cairo, 26 Oct. 1880, F.O. 141/140.

[2] *Memorandum by Consul Reade*, ibid.

[3] Felice to Borg, Zagazig, 1 Mar. 1882, F.O. 141/160.

[4] Cf. Borg to Vivian, Cairo, 23 Aug. 1878, F.O. 141/121.

[5] Cf. Holt, pp. 121–2, 148.

[6] *Correspondence respecting slavery in Egypt*, ibid.; *Report on the finances, administration, and conditions of Egypt, and the progress of reforms*, Egypt No. 1 (1896), C.-7978 pp. 22–24.

total population). True, some towns experienced a conspicuous growth, for instance Alexandria (from about 12,500 in the 1820s to 165,000 in 1864 and to 230,000 in 1882). Moreover, during the second and third quarter of the century some new towns were founded, among them Zaqāzīq and Port Said. But while these towns grew, others declined or stagnated (for instance Rosetta and Damietta).[1] Throughout the century fellahs left their villages and flocked into towns to escape conscription, oppression, famine, and epidemics, or to evade taxation. But in general they did not permanently stay in the towns: they were either sent back by force, or they returned of their own free will after conditions in the villages had changed for the better, or after they had gained enough money for a specific purpose.[2] By 1882 only 11·5 per cent. of the population lived in towns with more than 20,000 inhabitants, a very small increase compared with 1846, when the percentage was about 10 per cent.

During the last two decades of the century urbanization gained momentum. Between the censuses of 1882 and 1897 towns with more than 20,000 inhabitants grew by 68 per cent., while the total population grew by less than 43 per cent. By 1897 they comprised 13·6 per cent. of Egypt's population.[3] This was the period during which the guilds and slavery almost disappeared, with a few remnants left over for the twentieth century. During the first decade of this century the pace of urbanization slowed down: between 1897 and 1907 towns with more than 20,000 inhabitants grew by 17·2 per cent. as against 16·1 per cent. for the whole population, and by 1907 their inhabitants had not increased to more than 13·7 per cent. of the total population. This was certainly the result of the remarkable agricultural boom of the early years of the century. Nevertheless, by 1907 more than a third of the population of both Cairo and Alexandria were born elsewhere, and so were almost 60 per cent. of the inhabitants of Port Said. In the introduction to the 1907 census the director-general of the Census Department compared the growth of Cairo and Alexandria during the preceding decade with that of other towns in the world and arrived at the following conclusion: 'Considering the comparatively

[1] The different types of Egyptian towns in the nineteenth century, their social structure and municipal development, as well as the process of their respective decline, stagnation, or growth, will be analysed in a separate study.

[2] Baer, *Landownership*, pp. 28–33, and Rivlin, pp. 116–17, 204–5, 271–2 (sources mentioned in these two works are not repeated here); Bayle St. John, vol. i, pp. 35–36; Sāmī, Pt. II, pp. 325–6; Pt. III, vol. ii, pp. 451–2; Colquhoun to Russell, 24 June 1861, F.O. 78/1610 (on bedouins becoming urban workers because of the murrain of 1851); *Report by Mr. Beaman on the state of the Nile villages*, Cairo, 15 Mar. 1879, and Robertson Smith to Vivian, Cairo, 14 Mar. 1879, F.O. 141/131 (on fellahs flocking into towns of Upper Egypt because of the famine).

[3] For 1882 see *Recensement général de l'Égypte* (Cairo, 1884); for 1897—Boinet Bey, *Dictionnaire géographique de l'Égypte* (Cairo, 1899); Kremer, vol. ii, pp. 106–9; Colucci Bey in Hekekyan Papers, vol. xix, B.M. Add. MS. 37466, f. 100. It should be mentioned that most of these figures, except perhaps those for 1897, are unreliable, but there are many indications which corroborate the general trend expressed by the percentages given, even if the exact numbers may have been somewhat different

non-industrial character of both Cairo and Alexandria, it is surprising that the two cities are as high on the list as they are.'[1]

Most of the increase in Egypt's urban population was of course the result of the influx from the countryside which swelled the class of workers, petty traders, and people without any fixed occupation. It often happened that natives of a specific village or district migrated to a specific town and specialized in a particular occupation. In 1907 there lived in Cairo about 30,000 people born in Asyūṭ province, while a considerable part of the inhabitants of the Suez Canal towns had come from Qinā. Many of Cairo's porters were from Mūsha village (Asyūṭ province), many of the water-carriers from Dār al-Baqar (Gharbiyya), and a great part of the building workers were recruited in Tirsā (Giza).[2] Both government departments and private employers used to recruit their workers through contractors (*khawlī*, colloquial *khōlī*) who supplied the labourers, supervised their work, and paid their wages.[3] By the end of the first decade of this century the nucleus of a new working class had emerged, composed mainly of transport and building workers and of workers in the few industries which had been established: sugar refineries, ginneries, and cigarette factories.[4] However, a large proportion of the new urban lower classes consisted as yet of a fluctuating mass of people without any fixed employment.

The character of the middle class did not undergo profound changes, although as a whole it grew in size, and a shift took place in the relative importance of some of its components. We have mentioned that in the second half of the nineteenth century Egyptian artisans and merchants, especially small and medium ones, were severely hit by European competition. Even if their number did not decline, they certainly had no ample scope for expansion. Another group of the middle class that did not make much headway during that time was the liberal professions. According to the census of 1907, at that time Egypt had no more than 3,677 architects, engineers, and people with similar occupations, 2,237 lawyers and their clerks, 719 pharmacists and herbalists, 53 veterinary surgeons, and 1,271 physicians and surgeons, i.e. about 9,000 inhabitants per physician. Almost half of these were foreigners. Secular education was identified almost exclusively with entrance into government employment.[5] Moreover, once Egyptians were accepted as officials, government employment became the ideal of a large part of the Egyptian population because of the power and social status connected with it. In his autobiography Mubārak says: 'I chose not to become a *faqīh* . . . but

[1] Egypt, Ministry of Finance, *The census of Egypt taken in 1907* (Cairo, 1909), p. 26.

[2] Mubārak, vol. x, pp. 31, 100; vol. xvi, p. 90.

[3] J. F. Nahas, *Situation économique et social du fellah égyptien* (Paris, 1901), p. 170; J. Vallet, *Contribution à l'étude de la condition des ouvriers de la grande industrie au Caire* (Valence, 1911), pp. 23–24.

[4] For details on their conditions, organization, etc., see Vallet, *passim*.

[5] See M. Berger, *Bureaucracy and society in modern Egypt* (Princeton, 1957), pp. 28–29.

a clerk (*kātib*) because I saw that clerks were good-looking in appearance, regarded with respect, and near to the rulers.'[1] This development is reflected in the comparison between census figures for 1882 and 1907: while the total population grew by 66 per cent., the number of people employed in public administration grew by 83·7 per cent.: the total number of persons engaged in liberal professions (clergy, lawyers, physicians, artists, etc.) grew by only 35·6 per cent.[2]

The main change that occurred in the upper classes (disregarding for the moment foreigners on whom more will be said below) was the merging of formerly well-defined units in one group. We have seen that in the course of the century differences between 'Turks' and 'Arabs' were blurred; a parallel process took place in the socio-economic field. At the end of the eighteenth and the beginning of the nineteenth century the governing class of officials was strictly separated from the urban craftsmen and merchants, and the latter were never landowners. Nor did the governing class own land in the modern sense of the word, although it acted as tax-farmers. During the nineteenth century interpenetration between these different socio-economic groups developed in several ways.

First, in the course of the century high officials became large landowners, mainly by receiving land grants from the rulers. On the other hand, village notables and former bedouin shaykhs who had become large landowners were appointed in the civil service and moved to towns.[3] Sometimes these landowner-officials also entered other economic spheres, especially as contractors for supplies for the government, transport, etc.[4] At the end of the century officials were forbidden to have a share in government contracts, or to acquire land sold by the government,[5] but a considerable proportion of the high civil service continued to be recruited from landowners.[6]

At the same time rich merchants began to acquire large estates, both because agricultural development made investment in land a profitable business and because landownership had become the most important criterion of social status. Two outstanding cases, those of the al-Hajīn and al-Ṭarazī families, have been related in detail by Mubārak.[7] Others were the al-Shanāwīs

[1] Mubārak, vol. ix. p. 38. *Fāqīh* may have been used in the literary sense, i.e. a person versed in religious law, or in the colloquial Egyptian meaning of teacher in a Qur'ān school (*fiqī*).

[2] Figures for 1882 according to the unpublished third volume of the census as quoted by A. von Fircks, *Aegypten* (Berlin, 1895), vol. i, p. 187. These figures are known to be inaccurate, but the comparison certainly indicates the general trend.

[3] For detailed treatment of this development see Baer, *Landownership*, pp. 13–15, 17, 45–60.

[4] See, for instance, the interesting biography of 'Alī Bey al-Badrāwī, Mubārak, vol. xii, pp. 49–50. Cf. also Rogers to Stanton, Cairo, 3 Nov. 1871, F.O. 141/75, Pt. 3.

[5] Cf. Order of 28 June 1896, *Majmū'at al-qarārāt wa'l-manshūrat*, xxii (Cairo–Būlāq, 1896), pp. 333–4.

[6] See Berger, pp. 45–46.

[7] Mubārak, vol. iii, pp. 54–55; vol. xv, p. 96. Cf. Baer, *Landownership*, p. 23. On the interpenetration between landownership and urban business in the twentieth century see ibid., pp. 138–42.

and Mutawallī Bey Nūr of Manṣūra, Sayyid Aḥmad Bey al-Dīb, Rizqallāh Bey Shadīd and the Abāẓas of Zaqāzīq, Maḥmūd Pasha Sulaymān of Asyūṭ, and Muḥammad Bey Abū Ḥusayn and many others of Cairo.[1] Many of them, or members of their families, also served as government officials.

As a result of this interpenetration, no urban *bourgeoisie* in the European sense emerged in Egypt. There was no social class of Egyptians whose principal interest concentrated in the towns and in the promotion of urban economy. This is well illustrated by the lack of independent municipal development. Between 1890 and 1911 municipalities were established in many Egyptian towns, but most of their members were appointed by the central government or were government officials, the governor of the province had a decisive vote, and their powers were confined to a small range of activities. Moreover, foreigners were represented in a much higher proportion than their percentage in the population. Indeed, the only municipality with some tradition of independence and a larger scope of activity was that of Alexandria in which foreigners constituted the majority during the whole period under discussion.

Foreigners and westernization

At the end of the eighteenth century there were in Egypt no more than a few hundred Europeans, including Greeks. During the rule of Muḥammad ʿAlī the number of Europeans grew to about 10,000, at least half of them Greeks and about 2,000 Italians.[2] The great influx of Europeans occurred during the time of Saʿīd and Ismāʿīl, especially in the early 1860s, as a result of the great financial and commercial opportunities connected with the cotton boom and the manifold projects of these two rulers.[3] By 1878 their number had risen to 68,653, by 1897 to 112,574, and by 1907 to 151,414, of whom 62,973 were Greeks, 34,926 Italians, and the rest (53,515) others (excluding Ottoman subjects).[4] A proper evaluation of these figures should take into account that even after the great influx the number of foreigners did not rise above 1·3 per cent. of the total population (from less than one half of one per cent. in the 1840s), and that about a third of the 'other foreigners' (16,000 in 1907) were Asians, Maltese, or North Africans.

The contact of the Egyptian population with these foreigners was not the only channel of Western influence on Egyptian society. Between 1813 and 1919 about 900 Egyptians were sent on educational missions to Europe,[5] and

[1] For details on their landed property and urban business see Wright and Cartwright, pp. 384, 389, 481–2.

[2] Estimates vary considerably. Our estimate is based on Mengin, *Histoire de l'Égypte*, vol. ii, pp. 269 ff.; Clot, vol. i, pp. 167, 243 ff.; Bowring, pp. 4, 9; *Campbell report.*

[3] Cf. D. S. Landes, *Bankers and Pashas* (London, 1958), pp. 87 ff.

[4] Figures for 1878 according to F. Amici, *Essai de statistique générale de l'Égypte* (Cairo, 1879); for 1897—Gouvernment Égyptien, *Recensement général de l'Égypte 1. 6. 1897* (Cairo, 1898); for 1907—census quoted above (see n. 1, p. 156).

[5] M. M. Mosharrafa, *Cultural survey of modern Egypt*, vol. ii (London, 1948), p. 54;

many others visited Europe on their own. Thousands were educated at foreign schools in Egypt: the number of pupils at these schools was 7,450 in 1875 and 48,204 in 1913–14, many of them Egyptians.[1] In the course of the century hundreds of works were translated from European languages into Arabic, technical and scientific books as well as novels, plays, etc. Many Europeans were employed in controlling positions of the Egyptian administration, especially after the British occupation.

The contact with foreigners and with Europe expressed itself in many fields with which we are not directly concerned here. During the nineteenth century, especially after 1882, an extensive network of communications was established, parts of Cairo and Alexandria were built or rebuilt after the model of Paris, and supplied with water, gas, and electricity, the administration of Egypt was modernized, and important changes took place in legislation and the administration of the law. However, it would seem that the most important social change brought about by this contact was the development of education.[2] At the end of the eighteenth and the beginning of the nineteenth century there was no secular education, and learning was confined to the small class of people who were destined to become part of the religious establishment. There are no reliable figures for that period, but the few existing estimates indicate that at the time of Muḥammad ʿAlī not more than five per cent. of the children between 6 and 12 years of age received any formal education at all.[3] In the course of the century this percentage rose to about 17·5 in 1875 and a little less than 25 in 1913–14.[4] Part of the elementary and primary education was secularized, and a variety of institutions for secondary, vocational, and higher education was established. According to an estimate by Artin Pasha, the percentage of literate adults increased from one in 1830 to three in 1850 and to ten in 1881.[5] Thus a growing number of Egyptians were able to read the newly founded newspapers and the growing output of the Arabic printing presses, also an innovation of the nineteenth century.

However, although the above figures indicate progress, they also stress the fact that even at the end of the period under discussion only a very small layer of Egyptian society received any formal education; the number of those who did not forget what they had learned because of lack of practice must have been even smaller. Still smaller was the number of literate people whose education brought them into contact with Western society capable of changing

J. Heyworth-Dunne, *An introduction to the history of education in modern Egypt* (London, [1939]), pp. 253, 304, 326, 394.

[1] Sāmī, Pt. III, vol. iii, p. 1286; R. D. Matthews and M. Akrawi, *Education in Arab countries of the Near East* (Washington D.C., 1949), p. 34; Heyworth-Dunne, Appendix.

[2] See Heyworth-Dunne, *passim.*

[3] Cf. ibid., p. 360; Bowring, p. 137. Children in this age group are taken to have constituted 15 per cent. of the population.

[4] Figures for 1875 and 1913–14 according to Sāmī and Matthews and Akrawi as quoted in n. 1, above.

[5] Boktor, p. 139.

their social attitudes. Education as an instrument of westernization of Egyptian society was therefore confined to a very small part of the population.

Moreover, many factors reduced the social influence of contact with foreigners residing in Egypt. The overwhelming majority of foreigners lived in Alexandria and Cairo, and, except for the Greeks, most of the rest lived in Port Said and Ismailia. Thus only inhabitants of these towns had the opportunity of continuous contact with foreigners. But even in these towns foreigners generally lived in their own quarters, often secluded from the Egyptian population. In Cairo there was a striking difference between the appearance of the quarters in which the foreigners were concentrated and that of the Egyptian quarters: the former were lighted by electricity and gas while the latter were not, and in summer the European quarters were deserted.[1] In Alexandria the two elements mixed to a larger extent, but then the character of the population of Alexandria was typical of that of any Mediterranean port rather than of Egyptian society.[2]

Conclusion

As a result of all these factors 'westernization' was confined to a very small layer of Egyptian society. Moreover, the fact that this layer tried to adopt a foreign culture and civilization alienated it more and more from the bulk of the Egyptian population. While at the beginning of the century there were no significant cultural differences among Egyptians, the impact of the West created a gulf between the europeanized and educated Egyptian officials and other parts of the upper classes, and the great mass of fellahs and town-dwellers, including the lower middle classes.

As we have seen, the contact with Europe and the economic and administrative development in the nineteenth century changed only partly the life and organization of Egyptian society. The traditional family and religious community remained intact and the position of women in society did not change. Neither wealthy Egyptians nor the lower classes acquired the mentality of an industrial society. The social change brought about consisted almost entirely in the destruction of the traditional socio-economic framework: the dissolution of the tribe and the village community, the disappearance of the guilds, and the abolition of slavery. Most of these developments occurred during the last two decades of the century. But the creation of modern groupings, such as modern parties or labour trade unions, was left for the twentieth century.

As a result of the destruction of the traditional socio-economic framework the rigid separation between different units of the socio-economic structure vanished. We have seen that different groups of the upper class merged into one: similarly, mobility between the classes grew. In the eighteenth century everybody was born into his occupational group and there were very few

[1] Wright and Cartwright, pp. 333, 335–6.
[2] Ibid., p. 429. See also Landes, pp. 86–89.

chances for a poor man to become rich. Urbanization, the disappearance of the guilds, the growing demand for officials, the development of private ownership of land, and the great expansion of agriculture created opportunities which greatly increased social mobility. We have mentioned that in the second part of the century many officials and army officers were of fellah origin. Throughout the century not a few people of humble and poor origin became rich landowners, high officials, wealthy merchants, or even physicians.[1] However, lack of entrepreneurship among Egyptians, and lack of industrial development, confined mobility within limits which began to disappear only much later.

[1] See biographies in Mubārak, vol. ix, pp. 92–93; vol. xi, p. 88; vol. xxi, p. 49; vol. xvii, p. 4, etc.; Wright and Cartwright, p. 389 (Abū Ḥusayn); Mackenzie Wallace, pp. 197–9; cf. Baer, *Landownership*, pp. 49–50; Berger, pp. 45–46 (pointing out that the Egyptian higher civil service draws heavily upon the lowest socio-economic groups).

The Long-Term Growth of Agricultural Production in Egypt: 1821–1962

PATRICK O'BRIEN

INTRODUCTION

FOR most of its history the Egyptian economy has been dominated by farming. Even today (1965) agriculture still provides just over a third of national output and employment for about half the labour force.[1] As we move backwards in time the importance of agriculture becomes still more pronounced: just before the Second World War half of the net national output originated in agriculture and the ratio of both production and employment to their national aggregates was undoubtedly much higher for the nineteenth century.[2] In the absence of anything like reliable statistics of real national product for all but the years since 1939, the growth of agricultural output serves as an index of Egyptian economic progress in general. This is not to argue that it provides a very accurate indicator because from 1930 onwards manufactures assumed a growing importance in the economic life of the country. Moreover, long before industry made a noticeable contribution to national output, in fact as soon as agriculture lost its predominantly subsistence character and entered the market economy, services of various kinds accounted for a significant proportion of total product and employed a substantial share of the labour force. But the familiar division of an economy into three major sectors (primary produce, industry, and services) while convenient for certain analytical purposes often conceals the true character of a productive system. Services, in an economy where physical production is dominated by farming, are usually roughly commensurate with services to farmers. That is to say internal and external trade, financial institutions, transport, and even large areas of public administration, are geared to the work on the land. The output of the service sector normally moves in sympathy with the primary sector and it is the growth of agricultural production which both necessitates and makes possible the expansion of roads, railways, banks, insurance companies, storage facilities, as well as trade in both the inputs and output of farmers. In turn the existence of such facilities encourages further expansion of agricultural output.

Furthermore, until very recent years, Egyptian industry could hardly be defined as an autonomous sector of the economy because the great bulk of

[1] B. Hansen and D. Mead, *The national income of Egypt 1939–1962*, Memo. 355, National Planning Institute (Cairo, 1962).

[2] M. Anis, 'The national income of Egypt', *L'Égypte contemporaine* (Dec. 1950).

its activity consisted mainly of transforming agricultural produce, and the value added by manufacturing usually represented only a minor proportion of the value of finished products. As late as 1952 no less than 57 per cent. of net value added by industry emanated from processing foodstuffs, ginning, pressing, spinning and weaving raw cotton, tanning leather, and the manufacture of fertilizers and implements utilized by farmers. Even at that date 39 per cent. of total inputs of Egyptian industry represented raw materials purchased from local farmers.[1] Not only was agriculture the source of supply for a substantial share of raw materials utilized by industry but manufacturers sold most of their output to the bulk of the population who resided and worked in villages.

Thus, for most of its modern economic history, Egyptian agriculture has maintained intimate connexions with both the service and industrial sectors of the economy. Either through forward linkage, as a market, or backward linkage, as a source of supply for raw materials, the progress of the agricultural sector has, to a considerable degree, determined secular movements in the output of both services and industry. Any investigation of the long-term growth of the Egyptian economy should therefore logically begin with agriculture, and then the massive and persistent contribution made by farming to national output, as well as its close links with other sectors, will enable us to draw qualified conclusions about movements in production as a whole.

The primary concern of my paper will be to measure changes in total and *per capita* agricultural production from 1821 to the present day. It is divided into four parts: the first contains a discussion of the quantitative data now available in published form on output, area, and yield per feddan of the crops cultivated in Egypt and also on population figures. Part 2 will utilize this evidence to chart the course and secondarily to elucidate some of the causes of economic change in Egypt between the second and seventh decades of the nineteenth century. Part 3 discusses agricultural development from 1872–8 to 1895 and Part 4 the period 1895 to date. These periods have no strict analytical significance as cycles or long waves, they are simply convenient ways of arranging the data.

PART I. THE BASIC INFORMATION

Ideally, in order to trace changes in agricultural production over time, we require statistics of physical output and the corresponding market value for everything produced by Egyptian farmers. Needless to say such information is just not available except for a very limited number of years of the present century. Data on output in value terms are particularly scarce, and even if

[1] Central Statistical Committee, *Basic statistics* (Cairo, 1962), pp. 90–91; Ministry of Industry, *Census of industrial production, 1952* (Cairo, 1954), and G. Eleish, *The applicability and utilisation of an input–output model*, Memo. 168, National Planning Institute (Cairo, 1962). Eleish's figures refer to 1954.

published in quantity would raise awkward problems of price deflation. Furthermore, it soon became obvious that comprehensive coverage of farm production would not be possible because long runs of statistics had been published for only eight crops cultivated in Egypt during the last century and a half. Fortunately, the commodities concerned (cotton, wheat, maize, beans, barley, lentils, sugar, and rice) have consistently accounted for the bulk of *gross* agricultural production.[1] I therefore thought it would be advisable to build up time series of production figures, expressed in physical units, for these eight commodities which would then be used to represent the development of agricultural output as a whole since 1821.

For the years after 1895 the government has published comprehensive figures related to almost all crops cultivated in Egypt.[2] Before that time information, except for cotton, is definitely scarce and generally unreliable. The distinction between evidence for the nineteenth and twentieth centuries is pronounced enough to warrant separate discussions of the data published before and after 1895.

1. *Agricultural Production Statistics before 1895*

I made no attempt to collect statistics for the period before the reign of Muḥammad ʿAlī. Even so the amount of information available in Britain on nineteenth-century Egyptian agriculture is extremely limited. My search covered all relevant books and articles in Arabic, English, and French, traceable in London, and cited in the bibliographies of Egyptian historical literature compiled by Maunier, the British Museum, the London School of Economics, and the School of Oriental and African Studies.[3] I also checked through the appropriate Foreign Office reports and papers at the Public Record Office and reports from British consuls and administrators in Egypt published in Parliamentary Papers.[4] From this fairly exhaustive, not to say exhausting, foray among published and unpublished sources I came up with the meagre and very disappointing haul presented in Table 1. For the sake of clarity I have preferred to reference and comment on the sources utilized as an appendix to each table.

[1] The proportion of the gross value of the eight crops to total gross value in agriculture can be calculated from the following sources: P.R.O., F.O. 78/583 and F.O. 141/96; J. McCoan, *Egypt as it is* (London, 1878), ch. 9; J. Robino, 'Some statistics of Egypt', *Journal of the Royal Statistical Society*, Sept. 1884; I. Levi, 'L'Augmentation des revenus de l'état', *L'Égypte contemporaine*, vol. lxviii (1922); E. Minost, 'Essai sur le revenu agricole', ibid., vol. cxxiii (1930); H. Azmi, 'A study of agricultural revenue in Egypt', ibid., vol. clii (1934); J. Schatz, 'Mesures pour alléger l'endettement', ibid., vol. xxxiii; M. Anis, op. cit., and *Basic statistics*, pp. 67–69.

[2] Ministry of National Economy and (later issues) Department of Statistics and Census, *Annuaire statistique* (Cairo, annually or semi-annually).

[3] R. Maunier, *Bibliographie géographique de l'Égypte*, 2 vols. (Cairo, 1928); British Library of Political and Economic Science, *London bibliography of the social sciences* and School of Oriental and African Studies, *Library catalogue*.

[4] P.R.O., F.O. 24, 141, and 142. *Commercial reports from H.M. consuls in Cairo, Port Said and Alexandria* in British Parliamentary Papers 1862 to 1886 *passim*.

TABLE I. *Agricultural statistics, 1821–89*

	Cotton		Wheat		Millet and Maize		Barley		Beans		Lentils		Rice		Sugar-cane	
	Area	Prodn.	Area	Prodn.	Area	Prodn.	Area	Prodn.	Area	Prodn.	Area	Prodn.	Area	Prodn.	Area	Prodn.
1821				1,200		950		600		1,200		120		116		530
1821				1,156		874		552		1,152		104		165		
1832		136		1,001		1,221		897		966		193		110		
1833		56		1,450		910		650		700		70		80		180
1833		214		1,344		837		598		644		129		147		1,060
1835		144		950		1,010		560		800		70				
1844		153	914	2,534	799	4,495	874	3,109	839	2,243	158	163	98	490	12	
1871	699	2,044	1,200						1,070							
1872		2,299												445		
1875		2,928		6,662	1,884	10,503	521	3,103	1,320	4,575	89	312		98	71	
1877		2,594	891		601		491		617		121		41		46	
1878		1,686	1,150		1,884		521		1,220		150		50		30	
1879	950	3,199	890		1,900		541		600				240		34	
1886	1,051	2,932		4,000						3,000		800			34	38,251
1889	1,058	3,183	1,241		683		520		756						27	32,949

Notes and sources to Table 1

The figures for area are in thousands of feddans and for production in thousands of ardebs, except for sugar-cane and cotton which are expressed in thousands of cantars.

As far as possible I attempted to trace all figures back to their original sources. I have included under the relevant note any discussion found as to the nature of the source or the accuracy of the figures. If no comment is made that is because the original source contained no further information.

Where the quantities were expressed in an alien or uncommon standard (kilogrammes, hectolitres, bushels, etc.) they have been converted into the usual Egyptian measures of ardebs, cantars, and quintaux. The conversion ratios utilized were:

1 ardeb	=	5·44 bushels	=	198 litres
1 cantar	=	99·05 lb.	=	44·9 kg.
1 quintal	=	100 kg.	=	1·968 cwt.

The figures for maize include millet and sorghum. They are likely to be more inaccurate than the figures for any other crop because of the great difficulties involved in the collection of information related to food crops largely consumed on the farm and also because sometimes maize is defined to include millet or sorghum and sometimes the latter crops are excluded from the definition, often without warning.

All cotton production figures have been copied from a single source, Ministry of the Interior, *Cotton report for 1905* cited in *Annuaire statistique* (Cairo, 1910). They are in line, but not identical, with the figures published by A. E. Crouchley, *The economic development of modern Egypt* (London, 1938), t. 5b and F. Charles-Roux, *La Production du coton en Égypte* (Paris, 1908), pp. 42, 72, 82, and 106. The figures for earlier years of the century probably represent exports of long staple cotton and exclude short staple or *baladī* cotton as well as longer staple cotton consumed locally but the bulk of the crop was exported. The area figure for 1871 is from Muḥammad Fahmī Lahīṭa, *Ta'rīkh Miṣr al-iqtiṣādī fi'l-'uṣūr al-ḥadītha* (Cairo, 1944), p. 287 and the area figures for 1879, 1886, and 1889 are from Crouchley, op. cit., t. 5b.

Figures for sugar-cane production for 1821, 1833, and 1835 are based on production figures for refined sugar and have been calculated on the assumption (which rests upon figures in J. Mazuel *Le sucre en Égypte* (Cairo, 1937), p. 61, that the conversion ratio between sugar-cane and refined sugar is 10:1. The figures for 1886 and 1889 are the reported totals for sugar-cane.

1821. F. Mengin, *Histoire de l'Égypte sous le gouvernement de Mohammed-Aly* (Paris, 1823), vol. ii, pp. 373–4.

1821. G. Douin, *La Mission du Baron Boislecomte en l'Égypte et la Syrie en 1833* (Cairo, 1927), p. 86. Boislecomte, a French diplomat, referred to an official document for 1822.

1832. Douin, op. cit., p. 86. Douin said the figures for 1832 emanated from the Ministry of the Interior.

1833. F. Mengin, *Histoire sommaire de l'Égypte, 1823–1838* (Paris, 1839), pp. 161–3.

1833. A. -B. Clot-Bey, *Aperçu général sur l'Égypte* (Paris, 1840), p. 287. Clot was a doctor employed by Muḥammad 'Alī.

1835. J. Bowring, *Report on Egypt and Candia*, British Parliamentary Papers 1840 (xxi), p. 17. Bowring mentioned that his statistics came from papers of the consul general. He also pointed out that Egyptian statistics are unreliable. He cited a yield figure for sugar cane of 270 cantars a feddan which was based upon two estates only.

1844. P.R.O., F.O. 141/96 and F.O. 78/583. The former consists of an unsigned collection of tables. The latter transcribed by H. A. B. Rivlin, *The agricultural policy of Muḥammad 'Alī in Egypt* (Cambridge, Mass., 1961) Appendix 1, contains substantially the same information and is a consular report dispatched by the British consul in Cairo to the Foreign Office in December 1844. The consul said the tables were 'copied from official documents, they may be relied upon as showing approximately the vast resources of this country'. It is clear from the notes to several tables that the figures represent *optimum* rather than *actual* production. This optimum was based on assumptions about the height of the Nile flood. Moreover the notes pointed out how difficult it was to calculate production for Upper and Middle Egypt and mentioned that maize production is probably understated and cotton overstated. Finally the sub-totals in several tables are sometimes not consistent with aggregated totals. In all these figures should be regarded as only rough estimates of *potential* production. The documents contain further information on landholding, population, revenue and prices, and value of agricultural production.

1871. Lahīṭa, op. cit., p. 546.

1872. J. Robino, 'Some statistics of Egypt', *Journal of the Royal Statistical Society*, September 1884, pp. 421 and 433. Robino cited E. de Régny, *Statistique générale de l'Égypte* (1872) as his source. He also gave the following figures of yields per feddan in ardebs: wheat, 2·21; barley, 2·02; beans, 1·84; and lentils 1·84.

1875. J. McCoan, *Egypt as it is* (London, 1878), pp. 192–202. McCoan in his preface said he had resided for many years in the Levant and thanked two high-ranking Egyptian officials (Mubārak and Dor) for information. Robino, op. cit., p. 432 asserted that McCoan's figures come from Mouffettish, *Statistique agricole et animale* (1876), a book compiled to impress the khedive's creditors with the wealth and income of Egypt. They certainly appear exaggerated when compared with other information for the 1870s and McCoan posited yield figures for 1875 much higher than those achieved during the twentieth century. In all the figures appear to be unreliable. The area for sugar-cane is from Mazuel, op. cit., p. 61. Mazuel obtained the figures from W. Willcocks, *Egyptian irrigation* (London, 1913), p. 15. Mazuel also cited a yield figure for sugar of 300–50 cantars a feddan.

1877. Ministère de l'Interieur, *Essai de statistique de l'Égypte* (Cairo, 1879), vol. ii, t. 27. These figures were collected and compiled by the Bureau of Statistics under the direction of F. Amici. Amici is often cited as the author.

1878. J. Robino, op. cit., p. 432. Robino stated these figures were from Amici, *Essai sur la statistique d'Égypte* and relate to 1878. The sugar area is from *al-Muqtaṭaf*, vol. ii, no. 5 (Cairo, 1887), p. 292 and were originally taken from a report by Colonel Moncrieff of the Irrigation Department.

1879. Rāshid al-Barāwī and Muḥammad Ḥamza ʿUlaysh, *al Taṭawwur al-iqtiṣādī fī Miṣr fi'l ʿaṣr al-ḥadīth* (Cairo, 1945), pp. 142–7. The sugar area is that cited in *al-Muqtaṭaf*, vol. ii, no. 5, p. 292.

1886. J. Stadelman, *Annuaire Égyptien* (Cairo, 1886). Stadelman's book is a general work of reference. His figures do not appear reliable. Certainly the rounded totals do not inspire confidence that the figures are anything but guesses. The totals for maize and lentils are completely inconsistent with other figures. The figure for sugar area is from Mazuel, op. cit., p. 61. The figure for sugar-cane production is from Lahīṭa, op. cit., p. 438.

As the above table shows, information was discovered for only fifteen years of the nineteenth century, and my explanatory notes attempt to distinguish the more reliable from the untrustworthy statistics. Many of the tabulated figures are, however, impossible to appraise except in terms of their consistency one with another and with later official and more accurate information. For example, any statistic which asserts or posits a yield per feddan in the first half of the nineteenth century higher than that achieved 50 or 100 years later is almost certainly an exaggeration. Alternatively we may legitimately view with suspicion any very rapid increases in output over short periods of time. Again it seems reasonable to regard the 'odd' figure or figures for a series of successive years either as untrustworthy or as a reflection of a high or low Nile flood.

But in the light of such poor and sparse statistics my conclusion can only be the rather negative one that much more research will be required before we are in a position to say anything definite about variations in agricultural output, and by implication the whole course of economic change, over the nineteenth century. Some of the figures do, however, appear sufficiently reliable to establish limits to possible increases in output, and in Part II of this paper I have ventured to utilize the more plausible statistics, for 1821, 1832–5, and 1872–8, in an attempt to measure the rate of change of agricultural production over a fifty-year time span. Alternatively, nearly all the figures could be used as relatives to estimate the proportion of total area devoted to particular crops for given years or to gauge the importance over time of different products within aggregate farm production. It may be that published, or more likely, archival material in Cairo or Paris will yield further information. If not, major historical questions about the path and causes of economic development in nineteenth-century Egypt, and by implication about changes in the material welfare of the mass of the Egyptian people, will remain open. Of course, more or less plausible answers to such questions may still be offered by generalizing from the experience of particular areas or estates, but this way the construction of Egyptian economic history will require lengthy and painstaking research and even then will probably remain inconclusive.

2. *Agricultural production statistics since 1895*

From 1913 the *Annuaire statistique* contains fairly complete statistics related to the quantity, prices, area cultivated, and yield of all the major field-crops as well as a periodic census of animals owned by farmers. The data are well known and accessible and do not warrant reproduction here. For the period 1895 to 1909 production totals for agricultural commodities, other than cotton are, however, not available although the *Annuaire* includes figures of the area devoted to the various crops. In addition official information is fortunately available on the average yield of wheat, beans, and barley cultivated on state domains.

TABLE 2. *Average yield in ardebs per feddan on the state domains for wheat, beans, and barley, 1879–1911*

Year	Wheat	Beans	Barley
1879	2·96	3·03	1·90
1880	3·05	2·75	2·66
1881	3·58	2·50	2·00
1882	3·58	2·58	2·54
1883	3·58	2·20	2·25
1884	3·20	1·83	2·20
1885	2·88	2·17	2·06
1886	3·00	2·42	2·42
1887	3·96	2·54	3·03
1888	3·88	2·20	3·25
1889	4·00	2·83	3·66
1890	4·25	3·29	4·29
1891	4·80	2·42	3·58
1892	3·63	3·33	3·05
1893	5·17	3·63	4·38
1894	4·90	3·46	3·96
1895	5·00	2·75	4·50
1896	4·17	3·63	3·50
1897	4·46	3·54	3·66
1898	6·42	3·79	4·20
1899	5·58	4·08	3·79
1900	5·17	3·96	3·33
1901	5·75	3·38	3.75
1902	5·00	3·46	3·42
1903	5·94	4·17	4·33
1904	6·42	3·96	3·75
1905	5·88	3·17	3·54
1906	5·42	3·58	3·42
1907	5·83	3·54	3·83
1908	5·25	3·42	3·15
1909	6·06	3·46	3·23
1910	5·05	2·92	3·20
1911	5·11	3·92	4·00

Note to Table 2

Ministry of Finance, *Monthly return on the state and prospects of the cotton crop*, vol. i, no. 10 (Cairo, 1913), pp. 14–15, and Department of Statistics, *Annuaire statistique* (Cairo, 1913), pp. 486–7. The original figures were expressed in ardebs and roubks.

If we assume that average yields on state domains represent an average yield for the whole of Egyptian agriculture then production totals for wheat, beans, and barley can be easily calculated for the period 1895 to 1909. The question naturally arises as to how far it is plausible to regard yields on state domains, which then formed only a portion of the total cultivated area, as equivalent to yields throughout Egyptian agriculture. The point is certainly difficult to establish.

For a single but very important crop, cotton, average yields on state domains and average yields for all farmland can be compared for the five-year period 1894 to 1899. This comparison shows that the annual average yield on state domains at 5·14 cantars to the feddan was slightly lower than the average yield of 5·37 cantars per feddan throughout agriculture as a whole.[2] In the absence of evidence to the contrary cotton statistics support our using average yields for wheat, beans, and barley cultivated on state domains to represent average yields for all Egyptian farmland.

For the other major field crops, maize, rice, and sugar, no production or yield statistics appear to have been published until 1913, although the area devoted to each of these commodities is contained in the *Annuaire statistique*. If we assume that the published average yields per feddan for each of these crops over the period 1913 to 1923 was equivalent to the average yields for the period 1895 to 1913, production totals for maize, rice, and sugar-cane can then be calculated by multiplying this estimated yield by the published area.[3] Again the assumption may not be valid but the published evidence of yields on state domains for wheat, beans, and barley suggests that average yields per feddan were not significantly different between these two periods. If anything productivity per feddan was probably slightly higher before the First World War than over the subsequent decade.

By making bold assumptions about yields it proved possible to estimate the total quantity produced of eight field-crops (cotton, wheat, maize, barley, beans, lentils, sugar, and rice) for the period 1895 to 1913. After 1913 the *Annuaire statistique* published all required information. But the problem still remained of evaluating the data as published by the *Annuaire statistique*. Although economists and historians have often utilized this official source, I have nowhere come across a satisfactory appraisal of methods used

[1] Ministry of Finance, *Monthly return on the state and prospects of the cotton crop*, vol. i, no. 10 (Cairo, 1913), pp. 14–15; *Annuaire statistique* (1909), and Muḥammad Fahmī Lahīṭa, op. cit., p. 494.

[2] The yields for 1913 to 1923 are cited in the *Annuaire statistique*.

by government departments in the collection and collation of agricultural statistics.

We do know that before the First World War *ṣarrāfs* (tax-collectors) made returns to the Ministry of Finance of the area devoted to agriculture and the production of crops grown in their villages. Their reports were not based upon direct observation and measurement but upon the oral evidence of cultivators and their accuracy depended very much upon the efficiency and diligence of the *ṣarrāfs*. Several sample checks by the Survey Department, attached to the Ministry of Public Works, revealed quite serious errors in the statistics for 1908–10 and the government felt it necessary to warn *ṣarrāfs* that their returns would be subjected to periodic checks and that gross errors would be punished.[1] No doubt over time the quality of the returns improved, while the direct and comprehensive enumeration of the censuses of agricultural production conducted in 1929, 1939, and 1960 acted as a check on the methodology employed in the collection of agricultural statistics and provided a basis for revising the more inaccurate figures.[2]

3. *The cropped and cultivated area*

Egyptian farmland is usually classified into two totals—cultivated and cropped area. The former explains itself and the latter reflects the fact that most Egyptian land produces more than one crop per year. Over time Egyptian farmers have raised agricultural output both by cultivating more land and also by cropping the land two and in some cases three times annually. Cropped area is thus the surface equivalent of land which yields only a single crop and is the land input to be related to farm output.

Figures of cropped and cultivated areas for the period 1893–4 to date are published in the *Annuaire statistique*. Before that date scattered and often unreliable totals for the cultivated area only are available. As the information for the years after 1893–4 is well known and accessible it warrants no further comment here, but I thought it appropriate to reproduce and appraise the published figures of cultivated area for the period from 1813 to 1892.

Our survey of the evidence for the area of land cultivated in Egypt between 1813 and 1894 reveals that a mixture of fairly reliable and obviously untrustworthy estimates have been published. Statistics for 1813 and 1852 emerged as a result of cadastral surveys and are, therefore, probably exact enough for most purposes. Figures which are based on land-tax returns for the years after 1876, when the tax became more equitable and comprehensive, may

[1] H. Lyons, 'Some agricultural statistics of Egypt'; J. Haines, 'Sarraf's crop returns'; G. Morgan, 'Collection of crop statistics'; and A. McKillop, 'The cotton statistics', all printed in the *Cairo Scientific Journal*, Feb., 1907, May, 1908, July, 1909, and Jan. and Mar., 1910.

[2] Ministry of Agriculture, *The agricultural census*, 1929 and 1939 (Cairo, 1934 and 1946), pp. xii and i, ii, and iii respectively, and Azmi, op. cit.

also be regarded as a fair approximation to the area actually cultivated for those years. On the other hand the coverage and basis of the figures offered by Mengin and the British consul for 1821 and 1844 respectively are so impossible to interpret that they cannot be regarded as even a rough measure of the cultivated area. All other figures (for 1833, 1835, 1843, 1852, and 1862–79) seem to represent the estimates of informed contemporaries or were published by the Bureau of Statistics and while difficult to appraise, as part of a whole sequence of statistics, none appears implausible.

TABLE 3. *Cultivated and cropped area 1813 to 1895*

Year	Cultivated area (thousand feddans)	Cropped area (thousand feddans)
1813	3,054	
1821	1,956	
1821	2,032	
1833	3,856	
1835	3,500	
1843	3,672	
1844	3,569	
1852	4,160	
1862	4,053	
1863	4,395	
1869	4,500	
1873	4,624	
1875	4,804	
1875	4,703	
1877	4,742	4,762
1879	4,810	
1880	4,719	
1881	4,714	
1882	4,758	
1883	4,785	
1884	4,803	
1885	4,840	
1886	4,880	
1887	4,878	
1888	4,886	
1889	4,913	
1890	4,941	
1891	4,967	
1892	4,942	
1893	4,970	
1894	4,805	6,350
1895	4,874	6,431

Notes and sources to Table 3

1813. Y. Artin, *The right of landed property in Egypt* (London, 1885), p. 209. Artin pointed out that this total is from the cadastral survey of 1813–14. It is accepted by Lyons, who conducted the cadastral survey of 1897, as a reasonable estimate—H. Lyons, *The cadastral survey of Egypt* (Cairo, 1908), p. 75.

1821. Mengin, *Histoire de l'Égypte sous le gouvernement de Mohammed-Aly*, vol. ii, pp. 342–4. Mengin's figure is *taxed* land only. Rivlin, op. cit., Appendix 2, suggested this total is based upon a cadastral survey and attempted to account for the discrepancy between the area cultivated in 1813 and 1821. There is no evidence that a comprehensive cadastral survey was conducted in 1821 or that *taxed* land at that time was equivalent to *cultivated* land. Y. Artin, op. cit., p. 220 in fact stated that certain provinces of Upper Egypt paid taxes on *sāqiya* and *shādūf* and not on the basis of land. There is no need to explain the differences between the figures for 1813 and 1821. They are simply collected on a different basis and are, therefore, not comparable.

1821. O. Tousson, *Mémoire sur les finances de l'Égypte* (Cairo, 1924), p. 167. Tousson cited Mengin as his source and makes it clear that the total refers to *taxed* land only.

1833. Clot, op. cit., p. 264. Clot does not in fact relate this total to a particular year, but since so many of the statistics cited in his study relate to 1833, I concluded this figure also referred to 1833.

1835. Bowring, op. cit., p. 13. Bowring called his total *cultivatable* land and observed that the actual total cultivated depended on the height of the Nile.

1843. E. de Régny, *Statistique de l'Égypte* (Alexandria, 1870), p. 67. Régny was in charge of the Bureau of Statistics of the Ministry of the Interior.

1844. P.R.O., F.O. 78/583 and F.O. 141/96. The reports refer to *taxed* land. Rivlin, op. cit., Appendix 1, has attempted to use these documents to estimate the area cultivated in 1844. Her attempts are both confusing and unconvincing because *taxed* land does not equal cultivated land and the reports in any case make it clear that the figures cited refer to the *optimum* cultivable area and not the *actual* area cultivated. Rivlin's conclusion (p. 270) that the area of cultivated land declined between the French occupation and 1844 cannot be supported by these figures. Her assertion that Muḥammad ʿAlī increased the cropped area is not based on any statistics at all and to describe this as 'qualitative' rather than 'quantitative' improvement defies interpretation since an increase in the cropped area normally leads to an increase in the *quantity* produced.

1852. Lyons, op. cit., p. 75. This total was based upon a cadastral survey conducted between 1853 and 1859.

1862. Lahīṭa, op. cit., p. 290. The source of this total is probably Ministère de l'Interieur, *Essai de statistique générale de l'Égypte* (Cairo, 1878–9). The same figure is cited by S. Cave, *Report on the financial conditions of Egypt*, British Parliamentary Papers 1876 (lxxxiii), Appendix 2. Cave refers to the total as land cultivated under Saʿīd for 1854–63.

1863. Artin, op. cit., p. 219. Artin's figures were carefully and informatively set out and bear the stamp of reliability.

1869. Régny, op. cit., p. 67.

1873. Crouchley, op. cit., t. 3. Crouchley referred to a report by the American consul, Beardley, for this total. Several of the figures cited in this table are also contained in Crouchley's table. I have, however, preferred to return to the original sources in order to make a new appraisal of the data.

1875. Cave, op. cit., Appendix 2. The figures refer to land subject to tax.

1875. Artin, op. cit., p. 219.

1877. *Essai de statistique*, vol. i, p. 132. The year the figures relate to is not obvious. This compilation was published in 1878 and I, therefore, assumed the total related to the previous year. The statistic was in fact collected by Amici who also offered an implausible figure of cropped area for the same year. The Bureau of Statistics gave no indication of how the figures were compiled.

1879. ʿAbd al-Raḥmān al-Rāfiʿī, *ʿAṣr Ismāʿīl* (Cairo, 1932), p. 222.

1880–93. Government of Egypt, *Statistical returns, 1881–97* (Cairo, 1898), p. 12. The figures relate to taxed agricultural land. Taxed land for this period is probably a fair measure of cultivated land.

1894–5. Department of Statistics and Census, *Annuaire statistique* (Cairo annually or semi-annually from 1909).

Unfortunately no reliable figures for the cropped area seem to exist for the period before 1894. The solitary figure published by Amici for 1877 appears unreliable. Assuming that cropped and cultivated areas were approximately equal at the beginning of the nineteenth century, I find it difficult to accept the implication of this figure that all the investment in the irrigation system during the reigns of Muḥammad ʿAlī, Saʿīd, and Ismāʿīl made virtually no difference to the ratio of cropped to cultivated land.

4. *Population statistics*

No systematic enumeration of the populace was undertaken in Egypt until 1882 and that census is considered sufficiently inaccurate for observers to regard the second census of 1897 as the first *reliable* estimate of the Egyptian population. Since 1897 the government has conducted inter-decennial figures of total population based upon the registration of births and deaths.[1] These

TABLE 4. *Estimates of population, 1800–82*

Year	Total population (thousands)	Total urban population (thousands)
1800	2,489	412
1821	2,514	258
1830–5	2,500–3,500	
1844	1,954	315
1846	4,463	482
1855	4,402	
1869	5,215	
1872	—	566
1875	5,252	648
1878	5,517	569
1882	6,806	

[1] Department of Statistics and Census, *The census of population* 1897 et seq. and *Annuaire statistique*.

Notes and sources to Table 4

1800. E. Jomard, 'Mémoire sur la population comparée de l'Égypte ancienne et moderne'. *Description de l'Égypte* (Paris, 1818), vol. ii, pp. 95–100. This appears to be a more or less careful enumeration by one of the savants with the French expedition. The methodology employed was to obtain returns from every *shaykh al-balad* of the number of males resident in his village and to apply a coefficient, based upon sample surveys, of the ratio of males to females and children. The urban population was based upon estimates submitted to Jomard by French officers. Y. Artin, 'Essai sur les causes du renchérissment de la vie materielle au Caire dans le courant du 19me siecle', *Mémoires de l'Institut Égyptien*, vol. v, 1908, pointed out that the French estimate did not include the whole of Egypt but covered the country as far down the Nile as Aswān—cited by Rivlin, op. cit., Appendix 6.

1821. Mengin, *Histoire de l'Égypte sous le gouvernement de Mohamed-Aly*, vol. ii, p. 317. Mengin's estimate was based on the number of houses enumerated for purposes of the house tax. Given the number of houses Mengin supplied coefficients, based upon his own observations and information received from the *shaykh al-balad*, of eight persons per house in Cairo and four persons per house in the rest of Egypt. M. El-Darwish, 'A Note on the Population of Egypt', *Population*, February 1934, p. 43 considered Mengin's figure to be too low but offered no evidence to support his assertation.

1830–5. There are a number of estimates for these years offered by French and Russian diplomats resident in Egypt and discussed by Rivlin, op. cit., Appendix 6. Bowring, op. cit., p. 4 cites an official estimate for 3·2 millions which he thought was too high. Bowring goes on to say the 'best informed opinion' placed the population between 2 and 2½ million. The most explicit estimate is that by Clot, op. cit., vol. i, p. 167. Clot's estimate is 2,890,000 and is calculated on the same basis as Mengin's, that is by the application of Mengin's coefficients to official figures of the number of houses subjected to tax.

1844. P.R.O., F.O. 141/96 and 78/583. No indication is provided in the reports how these estimates were compiled. Rivlin, op. cit., Appendix 1 amends the figures to reach a total of 2,159,000, but when she considered estimates of population in Appendix 6 she preferred to disregard these figures as a serious estimate.

1846. Régny, op. cit., p. 11. Régny does not say how this estimate was compiled, but Darwish, op. cit., p. 43 asserts that the estimate was made in the same way as Mengin's, from house-tax data. Darwish considers it to be a more careful estimate than that of 1821, but he produces no evidence in support of this statement. I have not been able to trace the estimate back to its original source.

1855. Robino, op. cit., p. 148. This estimate was made by Calucci, President, Intendance Sanitaire of Alexandria.

1869. Régny, op. cit., pp. 13–14. Régny applied officially registered birth and death rates to the estimate for 1846 to arrive at this estimate.

1872. Ministère de l'Intérieur, *Essai de statistique générale de l'Égypte* (Cairo 1879), p. 8.

1875. Robino, op. cit., p. 419. Robino cites Rossi as his source. This is the figure given in the *Statesman's yearbook* (London, 1879), and copied from consular reports. The figure for urban population is also from the latter source.

1878. *Statesman's yearbook* (London, 1880), p. 635 refers to an official estimate made by Amici, chief of the Statistical Department of the Ministry of the Interior on 31 December 1878.

1882. Ministère de l'Intérieur, *Recensement général de l'Égypte* (Cairo, 1884). This census was conducted during the period of the 'Urābī revolt and is considered to be unreliable: J. Craig, 'The Census of Egypt', *L'Égypte contemporaine*, 1917, p. 212. Even so it is probably a more accurate estimate than all previous attempts based upon tax data and the imperfect figures of the registration for births and deaths.

demographic statistics are well known and accessible, but the random and dubious estimates published for earlier years in the nineteenth century warrant detailed examination.

Population estimates are extremely difficult to evaluate because very few of the figures are supported by anything like a detailed description of the methods of enumeration employed. Moreover, the whole series has suffered from errors in transcription and quite arbitrary amendments to the original totals in secondary sources. Apart from the obviously untrustworthy total for 1844 most commentators have been puzzled by the apparent rise and then sharp fall in the natural rate of increase of the population before and after 1846. Calculations by Craig and Boinet postulated the following rates of increase between 1800 and 1882:

Period	Rates of increase per thousand of the population	
	Craig	Boinet
1800–21	1·45	1·50
1821–46	22·98	31·40
1846–82	11·81	13·00
1800–82	—	20·30

In the light of such fluctuations in the natural rate of increase Boinet, Craig, and Darwish have made a number of *a priori* assertions about the estimates. They all accept the total for 1846 and are consequently pushed into concluding that the total for 1821 is too low or attempt to account for the rise and subsequent fall in the rate of increase as Boinet does, in terms of net immigration.[1] But there seems to be no evidence that Egypt experienced net immigration

[1] A. Boinet, 'L'Accroissement de la population en Égypte', *Bulletin de l'Institut Égyptien*, No. 7 (1886); J. Craig, 'The census of Egypt', *L'Égypte contemporaine* (Apr. 1917) and M. El-Darwish, 'A note on the population of Egypt', *Population* (Feb. 1934).

between 1821 and 1846 on the scale suggested by Boinet; nor is there evidence for accepting the figure for 1846 and rejecting that of 1821. Furthermore, I can find little in the social and economic history of the period 1821 to 1882 which accounts for the fall in the rate of increase after 1846. On the contrary the statistics of agricultural output presage the possibility of accelerated rate of growth for the entire half-century after 1821. Finally, if we accept Calluci's estimate for 1855 it then appears that the population suffered an absolute decline between 1846 and 1855. A more plausible hypothesis is that the population increased at a gradually accelerating rate over the entire period between 1821 and 1882 that the figure for 1846 is inconsistent with the rest of the series of estimates and also with other evidence on trends in economic and social development for the period.

PART II. THE DEVELOPMENT OF AGRICULTURAL PRODUCTION 1821 TO 1872–8

1. *Methodology*

Our survey of the evidence revealed that more or less satisfactory statistics exist on the physical production of eight major farm commodities, the cropped and cultivated areas as well as the total population for the period since 1895. It has also shown that a few but dubious figures are available for the other years of the nineteenth century. Many of the facts collected for the period before 1895 had, however, to be rejected as implausible or obviously inconsistent with other more reliable data. The process of elimination left information on output for just three periods: 1821, the years from 1830 to 1835, and a final set of figures related to the years 1872–8. Given the scarce and untrustworthy data for this earlier period the construction of a single composite index of agricultural output covering the entire time-span from 1821 to 1962 did not appear to be sensible. I thought it less misleading to trace the development of agricultural output over three periods: 1821 to 1872–8, 1872–8 to 1895, and 1895 to 1962. Any conclusions reached about developments before 1895 are vitiated by the quality of the statistics utilized and may be rendered obsolete by the discovery of new evidence. For the later period it proved possible to measure with some accuracy the course of change from official data contained in the *Annuaire statistique*.

In order to trace the development over time of agricultural output as a whole the figures related to the physical output of our eight crops had to be aggregated into an index number. Output totals for six crops were published in ardebs or at least units convertible to ardebs, but cotton and sugar-cane were measured in cantars. Simple aggregation thus proved impossible, and the method adopted involved the conversion of each separate quantity into a relative and the subsequent addition of the relatives. Before summation each relative had, however, to be weighted by the importance of the crop concerned measured in value terms, otherwise changes in over-all agricultural production would have been determined by the *heavier* not the most *valuable* crops.

Weights were selected which expressed the proportionate contribution made by individual crops to the aggregated gross value of all eight crops. Over time the total value and relative importance of different farm products varied considerably. For example, cotton made but a small contribution to the gross value of output during the second decade of the nineteenth century, but by the end of the century it had become the single most valuable crop grown in Egypt. Furthermore, the prices of some products like wheat seem to have risen relatively to the prices of other crops like beans and maize. It thus seemed desirable in constructing indices of output concerned to cover time-spans as long as 1821 to 1872–8 and 1895 to 1962 to weight each crop by its relative importance, not for a given year or groups of years as in the Laspeyres method (where $Q = \sum Q_n P_o / Q_o P_o$), but by its relative contribution to gross output over all years covered by the index.

Unfortunately the required information was not available. Price and value data for the period before 1913 proved to be very scarce and I had to compromise by weighting each crop by its contribution to the total gross value of all eight crops for selected years for which information happened to be published. In the case of the third index, covering 1895 to 1962, I managed to gather or to calculate total gross value for every crop for nearly all the years 1913 to 1962. (Gross values for 1913–18 were calculated by the application of average prices to the quantities published in the *Annuaire statistique*. Prices were measured with the aid of price indices from the same source and actual price data published by Schatz.)[1] I found insufficient evidence for the determination of weights for the years 1895 to 1913, but there is no evidence from figures on the allocation of land or the relative rates of growth of production for different crops that the weights for 1895–1913 would vary significantly from average weights for 1913–62. I also used the same weights (for 1913–62) to construct the second index covering 1872–8 to 1895. This solution is far from ideal but is a necessary compromise based on the absence of published price data for the last three decades of the nineteenth century. For the final index, 1821 to 1872–8, I found only scattered and often unreliable data on prices and gross value related to the years 1821, 1832, 1844, 1875, and 1878, which, in the absence of other information, formed the basis for the calculation of weights.[2] Given the weights which represent, somewhat crudely, the importance of each crop in value terms over the

[1] See n. 1, p. 164 and Schatz, op. cit.

[2] See references in n. 1, p. 164; Artin, 'Essai sur les causes du renchérissement de la vie matérielle', op. cit.; Tousson, op. cit., p. 169; Rivlin, op. cit., pp. 144, 152, 154, 157; R. Cattaui, *Le règne de Mohammed Aly d'après les archives russes en Égypte* (Rome, 1931–6), vol. ii, p. 408; Douin, op. cit., p. 87. W. Yates, *The modern history and conditions of Egypt* (London, 1843), vol. i, p. 462, and Barāwī and 'Ulaysh, op. cit., p. 68.

periods 1821 to 1872–8 and 1895 to 1962 I was able to calculate three index numbers of the following form:

$$\frac{q^n qp^t}{q^o qp^t}$$

(where qp^t is average gross value for selected years 1913 to 1962 or for selected years 1821 to 1872–8) designed to measure changes in the *volume* of farm output from 1821 to date. The indices measure gross output produced in the agricultural sector per unit of time. They do not trace changes in real value added (gross output minus inputs) and are, therefore, of only limited use for the measurement of efficiency in agriculture.[1]

2. *Statistics on the development of agriculture 1821 to 1872–8*

TABLE 5. *Quantities produced of eight crops, 1821 to 1872–8*

Year	Cotton (thousand cantars)	Sugar-cane (thousand cantars)	Wheat (thousand ardebs)	Maize (thousand ardebs)	Barley (thousand ardebs)	Beans (thousand ardebs)	Lentils (thousand ardebs)	Rice (thousand ardebs)
1821	51	530	1,151	912	576	1,152	112	141
1830–5	224	620	1,186	995	676	778	115	117
1872–8	2,540	41,588	3,780	6,113	1,277	2,520	221	127

TABLE 6. *Indices of production for eight crops, 1821 to 1872–8*

Year	Cotton	Sugar-cane	Wheat	Maize	Barley	Beans	Lentils	Rice
1821	100	100	100	100	100	100	100	100
1830–5	440	115	103	109	117	67	104	83
1872–8	5,000	785	330	670	220	219	194	90

Notes to Tables 5 and 6

Table 6 is calculated from Table 5.

1830–5 and 1872–8 cover the average output for those years. 1821 has been used as the *reference* base. I have discovered no evidence which suggests 1821 was a year when the harvest rose considerably above or fell substantially below other neighbouring years.

The sources for the data utilized in the construction of Table 5 are recorded in Table 1. Figures for cotton production emanate from a single source. Output totals for 1872–8 were calculated by the application of yield coefficients to the published figures for area devoted to several crops.

The figures indicate that over the half-century from 1821 to 1879–8 Egyptian farmers made very impressive additions to the output of cotton and sugar-cane, that the production of maize grew rapidly and other crops, except rice, rose at more modest but still commendable rates of increase.

[1] B. Hansen, *Output productivity and value added productivity*, Memo. 163, National Planinng Institute (Cairo, 1962).

TABLE 7. *Indices of agricultural development*

Year	Agricultural output	Total population	Rural population	Cultivated area	Cropped area
1821	100	100	100	100	100
1830–5	164	119	118	109	—
1872–8	1,208	209	206	156	178

Notes to Table 7

The sources for the above indices are contained in Tables 3, 4, and 5. The index of agricultural output is the *weighted* index of production described in Section 1 of this part of the paper. The total population for 1830–5 was taken to be the mean of available estimates, namely three million. This is close to the only explicit estimate for the early 1830s, namely Clot's figure for 1833, which was described in Table 4 above. I took as the area *cultivated* for 1821 the area recorded as cultivated in the cadastral survey of 1813–14. All other estimates for that year I rejected as unreliable. The figures for 1830–5 and 1872–8 again represent the average of information available for those years. No figures for the cropped area exist before 1893–4. I made the assumption that the ratio of cropped area for 1872–8 was equal to the cultivated area plus the area devoted to *sayfī* or summer crops recorded in Ministère de l'Intérieur *Essai de statistique de l'Égypte* (Cairo 1879), vol. ii, t. 27. Since the cropped area expanded mainly through the introduction of summer crops like rice and cotton the assumption is plausible. I further assumed that the cropped and cultivated areas were equal in 1821. This undoubtedly understates the cropped area for that year.

TABLE 8. *Indices of agricultural development 1821 to 1872–8*

Year	*Per capita* farm output	Farm ouptut per head of the rural population	Farm output per unit of land cultivated	Farm output per unit of land cropped
1821	100	100	100	100
1830–5	138	139	150	—
1872–8	578	586	774	679

Notes to Table 8

Table 8 is calculated from the relatives cited in Table 7 simply by dividing the weighted index of agricultural production by the indices for the total population, rural population cultivated, and cropped area.

3. *The Course of Agricultural Development 1821 to 1872–8*

According to my figures between 1821 and 1872–8 the volume of Egyptian farm output increased just over twelve times, while *per capita* production rose nearly six times. If the term 'revolution' in economic history is defined as a positive and sustained acceleration in the rate of growth, then during this half-century Egypt seems to have passed through an agrarian revolution. Moreover, since agriculture so dominated the economy, a rise in *per capita* farm output of such dimensions indicates a comparable rise in the standard of living and profound changes in almost all areas of economic activity.

One possible rejoinder to this hypothesis is to maintain that the figures are just too scarce and unreliable for the measurement of economic change over the nineteenth century. Certainly the data are far from ideal, and the first part of the paper was concerned to appraise their utility, but I would argue that all the statistics used in Table 7 provide a more exact notion of the pace of agricultural and general economic development than mere description. Nor does there seem to be any qualitative evidence to suggest that the figures are positively misleading.

In fact most other quantitative series now published tend to support the case for an agrarian revolution. Thus, if we accept Bowring's estimates for the early 1820s, exports, at current prices, appear to have increased by roughly the same proportion as farm output while imports rose at approximately the same rate as *per capita* agricultural production.[1] In addition government revenue increased from £1·2 million in 1821 to an average annual sum of £9·1 millions during the seventies.[2] Unfortunately no price indices exist which would permit the conversion of these totals of exports, imports, and revenue, into real terms, but there is nothing in the somewhat random price data now published to indicate that inflation occurred over the same period.[3] But the rapid increase in trade and public revenue does not necessarily imply a corresponding increase in farm output. On the contrary the indices can theoretically move in opposite directions, but in this case such a possibility is unlikely. Egyptian society in the early nineteenth century probably operated at or near subsistence level and was, therefore, not able to support a rapid increase in the export of farm produce without either purchasing more basic foodstuffs from overseas or depressing the consumption of sections of the rural population to the point of starvation. But imports consisted for the main part of manufactured commodities and luxury foodstuffs.[4] Of course to European travellers the poverty of the *fallāhīn* appeared shocking, but even they seldom suggested that villagers suffered from starvation.[5] The steady rise in total population over the period also counters

[1] Bowring, op. cit., p. 19, and Crouchley, op. cit., Table 6.

[2] Ibid., Table 10.

[3] All references to price data, which are far from plentiful or satisfactory, are cited in n. 1, p. 164 and n. 2, p. 178.

[4] Muṣṭafā Muḥammad al-Qūnī, *Taṭawwur Miṣr al-iqtiṣādī fi'l-'aṣr al-ḥadīth* (Cairo, 1944), pp. 68–72.

[5] See, for example, J. St. John, *Egypt and Mohammed Ali* (London, 1834); H. Martineau, *Eastern life* (London, 1848); T. Boaz, *Egypt, a popular description of the land, people, produce* (London, 1850); R. Whately, *The present state of Egypt* (London, 1858); E. About, *Le fellah, souvenirs d'Égypte* (Paris, 1869); W. Adams, *The land of the Nile* (London, 1871); C. Klunzinger, *Upper Egypt* (London, 1878). These travellers' tales are a diverting and rich

the possibility that exports may have been at the expense of the already low consumption standards of the mass of the people. Furthermore, peasants at low income levels do not usually acquiesce in such a substantial rise in taxes collected by the central government. If, as the figures show, Ismāʿīl found it possible to raise eight times more revenue than the ruthless founder of his dynasty this was surely not because Muḥammad ʿAlī imposed lower real rates of taxation on the *fallāhīn* but almost certainly because the effective burden of taxation declined or at least remained stable with the rise in real *per capita* incomes. Thus the conclusion must be that the substantial additions made, between 1821 and 1872–8 to exports, imports, and public revenue rested upon and indicate a corresponding rise in farm output.

Population figures do not, however, lend very much weight to the supposition that production increased something like twelve times over fifty years. The numbers of people resident in towns apparently grew more rapidly than those who resided in rural areas.[1] The development of towns in agricultural societies depends upon the expansion of farm production and the transfer of the surplus produce to urban dwellers either as payments for services rendered to farmers or as rents to landowners who live in towns and whose expenditures support the further expansion of an urban proletariat. At stages of economic development, comparable to that attained by Egypt from 1821 to 1872–8, the growth of towns thus reflects an increase in farm output and the purchase by the rural population of the services and products of the urban labour force. In turn the expansion of urban production encouraged the further growth of farm production.

On the other hand the comparatively modest growth in total population of about 1·4 per cent. per annum does not prima facie support the argument that a 'revolutionary' expansion of production occurred between the twenties and the seventies. Unfortunately any discussion about the nineteenth-century population suffers from an almost complete lack of reliable information about birth- and death-rates, but the view that the incidence of diseases like bilharzia and amoebia, which were closely associated with the spread of irrigation canals, maintained the death-rate at a very high level seems plausible enough.[2] Investment in the irrigation system seems to have had dual effects: first it raised the supply of food and created conditions for a higher population, but at the same time the augmented volume of water spread diseases which kept

source for the social history of Egypt and for comment on the mentality of European travellers in the nineteenth century.

[1] See Table 4. The figures for urban population are not, however, at all reliable. The definition of urban changed from author to author and for some estimates I simply averaged different figures of the population resident in the major towns.

[2] W. Cleland, *The population problem of Egypt* (Lancaster, 1936) pp. 80–83, and B. Schnepp, 'Considérations sur le mouvement de la population en Égypte', *Mémoires de l'Institut Égyptien*, vol. i, 1862. I am indebted to Professor B. Lewis for drawing my attention to this point.

the death-rate high and thereby prevented the population from increasing at a rate commensurate with the rise in output. Not until the government introduced antibiotics, pesticides, and improved village sanitation during the fourth decade of the present century did the death-rate exhibit any positive tendency to decline.[1]

4. *The causes of the rapid expansion in agricultural output 1821 to 1872–8*

All available evidence appears to support the view that agricultural output increased at a very rapid rate from 1821 to 1872–8. Economic historians have already described the causes of this development in general terms but the relationships between inputs and outputs for the agricultural sector have not been investigated quantitatively.[2] A production function for Egyptian agriculture would take the familiar form of $P = f(a, n, k, \text{and } g)$, where P is total production, a is land, n is labour, k is capital, and g is fertilizer. Land must contain all land utilized to grow farm produce and when a feddan grew two crops a year it should count as two feddans. In other words the land input should be the cropped and not the cultivated area. Unfortunately no statistics for cropped area exist before 1894 and the estimate in Table 7 is based on the assumption that the cropped area for 1872–8 was equal to the cultivated area plus the area devoted to summer crops. Ideally, labour should include the number of man-hours employed in the cultivation of farm output but again no such information exists. As a very crude approximation, changes in the rural population can be used to measure changes in the input of labour time because a high degree of correlation usually exists between movements in the rural population and movements in the agricultural labour force. Investment in agriculture took a variety of forms—implements, some rudimentary machinery, animals, and working capital, but above all it consisted of irrigation facilities, such as dams, barrages, canals, and drains. Unfortunately no data exist from which a series to represent capital input, either in physical or monetary units might be constructed, but virtually no capital apart from implements and animal power was directly employed in the process of production.[3] Agricultural investment was overwhelmingly concerned to increase the supply of water available to farmers and it resulted in additions to the cropped or cultivated area. The input land, therefore, embodied capital. During this period chemical fertilizers were not employed on any scale by the *fallāḥīn* and no facts exist about the quantities of animal manure they used in cultivation.

The information published for the half-century 1821 to 1872–8 thus permits us to relate output to only two inputs: labour and land which embodied

[1] ʿAlī al-Jirītlī, *al-Sukkān wa'l-mawārid al-iqtiṣādiyya* (Cairo, 1962).

[2] See C. Issawi, *Egypt in revolution* (London, 1963); Lahīṭa, op. cit.; Crouchley, op. cit.; P. Arminjon, *La situation économique et financière de l'Égypte* (Paris, 1911); also Barāwī and ʿUlaysh, op. cit.

[3] Ibrāhīm ʿĀmir, *al-Arḍ wa'l-fallāḥ* (Cairo, 1958).

capital. Nevertheless the figures show that average returns per unit of land and per unit of labour increased very substantially over the period. Real output per worker was probably nearly six times higher in the seventies than in 1821 while output per unit of land cropped had risen by 579 per cent. The information does not allow us to estimate the relative contribution made by each factor to the addition to total product. Furthermore, to account for such a huge increase in output simply in terms of an approximate doubling of the inputs of land and labour does not seem reasonable unless we attribute the rise in output either to economies of scale and/or a considerable increase in the marginal productivity of land and labour as a result of technical progress or complementary investment outside the agricultural sector. But there is no reason to suppose that the quality of either factor rose very much over this period. The level of education and expertise among the rural labour force improved only slightly if at all, while the probable improvement in the health and energy of the *fallāḥīn* as a result of the increased intake of food was partly outweighed by the spread of debilitating diseases which accompanied investment in the irrigation system. Nor is there any reason to expect that reclaimed land or land irrigated during the season of low Nile flood was more fertile than the old inundated land. On the contrary the fertility of the soil may well have been impaired by excessive watering during summer months and the practice of multiple cropping, while yields per feddan, measured in physical units, certainly displayed no tendency to rise from 1844 to 1872–8.[1] Thus the substantial increase in average returns per unit of land and labour must be sought either in terms of the rapid expansion of other complementary inputs such as animal power and manure, or in the reallocation of the land itself to more valuable crops. Unfortunately my information on inputs is exhausted by the data on land and labour, but it does not seem plausible to attribute much of the rise in output to the application of more manure and animal power.

We can, however, measure in a rough way the effects of re-allocation. The outstanding feature of Egyptian agricultural development over this half-century is the introduction and very rapid expansion in the cultivation of cotton for sale on world markets. Table 6 shows that the production of cotton rose fifty times between 1821 and the seventies. If we suppose that Egyptian farmers were not given the opportunity to grow cotton for sale to the industrializing countries and recalculate our index on the further assumption that the land under cotton in 1872–8 could have been reallocated to grow an alternative crop, such as maize, the index then shows that the volume of agricultural production during the seventies would have been only about 206 per cent. larger than the total for 1821. Without cotton, and on the unrealistic assumption that the labour force and cropped area would have increased by

[1] This is based on a comparison of yields cited in F.O. 141/96 (which exaggerated the actual productivity of the land) and, Robino, op. cit., who obtained his data from Régny.

an equivalent amount, the rates of growth *per capita* and total agricultural output would have fallen to something like the more modest figures of 0·5 per cent. and 1·25 per cent. per annum. Egypt's agrarian revolution rested overwhelmingly upon the introduction and expansion of a single cash crop.

PART III. THE DEVELOPMENT OF AGRICULTURE 1872–8 AND 1894–9

Data for the two decades before Egypt's statistical services began to publish regular and comprehensive information about the agricultural sector remains meagre. Figures exist for cotton and sugar-cane production, the cultivated area, and yields per feddan on state domains related to wheat, beans, and barley.[1]

TABLE 9. *Indices of the Development of Agriculture 1872–8 to 1895–9*

Year	Total output	Total population	Cultivated area	Cropped area	*Per capita* output	Output per unit of cropped land	Output per unit of cultivated land	Cropped area *per capita*
1872–8	100	100	100	100	100	100	100	100
1895–9	186	165	104	116	113	160	178	70

Notes to Table 9

The Output Index has been calculated from the data for 1872–8 cited under Tables 1 and 7 and for 1895–9 described in Part II, section 1 of this paper. The weights used were those employed for the index for 1895–9 to 1962. This index is, therefore, a base-weighted index of the form $\sum q^n qp^t / \sum q^o qp^t$ where qp^t is the average gross output in value terms for 1913 to 1962.

Total Population. No census of population was taken until 1882 and that census is regarded as unreliable. A further census was conducted for 1897. The figures used are from the *Annuaire statistique* (1920).

Cultivated Area is cited in Government of Egypt, *Statistical returns 1881–97* (Cairo, 1898), p. 21 and *al-Muqtaṭaf*, vol. xiii, no. 4, p. 253. It is land subject to land-tax.

Cropped Area has been estimated on the assumption that it was equivalent to cultivated area plus land devoted to cotton. Official estimates for the cropped area are available from 1893–4 and they reveal that the assumption provides us with a reasonably accurate indication for earlier years. The cotton area is cited by Crouchley, op. cit., t. 5b.

Compared with the previous half-century the data presented above suggests that this period was one of steady but much less spectacular advance. Output grew at the annual average rate of 3½ per cent. compared to a very

[1] Cotton production figures are published in *Annuaire statistique* (1910); sugar production in Lahīṭa, op. cit., p. 438, and Mazuel, op. cit., p. 61. For cultivated area see Table 9 and the yields for wheat, beans, and barley are in *Monthly return* (1913).

much faster rate of increase for the years between 1821 and 1872–8. Understandably the slackening rate of growth provoked no apparent anxiety among Egypt's rulers because in absolute terms output continued to rise and they probably expected production to grow at a diminished rate when cotton became established as the major crop cultivated by Egyptian farmers, and as the confines of the rotation system rendered it progressively more difficult to reallocate further land to cotton. Moreover, the output of cotton regarded by the government as *the* indicator of economic progress, still more than doubled over these two decades.[1]

Yet signs of the crisis which afflicted Egyptian agriculture during the following century were already in evidence. While demographic statistics for this period are by no means accurate, all the published estimates do point to a definite quickening in the natural rate of increase, which culminated in the population explosion of the twentieth century.[2] *Per capita* farm output rose only slightly during the closing decades of the last century and since the economy continued to depend to an overwhelming degree upon agriculture, this trend probably reflects the movement in *per capita* real income as a whole. Furthermore, if we assume that the agricultural labour force increased at the same rate as the population, it seems likely that marginal product per man employed in agriculture may have fallen. The small increment to average output per head (per worker) suggests that diminishing marginal returns to labour probably set in sometime during these two decades. Moreover, according to the *Annuaire statistique* the urban population grew by nearly 60 per cent. between the census years 1882 and 1897 which implies that the rate of internal migration was too slow to offset the declining growth of output per worker in agriculture.

In general terms, an explanation for the slower pace of development during the closing decades of the nineteenth century is not difficult to find. An agrarian revolution, precipitated by the introduction and spread of cotton, had occurred during the half-century from 1821 to 1872–8 but over time possibilities for the allocation of more land to cotton naturally diminished and thereby decreased the overall rate of growth of farm output. Production might however have grown somewhat more rapidly if further supplies of land had been made available to Egyptian farmers or if yields per feddan had increased more substantially. Investment in the irrigation system during this period did not occur on a scale sufficient to add more than 4 per cent. to the cultivated area and perhaps 16 per cent. to the cropped area. From 1821 to 1872–8 the input of land available to Egyptian cultivators had grown at a rate of about 1·25 per cent. per annum but during this period it had grown by only 0·75 per cent. a year. Throughout the nineteenth century the amount of land per

[1] *Reports on the finances, administration and condition of Egypt* (British Parliamentary Papers 1876 to 1894–5 *passim*).

[2] See Table 4 and *Annuaire statistique* (1920).

unit of labour employed in agriculture fell steadily but from the seventies on the rate of decline proceeded more rapidly. By the end of the century the cropped area per cultivator was probably something like one third less than it had been three decades earlier. In the absence of economies of scale, the law of diminishing returns leads us to anticipate decreasing returns to any factor the input of which increases at a faster rate than other factors, and also the obverse: increasing returns to the factors increasing more slowly in supply. Indeed, the deterioration in the ratio of land to labour during this period was accompanied by a considerable addition to average product per unit of land, both cropped and cultivated, and a much slower rise in the average product per input of labour. As the evidence for wheat, beans, barley, and cotton shows, physical yields per feddan began to rise.[1] Give the relative scarcity of land and the limited possibilities for the reallocation of farmland the *fallāḥīn* turned to more intensive and scientific cultivation.

PART IV. THE DEVELOPMENT OF AGRICULTURE 1895 TO 1962

1. *The course of agricultural development, 1895 to 1962*

For the sixty-seven years from 1895 to 1962 quantitative data is much more comprehensive and accessible and several indices of agricultural output, official and private, have been constructed designed to measure the course of change from 1913.[2] They often include a wider range of products than the eight field crops contained in my index. I preferred, however, to use a single index throughout this paper in order to facilitate comparisons with the years before 1913 and also to avoid certain disadvantages associated with base weighting which are often built into other indices. Moreover, the broad trends measured by alternative index numbers are certainly revealed by my index and it is in any case sufficiently comprehensive to cover never less than 63 per cent. of gross agricultural output for any year since 1913.

The following tables summarize the data on production and selected inputs for the agricultural sector over this period.

Table 10 and the graph show that the trend of agricultural production continued upward throughout the twentieth century but at a much slower rate than during the nineteenth century. Nevertheless, for a fairly developed agricultural sector to achieve an average compound growth rate of 1·2 per

[1] See Table 2 and n. 1, p. 169.

[2] M. El-Darwish, *Index numbers of agricultural production, 1913–29* (Cairo, 1932). Darwish's index covers eight crops and is a base-weighted index, weighted by average values for 1913–14. C. Issawi, 'Agricultural production index', *L'Égypte contemporaine* (Apr. 1942). Issawi's index is a base-weighted index covering 14 main crops. The Department of Statistics and Census publishes an index of the volume of agricultural output which includes nearly all agricultural production. It is a base-weighted index with average values for the period 1935–9 used as weights. The National Bank of Egypt also publishes a volume index with a fairly comprehensive coverage weighted by average total value of each crop 1946–50. This index is described in *Economic bulletin of the National Bank of Egypt*, 4 (1957).

TABLE 10. *Indices of Agricultural Growth, 1895–9 to 1960–2*

Years	Total output	Total population	Rural population	Agricultural working force	Cropped area	Cultivated area	Input of chemical fertilizers
1895–9	100	100	100	100	100	100	
1900–4	110	108	108	108	109	108	
1905–9	116	116	117	118	113	109	
1910–14	121	124	125	126	114	107	
1915–19	103	132	131	136	115	107	100
1920–4	113	140	138	153	120	107	144
1925–9	133	147	143	169	127	113	387
1930–4	135	156	150	186	126	111	474
1935–9	153	166	156	207	123	107	910
1940–4	131	177	162	205	133	108	397
1945–9	140	197	173	204	136	116	600
1950–4	150	222	188	206	140	115	1,246
1955–9	184	250	208	209	151	118	1,528
1960–2	204	271	213	212	152	119	—

Notes to Table 10

Total Output is the weighted index of eight crops described in Part II, section 1 of this paper.

Total and Rural Population figures are published in the *Annuaire statistique* and *Statistical pocket yearbooks*.

The definition of 'rural' is by no means unambiguous but the series is adequate for my purposes.

The Agricultural Working Force is the figures published in the *Censuses of population* for 1897, 1907, 1917, 1927, 1937, 1947, and 1960. The Inter-census figures have been estimated on the assumption that the agricultural labour force grew at a constant annual rate.

Cropped and Cultivated Areas are the figures published by the *Annuaire statistique.*

The index for fertilizer input has been copied from M. El-Imam, *A production function for Egyptian agriculture*, Memo. 259, National Planning Institute (Cairo, 1962). It has been brought up to date from the figures in Central Statistical Committee, *Basic statistics* (Cairo, 1962), p. 78. I could trace no figures for fertilizer input for the years before 1913. Fertilizers mean chemical fertilizers only, and exclude natural manures.

cent. per annum is a commendable achievement, particularly as output fell sharply during both World Wars when Egyptian farmers were cut off from essential imports of fertilizers, farm implements, and irrigation machinery. Recovery from the effects of the Second World War was even more protracted than recovery from the First, for it was not until the fifties that output attained the level of 1935–9. The growth of agricultural production appears to have accelerated since the Revolution and between 1950–4 and 1960–2 grew more rapidly than at any other comparable period this century, but it should be noted that the trend of production was upward even before 1952. Since then agricultural output has simply continued to rise but at a slightly faster rate.

On the other hand, the trend *per capita* farm income which moved steadily downwards often gives rise to descriptions of recent Egyptian economic history in Malthusian terms.[1] But such a trend may not be unfortunate, provided alternative opportunities for production and employment are created outside agriculture on a scale at least sufficient to compensate for the lack of advance in the primary sector. By 1960–2 farm output per person had fallen to 24 per cent. below the level attained in 1895–9 which implies that the rest

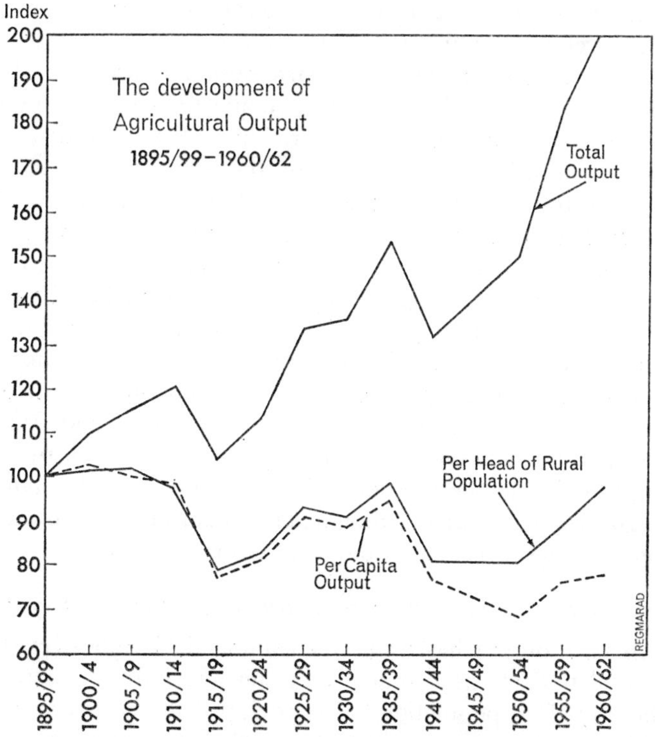

of the economy needed to expand at an annual average compound rate of about 0·5 per cent. in order to maintain *per capita* real income at the 1895–9 level. *A fortiori* to raise the standard of living required even higher rates of growth in industry and services, but there is every indication that these sectors have developed rapidly enough to raise average real incomes. These figures lend no support to the gloomy view that real income per person in Egypt is lower today than before the First World War.[2] It is, however, interesting to reflect that if the population had remained at the level of 1900 the Egyptian

[1] H. Riad, *L'Égypte Nassérienne* (Paris, 1964), ch. ii, and F. Harbison and I. Ibrahim, *Human resources for Egyptian enterprise* (New York, 1958), pp. 14–19.

[2] A. Mahhouk, 'Trends in Egypt's national income, 1913–1956', *Middle East Economic Papers* (1962), and A. El Sherbini and A. Sherif, 'Marketing problems in an underdeveloped country', *L'Égypte contemporaine* (July 1956).

standard of living could possibly have doubled during the present century, but we can hopefully observe that since 1950–4 *per capita* agricultural output has, in fact, risen slightly and is now approaching the level of 1915–19.

The figures certainly support the case for rapid industrialization. Moreover, since the trend also represents a decline in the *per capita* output of foodstuffs it indicates that Egypt has obviously become less and less self-sufficient in food and must export a rising amount of cash crops and manufactured commodities in order to maintain average consumption at a constant level. To raise the level will require even more exports.

Finally the relatively slow growth of farm output compared with the rapid rate of increase in population immediately affected the mass of Egyptians whose livelihood depended directly on agriculture. Farm output is not equivalent to real income which also depends on the terms of trade between agriculture and the rest of the economy, but as farm prices have not increased more rapidly than other prices, trends in the output provide a reasonable indication of changes in the standards of consumption of those who live from the land.[1] Moreover the national accounts indicate that since the First World War at least, the share of the national income received by the farming community has declined more rapidly than the size of that community.[2] Output per head of the rural population has remained consistently but not appreciably below the level of 1895–1904 but fell sharply in both World Wars. Since 1950–4 it has, however, risen rapidly and is now back roughly to the level of 1935–9. Under the present régime not only have the *fallāḥīn* benefited from government measures designed to redistribute agricultural income, but the figures suggest that the real output has risen as well.

2. *The causes of the decline in* per capita *farm output from 1895–9 to 1960–2*

Although farm output has risen at a commendable rate over the present century, population has risen at an even faster rate and the question arises as to why the growth of population has outstripped the growth of production. This paper is not, however, concerned with the population side of the ratio, but will suggest some of the reasons why farm output failed to increase more rapidly.

The elements of a production function for agriculture became much more complex during the present century because local cultivators began to utilize new inputs, such as fertilizers, selected seeds, machinery, modern implements and improved systems of drainage and crop rotations, on a far greater scale.[3] Data on the entire range of inputs employed in agriculture apart from land,

[1] U.N.O., *The development of manufacturing industry in Egypt, Israel and Turkey* (New York, 1958), t. x; A. El Tanamli, 'Évaluation de l'économie rurale Égyptienne', *L'Égypte contemporaine* (Oct. 1960), Appendix 3, and *Annuaire statistique*.

[2] See n. 1, p. 164 and P. O'Brien, 'Industrial development and the employment problem in Egypt', *Middle East Economic Papers* (1962).

[3] Azmi, op. cit.

labour, and fertilizers are scarce and a complete analysis of the process of transforming farm inputs into output is probably not possible at the macro level.[1] Instead Table 11 merely points out some of the more general but salient factors involved in the process.

TABLE 11. *Indices of Agricultural Development, 1895–9 to 1960–2*

Years	Output per worker in agriculture	Output per unit of land	Output per unit of fertilizer	Land-labour ratio in agriculture	The ratio of cropped to cultivated land
1895–9	100	100		100	100
1900–4	102	101		101	101
1905–9	98	103		96	104
1910–14	96	106		90	106
1915–19	76	90	100	85	107
1920–4	74	94	76	78	112
1925–9	79	105	33	75	112
1930–4	73	107	28	68	114
1935–9	74	124	16	59	115
1940–4	64	98	32	65	123
1945–9	69	103	23	66	117
1950–4	73	107	24	68	122
1955–9	88	122	14	72	128
1960–2	95	134	13	72	128

Notes to Table 11

These indices have been calculated from the information contained in Table 10.

The first point to observe is the almost continuous decline in the average output per worker employed in agriculture. This ratio reflects the rapid growth of rural population and, in the absence of a shift to more labour intensive crops and techniques of cultivation, the emergence of underemployment in the countryside. In other words, the tasks of producing a given output were shared among a greater number of people and some labour could have been removed without any loss of production. Output per worker fell because the input of labour increased much more rapidly than other factors of production, particularly land. Thus, apart from periods of war and its aftermath, the average product per unit of land rose steadily and in 1960–2 was 34 per cent. above the level of 1895–1900 whereas the average product of labour had fallen to 5 per cent. below the level reached during the base period.

One by no means unimportant reason for the fall in the average productivity of labour is that not until the fifties did the government make serious efforts to raise the health, nutritional, and educational standards of the rural population.[2] Such investment will, in time, undoubtedly yield returns in the

[1] See, however, A. El Imam, *A production function for Egyptian agriculture*, Memo. 259, National Planning Institute (Cairo, 1962).

[2] See my book, *The revolution in Egypt's economic system* (London, 1966), ch. 2.

form of higher output per man employed in agriculture. But the fundamental reason for the decline in farm output *per capita* and per worker is the persistent downward trend in the ratio of land to labour. Looked at in absolute terms the efforts of the government resulted in a 52 per cent. addition to the cropped area since 1895–9 and over the present century almost the whole of Egyptian farmland became perennially irrigated and the ratio of cropped to cultivated area rose by 28 per cent. to reach a level where, according to some agronomists, it began to impair the fertility of the soil.[1] But Table 11 shows that the amount of land per cultivator in 1960–2 was 28 per cent. lower than the amount available to his forebears at the beginning of the century. Over the past 90 years public investment in the irrigation system has resulted in the expansion of the cropped area at the average compound rate of approximately 0·72 per cent. per annum. The annual rate of expansion of farmland showed no tendency to rise during the twentieth century compared with last century when the pressure of population on the land was less strong. No doubt the capital required to add one more unit to the cropped or cultivated areas increased over time, when all the more obvious and profitable irrigation projects became completed, but the fact remains that public and private investment, particularly in the field of land reclamation, was just not sufficient to obviate a persistent decline in the land–labour ratio. From 1935–9 the ratio has, however, risen again; probably as a result of the migration of rural labour to towns as well as increased government investment in irrigation facilities. When the High Dam becomes operational, the amount of land available per cultivator is expected to rise sharply and the land–labour ratio may rise to a level not witnessed in Egypt since last century.[2]

As a reaction to the shortage of land Egyptian farmers naturally attempted to raise yields per unit of the scarce factor. Their efforts took two forms. First they attempted to reallocate land to more valuable products such as cotton, rice, sugar-cane, fruit, and dairy produce. The output of these products certainly expanded faster than the output of more traditional grain crops like wheat, maize, beans, and barley. However, it may well be that the conservatism of farmers and landowners prevented the adoption of the new crops at anything like the optimal rate. Critics of Egyptian farmers on this score should however bear in mind that with a given technology and factor endowment the real possibilities for the reallocation of land were much more limited than they were in the nineteenth century when a presumably more traditional body of peasants were able to adapt very quickly to world demand for cotton.

Next the *fallāḥīn* attempted to raise the physical yields per feddan through the application of chemical fertilizers, the employment of more scientific techniques of cultivation and to a more limited degree by mechanization. Only

[1] S. Saffa, 'L'exploitation économiqe et agricole d'un domaine rural Égyptienne', *L'Égypte contemporaine* (July 1949).

[2] Lajnat al-Takhṭīṭ al-Qawmī, *Mashrūʿ al-Sadd al-ʿālī* (memo. 26, Cairo, 1958).

data on chemical fertilizers lend themselves to direct comparison with the output index. Table 11 shows that the application of phosphates and nitrogen to Egyptian farmland increased so rapidly over the present century that the average product per unit of fertilizer input fell by 87 per cent. between 1915–19 and 1960–2, and at the present time it looks as if Egyptian agriculture is close to the point of negative returns as far as the further application of fertilizer is concerned. The increased output of fertilizers and the adaptation of other new techniques has, however, resulted in additions to the yields per feddan of several major crops since 1913. Tanamli's figures indicate that the average yield of cotton increased by 21 per cent. between 1913–19 and 1950–4, rice by 17 per cent., wheat by 14 per cent., and sugar by 13 per cent. On the other hand the yields per feddan for maize, beans, lentils, and onions failed to exhibit any increase at all.[1] But overall the increase in yields per feddan does not seem impressive and it stands as an important part of the explanation for the decline in *per capita* farm output. Responsibility rests to some extent with the lack of enterprise displayed by conservative Egyptian farmers and landowners and partly with the quality of land at their disposal. As sub-marginal land was brought into cultivation and as the ratio of the cropped to cultivated area increased, the fertility of the soil declined and it became progressively more difficult for Egyptian farmers to maintain average yields. Thus a part of the massive application of fertilizers reflects their attempt to preserve the fertility of land subject to multiple cropping and the deleterious effects of too much water.

CONCLUSION. THE DEVELOPMENT OF EGYPTIAN AGRICULTURE: THE LONG VIEW

My conclusions must be prefaced by the now all too familiar warning about the quality and quantity of the data for the period before 1895. I have, however, argued throughout the paper that statistics do not seem to be either unuseable or of a quality low enough to produce misleading results.

Over the long run from 1821 to 1962 the volume of Egyptian agricultural output appears to have increased continuously year by year to attain a level approximately sixteen times that of the base period. The half-century from 1821 and 1872–8 was one of quite exceptional growth which warrants the appellation of agrarian revolution. Thereafter output increased at a much more modest and steady rate. At the same time the population rose from about 2½ millions in 1821 to the present total of 26 millions. Despite such a huge addition to the numbers of Egyptians, the increase in agricultural output has been sufficient to raise farm output *per capita* nearly five times during the same period. Very impressive additions to *per capita* product were achieved over the nineteenth century but the years since 1900 have witnessed an almost

[1] Tanamli, *L'Égypte contemporaine* (Oct. 1960).

uninterrupted decline in agricultural output per head which seems, however, to have been more than offset by the increased production in other sectors of the economy, particularly in industry.

The main factors behind the progress of Egyptian agriculture have been the large-scale investment by the state which tripled the supply of land, and a sevenfold increase in the labour supply which was both the result and condition for the expansion of farm output. But all the efforts made by the government in the creation of dams, barrages, canals, and drains have at no point over the past 140 years succeeded in augmenting the land–labour ratio. The amount of land (cropped area) per cultivator in 1960–2 was probably something like 50 per cent. less than in 1821.

Thus most of the long-run expansion of agricultural output depended upon the expansion of average yields per unit of land. Between 1844 and 1960–2 the yields per feddan of cotton, wheat, lentils, and rice rose approximately three times, barley about twice, sugar nearly four times, and maize by 40 per cent. But, to an overwhelming extent, the increase in Egyptian agricultural output has rested upon the reallocation of land to more valuable crops for sale on world markets. In the absence of international demand for rice, fruit, vegetables and, above all, cotton, the long-run development of Egyptian agriculture would hardly excite comment.

Yet from the perspective of the present day, the Egyptian government and some academic commentators upon Egyptian economic development, are inclined to decry such 'lop-sided development' and regret the failure of Muḥammad 'Alī's experiment to inaugurate an industrial revolution over a century ago.[1] Quite apart from the question of whether, given Egypt's resource endowment at that time, Muḥammad 'Alī could have succeeded in his attempt to build up modern industry, it is still difficult to see what alternative pattern of economic growth could have raised *per capita* output at anything like the same rate as that achieved by the concentration on cotton. Furthermore, the 'spillover effects' from the development of agriculture were enormous. Harbours, railways, roads, trade, and storage facilities, financial institutions; the whole complex edifice of a modern infra-structure was built up to serve agriculture. Industry certainly did not grow, and given present needs and efforts to industrialize it may *now* seem unfortunate that at least the foundations of a modern manufacturing sector were not laid earlier. On the other hand Egypt's long-run comparative advantage for most of the nineteenth century seemed to remain very clearly with agriculture, unless of course one defines the long run as a perspective of over fifty years' duration. The modern case for industrialization rests upon diminishing returns to labour in agriculture which emerged as a result of the population explosion of the

[1] C. Issawi, 'Egypt since 1800: a study in lop-sided development', *Journal of Economic History* (Mar., 1961); F. Jirjis, *Dirāsa fī t'arīkh Miṣr* (Cairo, 1958), pp. 112–16, and A. Abdel-Malek, *Égypte: société militaire* (Paris, 1962), pp. 17–23.

twentieth century. This did not become obvious until the thirties, and from that point on the state afforded private industry every encouragement to expand. To criticize those in charge of Egypt's economy for their failure to diversify production at a much earlier period seems to be an unwarranted indulgence in hindsight.

The Jews in Nineteenth-century Egypt
Some Socio-economic Aspects

JACOB M. LANDAU

Introduction

It appears that one of the most neglected areas in research on modern Egypt is its Jewish community. While Egypt's Copts, Italians, and Greeks have been the subject of fairly extensive research,[1] its Jews have been considered in only one monograph[2] and a number of articles, some of them of general interest only. There are two explanations for this vacuum.

First, historiography on modern Egypt has for some time concentrated on the political and literary aspects:[3] only in very recent years have substantial studies treated the socio-economic history of Egypt. Throughout the nineteenth century, Egyptian Jews had a totally insignificant share in Egypt's political life. They seem to have preferred their isolation and shunned politics almost intentionally. For all practical purposes, their influence in Egyptian politics was nil, probably owing to their small number and to the inability of the wealthy few to turn their financial standing into a political asset even in the rare instances where the wealthy did have connexions with some political group. James Sanua, the only Jew to play an important role in the nationalist propaganda, during the last quarter of the nineteenth century,[4] was an exceptional case, and his political activity, anyway, had little if anything to do with his Jewishness, which he mentions but rarely in his extensive writings.

Secondly, the scarcity and non-availability of the materials relating to Egypt's Jews in the nineteenth century is such as to discourage many scholars, whether investigating modern Egypt or the Jewish communities in the Middle East.[5] Nevertheless, it seems that a preliminary report on some socio-

[1] Edward Wakin, *A lonely minority: the modern story of Egypt's Copts* (New York, 1963); L. A. Balboni, *Gl'Italiani nella civilità egiziana del secolo XIX°* (Alexandria, 1906); A. G. Politis, *L'Hellénisme et l'Égypte moderne* (2 vols., Paris, 1928–30); and other works.

[2] Maurice Fargeon, *Les Juifs en Égypte depuis les origines jusqu'à ce jour* (Cairo, 1938). This is a valuable work, but—as its title also implies—surveys a very long span of time.

[3] In this, some of the blame attaches to me, too, as evidenced by my *Parliaments and parties in Egypt* (Tel-Aviv, 1953; New York, 1954) and *Studies in the Arab theater and cinema* (Philadelphia, 1958): French revised translation, *Études sur le théâtre et le cinéma arabes* (Paris, 1965).

[4] See *Abū Naḍḍāra*, in *EI*², s.v.; and my *Abū Naḍḍāra: an Egyptian Jewish Nationalist*, in *The Journal of Jewish Studies*, vol. iii. 1 (1952), pp. 30–44, and vol. v. 4 (1954), pp. 179–80. A more recent study is I. L. Gendzier, *The practical visions of Ya'qub Sanu'* (Cambridge, Mass., 1966).

[5] Painstaking research on these communities is being carried out at the Ben-Zvi Institute, Hebrew University, Jerusalem, directed by Dr. M. Benayahu. Very little of this, however, deals with the Jews in modern Egypt.

economic aspects of Egypt's Jews can be presented, based on reported materials in the archives of the Cairo Jewish community (which however contain but very few documents of the nineteenth century);[1] the archives of the British, French, and Italian Foreign Offices; and on those of the Alliance Israélite Universelle, the Jewish philanthropic–educational society in Paris, which was actively interested in assisting Oriental Jews since its foundation (1860). When these archival materials are combined with the extremely rare references in Arabic sources, and the rather scanty information scattered in memoirs, travel-accounts, and the press, there emerges a not uninteresting picture of Jewish socio-economic activities in nineteenth-century Egypt. For the purpose of this paper, the nineteenth century ends in Egypt with the First World War, which was to be followed by many profound changes in Egypt affecting also its Jewish community.

Statistics

It has been asserted above that the Jewish community in nineteenth-century Egypt was small in numbers. Actually, for most of that century, nearly up to its very end, we have no reliable figures for the size and division of the Jewish community, in much the same way that we have very few exact demographic data for Egypt at the time. Reports of observers and travellers, not all of them trustworthy, are perforce a main source for these data.

In the 1830s Edward William Lane estimated the number of Jews in Egypt at some 5,000 out of a population of two million, approximately.[2] A few years later, about 1840, Clot-Bey[3] gave their number as 7,000. The difference between the data may have been caused by the 1,200 Karaites whom Clot included in his estimate;[4] alternatively, it is possibly a sign of rise in numbers, more obvious later. In the beginning of the second half of the nineteenth century, the Jewish traveller Yaʿaqōv Sappīr[5] calculated their number at 6,000–7,000. At the same time, the Roumanian Jewish traveller, Benjamin[6] estimated the Jews of Cairo and Alexandria—almost the whole Jewish community in Egypt—at 1,500 families, that is, more or less like Sappīr. A French tourist, Gellion-Danglar,[7] in a letter from Egypt dated September 1867, estimated that the Jews numbered between 7,000 and 8,000 people.

[1] As reported by I. Ben Zĕ'ev, *Arkhiyyōn ha-qĕhilla ha-yĕhūdīt be-Qahīr*, in *World congress of Jewish studies (summer 1947)*, vol. i (Jerusalem, 1952), pp. 435–8; and idem, *ha-Tĕʿūdōt ha-ʿivriyyōt she-bĕginzey ha-qĕhilla ha-yĕhūdīt be-Qahīr*, in *Sĕfūnōt*, vol. ix (1964), pp. 265 ff.

[2] E. W. Lane, *An account of the manners and customs of the modern Egyptians* (Everyman edn.), pp. 23, 558. Cf. also Fargeon, op. cit., pp. 157, 305.

[3] A.-B. Clot-Bey, *Aperçu général sur l'Égypte* (Paris, 1840), vol. i, p. 243.

[4] Ibid. Later, the number of Karaites rose, and around the year 1877 it reached about 2,000—cf. J. C. McCoan, *Egypt as it is* (London, 1877), p. 35.

[5] Quoted by Fargeon, op. cit., pp. 167–8, 305.

[6] J. J. Benjamin, *Acht Jahre in Asien und Afrika von 1846 bis 1855* (2nd edn., Hanover, 1858), pp. 222–5.

[7] E. Gellion-Danglar, *Lettres sur l'Égypte* (Paris, 1876), p. 69, letter 4.

A Jewish traveller, Deynard,[1] who visited Egypt in the years 1881–2, estimated them at 50,000, while a German writer, Vogt,[2] thought at about the same time that the figure was nearer to 30,000. The latter would seem closer to reality, as it is given, also, by other visitors to Egypt, Neumann[3] in 1892 and von Fircks[4] two years later, and, more significantly, partly corroborated by the census at the end of the nineteenth century.

The population census of 1882, the first in Egypt which was relatively systematic, did not allow for a count by religions, so that the earliest methodical data for the size of the Jewish community in Egypt are from 1897: the population census of that year counted 25,200 Jews, out of a total population in Egypt of 9,734,137. This is a considerable growth, compared to the 7,000–8,000 Jews who lived in the country around the middle of the century. This upward trend continued in the Jewish community, which grew to 38,635 in the year 1907, and to 59,581 in the year 1917.[5] This increase is remarkable percentage-wise, too: the Jewish community in Egypt grew from 1897 to 1907 by 53·3 per cent., and from 1907 to 1917 by 54·2 per cent., by far more than any other denominational group in Egypt, during that period.

Growing urbanization

The growth of the Jewish community in Egypt was mainly due to immigration, both as a part of the influx to Egypt of newcomers, taking advantage of favourable economic and financial conditions, and as a partial answer to refuge-seeking Jews, fleeing persecution in eastern Europe.

Most of the Jewish immigrants settled in the cities, chiefly Alexandria and Cairo, thus adding new force to the process of urbanization (which in this context means, mainly, concentration in the cities); this process was evident in the Jewish community in Egypt throughout the nineteenth century. Lane[6] had already noted that a majority of Egyptian Jews, some 3,000–4,000, lived in Cairo; this was reiterated by Clot.[7] Various travellers, a few years later, estimated the number of Cairene Jews at 3,000, too.[8] Alexandria, which appa-

[1] Efrayim Deynard, *Massa' lĕ-ereṣ ha-qedem* (Pressburg, 1882), p. 22.

[2] Hermann Vogt, *Die kriegerischen Ereignisse in Ägypten während des Sommers 1882* (Leipzig, 1882), p. 30.

[3] Theodor Neumann, *Das moderne Ägypten mit besonderen Rücksicht auf Handel und Volkswirtschaft* (Leipzig, 1893), p. 34.

[4] A. R. G. H. T. von Fircks, *Aegypten 1894. Staatsrechtliche Verhältnisse, wirtschaftlicher Zustand, Verwaltung* (Berlin, 1895–6), vol. i, p. 180.

[5] In addition to the official reports of the censuses, see L. Mboria, *La Population de l'Égypte* (Cairo, 1938), p. 125, table 39; *L'Égypte aperçu historique et géographique, gouvernement et institutions, vie économique et sociale* (Cairo, 1926), p. 373; Jewish Agency for Palestine—Economic Research Institute, *Statistical handbook of Middle Eastern countries* (Jerusalem, 1944), p. 54, table 3.

[6] Op. cit., pp. 23–24.

[7] Op. cit., vol. i, p. 243.

[8] John Gadsby, *My wanderings being travels in the East* (London, 1860), p. 211—refers to the year 1847, approximately; *Journal of a deputation sent to the East by the committee of the Malta Protestant college in 1849: by a lay member of the committee* (London, 1854), vol. i, p. 10—refers to 1849.

rently was the home of only a few hundred Jews at the beginning of the nineteenth century,[1] had about 1,200 in the year 1847[2] and 2,000 a few years later.[3] Hence, the estimate of Samuel,[4] in 1880, who thought Cairo's Jews numbered but 3,000, is too low, just as Deynard's appears inaccurate, too, when, in 1880–1, he estimated their number at 15,000, and an equal number for Alexandria.[5] More accurate is the evaluation of Borg, the British consul in Cairo, who out of his long-standing knowledge of that city, estimated their number at 7,000–8,000 in the year 1890.[6] This is corroborated by the data of the official censuses of 1897 and 1907:[7]

Jewish population in Egypt, by settlements, 1897–1907

Locality	1897	1907
Cairo	8,819	20,281
Alexandria	9,831	14,475
Ṭanṭā	883	1,104
Manṣūra	508	522
Port Said	400	378
Suez	120	74
Ismailia	39	11
Other	4,600	1,790
Total	25,200	38,635

From all the above data, one may deduce that not only did the Jews of Egypt concentrate in the cities and towns, but also that this preference was on an upward trend. The process of urbanization was mostly marked at the end of the nineteenth century and the beginning of the twentieth, concurrently with similar trends among the non-Jews in Egypt; it particularly applied to Cairo and Alexandria:[8]

[1] Noury Farhi, *La Communauté juive d'Alexandrie* (Alexandria, 1946), p. 20. *Encyclopaedia Judaica*, s.v. *Alexandrien*, estimates their number at even less.

[2] 'The history and state of the Jews in Alexandria', reported in *The Jewish Chronicle* (London), 10 Aug. 1849, pp. 350–1.

[3] Sappīr, op. cit. (Lyck, 1866), p. 3, *recto*.

[4] S. M. Samuel, *Jewish life in the East* (London, 1881), p. 6.

[5] Deynard, op. cit., pp. 14, 17.

[6] Public Record Office in London, Foreign Office (further: F.O.) 78/4310, R. Borg's no. 15 to Baring, dated Cairo, 24 June 1890, encl. in Baring's no. 207 to Salisbury, dated Cairo, 25 June 1890.

[7] Ministry of Finance, Egypt, *The census of Egypt taken in 1907 under the direction of C. C. Lowis* (Cairo, 1909), pp. 118–19; Jewish Agency for Palestine, op. cit., p. 54, table 3; E. A. Wallis Budge, *Cook's handbook for Egypt and the Sudan* (2nd edn., London, 1906), p. 73; Fargeon, op. cit., pp. 306–8; George Steindorff, *Ägypten in Vergangenheit und Gegenwart* (Berlin 1915), pp. 211–12.

[8] Sources in n. 7 above, and the official results of the 1917 census. The figures in N. Leven, *Cinquante ans d'histoire: l'Alliance Israélite Universelle (1860–1910)* (Paris, 1911–20), vol. ii, p. 127, are actually lower than the census results.

Jews in Cairo and Alexandria, as compared to their total number in Egypt, 1897–1917

	1897	1907	1917
Cairo	8,819	20,281	29,207
Alexandria	9,831	14,475	24,858
Total in Cairo and Alexandria	18,650	34,756	54,065
Number of Jews in Egypt	25,200	38,635	59,581
Percentage	74·01	89·96	90·74

The influx of Jews to the main Egyptian cities, number-wise and percentage-wise, was coupled with a very marked abandonment of the smaller towns and villages.[1] From the statistical data listed above, one sees that Jewish numbers were reduced in Port Said, Suez, and Ismailia—the gainers being, very probably, Cairo and Alexandria. When the chief rabbi of Egypt, Elī Ḥazzan, travelled in Upper Egypt during the year 1908 he found but few Jews in the smaller towns, while in the villages he found only several Jewish families, scattered here and there: five families in Aswān, two in Luxor, etc.[2] These figures are corroborated by the official censuses. The exodus towards Cairo and Alexandria was apparently not caused by insecurity or persecution, for under British rule life and property were well protected (there were only isolated cases of anti-Jewish violence). The main reason appears to be, in addition to the attractions of city-life (which affected non-Jews, also), the occupational characteristics of Egyptian Jews at the time, which induced many of them to move to the cities. This applies, in a great measure, to many Jewish immigrants, who came to settle in Egypt at the end of the nineteenth century and early in the twentieth: many of these remained in their port of entry—Alexandria—a feature common to immigrants everywhere, particularly to those who have no prearranged source of livelihood elsewhere.

Occupational trends

The information concerning the occupations of the Jews in Egypt during the nineteenth and early twentieth centuries is not always reliable, for most sources were naturally apt to mention, if at all, only the occupations of those Jews with whom they came into contact—which was not necessarily a representative cross-section.

Nevertheless, one feels that S. M. Samuel, after touring Egypt during 1879, came close to the truth, when he wrote that 'a Jewish servant, or labourer, is almost unknown in Egypt, our people here, as elsewhere, being infected with that dislike for manual labour and that preference for earning their living with

[1] Details in Fargeon, op. cit., *passim*.

[2] Information supplied by the chief rabbi's secretary, to B. Tarragan, who published it in the periodical *ha-Hashqafa* and reprinted it in his book *lĕ-Qōrōt ha-qĕhilla ha-yĕhūdīt bĕ-Aleksandriyya bĕ-arbaʿīm ha-shanīm ha-aḥarōnōt* (Alexandria, 1947), pp. 24–26.

their heads, rather than with their hands . . .'.[1] Although rather a sweeping statement, Samuel's impression is not inaccurate.

During most of the nineteenth century, Jews were known in Egypt as businessmen, money-changers, money-lenders, and pawnbrokers. This description, in full or in part, is oft-repeated. Actually, it is not wholly correct: while Jews did make a living by exchanging money or lending it, most of this was on a small scale, since very few Jews in Egypt, until the end of the nineteenth century, possessed the necessary funds for larger transactions. This, incidentally, did not impede a general belief in Jewish wealth from spreading in Egypt. As a matter of fact, E. W. Lane, in describing Egypt's Jews in the early 1830s, was much closer than others to the mark. He maintained[2] that many of them were poor, living on public charity, while a number of others were money-lenders, money-changers, goldsmiths, silversmiths, retail grocers, or fruiterers. This information was reiterated by Clot, who aptly defined their occupations as 'les professions qui demandent le plus d'activité et dont les profits sont les plus difficiles et les plus périlleux'.[3] One wonders, if what Clot meant was that money transactions, although advantageous, were often unsafe (in so far as the investor or creditor was concerned) in Muḥammad ʿAlī's days.

A few Jews took a part in the European trade and had their own shops at the side of other merchants in the bazaars[4] of the larger towns. By and large, in addition to the above money transactions, retail trade was the mainstay of Jewish business in Egypt, as observed by Lane. Benjamin noticed this, too, when visiting Egypt at mid-nineteenth century; he mentioned that their retail business relied chiefly on trade in fruit (particularly dates), tobacco, cotton, and silk.[5] In the second half of the nineteenth century, with the growth of tourism, an increasing number of Jews joined the local antique commerce, as well as the supply of commodities for the tourist trade, in Cairo and the country's ports; some Jews began to be active, also, in the import and export of tourist commodities, near the end of the century.[6]

The growth of tourism gave a further impetus to money-changing; at the end of Saʿīd's rule, one hears of at least one Jew, Yaʿaqov Qaṭṭāwī, who was appointed chief of the money-changers.[7]

Contrary to Samuel's above-mentioned characterization of the Jewish

[1] Op. cit., p. 6. [2] Op. cit., pp. 561–2. [3] Op. cit., vol. ii, p. 142.

[4] Cf. H. A. B. Rivlin, *The agricultural policy of Muḥammad ʿAlī in Egypt* (Cambridge, Mass., 1961), pp. 100, 179.

[5] Op. cit. (2nd edn.), p. 229. Some were indigo merchants, e.g. Yaʿaqov Rōlō—see F.O. 84/1290: List of slaves freed by T. F. Reade, being encl. in Consul Reade's Memorandum on slave-trade in Egypt, dated London, 13 Aug. 1868.

[6] For the year 1888, for instance, see further details in E. N. Adler, *Jews in many lands* (London, 1905), p. 25.

[7] Shāhīn Makāryūs, *Taʾrīkh al-isrāʾīliyyīn* (Cairo, 1904), pp. 223–4. If this is correct, it is a noteworthy achievement, as a sizeable number of the money-changers was made up of Copts.

occupational structure, we do find in Egypt an increasing number of Jewish artisans, most of whom indeed, seem to have come to Egypt with the immigration waves from Europe. One reads of Jewish silk-dyers[1] and a number of other artisans. Typically, these are practically always the easier crafts—tailoring, cigarette-rolling, and chair-making[2]—all remote from those industries requiring greater physical efforts. In addition to these and a few other crafts, as well as all sorts of retail trade,[3] a number of Jews was employed in the service of the community, while others found a living in trades necessitated by the dietary laws, such as butchers and sellers of kosher meat.[4]

All the above goes to show that previous occupational patterns were being followed, even intensified. An innovation, however, consisted in that an increasing number of younger Jews found employment as clerks, book-keepers, and agents in local and foreign commercial enterprises, as well as in foreign consulates[5] and the service of the Egyptian government. In the latter, some reached important positions, such as Victor Harārī, Efrayim ʿĀdeh, and Marc Ḥayyīm Biyālōs,[6] to mention a few. While the Copts and other Christian minorities in Egypt had a longer tradition of employment in the civil service, Jewish penetration into this field can well be attributed to the relatively high standards of Jewish education in Egypt,[7] which brought forth subsequent generations of officials and clerks.

Another new phenomenon, also due to education, at least partly, is the growing Jewish participation in Egypt's finances, mainly since the end of the nineteenth century. It has already been said that Jewish capital played a very limited role in Egypt's public finances during the first half of the nineteenth century. Later, during Khedive Ismāʿīl's rule, Egyptian Jews did show some interest in investing in a number of state-encouraged industrial projects. In the 1880s, in contradistinction to a very restricted political participation of the

[1] F.O. 141/11, petition of Abramo Pinto to Consul Walne, dated Cairo, 18 July 1844.

[2] McCoan, op. cit., p. 35; Adler, op. cit., p. 25. ʿAlī Mubārak, *al-Khiṭaṭ al-tawfīqiyya al-jadīda*, i, p. 100, writes that out of two guilds of chair-makers, in Cairo, one was composed of 337 Copts and Jews.

[3] Mentions are numerous e.g., Gellion-Danglar, op. cit., pp. 68–69 (for the year 1867); M. Lüttke, *Aegyptens neue Zeit* (Leipzig, 1873), vol. i, pp. 98–99 (for 1872); Deynard, op. cit., p. 18 (for 1880–1); Guglielmo Godio, *Cose d'Egitto* (Torino, 1882), p. 41 (for 1882); and others.

[4] See the materials in H. [H.] Dodwell, *The founder of modern Egypt* (Cambridge, 1931), p. 240 (for the year 1840).

[5] Among these, one might mention Augustus Cohen, an Egyptian Jew who was the secretary of Colonel Stanton, the British consul-general in Egypt, and then, in 1866, remained in charge of the British Consulate in Cairo—cf. F.O. 78/1942, Consul Reade to Lord Clarendon, dated Cairo, 14 Mar. 1866. Another case was that of Moïse Franco, another Egyptian Jew, who in 1870 was in charge of the French Consulate in Cairo—cf. the Paris archives of the Affaires Étrangères (further: AÉ), Correspondance Politique, Égypte, vol. xlviii, fol. 328, dated 24 Mar. 1870.

[6] See Makāryūs, op. cit., pp. 251–9.

[7] A topic on which one may consult, *inter alia*, my 'Manuscript materials on the teaching of Hebrew in the Egyptian schools of the Alliance Israélite Universelle', in *Dōrōn, Hebraic studies, essays in honor of Professor Abraham I. Katsh* (New York, 1965), pp. 26–36.

Jews in the national movement, a number of Jewish bankers were in touch with the nationalists, and even assisted them with funds.[1] Near the end of the century, Jewish bankers in Egypt began to rise in number and importance.[2]

This emerging class of Jewish businessmen did not supplant the trades in which the Jews of Egypt had been engaging throughout the nineteenth century. In the year 1899, S. Somekh, a teacher in the Egyptian schools of the Alliance Israélite Universelle, reported that[3] many Alexandrian Jews made a living as tailors, jewellers, cigarette-rollers, and (for new immigrants from Roumania) innkeepers and barmen. Lord Cromer's report for 1905 attributes to Jews most of the tailoring business and, relevantly, the cloth-trade. Other Jews, about the same time, made a profit by the sale of lottery tickets.[4] Still others, both local Jews and new immigrants, increased the steadily growing number of Jewish physicians,[5] lawyers,[6] and other professional workers.[7]

During the period of British rule, one finds the Jewish professional intelligentsia more active in public matters, social and economic. Besides the retail trade, Jews began to penetrate wholesale commerce, both internal and external; a growing number of Jewish shops catered for the refined and well-to-do.[8] As the years passed, Jews participated increasingly in the development of banking, commerce, and certain industries—mainly sugar, cotton, coal, and railways, to most of which they offered credits on easy terms.[9] Wealthy local Jews, chiefly of the Qaṭṭāwī, Harārī, Rōlō, Mōṣērī, and Suwāres families, took a part, early in the twentieth century, in directing large Egyptian companies, such as that of Kom Ombo, which managed large tracts of land and their cultivation.[10] Exceptionally, some members of these families had distinguished themselves, financially or professionally even before that,[11] even as far back as the mid-nineteenth century;[12] anyway, from the end of the nineteenth century, these families and some others from within the Jewish community vigorously entered the realm of big business.

[1] AÉ, Corr. Pol., Égypte, vol. lxxii, fol. 227, Consul-General Sienkiewicz's no. 126 to the French foreign minister, dated Cairo, 29 Jan. 1882.

[2] Von Fircks, op. cit., vol. i, pp. 179–80.

[3] Archives of the Alliance Israélite Universelle (further: AIU), Égypte, IX, E. c., Somekh to the President of the AIU, dated 7 Sept. 1899.

[4] Tarragan, op. cit., pp. 7–8.

[5] Maurice Fargeon, *Médecins et avocats juifs au service de l'Égypte* (Cairo, n.d.), pp. 27–48.

[6] Tewfik Soliman Abu Heif (pseudonym of Maurice Fargeon), *Les Relations entre égyptiens et juifs* (Alexandria, 1939), pp. 31–33, 47–48.

[7] For examples—agronomists, etc.—see Makāryūs, op. cit., pp. 247–8 and *passim*. Cf. Arnold Wright, *Twentieth century impressions of Egypt* (London, 1909), *passim*.

[8] Charles Issawi, *Egypt: an economic and social analysis* (London, 1947), p. 112. Later editions of this study (1954, 1963) add no details about Egypt's Jews.

[9] Murray Harris, *Egypt under the Egyptians* (London, 1925), pp. 163–5; Don Peretz, *Egyptian Jews today* (New York, 1956), pp. 8–9.

[10] Gabriel Baer, *A history of landownership in modern Egypt 1800–1950* (London, 1962), p. 130.

[11] Makāryūs, op. cit., cites a number of such instances, see e.g., pp. 223 ff., 238 ff.

[12] As is the case of Moïse Valensin, the Jewish banker in Alexandria, see AÉ, Corr. Pol., Égypte, vol. xxiv, fol. 97, A. Le Moyne's no. 208 to the French foreign minister, dated Cairo, 6 June 1852.

It should be stressed again that this was a new phenomenon. During most of the nineteenth century, in so far as Jewish-owned banking firms invested in Egypt, these were *European firms*, acting through their branches or representatives in Egypt.[1] At the end of this century, however, the general prosperity in the country, as well as the security of life and property ensured by British presence, was instrumental in Jewish penetration into the banking business. Early in the twentieth century, one finds quite a few Jews in key positions in the Anglo-Egyptian Bank, the Agricultural Bank, the National Mortgage Bank, Bank Misr, and some others;[2] in a number of investment companies, some of which dealt in banking business, such as the Crédit Foncier d'Égypte; and in some commercial firms, which were among those most active in fostering business connexions between local and foreign companies.[3]

The very same prosperity was tied up, early in the twentieth century, with a marked rise in the cost of living, particularly in food prices and rent, as well as in the value of real estate. This, as Tarragan aptly noticed in the year 1906, 'increased the wealth of the rich and the poverty of the needy'[4] in the Jewish community. The already existing cleavage between the financially successful and the masses was deepened, and later was to cause social friction. At the period under survey, however, the main tensions were not so much within the Jewish community itself but, rather, between Jews and non-Jews.

The Jews and their neighbours

The peculiar demographic features of the Jews in Egypt, their settlement in the larger towns and cities, their preference for commerce-oriented means of livelihood, clerical work (and, only later, the professions and banking) were often a result of their lowly political and socio-economic status.

Indeed, during the nineteenth century there occurred a marked change for the better in the pressures previously exerted on them: the Jews began to be regarded as just one component in the large mass of minority groups in Egypt, and very often their status was related to the general conditions of all these minority groups. Thus, while heavy fines and taxes had been repeatedly imposed upon the Jews (either alone, or along with others) during the Mamluk[5] and Ottoman[6] periods, the French occupation of Egypt,[7] and early in

[1] D. S. Landes, *Bankers and pashas, international finance and economic imperialism in Egypt* (Cambridge, Mass., 1958), p. 61 and *passim*.

[2] Harris, op. cit., pp. 163 ff.; R. Lambelin, *L'Égypte et l'Angleterre vers l'indépendance, de Mohammed Ali au roi Fouad* (Paris, 1922), pp. 194–8.

[3] Makāryūs, op. cit., p. 217.

[4] Op. cit., p. 14; cf. pp. 20–22.

[5] Examples in Fargeon, *Les Juifs en Égypte*, pp. 157, 160.

[6] S. J. Shaw, *Ottoman Egypt in the age of the French revolution* (Cambridge, Mass., 1964), pp. 64, 172.

[7] Details in Fargeon, *Les Juifs en Égypte*, pp. 153–4. Further materials in an interesting manuscript, *Administration des finances de l'armée d'Égypte an VI—an IX par A. Peyrusse*, in AÉ, Mémoires et Documents, Égypte vol. xix, fol. 34. The author was general secretary of the Directorate of Finances in the French army in Egypt.

Muḥammad ʿAlī's rule,[1] later in the nineteenth century, the fiscal policy regarding the Jews was related to that towards the Christian minorities. This was evidenced by the abolition of the *jizya*—which both Jews and Christians were paying[2]—early in the year 1855,[3] as well as by the proper apportionment of official money-gifts between the communities.[4] With the British occupation, moreover, formal discrimination against the Jews ceased.

This gradual improvement in the formal status of the Jews was not necessarily reflected in their socio-economic conditions, nor in the attitudes of Muslims and Copts towards Jews in Egypt. Lane[5] has already told us that, in his time, Egyptian Muslims both hated and despised the Jews more than they did the Christians. They would beat Jews without any provocation; and sometimes wrongly accuse them of having insulted their Prophet or the Qur'ān, thus bringing upon their heads the death penalty. Lane's description is partly corroborated by Clot.[6]

Again and again, tourists in Egypt and residents, Jews and non-Jews alike, wondered at the continuing prevalence of these feelings. They defined it as strong hostility and lack of tolerance.[7] This attitude was common to many *fallāḥīn*, too, despite the fact that some of them had very probably never met a Jew.[8] These feelings of hostility were not necessarily expressed in active violence. On the contrary, physical attacks on Jews, so prevalent in the 1830s, as already cited by Lane, became infrequent in the 1840s,[9] and rarer in the second half of the century. However, this latent animosity proved a fertile ground for repeatedly joining anti-Jewish riots, during the latter part of the nineteenth century.

Anti-Jewish riots in Egypt were regularly tied up with fantastic accusations of blood-ritual murder. Such an accusation was levelled against the Jews of Cairo, in 1844; and only the authority of Muḥammad ʿAlī prevented a riot.[10] This may have been a residue of the hatred and suspicion left by the much-bruited accusations against the Jews of Damascus four years previously. It was however during the last generation of the century that these accusations

[1] See *Mudhakkirāt Niqūlā Turk* (ed. G. Wiet; Cairo, 1950), p. 151. According to Wiet's French translation of these memoires, this 1803 tax referred to the Jews and others in Cairo.

[2] Some figures in Rivlin, op. cit., p. 333, n. 64.

[3] Amīn Sāmī, *Taqwīm al-Nīl* (Cairo, 1936), Vol. III, part i, p. 106. I am indebted to Professor Gabriel Baer for this reference.

[4] For Sultan Abdülaziz's gift, upon visiting Egypt in 1863, cf. AÉ, Corr. Pol., Égypte, vol. xxxi, fol. 221, App. 1–8 to E. Tastu's (French political agent in Egypt) report dated Alexandria, 18 Apr. 1863. Cf. *The Jewish Chronicle*, 26 June 1863, p. 2.

[5] Op cit., pp. 559–61.

[6] Op. cit., vol. ii, p. 141.

[7] See, e.g., Lüttke, op. cit., vol. i, pp. 95–100, for examples.

[8] Cf. F.O. 78/4145, Baring's 'secret' no. 138 to Salisbury, dated Cairo, 24 Mar. 1888, encl., being Foster's report to Baring, dated Alexandria, 21 Mar. 1888. Foster was an agricultural engineer in Egypt who knew the *fallāḥīn* well.

[9] For an apparently isolated instance, see *The Jewish Chronicle*, 5 Jan. 1849, p. 104 (two Jewish pedlars robbed and murdered on their way to Damietta).

[10] Details ibid., 18 Oct. 1844, pp. 6–7.

grew more frequent and resulted in actual violence.[1] In the years 1870, 1880, 1881, 1882, 1890, and 1892, there occurred such accusations against the Jews, just before the Feast of Passover, always exploiting the alleged disappearance of a Christian boy or girl.

While the 1870 accusation may have been tied up with the rising tide of Islamic feeling in Egypt, it might just as well have happened in some other year. Not so the 1880–1881–1882 accusations, distinguished by both their annual frequency and physical violence against the Jews; these years were the peak of anti-foreign agitation, and the general excitement proved a suitable backdrop for passion and violence.

Characteristically, Muslim Egyptians were in all cases the followers, rather than the prime movers of anti-Jewish incitement and riots. The instigators and leaders were, in all early cases, local Greeks, and, in the later ones, Christian Syrians. The facts that some of the Greek notables in Alexandria participated and that the local Greek press supported the accusations show that this was not something confined to the mobs. Very probably, the deterioration of authority in Egypt was being exploited by a national group enjoying capitulatory protection from too severe prosecution. Furthermore, sharp economic competition between the two communities conditioned both of them for violence; an added impetus was provided by both communities engaging, to a great extent, in the same occupations and trades, such as money-changing.[2]

The Christian Syrians, who were active in anti-Jewish propaganda, contributed their share of blood-ritual accusations in 1890, 1892, and ably employed the press for this purpose. Needless to say, the whole press did not follow this lead, but Syrian influence on journalism in Egypt at the time was considerable. Again, the same reasons that aroused the Greeks against the Jews in Egypt were applicable to the attitude of many Christian Syrians: economic competition was apparently whetted by debt to Jewish creditors, and abetted by the consciousness of a minority group attempting to transfer to another minority group, the Jews, the antagonism of the majority in Egypt.

The fact that the first three blood-ritual murder accusations were in Alexandria (1870, 1880, 1881) and two of the others in Port Said (1882, 1892) is also due to the relatively large Jewish concentration in these two cities: the Jews formed 3 per cent. of Alexandria's and 1 per cent. of Port Said's population; their presence was emphasized there through living and trading at close quarters. In these very cities, too, there was a large concentration of those very elements of the population who were competing with the Jews in business and trade.

[1] Of these, only a brief summary will be given here, as I have dealt with them at some length—including a number of relevant documents from the archives of the British and Italian Foreign Offices—in my Hebrew paper, *'Alīlōt dam w-rĕdīfōt yĕhūdīm bĕ-Miṣrayim bĕ-sōf ha-me'a ha-19*, in *Sĕfūnōt*, vol. v (1961), pp. 417–60.

[2] Cf. Godio, op. cit., p. 41 (for 1881–2, approximately).

The Jews in Egypt usually reacted to the accusations and to the bodily violence which often followed them by petitioning foreign consuls or the Egyptian authorities. However, a difference in tenor can be noticed: while the style of the earlier petitions was submissive and even imploring, this changed during the British occupation to a more assertive, sometimes aggressive, tone. In these later petitions, the Jews *demanded* protection, and reinforced their petitions with stormy meetings sponsored by the leadership of the community. This was very likely a consequence of the confidence the Jews felt in the ability and willingness of the British forces in Egypt to protect them.

Conclusion

The beginning of the British occupation in 1882 may well be considered the starting-point of the changes in status of the Jews in modern Egypt. These changes varied in nature and vigour. Before the British occupation, many observers and travellers[1] agreed that the Jews kept the exterior of their houses poor and dirty, and that this was done intentionally—to avoid the envy of their neighbours; also, that they dressed shabbily, for the same reason, often imitating the fashions of the non-Jews in Egypt; Jewish women sometimes imitated their Muslim counterparts, by wearing the veil in the street (but not at home). These reports about the Jews, although exaggerated in the case of the wealthier Jews, are essentially correct, and indicate a general state of apprehensive caution among Egypt's Jews. Some of this atmosphere continued to prevail under British rule, as the Jews felt repeatedly the shock of blood-ritual murder accusations. However, the Jewish upper class, followed by the middle class, gradually felt more secure, and openly imitated the British or French in all ways of life; indeed, it contributed actively to the westernization of Egypt. Side by side with steadily growing investment in Egypt's business, industry, and agriculture—as mentioned above—the upper Jewish strata passionately entered the swirl of social life in Cairo and Alexandria, vying with their neighbours for social elegance, increasingly so in the twentieth century.[2]

It is difficult to determine exactly how fully secure, socially and economically, Jews felt in Egypt, during the British occupation. The fact that their strenuous, often frantic, attempts to obtain foreign protection continued,[3] and that in 1897, about a half of Egypt's Jews were foreign nationals,[4] a ratio

[1] Lane, op. cit., pp. 558, 561–2; Clot, op. cit., vol. ii, pp. 139–40; Gadsby, op. cit., p. 243; Benjamin, op. cit., pp. 228–9; L. A. Frankl, *Aus Aegypten* (Vienna, 1860), p. 131; Gellion-Danglar, op. cit., p. 68; Lüttke, op. cit., p. 99; McCoan, op. cit., pp. 34–35; von Fircks, op. cit., vol. i, p. 180.

[2] For descriptions immediately following the First World War, cf. R. Lambelin, op. cit., esp. pp. 192–9; M. Harris, op. cit., pp. 163–6.

[3] The archives of the British and French consulates in Egypt preserve many traces of these attempts.

[4] Cf. the data in Fargeon, *Les Juifs en Égypte*, p. 306.

maintained until 1927[1] and changed only in the following decade,[2] would point at a certain reserve on their part to complete integration in Egypt.

[1] Official data of the census, summed up, also, in Jewish Agency for Palestine, op. cit., p. 56, table 6.

[2] Ibid., for 1937. Jacques Nantet, *Les Juifs et les nations* (Paris, 1956), pp. 192–3, asserts that close to the Second World War, only 7 per cent. of Egypt's Jews were Egyptian citizens; he brings however no proof for this statement.

Law Reform in Egypt: 1850–1950

J. N. D. ANDERSON

1. *Introduction*

THIS brief survey of legal reform in Egypt from the middle of the nineteenth till the middle of the twentieth century takes as its point of departure the withdrawal from government of Muḥammad ʿAlī Pasha, followed by the death of his son Ibrāhīm, in 1848. At that time the total population of Egypt amounted to about two and a half millions, some 80 per cent. of whom were illiterate peasants:[1] but much had already changed since the beginning of the century, and the foundations of the new Egypt had already been laid.

Constitutionally, Egypt was still, of course, part of the Ottoman Empire. Indeed, the *ferman* from the Porte which vested hereditary rights to the governorship of Egypt in the descendants of Muḥammad ʿAlī in 1841 also provided that the provisions of the *Hatt-ı Şerif* of Gülhane, 1839, regarding civil rights, and the provisions of all treaties concluded by the Porte with foreign powers, were to be applied in Egypt. An early version of this *ferman* had also required that all laws promulgated and to be promulgated by the Porte should be similarly executed in Egypt, but this was changed to a provision that all administrative regulations issued by the Porte should be applicable in Egypt 'in accordance with the requirements of the locality and the principles of justice'.[2] This phrase clearly gave the governors of Egypt considerable scope for local variations.

Muḥammad ʿAlī's programme of industrialization proved a failure, but he had been more successful in the sphere of agriculture. At the beginning of his reign almost all agricultural land in Egypt was theoretically owned by the state, and let out to *multazims* in the form of tax farms (*iltizāms*). In practice, however, it was often difficult to distinguish these holdings from land held as private property, while a considerable proportion of the land concerned had been made into *rizaq aḥbāsiyya*, or agricultural *awqāf*. But all this stood very much in the way of Muḥammad ʿAlī's plans for a centralized administration and economic development, so he proceeded to abolish the whole *iltizām* system and to gain control of almost all the land in Egypt, including the agricultural *awqāf*, in some cases by confiscation, and in others for compensation (whether real or promised); and he then redistributed the

[1] C. P. Harris, *Nationalism and revolution in Egypt* (The Hague, 1964), p. 20.

[2] Cf. R. A. Debs, *The law of property in Egypt: Islamic law and Civil Code* (Ph.D. thesis, Princeton, 1962), pp. 73 f.

greater part to peasant cultivators. Their right of cultivation normally passed from father to son (which accounts for the fact that the lands concerned were sometimes termed *athariyya*), but they had at first no legal right of inheritance; and on all such land a *kharāj* tax was levied (whence their name of *kharājiyya*)—though this tax was also levied by Muḥammad ʿAlī on the small amount of land which was still held by individuals in full ownership (*rizqa*). From 1829, moreover, Muḥammad ʿAlī began to grant to individuals uncultivated land not included in his cadaster. At first the recipients held only usufructuary rights (*taṣarruf*); but in 1836 such rights were decreed to be heritable by the eldest son, and in 1842 the sale or transfer of these *ibʿādiyyāt* was also permitted. In 1846, moreover, the peasants were allowed to pledge or transfer their *athariyya* land. This was not yet full ownership (although it got very close to it, in the case of the *ibʿādiyyāt*), but the foundations for future developments had been laid.[1] The Ottoman land law of 1839 was never applied in Egypt.[2]

But it was not only in regard to agricultural land that Egypt had gone her own way, even prior to 1850; for the same was also true of the criminal law. Characteristically enough, the first code on this subject, promulgated by Muḥammad ʿAlī in 1830, was primarily concerned with agriculture and village life. It was called the *Qānūn al-filāḥa*, was based on the latter part of *Lāʾiḥat zirāʿat al-fallāḥ* published a few weeks earlier, comprised fifty-five articles, and did not diverge from the principles of the *Sharīʿa* in any substantial way except in the punishment prescribed for theft. This was followed in 1837 by the *Qānūn al-siyāsa al-malakiyya*, which was concerned primarily with offences committed by officials. When the *Hatt-ı Şerif* of Gülhane was sent to Muḥammad ʿAlī in 1839 he replied that he had already implemented the main provisions regulating capital punishment and prohibiting talion, and that he would supplement these by further reforms. But the Ottoman Penal Code of 1840 was never applied in Egypt; instead, Muḥammad ʿAlī continued to promulgate penal legislation of his own. The most comprehensive of these laws was the *Jamʿiyya ḥaqqāniyya* of 1844, which also went further than any previous law in its departure from the *Sharīʿa*. A compilation of these penal laws enacted between 1830 and 1844 was published in 1845 as the *Qānūn al-muntakhab*, or 'Code de Mehemet Ali'. Some six months after Muḥammad ʿAlī's death, moreover, a popular summary of his penal legislation (which seems to have been originally issued in 1844) was published, and came to be named after his successor 'Code d'Abbas'.[3]

In matters of commerce the interests and influence of foreigners were of particular importance, but here—as, indeed, in regard to criminal offences

[1] Cf. Gabriel Baer, *A history of landownership in modern Egypt 1800–1950* (London, 1962), pp. 1–7.

[2] Nor, it seems, was this ever in fact intended.

[3] See Baer, 'Tanzimat in Egypt—The Penal Code', in *BSOAS*, vol. xxvi. 1 (1963), pp. 29–32.

committed by foreigners—the Egyptian courts had no jurisdiction whatever. This was due to the way in which the capitulatory system had developed in Egypt. This system, in origin, had its roots in the principle of the personal, rather than territorial, nature of law—a principle which was widespread in antiquity, which revived in the Mediterranean area with the disintegration of the Roman Empire,[1] and which harmonized closely with the Islamic view of law as basically religious and the Islamic system of leaving non-Muslim communities largely to follow—and administer—their own law. This principle was reinforced by the practice of the Crusaders and by the commercial activities of Venice, Pisa, and Genoa; and in due course it was extended to parts of the Muslim world such as Morocco and Egypt. It was inherited by the Ottoman Empire, and confirmed by a series of treaties starting in 1454.[2]

In the Ottoman Empire as a whole these privileges came to mean that cases involving foreigners of the same nationality would be heard in their own consular court; cases involving foreigners of mixed nationalities would be heard in the defendant's consular court; and cases involving foreigners and Ottoman subjects would be heard in Ottoman courts—whether 'mixed' courts, where these existed, or ordinary Ottoman tribunals. But in Egypt a different rule prevailed—partly as a result of the policy of encouraging Western contacts, and partly as a result of an unjustifiable extension of privilege by many of the seventeen Capitulatory Powers. As a result, the principle was established that the defendant's court had jurisdiction in all cases, so that the jurisdiction of the territorial Egyptian courts was restricted to actions in which the defendant was an Egyptian; and the consular courts normally applied the laws of their own countries.[3] In criminal cases this meant that the consular courts claimed jurisdiction in any case in which one of their nationals, or even 'protected persons', was accused. It was only where a foreigner accused an Egyptian of an offence that he had recourse to the Egyptian courts, which could not even compel a foreigner to give evidence before them—while the Egyptian police were precluded from searching a foreigner's house without the presence of a representative of his consulate. It can readily be realized how this system hampered the proper administration of justice, and could find its only possible justification in the exceedingly unsatisfactory state of the indigenous courts and the law they administered.

In 1845 there was a new development. Special courts were set up, in Alexandria and Cairo, to deal with commercial cases between foreigners and Egyptians; and in 1856 the Ottoman Commercial Code, which had been promulgated in Istanbul in 1850, was made applicable to these cases. From

[1] e.g. the laws of the Visigoths, of the seventh century.

[2] See Herbert J. Liebesny, 'The development of western judicial privileges', in Majid Khadduri and Herbert J. Liebesny (edd.) *Law in the Middle East* (Washington, D.C., 1955), pp. 309–33.

[3] Debs, op. cit., p. 76.

such a modest beginning the whole system of Mixed Courts, as set up some thirty years later, was destined to evolve.[1]

Basically, however, the fact remains that the courts of general jurisdiction in Egypt—as in the Ottoman Empire as a whole—were the *Maḥākim Sharʿiyya*, and the *Sharīʿa* law was still the fundamental law. It was not, indeed, invariably applied in practice, but in theory its position was unique and unassailable.

2. *From 1850 to the British occupation in 1882*

Constitutionally, Egypt continued to progress, during these years, towards an independence which was increasingly *de jure* rather than purely *de facto*. In 1867, for example, a *ferman* accorded Ismāʿīl Pasha the title of khedive, very considerable rights of internal legislation, and certain rights of negotiation with foreign powers. Successive *fermans* extended these privileges, and by 1873 the independence of Egypt in matters administrative, financial, and judicial was virtually complete, although she remained, of course, juridically part of the Ottoman Empire until the beginning of the First World War. But in the last few years before the British occupation, Egypt became more and more subject to European intervention.

These years were also marked by a certain tentative progress towards democracy and representative government. In 1866, for example, two decrees were promulgated constituting a Chamber of Deputies (*Majlis Shūrā'l-Nuwwāb*); and this *Majlis* met in 1867. Then, in 1878, another decree was issued establishing a responsible Cabinet, called *Majlis al-Nuẓẓār*. The Chamber was completely subservient to the khedive, and was suspended in 1879; but in 1881 Tawfīq resuscitated it, and during the ʿUrābī revolt it even went so far, meeting as a 'National Constituent Assembly', as to draw up and promulgate, in 1882, an elaborate constitutional charter, *al-Lā'iḥa al-Asāsiyya*.

In regard to land, it has already been noted that the Ottoman land law of 1839 was never applied in Egypt, and the same also applies to that of 1856. Agricultural developments had come to a stop under ʿAbbās I; but when Saʿīd succeeded in 1854 he resumed the policy of modernization. It was, indeed, his Land Law of 1858 which played the major role in establishing rights of private ownership in land over a great part of the country. By this law *rizqa* and *ibʿādiyya* land (together with those lands which, since 1854, had been termed *ʿushūriyya*) became the 'full property' of whoever received them;[2] he could deal with them in every way as their owner, endow them as *waqf*, and claim compensation if they were requisitioned for public use. As for the *athariyya* or *kharājiyya* land, this was henceforth to be subject to the Islamic law of inheritance,[3] and it might be pledged, mortgaged, sold, exchanged, or transferred (provided the local authority was duly informed)

[1] Debs, op. cit., p. 75.
[2] Art. 25. See Baer, *Landownership*, p. 8.
[3] Rights of inheritance under different principles had, in fact, first been granted in 1855.

and even leased for a period of up to three years (or longer, subject to review by the local authority); but this land could not yet be regarded as held in full ownership, since there was no right to compensation if the land was requisitioned for the public use, nor was any provision made for its free bequest or endowment as *waqf*.[1] Further advances were made under Ismāʿīl, for a decree of 1866 permitted owners of *athariyya* or *kharājiyya* land to bequeath it by will, although it expressly forbade them to endow it as *waqf* except with the khedive's permission. The *Muqābala* Law of 1871, moreover, hastened the process by which Ismāʿīl had started to sell the *raqaba*, or full ownership, of *kharājiyya* lands to the holders of usufructuary rights over them, for by this law anyone who paid six years' taxes in advance was not only freed from half his liability for taxes but was also granted rights of full ownership; and in 1874 this *muqābala* payment was made compulsory. The *Muqābala* Law was repealed in 1876, re-enacted in the same year, and repealed once more in 1880; but the Liquidation Law of 1880 which followed, although itself soon repealed, had recognized rights of full ownership over land for which the *muqābala* had been fully or partially paid.[2] In all this, Egypt had gone her own way, although it is noteworthy that the Ottoman legislation in 1867 about the ownership of land by foreigners, and in 1869 about mines, were both applied in Egypt.[3]

When we turn to the actual distribution of land among the population, we face a very complicated and obscure story. We have seen how Muḥammad ʿAlī abolished the *iltizām* system and divided up the land among the cultivators, and how these holdings gradually became the peasants' private property. It was not long, however, before the creation of vast estates on the one hand, and the progressive diminution of the number of peasant proprietors on the other, began to transform the whole situation. This was partly due to the introduction of the *ʿuhda* system in the last years of Muḥammad ʿAlī and in the succeeding reigns; partly to the impoverishment of the peasants and their inability to pay their taxes; partly to the fragmentation of their holdings by the operation of the Islamic law of inheritance; partly to the creation of large estates out of uncultivated land (i.e. the *ibʿādiyyāt*); and partly to the institution of the *jiflik* system, chiefly in the interests of the ruling family. But whatever the cause, there can be no doubt that the steady evolution of different systems of land-holding in Egypt into a more or less uniform concept of private property (except, that is, for the *awqāf*) was accompanied by the widespread expropriation of the peasant proprietors and the concentration of the vastly greater part of the land in the hands of a comparatively small number of rich landowners. Chief among these stood the ruling family, whose estates increased by leaps and bounds up to 1878,[4] after which the greater part were

[1] Baer, *Landownership*, p. 9.
[2] Ibid., pp. 10 f.
[3] Debs, op. cit., p. 75.
[4] When much of this land was relinquished to the state as security for the Rothschild loan.

transferred to the state. Next, in the early days of our period, came high officials, village notables, and the *'ulamā'*; but all of these tended, as time went on, to decrease in influence. Their place was taken, to some extent, by bedouin shaykhs, as a result of the settlement of the nomad tribes. But the major beneficiaries, from about 1880 onwards, were the new class of 'urban rich', whether lawyers or businessmen—including foreigners and members of the local minorities.[1]

In criminal law, the year 1851 saw the promulgation of the second Ottoman Penal Code. This was both less comprehensive and less severe than the Egyptian law of 1844, and the only point of outstanding significance was that it provided that, all over the Empire, no murderer might be executed until the death sentence had been confirmed by the sultan himself (a point which proved the main bone of contention between Cairo and the Porte for a number of years). But neither pressure by the Porte nor by Britain induced 'Abbās to introduce this Ottoman law in Egypt; instead, negotiations dragged on for some years, and it was not until Sa'īd ascended the throne in 1854 that a modified form of the Ottoman Penal Code of 1851 was published in Egypt, in 1855, under the name *Qānūn-nāmah al-sulṭānī*.[2] It seems clear, moreover, that under Sa'īd penalties were often imposed in an arbitrary way and that some of those prescribed in the Code were specifically increased in 1858; but the Code remained in force until the end of 1862—i.e. some four years after the promulgation in Istanbul of the Penal Code of 1858, a code which, unlike its predecessors, was firmly founded on French law.[3] It was not until after Ismā'īl had succeeded 'Abbās that orders were given, in 1863, that this new Ottoman Code was to be applied to Egypt; but this order was soon modified by instructions that those parts of the former Code which were peculiar to Egypt should be added to the Ottoman legislation.[4]

In the event, it took some twelve years to edit this new Egyptian code; but in the meantime other steps had been taken which eventually led to a radical change in the whole situation. For in 1867 the khedive took advantage of his newly recognized right of negotiation with foreign governments to address notes to each of the Capitulatory Powers expressing the desire of the Egyptian people for immediate judicial reform. This was the outcome of a report made by Nubar Pasha to the khedive which reviewed the abuses of the system of

[1] Cf. Baer, *Landownership*, pp. 13–70.

[2] Baer, 'Tanzimat', pp. 33–38.

[3] Previous codes had been much closer to the basic concepts of the *Sharī'a*, in which what we should term criminal law is characterized (*a*) by a clear-cut distinction between a small number of offences which are precisely defined and subject to fixed—and very severe—penalties, on the one hand, and all other wrongdoing, the punishment of which is left to the discretion of the court, on the other; (*b*) by the fact that some of these offences (of both categories) are regarded as primarily infringing the rights of the Almighty, and others as infringing those of some individual victim, who may decline to prosecute, may settle the case, or may remit the penalty; and (*c*) by the fact that homicide and wounding are treated, in most cases, more as torts than as crimes.

[4] Baer, 'Tanzimat', p. 45.

Capitulations as it had developed in Egypt and proposed its abolition; but which recognized that this would never be accepted by the powers unless their interests were secured under a judicial system which merited their confidence and respect. Such a system manifestly did not exist in either the *Sharīʿa* courts (which administered a law which Christians regarded as essentially based on an alien religion) or in the hierarchy of indigenous *majālis* (which administered a distinctly haphazard and arbitrary justice in a variety of matters, both criminal and civil).[1] Nubar Pasha suggested, therefore, the creation of courts organized along the lines of the existing 'mixed' courts of Alexandria and Cairo, staffed by foreign as well as Egyptian judges, to exercise jurisdiction in all cases[2] in which foreigners were involved—whether commercial, civil, or criminal—regardless of the nationality of the defendant or accused person. In commercial cases, these courts would apply the existing commercial law; in civil cases, they would administer a new civil code which was being drafted in Egypt and which was described as a 'reconciliation' of French and Egyptian law; and in criminal cases they would apply the new criminal code which was also in course of compilation.[3] Such courts, it was emphasized, would benefit Egyptians and foreigners alike, and would substitute a single jurisdiction, under competent judges, for the chaos and near anarchy of the existing situation.

This proposal received outspoken support from Britain,[4] but met with considerable opposition from France and most of the other powers. For a considerable time the issue was in doubt, while the work of drafting the necessary codes went steadily forward. These were duly promulgated in 1875; but in the event the Penal Code remained virtually a dead letter, since the opposition of the Capitulatory Powers brought it about that the Mixed Courts, when eventually established in 1876,[5] were deprived of almost all criminal jurisdiction. The only exceptions were 'contraventions' and the punishment of certain 'crimes' committed against these courts or their personnel in the exercise of their proper duties. For the rest, the consular courts were confirmed in their criminal jurisdiction for more than another half-century—as also in cases of personal status which concerned their nationals.

But in spite of this bitter setback to Nubar Pasha's proposals, it is almost impossible to over-emphasize the importance of the creation of the Mixed

[1] e.g. the *Majālis daʿāwī'l-balad*, the *Majālis daʿāwī'l-markaz*, the *Majālis maḥalliyya* and the *Majlis ʿālī*. Cf. Sarofim, *England and the criminal legislation of Egypt from 1882* (D.Phil. thesis, Oxford 1949), pp. 3 f., who summarizes the objections to these courts as incompetence, irregularity of sessions, lack of uniformity in procedure, variance of treatment according to rank, etc.—besides the intervention of executive authorities.

[2] Except only for litigation about real property, which was to be left to the Egyptian courts. But this was not accepted by the powers, and such cases came to be within the competence of the Mixed Courts wherever a foreigner was concerned.

[3] Debs, op. cit., pp. 77 f.

[4] Cf. Sarofim, op. cit., pp. 8 f.

[5] Originally under the name of 'Tribunals of the reform' (cf. Debs, op. cit., p. 79). They were organized under Egyptian law, but their status was also defined by international agreements.

Courts. First, this meant the unification of much jurisdiction which was previously in a state of chaos—which itself, of course, made a vital contribution to the slow growth of the concept of the 'rule of law' in the modern sense. Another immediate effect was the raising of the standing and prestige of the judges.[1] It is true that the *'ulamā'* had always enjoyed a prestige of their own; but the personnel of the 'secular' courts—and even, to some extent, of the *Sharī'a* courts—had been regarded, all too often with reason, as the agents of the executive. Now, however, foreign judges of learning and repute were nominated by the powers, at a salary far exceeding that in most European countries; their tenure of office was for life, and their discipline and impeachment in the hands of their colleagues; and their jurisdiction was exercised without fear or favour, even over the highest in the land.[2] Of their complete independence there could be no question whatever. But there was yet another result which, in course of time, had an even greater influence on the history of Egypt: the fostering of the growth of a large group of professional lawyers, trained in the modern way (for the standards set by the European judges demanded a corresponding standard from their Egyptian colleagues and from the advocates who appeared before them), and with a tradition of intellectual and political independence—for the influence of this group was by no means confined to the law, but permeated the whole structure of society. In particular, it was from this group that an enormously high proportion of the politicians was drawn.[3]

The establishment of these courts had been dependent, on the one hand, on the consent of the Capitulatory Powers and, on the other, on the promulgation of suitable codes for them to apply. It has already been noted that this was achieved in 1875, some two years after the khedive's right to legislate had been recognized in an Imperial *ferman*. The Penal Code, dead letter though it largely remained, was firmly founded on French law, like the Ottoman code on which it was primarily based; and it has been remarked that it went further than the Ottoman code in excluding any references whatever to the *Sharī'a*.[4] But this is largely explained, no doubt, by the fact that it was designed for the mixed courts and had, therefore, to be acceptable to foreign opinion; and it seems unlikely that the concessions to Islamic law and Muslim sentiments, which reappeared in the codes which were subsequently promulgated for the native courts, represent so much any significant resurgence of orthodox

[1] See Farhat Ziadeh, 'The case of lawyers in Egypt', in *Enterprise in the emerging socialist countries of the Near East* (Sixteenth Annual Near East Conference of Princeton University), privately printed for members of the Conference (Princeton, 1964), p. 25.

[2] Not even the private estates of the khedive were exempt.

[3] To mention only a handful of lawyers who played a leading role in politics, they included Muṣṭafā Kāmil, Muḥammad Farīd, Sa'd Zaghlūl, 'Abd al-Khāliq Tharwat, Muṣṭafā al-Naḥḥās, and Makram 'Ubayd. Lawyers were prominent in the 'rebellion' of 1919, the protracted negotiations with Britain, and every constitutional development in Egypt. They were also in the vanguard of liberal thought and even literature. Cf. Farhat Ziadeh, op. cit., pp. 26 f.

[4] Cf. Baer, 'Tanzimat', pp. 46 f.

influence as a recognition of the different milieu in which they were to be applied.

It is the Civil Code of 1875 which represents by far the most radical departure from Ottoman precedents, for it was promulgated at a time when the civil code of the Ottoman Empire—the *Mecelle*—was in course of compilation. And the most significant features in the *Mecelle* were, first, that it was derived, not from French law (like most of the Tanzimat reforms),[1] but from the principles and precepts of the *Sharīʿa*; secondly, that it represented the first example in history of the promulgation by a Muslim government of an official codification of such precepts; and, thirdly, that it took the form, not of a compilation of the most authoritative opinion, in each matter, in the Ḥanafī school, but rather of an eclectic choice, in accordance with contemporary needs, from the comparatively wide variety of opinions which had received any sort of recognition by Ḥanafī jurists.[2] It was in sharp contrast to this procedure that the Egyptian government, in its newly recognized legislative independence, promulgated a law which was frankly French in the origin of the vast majority of its precepts, although 'reconciled' to local needs by the fact that it incorporated a number of short sections derived from the *Sharīʿa*—e.g. the principles applicable to 'death sickness' (with the important exception that these principles were not to be applied to the prejudice of a third party who had, in good faith, acquired a right in some piece of property for valuable consideration); to lesion (*ghubn*) in the sale of immovable property to a person who is legally incapable, in the lease of *waqf* property, in the partition of property held in common ownership, or in the distribution of an estate; to the party at whose risk purchased property remains; to planting or building on leased land; to the ownership of different storeys in the same building, or of a party wall; and to the right of pre-emption (*shufʿa*); to gifts; or to the doctrine that there cannot be any inheritance until after the payment of debts.[3]

In addition to the Civil Code and the Penal Code, the Commercial Code, the Code of Maritime Commerce, the Code of Civil and Commercial Procedure, and the Code of Criminal Procedure were all promulgated in the same year. And from 1889 the Mixed Courts were also empowered to apply all such laws of Egypt with regard to lands, embankments, and canals, etc., as were agreed by the General Assembly of these courts (i.e. in effect by the signatory powers).[4]

Meanwhile the *Sharīʿa* courts, and the sacred law which they applied in the old traditional way, remained largely unchanged. It is true that the year

[1] A considerable body of opinion had, indeed, favoured the compilation of an Ottoman civil code based on the French model, but the contrary view had eventually prevailed.

[2] Some of which were, in reality, of other than Ḥanafī inspiration, although they had been adopted by later Ḥanafīs.

[3] See my article 'The Sharīʿa and civil law (the debt owed by the new civil codes of Egypt and Syria to the Sharīʿa), in *The Islamic Quarterly*, vol. i (1954), pp. 29–46.

[4] Cf. Debs, op. cit., p. 81.

1873 saw the establishment of the *Majālis Ḥisbiyya*, to supervise the financial interests of those Muslims who did not themselves enjoy full legal competence. This jurisdiction had previously belonged to the *Sharīʿa* courts; so the Decree of the *Ḥisbiyya* Courts, in 1873, may be regarded as the first step[1] in the progressive reduction of the scope of these *maḥkamas*[2] from courts of general jurisdiction to courts with a strictly limited competence.

This was followed, in 1880, by a Law of the *Sharīʿa* Courts. Comprised of no less than 190 articles, this covered such matters as the appointment, duties, and discipline of the judges and other personnel and the organization of the courts. But the only points of outstanding significance in this law (which was accompanied by another fixing the fees chargeable in these courts) are the fact that it specifically confines their competence to matters of personal status (and all that stem from this or is connected with it) and questions of homicide;[3] that it provides that they must always apply the dominant opinion in the Ḥanafī school except in matters of homicide, when—'in order to prevent corruption and in view of the frequency with which people do not hesitate to shed blood'—the doctrine of the 'Two Companions' was to be preferred to that of Abū Ḥanīfa himself in regard to the definition of what may be termed 'capital' homicide;[4] and that it provided for periods of prescription—of fifteen years in most cases, and of thirty-three years in cases regarding *awqāf*.[5]

3. *From the British occupation till 1923*

The British occupation in 1882 made no difference whatever to the juridical status of Egypt, which remained, in law, a part of the Ottoman Empire which had attained a very high degree of autonomy. But it had a profound effect on the actual government of the country, where the work of the different ministries was made subject to the control of British officials.

Security of the person, of possessions, and of honour had been guaranteed to all subjects of the Porte, without distinction of religion, as early as the *Hatt-ı Şerif* of Gülhane in 1839, and this had been specifically applied to Egypt by *fermans* of 1841 and 1867. At the time of the British occupation, therefore, the civil rights and liberties of Egyptians had received official recognition, but it was not until 1 May 1883 that the political right of universal suffrage was accorded to all Egyptians over twenty years of age,[6] by the Organic Law of Khedive Tawfīq, which reorganized the whole constitutional framework of Egypt. This provided for Provincial Councils, a Legislative Council, and a Legislative Assembly—the latter composed of 82 members, made up of six ministers, the 30 members of the Legislative Council (16 of

[1] Except, that is, for the *majālis* to which reference has already been made.
[2] Properly *maḥākim*: this was the name used for the *qāḍīs*' courts in Egypt.
[3] Art. 53. [4] Art. 10. [5] Art. 14.
[6] Cf. Henri Lumba, *Droit public et administratif de l'Égypte* (Cairo, 1909), pp. 20, 82, etc.

whom were elected by the Provincial Councils and 14 appointed by the government), and 46 delegates elected by the people. No new direct taxes could be imposed without its approval, and it had to be 'consulted' on a large number of other subjects. In 1913 its composition was somewhat changed and its powers considerably increased; but in 1915 it was suspended.

There can be no doubt, moreover, that the protection of the civil right to equality before the law and before the courts was greatly strengthened by the establishment, in 1883, of the National Courts and by the promulgation of civil and penal codes, together with codes of civil and criminal procedure, for these courts to apply. Henceforth it was only in the *Sharī'a* courts, and the community courts of the non-Muslim communities, that an uncodified law was still applied in the old, traditional way; but these courts were strictly confined to matters of family law in its widest connotation (marriage, divorce, paternity, guardianship, and succession) and the law of *waqfs* and gifts.

The codes of 1883, moreover, were modelled on those promulgated in 1875 for the use of the Mixed Courts. First came the Decree for the Reorganization of the National Courts, followed by six codes. Two of these—the Commercial Code and the Code of Maritime Procedure—were almost identical with those promulgated in 1875 for the Mixed Courts; but the others—the Penal and Civil Codes, and the Codes of Civil and Criminal Procedure—included certain very minor differences. Thus the Code of Criminal Procedure of 1883—designed, as it was, for the National Courts—included provisions that the death sentence should not be imposed unless the accused had been convicted on the testimony of at least two witnesses; that before a capital sentence was executed the *muftī* must confirm that such a sentence was not, in the circumstances, contrary to Islamic principles;[1] and that the dispositions of the code were not to be so construed as to derogate from those personal rights (e.g. to blood money) which were recognized by the *Sharī'a*.[2] This last point duly reappeared, moreover, in the revised codes of 1904 and even 1937.[3]

In general terms, however, all these codes were substantially French in origin, and the Civil Code of 1883 included little more indigenous material, and little more that was derived from the *Sharī'a*, than the Civil Code for the Mixed Courts promulgated in 1875. At first sight this may seem somewhat surprising, from two different angles. First, it might have been expected that the British would have tried to secure the adoption of English, rather than French, principles—and there can, indeed, be no doubt that they did, at times, exert considerable pressure in this direction. But the pre-eminent influence of French law in the Ottoman Empire as a whole, the recent

[1] This provision had, in fact, also been included in the Decree of the Reorganization of the National Courts, Art. 15. It continued in force right up till 1937.

[2] See my article 'Homicide in Islamic Law', *BSOAS*, vol. xiii. 4 (1951), pp. 811–28.

[3] Cf. in both cases, Art. 7. Cf. also, in this context, Art. 216. Another example is a husband's right, under the *Sharī'a*, to submit his wife to mild corporal punishment in certain circumstances.

promulgation in Egypt of the special codes for the use of the Mixed Courts, and the obvious advantages in establishing a more or less uniform law for foreigners and Egyptians alike, precluded any such attempt in 1883. Secondly, it may seem strange that no greater attempt was made to devise codes of law derived from Islamic principles—as had, indeed, been done in Istanbul in regard to the *Mecelle* (which was unique, in this respect, among the Tanzimat reforms). It seems, however, that the ruling circles in Egypt were, at this period, even more firmly set on the path of modernization and reform than were the corresponding Ottoman circles, and that the influence of foreigners was considerably more pronounced. It is clear, moreover, that at this period Muslim opinion, both in Cairo and in Istanbul, felt that it was preferable to preserve the *Sharīʿa* intact and inviolable as the ideal law—even if this meant that it must in large part be quietly superseded, in practice, by an alien system—rather than allow any profane meddling with its immutable provisions. It was not until many years later that opinion came to change in this respect.

As a result, the dichotomy in the courts, and in the law which they administered, became even more clear-cut in Egypt than in the rest of the Ottoman Empire. On the one side stood the new courts, both Mixed and National, applying a codified law which was of composite origin, but in which Western influence greatly predominated; and these were staffed by lawyers trained in the modern way, who came to constitute one of the most influential, liberal, and progressive elements in the population. On the other stood the *Sharīʿa* courts, in which the dominant opinion in the Ḥanafī school, still uncodified, had to be sought in the multifarious classical texts by judges and lawyers who were still trained in the traditional manner. As for the non-Muslim community courts, these too applied an uncodified law and often followed a procedure which was of questionable propriety.

But although the codes of 1883, like those of 1875, were basically of French inspiration, the influence of English legal concepts was by no means negligible at this time. Even before the codes were promulgated an Englishman (Sir Benson Maxwell) had been appointed procureur-général, and another (Clifford Lloyd) was sent out to Egypt as director-general of reforms—and both did their best to get the draft code of criminal procedure modified in accordance with English concepts.[1] The same policy was followed, with greater insistence, by Sir Raymond West, a former Anglo-Indian judge, when he assumed office as procureur-général; and it was Nubar Pasha's resistance to such pressure which led to the appointment of a Belgian, Le Grelle, in his place. It was not long, however, before the British position in Egypt was strengthened, in 1888, by the failure of the Porte to ratify the Drummond Wolff Convention; and the new British consul-general insisted on the

[1] See Sarofim, op. cit., pp. 28–34, where the suggestion is made that traces of English influence can be detected also in the Penal Code of 1883.

appointment of an Englishman (Sir John Scott) as adviser to the Ministry of Justice and of English judges to the National Courts.

In due course Scott gave way to Sir Malcolm McIlwraith, a Scotsman who had been trained in French law. He recognized that the Egyptian codes had been 'more successful than one would have been entitled to expect',[1] but that the modifications introduced by his predecessors had made them diverge more and more from their French models; so he set up a commission to revise the Penal Code and Code of Criminal Procedure, and new codes were promulgated in 1904. These followed the general lines of the legislation of 1883, for the policy of 'grafting' those piecemeal reforms which seemed necessary into the existing law, rather than any wholesale substitution of English principles, had come to prevail; but the Penal Code of 1904 incorporates verbatim certain sections of the Sudan Penal Code of 1900, which had been largely drafted in Egypt, probably by the same draftsmen.[2] A proposal to anglicize the Egyptian criminal legislation still further, laid before the Legislative Council in 1914, was shelved on the outbreak of the First World War; but in 1916 Sir William Brunyate, who had succeeded McIlwraith, returned to the attack. His object was 'to correct errors, clear up obscurities and fill up lacunae in the Egyptian penal code, having sought inspiration chiefly from the Indian penal code, which has already been adopted in a modified form in the Sudan'. But Brunyate's draft code aroused the strong opposition of the legal profession, which had (as we have seen) attained great political influence in Egypt, and had been trained in the French tradition; and the growth of the nationalist movement in Egypt led to the abandonment of this draft.[3]

When we turn to the *Sharīʿa* courts we find that this period (1882–1923) witnessed a radical transformation, not only in their position *vis-à-vis* other courts and in the scope of their jurisdiction, but also in the jurisprudential approach to the law they must apply. We have already observed that the Law of *Ḥisbiyya* Courts, 1873, may be regarded as a modest step in the progressive reduction in the scope of the *maḥkamas* from courts of general jurisdiction to courts with a strictly limited competence; and this process was, of course, enormously advanced by the establishment of the National Courts in 1883.

In historical fact the *qāḍīs*' courts have seldom if ever enjoyed a complete monopoly of jurisdiction in the Muslim world. Always and everywhere, in general terms, there have existed other and rival jurisdictions—the court of the inspector of markets (the *muḥtasib*), for example, the police (*shurṭa*), and the Court of Complaints (*nāẓir al-maẓālim*). Long before our period, moreover, criminal justice in Egypt was in great part administered by the hierarchy of *majālis* to which reference has already been made. But the fact remains that before 1883 the *maḥākim* were the courts of general and

[1] Ibid., p. 54.

[2] Cf. ibid., pp. 85 f.

[3] Which was subsequently promulgated as the Penal Code of Baghdād.

residuary jurisdiction, while after that date they were virtually restricted to the sphere of the law of personal status in respect of Muslim litigants.

Much the same, moreover, may be said about the *Sharīʿa* law. It was not that, in the past, this had in fact been universally applied. In the spheres of crime and commerce, in particular, the *Sharīʿa* had never in fact consistently prevailed, but had always fought an uphill and often losing battle with executive decrees (or even caprice) and with commercial practice. But it was only very rarely that such decrees had reached the dimensions of codes of law, and the *Sharīʿa* had always enjoyed a pre-eminent status as the basic law to which all paid their homage. But from 1875 the situation in Egypt radically changed, for in the National as well as the Mixed Courts the administration of justice was based on a whole series of codes some of which owed little, and some nothing, to the *Sharīʿa*; and these codes were applied by a class of lawyers trained in the European tradition. Apart, therefore, from those limited chapters in the Civil Code which consisted of provisions based on the *Sharīʿa* and those very minor concessions to Islamic principles included in the Code of Criminal Procedure, the sacred law of Islam was largely confined to the *qāḍīs'* courts and the subjects within their competence.

Into this sphere the spirit of reform was slow to penetrate. First, as we have seen, a strictly limited part even of the family law was taken from the *Sharīʿa* courts in 1873 and given to the new *Ḥisbiyya* Courts; and the jurisdiction of these latter courts was extended and consolidated by a new law of *Ḥisbiyya* Courts in 1896.[1] Under this the jurisdiction of the Public Treasury, or *Bayt al-Māl*, in any matter of inheritance was brought to an end; the *Ḥisbiyya* Courts were reorganized in various ways, including the provision of channels of appeal; their jurisdiction was extended to cover the protection of the financial interests of absent persons, as well as minors, and to all native Egyptians, whether Muslims or not; and the minimum age of majority was fixed at 18 years, instead of being left to the physical and mental maturity of the individual concerned.

In 1897, moreover, a new Law of the Organisation and Procedure of *Sharīʿa* Courts was promulgated; and this was followed, in 1910, by an amending law on the same subject,[2] which was brought into effect in 1911, constituted a major piece of legislation, and ran to no less than 384 articles. Under these laws a whole hierarchy of courts was organized, and the competence of each, together with the proper channel for appeal or 'revision', was precisely defined. Questions of homicide ceased to be within their competence, which was now confined exclusively to questions of personal status, family law, gifts, and *awqāf*. Detailed rules of procedure were also included, and covered such matters as documentary evidence[3] and the swearing and cross-examina-

[1] Brought into operation in 1897.
[2] No. 31 of 1910. There were also minor additions and amendments between 1897 and 1910.
[3] Under the classical *Sharīʿa* the proof *par excellence* is oral testimony, and documentary

tion of witnesses,[1] instead of the ancient process of investigating their characters (*tazkiyya*), while any attempt to impugn their characters by the other side was kept within strict limits.[2] More significant still, the courts were expressly precluded from entertaining litigation at all, in certain specified circumstances, in the absence of documentary evidence—e.g. when the claim was based on an oral confession alleged to have been made outside the court;[3] on a *waqf* which was not evidenced by a notarial act;[4] on a marriage or divorce, after the death of one of the parties, for which no documentary evidence could be produced;[5] or on a bequest, if denied by the heirs, which was not similarly supported.[6] The detailed requirements in such cases tended, indeed, to become more exacting with each successive code. Nor should this be regarded as in any way fortuitous; on the contrary, this procedural device—which does not attempt to make any change whatever in the substantive law, but which quietly deprives it, in specified circumstances, of its primary effect by the denial of all judicial enforcement—should be recognized as perhaps the earliest, and certainly the least controversial, of the expedients of reform.

But more radical suggestions for reform were also in the air around the turn of the century, sponsored by such names as Muḥammad Shākir, Qāsim Amīn, and Muḥammad ʿAbduh. Why, they argued, should the courts always be required to follow the dominant opinion in the Ḥanafi school—particularly in matters such as the judicial divorce of misused wives, where the dominant Ḥanafī doctrine is rigid in the extreme, and some of the other schools much more liberal? Had not the individual Muslim in his private life always enjoyed considerable latitude as to which school he would follow, whether in general or in any particular question; and, while it was true that a similar discretion was commonly denied the *qāḍī* in his official capacity, was there not considerable authority for the proposition that it was within the competence of the ruler, when the public interests so required, to require his courts to abandon the dominant opinion of the school they normally followed in favour of the ruling of some other reputable juristic authority of the past?

It will be recalled that as early as 1880 the Law of *Sharīʿa* Courts included one such provision, whereby the courts were required to follow the view of the 'Two Companions and three *Imāms*',[7] instead of the dominant view in the Ḥanafī school, in regard to the definition of 'capital' homicide.[8] This expedient was, indeed, applied by the Ottoman sultan to two urgent problems of divorce

evidence is largely discounted. In practice, on the other hand, documentary evidence has been comparatively widely used—and provision for this was made in the Law of 1897 (cf. Arts. 25, 27, etc.) and, in more detail, in 1910.

[1] Cf. Code of 1910, Arts. 171, 180, and 181.

[2] Ibid., Art. 183.

[3] Cf. Law of 1897, Art. 29; Law of 1910, Art. 129.

[4] Cf. Law of 1897, Art. 30.

[5] Cf. Law of 1897, Art. 31; Law of 1910, Art. 101.

[6] Cf. Law of 1897, Art. 32; Law of 1910, Art. 100.

[7] i.e. Abū Yūsuf and Muḥammad al-Shaybānī, on the one hand, and Mālik b. Anas, Muḥammad al-Shāfiʿī and Aḥmad b. Ḥanbal, on the other.

[8] See above, p. 218.

in 1915; it was considerably more widely used in 1916 in the then Anglo-Egyptian Sudan, where the grand *qāḍī* (an Egyptian) put into force several reforms which had for long been under discussion in Egypt; and in 1917 it formed the major basis of the widespread reforms included in the Ottoman Law of Family Rights. But although the pressure for reform was no less strong in Egypt, the period of the First World War was not considered suitable for such an innovation, and it was not till after it was over that the first reforms in family law were enacted by Law No. 25 of 1920.

Meanwhile the juridical status of Egypt had been changed in 1914 by act of the British, who not unnaturally reacted to the war with Turkey by repudiating the suzerainty of the Porte over Egypt and by the transformation of their *de facto* occupation of that country into a *de jure* protectorate. But the people of Egypt, little though they cared, in general, for the Porte, reacted sharply, in 1919, to British control; and it is noteworthy that the nationalist cause was largely led by lawyers. So in 1922 Britain recognized the independence of Egypt, although she reserved to herself questions of defence, the control of imperial communications, the protection of foreigners, and the Sudan; the sultan of Egypt assumed the title of king; and next year a constitution was promulgated.

4. *From 1923 to 1950*

The new constitution was based on Belgian and Ottoman models. It provided for a Senate and Chamber of Deputies under a monarchy in which the king had the right to select and appoint the prime minister, the president of the Senate, and half the senators; to dismiss the Cabinet and dissolve Parliament; and to return draft laws to Parliament for reconsideration. The Cabinet was drawn from the two Chambers and was collectively responsible to the Lower House, which was elected on the basis of universal male suffrage. This constitution was partially suspended by royal decree in 1928 and replaced, in 1930, by another, which somewhat restricted the powers of Parliament, increased those of the executive, and provided for elections in two stages, under a new Electoral Law. This remained in force until 1935, when the king—under nationalist pressure, just before the conclusion of the treaty of alliance with Britain—restored the constitution of 1923, which then remained in force until the Revolution. But throughout this period the average life of a Cabinet was less than one year, and there were general elections in 1924, 1925, 1926, 1929, 1931, 1936, 1938, 1942, 1946, and 1950. In addition, the king frequently acted in a very high-handed and arbitrary way.

A significant feature in this last part of the period under review is the steady enlargement of the area of reform in regard to the law administered by the *Sharīʿa* courts. Law No. 25 of 1920 had introduced some very welcome reforms in the sphere of marriage and divorce by the simple expedient of adopting a 'weaker' Ḥanafī view, or the dominant view of one of the other

Sunnī schools, in place of the dominant Ḥanafī doctrine. This was enough to give considerable relief to ill-used wives whose needs could be met by a judicial dissolution of their marriages, but it would not suffice to restrict the evil of child marriage or to provide any limitation on the ridiculously wide validity accorded to formulae of repudiation uttered by Muslim husbands.

The problem of child marriage could, however, find at least a partial solution by the procedural expedient which we have already described. Thus under the Law of the Organisation and Procedure of *Sharī'a* Courts, 1931, these courts were precluded from entertaining any litigation in respect of a disputed marriage[1] which had not been registered, and already, in 1923, the registrars of marriages had been forbidden to register any union in which the bride and bridegroom had not reached the age of 16 and 18 respectively; and they were also precluded from hearing any matrimonial cause whatever where the parties had not reached these ages at the time of litigation. As for a husband's unilateral repudiation of his wife, the expedient of an eclectic choice between the doctrines of the different schools and jurists was stretched, in the provisions of Law No. 25 of 1929, to include certain dicta attributed to early jurists before the schools had crystallized, together with opinions put forward by certain radical thinkers of a rather later period, with the result that most forms of repudiation which the husband did not really intend to be effective were henceforth deemed not to end the marriage relationship.

It did, indeed, seem probable, in 1927, that the reforms would go considerably further than this, for the Cabinet approved draft legislation to restrict polygamy and actively to restrain a husband from exercising his right of repudiation. The provisions designed to this end were based, in the main, on the views of Muḥammad 'Abduh, and constituted not so much a choice between the variant views of the past as a contemporary exercise of the right of *ijtihād*, or the faculty of going back to the original sources of the law and interpreting and applying them by one's own exertions. This faculty, which was freely exercised during the first three centuries of the Muslim era, has been commonly considered by Sunnīs to have then fallen into abeyance; but many modern Muslims deny this, and claim that there can be no objection to its resuscitation. In the event, however, King Fu'ād refused to approve these particular provisions, and they were not included in Law No. 25 of 1929.

But all these reforms—except only in the field of organization and procedure—were fragmentary and piecemeal. They tackled, indeed, the points which seemed most urgent, sometimes in a surprisingly radical way; but they could in no sense be regarded as comprehensive codes. So it was a new departure[2] when, in 1943, the Law of Intestate Succession was promulgated, followed in 1946 by the Law of Testamentary Dispositions and the Law of

[1] Except only a claim of legitimacy.

[2] For the three codes drafted by Qadrī Pasha (Personal Status, *Waqfs*, and Contracts and Property) were never officially promulgated.

the Provisions of the *Waqf*.[1] In these comparatively comprehensive codes little or no claim was made to the faculty of *ijtihād*; but the principle of an eclectic choice between the variant opinions of the past was sometimes taken to the utmost limits in the process known as *talfīq*, namely the combination of part of the view of one school or jurist with part of the opinion of another in a composite whole which is really new, although each of its component parts can claim the most respectable ancestry.

Meanwhile, however, the most significant developments had taken place in regard to the Mixed Courts and the Consular Courts, as a result of sustained pressure[2] from politicians of almost all parties in Egypt that the Capitulations must be brought to an end and that Egypt must attain juridical as well as political independence. This demand enjoyed British support, and a conference of the Capitulatory Powers at Montreux led to the Montreux Convention of 8 May 1937, under which the Capitulations were abolished, the Consular Courts were deprived of their extra-territorial jurisdiction in all criminal matters, and the Mixed Courts were to be brought to an end after a 'transitory period' of twelve years (during which they were to take cognisance of all criminal proceedings against foreigners, in addition to continuing with their civil jurisdiction).

Realizing that the abolition of the Capitulations and the administration of all criminal justice in regard to foreigners by the Mixed Courts would necessitate certain amendments to the existing criminal law—for the Criminal Code drafted for the Mixed Courts in 1875 had remained virtually a dead letter, and the Criminal Codes of 1883 and 1904, drafted for the National Courts, were not regarded as altogether suitable for foreigners—the Egyptian government had appointed a commission to make the necessary preparations. The result was the Penal Code of 1937, promulgated for use in both the Mixed and National Courts and applicable to all residents in Egypt. This was firmly based on the Code of 1904, with such minor modifications as seemed necessary.[3]

But a much more difficult task confronted the government during the 'transition period'—namely, the preparation of a new Civil Code for use in the National Courts in 1949, when they would inherit a monopoly of all jurisdiction, civil and criminal. The Civil Code of 1883, drafted for the National Courts, was almost as French in its inspiration as that promulgated in 1875 for the Mixed Courts; and there was considerable pressure in Egypt that the new code should not represent any slavish adoption of an alien

[1] The most noteworthy feature of this law was the fact that it decreed that private or family *awqāf* must never be created in future to last for more than sixty years, or two series of beneficiaries, after the death of the founder; and that public or 'charitable' *awqāf* might in future be either permanent or temporary, except only in the case of mosques or cemeteries.

[2] In which lawyers, again, played a leading role.

[3] Cf. Sarofim, op. cit., pp. 60 f. This Commission was composed of one Englishman, Sir Arthur Booth, and two Egyptians, 'Abd al-Ḥamīd Badawī Pasha and Ṣabrī Abū 'Alam Pasha. Sir Arthur Booth was the last Englishman to hold the post of judicial adviser.

system, but should rest on a much more indigenous foundation. There was, indeed, an extremely vocal minority which asserted that, now that ways and means had been found of codifying the precepts and principles of the *Sharīʿa* on an eclectic basis, and with a new freedom of interpretation and application, there was no reason why a comprehensive code of civil law should not be derived exclusively from this source.

The responsibility for drafting this new code was entrusted to a committee under the chairmanship of ʿAbd al-Razzāq Aḥmad al-Sanhūrī Pasha. Their work was much discussed, both in the press and among experts; their draft was extensively debated, both in the Senate and the Chamber of Deputies; and the code was eventually promulgated in July 1948, and brought into operation on 15 October 1949. Considerable publicity was given at the time, moreover, to the fact that the new code had drawn extensively on 'the decisions of Egyptian courts, comparative legislation and the *Sharīʿa*' as its sources of amendment and enrichment; but this must not be allowed to obscure the fact that Sanhūrī Pasha himself stated, in the course of its discussion before the Committee of Civil Law set up for that purpose by the Senate: 'I put on record now that three-quarters, or five-sixths, of the provisions of this Law are based on the decisions of Egyptian courts and on the existing legislation.'[1] All the same, the Explanatory Memorandum states unequivocally that its authors derived from the *Sharīʿa* 'many of its general concepts and many of its detailed provisions';[2] the Report of the Committee of Civil Law reiterated this claim and remarked that 'the strengthening of the links between this draft code and the provisions of the *Sharīʿa* represents a retention of a spiritual heritage which deserves to be preserved and used';[3] and Sanhūrī, when challenged as to why he had not based it more firmly on the *Sharīʿa*, stated categorically: 'I assure you that we did not leave a single sound provision of the *Sharīʿa* which we could have included in this legislation without so doing. . . . We adopted from the *Sharīʿa* all that we could adopt, having regard to sound principles of modern legislation; and we did not fall short in this respect.'[4]

What, then, is the debt that this code does in fact owe to the *Sharīʿa*? This can, perhaps, be classified under four headings:

(*a*) That the *Sharīʿa* is specifically mentioned as one of the sources from which judges should derive a rule to decide any point not covered by the provisions of the code. This is chiefly enshrined in Article 1, which enacts that 'The provisions of this code govern all matters to which they apply in letter or spirit. In the absence of any provision that is applicable, the judge will decide according to custom and, in the absence of this, in accordance with the principles of the *Sharīʿa*. In the absence of these, the judge will apply the principles of natural justice and the dictates of equity'. Opinions may, of

[1] *al-Qānūn al-madanī: Majmūʿat al-aʿmāl al-Taḥḍīriyya*, vol. i, p. 70.
[2] Ibid., p. 20. [3] Ibid., p. 159. [4] Ibid., pp. 85, etc.

course, differ as to the real significance of this provision; but I must confess that I myself regard it as of more value for purposes of propaganda and sentiment than practical application. But it is important to note that subsequent articles expressly provide that 'Missing persons and absent persons are subject to provisions enacted in special legislation, in the absence of which the *Sharī'a* will be applied';[1] that 'The establishment of the heirs, the computation of their shares in the inheritance, and the devolution upon them of the items of the estate, is governed by the provisions of the *Sharī'a* and by the legislative enactments concerning inheritance and estates',[2] and that 'Wills are governed by the provisions of the *Sharī'a* and by legislative enactments concerning wills'.[3] Here the mention of legislative enactments refers to Laws No. 25 of 1920 and 1929, to the Law of Intestate Succession, 1943, and to the Law of Testamentary dispositions, 1946—all of which have already been discussed; but the Explanatory Memorandum to the new code remarks that these articles have resolved certain points of dispute and have made it clear that the Islamic law of testate and intestate succession applies to all Egyptians, irrespective of their religion or sect.

(*b*) That a natural inclination in favour of conformity with the *Sharī'a* has sometimes influenced the choice between certain concepts on which European codes are themselves divided. Alleged examples of this principle may be found in an objective rather than subjective tendency in regard to the treatment of obligations and contractual rights;[4] the principles applicable to 'abuse of rights';[5] the legal consequences of exceptional and unpredictable events;[6] and provisions regarding the assignment of debts.[7] The last of these may be regarded as essentially Islamic, although a parallel may be found in Germanic codes; but in each of the other cases the primary source was almost certainly European law.

(*c*) That in a few points new borrowings have in fact been made from the *Sharī'a*. Instances quoted for this are the principles governing the *majlis al-'aqd*,[8] legal capacity,[9] the lease of *waqf*,[10] the contract of *ḥikr*,[11] the lease of agricultural land,[12] the termination of a lease on the death of the lessee or the occurrence of 'serious and unforeseen circumstances',[13] and the release of debts by unilateral declaration.[14]

1 Art. 32. 2 Art. 875. 3 Art. 915.
4 Cf. *al-Qānūn al-madanī*, vol. i, pp. 20 f. Also vol. ii, pp. 5 ff.
5 Arts. 4 and 5. Cf. ibid., vol. i, p. 91.
6 Arts. 147 and 608. Cf. ibid., p. 89.
7 Arts. 315–22. Cf. ibid., vol. iii, pp. 136 ff.
8 i.e. the 'meeting' at which a contract is concluded. Cf. Art. 94 and ibid., vol. ii, pp. 39 ff.
9 Arts. 45–47, 110–16, 118–19. Cf. ibid., vol. i, pp. 357–62; vol. ii, pp. 112–28 and 132–40.
10 Arts. 628–34. Cf. ibid., vol. iv, pp. 648–63.
11 Arts. 999–1014. Cf. ibid., vol. vi, pp. 560 ff.
12 Arts. 610–27. Cf. ibid., vol. iv, pp. 602–45.
13 Arts. 601–2, 608–9. Cf. ibid., pp. 580–4 and 597–601.
14 Arts. 371–2. Cf. ibid., vol. iii, pp. 294 ff.

(*d*) That those provisions in the previous codes which were derived from the *Sharīʿa* have been retained.[1]

Little remains to be said. Yet another Law of *Ḥisbiyya* Courts was promulgated in 1949, and a new Criminal Code and Criminal Procedure Code in 1950[2]—and it is noteworthy that the consent of the *muftī* is no longer required before a death sentence is executed.

5. *Postscript*

The period under review does not, of course, include the Revolution, so no attempt has been made in this paper to review the legislation which has governed the programmes of land reform, nationalization and socialization. But it is germane to this paper to note that in 1952 private or family *waqfs*, which had been severely restricted in their scope and duration in 1946,[3] were abolished; and that in 1955 the same fate befell both the *Sharīʿa* Courts and those of the non-Muslim communities. This does not mean that the *Sharīʿa* law[4] is not still applied in all that concerns the personal status and family law of Muslim litigants, or the law of the non-Muslim communities in so far as the family law of their members is concerned (but excluding, in their case, matters of testate and intestate succession, in which the Islamic law is now applied to all Egyptians); but it does mean that all litigation in Egypt, without exception, has now been entrusted to the National Courts. It is true that most of the *qāḍīs* of the former *Sharīʿa* Courts were taken over by the National Courts and still exercise jurisdiction in such cases; but these will inevitably be eliminated by the passage of time, and it seems most unlikely that any future judges will be recruited from personnel trained in the old, traditional way.[5]

This clearly makes it the more imperative that the law of personal status, as applied by the courts, should be reduced to a comprehensive code—as has already happened in Syria, Tunisia, Morocco, and Iraq. But although such a code has, in fact, been in draft in Egypt for some years, the dispute between the conservatives and the progressives still continues, and the expected date of promulgation has been repeatedly postponed. It seems unlikely, moreover, that any decision will be taken in this matter in the immediate future, since the present régime may well hesitate, at this juncture, to offend conservative opinion inside Egypt regarding such matters as polygamy and divorce, on the one hand, or to forfeit its international reputation as progressive and

1 Cf. above, pp. 217, 219. For this whole subject see my 'The Sharīʿa and civil law'.

2 Brought into operation in 1951. It has, indeed, been remarked that under these codes the procedural law of Egypt has gone back rather more closely to French models and discarded certain 'British' adaptations.

3 See above, p. 226.

4 Now in its partially codified form, of course.

5 It is noteworthy that lawyers, once again, took a leading part in advocating the abolition of communal jurisdiction.

enlightened by lagging behind Tunisia, Morocco, Iraq, and even Syria, on the other.

But, however this may be, the future administration of the Islamic law by personnel trained in the modern, rather than the traditional, fashion can scarcely fail to exercise a certain influence on the law they apply. It seems reasonably certain, moreover, that it is only a question of time before the law in Egypt is not only administered by unified courts, staffed by personnel trained in a unified way, but is itself based either on a unified code, or at least on a series of codes which are closely integrated. In everything except the personal and family law these codes will represent an amalgam between Western and Islamic concepts, with the basic emphasis on the former—but with the whole permeated, if the present trend continues, with the ideology and objectives of Arab Socialism; and even in the sphere of family this amalgam will in fact subsist, but in a form which is much more distinctively Islamic.

The Impact of Egypt on Britain
A Study of Public Opinion

H. S. DEIGHTON

THERE can be no exercise more certain to disabuse a student of history of the illusion that his study is an exact science, than an essay into the history of opinion. Opinion sways almost everything in public life, it can be identified easily but quantified only with difficulty, so that the history of opinion is itself, more evidently than with other forms of historical writing, the expression of opinion. Yet to say following from this that the history of opinion is necessarily so insubstantial as to be scarcely worth writing is almost to set aside the possibility of writing history at all, especially the sort of political history which concerns itself with the relationships of nations, so generally does the picture of their relationships spring not from any set of objective facts but from what people have believed—or have chosen to believe—to be the facts.

Within these limits the study of the way in which one society has seen itself in relation to another has attracted close and fruitful attention during the past twenty years—notable are Professor Southern's brilliant and luminous essay on *Western views of Islam in the Middle Ages*, and Dr. Daniel's *Islam and the West*, which he significantly sub-titled 'The making of an image'.[1] No less appropriate as being concerned with the image current from time to time in one nation–state or another, is recent work on the English picture of Russia—by Dr. M. S. Anderson and Dr. Gleason.[2] Dr. Gleason felt the need for a basic theory upon which to depend his argument, and made use of that which was first set out by Mr. Walter Lippman.[3] From this he took the concept of 'stereotypes'—of the standard images of other peoples which tend to gain currency—the 'well worn moulds into which . . . remote and unfamiliar objects tend to fall at all times and in all societies'.[4] It is with such images of Egypt and of Britain's role there as have been current among British people since the two first became important to one another that this paper is concerned—with the images themselves and not with any attempt to put a value upon their accuracy. This is an exercise not in Egyptian but in British history—important to the history of Egypt only because for a short period of

[1] R. W. Southern, *Western views of Islam in the Middle Ages* (Cambridge, Mass., 1962); and Norman Daniel, *Islam and the West. The making of an image* (Edinburgh, 1960).

[2] M. S. Anderson, *Britain's discovery of Russia, 1553–1815* (London, 1958) and J. H. Gleason, *The genesis of Russo-phobia in Great Britain* (London, 1940).

[3] Walter Lippman, *Public opinion* (New York, 1929).

[4] Gleason, op. cit., p. 7.

her long history Britain was herself of the first importance to Egypt. In it we may safely look for 'images' and 'stereotypes', though we must expect to find that these things are susceptible to change. We shall find that it is possible for two different and conflicting images to exist side by side in the same society, reflecting conflicts between those who hold them.

Egypt remained 'remote' so far as the British people were concerned, until the middle of the nineteenth century. By 1848, a reviewer could remark that a tour of Egypt was 'no greater novelty than a tour of Italy before the first French Revolution', and that it 'would be a weary task to enumerate [the travel books on the eastern Mediterranean in the preceding twenty years] . . . especially since steam and the liberal rule of Muhammad Ali'.[1] A hundred years later, after the troop movements of two world wars, the number of living British men and women who had served in Egypt and had thereby acquired a picture of the country which was none the less vivid and significant for being partial and distorted, was probably greater than the total number of British people who had ever visited India. This fact may help to explain the reluctance of the nation which had, in 1947, watched the surrender of the empire of India with hardly a murmur of protest, to allow that they did not any longer stand in a special relationship, at once privileged and tutelary, to Egypt. For the rest of the explanation of this curious fact we must look to the previous history of the relationship between the two countries, and in particular to the almost incessant barrage of opinion, sentiment and propaganda about that relationship to which the British people had been subjected for a hundred years.

This stream of opinion-forming material began to flow in the time of Muḥammad ʿAlī. But the 'liberal rule' of Muḥammad ʿAlī was not an expression to which all his contemporaries would have assented. A decade earlier, in 1838, Englishmen who were concerned about politics had been obliged to take a view about the Egypt of Muḥammad ʿAlī because of the great crisis brought about in international, and in English domestic, politics, by Lord Palmerston's determination to treat the pasha as a danger to the Ottoman Empire which it had become a cardinal point of his policy to defend. Palmerston had decided to drive the pasha's forces out of Syria and to confine him for the remainder of his life, and that of his dynasty, which Palmerston did not expect would long survive him, to what he called 'his shell of Egypt'. Englishmen at that time—and since then—were unhappy at, even incapable of accepting, mere considerations of power—reasons of state—as the sole bases of national policy. They wanted—and Palmerston himself was not less characteristically one of them in this, than in so many other respects—not only to have, and to be seen to have, sufficient power to make it probable that they would emerge on the winning side in any likely

[1] *The Spectator*, 20 Apr. 1848, in a review of Harriet Martineau, *Eastern life, past and present.*

conflict. They wanted too the feeling that they were on the right side in a moral, humane, sense.[1]

Their principles were the belief in ordered freedom and in the systematic removal of anomaly and injustice—'reform' which it was confidently believed would result in a continuing tide of human betterment—'progress'. 'Palmerston', wrote an historian in this century, 'could not try to advance British interests without associating them with an attempt to improve the lot of those who were to be used as the instruments of that purpose'.[2] This was true both of Palmerston himself and of the British electors, whose opinions he came to know so well and to manipulate so skilfully. The British public demanded of their leaders the sense both that they were strong and that the policy of their country was an instrument of progress throughout the world. In the East, where the British government had decided—after understandable hesitations but with good show of reason—that peace and British interests would both be best served by sustaining the Ottoman Empire, the first of these requirements was easily come by—the second very much less so.[3] Palmerston's domestic problem was to convince his fellow-countrymen that the prospects of 'progress' were greater in Turkey than in Egypt. It was not an easy undertaking, for the achievements of the 'founder of modern Egypt' had caught the eye and attracted some sympathy in England. Jeremy Bentham, the most conspicuous prophet of reform, had written to Muḥammad ʿAlī in 1828, addressing him as 'Le plus éclairé et le plus bienfaisant, qui fut jamais parmis les sectateurs de l'Islamisme' and offering to make permanent his beneficient régime by undertaking personally the education of 'Votre petit-fils Abbas'.[4] But when Egypt became for the first time a preoccupation of politically minded Englishmen, Palmerston saw to it that she was presented to them as a country in the grip of an indefensible, and probably transient, tyranny.

There is little reason to suppose that he was being less than honest in propagating this view. His private letters make clear the reality of his personal dislike of Muḥammad ʿAlī and all his works. And it is worth while to draw attention to his sincerity, if only to make the point that Egypt has conspicuously been a country of which many Englishmen have found it easy to believe what it was convenient for them to believe. Palmerston attacked the Muḥammad ʿAlī régime on grounds of policy, but he had good 'ideological' reasons for doing so. He certainly did not share the view of Jeremy Bentham that Muḥammad ʿAlī was the Peter the Great of the Muslim world. Indeed, for all that his professions of faith in the regenerative capacity of Constantinople seems to have owed as much to necessity as to judgement, the signature,

1 C. K. Webster, *The foreign policy of Lord Palmerston, 1830–1841* (London, 1951), p. 577.
2 Ibid.
3 Bernard Lewis, *The emergence of modern Turkey* (London, 1961), chapter iv and *passim*.
4 B.M. Add. MS. 25663, f. 139.

in 1838, of an Anglo-Turkish Commercial Treaty was in close accord with the economic doctrines of the British Liberals and seemed to Palmerston to be a genuine and major reform, a step without which progress would be impossible and from which it could not fail to flow. It was also a weapon against Egypt, for its application of qualified free trade principles to the entire Ottoman Empire included Egypt and could, therefore, not fail to strike at the monopolies which were still the bases of Muḥammad 'Alī's economy. These monopolies were anathema to Palmerston's Englishmen and it was not difficult to persuade them, especially those who had no experience of Egypt at first hand, of the truth of Palmerston's own private judgement that 'Mehemet Ali has divided the population of Egypt into two classes, the Rich and the Poor. The rich class consists of Mehemet Ali himself single and alone, the poor class all the other inhabitants of Egypt'.[1] Add to this the fact that the existence of domestic slavery in Egypt was well known and that the conquest of the northern Sudan was widely regarded as a large-scale, long-term, slave hunt, and it is easy to see why such denunciations of the Egyptian régime found ready listeners in England. Yet this first British 'official view' of Egypt did not go unchallenged. Two conflicting views about Egypt and her rulers were to characterize British opinion from that day to this. The challenge to Palmerston's interpretation came notably from some of his own officials in Egypt[2]—yet the effective persistence of his own view can best be illustrated by the words with which Sir Charles Webster, writing over a hundred years later, chose to express that fact. 'Nearly all . . . [Palmerston's] agents' he wrote, 'succumbed to the wiles of Mehemet.'[3]

The Eastern crisis of 1839 was not only an international crisis in which Great Britain was intimately concerned. It involved a major and memorable conflict in British domestic politics. Palmerston contrived a general acceptance of the view that Egypt had undergone no more than a 'spurious regeneration'.[4] But the real issue—as so often in the history of Anglo-Egyptian relations—lay elsewhere. Co-operation with France, cautious and qualified, but genuine, had been a central feature of Palmerston's policy, as of his immediate predecessors. But, by 1838, Palmerston had decided that the integrity of the Ottoman Empire was of more consequence to England even than the friendship of France—which was thus placed in jeopardy because the most voci-

[1] Palmerston–Ponsonby, 23 June 1838, quoted in Webster op. cit., p. 275.

[2] See F. S. Rodkey, 'The efforts of Briggs and company to guide British policy in the Levant, 1821–1841' in *Journal of Modern History* vol. v (1933), pp. 324 ff.; V. J. Puryear, *International economics and diplomacy in the Near East, 1834–1853*, especially pp. 23 ff.; Webster, op. cit., p. 607, for the views of the British consul-general, 'Campbell grew more and more favourable to Mehemet', and, of a special envoy, in B38, 'Bowring . . . too, fell under Mehemet's spell'.

[3] Webster, op. cit., p. 607.

[4] The phrase is Lord Ponsonby's. In the dispatch in which he described the proclamation of the Edict of Gülhane, he seized the opportunity for a side-blow at Muḥammad 'Alī. Ponsonby–Palmerston, 5 Nov. 1839; quoted by Webster, op. cit., p. 656.

ferous elements in French politics and in the French press, had long found an outlet for their national pride in the patronage of Muḥammad ʿAlī. Since the more radical members of the British Cabinet were essentially anti-Russian, and anxious not to quarrel with France, the result was a conflict which went near to bringing the government down. And this in such circumstances as, wrote the prime minister, while the struggle was at its height, 'will be an evil for the country because it will appear, and it will be, that the English government will have been changed by the outcry of the Press and populace of Paris, and by the mere apprehension of a serious difference with France'.[1] When Palmerston had triumphed and Muḥammad ʿAlī was once more contained within his 'shell of Egypt', the affairs of that country had finally come to be a concern of the powers of Europe, and the English people had acquired a habit of which they have only recently begun to break themselves—that of looking to the extent of their influence in Egypt as one measure of their status in world affairs.

The next phase of Anglo-French conflict in Egypt arose over the building of the Suez Canal.[2] This struggle for influence was fought out against the hectic background of the Egypt of the reign of Saʿīd Pasha and the first part of that of Ismāʿīl, and introduced new elements into the Englishman's image of Egypt from which at the same time, there gradually arose a concept, attractive to many Englishmen, of an English role there.

Among the steady flow of books upon Egypt which came from the English presses from the time of Muḥammad ʿAlī, one remained pre-eminent, both for its quality, and for the extent and persistence of its influence. That was Lane's, *Modern Egyptians*.[3] Lane had been one of a small but distinguished band of Englishmen who, attracted principally by the dramatic unfolding of the life of ancient Egypt, had gone to live and study there during the 1820s.[4]

[1] Lord Melbourne, quoted by Webster, op. cit., p. 712. For a coherent expression of the place which Egypt held in the conspectus of French Radical thought, see Louis Blanc, *The history of ten years, 1830–1840* (London, 1844–5), especially vol. ii, pp. 197 ff.

[2] The Duke of Argyll, *Autobiography and memoirs* (London, 1906), vol. i, p. 568: 'On the 20th August (1855) we heard for the first time in the Cabinet of an idea which ultimately took form in one of the greatest events of our time. This was the idea of cutting a canal to join the Mediterranean and the Red Sea. It was a French idea and was urged upon us by our ally Louis Napoleon. Palmerston surprised me and others by the most vehement opposition. It would, he said, cut off Egypt from Turkey, stop the advance of the troops of the Suzerain Power and place British interests in Egypt and India at the mercy of the French. . . . All my colleagues and I thought the proposal itself was one which could not be creditably or successfully opposed. . . . But Palmerston remained hostile. . . . He seemed quite ready for us to quarrel with France rather than to consent to any such canal.' Such was Palmerston's personal influence at that time that he carried his unwilling colleagues with him and committed successive British governments to a policy whose signal and public failure was marked by the opening of the canal in the exhilarating days of 1869 when the first convoy steamed through the isthmus, headed by the Empress Eugénie herself in the Imperial yacht on what was to be the swan song of the diplomacy of the Second Empire.

[3] Edward William Lane, *An account of the manners and customs of the modern Egyptians* (London, 1836).

[4] Some of their names, Wilkinson, James Burton (later Haliburton), Linant, and Bonomi, have their places in the history of Egyptology.

But Lane was soon strongly attracted by the life of Egyptians in his own day. In 1833, apparently at the prompting of Lord Brougham, he returned to Egypt for another two years to complete an account of contemporary Egyptian society. First published in December 1836, *Modern Egyptians* was sold out in two weeks and the first printing of a second and cheaper edition had gone before the end of the next year. The process continued throughout the nineteenth century until, in 1908, the book found a place in the Everyman Library with an edition which had been four times reprinted by 1936.[1] This remarkable publishing history is scarcely surprising, for the work was, and remains, a model for the accurate description of the life of a whole society. Its great and continued success is at once a tribute to the appetite of Victorian Englishmen for serious and detailed information, and a comment on the extent to which they were interested in Egypt. It is safe to say that a comparable book on India—if one had ever appeared—would have had a far less general success.

It was upon the basis of Lane's book that all serious attempts by Englishmen to understand Egyptian society rested for a hundred years. It was certainly no bad basis. But in one very important respect the picture of Egypt left upon the English mind by Lane was changed during the years between the Crimean War and the occupation of 1882. During those years there grew up, partly as a by-product of the course of British policy, and partly through the comments of influential observers, a greater degree of understanding of the real native Egyptians, the *fallāḥīn*, who attracted a growing sympathy. In part, this new attitude to the native people of Egypt was a direct result of Palmerston's determination to resist the French project for digging the Suez Canal. Frustrated in the attempt to secure, by diplomatic means, the repeal of the *ferman*, which gave de Lesseps the necessary authority to go ahead with his project, successive British governments switched their attack to its likely social effects in Egypt itself. The Canal, it was argued, would not benefit Egypt at all, and would do incalculable harm to the native Egyptians, both during its construction by the ruthless use of forced labour, and afterwards by increasing and making permanent the European community in the country, which was represented as being for the most part rapacious, unscrupulous and, from the point of view of Egyptian interests, thoroughly undesirable.

Lane had been affectionate and interested rather than respectful towards the native Egyptians, whose way of life he described in such detail. He wrote of the word *fallāḥ* that 'the Turks often apply this term to the Egyptians in general in an abusive sense as meaning the "boors" or "the clowns"',[2] but he himself showed little respect for them. Rather, for all his detailed study of, and long sojourn with, the Muslims of the towns, he was an early example of the Englishman infected with nostalgia for the dwellers in the desert. 'The

[1] Five thousand copies were sold in serial form in Knight's 'Weekly Volumes' in the 1840s and an edition in two volumes, first issued in 1871, had sold more than 17,000 copies by 1877.

[2] Lane, op. cit. (Everyman edn.), p. 27.

Felláḥeen of Egypt', he wrote, 'cannot be justly represented in a very favourable light with regard to their domestic and social condition and manners. In the worst points of view, they resemble their Bedawee ancestors, without possessing many of the virtues of the inhabitants of the desert.'[1] But another observer, whose book first appeared a few years earlier, expressed a view which was eventually to achieve wider (and highly influential) acceptance in England. James Augustus St. John's *Egypt and Mohammed Ali, or travels in the valley of the Nile* (1834) was an ephemeral work. An important reviewer[2] made it plain that he thought so. But a generally hostile notice found in St. John's judgements the 'merit . . . of having deigned to pay some attention to the poor oppressed fellahs whom preceding travellers have treated very much in the spirit of their tyrannical oppressors', and praised him for having 'had the courage to show the many admirable qualities which, amidst their desolation and misery, still distinguished the Arab population of Egypt'. The *fallāḥīn* were naturally industrious and active but they had been so preyed upon by the pasha (Muḥammad ʿAlī) and by 'a class of foreign mechanics and adventurers' that 'in a land which ought to be the realm of plenty want universally prevails; the whole mass of the population have been reduced to the state of paupers'. Thus early, and little noticed, was sounded a note which accorded very well with the views of Lord Palmerston and which was to grow louder and more influential in the decades after his death.

As early as 1855, in instructing the British ambassador in Paris to ask the French government not to back the Canal project, the British government had drawn attention to the 'disastrous effects' which would follow the inevitable large-scale use of forced labour.[3] Once adopted, the policy of resistance to the use of the corvée was consistently upheld and vigorously prosecuted, and information about forced labour was carefully collected and sent home by the official British representatives in Egypt.[4] Such ammunition was then, as it were, loaded in the drafting departments of the Foreign Office and fired at points deemed appropriate. Thus, in February 1863, Lord John Russell from the Foreign Office, instructed Lord Bulwer, ambassador in Constantinople, that he should impress upon the Turkish, and they in turn upon the Egyptian, authorities, that care should be taken that temporary compulsion to keep open certain essential irrigation ditches 'is not made a precedent for the employment of forced labour on the Suez Canal or on other speculative enterprises'. Forced labour, he added, had long since been abolished in Turkey, and was

[1] Lane, op. cit., p. 201.

[2] *Edinburgh Review*, July 1834, pp. 404 ff.

[3] P.R.O., F.O. 27. To Cowley (in Paris) No. 761 of 18 July 1855. This was not inconsistent on the part of a government which had, with the full support, and sometimes perhaps in fear, of English public opinion, consistently fought the slave-trade. Yet it did represent something of a sudden conversion, for there is little evidence of any British embarrassment at the use of forced labour in the construction of the Alexandria–Suez railway line which was the preferred British alternative to the Canal.

[4] P.R.O., F.O. 198/27. Volume of Confidential print dated 19 Dec. 1865. *Correspondence relating to the Suez Canal: 1859–1865*. Colquhoun's No. 146 of 1 Apr. 1862.

'a remnant of barbarous times . . . it is impossible to suppose that the fellahs of Egypt differ so much from the rest of mankind as to be unwilling to labour for wages if sufficient wages were offered to them. . . . This forced labour system degrades and demoralises the population and strikes at the root of the productive resources of the country.'[1]

When, as the result of the arbitration of the Emperor Napoleon III, the battle against the Canal was finally lost, the British government took comfort and credit, with British opinion, for the fact that forced labour, which had at one time involved 60,000 *fallāḥīn* on the Canal, was to end 'essentially owing to the exertions of Her Majesty's Government'.[2]

Alongside this official picture of the plight of the native Egyptians, widely presented in the British press, stood another; that of the exploitation of Egypt and her peoples by rascally aliens, many of them French. The exploitation and abuse of Egypt by foreign residents sheltering under the privileges conferred upon them by the indiscriminate extension of the system of Capitulations, has often been described.[3]

In 1865, Lord Bulwer, the British ambassador at Constantinople, left his Embassy under a cloud, which had nothing to do with the affairs of Egypt. Just before he did so he visited Egypt and wrote, in analysis and instruction, a paper to the consul-general in Alexandria which remains as lucid and accurate a statement of the British view of Egypt, and of British policy towards Egypt in those years, as can be found.[4] At this time, and indeed for nearly a hundred years after it, what the British most feared was a drastic and incalculable change in the status and situation of Egypt. To make the pasha 'independent of the Porte', he wrote, 'would be to withdraw from Egypt the protection which it derives from being part of the Ottoman empire. To sink him down to an ordinary Pasha would be to make the fate of Egypt entirely dependent on that of Turkey; whereas if any catastrophe befell other Turkish provinces it might still be our . . . policy to preserve the territory . . . from a foreign yoke. And in such case it would be a great help to find a government constituted and accustomed to exercise a sort of national authority.' 'Our aim . . . is to build up the native Government and not to pull it down.' 'At this instant, a Frenchman can walk into a crowd with a revolver and shoot the first three Arabs he sees. The Egyptian government can neither inflict punishment upon him nor have any share in his trial; the French Consul takes the whole affair into his own hands . . . nor are there wanting daily examples of new attempts to interfere in the local Government. . . .' Opportunities for such

[1] P.R.O., F.O. 198/27. Russell to Bulwer, No. 8 of 11 Feb. 1863.

[2] P.R.O., F.O. 198/27.

[3] Notably, and most recently, by D. S. Landes, *Bankers and pashas* (London, 1958).

[4] Lyons to Russell No. 8 of 25 Oct. 1865, from Constantinople, enclosing a copy of Bulwer to Stanton (at Alexandria) of 10 Oct. 1865. The quotations are from the latter document which Lyons, who had just succeeded Bulwer as ambassador at Constantinople, described as 'a very able and important State paper'.

interference were, naturally enough, eagerly sought by consuls anxious to demonstrate the extent of their influence in Egypt. The consequent erosion of the authority of government was bad for Egypt and, he argued, consequently bad for England, though 'even our own Consuls have at times fancied that English influence was to be exhibited and extended by these means'. This was unwise for 'It is true that if the Egyptians permit other nations to usurp unduly, certain privileges for ours must be claimed; but it is far more desirable that the Viceroy should exercise those powers that justly belong to him than that we should share in the general spoliation of his legitimate rights'. And he pointed with an accuracy which the advantages of hindsight serve only to emphasize, to the complications which the affairs of Egypt brought to relations between England and France: '. . . our general policy and the tendency of public opinion in England is favourable to what is called a French alliance. . . . It is not desirable therefore for us to have a quarrel with France on Egyptian matters. . . . But . . . we cannot make it too clear . . . that we will not allow France to assume, directly or indirectly . . . a predominant situation in Egypt.' There are few better accounts of the problems and considerations which were to underlie the British attitude to Egypt, at least, until the making of the Anglo-French *Entente*, in 1904.

Thus for British opinion, public no less than official, Egypt was a country suffering from exploitation by privileged foreigners: Egypt was a country whose people deserved sympathy and whose limited but effective independence was something to be encouraged and sustained, so long as it was put to no very great use. Bulwer's last injunction in this dispatch was to try to gain the confidence of the Egyptians by showing interest in them. 'A swaggering and bullying system can never succeed but for a moment, and is always followed by reaction.'

The interest in Egyptians, for which Bulwer called, had in the same year received much stimulus in the publication of a book which was to become a minor classic of later Victorian England. Upper Egypt had become a winter resort for well-to-do English people. But Lady Lucie Duff Gordon, who went to live at Luxor in the hope of curing herself of tuberculosis, was no ordinary tourist. Like Lane, she lived with the people and far more than he, she grew to love, to understand, and to sympathize with them. But she was not only sympathetic, she was highly articulate, and her *Letters from Egypt* (London, 1865), with its vivid picture of an Egyptian society that lost nothing in appeal for Victorian England by being recognizably 'Biblical', planted a sympathy for the *fallāḥīn* in many English minds. Favourably and influentially reviewed,[1] it was widely read and often republished. One reviewer seized upon its publication as an occasion to publicize both a new and more sympathetic understanding of the Orient and the idea that the East offered a unique role for Englishmen.[2]

[1] e.g. *Edinburgh Review*, July 1865, pp. 217–38.

[2] 'The Asiatic', he wrote, 'can never be understood by those who hate him and the woman

This reviewer was Meredith Townsend (1831–1911) and he exercised a considerable influence on English opinion, both personally through his friends, of whom Walter Bagehot, then editor of *The Economist*, was one, and anonymously through the columns of *The Spectator*, of which he was editor and part-owner. He seems to have been one of the now forgotten prophets of that age of prophets.[1] Early years in India had left him with a respect and understanding of societies other than his own in the tradition of Sir William Jones and Sir Thomas Munro. More characteristic of his contemporaries was his robust belief in the capacity of his fellow countrymen to govern and lead, although he was far from being what was soon to be known as a 'jingo'. He believed that the growing physical superiority, and the continued rivalry, of the European great powers, made necessary, for the time being, some sort of European control over the greater part of the Orient. He had no illusions that such controllers would be loved by those they controlled. In the interests of the self-respect, both of the Oriental peoples and of their European rulers, he wished the alien hand to be as honest and as light as possible. He was expressing a feeling which he had done much to popularize when he wrote: 'If anything is clear it is that Englishmen have a talent for governing Oriental peoples . . . without pressing too severely upon their social freedom'.[2] At the outbreak of the American Civil War, Townsend had committed his paper to the Northern cause, principally because he hated slavery. The North was, at first, not popular with the kind of Englishman who bought *The Spectator*, and for a while the paper's very existence was in jeopardy. But its fortunes were restored by the military success of those it supported and, when the war was over, *The Spectator* was committed to a course of continuous but reasoned advocacy of a British 'guardianship' of Egypt. It was a fruitful field of advocacy for a man who stood squarely, though far from aggressively, in the tradition of Palmerston, for it fulfilled the two requirements of national political interest and of broad humanity. England was to sustain at one and the same time her own interests and those of the general peace, by keeping other alien hands away from Egypt and, by her guardianship, to protect and raise the *fallāḥīn*, whose plight was becoming increasingly well known.

The idea of the English as protectors of the native Egyptians, was already in the air.[3] It was believed, and not unjustly according to Dr. David Landes, that the British residents were juster and less rapacious than most of their fellow Europeans. During the 1860s, events to the south of Egypt did much

who thinks every Arab graceful and dignified will understand him far better than one who is only impressed by his . . . squalor.' *The Spectator*, 22 July 1865, p. 813.

[1] The absence of a biography is surprising. It was reported of his friend and close collaborator, R. H. Hutton, that he strictly forbad any sort of obituary. 'Remember,' he said to his successor on *The Spectator*, John St. Loe Strachey, 'if you ever write anything about me . . . I will haunt you.' J. St. L. Strachey, *The Adventure of living* (London, 1922), p. 220. Perhaps Townsend felt the same way.

[2] *The Spectator*, 3 Feb. 1876.

[3] Landes, op. cit., pp. 94–95, especially note 3, p. 94.

to encourage in Englishmen the idea that this protective role could be, with advantage to almost all parties, made at once more authoritative and more extensive. This was the age of the opening-up of Africa, a process to which attention had been drawn by Muḥammad ʿAlī's conquest of the Sudan. The 1850s and 1860s were the decades of the early exploration of central Africa, of Livingstone's journeys and of the successful search for the sources of the Nile. These exploits, many of them conducted by Englishmen, were widely reported in England and avidly followed by English readers.[1] Not surprisingly the success, or supposed success, of these Englishmen in their relations with the native peoples they had to do with, and in particular the extent of the influence they often claimed to have established over them, did not escape notice. This was so particularly in the context of their frequent references to the horrors of slavery and the slave-trade. It followed that this influence was seen as the appropriate instrument for the mitigation of slavery and for the 'civilizing' of the whole vast area. Townsend was quick to take the point, which he stressed in a review of Samuel Baker's *Albert N'yanza*,[2] in 1866. He seized upon the extent of influence which Baker had achieved and drew attention to the personal qualities which in his view had accounted for it.[3] For Townsend and those who thought like him in this matter, Samuel Baker was an excellent example of a type of Englishman of whom they believed there to be many. He advocated the use of their talents to bring these 'glorious regions' within the reach of 'civilization'. 'With 5,000 Arabs thoroughly disciplined . . . a man like Mr. Baker would ensure order from Khartoum to the lake and that must one day be the first step towards the utilisation of these vast regions which now yield only elephant tusks to Europe and female slaves to the harems of Egypt, Turkey and Africa.'[4]

In 1869, the idea of employing English talent in this way was given reality

[1] e.g.: D. Livingstone, *Missionary travels and researches in South Africa*, 1857; Richard Burton, *The Lake regions of central Africa*, 1860; J. H. Speke, *Journal of the discovery of the source of the Nile*, 1863; Richard Burton and James M'Queen, *The Nile basin*, 1864; J. H. Speke, *What led to the discovery of the source of the Nile*, 1864; James Grant, *A walk across Africa*, 1864; D. Livingstone, *Narrative of our expedition to the Zambesi and its tributaries*, 1865; Samuel W. Baker, *Albert N'yanza, great basin of the Nile*, 1866; Samel W. Baker, *The Nile tributaries of Abyssinia*, 1867; H. M. Stanley, *How I found Livingstone*, 1872; Georg Schweinfurth, *The heart of Africa*, 1873; D. Livingstone, *Last journals*, 1874; Samuel W. Baker, *Ismailïa, A narrative of the expedition to central Africa for the suppression of the slave trade*, 1877. Circumstances combined to give these books a wide popular appeal. Interest in missionary enterprise and the scope for it was general and persistent, as was that in slavery. Livingstone was a national hero. The dispute about the 'rescue' of Livingstone had a high news value as had, earlier, that about the sources of the Nile, and Abyssinia, at the time of the dispute with Theodore.

[2] See n. 1, above.

[3] *The Spectator*, for 9 June 1866. He was 'severely just' and 'careful to prevent oppression'. He was careful to keep his word 'even to his own hurt', and 'if he killed, as he did occasionally, it was in fair fight against those who would have killed him and if he struck it was to maintain an absolutely essential discipline'.

[4] Ibid.

with Ismāʿīl's appointment of Baker to the governor-generalship of the equatorial provinces of the Sudan. There is good ground for regarding what followed as a clumsy failure. 'The expedition degenerated into a sorry affair of hand to mouth administration, tribal warfare and seizure of grain.'[1] The results were disappointing to Ismāʿīl, and accounts of Baker's activities did not win him the unqualified approval of powerful anti-slavery elements in British society. But what they learned of Baker's proceedings in the Sudan served substantially to reinforce the growing belief of the British public in 'the governing power of an Englishman when he chooses to exercise it'.[2] Ten years later the novelist, H. Rider Haggard, expressed what he knew to be a widely acceptable sentiment when he wrote: 'We alone of all the nations in the world appear to be able to control the coloured races without the exercise of cruelty. . . . It is our mission to conquer and hold in subjection, not from thirst of conquest but for the sake of law, justice and order.'[3]

This growing and, as it may now seem, fanciful, concept of a specifically and peculiarly English role in the non-European world, needs to be understood in the light of the substantial changes which came over Great Britain's position in the international community during the 1860s. The policies of Palmerston—in fact a good deal less aggressive in practice than they were bombastic in expression—had suited the British people of his day, although they had never gone unchallenged. But in the years just before his death in 1865, they grew less appropriate to the changing situation on the continent of Europe. From 1863 successive British governments pursued policies to which the far from well-defined term, 'non-interventionist', was often applied. This 'non-intervention', which in effect was a sort of isolationism, was not inappropriate to the position in which Britain found herself in Europe, but it was not a very gratifying role for those Englishmen, and they were still many, who wished to think of their country as exercising a powerful and benevolent influence upon human affairs. Like other 'isolationisms' in other places and since those days, it flourished alongside a tendency to lecture and feel superior to those neighbours with whose affairs the withdrawn neighbour disdained to mix. It was made less bearable by reason of the lurking, and not unjustified, suspicion that the British government's failure to exercise a commanding influence was not entirely a matter of choice. It was especially unsatisfactory to those who felt that their country's influence upon mankind ought to be exercised by some means more tangible and more immediate than that afforded by the example of what many contemporary Englishmen were self-satisfied enough to consider a model, progressive, society. Its two most consistent and effective critics were Townsend, who combined attacks upon the

[1] The judgement is that of P. M. Holt, *The Mahdist state in the Sudan, 1881–1898* (London, 1958), p. 27. See also Richard Hill, *Egypt in the Sudan, 1820–1881* (London, 1959), p. 136.

[2] In a review of Samuel W. Baker, *The Nile tributaries of Abyssinia* (London, 1867), published in *The Spectator*, 1867, p. 1322.

[3] Quoted by Morton Cohen, *Rider Haggard: his life and works* (London, 1960).

'irresponsibility' and 'immorality' of inaction in Europe with the call for an English *mission civilisatrice* in north-east Africa, and Lord Robert Cecil, the principal political writer in the *Quarterly Review*, and subsequently, as Lord Salisbury, foreign secretary and prime minister, the most important single influence upon Anglo-Egyptian relations.

In 1870 events brought an abrupt end to the short reign of non-intervention in the British mind. The Franco-Prussian war which transformed the power structure of Europe in apparent disregard either for British influence or British interests and, still more the Russian denunciation of the Black Sea Clauses of the Treaty of Paris in the same year, ended the phase of popular indifference to foreign affairs, by the time that the public were first able to read, and take pleasure in, Samuel Baker's account of his stewardship in the Sudan, published in 1874 as *Ismailïa*. A year before Georg Schweinfurth in *The heart of Africa* (with an introduction by Winwood Reade, author of the *Martyrdom of man*) had attracted attention, not least by his account of Baker's activities and his speculation as to the chaos which would follow when 'the English Pasha' was withdrawn. In the upshot Gordon, the uneasy hero of this concept of the Englishman's role in the Orient, went to the Nile valley to take over where Baker had left off, and the ingredients of the situation which was to dominate the ruling English idea of England's relation with Egypt, already existed.

This, then, at the outset of the period of special relationship and occupation, was the place of Egypt in the English political imagination. Its strategic importance long recognized, had been enhanced by the opening of the Suez Canal and by the palpable decline in Turkish power. It was 'the key to our house in the East' and as such no government would be permitted either by its advisers or by public opinion, to disregard the course of events there. It was a territory upon which, by comparing degrees of influence, Englishmen were apt to think that they could measure the national standing on the international scene—could see what kind of a figure they were cutting. It was the principal arena for the more or less endless rough-and-tumble which arose from the love–hate relationship between England and France. And it contained a society in which the great bulk of the people—the 'wretched *fellaheen*' whose sufferings were so widely publicized in England—seemed to be crying out for just that sort of beneficent authority which so many Englishmen were coming to regard their fellow-countrymen as peculiarly qualified to provide.

In 1875 the dramatic purchase, by the British government, of the khedive's shares in the Suez Canal, caught the maximum of public attention and involved all these factors. It had in no sense been planned. It was a reaction to an unexpected circumstance—the discovery or belief, that Ismāʿīl was contemplating the sale of his shares and the fear that they might fall into French hands. But it proved, at once, to be surprisingly popular.[1] Disraeli had made

[1] Gladstone wrote 'A storm of approbation seems to swell even to rage on every side'

a good deal of play before the election of 1874 with the need for a more positive assertion of Britain's role in foreign affairs. In office, at first, he did little about it and his foreign secretary was the leading non-interventionist, Lord Derby. It was the unexpected outburst of exhilaration which followed the announcement of the purchase, that transformed the Disraeli government into an administration of foreign affairs, the light in which it has since been regarded. In that sense this first step into Egypt—as it proved, but was not intended, to be—was not so much a consequence as a cause, of policy. It showed that national self-assertion abroad could be good politics at home. It began the revival, following the quiescent aftermath of the war, of French jealousy—and of jealousy of France. It fixed in British minds the concept of Egypt as a major British interest—and it gave full reign to those Englishmen who looked for a British role in the regeneration of Egypt and in the succouring of the *fallāḥīn*.

The next episode was the deposition, in 1879, of the Khedive Ismāʿīl. Lord Salisbury, who had been foreign secretary for more than a year, was concerned principally to achieve a settlement of a difficult situation without arousing the hostility of France—and to prevent her from acting alone. There were reports that a squadron was preparing at Brest[1] and Lord Lyons, the British ambassador in Paris, warned that 'French power and French feeling are very different from what they were seven years ago when the French would have let us do almost anything we chose in Egypt if we would have taken care of the interests of their Bondholders'.[2] French diplomatists abroad and the French public were 'beginning to think that France has become too strong to play a secondary part any longer'.[3]

The crux of the matter was public opinion—both in France and in England and so it was to remain for a quarter of a century. Gambetta—in his period of power without responsibility—was attacking Waddington, the premier, through the press and by organized interpellations in the Chamber of Deputies, for weakness towards Egypt—and England. And the British press was not slow to reply.[4] Before, and after, the occupation of 1882, under the leadership of the 'Fourth Party', it became a stock-in-trade of political troublemakers in the House of Commons to harass the government of the day with accusations

(to Lord Granville, 22 Nov. 1875). Lord Salisbury later told a meeting of the Associated Chambers of Commerce that 'Foreign countries have thought that a new spirit altogether strange has come over the country' and agreed that 'there is a kind of sensation, a thrill'. Reported in *The Spectator* for 19 Feb. 1876, which remarked, in the same issue that 'The House . . . cheers every allusion to British interests in Egypt'.

[1] Salisbury Papers: Lyons to Salisbury, 18 Apr. 1879.

[2] Ibid., 22 May 1879.

[3] Ibid., 10 June 1879.

[4] Ibid., 20 June 1879, for an account of the French press campaign against England; and vice versa, 29 May 1879, for the complaint that the attitude of the English press 'patronising and pedagogical' had made things worse. In a situation strikingly similar to that of 1838–9, Waddington privately warned Salisbury that, as Salisbury put it, 'any language used in the

of weakness towards France in Egypt, and they never lacked vociferous support in sections of the British press.

The more closely the story of the occupation is examined the more plainly does it come to be seen as a tragedy of circumstance, of conflicting readings of the situation, and of conflicting personalities, in which, in the upshot, the politicians' concern for public opinion exercised the final say. Wilfrid Blunt, to whose access to influential circles in England there were few limits, had the ear of the prime movers in Gladstone's second government.[1] He was an experienced traveller who knew Arabic, and loved Egypt and Egyptians, and he was severely critical of Abdülhamid II (which could not fail to commend him to Gladstone at that time)[2]—but he failed to persuade the prime minister that 'Urābī and his supporters represented a genuine patriotic movement.

Early in 1882 there seemed a chance that he might succeed. In January Hamilton, one of the prime minister's private secretaries, wrote in his diary that it seemed as though the consul-general, Malet, had lost his head and misled the government; that Gladstone was surprised at 'the development of the national sentiment' in Egypt, and that he would like to give scope to 'Egypt for the Egyptians' were this feasible and attainable without risk.[3] Towards the end of May the feeling was that it 'will be requisite to bring the nationalist-military party to their senses', and there was 'no doubt that the country from the Chamber of Notables downwards, is against them and will be glad to be free of their military despotism'.[4] Yet the puzzle persisted. Barely twenty-four hours after the news of the riots in Alexandria the government is described as 'regularly sandwiched between Wilfrid Blunt and his nationalists and the Foreign Office and their clientele headed by Malet'.[5] Ten days later the doubts were back again. In an atmosphere in London in which expressions like 'We have been kicked out of Egypt' were commonplace, and in which intervention in one form or another was now held to be inevitable and likely to be met with resistance, Hamilton was able to write 'and all for what? . . . compare our aims with those of the new Ministry accepted by Arabi . . . and they will be found practically identical. But by the policy we have pursued we have landed ourselves in this dilemma' that to recognize the new ministry would be eating our words.[6] Three days later the die seems certainly cast. Reflecting, at a time when the government was widely unpopular, that a 'Jingo policy would be temporarily popular', Hamilton reflects the moral dilemma of the government and the amoral way which was chosen out

House of Commons about Egypt such as we had hitherto used would probably cost him his place'. (Iddesleigh Papers; B.M. Add. MS. 50019, Salisbury to Iddesleigh, 20 June 1879.)

[1] Hamilton Papers; B.M., Add. MS. 48430, entry for 25 July 1880 *et al.*

[2] He urged 'the deposition of the Sultan and the substitution of a less powerful, less clever and less deceitful man—a nonentity in fact, after the fashion of what has been done in Egypt'. Hamilton Papers; B.M., Add. MS. 48630, entry for 27 June 1880.

[3] Entry for 20 Jan. 1882.

[4] Entry for 23 May 1882.

[5] Entry for 13 June 1882.

[6] Entry for 25 June 1882.

of it. 'What right', he wrote, 'have we to interfere at all? Our plea must be to rid the country . . . from a military dictatorship.'[1] And that was the way that things went. England did assert herself at Alexandria and later at Tel el-Kebir. The government won unwonted popularity, upon which Gladstone capitalized with skill.[2] Once committed to the concept of 'Urābī as a military dictator and nothing else, Gladstone rode it hard. He was apparently genuinely shocked by evidence that 'Urābī had been in communication with Abdülhamid and after Tel el-Kebir was so far consistent in this attitude that Hamilton could write 'Mr. Gladstone would be glad if Arabi could be hung without *real* inclemency'.[3]

The intervention in Egypt had restored the fortunes of the government in a moment of extreme difficulty. It may indeed have saved it from division and defeat. But the cost was very heavy. It was to prove much easier to go into Egypt than to get out of it. There can be no doubt that the wish of all the responsible English statesmen for at least, the next ten years, was for evacuation. But to evacuate became increasingly difficult. The verbal conflict with France, in the press and in the parliamentary chambers in London and Paris, grew hotter and Salisbury, as he well knew, would have had difficulty in getting the approval of Parliament for the Drummond Wolff agreement if it had not been destroyed from without.

By 1890 it was plain that evacuation was, politically, no more than a remote possibility. In this situation the second of the two principal political requirements of a British foreign policy came into play. If Englishmen looking at Egypt could feel themselves to be strong because of their national presence there, they required also the feeling that good was coming from their presence. The task of giving them that assurance was not a difficult one. If the benefits conferred upon the *fallāḥīn* by the régime of British control were palpably and deliberately exaggerated, they were also, and demonstrably, real ones. The desire to help the *fallāḥīn* and the belief that Englishmen were particularly well qualified to do so, were still strong. From 1890, or thereabouts, the emphasis was upon the good that England was doing in Egypt. This emphasis had been suggested by Baring five years before. In 1885, during the last months of the Liberal government, he wrote to the foreign secretary, Lord Granville, a private letter suggesting the lines of defence which the government might adopt when its Egyptian policy was attacked in Parliament. He foresaw that 'all the Jingoes and many who should not be Jingoes, will advocate what is virtually an annexation policy', and deprecated this. He suggested that stress should be laid upon the benefits which British predominance had already conferred upon the Egyptian people, notable in respect

[1] Entry for 28 June 1882.

[2] After Tel el-Kebir he arranged for a nation-wide series of thanksgivings, and the diarist felt able to remark, on 31 Dec. 1882, that the government's position was 'so much brighter than a year ago'.

[3] Entry for 23 Sept. 1882.

of kourbash and corvée, and added 'Egypt, in spite of its present difficulties, is on the high road to progress and has a future before it'.[1] This was to be the note of the future, a note deliberately selected and consciously struck, in the knowledge that it would appeal to the pride of many Englishmen and serve to appease the consciences of others.

Throughout the 1890s great care was taken with the way in which events in Egypt were presented to the British public. The evils of Dervish rule in the Sudan[2] and the blessings of British paramountcy in Egypt were kept steadily and deliberately before the public eye. In this process the great set-piece was Alfred Milner's *England in Egypt*, which was first published in 1892 and quickly ran through many editions. There seems little room for doubting that its production was the principal objective of those who appointed Milner (a professional journalist who had once edited the *Pall Mall Gazette*[3] before he moved into the upper regions of the Civil Service) to his short-lived term of office at the Ministry of Finance, at Cairo. In the summer of 1891, when *England in Egypt* was being written, Baring told him 'foreign policy is pre-eminently a matter about which the crowd not only should but need to be guided. . . . I am sure that as regards Egypt and other matters the only plan is to follow Cobden's Corn Law system—i.e. to go on drumming the same thing into their heads over and over again. You have done your part of the work well.'[4] Milner's picture of a beneficent England, operating at her most effective in Egypt, struck a deep chord. Although the other view survived—it was kept assiduously alive for thirty years and more by Wilfrid Blunt—this was altogether too attractive not to gain and retain a general currency. It was certainly one of the most successful pieces of official propaganda in British history. It was, no less certainly, one of the least fortunate in its eventual consequences. For in keeping with the ironic fate which had dogged Anglo-Egyptian relations since 1882, the more widely the Milner view of Egypt came to be accepted in England, the less true to the facts it became. Indeed it was, as one of Milner's correspondents wrote to him from Egypt, out of date before it was published. Its publication coincided with the crisis of 1892, in which Baring, supported by Lord Rosebery at the Foreign Office, overrode the new khedive. 'Your book', wrote Eldon Gorst to Milner,[5] 'describes the situation which had ceased to exist two months before the book was published.'

1 Granville Papers; P.R.O. 30/29/167, Baring to Lord Granville, 25 Jan. 1885.

2 As Richard Hill has recently shown; see Richard Hill, *Slatin Pasha* (London, 1965), 30–42; and cf. P. M. Holt, 'The source-materials of the Sudanese Mahdia', *St. Antony's papers*, No. 4; Middle Eastern affairs, No. 1 (London, 1958), at pp. 112–13.

3 During the imprisonment of the editor, W. T. Stead, in connexion with the 'Modern Babylon' campaign which he had conducted in that newspaper. For a visit to him in that capacity by Wilfrid Blunt, see W. S. Blunt, *Gordon at Khartoum* (London, 1911), p. 487. It is interesting that after that meeting Blunt could write, 'I like Milner', and that the *Dictionary of National Biography* should credit Stead 'with Milner' with inaugurating the 'new journalism'.

4 Milner Papers; Cromer to Milner, 27 June 1891. Private.

5 Milner Papers; Eldon Gorst to Milner, 3 Feb. 1893.

Wingate told Milner that 'The whole affair shows a spirit of absolute enmity between English and Egyptians'.[1]

This perhaps exaggerated the hostility of all but a few Egyptians, but, as we know, the hostility did grow, and as it did so English apologists fell back more and more upon reference to the good which England was doing to Egypt. Lord Cromer, as Baring became, and his achievements came, particularly after the publication of his *Modern Egypt*, in 1908, to be regarded as the model of benevolent British imperialism. This book was described by one reviewer as a 'splendid record . . . of the governing instinct of our race',[2] and Cromer and his colleagues were 'our new crusaders. We wish them luck; their glory is our own'.[3] This view did not, of course, go unchallenged. The publication of Wilfrid Blunt's *Secret history of the British occupation of Egypt*, in 1907, and the publication at intervals of his other books, saw to that. But if not unchallenged, it certainly prevailed, notably, and most important, with the young Winston Churchill. During the years before the First World War, Churchill was several times a guest of Wilfrid Blunt in Sussex. Blunt's records of their many conversations, if accurate, are fascinating. They show the young politician warm with admiration for courageous oriental nationalists, even though their enemy was Britain. He spoke of the last speech of the young Indian, Dingra, who was executed in 1909 for assassinating a British Indian official in London, as 'the finest ever made in the name of patriotism'.[4] In the same year he is reported as saying of the British empire 'we get no advantage from it and it's a lot of bother. The only thing one can say for it is it is justified if it is undertaken in an altruistic spirit for the good of the subject races'.[5] But in the end he adopted the view which Milner had set about—he believed in the beneficent empire. In October 1910 he again visited Blunt and 'his last word to me was "You must not quarrel with me if I annex Egypt"'.[6] He remained the principal, and sturdy, defender of that view. During the Cabinet battle about Lord Milner's proposals of 1921, Churchill was the chief protagonist of conceding nothing. 'I am not at all prepared', he wrote, 'to sit still and mute, and watch the people of this country being slowly committed to the loss of this great and splendid monument of British administrative skill and energy.'[7]

[1] Milner Papers; Wingate to Milner, 18 Jan. 1893.

[2] In keeping with its tradition, in *The Spectator*, 1908, pp. 374 and 470.

[3] *Edinburgh Review* (207), pp. 487–511. *The Nation* with a review in two instalments (28 Mar. and 18 Apr. 1908) was much less fulsome, saw a valid future for Egyptian nationalism, which might give rise to an independent Egypt that could 'represent no mean addition to the circle of self-sustained and civilising nations', and blamed Cromer for never having learned Arabic: this fact 'helps me to understand why he, who won so many things for Egypt, never won its heart'.

[4] W. S. Blunt, *My diaries*, vol. ii (London, 1919), p. 288; entry for 3 Oct. 1909.

[5] Ibid., p. 295; entry for 25 Nov. 1909.

[6] Ibid., p. 337; entry for 14 Oct. 1910.

[7] Churchill to Curzon, 13 June 1921, quoted in Lord Beaverbrook, *The decline and fall of Lloyd George* (London, 1963), p. 42.

Notes sur la hiérarchie sociale en Égypte à l'époque de Muḥammad ʿAlī

NADA TOMICHE

Au début du XIXème siècle, au moment où, sous l'impulsion énergique de Muḥammad ʿAlī, l'Égypte s'industrialise à une allure accélérée, elle souffre particulièrement des difficultés des pays sous-peuplés.

Les estimations de la population, établies au début du XIXème siècle, encore que très approximatives, montrent bien la pénurie de la main-d'œuvre. De 1799 à 1802, pendant trois ans, la commission des lettres et des arts, venue avec l'expédition française, tient des registres des naissances et des décès. Elle évalue la population à 2 466 950 âmes.[1] En 1821 Mengin avance le chiffre de 2 514 000 sédentaires et environ 42 000 bédouins « combattants »,[2] soit en tout 2 530 950 âmes — sans compter les bédouins « non-combattants » dont le nombre devait s'élever à environ 80 000 âmes. Vers 1833, Muḥammad ʿAlī fait faire le recensement des habitations (870 000 maisons). Sur la base de quatre personnes par maison, l'estimation de la population atteint à cette époque 3 480 000 habitants, encore que, d'après Duhamel, consul général de Russie en Égypte, elle ne dépassât pas 2 500 000, les employés du Pacha ayant « porté sur les registres tant des maisons abandonnées que des étables et des pigeonniers, qui, il faut le dire ressemblent à s'y méprendre aux habitations humaines ».[3] En gros, pendant la première moitiè du XIXème siècle, la population ne semble pas avoir dépassé 3 000 000 d'habitants.

En 1821 d'après Mengin,[4] les principales villes sont désertes. Le Caire (avec le Vieux Caire et Boulaq) compte 218 560 habitants, Damiette 13 600, Rosette 13 440, et Alexandrie 12 528 habitants seulement. Alexandrie est alors à la veille de prendre son essor et de parvenir au premier rang des cités commerçantes d'Orient. De 1821 à 1846 (quand elle comptera plus de 150 000 habitants), l'immigration intérieure et étrangère et le transfert de la résidence du souverain[5] transforment la petite ville en centre de civilisation et souvent

[1] F. Mengin, *Histoire de l'Égypte sous le gouvernement de Mohammed-Aly* (Paris, 1823), T. ii, p. 616, note de Jomard.

[2] Ibid., T. ii, pp. 307–10.

[3] R. Cattaui, *Le Règne de Mohamed Aly d'après les archives russes en Égypte* (Le Caire–Rome, 1931–6), T. ii, 2e partie (Rome, 1934), p. 350.

[4] Mengin, *Histoire*, T. ii, p. 317.

[5] Malgré une préférence marquée pour Alexandrie où il résidera continuellement jusqu'en 1826, Muḥammad ʿAlī se rendra souvent au Caire après cette date, la situation de cette ville, pour diriger le pays étant « plus favorable parce qu'elle est presque centrale » (Section des manuscrits aux Affaires Étrangères, Paris, AÉ. Correspondance politique des Consuls, Le Caire, 1803–28, vol. 26, fol. 320 verso). Ses déplacements se multiplieront dès lors de telle sorte

en capitale effective du pays. Rosette et Damiette également se développeront mais à une allure beaucoup plus lente, éclipsées la première par Alexandrie et la seconde, dans la dernière moitié du siècle, au moment du percement de Suez, par Port-Said. En 1846, elles compteront respectivement près de 18 000 et de 37 000 habitants. Le Caire, cependant, après avoir connu un accroissement de population (260 000 en 1831), retombe à 110 000 après la peste de 1835[1] pour remonter à 250 000 environ en 1846.

La majorité de la population sous Muḥammad ʿAlī est formée par les «indigènes», Musulmans de race blanche descendants des Coptes et des tribus arabes venues par vagues successives arabiser le pays. Elle peut être estimée à 2 750 000 âmes environ après déduction de la population minoritaire.

Les minorités vers 1835 semblent se décomposer ainsi: 32 000 Turcs et 5 800 Mamelouks,[2] 29 500 Nubiens et Abyssins servant chez les particuliers riches ou comme soldats dans l'armée.[3] Ces groupes représentent un total de 67 300 Musulmans. Le nombre des Européens, techniciens et grands commerçants, s'accroit sensiblement depuis que Muḥammad ʿAlī a entrepris d'industrialiser le pays. En 1821, Mengin[4] les estime à 1 200 passés à 5 000 vers 1835.[5] En y ajoutant 2 000 Arméniens,[6] orthodoxes pour la plupart,[7] 5 000 Grecs (catholiques et orthodoxes),[8] 3 750 Syriens[9] et 160 000 Coptes,[10]

que le consul général de France résidant à Alexandrie recevra en 1828 une augmentation de traitement pour pouvoir habiter alternativement Alexandrie et le Caire, AÉ, Corresp. commerciale Alexandrie, 1828–9, vol. 23, fol. 2.

[1] J. Michaud et B. Poujoulat, *Correspondance d'Orient, 1830–1831* (Paris, 1833–35), T. v, p. 238.

[2] F. Mengin, *Histoire sommaire de l'Égypte sous le gouvernement de Mohammed Aly* (Paris, 1839), pp. 156–9. Les Mamelouks, anciens esclaves blancs libérés par leurs maîtres étaient auparavant importés de Géorgie, Circassie, du Caucase, etc., territoires libérés par la Russie à la fin du XVIIIème siècle et d'où l'importation d'esclaves avait pratiquement cessé. Le nombre des Mamelouks était tombé de 10 000 sous ʿAlī Bak, à 2 000 au début du règne de Muḥammad ʿAlī (voir les excellentes études d'Ayalon, «Studies in al-Jabartī» *Journal of the economic and social history of the Orient*, vol. iii, parts 2 et 3). Après la guerre de Morée, de jeunes esclaves grecs avaient été amenés en Égypte. En 1829, Gros, envoyé en mission de rachat par la France, estimait leur nombre à huit ou neuf mille. Il précisait que si la situation des esclaves était généralement peu enviable, ceux d'entre eux qui se trouvaient placés chez les Turcs et qui avaient accepté de changer de religion, étaient bientôt libérés et ces nouveaux Mamelouks richement vêtus, bien traités devenaient pour la plupart des hommes puissants dans le pays (G. Douin, *L'Égypte de 1828 à 1830, correspondance des consuls de France en Égypte* (Rome, 1935), p. 97.).

[3] Mengin, *Hist. sommaire*, pp. 156–9. Dans Cattaui, *Arch. russes*, T. ii, 2e partie, p. 353. Duhamel accepte les estimations de Cadalvène, à savoir 7 000 Barbarins venus du Soudan et 18 000 Noirs amenés d'Afrique Centrale.

[4] Mengin, *Hist.*, T. ii, p. 269. [5] Cattaui, *Arch. russes*, T. ii, 2e partie, p. 353.

[6] Mengin, *Hist.*, T. ii, p. 271 et A.-B. Clot-Bey, *Aperçu général sur l'Égypte* (Paris, 1840), T. i, p. 245.

[7] Clot, *Aperçu*, T. i, p. 245.

[8] Mengin, *Hist.* T. ii, p. 276; évalués à 7 000 par Clot, *Aperçu*, T. i, pp. 244–5.

[9] Mengin, *Hist.*, T. ii, p. 276.

[10] Ibid., T. ii, p. 282; Michaud et Poujoulat, *Correspondance*, T. v, p. 240. Duhamel les évalue à 145 000 (Cattaui, *Arch. russes*, T. ii, 2e partie, p. 353) et Clot, *Aperçu*, T. i, pp. 243–4, les distingue en 150 000 Coptes jacobites et 5 000 Coptes 'catholiques'.

qui forment une minorité autochtone de langue arabe ayant perdu son parler traditionnel, on obtient un ensemble de 175 000 Chrétiens. Les 7 000 Juifs[1] dont 1 200 Caraïtes[2] portent le total de la population des «minoritaires» à près de 250 000 âmes, soit environ 9 pour cent de l'ensemble des habitants de l'Égypt dans la première moitié du XIXème siècle.

Pendant plus de trente ans, Muḥammad ʿAlī va faire travailler la grande majorité de cette population au bénéfice de ses monopoles. Après 1808 en effet, la presque totalité des terres cultivés de l'Égypte (2 millions de feddans) appartient à l'État ou au souverain dont le dirigisme agricole favorisera, dès 1822, l'introduction et la culture intensive du coton à longue fibre, la plantation des dattiers (5 à 6 millions), d'oliviers (310 000 pieds), du mûrier en 1817, de l'opium (pour l'exportation). Il donne un nouvel essor à la culture de l'indigo, de la canne à sucre, du lin, du chanvre, du riz, des pois, des fèves. La récolte des céréales passe de 8 millions d'hectolitres en 1812, à 11 millions en 1832. Elle est exportée au deux tiers.

Dès 1816, le gouvernment s'adjuge également le monopole de l'industrie qu'il tente de développer et d'élever au niveau européen, au détriment des artisanats locaux. En 1836, on dénombre en Égypte: 29 ateliers de filature et de tissage, 14 fabriques d'armes, 12 indigoteries, 4 moulins à décortiquer le riz, 1 fabrique de fez, l'arsenal à Alexandrie, 3 raffineries de sucre et distilleries de rhum, 6 salpêtrières, 300 pressoirs pour l'huile de lin, de carthame, de sésame, d'olive, et de laitue, 164 entreprises de couveuses artificielles, 1 imprimerie nationale.[3]

Le souverain attribue de même à l'État le monopole des ventes destinées à l'étranger. L'ensemble de cette économie «dirigée» se développe à l'abri d'une sévère protection douanière.

A son arrivée au pouvoir en 1805, Muḥammad ʿAlī venait d'assister aux réalisations que la technique française moderne avait permises à une petite armée coupée de la mère patrie et tenant en respect les forces ottomanes liguées à celles des Mamelouks. Militaire de par le hasard de la guerre mais commerçant en tabacs de par son métier, le nouveau souverain de l'Égypte, libre de toute tradition militaire, est déterminé à s'appuyer sur une armée formée à l'exemple de celle qu'il avait vue à l'œuvre, et à diriger l'Égypte comme une entreprise privée dont il serait l'heureux propiétaire. Il y parvient jusqu'au moment où les pressions étrangères, l'«hérédité» accordée à sa famille et les menaces le contraindront, aux environs de 1840, à plus de conformisme. Auparavant, animé de l'esprit novateur des pionniers du

[1] Estimation de Clot, *Aperçu*, T. i, p. 243, vers 1835 et de V. Schoelcher *L'Égypte en 1845*, (Paris, 1846), p. 200. Michaud et Poujoulat, *Correspondence*, T. v, p. 240, évaluent leur nombre à 3 000. Mengin vers 1821, *Hist.*, T. ii, p. 281, et Duhamel dans Cattaui, *Arch. russes*, T. ii, 2e partie, p. 353, vers 1836, l'estiment à 3 500; E. W. Lane, vers la même époque, *An account of the manners and customs of the modern Egyptians* (Everyman edn.), pp. 23, 558, l'estime à 5 000.

[2] Mengin, *Hist.*, T. ii, p. 281.

[3] Cattaui, *Arch. russes*, T. ii, 2e partie, p. 381 sv., Clot, *Aperçu*, T. ii, p. 293 sv.

capitalisme, aventurier ne s'embarrassant ni de coutumes ni de routine, il gouverne seul, après avoir écarté l'ancienne noblesse dirigeante et en affaiblissant systématiquement toutes les forces groupées, corporations ou institutions privilégiées susceptibles de mettre des limites à son absolutisme.

Hiérarchie et organisation sociale

Au sommet de la hiérarchie, il y a donc Muḥammad ʿAlī.

Au dessous de lui, parfaitement soumise, la minorité non autochtone de Turcs et de Mamelouks forme, d'après Duhamel, «la classe privilégiée et pour ainsi dire l'aristocratie du pays».[1] Elle compose la cour du pacha et le corps des hauts fonctionnaires qui, assistant le souverain, sont à la tête de l'administration et de l'armée.

L'armée représente un ensemble social situé en marge des classes. Les soldes des troupes sont faibles, les paiements se font avec de longs retards atteignant parfois une année, entraînant désertions et profond mécontentement. Mais les officiers haut gradés, par contre, sont bien payés. «En payant largement les officiers supérieurs, Méhémet Ali a voulu s'assurer de leur dévouement. . . . En payant faiblement les sous-officiers et soldats, il a pensé que le dévouement des chefs répondrait de l'obéissance des subalternes et que ceux-ci étaient d'ailleurs assez payés s'ils comparaient le bien-être qu'ils ont sous les drapeaux à la misère de leurs village» écrit le consul général Cochelet au Ministre des Affaires Étrangères de France, le 26 février 1838.[2]

Solde du simple soldat	15	piastres	par mois
Solde du caporal	25	”	”
Solde du sergent	30	”	”
Solde du sergent-major	40	”	”
Solde de l'adjudant sous-officier	60	”	”
Solde du sous-lieutenant	250	”	”
Solde du lieutenant	350	”	”
Solde du capitaine	500	”	”
Solde de l'adjudant major	1 200	”	”
Solde du chef de bataillon	2 500	”	”
Solde du lieutenant-colonel	3 000	”	”
Solde du colonel	8 000	”	”
Solde du général de brigade	11 000	”	”
Solde du général de division	12 500	”	” [3]

Les effectifs de cette armée augmentent d'abord regulièrement, avant d'être réduits à 18 000 hommes par les firmans de 1840. Vers 1821, formée de Turcs et d'étrangers, elle compte environ 20 000 hommes: 10 000 fantassins, 9 000 cavaliers et 1 200 canonniers.[4] En 1832, les Mamelouks formés par le

[1] Dans Cattaui, *Arch. russes*, T. ii, 2ᵉ partie, p. 352, lettre datée de juillet 1837.
[2] AÉ, Corresp. politique des Consuls, Égypte, 1837–8, vol. 6, fol. 233.
[3] Clot, *Aperçu*, T. ii, p. 225.
[4] Mengin, *Hist.* T. ii, p. 265.

colonel français Sève (Sulaymān Pacha) représentent les cadres d'officiers. Les troupes se composent d'esclaves noirs achetés au Kordofan et au Sennâr. Mais les noirs résistent mal à la fatigue et on a alors recours au recrutement indigène. En 1837, d'après Duhamel, l'armée est formée entièrement d' «Arabes» pour les grades subalternes; elle est dirigée par des officiers turcs. Elle compte — à en croire les estimations officielles — 92 800 fantassins, 13 440 cavaliers, 6 912 artilleurs (avec 36 batteries) et 1 600 sapeurs, soit en tout 114 752 soldats. Mais Duhamel jugeant ce chiffre d'un tiers trop élevé le ramene à 76 500 hommes.[1] En 1838, Cochelet écrit à Molé que l'armée égyptienne se compose «de 55 régiments de troupes régulières dont le nombre total est évalué à 116.660 hommes et de troupes irrégulières montant à 20.162 individus».[2] Soit en tout 136 822 hommes.

La marine, de même, se développe rapidement. Dès 1824, «les premières frégates du Vice-roi furent construites à Livourne, Marseille et Trieste».[3] En 1829, après le désastre naval de Navarin (1827), l'arsenal d'Alexandrie est aménagé et permet de construire une nouvelle flotte égyptienne composée, en 1838, de 12 vaisseaux de ligne, 7 frégates, 4 corvettes, 3 bricks, 5 goélettes, un cutter, un bateau à vapeur et 40 bâtiments de transport. La marine compte plus de 18 000 matelots et l'arsenal 5 600 ouvriers.[4] Les cadres formés par le Français Besson se composent de Turcs, de Mamelouks et de quelques Européens.

Les dépenses militaires de l'Égypte en 1833 et en 1834 sont les suivants:[5]

Budget de l'armée	60 000 000	piastres
Traitement des grands officiers[6]	8 000 000	,,
Budget du personnel de la marine	30 000 000	,,
Solde de la cavalerie turque irrégulière	3 250 000	,,
Solde des Arabes bédouins	2 500 000	,,
Dépenses de l'École militaire	750 000	,,
Pour le matériel de guerre	7 000 000	,,
Construction des bâtiments de guerre	7 500 000	,,
Total	119 000 000	piastres

[1] Cattaui, *Arch. russes*, T. ii, 2e partie, p. 397. D'après Clot, *Aperçu*, T. ii, pp. 229–35, les forces militaires de l'Égypte «avant la dernière guerre» s'élevaient à environ 180 000 hommes. Depuis, elles s'élevaient à 130 000 hommes auxquels s'ajoutaient 41 678 combattants des troupes irrégulières, 47 800 gardes nationales, soit en tout 219 478 hommes. Son estimation diffère de celle de Duhamel du simple à près du triple.

[2] AÉ, Correspond. politique des Consuls, Égypte, 1837–8, vol. 6, fol. 230–230 verso.

[3] Cattaui, *Arch. russes*, T. ii, 2e partie, p. 401.

[4] Cf. Clot, *Aperçu*, T. ii, p. 254 = effectif égyptien 15 463 hommes, plus 4 076 ouvriers enregimentés de l'Arsenal d'Alexandrie. Au total 19 539 hommes. D'après Cochelet, le nombre des «officiers, soldats, matelots, ouvriers de la marine» se chiffrait à 25 000 hommes (AÉ, Corresp. politique des Consuls, Égypte 1837–8, vol. 6, fol. 230–230 verso.).

[5] D'après le rapport envoyé par Ferdinand de Lesseps, du Caire, le 19 novembre 1834, AÉ, Corresp. commerciale, Le Caire, 1833–42, vol. 27, fol. 12–12 verso. Repris par Mengin, *Hist. sommaire*, pp. 153–5 et Clot, *Aperçu*, T. ii, pp. 210–11.

[6] En fait cette ligne comporte le titre suivant: «Traitement des grands officiers et chefs

Ce montant, sur des dépenses budgétaires totales d'environ 200 000 000 de piastres, montre que 60 pour cent des recettes de l'État sont affectés aux dépenses militaires. Duhamel pouvait donc écrire à juste titre qu'« une des grandes plaies de l'Égypte est sans contredit son état militaire, qui est hors de proportions avec la population du pays et qui absorbe plus de la moitié de ses revenus ».[1]

A côté de ces grands corps de l'État, et ne considérant semble-t-il que la société purement « indigène » de l'Égypte, Clot-bey[2] relève, vers 1835, quatre « classes » (le mot est de lui):

> La première est celle des ulémas, les hommes de loi et de la religion. . . . Quoique tout Musulman puisse entrer dans le corps des ulémas, ils se transmettent héréditairement leurs charges et forment une espèce de caste aristocratique. . . . Leur haut ascendant a été détruit par le vice-roi qui leur a enlevé les grandes richesses territoriales qu'ils devaient à la superstitition et à l'ignorance de leurs compariotes. Ils ont maintenant peu d'influence et n'exercent aucune action sur le gouvernment, qui se trouve entièrement concentré entre les mains des Turcs.

Bien que privés des revenus des *waqfs* et *rizaq*, les shaykhs et les ulémas reçoivent, sous Muḥammad ʿAlī, une pension viagère de compensation. Après avoir contribué à amener Muḥammad ʿAlī au pouvoir, leurs chefs avaient été exilés, voire assassinés (tel al-Jabartī, l'historien, abattu, dit-on, sur les ordres du souverain). Désormais, ils ne donnent « en aucune manière l'idée d'un corps politique à peine celle d'un corps religieux ».[3] Mais encore qu'ils aient perdu tout pouvoir temporel ils conservent un prestige inaltéré aux yeux de la population dont ils forment le seul groupe indigène ayant sa place dans les rangs les plus aisés de la société égyptienne. Ils bénéficent aussi de la force du sentiment religieux populaire qui « remplace d'une manière exclusive et absolue le sentiment national qui manque à ce pays ».[4] Muḥammad ʿAlī leur manifeste considération et respect afin de tirer parti de l'emprise qu'ils conservent sur les masses musulmanes.

d'administration, 19 929 500. » Mais d'après Cochelet (AÉ, Corresp. politique des Consuls, Égypte, 1837–8, vol. 6, fol. 232 verso), l'État-major de l'armée était « composé de 65 officiers généraux et colonels dont un général en chef, 10 généraux de division, 14 généraux de brigade et 40 colonels ». D'après les traitements mentionnés plus haut, la somme peut être évaluée à 8 000 000, chiffre adopté ici.

[1] Cattaui, *Arch. russes*, T. ii, 2e partie, p. 420.

[2] Clot, *Aperçu*, T. i, p. 259 sv. Intéressant à comparer avec la hiérarchie établie par Maqrīzī, *Ighātha*, 73. 6 et sv. (*Ighāthat al-umma bi-kashf al-ghumma* (ouvrage rédigé en 1405) trad. franç. de G. Wiet, *Le traité des famines* (1962): La première classe comptait les membres du gouvernement et toute l'armée jusqu'au plus bas grade; la deuxième, les grands négociants (importateurs d'épices et d'esclaves par ex.); la troisième classe comprend les petits marchands et boutiquiers; la quatrième les paysans et les fermiers, aisés aux époques de prospérité et d'inondation ou décimés par les famines et les sécheresses; la cinquième classe était celle des intellectuels (savants, professeurs, étudiants, petits propriétaires et salariés du Sultan): la sixième classe celle des artisans, et la septième et dernière comprenait les pauvres et les mendiants.

[3] G. Douin, *La mission du baron de Boislecomte* (Le Caire, 1927), p. 143.

[4] Ibid., p. 144.

« La deuxième classe », poursuit Clot, « est formée par les propriétaires, les négociants, les marchands: elle est peu nombreuse; elle ne contient en général que des fortunes médiocres. » Les maisons et logements sont demeurés propriétés privées, le pouvoir laissant aux propriétaires d'immeubles le bénéfice des loyers. La distinction que semble faire Clot entre « négociants » et « marchands » pourrait se rapporteur aux « exportateurs-importateurs » d'un côté et aux individus adonnés au commerce intérieur de l'autre. Les exportateurs sont en très grande majorité des étrangers représentants d'établissements européens. Ils résident surtout à Alexandrie. Alors qu'en 1821 on comptait à Alexandrie 21 maisons de commerce étrangères (3 françaises, 2 anglaises, 1 maltaise, 4 toscanes, 5 vénitiennes, 1 allemande et 5 grecques), en 1835, il y en a 44 (13 françaises, 7 anglaises, 9 autrichiennes, 8 toscanes, 2 sardes, 1 suédoise, 1 danoise, 1 hollandaise, 1 prussienne, 1 grecque) soit un accroissement de 228 pour cent de 1821 à 1835 et seulement 6 négociants musulmans et 4 Syriens.[1]

Au Caire, par contre, en 1821 on comptait 20 établissements européens (3 français, 1 anglais, 4 toscans, 2 vénitiens, 2 de Trieste et 8 grecs).[2] En 1835, il n'y en a plus que 18 (1 anglais, 9 autrichiens, 4 toscans, 2 sardes, 2 grecs), mais il y a aussi 10 établissements grec-catholiques généralement Syriens, et 63 établissements turcs, maghrébins et égyptiens.[3] Un net déplacement du grand négoce européen s'est opéré vers Alexandrie et son port: les opérations de l'Égypte avec l'Europe, note Boislecomte en 1833, « se font presqu' exclusivement avec les négociants européens et la navigation du port d'Alexandrie est toute européenne ».[4] Si Muḥammad ʿAlī favorise l'établissement de maisons européennes au détriment des indigènes, c'est que les besoins de sa jeune industrie exigent des importations nouvelles et accrues de biens d'équipement et de matières premières et que les Musulmans connaissent mal les sources d'approvisionnement en Europe. Sachant gré aux Européens de l'apport qu'ils fournissent au pays, Muḥammad ʿAlī contraint les autochtones à étouffer toute manifestation de xénophobie non seulement en Égypte mais aussi en Syrie, quand il conquiert le pays. Il abolit les signes distinctifs que les non-musulmans étaient obligés de porter sur leurs vêtements dans les deux pays et montre un esprit de tolérance qui ne se démentira jamais. Les négociants arabes et musulmans se trouvent circonscrits dans le centre commercial de second ordre qu'est devenu le Caire. Ce sont souvent les agents à l'importation et pour la distribution des négociants étrangers établis à Alexandrie:

Les commissionnaires en qui [ces derniers] placent leur confiance pour le débit de leurs marchandises sur cette place [Le Caire] sont des personnes établies sur le

[1] Mengin, *Hist. sommaire*, p. 225. Clot, *Aperçu*, T. ii, p. 328. En 1826 déjà, Malivoine comptait 10 établissements français à Alexandrie (lettre du 4 janvier 1826; AÉ, Corresp. consulaire, Le Caire, 1803–28, vol. 26, fol. 272 verso).

[2] Mengin, *Hist.* T. ii, pp. 417–18.

[3] Mengin, *Hist. sommaire*, pp. 225–66. Clot, *Aperçu*, T. ii, p. 328.

[4] Douin, *Boislecomte*, p. 97.

pays depuis nombre d'années, qui ont l'habitude de traiter avec les habitants et qui trouvent dans ce travail un moyen d'existence. Le commerce d'importation s'exploite en grande partie dans cette ville; il diffère en cela de celui d'extraction [*sic*] qui ne peut se traiter qu'à Alexandrie.[1]

Les «marchands», dans le cadre du commerce intérieur, sont en grande majorité indigènes. L'État n'a pas étendu son monopole au commerce de détail trop fragmenté et s'est contenté de fixer les prix de vente afin de limiter les hausses. Les marchands conservent des vestiges appréciables de leur ancienne autonomie. Ils se groupent encore souvent par quartier, selon leurs origines religieuses ou ethniques et ils jouissent parfois de quelques privilèges. Au Caire, vers 1831, «les Israélites payent une certaine redevance pour n'avoir pas à recevoir la visite du *Moḥtesib* dans leur quartier. Ayant donc le privilège de vendre leurs denrées à un prix plus élevé que les autres habitants de la capitale, ils peuvent eux-mêmes les acheter plus cher et avoir en boutique de meilleures qualités que partout ailleurs, surtout en ce qui concerne les fruits».[2] Les Coptes, dix mille environ, commerçants pour la plupart, vivent dans «deux des quartiers les plus populeux du Caire».[3] Les Grecs-orthodoxes habitent aussi deux quartiers du Caire; beaucoup d'entre eux sont des détaillants.[4] Les Grecs-catholiques, venus depuis près de cent ans de Syrie, ont créé des établissements prospères et sont «marchands, drapiers, merciers, quincailliers».[5] Relativement groupés, ils conservent encore leurs anciennes corporations, leurs coutumes et ont à leur tête le *shāhbandar* qui sert d'arbitre et de juge entre ses collègues dans les litiges professionnels.[6]

«La troisième classe», écrit Clot, «est celle des artisans.» Profondément affectée par les transformations économiques du règne de Muḥammad ʿAlī, elle comprend deux types de travailleurs urbains. Le premier encore imbriqué dans l'ancienne organisation corporative, et le second perdu dans la masse nouvelle d'ouvriers salariés, sans protection d'aucune sorte. Un groupe de transition, formé d'anciens artisans, continue à détenir ses instruments de travail mais ne peut plus disposer de sa production que l'État achète à un prix fixé unilatéralement.

L'ancien type d'artisan se maintient dans le secteur de la distribution et des services: boulangers, bouchers, pâtissiers, tailleurs, barbiers, chameliers, âniers, relieurs, potiers, nattiers, bijoutiers, etc. L'appauvrissement des milieux de commerçants, de maîtres-artisans et d'ulémas, ainsi que la disparition de la riche aristocratie de Mamelouks a provoqué la décadence du petit artisanat

[1] Malivoine au baron de Damas, Le Caire, 4 janvier 1826, AÉ, Corresp. politique des Consuls, Le Caire, 1803–28, vol. 26, fol. 272 verso-273.

[2] Lane, *Manners*, p. 559.

[3] Mengin, *Hist.* T. ii, 282–3.

[4] Ibid., p. 276.

[5] Ibid., p. 271–2.

[6] Jabartī, *ʿAjāʾib*, T. iv, p. 176; traduction française, T. ix, p. 90.

de luxe. Certains, tels les relieurs[1] se groupent encore par quartiers distinctifs et en corporations tolérées mais non plus obligatoires.

La corporation est alors une sorte d'aristocratie formée de maîtres-artisans. L'apprenti n'y pénètre qu'après un stage plus ou moins long, sur recommandation de son patron, après une brève cérémonie devant le shaykh de la corporation. Aucune présentation de chef-d'œuvre n'est exigée.[2] La corporation a à sa tête un shaykh qui s'adjoint « des espèces de lieutenants » (*naqīb*).[3] Le shaykh est désigné par les autorités. En fait son rôle principal consiste à servir d'intermédiaire entre les autorités administratives et les travailleurs. Il assure, pour le compte du gouvernement, la police de la corporation, le prélèvement des impôts après avoir décidé de leur répartition entre les artisans placés sous sa juridiction, et il aide le pouvoir central à enrôler des hommes dans l'armée.

Cependant une nouvelle catégorie de travailleurs se développe: celle des ouvriers anonymes de la grande industrie. Se superposant à l'artisanat corporatif déclinant, une société ouvrière, salariée, non organisée, se forme, absorbant les ancien artisans des métiers étatisés. Pendant une étape transitoire, les travailleurs du bâtiment,[4] du textile,[5] etc., reçoivent l'ordre de ne travailler que pour un seul client, l'État. Continuant à détenir leurs instruments de travail, ils reçoivent la matière première brute et la rendent aux agents du gouvernement sous forme de produits travaillés, en quantités déterminées par les expériences préalables. Ils sont payés à la pièce et les déchets sont déduits de leurs salaires. Estampillés pour empêcher toute fraude,[6] les produits sont revendus au double du prix de production et nul, pas même l'artisan, ne peut conserver de pièce qui ne portât pas la marque du gouvernment.[7]

Comme les hommes, les femmes qui filent à domicile sont « réquisitionnées » par le gouvernment,[8] payées à la pièce par le *shaykh al-balad* et soumises aux mêmes obligations que les hommes. En cas d'abus, elles peuvent porter plainte auprès du *nāẓir* et reçoivent éventuellement satisfaction.[9]

Les artisans semblent supporter généralement mal ce nouvel état de choses et l'on voit des maçons et des menuisiers abandonner leurs métiers. Le chef de

[1] Michaud et Poujoulat, *Correspondance*, T. vi, pp. 299–300.

[2] Clot, *Aperçu*, T. ii, pp. 301–2.

[3] Ibid., pp. 300–1.

[4] Jabartī, *'Ajā'ib*, T. iv, p. 159; trad. fr., T. viii, p. 357.

[5] Ibid., T. iv, p. 282 (Année 1232/1816–17) Douin, *Boislecomte*, p. 90 sv.

[6] Mengin, *Hist.*, T. ii, pp. 376–7.

[7] Jabartī, *'Ajā'ib*, T. iv, p. 282; Mengin, *Hist.*, T. ii, p. 377; Schoelcher, *L'Égypte*, pp. 54–55; cf. décision parue dans le *Journal Officiel d'Égypte*, no. 353 (février 1831) et citée par M. Fahmy, *La Révolution de l'industrie en Égypte et ses conséquences sociales au 19e siècle (1800–1850)* (Leide, 1954), p. 17.

[8] Ordre émis par le Ministère des Finances, Abdine, Registre 3, Document 228, 5 rabī' 1234/février 1819, cité par Fahmy, *Révolution*, p. 93.

[9] C'est ce qui se passait en 1823 dans la province de Sharqiyya où elles accusaient le *shaykh al-balad* de détourner leurs salaires. Cf. Document 426, Abdine, Registre, 12, 3 rabī' al-awwal 1239/7 novembre 1823, cité par Fahmy, *Révolution*, p. 93.

la corporation reçoit alors l'ordre de retrouver les fuyards et de les remettre aux autorités.[1]

Quand les nouvelles fabriques d'État sont construites, l'étape transitoire prend fin. Les ouvriers vont travailler dans les entreprises gouvernementales. Ils sont indistinctement choisis par le gouverneur de la province, et non par le directeur de la fabrique. Ce dernier se contente d'inscrire les noms et salaires dans les registres et d'effectuer les paiements.[2] Le nouveau «prolétariat» ainsi constitué est relativement concentré: la plupart des trente fabriques de coton existantes ont «des dimensions très étendues».[3] Dans les villes telles que Rosette, Damiette, al-Manṣūra, Qaliyūb, Manūf, al-Maḥalla al-Kubrā, Zifta et autres, «la presque totalité de la population apte au travail, est employée par les fabriques et les manufactures d'État».[4]

À al-Maḥalla al-Kubrā, sur une population de 8 000 à 9 000 âmes, près de 3 000 ouvriers, y compris femmes et enfants, travaillent dans les diverses manufactures.[5] En 1829, dans l'arsenal d'Alexandrie, 8 000 fellahs sont «transformés d'un seul coup en maçons, charpentiers, menuisiers, forgerons, mécaniciens, cordiers, etc.»[6] Il n'en reste plus, il est vrai, que 1 000 en 1845.[7] De même, les 400 ouvriers de la fonderie de Būlāq près du Caire sont réduits à 150 en 1845.[8] Fuwwa compte 400 à 500 ouvriers dans la fabrique de fez.[9] Il y a 1 000 ouvriers dans la filature de Damanhūr,[10] 1250 dans la filature de coton à Shibīn,[11] 4 000 dans les 4 fabriques de al-Manṣūra.[12] Il y a à Qaliyūb, 600 ouvriers dans la filature de coton[13] et 300 dans la manufacture de Khurunfish. Selon Mengin,[14] le nombre des ouvriers dans l'ensemble des industries d'État, en Égypte, aurait atteint 31 000, auxquels s'ajouteraient 40 000 ouvriers du bâtiment, occupés à construire de nouveaux ateliers, soit en tout 71 000 personnes. Ce total semble avoir été inférieur aux besoins. Il n'est pas jusqu'aux femmes que, faute de main d'œuvre, on n'embauchât dans les nouveaux ateliers. Boislecomte en compte 150 à Damiette et autant à al-Manṣūra: elles travaillent voilées, à côté de leurs compagnons qui sont «plus

[1] Jabartī, *'Ajā'ib*, T. iv, p. 159, trad. fr., T. viii, p. 357.

[2] Cf. ordre de Muḥammad 'Alī au directeur de la fabrique de Fuwwa, juillet 1825 (registre n° 19, document 188 cité par Fahmy, *Révolution*, p. 65).

[3] Douin, *Boislecomte*, p. 92.

[4] A. Rafalovitch, *Putechtchestvie po Nijnemu Egyptu i Vnutrennim Oblastiam*, CPb. 1850 (Voyage en Basse-Égypte et dans les régions intérieures du Delta), p. 253, fréquemment cité par F. M. Atsamba, «Sostoianie Promitchlennosti i Polojenie naemnikh rabotchikh v Egipte v. XIX veke» («L'état de l'industrie et la situation des ouvriers salariés en Égypte, au XIXe siècle»), dans *Otcherki po istorii Arabskikh Stran* (*Sbornik Statei*) (Recherches sur l'histoire des pays arabes — Recueil d'articles —) éd. de l'Université de Moscou, 1959, p. 20.

[5] Michaud et Poujoulat, *Correspondance*, T. vii, p. 34.

[6] Schoelcher, *L'Égypte*, p. 51.

[7] Ibid., p. 52. D'après Michaud et Poujoulat, *Correspondance*, T. v, p. 10, il y en avait 1 200 à 1 500 vers 1835.

[8] Schoelcher, *L'Égypte*, p. 53.

[9] Rafalovitch, p. 43; Atsamba, p. 20.

[10] Rafalovitch, p. 404; Atsamba, pp. 19 et 20.

[11] Rafalovitch, p. 307; Atsamba, p. 20.

[12] Rafalovitch, p. 366; Atsamba, p. 20.

[13] Rafalovitch, p. 275; Atsamba, p. 20.

[14] Mengin, *Hist. sommaire*, p. 212.

qu'à demi-nus »,[1] Rafalovitch en voit 150 sur les 400 ou 500 ouvriers de Fuwwa.[2] Cette contribution officielle de la femme comme ouvrière à la production industrielle est un phénomène unique dans le monde musulman de l'époque.

Les salaires de l'industrie semblent avoir été médiocres. Le traitement d'un directeur d'usine se compare à celui d'un capitaine dans l'armée, avec cette différence que le premier ne profite pas des rations supplémentaires octroyées au second. Les salaires nominaux ouvriers sont supérieurs à ceux de la troupe, mais le revenue réel de l'ouvrier est inféreur à celui du soldat puisqu'il n'est ni logé, ni nourri, et que, le plus souvent, on le paie à la pièce, rarement à la journée.

En 1821, dans la fabrique de plaques de cuivre servant au doublage des vaisseaux à la Citadelle du Caire, le *nāẓir* (directeur) reçoit 500 piastres par mois, le peseur 300 piastres par mois, le premier écrivain 300 piastres, le magasinier 200 piastres, le second écrivain 120 piastres, le portier 30 piastres par mois et les vingt ouvriers arabes, 4 piastres par jour et un supplément pour le travail de nuit. Par contre, les 4 « ouvriers-maîtres » anglais touchent respectivement, par mois, 1 875 piastres, 1 500 piastres et 500 piastres pour chacun des deux derniers.[3] Un tisserand, à Sittī Zaynab au Caire, tisse 8 pics par jour en été et 6 en hiver, car les journées sont plus courtes. Payé à la pièce de 32 pics, il gagne, selon les saisons, une piastre et demi à deux piastres par jour.[4]

A comparer les salaires des débuts de l'industrialisation à ceux de la fin du règne, on relève une apparente stabilité.

En 1845, en effet, le directeur de la *Mabyaḍa* (teinture et impression des tissues) du Caire, Égyptien ayant étudié en Europe, l'un des employés les mieux payés, ne gagne pas plus de 500 piastres par mois, et un technicien à la fonderie de Būlāq, près de la capitale, après avoir été envoyé se spécialiser en Europe, touche 125 piastres par mois:

> Les premiers ouvriers, ceux qui conduisent les métiers, ne gagnent pas au-delà de deux piastres 30 paras par jour. Le tisserand a 8 piastres 30 paras pour une pièce. Or le plus habile n'en peut faire plus de sept par mois. La moyenne est de six. ... A la fabrique de toile peinte de Mabiadah les artistes qui gravent les bois pour imprimer reçoivent 3 piastres par jour. Le taux de la tache est calculé de façon que l'ouvrier le mieux rétribué ait 60 piastres par mois, et celui qui gagne le moins 20 piastres. La moyenne est de 40 piastres par mois. . . .[5]

Il est difficile de juger du pouvoir d'achat de ces salaires. En général les prix sont indiqués, selon les sources, tantôt par ardebs de 145 okes (l'oke =

[1] Douin, *Boislecomte*, p. 91, 29 juin 1833.
[2] Rafalovitch, p. 43; Atsamba, p. 20.
[3] Mengin, *Hist. somm.*, p. 223. Une bourse = 500 pt, un talari = 25 pt, 1 pt = 40paras, 1 pataque = 2 pt 10 paras. En 1833, une piastre = 25 centimes.
[4] Mengin, *Hist. somm.*, p. 203.
[5] Schoelcher, *L'Égypte*, pp. 54–56. Cf. Michaud et Poujoulat, *Correspondance*, T. v, p. 10.

1 kg 248)[1] tantôt par ardebs de 138 kg[2] tantôt en hectolitres (pour les grains) tantôt au prix de vente à l'exportation, au prix d'achat au fellah producteur, au prix de gros sur le marché intérieur ou au prix de détail. Par ailleurs, les prix varient considérablement entre les grandes villes (Le Caire et Alexandrie)[3] et du simple au double entre les villages et les villes.[4]

Aussi est-il difficile de conclure à la stabilité des prix quand, en comparant deux auteurs,[5] l'on note qu'en 1830, l'ardeb de fèves ou d'orge coûtait 32 pt et l'ardeb de blé 56 pt, alors qu'en 1836, l'ardeb de blé coûtait 51 pt, celui de fèves 54 pt et celui d'orge 63 pt. En 1830, le maïs coûtait 27 pt l'ardeb (de 145 okes); en 1846, l'ardeb (de 138 kg précise-t-on) valait 40 à 45 pt, soit 27 à 32 pt l'ardeb de 145 okes.[6] A ces causes d'imprécision s'ajoutent les fluctuations dues aux mauvaises crues et aux épidémies, et la dévaluation de la piastre égyptienne. En effet le franc vaut: en 1805, 0 pt 62; en 1812, 1 pt; en 1821, 1 pt 4; en 1825–6, 2 pt; en 1829, 2 pt 55; en 1833, 3 pt 33;[7] en 1843, 4 pt.[8]

A supposer qu'un ouvrier gagnant 2 pt par jour (= 80 paras) eût à faire vivre sur son salaire trois enfants — et en considérant que les gains de la femme pussent faire vivre le restant de la famille — il aurait eu à payer, en 1836, d'après les prix relevés par Lane au Caire, 10 à 20 paras, soit près du cinquième du salaire de sa journée pour une outre de peau de mouton remplie d'eau: 6 à 7 paras pour 1 oke de fèves, 9 paras pour le même poids de blé, 10 paras pour 6 œufs. Sans compter les légumes et fruits, le vêtement, le logement et les soins.

Les salaires ne sont pas toujours versés intégralement aux ouvriers. « On leur fait souvent des retenues pour les faux frais de la manufacture, pour remplacer un buffle ou un mulet du manège, qui meurt, pour réparer un métier brisé, etc. . . . Quelquefois, enfin, ce qui leur reste dû de salaire est payé au bout de six mois en produits mal réussis de la fabrique qu'ils revendent à moitié prix pour réaliser de l'argent comptant. »[9]

[1] Cattaui, *Arch. russes*, T. ii, 2e partie, p. 409.

[2] AÉ, Corresp. commerciale, Le Caire, 1843–9, vol. xxviii, fol. 265 verso. D'après Mengin, *Hist.* T. ii, p. 359 « L'ardeb de riz de Damiette pèse 225 okes, à Rosette, il n'en pèse que 155 ». Pour E. de Cadalvène et J. de Breuvery, *L'Égypte et la Nubie* (Paris, 1841), T. i, p. 381, l'ardeb de blé, maïs fèves, orge ou pois équivalait à 145 okes, mais l'ardeb de riz équivalait à 225 okes et l'ardeb de sel à 240 okes.

[3] AÉ, Corresp. commerciale Alexandrie, 1830–1, vol. 24, fol. 180; d'après Mimaut, consul général de France écrivant d'Alexandrie le 5 février 1831, le prix du blé au Caire était de 52 pt l'ardeb et à Alexandrie de 66 pt l'ardeb, soit 1/3 plus cher.

[4] Lane, *Modern Égyptians*, p. 320.

[5] Cadalvène et Breuvery, *L'Égypte*, T. i, p. 381 donnent les prix vers 1830 et Duhamel, dans Cattaui, *Arch. russes*, T. ii, 2e partie, p. 409, en date de juillet 1837.

[6] Cadalvène et Breuvery, *L'Egypte*, T. i, p. 381 et AÉ, Corresp. commerciale, Le Caire, 1843–9, vol. 28, fol. 265 verso.

[7] Douin, *Boislecomte*, p. 128.

[8] Dès le 10 mai 1836, Mimaut écrivait à Thiers: «Notre pièce de 5 francs serait admise à 19 pt. 10 paras et celle de 20 à 79 pt 6 paras.» AÉ, Corresp. politique des Consuls, Égypte, 1835–6, vol. 5, fol. 180. En 1846, le franc était régulièrement converti à 4 pt. AÉ, Corresp. commerciale, Le Caire, 1843–9, vol. 28, fol. 265 sv.

[9] Schoelcher, *L'Égypte*, pp. 55–56.

Si cette situation ne semble pas avoir provoqué de révolte chez les ouvriers encore totalement désorganisés et privés de la protection de leurs anciennes corporations, du moins a-t-elle dévoloppé en eux une forte «répugnance à s'enfermer dans les ateliers et à s'astreindre à un travail journalier».[1] Arrachés à leurs habitudes et à leur milieu, parfois même à leurs familles, battus et enfermés dans les locaux sans air et sans lumière, dans des conditions auxquelles ils s'habituent mal, surtout s'ils sont passés de l'état de maître-artisan ou de paysan à celui d'ouvrier, ils gardent au fond du cœur la haine des nouvelles techniques[2] qu'ils rendent responsables de leurs malheurs. Ils opposent une résistance acharnée à la modernisation de l'outillage: «Des vingt-trois ou vingt-quatre fabriques de coton qui existent en Égypte», écrivait un observateur anglais en 1834, «il n'en est pas une qui n'ait été à un moment ou l'autre, accidentellement ou volontairement mise à feu».[3]

Pour contraindre les anciens artisans expropriés à accepter la discipline du travail salarié, le gouvernement met sur pied une police sévère, interdisant tout déplacement d'un village à l'autre sans permis spécial, recrutant, par la force, des ouvriers pour les fabriques d'État, les accablant de punitions et de coups.[4] L'enrôlement dans certaines fabriques est même parfois imposé comme sanction pénitentiaire: «Les peines prévues contre quiconque ne respecterait pas les monopoles d'État sont les coups, la mort ou le travail à la fabrique de Boulac. Mentionnez le village du ressortissant coupable, noms et prénoms et livrez-le à vos agents qui le remettront à l'usine de fer».[5] Ces forçats ne reçoivent, pour tout salaire, que du pain et de l'eau.

Pourtant, quand les ouvriers acceptent leur nouveau mode de travail, ils se montrent aptes à assimiler les méthodes modernes, «la promptitude de leur intelligence, leur extrême adresse manuelle furent un sujet d'étonnement pour leurs instituteurs».[6] Un observateur anglais, J. Bowring, à la suite de nombreuses visites dans les entreprises d'État, va jusqu'à dire que «tous les ouvriers préfèrent le travail dans les usines au travail dans les champs».[7] Affirmation à première vue surprenante qu'explique peut-être le fait que l'ouvrier agricole gagne moins que l'ouvrier d'industrie (environ 30 paras par jour) et que, plus lourdement chargé d'impôts, il craint davantage encore la réquisition pour l'armée.

«Enfin la quatrième classe», écrit Clot, «est formée par les agriculteurs, les paysans, connus sous le nom de *Fellahs*, qui composent la masse de la nation.»

[1] Douin, *Boislecomte*, p. 91, 29 juin 1833.

[2] Pezzoni à Ribeaupierre, 4 septembre 1827, dans Cattaui, *Arch. russes.*, T. i, p. 95.

[3] J. A. St. John, *Egypt and Mohammed Ali* (Londres, 1834), T. ii, pp. 420–2, 412–13, 421.

[4] Schoelcher, *L'Égypte*, p. 53; Douin, *Boislecomte*, p. 91, 29 juin 1833.

[5] Muḥammad ʿAlī à son représentant à Jirjā, registre n° 3, document 257, en date du 12 jumāda 'l-awwal 1238 = 25 janvier 1823 cité par Fahmy, *Révolution*, p. 17 (avec une concordance erronée: 12 jumāda 'l-awwal 1238 = mars 1823). Voir aussi Douin, *Boislecomte*, lettre du 29 juin 1833, p. 91.

[6] Schoelcher, *L'Égypte*, p. 52.

[7] J. Bowring, *Report on Égypt and Candia* (Londres, 1840) p. 36.

Ces paysans-fellahs forment près des neuf dixièmes de la population de l'Égypte. Leur sort semble avoir été, comme toujours, très misérable. Muḥammad 'Alī avait bien tenté d'améliorer leur condition, s'il faut en croire le consul de France, Drovetti, qui écrit le 4 avril 1812: « Cette année comme dans la précédente, les contributions foncières se sont perçues en grains à un taux supérieur à celui du marché, ce qui, joint à un régime moins vexatoire introduit dans les provinces, place les agriculteurs dans une position beaucoup plus agréable que celle où ils se sont trouvés jusqu'à présent. »[1]

En fait, soumis à la « planification » établie par les autorités, le fellah, véritable ouvrier agricole salarié, plante, aux dates indiquées, les semences distribuées par les autorités. Il reçoit les instruments aratoires et les bestiaux nécessaires à l'irrigation. Sa paye journalière est d'environ une piastre en nature ou en argent.[2] Écrasé de charges et responsable en sus de l'impôt du voisin, de par la pratique de « l'impôt solidaire », sa misère matérielle et morale est accrue par la pratique des réquisitions forcées pour l'armée où il peut servir toute sa vie, aucun règlement n'ayant été édicté quant à la durée du service militaire.[3] Arraché à sa famille, il peut aussi être enrôlé de force à l'arsenal, à la fonderie ou dans les industries d'État.[4] Les corvées représentent encore l'épreuve la plus pénible:

> quand le gouvernement a des constructions ou des travaux à faire, il donne aux chefs des provinces des ordres pour qu'ils lui amènent tel nombre d'hommes dont il a besoin: alors les populations tout entières de plusieurs villages, hommes, femmes, enfants, jeunes filles sont prises et garrotées et s'acheminent péniblement aux lieux marqués sous la conduite du cheik el-balad; l'autorité ne s'inquiète point de fournir à leurs besoins, de donner à manger à ceux qui ont faim durant la route: il arrive souvent que les plus pauvres meurent de faim et que des cadavres gisent sur les chemins où ces ces malheureuses bandes ont passé.[5]

La corvée du creusement du canal Maḥmūdiyya occupe ainsi 313 000 fellahs, amenés de sept provinces différentes. En dix mois, douze mille d'entre eux meurent de soif, de faim et de fatigue par suite de la mauvaise organisation du travail. Pendant cette période pour creuser plus de 80 km, ils sont payés 28 à 30 piastres chacun.[6] Le canal allant de Zaqāzīq au Wādī al-Ṭumaylāt (34 666 m.) provoque de même la réquisition de quatre vingt mille fellahs de la province de Sharqiyya. Les vingt premiers kms. sont terminés en 5 jours de travail intensif. En 1833, 200 km de canaux sont ainsi creusés dans toute l'Égypte par les corvéables.[7]

[1] AÉ, Corresp. politique des Consuls, Le Caire, 1803–28, vol. 26, fol. 207.

[2] A partir de 1834–6 seulement, il pourra disposer de ses récoltes en céréales contre un droit de compensation.

[3] P. N. Hamont, *L'Égypte sous Méhémet-Ali* (Paris, 1843), vol. i, p. 43; Clot, *Aperçu*, T. ii, p. 255 et sv.; Michaud et Poujoulat, *Correspondance*, T. vi, pp. 81–82.

[4] Schoelcher, *L'Égypte*, p. 55.

[5] Michaud et Poujoulat, *Correspondance*, T. vii, pp. 71–72.

[6] Mengin, *Hist.* T. ii, p. 335; Douin, *Boislecomte*, p. 83.

[7] Ibid.

Le mécontentement paysan se traduit de diverses manières; par la fuite d'abord: «Au commencement de 1822, la province de Charkyeh, d'après le recensement fait, comptait quatre-vingt-quatorze mille hommes en état de porter les armes, dont six mille étaient en fuite.»[1] Il se traduit également par des soulèvements en 1820–1, 1822–3, 1824, 1826, 1846,[2] sévèrement réprimés par les autorités et l'armée — dont les troupes, d'origine paysannes, refusent parfois de tirer et désertent les rangs.

Après 1836, une certaine liberté est rendue aux «chefs de villages» qui parviennent à percevoir l'arriéré des impôts dus à l'État. Ils obtiennent alors le droit de s'administrer eux-mêmes sans être soumis aux *nāẓirs*.[3] Cette amélioration de la situation des *shaykh al-balad* ne semble pas avoir amélioré sensiblement celle du paysan. A la suite des firmans de 1840, qui réduisent l'armée et mettent fin au système des monopoles d'État, les terres de la Moyenne et de la Haute Égypte sont rendues à la libre exploitation, ainsi que la moitié de celles de Basse Égypte. Alors seulement, le paysan retrouve quelque chance de posséder un lopin. Les risques surtout deviennent moindres pour lui d'être enrôlé dans l'armée ou l'industrie.

A côté des paysans, un petit nombre de bedouins turbulent sont sévèrement surveillés par Muḥammad ʿAlī qui les circonvient en tirant parti de leurs rivalités ancestrales et en favorisant les uns aux dépens des autres. Il leur enlève leur principale force en réquisitionnant hommes et chevaux pour ses expéditions militaires[4] et en tentant de les sédentariser.

Dans cette organisation sociale, on ne voit pas encore poindre de bougeoisie. Les circonstances ne sont pas favorables à la naissance d'une classe intermédiaire. A une économie de subsistance plusieurs fois centenaire, s'est trop brusquement substitué le monopole d'un souverain entreprenant, industrieux et jaloux de toute puissance autre que la sienne. Même quand il disparaîtra, le commerce et l'industrie seront laissés aux non-musulmans, phénomène qui se retrouvera dans les autres pays de l'Islam. Cette classe non autochtone ne pourra pas jouer le rôle qui incombe à la bourgeoisie dans une société moderne. Il faudra attendre les lendemains de la première guerre mondiale pour assister au développement d'une banque à capitaux nationaux, à un nouveau début d'industrialisation et à la naissance d'une bourgeoisie proprement égyptienne.

[1] Mengin, *Hist.*, T. ii, p. 317.

[2] Voir G. Baer, «The submissiveness of the Egyptian peasant», dans *New Outlook*, vol. v, nº 9 (49), novembre–décembre 1962, pp. 17–19. H. A. B. Rivlin, *The agricultural policy of Muḥammad ʿAlī in Egypt* (Cambridge, Mass., 1961), pp. 113–207.

[3] AÉ, Corresp. politique des Consuls, Égypte, 1835–6, vol. 5, fol. 251 verso.

[4] Mengin, *Hist.*, T. ii, p. 300.

The Role of the ʿulamāʾ in Egypt during the Early Nineteenth Century

AFAF LOUTFI EL SAYED

THE golden age of the power of the *ʿulamāʾ* in modern Egypt can be counted from the last few decades of Mamluk rule until the advent of Muḥammad ʿAlī to power; for during that period the political power of the *ʿulamāʾ* rose to unprecedented heights, only to fall low. In this paper we shall try to show that the political position of the *ʿulamāʾ* was a consequence of the social structure of Islamic society, and that when that society became exposed to westernizing influences, their once powerful position was jeopardized and eventually declined.

Traditional Muslim society admitted of two major groups who were set in authority over the people, these were firstly the military, 'the men of the sword', and secondly the religious, 'the men of the pen'. While the former group had charge of the administration, of ruling the state, the latter group, as a consequence of their being the guardians of religion, were in charge of the intellectual and social life, of the law and its application; that is, they were the teachers, the scholars, the *qāḍīs*, and the *muftīs*.

This division of society meant that within the Muslim community there were two potential sources of authority—one stemming from the use of coercive force and vested in the military, and the other stemming from the use of moral and religious sanctions and vested in the *ʿulamāʾ*. In the ideal state both these elements were to work in harmony and in close co-operation one with the other, but soon the military used their power of coercion to impose upon the religious authorities, and the latter, by the twelfth century had learned the harsh lesson that 'necessity makes lawful what is prohibited',[1] and developed a Sunnī tradition of submission to established authority, whenever they saw that they could not do otherwise. The strong ruler thus used the *ʿulamāʾ* either to legitimatize his actions *vis-à-vis* the community, or to help him rule the people, for in a society dominated by religion and tradition, the moral influence of the *ʿulamāʾ* was great, and their right to participate in matters of government recognized.[2] By the eighteenth century, when coercive power had become weak or diffused and when 'long established custom had given them a practical immunity from arbitrary execution and punishment, they could afford to brave the displeasure of *Paşas* and *Beys*',[3] and were

[1] Al-Ghazālī, *Kitāb al-iqtiṣād fi'l-iʿtiqād* (Cairo, 1320), p. 107.

[2] H. A. R. Gibb and H. Bowen, *Islamic society and the West* (London, 1950, 1957), vol. 1, pt. ii, p. 110.

[3] Ibid., p. 111; also Jabartī, *ʿAjāʾib*, vol. iii, p. 266.

able to oppose the rulers with some measure of success and even able to lead movements of opposition.

This was the case for as long as the Muslim community remained aloof from Western influences. For then the position of the *'ulamā'* as the intellectual *élite* was guaranteed, and their prestige and influence remained great. It was only when the traditional society broke up to admit westernizing influences that we notice the decline in the authority of the *'ulamā'*, and their displacement in all their functions, save the religious one, by a social group that formed a new *élite* of civil servants, lawyers, and journalists, an *élite* that replaced the *'ulamā'* both in their role as an instrument of authority over the people, and as a channel of popular opposition to the rulers.

Mamluk Egypt

The *'ulamā'* in Egypt held a special position by virtue of the Mamluk system of rule, and by virtue of the fact that rulers and ruled formed different ethnic and linguistic units. There was a gap between the groups, and the *'ulamā'* supplied the bridge that filled that gap. In the words of a rector of al-Azhar, the *'ulamā'* were there to serve as intermediaries with the rulers.[1]

In spite of the fact that the *'ulamā'* formed an opposition to the Mamluks, yet the relationship between both groups was, on the whole, an amicable one, not only as a result of the Sunnī tradition of submission to authority, but also because, according to al-Jabartī, the Mamluks had been reared in the laps of the *'ulamā'*, read the Qur'ān, studied the *Sharī'a* and went on the *Ḥajj*.[2] This, he claimed, instilled in them a veneration for the *'ulamā'* and a deference to their wisdom, as well as a respect for the established and traditional way of life. On the other hand, many of the *'ulamā'* regarded the Mamluks with favour. Some of them were dependent on Mamluks for their livelihood, they attached themselves to Mamluk houses, and were given livings by them. They visited those Mamluks who had religious tendencies, or literary pretensions, they intermarried with them, and some wealthy *'ulamā'* even came to possess *mamlūks* of their own. Both groups co-operated with each other, and the *'ulamā'* became the only restraining force, aside from the physical, on the Mamluks. The latter, who because of their excessive factionalism distrusted each other, often used the *'ulamā'* as mediators among themselves. In times of crisis they appealed to the *'ulamā'* to intercede for them, either with the Almighty through special prayers and readings of al-Bukhārī, or to use their influence over the people whenever they threatened a disturbance.

This influence which the *'ulamā'* had over the people, was one of the mainsprings of their power in Egypt. For as Mamluk influence waned, the antagonism of the Ottoman sultanate grew, and their power to curb the people was curtailed. Popular uprisings grew more frequent. Only the *'ulamā'* were able to preserve the peace without a show of force. To illustrate this al-Jabartī

[1] Ibid., vol. i, p. 187.

[2] Ibid., vol. iv, p. 49.

cites an incident in 1785 when Ibrāhīm Bey, then *Amīr al-Ḥajj*, made the rounds of the *'ulamā'*, namely Shaykhs al-Bakrī, al-'Arūsī, and al-Dardīr, and, making himself small (*tasāghara fī nafsihi*),[1] requested that they help him preserve the peace and prevent the populace from behaving in an unruly manner, and giving the Porte an excuse for intervention. Thus if the Mamluks respected the *'ulamā'* and deferred to them, it was not only because of their religious upbringing, but because they knew that the *'ulamā'* controlled the people and could both rouse and restrain them, and it was this dual role of rabble-rousers and peace-makers which was the source of their political power in Egypt.

In turn, many of the people respected and trusted the *'ulamā'*. Apart from the fact that there was no one else to trust, the *'ulamā'* were Arabic-speaking like the people, unlike the Turkish-speaking Mamluks, and al-Jabartī gives instances when *'ulamā'* told the Mamluks to translate their words because 'we do not know Turkish',[2] even though there were Arabic-speaking Mamluks and Turkish-speaking *'ulamā'*. Most of the *'ulamā'* came from the people, and lived with the people. They were accessible, even the most glorified amongst them. They were *awlād balad* rather than *mamālīk*. Since the people were religious and superstitious, and the *'ulamā'* were the representatives of religion, they were believed to possess *baraka*, to be capable of *siḥr*, or at least, as holy men who knew the Qur'ān, they were worthy of veneration. They were thus held in high esteem and received preferential treatment everywhere.[3] On the other hand, the *'ulamā'* regarded themselves as the quintessence of God's *élite*, '*khulāṣat khāṣṣat Allāh fī khalqih*', by virtue of the 'word of truth' which they diffused.[4]

In most villages the local shaykh often acted as *muftī*, *qāḍī*, and general peace-maker, but it was from the urban groups that the *'ulamā'* derived their main force, for although the *fallāḥīn* often appealed to the *'ulamā'* when they were taxed beyond endurance, yet they were too scattered to form an effective power-bloc, and more often than not were allowed to cry in the wilderness, unlike the urban groups who were organized.

We know that the merchants and artisans of Cairo were formed into guilds and corporations that were highly organized groups, each under the leadership of a shaykh who had authority to inflict fines and even corporal punishment on members of the corporation. These guilds had close connexions with the *'ulamā'* and with the Ṣūfī orders.[5] It was said that some guilds practised their trade from within the precincts of a mosque.[6] The *ijāza* given to an apprentice

[1] Jabartī, *'Ajā'ib*, vol. ii, p. 111.

[2] Ibid., p. 158.

[3] E. W. Lane, *An account of the manners and customs of the modern Egyptians* (Everyman edn.), pp. 218–19; also Jabartī, *'Ajā'ib*, vol. iv, p. 192 *passim*.

[4] Khalīl Shaybūb, *'Abd al-Raḥmān al-Jabartī* (Cairo, 1948), p. 28, quoting Shaykh Ḥasan al-Jabartī.

[5] See G. Baer, *Egyptian guilds in modern times* (Jerusalem, 1964), especially pp. 6–11.

[6] Ibrahim Salama, *L'Enseignement islamique en Égypte* (Cairo, 1939), p. 217. Also M. de

was couched in religious terms.[1] The *'ulamā'* and shaykhs of corporations frequently met; often the latter appealed to the former for assistance even with their own trade, for instance the father of al-Jabartī helped to correct the weights and measures,[2] and was himself adept at the art of marble inlay. Many guild members were also members of Ṣūfī orders as were many of the *'ulamā'*, for al-Azhar from the sixteenth century had become a centre of Sufism.[3] Thus the link between three urban and highly organized groups such as the *'ulamā'*, the guilds, and the Ṣūfī orders was an obvious one, and it would appear to have been a simple matter for the *'ulamā'* to rouse large groups of the population to action by calling upon either the corporations or the orders, especially since al-Azhar was in close proximity to the city's commercial artery, the Qaṣaba.

The danger-signal was a drum sounded from one of the minarets of al-Azhar, which could be heard within a wide radius, and since most of the guilds converged along topographic lines with the water-carriers inhabiting one street, the coppersmiths another, and so on, whole *sūqs* would then close, gates leading to the various quarters barricaded, the gates of al-Azhar would be shut, and a mob, armed with stout staves would assemble in front of al-Azhar to await the *'ulamā'*. This was the voice of public opinion. It could get out of hand and degenerate into a mob, but it could also become the core of popular resistance movements, as it did during the French occupation. But it was through the urban population that the *'ulamā'* were able to restrain the authorities, and it was to the *'ulamā'* that the urban population appealed when it wished to reach the ear of the said authorities.

But who were the powerful *'ulamā'* of Egypt? Firstly they were those who occupied an official position in the religious hierarchy such as the rector of al-Azhar, the *muftīs* of the four *madhhabs*, and the marshal of the Notables (*naqīb al-Ashrāf*).[4] Then came the heads of two Ṣūfī orders, Shaykh al-Bakrī and Shaykh al-Sādāt. Both these shaykhs were descendants of the Prophet and of Abū Bakr. Their titles were hereditary, and passed on to whichever member of the family the reigning shaykh chose to appoint. Traditionally, from the eleventh century of the Hijra, Shaykh al-Bakrī acted as the principal director and co-ordinator of the mystical orders in Egypt,[5] which meant that he not only led the orders on festival days, but also appointed the heads of the orders, and

Chabrol, 'Essai sur les mœurs des habitants modernes de l'Égypte', *Description de l'Égypte: État moderne*, vol. ii, p. 379.

[1] Jabartī, *'Ajā'ib*, vol. ii, pp. 214–15.

[2] Ibid., vol. i, p. 399.

[3] Salama, op. cit., p. 130.

[4] The *qāḍi*, being appointed by the Porte, was identified with the Ottomans, and was never regarded as one of the local *'ulamā'*. And since his appointment was a yearly one he never had any following, and his role was a minor one. Although in other Muslim lands *naqīb al-Ashrāf* was one of the leading religious personalities, in Egypt he had a lesser degree of importance. However, since the title was usually held by either Shaykh al-Bakrī or Shaykh al-Sādāt, who were powerful men in their own right, we are justified in including it amongst the religious power hierarchy, especially when 'Umar Makram occupied the office.

[5] Muḥammad Tawfīq al-Bakrī, *Bayt al-Ṣiddīq* (Cairo, 1905), p. 394.

even had a hand in choosing the rector of al-Azhar.[1] As for Shaykh al-Sādāt, he was the head of the Wafā'ī order, and disputed the right to *niqābat al-Ashrāf* with Shaykh al-Bakrī, and was in fact his chief rival for power.

The power these two men wielded is best described by two of their contemporaries. The first, Aḥmad Pasha al-Jazzār, wrote in the *Nizamname-i Mısır*:

> . . . there is His Excellency the *Şeyẖ ul-Bekrî* . . . who has many relatives, dependents, followers, and revenues. All the *'Ulemâ* of the Azhar and the *Emîrs* and elders of the corps and the merchants and other people kiss his hand and venerate and esteem him. After him [in rank] there is the greatly honored Excellency the *Şeyẖ ul-Sâdât* . . . All his circumstances are like those of the aforementioned . . . all the *'Ulemâ* of the Azhâr [*sic*], . . . the poor of the city, the *Rûm Ôşâğî*, and the North African merchants follow them and never contradict their words. In sum, they have the ability to assemble in a single day a powerful military regiment of at least seventy or eighty thousand men who are docile and loyal to them.[2]

Al-Jabartī supports al-Jazzār's estimate, and in his obituary of Shaykh al-Sādāt added that clerks worked for the shaykh and considered it a major sin (*min al kabā'ir*) to receive wages for their work.[3] The *amīrs* and even his colleagues treated him with such esteem that the *khaṭīb* had special *khuṭab* which he would deliver when the shaykh appeared at the mosque, and these were so eulogistic that al-Jabartī claimed he overheard a man saying that the *khaṭīb* might as well have ended his speech by saying 'kneel and bow down and worship Shaykh al-Sādāt.'[4] His house came to be regarded in the same light as that of a chief of the police, to be feared by some, and used as a place of refuge and appeal by others.[5]

Both Shaykh al-Bakrī and Shaykh al-Sādāt held their power over the people by virtue of their headship over the Ṣūfī orders. Both men had the aura of the *Ashrāf* about them, both were excessively wealthy by virtue of their being *nāẓirs* over very extensive *waqfs*, and also through their personal property.[6] They held *mūlids* (*mawlids*) which were lavish, and which were attended by the high and the mighty. Traditionally the Bakrī shaykhs celebrated the Prophet's birthday, while the Sādāt celebrated *mūlid Sayyidnā al-Ḥusayn*. These were privileges which had accrued with the ages, and with each privilege the shaykhs acquired a little more wealth, prestige and consequently, political influence. We can easily say that throughout the eighteenth and up to the middle of the nineteenth century these two men were involved in most of the major political incidents in the land.

On the other hand, the official *'ulamā'* in the country were headed by the

[1] Al-Bakrī, op. cit., p. 42; also de Chabrol, op. cit., p. 394, n.

[2] Stanford J. Shaw, *Ottoman Egypt in the eighteenth century* (Cambridge, Mass., 1962), pp. 22–23 (English text).

[3] Jabartī, *'Ajā'ib*, vol. iv, p. 187.

[4] Ibid., p. 192. [5] Ibid., p. 191. [6] Ibid., p. 189.

rector of al-Azhar, who was elected to the post by his fellow *ʿulamāʾ*, pending the approval of the ruler. Where the *ʿulamāʾ* were divided on their choice of rector an awkward situation could and did arise, and one such incident led to an impasse lasting seven months.[1] The influence of Shaykh al-Azhar was inherent in his position, but the manner in which he used this influence naturally depended upon his personality.

One of the strongest rectors of the time was Shaykh al-Sharqāwī (1793–1812). He was an intriguer, who could take the initiative and show courage at times of crisis. One such crisis arose in 1794 when *multazims* of Bilbays appealed to him, also a *multazim* of the area, to help them oppose a new tax. Al-Sharqāwī gathered the *ʿulamāʾ*, closed al-Azhar, summoned the mob, and marched to the house of Shaykh al-Sādāt. There the *ʿulamāʾ* discussed their grievances in general, and told the *defterdar* that they wanted 'justice, an end to tyranny, a return to the rule of the *Sharīʿa* and an end to the various new taxes innovated'.[2] The crisis lasted for three days, with the mob daily growing in size and the Mamluks becoming more alarmed, until finally they all met at the pasha's house, and the *qāḍī* drew up a document wherein the beys promised not to raise new taxes, but to deal fairly with the people. This incident was a potent example of the pressure which the *ʿulamāʾ* could bring to bear on the Mamluks, but unfortunately the Mamluks were never coerced for long, and soon returned to their former ways.

The second official personality in the hierarchy was *naqīb al-Ashrāf*. This title was usually held by either Shaykh al-Bakrī or Shaykh al-Sādāt, but from 1793 to 1809, save for a brief interim period during the French occupation, the post was occupied by Sayyid ʿUmar Makram. Very little is known about his antecedents, or even about his ancestry, for his sole claim to being a *sharīf* rested on two *ḥujjas* dated 1210/1795–6 and 1235/1819–20, the dates being subsequent to his appointment as *naqīb*. He springs into al-Jabartī's chronicles fully grown as a man who negotiated the return of Ibrāhīm and Murād with the Ottoman authorities, and who was rewarded for this service by being appointed to the position when the contemporary incumbent Shaykh al-Bakrī died. Makram seemed to have been a man of authority and means, and something of an adventurer. When the French occupied Egypt, he left the country and spent the years wandering in Gaza and Acre. When he returned to Egypt he became involved in a revolt and a *coup d'état* as we shall see later.

These were not the only *ʿulamāʾ* to wield power. Lesser *ʿulamāʾ* were capable of rousing the masses. For example, Shakyh al-Dardīr, the Mālikī *muftī*, once suggested to the mob, when they complained to him that the house of the head of the Bayyūmī order had been plundered by Ḥusayn Bey, that they all go and plunder the houses of the Mamluks, either gaining victory over them, or dying as martyrs.[3] He was only restrained from carrying out his

[1] This was the incident involving al-ʿArīshī and al-ʿArūsī in 1777.
[2] Jabartī, *ʿAjāʾib*, vol. ii, p. 258.
[3] Ibid., p. 103.

intention by the timely intervention of the *ağa* of Janissaries. It is an interesting sidelight on the Mamluks' image of themselves to note that when Ḥusayn Bey was reproached by Ibrāhīm Bey for his deed, he answered: 'We all plunder, you plunder, Murād Bey plunders, and I also plunder.'

From these incidents it is clear that the *'ulamā'* could and did exert a definite pressure on the political atmosphere under the Mamluks, and we are justified in talking about them as the popular leaders of the country, as distinct from its actual rulers. This popular leadership was hampered by its tradition of submission to authority, and by its lack of effective fighting power, for a mob, although dangerous, was not capable of standing up to Mamluk arms for long. The *'ulamā'* were thus too cowed by physical strength to do more than demonstrate against the Mamluks. In fact, when at one time they were incited by the *kapudan paşa* to rise against their rulers, they refused, saying 'the *amīrs* form a strong and powerful party . . . we are impotent, for their tyranny has weakened the people'.[1] Yet at the same time, was there not a sneaking sense of loyalty towards the Mamluks whose house were 'mingled' with those of the people?[2]

The role of the *'ulamā'* at this stage remained at the defensive and mediatory stage, for there was no better alternative to Mamluk rule; and although they complained bitterly of the situation, there was no justification or incentive for taking direct action to change it. The French expedition and its aftermath was soon to supply them with an alternative to the Mamluks, and with an incentive to action.

The French expedition and its aftermath

Bonaparte's occupation of Egypt, while it did not totally destroy the Mamluk system of rule, did suspend it in some parts of the country for a few years. When Bonaparte ousted the traditional ruling class from power, he had to find a native substitute to collaborate with him in ruling Egypt, and the obvious alternative was the *'ulamā'*, the only other *élite* in the land. Thus it came about that in composing his *Dīwān*, Bonaparte filled it with *'ulamā'* who were to help him legislate, maintain order, and act as an intermediary between the French authorities and the people.

This is not to suppose that overnight with the *Dīwān* the *'ulamā'* developed initiative and became the rulers of Egypt, and there is little reason to suppose that the French did so intend, but for the first time the ruling power in the country was making a show of governing in consultation with the *'ulamā'* as representatives of the local will and the local weal. And although the Mamluks also had had a *Dīwān* which included the *'ulamā'*, it had not been a *Dīwān* that pretended to be 'un essai pour accoutumer les notables d'Égypte à des idées d'assemblée et de gouvernement',[3] as Bonaparte intended his *Dīwān* should

[1] Jabarti, *'Ajā'ib*, vol. ii, p. 110. [2] Ibid.

[3] Napoleon, *Correspondance* (Paris, 1860), vol. v, no. 3423.

become. Thus with the defeat of the Mamluks, the *'ulamā'* who felt bitter against them, and who blamed them for the occupation,[1] came to see themselves, and to be seen by the people, as occupying a greater position of authority than before.

Bonaparte's reasons for choosing to rule through the *'ulamā'* were exposed in a memorandum which he wrote:

. . . I have preferred the ulema and the doctors of the law: first, because they are the natural leaders; secondly, because they are interpreters of the Koran, and the greatest obstacles we have met with and shall still meet with proceed from religious ideas; and thirdly because these ulema have gentle manners, love justice, and are rich and animated by good moral principles . . . they are not addicted to any sort of military manoeuvring and they are ill adapted to the leadership of an armed movement.[2]

But because they were the natural leaders, and the interpreters of the Qur'ān, and because the French were non-Muslims, the *'ulamā'* though ill-adapted to lead armed movements, could not desist from doing so. This they did on three different occasions within a period of seven years. The first occurred in October 1798. This was an abortive revolt, led by the Shaykh of the *Riwāq* of the Blind in al-Azhar, who was executed along with several other *'ulamā'* for his pains. The second revolt took place in March 1800, and was a combined operation of Ottoman forces, Mamluks, and the Egyptian populace led by 'Umar Makram. The third revolt took place in 1805 and placed Muḥammad 'Alī on the viceregal throne of Egypt.

Aside from 'Umar Makram, the *'ulamā'* who were involved in these revolts were Shaykh al-Sādāt, who was accused by Bonaparte of fomenting the first revolt, although al-Jabartī exonerates him. He was not punished, for fear of a popular reaction. But he was implicated in the second revolt and was fined, imprisoned, and beaten by the French.[3] This led to a heightening of his prestige amongst the people, and to the lessening of that of Shaykh al-Bakrī, who had befriended the French. When the French evacuated Egypt al-Bakrī was deposed from his order, and his daughter was killed for consorting with the French.[4]

The effect of the French occupation on the *'ulamā'* was to place them in an even greater position of authority than they had previously occupied, and to establish them as the actual leaders of the people, albeit not effectual ones, through sheer military ineptitude. They played a similar role to the one they had played under the Mamluks, but with the addition that their submission

[1] Shaykh al-Sādāt accused the Mamluks of bringing on the occupation by their misguided actions. Jabartī, *'Ajā'ib*, vol. iv, p. 192.

[2] C. de la Jonquière, *L'expédition de l'Égypte (1798–1801)* (Paris, 1899–1907), vol. v, p. 597. Translation quoted from F. Charles-Roux (tr. E. W. Dickes), *Bonaparte: governor of Egypt* (London, 1937), pp. 353–4.

[3] Jabartī, *'Ajā'ib*, vol. iii, p. 108.

[4] Ibid., p. 192.

to authority was one of necessity, and not of voluntary co-operation, and that they became the official ruling group, for most orders came to the people through the *Dīwān*, and were signed by the *'ulamā'*, even though planned and executed by the French.

After the French evacuated Egypt, and Ottoman forces and Mamluks once more began jockeying for power; that is with the return of a Muslim military caste, the *'ulamā'* went back to their basic functions, and left the military factions to fight it out between themselves. The result was four years of chaos and bloodshed.

During these years the bond between the *'ulamā'* and the Mamluks had weakened, and while the Mamluks still trusted only the *'ulamā'* when negotiating with their opponents, both *'ulamā'* and people realized the sheer ineptitude of the Mamluks and their inability to protect them from the ravages of either French or Ottoman. With loss of military power came loss of prestige, and in 1803 Shaykh al-'Arūsī could harangue Ibrāhīm Bey in the middle of the *Dīwān* and say:

> . . . Dieu se gardera d'éxaucer vos prières . . . car la tyrannie, l'injustice et la débauche règnent sur l'ensemble de notre pays. Nos gouvernants ne sont pas de vrais musulmans. S'ils étaient des croyants sincères, j'entends des hommes passionnés de justice et d'intégrité, ils aboliraient les taxes indirectes, les contributions irrégulières, supprimeraient les prélèvements arbitraires, rassureraient les populations: leur inculqueraient les intentions pures, régéneraient le pays et donneraient confiance aux habitants. Or que voyons nous ? Précisément le contraire de ce qu'exige la justice. Sous leur gouvernement, les troubles et les exactions s'étendent, le vice s'étale au grand jour . . . les mamlouks et les soldats, jour et nuit, pillent, ravagent, frappent, tuent, sans craindre ni chef ni notable.[1]

Nicolas Turc ended his account of this incident by saying, 'et le conseil convoqué par Ibrahim Bey se sépara de cette façon'.[2] A far cry from the days when the *'ulamā'* were co-operating with the Mamluks.

Not only was the political situation chaotic, but the economic situation continued to deteriorate to such an extent that people wept before 'Uthmān al-Bardīsī, head of Murād's faction, and shouted slogans such as 'Aysh takhud min taflīsī, yā Bardīsī'. While this was happening, Muḥammad 'Alī told the people and the *'ulamā'* that they should not have to pay such exorbitant taxes; that this was the result of bad administration, thereby implying that he could do better and projecting the image of an upright man of action and authority.

[1] Nicolas Turc (ed. and tr. G. Wiet), *Chronique d'Égypte: 1798–1804* (Cairo, 1950), pp. 193–4.

[2] Jabartī, *'Ajā'ib*, vol. iii, pp. 263–4 has a different version. The *'ulamā'* wished to offer a special prayer, *al-istisqā'*, but told Ibrāhīm that they could only do so if the forced loans were stopped and restitution made, etc. He answered that he could no nothing, for he had no influence on anybody. They then made answer that they would emigrate from Egypt, and he said he too would do likewise.

Matters reached a head when the *vali*'s troops ravaged the city to such an extent that, according to the French agent, they had 'indigné le peuple, qui s'est mis sur l'offensive. Les portes de la grande mosquée ont été closes, tous les bazars, tous les okelles ont été fermés et les habitants n'attendaient que le signal de leurs cheikhs pour fondre sur les delhis'.[1] The *'ulamā'*, being appealed to by the people, and unable to tolerate such anarchy, assembled in the house of Shaykh al-Sharqāwī in order to determine a course of action. Such open antagonism was being manifested towards the Ottomans that people went round saying, 'Ya Rabb, ya metgallī, ehlek el-'Osmānlī'.[2] While the *'ulamā'* were closeted together, Muḥammad 'Alī was wooing Sayyid 'Umar Makram, meeting him in secret, and promising him that he would do nothing without consulting the *'ulamā'*, if only they would choose him as the new *vali*.[3] In that sense the situation was similar to that of previous embryonic revolts, for prospective rulers always sought to gain the *'ulamā'*'s goodwill before their seizure of power, so Muḥammad 'Alī was acting along traditional lines, the only difference lay in the manner in which the *'ulamā'* themselves were acting.

The *'ulamā'*, finally reaching the end of their deliberations, presented a list of their complaints to the *vali*, and when the *vali* refused to comply with their terms, they rode up to Muḥammad 'Alī and said: 'We do not wish for the rule of this pasha, he must be deposed.' Muḥammad 'Alī asked whom they planned to put in his place, and they answered: 'We will have none but you, you will become *vali* over us, on our conditions, and from what we have seen of you of justice.'[4] Then Shaykh al-Sharqāwī clothed him in a *quftān* as an official act of investiture. This was by way of being a *coup d'état*, which, when the *vali* refused to accept deposition at the hands of *fallāḥīn*, turned into an armed revolt. The *'ulamā'* exhorted the people to prepare for combat, and organized resistance groups, and though the dynamo of the revolt was 'Umar Makram, the other *'ulamā'* assisted him as well.[5]

When the *vali* found himself besieged in the Citadel, he was forced to send a messenger, who demanded an explanation from 'Umar Makram, and asked why the *'ulamā'* had seen fit to disobey 'those set in authority over them', that is, the *vali*. Makram gave the following significant answer: 'Those in authority are the *'ulamā'* and the followers of the *Sharī'a* and the righteous sultan, but this is a tyrannical man, and it is the tradition from time immemorial that people (*ahl al-balad*) depose the *vali* if he be unjust.' Then the messenger asked, '. . . are we *kuffār*?' that they should be so ill treated, and Makram said: 'Yes, for the *'ulamā'* have decreed that it is righteous to fight you for you are rebellious (*'uṣāh*),'[6]

[1] Georges Douin, *Mohamed Aly: Pacha du Caire: 1805–1807* (Cairo, 1926), no. 21.

[2] Jabartī, *'Ajā'ib*, vol. iii, p. 329.

[3] Ibid., vol. iv, p. 32.

[4] Ibid., vol. iii, p. 329.

[5] Douin, op. cit., no. 32.

[6] Jabartī, *'Ajā'ib*, vol. iii, p. 331.

The short account given by al-Jabartī of this exchange is most illuminating on the new attitude the *'ulamā'* had adopted. They had just deposed the Ottoman *vali* with no other authority save the tenuous will of *ahl al-balad*. This was an unprecedented action for the *'ulamā'* in Egypt to take, and one which could only be justified by an appeal to Muslim tradition. *Valis* had often been deposed in Egypt, but only when the *Dīwān*, that is the Mamluks, had so decreed, for they possessed the power of constraint. This time the *'ulamā'* arrogated to themselves the power to depose the *vali* on religious grounds, based on their traditional power to declare a ruler 'rebellious'. Moreover, they themselves were the coercive force that was to make the deposition effective, for Muḥammad 'Alī's troops were divided amongst themselves, and were insufficient to carry out the coup successfully, especially as they were constantly defecting because of lack of pay, so that it was the people, who, armed by the *'ulamā'*, did all the fighting. Town-criers went round calling on the people to arm and report for action in response to 'the call of Sayyid 'Umar Makram and the *'ulamā'*".[1] And the French agent reported that this 'prouve à l'évidence qu'ils [the shaykhs] maîtrisent en ce moment les destinées du gouvernement du Caire'.[2] 'Umar Makram, assisted by the head of the greengrocers' guild, organized combat groups which took over whenever Muḥammad 'Alī's forces deserted their posts, which happened fairly regularly. 'On voit règner le même enthousiasme qu'en France dans les premiers moments de la Révolution',[3] commented the French agent. This had all the characteristics of a popular movement, called into existence and organized by the *'ulamā'*.

For one brief glorious moment the *'ulamā'* had taken the initiative and had posed as the rulers of the country, rousing the people into a resistance movement. 'Umar Makram levied a contribution from the wealthier citizens and bought arms to supply the populace, and even paid the poorer artisans a daily wage, as indemnity for leaving their trade and turning soldiers.[4] As a result, he could call upon nearly 40,000 armed men. As far as the inhabitants of Cairo, and indeed the other big cities, were concerned, Makram was their leader, and Muḥammad 'Alī, for the time being, took second place. Given Muḥammad 'Alī's later record, the suspicion that he stage-managed the whole crisis is not unnatural, but one must keep in mind that Makram was also a leader in his own way, and that Muḥammad 'Alī was relatively unknown to the Egyptians, so that his early position was weak. But whether he had managed the whole situation or not, does not take away from the *'ulamā'* the credit for organizing and carrying out the revolt. For Muḥammad 'Alī could not have succeeded without their aid, and the *'ulamā'*, had they so chosen, could have sat back and left the various factions to fight amongst themselves as they had always done, instead of which they chose to take an active part in the events.

[1] Jabartī *'Ajā'ib*, vol. iii, p. 332.
[2] Douin, op. cit., Drovetti, no. 33.
[3] Ibid., no. 32.
[4] Ibid., no. 37.

Muḥammad ʿAlī undoubtedly intrigued to get the *ʿulamāʾ* to appoint him as *vali*, but he could not have forced them to act had they not wished to do so themselves. They followed through by sending a petition to Istanbul asking the sultan to sanction their *coup d'état* and proclaim Muḥammad ʿAlī governor of Egypt. Eventually a *ferman* arrived from the Porte appointing him as *vali*, since 'the *ʿulamāʾ* and the people have so requested'.[1]

Muḥammad ʿAlī

The honeymoon period between the *ʿulamāʾ* and Muḥammad ʿAlī lasted for nearly three years. At first his position was still shaky and he needed the *ʿulamāʾ* to protect him from the intrigues of the Porte with the Mamluks, who were trying to return to power, But by 1809 he felt sufficiently confident in his position to turn against the *ʿulamāʾ*. They had chosen him on the understanding that he would abide by certain conditions, which basically were that no new taxes were to be levied, and the old unjust taxes to be repealed. But Muḥammad ʿAlī, who needed money even more desperately than did his predecessors, neither could nor would abide by these conditions, and found the *ʿulamāʾ*'s constant pressure irksome. For they had resumed their old role of mediators between the ruler and the people, and interfered whenever a loan was raised. Thus Muḥammad ʿAlī found himself in the position of having to placate and wheedle the *ʿulamāʾ* in order to raise taxes. In this last task he was ably assisted by Makram who helped him to distribute and collect the loans.[2] But when Muḥammad ʿAlī started taxing the *ʿulamāʾ*, who were traditionally immune from taxation, and when he began to change the established systems, then they opposed him. But this the new *vali* could not permit. And helped by their own cupidity, their sense of survival, and their reluctance to take on responsibility, he managed to remove them from his way.

When Muḥammad ʿAlī first came to power, he took an oath to rule with justice, and in consultation with the *ʿulamāʾ* (*bi-mashūrat al-ʿulamāʾ*).[3] Brought to its logical conclusion, this oath could have spelt the beginning of the *ʿulamāʾ* as an effective consultative body, and as the final arbiter of political power in the country, for the pasha had agreed to accept deposition were he to contravene the *ʿulamāʾ*'s wishes. But they were still unused to handling power, and were afraid of it, and hurriedly abdicated what power they had had into his hands. Telling him that he was the ruler of the land, they returned to their lessons in al-Azhar, and forced ʿUmar Makram to disband his men.[4] By this act they lost their right to anything more than the use of moral influence.

In the second place, the *ʿulamāʾ* had never shown a wholly united front in the face of adversity, or even a front that remained united for long. Previously there had existed a pattern of evenly balanced forces showing not one man,

[1] Jabartī, *ʿAjāʾib*, vol. iii, p. 336.
[2] Ibid., vol. iv, pp. 20, 22 *passim*.
[3] Ibid., p. 32.
[4] Ibid., vol. iii, p. 337.

but several, in positions of power and authority among the religious hierarchy. This meant a diffused leadership, but also provided a system whereby leaders rose and succeeded one another. But the recent events had distorted the pattern. Since Shaykhs al-Bakrī and al-Sādāt chose not to play an active part in the events, only two protagonists appeared, Shaykh al-Sharqāwī and ʿUmar Makram. Soon Makram began to intrigue against al-Sharqāwī, and in October 1808 al-Jabartī reported that al-Sharqāwī was put under house-arrest, at the instigation of ʿUmar Makram, 'because of intrigues and rivalry' (*ḍaghā'in wa-munāfasāt*).[1] Strangely enough, French reports of the time recount the arrest of two principal shaykhs of Cairo, who were accused 'd'avoir cherché à faire soulever les habitants',[2] whereas the reasons given by al-Jabartī for the arrest seem to have been material ones. The fact that the rector of al-Azhar could have been arrested without eliciting an outcry from the rest of the *ʿulamā'* showed that the centre of power had moved out of the rector's hands and into those of the *naqīb*, whose power had become paramount; according to al-Jabartī, 'l'influence de Sayed Omar devint considérable, et après l'avènement de Mohamed Aly, elle augmenta au point que c'était lui qui décidait les affaires les plus importantes'.[3] Even the sultan seems to have recognized this privileged position, for when Muḥammad ʿAlī repulsed the British attack on Alexandria in 1807, the sultan sent him gifts, and sent fur pelisses to his sons, the *kâhya*, the *defterdar*, and ʿUmar Makram.[4]

The rector's temporary disgrace revealed the basic weakness of the *ʿulamā'* as a body, and Makram in helping to degrade al-Sharqāwī, was merely hastening his own downfall and that of the whole class, for he showed Muḥammad ʿAlī that the *ʿulamā'* had less *esprit de corps* than the recent events might have led him to believe, and regarded its members as expendable and replaceable.

Thus so long as Makram proved a useful ally, he was Muḥammad ʿAlī's 'honoured father', but the minute he showed a spirit of opposition, he was quite ruthlessly set aside. Makram had been growing increasingly more restless at the ruler's economic reforms, and the last straw came in 1809 when a prospective tax was to be levied on hitherto untaxed land. The *ʿulamā'*, thoroughly disturbed at this move, called a meeting to discuss what action they could take to stop Muḥammad ʿAlī, and Makram, waxing indignant at what he regarded as a breach of faith on the part of the ruler, made the *ʿulamā'* take a solemn oath to oppose the ruler until he repealed all the vexatious taxes.

But by then the *ʿulamā'* had little power of coercion left; they had given in too many times in the previous years to be able to make an effective stand,

[1] Jabartī, *ʿAjā'ib*, vol. iv, p. 18.
[2] Douin, op. cit., no. 120.
[3] Jabartī, *ʿAjā'ib*, vol. iv, p. 93. Quoted from French translation, vol. ix, p. 56.
[4] Letter of thanks from Muḥammad ʿAlī to the sultan thanking him for the items and dated 4 Rajab 1222 7 Sept. 1807. Egyptian Government Archives (hereafter, E.G.A.), Maʿiyya Saniyya, *Daftar* i, 1222–8.

and Muḥammad ʿAlī succeeded in wooing some of the *ʿulamāʾ* away from Makram. These *ʿulamāʾ*, Shaykh al-Mahdī and Shaykh al-Dawākhlī, disliked Makram, and since many other *ʿulamāʾ* were jealous of his power, a cabal including Shaykh al-Sharqāwī and Shaykh al-Sādāt endorsed Muḥammad ʿAlī's attempts to get rid of Makram, who was then sent into exile. The reasons given for his exile were, ironically enough, his plotting against Shaykh al-Sharqāwī and Shaykh al-Mahdī, as well as his entering people falsely in the register of the *Ashrāf*.[1]

The downfall of Makram was also that of the *ʿulamāʾ* as a political force: al-Jabartī speaks of him as 'Sayed Omar qu'ils [the *ʿulamāʾ*] haissaient, et dont ils étaient jaloux; . . . cependant [il] était pour eux un appui et un défenseur. La preuve en est qu'après son départ leur influence alla toujours en diminuant'.[2] For a long time to come the people still continued to think that the *ʿulamāʾ* were powerful, and appealed to them for the redressment of their wrongs, but, as al-Jabartī sadly remarked, '. . . le public croyaient que les cheikhs gardaient encore quelque pouvoir et qu'ils pouvaient les protéger. Ils ignoraient qu'ils s'étaient tous rendus au maître qui faisait peser sur eux sa force, et que chacun d'eux avait quitté la bonne voie et suivi la mauvaise, celle de ses caprices'.[3]

With the exile of ʿUmar Makram the last vestige of opposition to Muḥammad ʿAlī disappeared, for the *ʿulamāʾ* were too cowed to attempt any further action, especially after the sudden end of a once influential man; and when the *waqfs* were confiscated, they became dependent on the pasha's bounty for survival, and in a greater position of subservience than they had ever been.

The fact that Muḥammad ʿAlī had dominated the *ʿulamāʾ* was not the beginning of their decline from power, for at different periods throughout history they had been cowed by powerful rulers, only to rise again, but we have earlier suggested that the introduction of westernizing influences was the cause for their permanent decline as against a customary rise and fall from power, and the first effective Western influences were introduced by Muḥammad ʿAlī.

It would be out of place here to go into details of his reforms, but let us briefly say that he saw the goal to his ambitions as attainable only through an efficient army modelled on European lines. To this end he increased the country's revenues, and changed its administrative and educational systems. He imported European advisers who helped him to reorganize his administration on Western lines, with a government bureaucracy divided into ministries, and ruling through provincial governorates, each having a hierarchy of civil servants responsible to a centralized authority. He introduced a

1 E.G.A., Maʿiyya Turkī, *Daftar* 16, no. 19, 15 Shaʿbān 1224 25 Sept. 1809.

2 Jabartī, *ʿAjāʾib*, vol. iv, p. 101. French translation, vol. viii, p. 223.

3 Jabartī, *ʿAjāʾib*, vol. iv, p. 204. French translation, vol. ix, p. 80.

Western-style system of education to provide his army with teachers, and his administration with officials, and finally, he became the sole landowner, merchant, and industrialist in the land.

Though some of these reforms were undoubtedly to prove beneficial, most of them had adverse repercussions on traditional social life. The need for an army meant conscription on a large scale, thereby depriving the countryside of its able-bodied men to the detriment of agriculture. His land-reform policy concentrated land in the hands of a few landlords, and left the fellah in just as bad a condition as under the Mamluks. His economic policies encouraged the penetration of European trade to the detriment of home industries, while his large-scale industries were mostly failures. Lastly, by becoming the sole monopolist in the land, he destroyed the merchant class.

The traditional social pattern of groups having a cohesive force and an internal organization of their own that was independent of a central authority, was rapidly changing to make way for a new social pattern, which depended on a government-appointed hierarchy, subservient to an overall centralized authority. The old Muslim pattern was making way for a new pattern in a Western style. This pattern provided for an administrative class which was not guided by the rule of tradition, and which, though inefficient and corrupt as well as tyrannical, became a new social *élite*, and the nucleus of a class of government officials who were eventually to rise to prominence as the result of the educational reforms introduced, a group that was eventually to displace the *'ulamā'* as the intellectual *élite* of the land.

But though Muḥammad 'Alī could ride roughshod over the *'ulamā'* he could not totally ignore tradition, for after all he was a Muslim ruler. Thus he set a pattern of behaviour that was to become the usual one for his successors to follow, a pattern which, while it paid honour to the *'ulamā'* as a religious class, gave them very little opportunity to share in the government of the land, and relegated them to a secondary position. Muḥammad 'Alī endowed *waqfs*, ordered al-Bukhārī to be read,[1] honoured the *'ulamā'* on feast-days, gave them gifts,[2] increased their funds when they complained of need,[3] made them members of his *Dīwān*,[4] and never openly tampered with the affairs of al-Azhar. He used them as students and teachers in his new schools, and he even used them as propagandists; a history of his reign written by Shaykh Khalīl al-Rajabī at the suggestion of the rector of al-Azhar, Shaykh al-'Arūsī was such a work, for one out of its seven chapters is devoted to extolling the benefits of conscription, supplying quotations from the Qur'ān and the Prophet to show that the reward of the *muqātil* is Paradise.[5] But slowly a machine

[1] E.G.A., Ma'iyya Turkī, *Daftar* 18, no. 768.
[2] Ibid., 21, no. 372.
[3] Ibid., 21, no. 85.
[4] Ibid., 1, no. 11.
[5] Khalīl b. Aḥmad al-Rajabī, *Ta'rīkh Muḥammad 'Alī*; unpublished MS., Dār al-Kutub, Cairo.

was being built up which toppled the *'ulamā'* from their pedestal and made them turn into an inward-looking, reactionary element.

Muḥammad 'Alī had started a social revolution, and in doing so he closed the one channel of opposition to tyranny that Egypt had known for centuries. The traditional bridge between ruler and ruled had gone, and there was nothing to replace it for many decades until a third estate once more grew to prominence. The *'ulamā'* might have found a new group of allies to work with, but the westernizing reforms inhibited that, for the new groups had little respect for tradition, and in fact were little aware of it since many of them were recent European and Turkish immigrants, and did not venerate the *'ulamā'* as the Mamluks were said to have done. Society was no longer divided into a military and a religious group; it now had civil servants and administrators who formed a new *élite*, having more knowledge of the governing process and more authority than the *'ulamā'*. And although al-Azhar supplied the raw material that formed the new intellectual *élite*, yet these too grew apart from the traditionalists because of their western training, and former *'ulamā'*, like Rifā'a Rāfi' al-Ṭahṭāwī, thought that al-Azhar should concentrate on teaching religion and the Arabic language, and leave the other branches of learning to those more qualified. Even rectors like Ḥasan al-'Aṭṭār felt the impending wind of change, and hinted that al-Azhar must perforce in the future reform itself.

The *'ulamā'* lost their standing as the intellectual superiors, and, instead of attempting to reform themselves and join in the current, because the current was a new and unknown one, tainted with European influence, they refused to have anything to do with it. Entrenching themselves even more rigidly behind their traditions, they devoted themselves to the arduous task of survival. Change, to them, became a reprehensible innovation. This rigidity only served to retard the intellectual development of al-Azhar, and justified the accusations of reaction that were later levelled at it.

Throughout the nineteenth century, the *'ulamā'* were gradually displaced in their functions as scholars and educators, and they were also to lose their functions as *qāḍīs* and legislators. Nonetheless they retained much of their influence over the people and the religiously minded elements of society, which meant the vast majority—but a majority that was politically negligible, even though it was used by absolute rulers whenever they wished to pose as liberals. Thus rulers continued to make a show of consulting the *'ulamā'*, as a means of sanctioning new or unpopular moves. Ismā'īl was specially able at wooing the *'ulamā'*, he even had Shaykh al-Bakrī draw up a *lā'iḥa waṭaniyya*, to be signed by *'ulamā'* and notables, to prove to Europe that he was supported by public opinion in Egypt.

Likewise the 'Urabists, when they sought to depose Tawfīq found that they needed the approval of the *'ulamā'*. But the *'ulamā'* were never to regain the power and authority that they had had under the Mamluks. Though their decline in power was hastened by Muḥammad ʿAlī's autocracy, it was an inevitable consequence of the westernizing current, for otherwise they would have regained their standing under ʿAbbās; but their supremacy depended on an Islamic pattern of society, and once this changed, then perforce their status had to change. Once education, law, and justice were removed from the hands of the *ʿulamāʾ*, their political influence waned. Once nationalism replaced the overall concept of the Muslim community as the focus of loyalties, the political influence of religion waned. When the modern Muslim relegated religion to the realm of the spiritual, and admitted that society could be ruled by a civil code of law, his dependence on the *ʿulamāʾ* as other than religious teachers disappeared, and their influence on him in matters other than religion disappeared likewise.

Egyptian-Yemeni Relations (1819–1840) and their Implications for British Policy in the Red Sea

ABDEL HAMID EL-BATRIK

EARLY in the sixteenth century the Egyptian Mamluk power in the Yemen was overthrown by Sultan Selim I, and the whole of the Red Sea coast acknowledged Ottoman sovereignty. In 1545 Sanʿāʾ became the seat of the pasha of the Yemen, but to maintain the occupation of the capital proved beyond Ottoman power. The Ottoman forces were unable to extract tribute from the Yemeni tribes, many of whom remained practically independent. In 1599 the inhabitants of the Yemen raised the standard of rebellion against the Ottoman government. Sinan Pasha, one of the foremost Ottoman commanders, was dispatched in 1569 to settle the matter with an army. The southern highlands were reduced quickly to temporary submission, but no progress could be made north of Sanʿāʾ. The *imām* acknowledged Ottoman sovereignty so long as neither an Ottoman soldier nor an Ottoman tax-gatherer showed himself in the highlands. In 1630 the Ottomans withdrew from Sanʿāʾ as a result of a revolution under the leadership of the famous Qāsim al-Kabīr, who freed the whole Yemen from the odious yoke of the Ottoman pashas. So *imām* succeeded *imām* without apparently performing any deeds to redound to their own praise, or raise the splendour of their country. Their lives were simply spent in keeping in order the turbulent tribes of the Yemen. From time to time tribes raised the standard of independence, but there seems to have been no organized attack upon the *imāms*, although the family was continually engaged in intrigues over the succession. But the country was still isolated from the outside world.

In 1762 King Frederick V of Denmark organized an expedition for the exploration of Arabia under the leadership of Carsten Niebuhr. Niebuhr twice interviewed the *imām* during his stay in Sanʿāʾ, and the second time greatly interested the *imām* by exhibiting and explaining his scientific instruments. The Yemen at this time had attracted a few European adventurers, who had become Muslims, and entered the service of the *imām*. Among these was a certain Scot named Campbell, who commanded the artillery of al-Mahdī ʿAbbās, the then *imām*. In 1799 a British force was sent to cruise in the Red Sea, as the French had taken possession of Egypt; and Perim, an island situated in the straits of Bāb al-Mandab, was occupied for a period of four months.

During the years 1804 and 1805 the Yemen suffered from continual raids by the Wahhābī leaders, who were chiefs of the ʿAsīr, a mountainous country lying between the Ḥijāz and the Yemen proper. When Muḥammad ʿAlī, in 1813, invaded the Ḥijāz and Najd, he sent an envoy to the *imām* of Ṣanʿāʾ, requesting his co-operation in stamping out the Wahhābīs. This was readily given, for the *imām* evidently saw that Muḥammad ʿAlī's eyes were turned in the direction of the Yemen; and although he protested that he himself was devoid of means to carry on warfare, he gave the envoy letters to the governor (*dawla*) of Mukhā to supply him with vessels and material, 'knowing full well that he possessed neither'.[1] The Egyptian troops took the town of Qunfudha, north of Luḥayya; but in 1819 Muḥammad ʿAlī entered into negotiations with the *imām* and made a treaty with him. The terms agreed upon were the restoration to the *imām* of the territories that had been usurped by the *sharīf* of Ḥudayyida (a Wahhābī), comprising Ḥudayyida, Luḥayya, Qunfudha, and Qamarān. The return of these possessions was offered to the *imām* on condition he supplied Muḥammad ʿAlī with twenty thousand *bahars* of coffee, ostensibly 'for the use of the Grand Signor'.[2] This was reckoned as tribute, and the Yemen was thereafter 'considered as in some degree under the protection of the Porte'. This quantity of coffee was claimed by Muḥammad ʿAlī on two grounds; first, he alleged that former *imāms* had been tributaries of the Porte, and had paid this tribute either in money or in coffee, through the pashas of Egypt; secondly, he had restored to the *imām*, after a costly war, nearly a whole province which had not for many years paid any revenue to Ṣanʿāʾ.[3] The *imām* was only too happy to accede to a proposal which would restore to him a territory which he himself could not have reclaimed, and which for many years had been in a state of insurrection.

After this agreement with the *imām* of Sanʿāʾ, Muḥammad ʿAlī abstained from interfering in the affairs of the Yemen. It was not until November 1820 that he began to be disturbed by news dispatched to him from Jedda about an expected British assault on Mukhā, the chief port of the Yemen. Rustum Ağa, the director of Customs in Jedda, informed him that about ten naval vessels had been sent by the British East India Company to blockade Mukhā, demanding reparation from the *imām* of Ṣanʿāʾ following an incident which arose out of the conduct of the governor of Mukhā.[4] An Arab was detained at the British factory there. He was released, but the factory guard, the captain of a merchant vessel, and the British resident were seized, beaten, and abused, while the factory itself was plundered. It was resolved to send a force to obtain satisfaction. The *imām* followed the usual policy of delay. Mukhā was

[1] R. L. Playfair, *A history of Arabia Felix or Yemen* (Bombay 1859), p. 131.

[2] Salt to the under-secretary of State for Foreign Affairs, 6 May 1819, One bahar = 222 lb 6 oz approx.

[3] Muḥammad ʿAlī to Aḥmad Yeğen, 23 Nov. 1821; Abdin Archives (subsequently abbreviated A.A.), Reg. 7., doc. 64.

[4] Muḥammad ʿAlī to the Porte, 19 Feb. 1821; A.A., Reg. 4, doc. 182.

therefore bombarded, the forts were attacked and destroyed;[1] and the *imām* yielded to force. He was compelled to sign a treaty (15 January 1821) by which the British resident was to have a guard of forty men, and to be allowed to appear in public on horseback; the customs dues payable by British traders were lowered to a rate less than that paid by the French; and that the British resident was to be the judge of all cases concerning British subjects.[2]

Muḥammad ʿAlī had meanwhile become uneasy at the success of the British, who had established their influence in the most important port in the Yemen. At Constantinople strong remonstrances were addressed to the British ambassador, while Muḥammad ʿAlī was reproached for not doing his utmost to check British imperialist schemes in the Yemen.[3] This crisis ended when the British government notified Muḥammad ʿAlī through the British agent in Cairo that they had no designs upon Yemen or any wish to interfere with the sultan's suzerainty there. Muḥammad ʿAlī was engaged in other campaigns for many years, and postponed his projects in the Yemen until a suitable opportunity arose.

The events which led to Egyptian expansion in the Yemen began simply enough, in a mutiny of some Albanian troops under Muḥammad Ağa (generally known as Türkçe-bilmez). He led a rebellion in Jedda in 1832, when the Syrian war had severely strained Muḥammad ʿAlī's finances, and caused the pay of the Albanian irregular soldiery to fall in arrears. In point of fact, Türkçe-bilmez was encouraged by the pasha of Baghdād, who was in secret correspondence with him and with the other Albanian leaders in the Ḥijāz.[4] During the conflict between the sultan and Muḥammad ʿAlī, these Albanian leaders received a letter from the pasha of Baghdād informing them that the Egyptian troops had been defeated in Syria. Türkçe-bilmez, 'calculating the possibility of Mohammad Ali ultimately being subdued by the Porte, considered that the moment had arrived, when by active opposition to the Egyptian rule, and thus showing fidelity to the Sultan he might rise to higher dignity and get in the progress of time the investiture of the Pashalic of Jidda'.[5] Türkçe-bilmez's hope, together with the encouragement which he was receiving from the pasha of Baghdād, fired his ambition. At Jedda, he seized all public property, as well as the Egyptian ships. Then he prepared to attack Mecca, but was forced to retreat to Jedda by superior Egyptian forces. Having been apprised of the approach of considerable forces from Egypt, and being no longer able to hold Jedda against the Egyptian forces coming from Mecca, Türkçe-bilmez fled with his rebels towards the Yemen.[6]

[1] Bruce to Salt, 20 Jan. 1821; I.O., Egypt and the Red Sea, 7.

[2] Aḥmad Yeğen to Muḥammad ʿAlī, 10 Mar. 1821; A.A., Reg. 7, doc. 139.

[3] Seyid Ali (grand vezir) to Muḥammad ʿAlī, 22 Rabīʿ I 1236/28 Dec. 1820; A.A., Case 7, doc. 7.

[4] This collusion resulted in Türkçe-bilmez's appointment as governor of Baṣra by the pasha of Baghdād, when the former eventually fled to Iraq.

[5] Campbell to Palmerston, 16 Apr. 1832; F.O. 78–227.

[6] *Sharīf* Muḥammad b. ʿAwn to Muḥammad ʿAlī, 4 May 1832; A.A., Reg. 44, Doc. 233.

Marching south, he invested Ḥudayyida. He opened fire upon the town walls, whereupon the place capitulated. Türkçe-bilmez did not remain there, however, but leaving a garrison of four hundred men, proceeded with the remainder of his force to Zabīd, and succeeded in taking possession of it by a stratagem. Then he proceeded towards Mukhā which also surrendered. Early in 1833, Türkçe-bilmez, having demanded and received the surrender of the governor of Aden, sent him a delegation of forty persons. These were well received, but during the night more than half their number were murdered, and the rest barely escaped. However, the rebels were now firmly established in the Yemen, making Mukhā their headquarters, and seriously interrupting the Red Sea trade.[1] This daring insurrection of Türkçe-bilmez afforded Muḥammad 'Alī an opportunity of attempting what had long been an unfulfilled project, that of invading the Yemen.

Muḥammad 'Ali calculated that the chaotic state of the Yemen would make the British government decide not to oppose his territorial claims there, as they would prefer his firm rule in the Red Sea ports to the comparatively weak rule of the *imām*. On 3 June 1833 Muḥammad 'Alī informed the British agent, Campbell, that, in consequence of intelligence he had received of the designs and proceedings of Türkçe-bilmez, he had resolved to send an expedition against him; and therefore he was seeking the acquiescence of the British government in his expedition to the Yemen.[2] When Muḥammad 'Ali knew that there would not be any objection on the part of the British government to the expedition he had already sent to Mukhā before receiving their communication, the pasha expressed his grateful thanks, and assured Campbell that 'he should not in any way militate against any agreement they had with the late Imam'. He added that the Yemen 'is now in a complete state of anarchy, and without any government; a state of affairs which was prejudicial to the interests of all, and more particularly to Great Britain and himself'.[3] Campbell supported the pasha's attitude, having noticed that when the late *imām* of Ṣan'ā', the *imām* al-Mahdī, died in 1832, while Türkçe-bilmez was invading the Yemen, two brothers of the *imām* were fighting for the succession. The Yemen was therefore torn by a civil war. The result of all this had been that in the Yemen there was hardly any commerce with the British during the year 1832 and nearly all the coffee of Mukhā was carried off in ships of the United States 'to the manifest detriment of British commerce'.

Simultaneous campaigns in the south then began in Arabia; the first, under Aḥmad Yeğen, towards the 'Asīr, and the second into the Yemen under Ibrāhīm Yeğen Pasha. The 'Asīr campaign was effected to protect the deep thrust into the Yemen. The most interesting information about the two armies sent to the south is to be elicited from the valuable report written by Captain Mackenzie about his journey through Egypt and Arabia during 1836. This

[1] Campbell to Palmerston, 27 Oct. 1833; F.O. 78–228.
[2] Ibid., F.O. 78–228. [3] Ibid., F.O. 78–228.

report reveals the importance Muḥammad ʿAlī attached to the Yemen campaign. The pasha evidently resolved to provide the expedition with the cream of his modern (*niẓām jadīd*) army.[1] However, before the Yemen campaign under Ibrāhīm Yeğen began, a conflict had broken out between two enemies of Muḥammad ʿAlī: the Albanian troops and the ʿAsīr tribes, who, under the leadership of ʿAlī b. Mijthal, appeared before Zabīd, and took the town by assault. Then they advanced to Mukhā and surrounded it on the land side. Türkçe-bilmez and his rebels attempted to make their escape by sea. The events which followed were reported by Robert Moresby (commander in the Indian Navy) thus:

> they attempted without sails or oars to reach the Benares and H.M.'s Brig-of-War *Tigris*. The wind and sea being strong against them, they found it impossible and were fast drifting out to sea, where they must inevitably have perished had we not sent out boats to their assistance. . . . Turkje Bilmez having claimed the protection of the British it remains with the India Government what to do with him.[2]

Thus Türkçe-bilmez escaped on the *Tigris*, and was conveyed to Bombay.[3] Muḥammad ʿAlī, conveniently rid of the Albanian mutineers, devoted his energies to subduing the ʿAsīrī tribes who were occupying Mukhā. Their leader, Ibn Mijthal, decided to withdraw, however, when he learned that an Egyptian fleet was approaching Mukhā, and that Ibrāhīm Yeğen Pasha with his well-disciplined army was advancing overland.[4] The fleet under the command of Ḥāfiẓ ʿAlī took possession, one by one of the main ports of the Yemen. At the same time, the main Egyptian army, under Ibrāhīm Yeğen, arrived at Bayt al-Faqīh, a considerable market for coffee. Although Mukhā was the main objective of the Egyptian expedition, Ibrāhīm Yeğen established his headquarters at Ḥudayyida, owing to the ruinous state of Mukhā which had resulted from the plundering of the town by the ʿAsīrī tribes. At the same time, he decided to make Ḥudayyida a centre for trade and a monopoly port for coffee. To all the Yemeni seaports Muḥammad ʿAlī appointed governors, who acted at the same time as directors of Customs. By the year 1837, Egypt was in actual possession of the whole of the Arabian coastline from Suez and ʿAqaba in the north to Mukhā, near the strait of Bāb al-Mandab at the southern extremity of the Red Sea. Egyptian troops garrisoned the Arabian ports of the Red Sea and the chief hinterland towns. The next step was to seize Taʿizz which was considered by Ibrāhīm Yeğen to be 'the key of Ṣanʿā'.[5] Being aware of the hatred between the governor of Taʿizz, Sayyid

[1] Sir Alexander Johnston to Palmerston, 4 July 1837; F.O. 78–3185.
[2] Robert Moresby to Campbell, Dec. 1833; F.O. 78–245.
[3] Six years later he reappeared as governor of Baṣra as a reward for his mutiny.
[4] Campbell to Palmerston, 27 Feb. 1834; F.O. 78–245. Muḥammad ʿAlī to Ibrāhīm Yeğen, 28 Feb. 1834; A.A., Reg. 211, doc. 477.
[5] Ibrāhīm Yeğen to Muḥammad ʿAlī, 26 Feb. 1838; A.A., case 262, doc. 299.

Qāsim, and the nephew of the *imām* of Ṣanʿā', Ibrāhīm Yeğen sent an envoy to win the former over to Egyptian interests. An arrangement was concluded between Ibrāhīm Yeğen and Qāsim to the effect that the latter should reside at Mukhā, receiving 10,000 dollars down and a monthly stipend of 4,000 piastres.[1] To take possession of Taʿizz, a force of one thousand men was sent; the town surrendered without any resistance, and an Egyptian governor was appointed. Ibrāhīm Yeğen then set about preparations for the investment of Ṣanʿā', the capital of the imamate. Meanwhile, an Egyptian contingent made its way south. In September 1837, Ibrāhīm Yeğen sent Major Ṣādiq to conquer the southern territories of the Yemen. This officer, in his advance, reached the town of Aden and reported to Ibrāhīm Yeğen Pasha that: 'With the victorious force of the khedive, we were able to enter Aden, where all the tribal sheikhs as well as those in the neighbouring districts paid homage to us. In view of the fact that the inhabitants of Aden were extremely discontented with the government of Ṣanʿā', they showed great joy on seeing us enter their town'.[2] This Egyptian force withdrew, however, from Aden after a few days. Dodwell states that Muḥammad ʿAlī 'was disposed to regard the ruler of Aden as a mere dependent, subordinate to the Imam of San'a, who had been compelled to recognise the viceroy's authority. Alternatively he claimed it as formerly part of the Turkish empire'.[3] But in point of fact, it was not possible to treat such claims seriously, as the *imām* of Ṣanʿā' had never exercised permanent control of Aden, and the Turkish claim there was equally nominal. From the economic point of view, Muḥammad ʿAlī did his utmost to exploit in every possible way the commercial resources of the Yemen. After the occupation of Ḥudayyida, Mukhā, and Taʿizz, a 'Coffee Department' was established in Ḥudayyida and the 'Council of Jedda' controlled the coffee trade of the Yemen after Muḥammad ʿAlī had decided to monopolize it. On 24 February 1838 Ibrāhīm Yeğen reported to Muḥammad ʿAlī that the revenues of Taʿizz province were estimated to be 70,000 dollars annually.

But before carrying out Muḥammad ʿAlī's economic projects in the Yemen, it was necessary to conquer Ṣanʿā'. In fact, the political and personal weakness of the *imām*, his reputation for extravagance, and his loose behaviour were factors which would have facilitated the success of the Egyptian invasion of Ṣanʿā'. While Ibrāhīm Yeğen was awaiting strong reinforcement from Mecca to effect his next move, an envoy, Sayyid ʿAbd al-Rabb, sent by the *imām* of Ṣanʿā', arrived at Aḥmad Yeğen's camp in the ʿAsīr, where he

[1] Ibrāhīm Yeğen to Muḥammad ʿAlī, 6 July 1837; A.A., case 262, doc. 259. Playfair, supported by records of the East India Company, says that: 'The money herewith to pay the treachery of Sidi Qasim was borrowed from the merchants of Mokha as the finances of Ibrahim Yakan were at a very low ebb.'

[2] Major Ṣādiq Efendi to Ibrāhīm Yeğen, 28 Sept. 1837; A.A., Case 261, enclosure doc. 399.

[3] H. [H.] Dodwell, *The founder of modern Egypt* (Cambridge, 1931), p. 145.

requested the pasha to send him to Egypt so that he might personally put to Muḥammad ʿAlī the *imām*'s views concerning Egyptian rule in the Yemen. Sayyid ʿAbd al-Rabb handed Aḥmad Pasha a letter signed by the *Imām* ʿAbdallāh al-Nāṣir li-Dīn Illāh, requesting him to send the envoy to 'the Sword of Islam, the defender of the Prophet's descendants, Muḥammad b. ʿAlī Pasha'.[1] Instead of sending him to Egypt, Aḥmad Yeğen elicited all the views of the *imām* from the envoy and reported fully to Muḥammad ʿAlī. The main point raised by the *imām* was that the areas already ceded to the Egyptians should continue under their control on condition that no further expansion took place, Ṣanʿā' remaining an integral part of the domain of the *imām*. Aḥmad Yeğen, reporting to Muḥammad ʿAlī, said that he told the envoy that the present *imām* had deliberately declared war on the Egyptian troops, and that 'it would be wise, on the *imām*'s part, if he allowed an Egyptian governor to administer Ṣanʿā', and agreed to receive a considerable salary, comparable to that received by the *sharīf* of Mecca. I am inclined to think that our Master may agree to such terms, as you will no doubt find out on reaching Egypt'.[2]

Sayyid ʿAbd al-Rabb's visit to Egypt was rendered nugatory by the developments immediately following the Egyptian advance towards Aden. The future of the Yemen, instead of being decided by the *imām* and Muḥammad ʿAlī, became dependent on British policy in Aden and the Red Sea, when Great Britain felt compelled to check the territorial ambition of the pasha.

The advance in the Yemen gave rise to rumours that the Egyptian forces would be sent to take possession of 'the shores at the entrance and on the outside of the Red Sea'. This caused a reorientation of the British attitude towards Egyptian rule in Arabia. Palmerston instructed Campbell 'to take an early opportunity to mention the subject to the Pasha of Egypt, and to intimate to him that such a movement of his forces would not be well looked upon in England or in India and might give rise to discussions between him and the British government'.[3] When Campbell brought the subject of the 'possession of the shores at the entrance of the Red Sea' before Muḥammad ʿAlī, he assured Campbell that he had never contemplated such an expedition. But his positive denials of Egyptian antagonism to British interests in the Red Sea and elsewhere failed to convince Palmerston of the integrity of his attitude, and every subsequent Egyptian move in Arabia was looked upon with suspicion.

By 1837 the operations of three Egyptian armies were brought under a fair degree of correlation; one, commanded by Khūrshīd Pasha, operated on the Persian Gulf; the second, that of Aḥmad Yeğen, in the ʿAsīr, which was regarded as 'the key of Yemen'; the third was that of Ibrāhīm Yeğen, whose

[1] Aḥmad Yeğen to Muḥammad ʿAlī; A.A., case 263, enclosure, doc. 179.
[2] Aḥmad Yeğen to Muḥammad ʿAlī (undated); A.A., case 363, doc. 179.
[3] Palmerston to Campbell, 4 Aug. 1837; F.O. 78–3185.

objective was later interpreted as the conquest of the whole of Yemen in order to monopolize the coffee, and to supply the whole country with the manufacture of Egypt.[1] During the early months of 1838 Egyptian influence extended to practically all the confines of Arabia, and the British government had reason to believe at that time that Muḥammad ʿAlī's ambition extended far beyond the peninsula.

In January 1839, however, the British occupation of Aden frustrated the pasha's ambition. The capture of Aden was a blow, not only to his schemes of domination in Arabia, but also to his prestige throughout the Yemen. The whole trade of Mukhā coffee would be removed from Mukhā to Aden; which would mean the loss of a very valuable monopoly. As Anglo-Egyptian relations in Arabia became more tense in consequence of developments in Syria, the Yemen continued to contribute occasions of bitterness.

At last, at the end of November 1839, Campbell informed Palmerston that he had told the pasha of the British government's desire that the Egyptian troops should evacuate the Yemen. The pasha replied that he would take the affair into consideration as soon as the Eastern Question 'now under discussion should be finally arranged'. But Campbell did not hesitate to assert that there was nothing in common between the Eastern Question and the Yemen, as the first was an affair of the great powers in general, whereas the second embraced British interests alone, and that in all matters connected with the pasha's proceedings in the Red Sea or in the Persian Gulf, the British government 'would not at all consult her allies, but consider it as a question solely concerning Great Britain'.[2] The pasha played for time, stating that 'he could not at the present moment take steps to evacuate the Yemen and that he would direct his Foreign Secretary to draft a reply'. A further reply stated that the pasha was very occupied in extremely urgent affairs of the moment and would deal with the Yemen question as soon as it became convenient.[3]

Before these discussions began in Cairo there was some British manœuvring in southern Yemen by Captain Haines, the British political agent in Aden. On 28 February 1839 Haines reported to Campbell that he had been 'successful in entering into treaties of peace and friendship with nearly all the near neighbouring States'. He stated that:

> the territory now acquired by the Pasha of Egypt extends but little beyond Ta'is, to the North Eastward and Southward of which he meets strong opposition, and is likely to do so from the country being mountainous and its passes strong—his principal force is now applied to the reduction of Sheikh Sherzebee [*sic*] territory—a rich coffee country called Haushereea, and as its position is conveniently situated for trade with this port [Aden], and the disposition of the Chieftain Sheikh Sherzebee having prompted him to apply to me to enter into a treaty of friendship and commerce.

[1] Haines to Campbell, 28 Feb. 1839; F.O. 78–373.
[2] Campbell to Palmerston, 2 Nov. 1839; F.O. 78–375.
[3] Boghos Bey (Egyptian foreign secretary) to Campbell, Oct. 1839; F.O. 78–375.

He stressed here that Ibrāhīm Yeğen Pasha, the commander-in-chief of the Egyptian expedition to the Yemen, would take a long time to reduce the territory near to Aden and would take still longer to conquer the country independent of the *imām* of Ṣan'ā'. Should, however, he succeed in conquering the tribes of Dhū Muḥammad and Dhū Ḥusayn, who were 'numerically strong, possess great activity, and have strong passes, . . . San'a, the capital of Yemen, will soon be within his reach'. Haines went on to say that in gaining influence in this area, bribery would play an important part. Haines pointed out that if Ibrāhīm Yeğen Pasha could be stopped from advancing, the roads across the Yemen would 'in the course of a few months, by friendly negotiation, be open for free intercourse and the exports of the country give a return for British import'. Now comes the crux of Haines's letter. If Ibrāhīm Yeğen succeeded in conquering the whole of Yemen, its whole commerce would be monopolised by Egypt, and even the Indian trade of Britain would be entirely ruined. Haines concluded: 'I have much pleasure in informing you that I have been successful in entering into treaties of peace and friendship with nearly all the near neighbouring States and that the roads from Aden into the interior are now open for supplies and commerce.'

At this stage, Palmerston decided to recall Colonel Campbell, who had then been serving in Egypt since 1833, and was accused of leniency towards Egypt. Colonel Hodges was appointed in his place on 30 October 1839. The new consul 'was intended to show a stiff upper lip to Mohammed Ali',[1] and had 'a prompt, unhesitating readiness to believe the worse'.[2] During this time, Ibrāhīm Yeğen was doing his utmost to induce his brother, Aḥmad Pasha, the governor of the Ḥijāz and commander-in-chief of the 'Asīrī expedition, to supply him with reinforcements to fulfil his task in the Yemen, but in spite of repeated requests, Aḥmad Yeğen insisted that he could not spare any men to send to the Yemen.[3]

While Muḥammad 'Alī, owing to the pressure of circumstance had ordered Ibrāhīm Yeğen on 17 February 1840 to evacuate the Yemen,[4] Hodges reported that the pasha's forces in Yemen had been lately strengthened by 2,000 infantry and cavalry from Jedda, and that the Arabs of the neighbourhood of Aden, instigated by the Egyptians, or, at all events, with the hope of their assistance, were again assembling, and likely to muster 20,000 men within a month. The report of a native agent, employed by the political agent at Aden, states 'that Mohammed Ali had sent a certain Sayyid Hussein as Ambassador to the Imam of San'a, with the proposition that he would assist the Imam with men, money, and supplies, if he would endeavour to drive the English from Aden, and engaging, on the part of the Pasha, that on the

[1] H. W. V. Temperley, *England and the Near East* (London, 1936), p. 109.
[2] Dodwell, op. cit., p. 181.
[3] Ibrāhīm Yeğen to Aḥmad Yeğen, 8 Oct. 1839; A.A., case 263, doc. 42, 166, 188.
[4] Ibid., 8 Apr. 1840; A.A., case 269, doc. 10/192.

expiration of the war he would yield the conquered territory to the Imam'. Another proposal was also made by the same Sayyid Ḥusayn, that the *imām* should make over his sovereignty of Ṣanʿāʾ to Muḥammad ʿAlī, who in turn, would grant him a suitable pension for life.[1] There is no mention, however, in the Abdin Archives of this proposed mission of Sayyid Ḥusayn.

By 1840, the political situation made Muḥammad ʿAlī yield to British pressure in Arabia, and by the end of the year all Arabia had been evacuated, except for some irregulars left with the native *amīrs* who had proved their loyalty to Muḥammad ʿAlī. These *amīrs* considered it incredible that the Egyptians should evacuate Arabia at the very moment when Egyptian prestige there was at its zenith. The Yemen was the first country to be evacuated. The territories which had been conquered by the Egyptians were invested in *Sharīf* Ḥusayn b. ʿAlī Ḥaydar of Abū ʿArīsh. Ibrāhīm Yeğen with his troops left the Yemen on 9 May 1840, whereupon the whole of this territory was plunged into local wars.

[1] Hodges to Palmerston, 22 Mar. 1840; F.O. 78–3185.

The Breakdown of the Monopoly System in Egypt after 1840

AHMED ABDEL-RAHIM MUSTAFA

THE reign of Muḥammad ʿAlī marks the end of Egypt's isolation and its integration into the world economy. It witnessed the beginnings of the shift away from closed to open economy, and was characterized by the state's control of the greater part of economic activities.[1]

Having destroyed the most formidable of his political opponents in 1811, the *vali* began to lay the foundations of a monopoly system, which in due time comprised all the economic activities of Egypt. He laid his hands on most of the lands of the country, and controlled both its commerce[2] and industry. The lands were sequestrated and then given to the *vali*'s sons, relatives, and officers, by no law but his own pleasure and without inquiry as to whom they had belonged in the times of the Mamluk beys, whom he had either massacred or driven out. He seems to have assumed as a principle that all the lands not actually possessed by a proprietor with a title belonged to the government; and these lands he either farmed out, or distributed, or cultivated on his own account, as he found most advantageous to the revenue.[3] The peasants working on these lands suffered much hardship and were reduced to a certain status of serfdom to the state, with the result that a great number of them fled from their villages, if not from Egypt altogether. The system of monopoly in the field of industry also bore very hard on the handicrafts, and killed whatever spirit of enterprise may have survived in them.[4]

Commerce, according to that system, functioned in two principal ways: by the system of *appaltos* (farms), and by government monopoly. Trade was conducted in the manner most profitable to the *vali*. He issued *fermans* ordering the sale of his commodities to merchants with whom he chose to deal. He also tried to keep the prices high by all the means at his disposal. The result was that all commerce among the native traders came to end; and nine out of ten of the merchants in 1818 were originally adventurers, who, in the first instance, had no capital of their own. They commenced on their arrival by making interest with one of the courtiers to prevail on the *vali* to grant them

[1] Ḥusayn Khallāf, *Al-tajdīd fi'l-iqtiṣād al-Miṣrī al-ḥadīth* (Cairo, 1962), pp. 4–5.

[2] 'On croit généralement que le monopole est étendu à toutes les productions de l'Égypte. On se trompe; il est plusieurs articles, et entre autres la plupart des céréales, dont le libre emploi est abandonné aux fellahs.' A.-B. Clot-Bey, *Aperçu général sur l'Égypte* (Paris, 1840), vol. ii, p. 198.

[3] P.R.O., F.O. 195/365, No. 10, Murray to Canning, 21 Apr. 1852.

[4] ʿAlī al-Jirītlī [el-Gritly], *Ta'rīkh al-sināʿa fī Miṣr* (Cairo, 1952); C. Issawi, *Egypt in revolution* (London, 1963), p. 43.

a *ferman* for a certain quantity of grain, payable some months after receipt. With this they entered into the market; and if they could manage by jobbing to realize a profit on that first occasion, all went well. This credit became established with the public treasury, and as it increased, they went on boldly speculating with its funds.[1] These few favoured merchants, Italians and Greeks, could in future assist the *vali* with loans of money or make him advances on account of grain to be delivered to them.[2] The government monopolies were aggravated by the interference of the foreign consuls, a great number of whom were agents of the *vali*, and indulged in an extensive commerce, from which they drew enormous profits.[3]

This monopoly system was also applied to the other possessions of the *vali*. In the Sudan, it proved to be so strict that the inhabitants ceased to bring their merchandise to the markets. The government, moreover, imposed taxes on the carrying of products from one place to another; and these taxes were so crushing that they in fact impeded commercial movement, since nothing was exempted from the government monopolies except slaves. In Crete,[4] oil was monopolized; in Syria, the same system was generally applied, especially as concerning silk; and it was also one of the major reasons that induced Muḥammad ʿAlī to follow an expansionist policy in Arabia, for his intention to control the coffee trade impelled him to send an expedition to the Yemen (1833–8).[5] This all resulted in the temporary deterioration of the transit trade of Africa and Arabia.[6]

Muḥammad ʿAlī drew large profits from these monopolies, which became, indeed, the keystone of his financial policy, and the means of equipping his army and navy, and paying for his military operations. As long as the monopoly system lasted, he was, practically speaking, the sole exporter of the country; and nineteen-twentieths of the export trade passed through his hands. But he had not the same control over imports as over exports, for an Imperial decree of 1820 came to remind him that by international convention with the Porte, foreign merchants had the right to introduce their goods for sale in all parts of the Ottoman dominions on a payment of an import duty of 3 per cent. The application of this rule put foreign merchants in an advantageous position, as Ottoman subjects, including non-Muslims, had to pay higher duties. But the *vali* was by far the biggest importer in the country. In 1836, for example, 40 per cent. of the imports were for the account of the government.[7]

[1] H. A. B. Rivlin, *The agricultural policy of Muḥammad ʿAlī in Egypt* (Cambridge, Mass., 1961), p. 175.

[2] F.O. 195/169, Barnett to Canning, 1 Dec. 1841.

[3] Muḥammad Fu'ād Shukrī and others, *Binā' dawla: Miṣr Muḥammad ʿAlī* (Cairo, 1948), p. 402.

[4] Zaynab ʿIṣmat Rāshid, *Krit taḥt al-ḥukm al-Miṣrī* (Cairo, 1964).

[5] *Binā' dawla*, pp. 55–57.

[6] Khallāf, op. cit., p. 345.

[7] A. E. Crouchley, *The economic development of modern Egypt* (London, 1938), pp. 88–89.

This monopolistic system, however, was developed at a time when free trade began to gain momentum in western Europe. Increased production in Britain had created a need for greater trading opportunities, and led the British government to examine trading conditions throughout the world with a view to revising existing treaties, and obtaining conditions more favourable to British trade.[1]

The Porte had other reasons which induced it to adhere to the British inclination. The sultan intended to destroy Muḥammad ʿAlī's greatest source of revenue, thus undermining his ability to maintain an army which might threaten Ottoman sovereignty over Egypt and her possessions. The Porte offered customs concessions and exemptions to European states, having in view to lay impediments in the way of the *vali* and to weaken his relations with the great powers. In 1834, for example, it issued a *ferman* declaring the end of the government monopolies in Syria; and on 16 August 1838 the Anglo-Turkish Convention, or the Treaty of Balta Liman,[2] was signed, aiming primarily at the destruction of the monopolistic practices in the Ottoman Empire. Its main stipulations were as follows:

i. The free exchange of products;
ii. British subjects were offered the status of the most favoured nation, and enjoyed all privileges conferred on the subjects of other countries;
iii. The duties on imports were fixed at 3 per cent. with an additional 2 per cent. on retail; and additional taxes on imports were abrogated;
iv. Export duties were fixed at 12 per cent., of which 3 per cent. were paid by foreign exporters.

The *vali*, after learning of the signature of the Treaty, said that he would comply with its stipulations, being conscious of his need of European sympathy and support in his ensuing struggle with Turkey. He only made a stipulation that British merchants were not to make advances to the grower for the purchase of the crop before it was gathered in, but that they could purchase it as soon as the crop was taken off the ground; and that the grower should have free and full liberty to bring his crop to the market, and to dispose of it how and to whom he pleased.[3] After the settlement of his conflict with the Porte, he said that he had no desire for monopolies, as he was himself satisfied that free commerce was to his interest.[4] But the new British consul-general, Colonel Barnett, expected that the *vali* would try by every means of evasion and procrastination to put off the hour when he should fairly and fully throw open the trade of Egypt. There were persons interested in seeing the prevalent state of things continue, and they had the most influence with the

[1] Rivlin, op. cit., pp. 182–3. Also Crouchley, op. cit., pp. 75–76.

[2] The text of the Treaty is to be found in J. C. Hurewitz, *Diplomacy in the Near and Middle East* (Princeton, N.J., 1956), vol. i, pp. 110–11.

[3] Rivlin, op. cit., pp. 185–6.

[4] F.O. 142/13, No. 5, Barnett to F.O., 19 Aug. 1841.

vali, whose interest was generally identical with theirs.[1] Barnett's anticipations proved to be true. The *vali* would not easily give up his monopolies, and offered all possible resistance before being forced, step by step, to adhere to the stipulations of the Turco-British Treaty and similar treaties concluded between Turkey and other European powers.[2]

From the beginning Lord Palmerston was of the opinion that a monopoly was not less a monopoly because it extended over a whole country instead of being confined to a part of that country; because such a monopoly was established by the governor and for his exclusive profit, instead of being granted to private individuals. The monopolies established by Muḥammad ʿAlī in Egypt, for his own profit, were just as much a violation of the Treaty as if they had been granted by him for the profit of other persons. Concerning the fact that the *vali* was the proprietor of a great part of the soil in Egypt, Palmerston observed that unless he had acquired that property by purchase, he could only be considered as holding it in his capacity of representative of the sultan, who was the sovereign, and not as the *vali*, who was only a subject.[3] In this respect we must note that the Treaty of London, concluded in 1841, stipulated that all commercial treaties made by foreign powers with the Porte were to be respected.

Muḥammad ʿAlī made some minor concessions to the merchants, allowing them to deal directly with the *fallāḥīn*; although he reserved for himself the right to fix the price of the produce, and to purchase produce at the price he fixed, if no one else bought it.[4] In August 1841, Barnett found the Treaty of 1838 a dead letter, which he attributed to the backwardness of individuals to prefer any distinct charge against the government of an infraction of the Treaty; some from a fear of displeasing the *vali*, to whom they owed their fortunes, others from a dislike of taking a prominent part, and a few perhaps from an idea that the case was a hopeless one, and that it was better to allow things to go on as they were. All this had rendered it extremely difficult for him to lay hold of any specific case upon which to found a complaint.[5] The monopoly of boats on the Nile and the Maḥmūdiyya Canal continued; and as long as the merchants were not permitted to possess nor able to hire boats, the liberty of purchasing the produce of the country, even though granted without any restriction, proved to be of no benefit. Barnett, together with the Russian and French consuls-general, as well as a good number of the British merchants, protested against that procedure, and the *vali* promised to comply with their protests. Barnett commented that much still remained to be done before anything like freedom of commerce obtained in Egypt, and that, unless Britain was supported by the Porte in enforcing the execution of

[1] F.O. 142/13, No. 18, Barnett to F.O., 19 Sept. 1841.

[2] Austria, Belgium, France, the Hanseatic League, Sardinia, Sweden, Norway, Spain, Holland, and Denmark all hastened to make similar treaties with Turkey. (Shukrī, op. cit., p. 59).

[3] F.O. 78/708 (copy), Palmerston to Campbell, 12 Oct. 1839.

[4] Rivlin, op. cit., p. 186.

[5] F.O. 195/169, Barnett to Canning, 1 Dec. 1841.

the Treaty of 1838 in Egypt, the *vali* would always find means to elude such provisions of the Treaty as affected his right of monopoly.[1]

To these remonstrances which Barnett was repeatedly called upon to make to the *vali*, he only received the same assurances of the latter's intention *gradually* to abolish the monopolies, and to throw open the trade of Egypt. Muḥammad ʿAlī pleaded the difficulty of making a sudden change in a system which had so long existed, although he took the advantage of the Treaty of 1838 to raise the import and export duties. Barnett declared to him that if the monopolies were not abolished, he (Barnett) would be under the necessity of notifying British merchants that they would no longer be bound to pay the additional duties on imports and exports, in virtue of the tariff of the Treaty of 1838. He at the same time urged upon the *vali* the necessity of explicit orders being given to the *mudīrs* (governors of provinces) and other officers not to throw impediments in the way of cotton, grain, and other produce of Egypt being purchased from the growers, and asked that the greatest publicity should be given to these orders throughout Egypt. Although he succeeded in obtaining the abolition of the *appalto* on wines and spirits, he had reason to suspect that an attempt would be made to renew the duty in another shape by levying a tax on the retailers in the towns.[2] The Austrian consul-general was instructed by his government to act with Barnett on this question; and the French consul-general received instructions to employ all his efforts, in concert with the consuls-general of Austria and Britain, to induce the *vali* to adhere to the system of public sales by auction which he had repeatedly engaged to adopt.[3]

But Muḥammad ʿAlī persevered in his monopolistic policy. He proposed to certain merchants to sell to them the cotton and corn crops of Egypt and of the Sudan at a reduced value, in consideration of certain pecuniary facilities to be afforded to him by those merchants in return.[4] He also intended a sale of a considerable quantity of wheat, which he had privately disposed of to certain parties.[5] Meanwhile, he was reaping the advantage of those articles of the Treaty which empowered him to raise the duties on the exports and imports. In Barnett's opinion the greatest evil which British commerce would have to contend against, supposing all minor difficulties to be removed, was the system still pursued by the *vali* of seizing the lands of the peasants, by which means he was gradually creating for himself a monopoly of all the produce of the country.[6] He made over to different members of his family nearly the whole of his *chifliks* in Upper Egypt, thus intending to evade the obliga-

[1] Barnett's dispatch to Canning, 20 Mar. 1843.
[2] F.O. 142/13, No. 3, Barnett to F.O., 17 Jan. 1842.
[3] F.O. 142/13, Nos. 9 and 39 from Barnett to F.O., 23 Feb. 1842 and 17 Nov. 1843.
[4] F.O. 141/7, No. 4, F.O. to Barnett, 26 Aug. 1841.
[5] F.O. 78/541, No. 6, F.O. to Barnett, 3 Apr. 1843.
[6] F.O. 195/209, No. 1, Barnett to F.O., 3 Jan. 1842.

tions of selling the produce of these lands by public auction, while he would at the same time be able to command the disposal of them to his friends.[1] He had, moreover, become the possessor of two-thirds of the cultivable lands of Egypt, and disposed of a great proportion of the produce of the *fallāḥīn*: a part was purchased by the government at the price it fixed, and another part was taken in lieu of taxes. If he were considered the possessor of the lands, he was free to dispose of the produce; but if he were considered as the ruler of Egypt, disposing of the lands on behalf of his suzerain the sultan, he was obliged to apply Article II of the Treaty of 1838[2] and to sell the produce of the lands by public auction. This procedure was applied at Istanbul to the produce disposed of by the Ottoman government.[3] He yielded to the pressure of the consuls-general and issued regulations granting permission to foreigners to build boats for their own use, and to carry the produce of the country in such boats on the Nile and the Maḥmūdiyya Canal, on condition that they were manned by Egyptian sailors, and carried the Turkish flag. But before the merchants could build boats, they found it difficult to hire any more ships; those who possessed their own boats could find no crews. It was said that the monopoly on boats had ended, but that the crews were the subjects of the pasha and could be disposed of as he saw fit.[4]

Barnett tried to induce the *vali* to give up the monopoly of transport, and to open the interior of the country to the navigation of foreigners, although British merchants seldom went into the interior to buy grain or other produce. They preferred making their purchases in Alexandria to the trouble and risk of bringing goods down the Nile.[5] Muḥammad ʿAlī did not commit himself to any promise concerning the monopoly of traffic. He even monopolized the overland route between Cairo and Suez; and the transit service was made over to the Egyptian government later in 1846. The whole of the European officials of the company were retained in the employ of the *vali*, and the fares of the passengers were reduced from £15 to £12. This resulted in the displeasure of both the British passengers and the British government, which had

[1] F.O. 78/582, No. 2, Barnett to F.O., 15 Jan. 1844.

[2] This article ran as follows: 'The subjects of Her British Majesty, or their agents, shall be permitted to purchase at all places in the Ottoman dominions (whether for the purpose of internal trade or exportation) all articles, without any exception whatsoever, the produce, growth, or manufacture of the said dominions, and the Sublime Porte formally engages to abolish all monopolies of agricultural produce, or of any other article whatsoever, as well as all *permits* from the local governors, either for the purchase of any article, or for its removal from one place to another when purchased; and any attempt to compel the subjects of Her British Majesty to receive such permits from the local governors, shall be considered as an infraction of Treaties, and the Sublime Porte shall immediately punish with severity any vezirs and other officers who shall have been guilty of such misconduct, and render full justice to British subjects for all injuries or losses which they may duly prove themselves to have suffered.'

[3] F.O. 78/541, No. 27, Barnett to F.O., 19 Aug. 1843.

[4] Rivlin, op. cit., p. 187.

[5] F.O. 142/13, No. 11, from the same, 20 Mar. 1843.

endeavoured to sign an abortive treaty with the *vali* as to the overland route between Cairo and Suez. The ships of the Peninsular and Oriental Company, which sailed on the Nile, were also bought by him.

Although Muḥammad ʿAlī had not disposed of his cotton by public auction, and had not shown any willingness to allow any purchaser, who might have been ready to give the price demanded to acquire possession of it, Lord Palmerston did not understand that the *vali* sought to evade the conditions of the Treaty. The manner in which the *vali* was content to receive payment for the cotton did not appear to Lord Palmerston to be a matter for any interference on the part of the British government. The bargain might have been a very provident one on the part of the *vali*, but until it could be shown that British subjects were precluded from dealing on the same terms as the subjects of other states, and from providing equally with them the means of payment, there would have been no ground for complaint which would have justified a demand for a change of the system.[1] Barnett, therefore, thought fit to notify to the British merchants in Egypt that they would not be bound to pay the duties specified in the Treaty until all the provisions of that act were carried into effect.[2] The British government supported him in this point of view; but as, however, Sir Stratford Canning said that the Porte had undertaken to induce Muḥammad ʿAlī to abolish monopolies and to refrain from giving cause of complaint to the British government, instructions were sent to Barnett not to take any further steps in order to obtain from the *vali* the execution of the Treaty, until further instructions to him from the Foreign Office or from Sir Stratford Canning, after the result of the promised intervention of the Porte had been ascertained.[3] The *reis efendi* did not deny the justness of British complaints; nor did he reject the demand which Canning had founded upon them. But he expressed a great reluctance to issue any public orders to the *vali* at that particular moment, alleging that Muḥammad ʿAlī had himself promised to abolish the monopolies as soon as the existing contracts expired. He at the same time noted that the grand vezir had written confidentially to the *vali* in the sense which Canning required.[4] But Barnett was not disposed to look for any very favourable result from the exertions which the Porte might make to enforce the execution of the Treaty in Egypt, since the *vali* had a strong party at Istanbul; and because the financial embarrassment of the Ottoman government would indispose them to use such language as would probably irritate Muḥammad ʿAlī, and perhaps induce him to delay the payment of the tribute.[5]

However, Muḥammad ʿAlī showed in May 1842 more readiness than heretofore to attend to the suggestions made to him by Barnett and the other

[1] F.O. 78/541, No. 10, F.O. to Barnett, 25 July 1843.
[2] F.O. 141/7, No. 3, F.O. to Barnett, 24 Mar. 1842.
[3] Ibid.
[4] F.O. 141/9, No. 2, Canning to Barnett, 5 Mar. 1842.
[5] F.O. 142/13, No. 18, Barnett to F.O., 21 Apr. 1842.

consuls-general. He consented henceforth to sell only by public auction the produce of the lands he held. A sale was held for forty thousand ardebs of the next crop of sesame seed; and the whole quantity of the seed which he expected to produce was disposed of at a lower price than it afterwards fetched to four or five of the merchants, whom he had been in the habit of favouring. Upon representations made to him by Barnett the sale was annulled. It is worth noting here that sesame seed had become an article of great demand in France, where the oil extracted from it was used in the manufacture of soap.[1]

At the same time, the *vali* consented to execute the Treaty of 1838 by his promise to give up the monopoly of cotton after the ensuing crop. Barnett then turned his attention to the question of the tariff which fixed the duties to be paid upon the different articles of export and import. He considered the tariff to have been made without a sufficient knowledge of the average prices of the articles exported, or of the quality and value of manufactured goods which formed by far the larger proportion of British imports into Egypt;[2] and all the articles of British manufacture which came to Egypt were heavily affected by the tariff. As the Treaty of 1838 charged a tariff of 5 per cent. on imports and 12 per cent. on exports, the *vali* at last agreed to the arrangement which Barnett proposed to him for the payment of the import and export duties;[3] and thus a great obstacle was overcome as to the application of free trade to Egypt. But although some of the duties levied on goods were abolished to the benefit of British trade, yet British merchants paid higher duties than the subjects of Russia, who were entitled by treaty to import goods into the Ottoman dominions, upon paying the import duty of 3 per cent. only, which the British merchant paid, in lieu of all other interior duties. These other and interior duties having been abolished, the Russian subjects enjoyed all the advantages of their abolition without paying any equivalent, thus giving them a clear advantage of 2 per cent. over the British merchant.[4]

The monopoly system was also applied to the Sudan, which continued to be under Egyptian administration after 1841 according to a special *ferman* granted to the *vali* who from the start, as we have seen, proposed to certain merchants to sell to them the cotton, and the corn crops of Egypt and the Sudan for the pecuniary accommodation they would afford him from time to time, and to give these crops at a price under that of the market. This meant that the *vali* was to be the monopolist of the produce of both Egypt and the Sudan, and that the few merchants to whom that produce was to be so trans-

[1] F.O. 142/13, No. 19, Barnett to F.O. 15 May 1842.

[2] The export duty upon cotton amounted to above 22 per cent.; on wool from 20 to 25; Mocha coffee 14; safflower 50 buffalo and ox horns 22; opium 15; on all kinds of grain much above 12; and on grey calicos the import duty amounted to 9 instead of 5. Ibid., No. 20, Barnett to F.O., 20 May 1842.

[3] Ibid., from the same, 26 May 1842.

[4] F.O. 141/8, Robertson to Barnett, 1 Mar. 1843.

ferred, would be the only sellers of it in detail, and it was supposed that not more than half-a-dozen merchants would be selected. This was tantamount to the establishment of two monopolies, and was destined to make impossible the competition of the body of merchants in the purchase or sale of products, by those who had acquired possession by such means. The *vali*, by organizing such a company of buyers, might be said to evade or violate his promise of submission to the treaties of the Empire with foreign powers. It was thus evident that the proposed measure was both mischievous to the general trade and hurtful to British trade itself, since the monopolists would not fail to sell to their own countrymen, at the highest prices, as well as to others, the moment they had no competition in the general market to restrain them.[1] A public notice was issued in March 1842 by Boghos Bey, the Egyptian secretary for Commerce and Foreign Affairs, that the *vali* had given orders to the governor of Sennar to throw open the trade in henna, gums, ivory, hides, and senna—the produce of that country. Other orders were at the same time sent by the *vali* to the same governor to buy all these articles for his account: thus beginning to claim the monopoly, and to enforce it in favour of himself.[2]

All the Sennar produce naturally sought for itself other outlets in order to avoid the enormous profits claimed by the viceregal monopolist. The principal of these outlets were the ports of Massawa and Suakin on the western coast of the Red Sea. The *vali*, being resolved to leave no means untried for securing his object, asked and obtained from the Porte the government of the two towns, whereby he effectually closed all outlets for the produce of Sennar, and made the European merchants at Jedda and other places, engaged in the gum-trade, dependent on him for their supply.[3] The policy of the *vali* was even more vulnerable in the Sudan than in Egypt; for while he ruled Egypt on a hereditary footing, he was only invested with the pashalic of Sennar during the pleasure of the Sultan, it being expressly stated in the *ferman* that it was a separate pashalic and '*sans hérédité*'. This was a subject of remonstrances on the part of Great Britain, France, and Austria in both Cairo and Istanbul. In June 1848, accordingly, the grand vezir addressed a *ferman*[4] to the *vali* of Egypt enjoining him to desist from his attempt to monopolize the produce of Sennar. The British consul-general, Murray, even suggested that if the *vali* hesitated or declined to fulfil fairly and without equivocation the stipulations of the Treaty, the Porte should be urged to bestow the pashalic of Sennar on some officer sent directly from Istanbul, and that the government of Massawa and Suakin should be resumed by the Porte on the death of Muḥammad ʿAlī.[5] In November of the same year the Egyptian government

[1] F.O. 141/7 (copy), No. 264, Ponsonby to Palmerston, 3 Aug. 1841.

[2] F.O. 195/209, Barnett to Canning, 6 Apr. 1842; also F.O. 78/708, No. 49, Murray to Palmerston, 10 Aug. 1847.

[3] F.O. 78/708 (copy), No. 14, Murray to Cowley, 15 July 1847.

[4] F.O. 141/15 (copy)—The grand vezir to the pasha of Egypt (translation), dated 6 June 1848.

[5] F.O. 142/16, No. 27, Murray to Palmerston, 3 July 1848.

agreed to put an end to the monopoly of Sennar after three months, 'in consideration of the Egyptian government engaging entirely and unreservedly to abandon it at the expiration of that period'.[1] Orders were accordingly sent to the governors of Massawa and Suakin not to raise difficulties in the way of exporting the gums and senna owned by British individuals.[2]

Under 'Abbās Ḥilmī I the Sennar monopolies were abolished, and the trade in gums, senna, and the other produce of those countries were made open.[3] 'Abbās also allowed the two towns of Massawa and Suakin to revert to Turkey, since they were remote from Egypt, and since Muḥammad 'Alī had obtained them solely in order that he might command the only eastern outlet for the produce of Sennar and the Sudan. They were then put under the authority of the pasha of Jedda. The British government immediately established a consular agent at Khartoum in order to protect British merchants, who, since the abolition of the monopoly of gums, senna, and other produce of Sennar, had embarked in that trade.[4]

During the late forties the condition of Egypt was not flourishing: Muḥammad 'Alī was losing his old vigour: the health of Ibrāhīm was deteriorating, and the government of the country passed into the hands of 'Abbās Ḥilmī I after the death of Ibrāhīm and the degeneration of the mental faculties of Muḥammad 'Alī. Commerce, both foreign and internal, was languishing; immense stores of produce, grain, and cotton, were lying in the government storehouses unsaleable at a price 60 per cent. below the average of the previous year; and while the productive resources of Egypt were thus stagnant, the unproductive expenditure of money and labour on the Barrage, canals, fortifications and other military preparations, continued with unabated activity.[5] The treasury was empty; all departments of the public service were in arrear of pay, and extreme severity was still resorted to in forcing back to the *vali*'s *chifliks* the *fallāḥīn* whom want and ill-treatment had induced to abandon them.[6] The Egyptian government, finding that there was no escape from the plain and obvious sense of the treaties, consented to suppress the duties heretofore levied at Būlāq,[7] the port of Cairo.

[1] F.O. 78/765, Draft from F.O. to Murray, 1 Nov. 1848.

[2] F.O. 78/757 (copy), from Artin Bey to Murray, 1 July 1848.

[3] F.O. 195/330, No. 6, Murray to Canning, 12 Mar. 1849.

[4] F.O. 141/17, Consular No. 4, F.O. to Murray, 12 Mar. 1850. While the two towns were held by governors appointed directly from the Porte, a very active commerce was carried on between them and Jedda, Bombay, and other places in which British and Anglo-Indian merchants largely participated (F.O. 142/16); No. 6, Murray to Canning, 25 June 1848.

[5] F.O. 78/757, No. 23, Murray to Palmerston, 17 June 1848, and another dispatch dated 3 July 1848.

[6] F.O. 78/623, Barnett to Canning, 14 Mar. 1845.

[7] F.O. 195/330 (copy), No. 29, Murray to Palmerston, 19 May 1849. Murray had had a conversation with Artin Bey, the Egyptian secretary for Commerce and Foreign Affairs, and to all the latter's observations on the difficulty of preventing smuggling, Murray replied that the same existed in a much greater degree in England and France, and that it was the

Under ʿAbbās many changes took place, and affected Egyptian commerce and foreign relations. For many years, there had been a regulation, first promulgated by Muḥammad ʿAlī, that no contract for the purchase of produce from the *fallāḥīn* by payment in anticipation should be held valid; and with at least the tacit consent of the consuls-general that regulation was rigorously acted on. At first it was the subject of some complaint on the part of petty traders and agents, who were in the habit of visiting the provinces to buy up small parcels of produce which they subsequently disposed of in the markets of Cairo and Alexandria. In later times no such complaints were made, and it was generally represented that under the more easy rule of ʿAbbās, the law, though still existing, had been designedly left in abeyance. This, in some districts, was the case with the cognizance of the local governors; and there was also a system of evasion which was very generally and successfully adopted. The person who made advances to the *fallāḥīn* for produce which was not yet harvested, took from the cultivator, instead of a contract in the ordinary form, a money bond for a sum that included not only the cash which he had advanced, but such further sum as would, by his calculation, meet the market price of the article at the expected time of delivery. There was a verbal understanding between the parties; and when the *fallāḥ* delivered the produce, the merchant's agent acquitted the former of his money engagement. If the cultivator failed to deliver the produce, the local tribunal could be called on to enforce the money bond, in the amount of which a large profit had already been included. This appeared to be an irregular but safe proceeding; and it was found to be generally effectual for the protection of the parties who were willing to make advances for cultivators.

On the large houses no bad effect whatever was duly produced so long as the government disposed of its produce by public auction; those auctions were fairly conducted and, whatever might be the state of the markets, took place at regular periods. Whereas Muḥammad ʿAlī had sold to about twelve houses, mostly Greek and French, and these to other merchants at high rates, ʿAbbās sold by auction.[1] The merchants became furious; and the consuls of Austria, Sardinia, and Tuscany protested at what they considered an attempt by the *vali* to monopolize the whole produce and interrupt the merchants' contact with the *fallāḥīn*, with the object of making it impossible for foreigners to compete with him.[2] He had in fact duly issued a circular stating that the system which had hitherto been in practice of the cultivators' disposing of their crops to commercial houses, when they had often not paid the taxes due to the government, was from henceforth to stop, and that any persons

duty of the government to meet and overcome such difficulties by establishing efficient custom-houses at frontier towns and sea-ports, not by establishing them at places in the interior, in violation of existing commercial treaties. F.O. 195/330, No. 6, Murray to Canning, 12 Mar. 1849.

[1] F.O. 78/966 (copy), Walne to Paget, 7 Jan. 1853.

[2] Ibid., No. 9, Paget to Russell, 30 Jan. 1853.

purchasing from cultivators so indebted might have their bargains declared null and void, and the goods confiscated.[1]

This meant a resort to the old monopoly system, and ran in contradiction to Article II of the Treaty of 1838. Bruce protested against that procedure; and the British government instructed their ambassador at Istanbul to state to the Ottoman government that the system adopted by the *vali* was clearly an infraction of the Treaty, and to ask that he might duly receive positive instructions for his future guidance.[2]

In September 1853, moreover, ʿAbbās forbade the export of grain, on the pretext that the Nile flood had destroyed a great proportion of the produce. The consuls-general protested; and the *vali* agreed to export the quantities that were already at Alexandria. But although he permitted the grain to be conveyed to Alexandria, the government did not allow free export; and nothing in the possession of the government or the *vali* was released in the market.[3] He also issued an order whereby the ships carrying corn were to stop at al-ʿAṭf, where the Nile and the Maḥmūdiyya Canal met. Bruce protested, pressed for the application of the treaties, and noted to the Egyptian authorities that the *vali* would place himself in a most critical position, since it would be made to appear that his separate administration of Egypt was incompatible with the strict observance by the Porte of its treaties. It was said that the *vali* adopted that measure with a view to getting the produce into his own hands at a low price, and selling it afterwards to his advantage, while other persons well acquainted with the country were of the opinion that he was afraid of large requisitions of grain being made upon him from Turkey. It was thought that he wished to arm himself, under pretext of security, with a plausible ground for refusing to comply.[4]

ʿAbbās himself said that the Ottoman government had demanded grain from Egypt, and had promised to pay 90 piastres per ardeb of wheat on delivery at Istanbul.[5] But as he had a great deal of cunning, and did not wish to make sacrifices for the war, he gathered all the cotton of the country, and did not sell it, being anxious that the notion should prevail that he had difficulty in providing funds for the internal improvements he was carrying on, and that he had done his utmost to assist the Porte. He, however, did not seem to recollect that the resources and condition of Egypt were thoroughly understood at Istanbul.[6]

[1] F.O. 78/966, No. 6, Paget to Russell, 8 Jan. 1853.

[2] F.O. 78/1034, Draft No. 36, from F.O. to Bruce, 16 June 1854.

[3] F.O. 78/1053, Dispatch from Bruce to Clarendon marked 'Separate'; 16 Feb. 1854.

[4] Ibid., No. 4, Bruce to Clarendon, 2 Feb. 1854.

[5] F.O. 78/1036, No. 28 from the same, 16 June 1854.

[6] Ibid., No. 34, from the same, 5 July 1854. A vezirial letter to ʿAbbās, on his late proceedings as the monopoly of the sale of grain, was not received by him because of his sudden death. F.O. 142/18, No. 7, Bruce to Stratford de Redcliffe, 4 Aug. 1854.

Finding out that the Greeks were the principal purchasers of produce in the interior of Egypt, ʿAbbās intended to expel them altogether from the country. That act was duly effected with great and unnecessary severity by the governor of Alexandria; and so little disposition was shown to attend to the representations of the consuls of the allied powers, when they asked for the prolongation of the term in favour of Greeks whose large dealings with commercial houses would have entailed heavy losses, that foreign protection was largely accorded to them.

The enterprise of the Greek traders, combined with their knowledge of the language and the habits of the Turks, made them very formidable competitors; and ʿAbbās, who was bent on monopolizing the produce of the country, found their presence a serious obstacle, and wanted to get rid of them altogether.[1] But the British ambassador at Istanbul issued a circular stating that: 'Hellenic subjects in the service of British commercial houses, or of British subjects in general, are to be allowed to remain for the present on the responsibility of their several employees . . . and furnished with *cartes de sûreté* by the Ottoman authorities, except in cases where the conduct of either party has warranted, or may in future warrant, a special complaint on the part of the police.'[2]

The *vali*'s attitude towards the Greeks was connected with his general internal policy. The property inherited by the sons of Muḥammad ʿAlī and Ibrāhīm consisted of *chifliks*, that is the former property of the Mamluks, and of *ʿuhdas*. The *chifliks* were secured by *ferman*, and paid no tax to the government. ʿAbbās did not take them away directly; but as he was bent upon ruining their holders, he effected his purpose in the following manner. The governors of the provinces took care that the proprietor should not get money to carry on the cultivation; the *fallāḥīn* finding the land uncultivated, entered upon it, and cultivated it on their own account. By law they were required to pay the proprietor an amount equal to the land-tax; but the governors were instructed not to enforce the proprietor's demands and consequently he derived no income from it whatever, thus soon being driven to abandon it. Ibrāhīm left upwards of seventy villages held as *ʿuhdas* which were in great part, if not altogether, taken from his sons. The holder of the *ʿuhda* advanced capital, and carried on all such cultivation as sugar and cotton, which required considerable outlay. The wealthy shaykhs, or headmen, in the villages played an equally important part in the cultivation of their districts. They were rooted out in great measure; and the government, by reducing them to debt, was able to seize their considerable funds. In lands thus deprived of the services of the capitalists, while the state did nothing to fill the vacuum, the description of cultivation which gave the best return degenerated. Where the land was of inferior quality, the *vali* did not resume it, and the *fallāḥīn*, deprived of native capitalists, looked for assistance to the agents of the

[1] F.O. 78/1035, Bruce to Clarendon, 16 May 1854. [2] Ibid.

mercantile houses, who had customarily made advances on the security of the crops. The *vali*, who was most anxious to cut off this resource, revived a circular originally issued by Muḥammad ʿAlī prohibiting the sale of unripe crops. He in fact dreaded these agents, who could encourage the *fallāḥīn* not to deal with the agents of the government, and who could invoke the Capitulations in defending themselves against his harshness.[1]

On his death, ʿAbbās left the public finances charged with an internal debt which amounted to a hundred million francs, and the coffers of the state were completely empty.[2] His successor Muḥammad Saiʿīd Pasha showed some liberal tendencies[3] and a toleration of foreigners which amounted to weakness. This toleration was partly due to his ambition of attaining independence; and, as the Muslim supremacy in Egypt was the sultan's hold on the country, he thought that by lowering that influence, and raising the Christian and European influence, he could weaken the sultan's authority and gain partisans and protectors for himself.[4] He was moreover devoid of the fanaticism which characterized ʿAbbās, and was inclined to adopt more cordially any suggestions of improvement.[5] In the eyes of those who knew him he was a man of kindly disposition and good intentions; but he had neither the health nor the energy to leave any lastingimpression on the condition of Egypt during hisreign.[6]

Saʿīd wished from the start to get rid of the mercantile character which his predecessors had too much affected. No difficulties were thrown in the way of the merchants who wished to deal with the *fallāḥīn* in the interior. The British consul-general commented that the carrying out of the system would enrich the peasant, and that the establishment of European agencies would eventually render necessary the adoption of more enlightened maxims of administration in the interior, and give the cultivator that security of property which had hitherto retarded the many plans of improvement in Egypt. He added that Saʿīd had good qualities and that his ideas of reform were just, but that he had some defects which made it difficult to realize them; being dazzled by magnificent projects, and without the perseverance and steadiness requisite to carry out social improvements.[7]

But the new *vali* indulged in a spirit of opposition to everything done by his predecessor to an extent which entirely contradicted all his professions in favour of improved administration. He seemed to think that the best way of reorganizing the different departments, which had already suffered considerable deterioration in the time of ʿAbbās, was to begin by abolishing them altogether; and justified these measures on the grounds of economy, and of the

[1] F.O. 78/1036, No. 24, Bruce to Clarendon, 1 June 1854.

[2] *Précis de l'histoire d'Égypte*, vol. iv, Angelo Sammarco, *Les règnes de ʿAbbas, de Saʿid et d'Ismaʿil (1848–1879)* (Rome, 1935), p. 8.

[3] J. Carlile McCoan, *Egypt as it is* (London, 1877), p. 81.

[4] F.O. 195/722, No. 7, Bruce to Russell, 4 Jan. 1863.

[5] F.O. 195/412, No. 15, Bruce to Stratford de Redcliffe, 17 July 1855.

[6] Edward Dicey, *The story of the khedivate* (London, 190), p. 222.

[7] F.O. 195/412, Bruce to Stratford de Redcliffe, 8 July 1855.

necessity of meeting the debts left by ʿAbbās. But he in fact reversed his predecessor's policy of reliance upon the Arab element to the detriment of the Turks. He told the British consul-general that he meant to have none but Turkish officers, and spoke of the unfitness of the Arabs for any high employment. This policy tended to throw him into the hands of the French party. It inclined him to consider them as having a claim upon him, in consequence of the disfavour shown to them by ʿAbbās, and gave them facilities to access which the British merchants did not enjoy.[1]

All this led to a series of liberal reforms, the foremost of which was the suppression of internal customs duties and all monopolies. Freedom of commerce was thus secured, and no obstructions were thrown in the way of persons dealing in the interior with the native producers.

The results were very favourable to the proprietors, and the prices of grain in the remote provinces, nearly as far as Aswān, fully shared in the advance consequent on the active demand at Alexandria for exports, especially since the internal customs-house at Būlāq, so long the subject of vexation and fruitless remonstrances, was abolished, and the pernicious system of octroi-duties done away with almost entirely.[2]

But since the monopoly system was thus abolished, the field for foreign adventurers was much narrowed, and the persons in favour with the *vali* directed their efforts to obtaining grants of exclusive privileges in favour of projects which had not previously been introduced into Egypt. Such a system led inevitably to the greatest abuses by giving advantages to the persons in the *vali*'s favour, by imposing a check on subsequent improvements, and by subjecting the people and the trade of Egypt to any scale of payment those monopolists might choose to exact.[3]

Saʿīd's weakness proved to be especially deleterious to the welfare of Egypt by giving much scope to the interference of the foreign consuls, many of whom made dishonest gains from their positions. The paid consuls-general were those of France, Austria, Greece, Prussia, Britain, Spain, the United States of America, Sardinia, and Russia. The unpaid and trading consuls-general were those of Holland, Belgium, Tuscany, Naples, Denmark, the Hanseatic League, Portugal, and Sweden. Most of the unpaid consuls-general were not even natives of the countries they represented; the Neapolitan consul-general, for example, was an ordinary Levantine who had made money. Some had purchased their appointment, and all had acquired it, not so much for the position, as for the opportunities it afforded for engrossing government business. They had received no education for the judicial duties they were called on to execute, and their object was naturally to keep on good terms with the local government and to turn to their own private account

[1] F.O. 195/412 (copy-private), from Bruce to F.O., 16 Dec. 1854.
[2] F.O. 195/522, copy No. 8, Bruce to F.O., 2 Feb. 1857.
[3] F.O. 78/1338, No. 21, Bruce to Clarendon, 13 Apr. 1857.

the facilities of access to the *vali* which belonged to the office of consul-general.[1]

The result was that such consuls played a decisive part in opening the doors of Egypt to the growing Western capitalism and to European immigration;[2] also in exercising pressure on the Egyptian government to exact indemnities, sometimes for imaginary losses. The British consul-general gives us the following vivid picture of the role played by such consuls:

> The language of these gentlemen on general questions accords rather with what is beneficial to their own interests, than with the policy of the governments they represent. When Said Pacha first came into power and was discussing the expediency of putting an end to the system of monopolizing produce in the hands of the government, which Abbas Pacha had lately attempted to re-establish, one of the chief opponents of his liberal views was the Belgian Consul-General. The language he held was certainly not in accordance with the policy of the Belgian government in such matters.[3]

This is why Bruce suggested to the British government that the interests of foreign countries, as well as those of Turkey itself, required that the extensive judicial powers exercised by the consuls representing foreign countries in the Levant should be bestowed exclusively on persons who were unconnected with trade, and who, forming part of the service of the country to which they belonged and properly paid, should present a sufficient guarantee for their independence, and for the conscientious discharge of their functions.[4]

Saʿīd was a Turk; and it was the habit of the Turks, seeing foreign agents engaged in claiming a share in profitable abuses for their subjects, and in supporting claims arising out of illegal transactions, to look upon them as linked with the jobbers who professed that their sole object was *exploiter les Turcs*. They naturally drew the inference that the best way to propitiate a consul-general, and insure through him the goodwill of the government he represented, was to give his countrymen an undue proportion of advantage at the expense of the general interests of commerce and of the government itself.[5] The result was that Saʿīd considered the body of foreign agents as his natural enemies whose only object was to make money out of him. But he could not resist the ever-increasing European pressure on Egypt, which was enhanced by the final collapse of the monopoly system during his reign. Moreover, persons in his favour were obtaining exclusive privileges for the exercise of particular branches of industry and were selling them to companies to be

[1] F.O. 78/1222, Nos. 13 and 21 from Bruce to Clarendon, 4 Apr. and 5 May 1856.

[2] Although accurate censuses were not available in Egypt until 1897, Issawi estimates the number of foreigners in Egypt as being about 3,000 in 1836 and more than 68,000 in 1878 and 221,000 in 1907. Issawi, op. cit., p. 29.

[3] F.O. 142/20, No. 6 (consular), Bruce to F.O., 14 Mar. 1857.

[4] Ibid., No. 6 (confidential), from the same, 24 Jan. 1857.

[5] F.O. 78/1222, Nos. 13 and 21 *supra*.

worked, thus entailing injustice on the Egyptian population, and tending to overpower and supersede the authority of the ruler, and thereby supplant the Turkish race in Egypt.[1]

Commerce, therefore, became based on the worst possible footing, since the merchants preferred investing their capital in treasury bonds; these paid interest from 15 to 18 per cent. Sa'īd took care that every bond as it fell due should be punctually paid, so that their reputation should stand high. Every person, high or low, who possessed any objects of value, parted with them to invest in these bonds. In spite of that, the amount of exports and imports was largely increasing.[2]

The way was thus paved for integrating Egypt as an agricultural colonial unit in the international politico-economic system;[3] and the collapse of Muḥammad 'Alī's schemes points out one of the major obstacles to economic development in Egypt; the lack of political autonomy. As we have seen, the tariff was fixed by conventions concluded between the Ottoman government and the great powers; and no direct taxes could be imposed on foreigners without the consent of their governments, because of the Capitulations.

Muḥammad 'Alī, by his monopoly system, had given an impetus to agriculture, industry, and commerce, and had defended Egypt's autonomy, while at the same time taking advantage of European experts and technicians, whom he encouraged to settle in Egypt. Thus the government monopolies impeded foreign activities in Egypt during the first half of the nineteenth century, with the result that the importation of European capital on a wide scale did not take place till the second half, after the opening of the Suez Canal and with the pressing need of financing the production of cotton and preparing it for exportation.

'Abbās was against European influences altogether; if he hated Europeans and secluded himself from their society, he did so in order to stem the tide of Western penetration, which had been encouraged during the last decade before his accession.[4] But Sa'īd's reign marks a transitional period in Egypt's history. His personality and his policy, at the time which witnessed the growth of European industrialism and capitalism, were responsible for the debts, the execution of the Suez Canal, mostly at the expense of the Egyptian government, and the pacific European invasion of Egypt—which all bore fruit in the ensuing generation.[5]

1 F.O. 142/20, No. 22, Bruce to Clarendon, 16 Apr. 1857.

2 F.O. 142/112, Colquhoun to Russell, 11 Nov. 1861.

3 Issawi, op. cit., pp. 19 and 24.

4 J. Heyworth-Dunne, *An introduction to the history of education in modern Egypt* (London, 1939), p. 289. See also, Ahmed Abdel-Rahim Mustafa, 'Some Aspects of Egypt's Foreign Relations under Abbas I' (*Annals of the Faculty of Arts, Ain Shams University*, vol. viii (1963), pp. 63–82.

5 Cf. Subḥī Waḥīda, *Fī uṣul al-mas'ala al-Miṣriyya* (Cairo, 1950).

The Egyptian Nationalist Party: 1892–1919

ARTHUR GOLDSCHMIDT, JR.

EGYPTIAN nationalism is one of the most frequently studied movements in modern Middle Eastern history. This has been particularly true at times when its aims have collided with the interests of other forces operating on the world scene. Despite Egypt's growing role in regional and world politics, a role she plays in a style clearly influenced by her past triumphs and frustrations, no professional historian[1] has yet written a coherent and integrated account of the Egyptian nationalist movement from the native resistance to the Bonapartist occupation until the present day. Certain phases of the movement, notably the revolutions of 1882 and 1919, whose leaders have now been securely enshrined in the pantheon of Egypt's political history, have been fairly well chronicled. This paper will be devoted to a phase that is not so well known, although it succeeded in disseminating the ideas of nationalism among the Egyptian upper and middle classes, namely the Nationalist Party[2] of Muṣṭafā Kāmil (1874–1908) and Muḥammad Farīd (1868–1919). It was this party which carried the standard of popular opposition to the British occupation of Egypt until the outbreak of the 1919 revolution.

After the final defeat of the first Egyptian nationalist revolution at Tel-el-Kebir by a British expeditionary force in 1882, the nationalist movement entered a quiescent phase. Indeed, it is commonly thought that the ensuing decade passed without any Egyptian resistance to foreign control, now clearly established by the presence of the British army of occupation and personified by Sir Evelyn Baring (later Lord Cromer), who served from 1883 to 1907 as the British consul-general in Cairo. Despite intermittent declarations by British ministers that the occupation of Egypt was only temporary, Cromer acting from day to day to solve Egypt's most pressing financial and administrative problems, gradually established a set pattern of government. Under this system, often called 'the veiled protectorate', the appearance of rule was retained by the khedive and his ministers, while the real power rested in the

[1] I use the qualifying adjective 'professional' in humble acknowledgement of the monumental work of the late amateur historian, ʿAbd al-Raḥmān al-Rāfiʿī (1889–1966), whose writings on Egypt encompassed nearly the entire span of recorded history and provide invaluable source material for the modern period. ʿAbd al-Raḥmān al-Rāfiʿī was trained in Cairo and Paris as a lawyer, was active in the Nationalist Party throughout its formal existence, and served Egypt as a deputy, senator, and minister, while writing his histories, memoirs, and other books.

[2] In Arabic, *al-Ḥizb al-Waṭanī*, also sometimes translated as National Party or Patriotic Party, and not to be confused with the Wafd, the main standard-bearer of Egyptian nationalism from 1919 to 1952.

hands of Cromer, aided by the British officers in the Egyptian army and in the army of occupation, and by a growing corps of advisers in the Egyptian ministries.

Although great advances were achieved in most phases of Egyptian administration under this system, it is hardly surprising that the time eventually came when Egyptians, especially the young men who had never known the old system, began to wonder whether they would ever be entrusted with the reins of political power in their own country. The growth of this feeling required many years. In 1882 the diehard ʿUrabists were silenced by the exile or imprisonment of their leaders. Other nationalists who had foreseen in time the outcome of the ʿUrābī revolution, made their peace with Khedive Tawfīq, who seems to have kept to himself any resentment he might have harboured against the British. Indeed, he managed to co-operate fairly amicably with Cromer until his sudden death in January 1892.

In the early years of the British occupation, the Egyptian Question was almost entirely international in nature. France, whose political, economic, and cultural interests in Egypt had been far greater than Britain's, but whose political leadership had refused at the critical moment to co-operate with Britain in upholding the khedive's authority against ʿUrābī, now pursued a spiteful 'policy of pinpricks' because of her consequent exclusion from power in Egypt. The French government repeatedly demanded a time-limit to the British occupation, while some of the French residents in Egypt blew upon the coals of opposition to Cromer's administration through their personal contacts with Egyptians or in the columns of such newspapers as *al-Ittiḥād al-Miṣrī* and *Le Bosphore Égyptien*.[1] The Ottoman government, nominally Egypt's suzerain, also opposed the British occupation, both in Istanbul and in Cairo, where the headquarters of the Turkish high commissioner was widely believed to be the centre of a network of anti-British spies.[2] But native opposition, especially after the suppression of the Society for Revenge[3] in 1883, was practically non-existent.

The turning point came when Khedive Tawfīq died, and was succeeded by his eldest son, ʿAbbās II, who was barely 18 years old by the Muslim lunar calendar. Educated at the Theresianum (the Princes' School) in Vienna,

[1] For *al-Ittiḥād al-Miṣrī*, about which I know nothing, see Jacob Landau, *Parliaments and parties in Egypt* (Tel Aviv, 1953), p. 104. For *Le Bosphore Égyptien*, see Jules Munier, *La presse en Égypte (1799–1900): notes et souvenirs* (Cairo, 1930), pp. 9–20, and the following published documents: France, Ministère des Affaires Étrangères, *Documents diplomatiques: 1885*, 'Affaire du journal Le Bosphore Égyptien' (Paris, 1885); Great Britain, Foreign Office, *Egypt, 1885, No. 12*, 'Correspondence concerning the suppression of the "Bosphore Égyptien"' (London, 1885).

[2] H. F. Wood, *Egypt under the British* (London, 1896), pp. 62 f.

[3] The Society for Revenge, or *Jamʿiyyat al-Intiqām*, was a secret, terrorist society, whose programme was to prepare for an armed insurrection to drive out the British and assassinate those Egyptians who had betrayed the ʿUrābī Revolution. One of its members was Saʿd Zaghlūl. See Aḥmad Shafīq, *Mudhakkirātī fī niṣf qarn* (Cairo, 1934–6), vol. i, p. 212, and ʿAbbās Maḥmūd al-ʿAqqād, *Saʿd Zaghlūl: sīra wa taḥiyya* (Cairo, 1936), p. 72.

the young khedive cherished ambitions of becoming the real ruler of Egypt, which soon led him into conflict, first with the Ottoman high commissioner and then with Lord Cromer, over his choice of a prime minister. Khedive ʿAbbās soon acquired an entourage of Egyptian and European advisers who were hostile to Cromer, and who encouraged him to dismiss Muṣṭafā Fahmī, an advocate of co-operation with the British, in favour of Ḥusayn Fakhrī (1843–1920), a man of quite different views. Cromer quickly acted, after obtaining the support of Lord Rosebery, Britain's Liberal foreign secretary, and assurances from the other foreign consuls in Egypt that they would not interfere, and forced the khedive to nullify the change. He then persuaded the khedive to appoint Riyāḍ Pasha, as a face-saving compromise.

This clash between the young khedive—eager to assert his right to rule Egypt without British interference, but apparently misled by his advisers as to the readiness of the other European consuls to oppose Britain on his behalf—and the more experienced and powerful British consul-general, is a convenient episode with which to mark the beginning of the new Egyptian nationalist movement. Shaykh ʿAlī Yūsuf (1863–1913), the talented editor of the hitherto obscure Arabic daily, *al-Mu'ayyad*, backed the khedive, as he was to do with tenacious loyalty until the end of his days.[1] Meanwhile, Yaʿqūb Ṣarrūf (1852–1927) and Fāris Nimr (1856–1951), graduates of the Syrian Protestant College in Beirut, sided with Cromer in the pages of *al-Muqaṭṭam*. Some of the students in the higher schools of Cairo, notably the Egyptian government-run School of Law, demonstrated in support of the khedive before the offices of *al-Muqaṭṭam*. Their leader was an articulate, 18-year-old law student named Muṣṭafā Kāmil.

Muṣṭafā Kāmil came from a middle-class Cairo family and was educated almost entirely in government schools. As a secondary-school pupil, he had organized a literary society, participated in several secret political societies, and gained prestige among his peers by becoming a protégé of ʿAlī Mubārak, the minister of education, who gave him a scholarship and frequently invited him to his house.[2] Upon completing secondary school in 1891, Muṣṭafā

[1] It is now generally believed that *al-Mu'ayyad* was begun with the support of a number of wealthy Egyptians (such as Saʿd Zaghlūl) in Dec. 1889 as a counterweight to *al-Muqaṭṭam*, which in turn had been founded that same year—with British moral although probably not financial support—to oppose the pro-French *al-Ahrām*. In Egyptian journalism, it is often the case that for every action you get an equal and opposite reaction. According to a contemporary English writer, however, *al-Mu'ayyad* was patronized at its birth by Riyāḍ Pasha and hewed closely to his political line, which tended to be pro-British until Riyāḍ quarrelled with Cromer over the appointment of a British adviser to reform the National Courts in 1890, whereupon both patron and paper changed sides. See Wood, op. cit., pp. 154–8. The early obscurity of *al-Mu'ayyad* is illustrated by the fact that W. Fraser Rae, writing on the Egyptian press in 1892, never mentions it. See W. Fraser Rae, 'The Egyptian newspaper press', *The Nineteenth Century*, vol. xxxii (1892), pp. 213–23.

[2] Alī Fahmī Kāmil, *Muṣṭafā Kāmil Bāshā fī 34 rabīʿan* (9 vols.; Cairo, 1908–11), vol. i, pp. 111–36. For economy of space and time, ʿAlī Fahmī Kāmil's biography of his brother will hereinafter be indicated by A.F.K.

chose to study law, which he believed to be 'the key to the knowledge of the rights of individuals and nations'.[1]

At the Khedivial School of Law Muṣṭafā was befriended by a classmate, Fu'ād Salīm al-Ḥijāzī (1874–*c.* 1940), who invited Muṣṭafā to his house and introduced him to his father, Laṭīf Salīm (d. 1907), who as head of the Military College had made the speech that sparked off the demonstration of the Egyptian army officers against the 'European Ministry' of Nubar Pasha in 1879. A former 'Urabist now in eclipse, Laṭīf Salīm ran a sort of political salon at his house, and invited Muṣṭafā to attend. This enabled him to meet some of the leading literary and political figures of the day, such as Shaykh 'Alī al-Laythī (1821–96), Ismā'īl Ṣabrī (1854–1923), Maḥmūd Sālim, and Ismā'īl Shīmī (d. 1912), whose common bond was their secret opposition to the British occupation.

After the ministerial crisis of 1893, Latīf Salīm organized this group into a secret society, which he called the Nationalist Party, the name that the 'Urabist officers' movement had once borne. Its purposes were to organize Egyptians to work for their country's independence and to present its cause to European, especially French, public opinion. Among its members were many young men who later became Muṣṭafā Kāmil's chief supporters, such as Aḥmad and 'Abd al-Laṭīf al-Ṣūfānī, Maḥmūd Anīs, Ḥasan 'Āsim, Muḥammad Khulūṣī, Ḥasan 'Abd al-Rāziq, and Muḥammad Farīd. Muṣṭafā Kāmil was in Paris for his first-year law examinations when the Nationalist Party was formed, but joined after his return to Cairo, and soon superseded Laṭīf Salīm as its leader.

The khedive, whose role in this particular avatar of the Nationalist Party remains obscure, went to Istanbul that summer to enlist the support of Abdülhamid. Anti-British feeling among Egyptian government and Palace officials intensified that autumn.[2] The crisis came to a head in the Frontier Incident of January 1894, in which Kitchener, the sirdar of the Egyptian army, attempted to resign when the khedive, while on an inspection tour of Upper Egypt, made some disparaging remarks about the British officers in such a way as to undermine the discipline of the native troops. Cromer supported Kitchener (who withdrew his resignation) and upbraided the khedive, who consequently nursed a grudge against both men for many years.

Meanwhile Muṣṭafā Kāmil continued his legal studies and also published a monthly students' magazine called *al-Madrasa*, through which he came under the influence of 'Abd Allāh Nadīm (1845–96), one of 'Urābī's most gifted orators and writers. Pardoned by Khedive 'Abbās and allowed to return to Egypt, Nadīm published from August 1892 to June 1893 a weekly magazine called *al-Ustādh*. Its bitingly satirical articles against the British occupation finally goaded Cromer into demanding his expulsion, but his influence

[1] Muṣṭafā Kāmil to 'Alī Fahmī Kāmil, Alexandria, 12 July 1891, from A.F.K., vol. i, p. 137.

[2] Earl of Cromer, *Abbas II* (London, 1915), pp. 45–49.

survived in his apt young pupil. According to Jurjī Zaydān, Nadīm sought out Muṣṭafā and advised him not to repeat the errors of the ʿUrabists, namely their opposition to the khedive and their reliance on the strength of the Egyptian army rather than on that of public opinion.[1] Whatever Nadīm may in fact have said, it is significant that he was—together with Laṭīf Salīm—the slender link from ʿUrābī to Muṣṭafā Kāmil,[2] and that his advice sums up the main differences between the two nationalist leaders. Indeed, some of the party's later difficulties arose because Muṣṭafā followed this advice too carefully.

The most fruitful contact for Muṣṭafā Kāmil—and the most crucial for the early development of his movement—was with Khedive ʿAbbās. How and when this contact was initially established remains obscure. The khedive's secretary, Aḥmad Shafīq, writes that the occasion was the visit ʿAbbās made in February 1892 to the Khedivial Law School, where he was welcomed by Muṣṭafā on behalf of the students.[3] It is also possible that the khedive first heard of Muṣṭafā when he led the student demonstration against *al-Muqaṭṭam* during the 1893 ministerial crisis. Although Muṣṭafā's lack of a private income is well-known, it has not been ascertained whether the khedive subsidized *al-Madrasa*, or gave Muṣṭafā a scholarship to complete his legal studies in France.[4] It is interesting to note, however, that Muṣṭafā managed to give an elaborate banquet for the Ottomans and Egyptians in Paris to celebrate the 1894 anniversary of the sultan's accession.[5] At this time ʿAbbās was still courting Ottoman support against the British in Egypt.[6]

After sustaining his final law examinations at the University of Toulouse in November 1894, Muṣṭafā Kāmil returned to Egypt, but not to practise law. During his homeward journey he made the acquaintance of Colonel Baring, Lord Cromer's brother. In the course of a long conversation the Colonel asserted that Britain intended to stay in Egypt indefinitely, regardless of what the other European powers might think.[7] Muṣṭafā published this conversation in *al-Ahrām*, which at the time followed a Francophile policy. The article aroused considerable controversy in Egyptian political circles, and gave Muṣṭafā some welcome notoriety.

[1] Jurjī Zaydān, *Tarājim mashāhīr al-sharq fi'l-qarn al-tāsiʿ ʿashar* (Cairo, 1922), p. 295.

[2] As far as we know, Muṣṭafā never met ʿUrābī, even after the latter's return from exile in 1901. ʿUrābī's praise of the accomplishments of the British occupation must have displeased the younger nationalists, and Muṣṭafā once wrote to Mme Adam of 'the shameful treason of Arabi', referring to his surrender after the battle of Tel-el-Kebir. See Juliette Adam (ed.), *Egyptian-French letters* (tr. Frederick Ryan; Cairo, 1909), p. 84.

[3] Shafīq, vol. II. i, p. 50.

[4] As alleged by Muḥammad Ḥusayn Haykal, *Tarājim Miṣriyya wa gharbiyya* (Cairo, 1929), p. 144.

[5] A.F.K., vol. ii, pp. 121–34.

[6] Cromer, p. 63.

[7] 'Ḥadīth dhū sha'n', *al-Ahrām* (28 Jan. 1895). Text in A.F.K., vol. iii, pp. 20–28; Shafīq, vol. II. i, pp. 192–5; Aḥmad Rashād, *Muṣṭafā Kāmil, ḥayātuhu wa kifāḥuhu* (Cairo, 1958), pp. 54–58.

In view of the khedive's early struggles with Cromer, it is not too surprising that Egyptians were increasingly turning against the British occupation. The British even found it necessary to make the Egyptian government promulgate a law providing for special courts to try cases of assault against occupation troops by Egyptians. Muṣṭafā Kāmil and the khedive tried to direct this mood of popular opposition into nationalist channels by creating a secret society, called *al-Jamʿiyya li-Iḥyāʾ al-Waṭan* (the Society for the Revival of the Nation), in which many Egyptian and European Palace functionaries, judges, and government officials took part.[1]

France's opposition to Britain's occupation of Egypt intensified in the 1890s as one aspect of the world-wide colonial rivalry between the two powers. It is illustrative of the lengths to which this rivalry was carried that a French engineer in the Egyptian civil service gave a paper in Cairo in 1893 on the feasibility of controlling Egypt's water supply by erecting barrages on the upper Nile. The speech attracted widespread attention in France, and many politicians urged the French government to send an expedition to seize control of the Sudan, put a dam across the upper Nile, and threaten to divert Egypt's water supply unless the British withdrew their forces or made special concessions to French interests in Egypt.[2] François Deloncle, a prominent French advocate of a forward policy in the Nile valley and a member of the Chamber of Deputies, visited Egypt in March 1895. He was met by Muṣṭafā Kāmil at Alexandria and fêted during his twenty-day visit by the nationalists and by the members of the khedive's entourage, with whom he evidently made an agreement to bring Muṣṭafā Kāmil to Paris, where they would work together to induce the French government to oppose the British occupation.[3]

Muṣṭafā, amply fortified with Palace funds, sailed for France in May, carrying a petition protesting against the creation of the special courts and requesting French aid in securing the evacuation of British forces from Egypt.[4] Deloncle was supposed to take young Muṣṭafā in hand and introduce him to some of France's leading politicians and journalists. Instead he tried to prevent Muṣṭafā from presenting his petition to the French Chamber of Deputies, belittled him in public by saying that he had brought him to Paris as his 'Arabic secretary', and refused to introduce him to any of his influential friends. Deloncle proved also to have many equally influential enemies, whom Muṣṭafā hardly wished to share with his mentor.[5] Eventually they quarrelled,

[1] Among its members were Aḥmad Shafīq, Ismāʿīl Shīmī, Maḥmūd Sālim ʿArafat, Louis Rouiller (the khedive's private secretary, a Swiss national), Yūsuf Ṣiddīq, and Aristide Gavillot (the Havas correspondent in Egypt). See Shafīq, vol. II. i, p. 190; also A.F.K., vol. ii, p. 243.

[2] William L. Langer, *The diplomacy of imperialism* (2nd edn.; New York, 1960), pp. 127 f.

[3] Shafīq, vol. II. i, pp. 197–9.

[4] Muṣṭafā presented the petition to the president of the Chamber of Deputies on 2 June 1895, together with a painting representing enslaved Egypt appealing, through Muṣṭafā, to France for her liberation. See A.F.K., vol. iii, pp. 75 f.

[5] Muṣṭafā Kāmil to Aḥmad Shafīq, Paris, 6 June 1895, taken from Shafīq, vol. II. i, p. 201. Also Muṣṭafā Kāmil to Shaykh ʿAbd al-Raḥīm Aḥmad, Paris, 8 June 1895, from Muḥammad

and although they were reconciled, much to the relief of their Egyptian and European supporters in the khedive's entourage,[1] they never again collaborated, and Muṣṭafā was left to steer his own course through the murky waters of French politics.[2] He made his first major speech on Egypt at Toulouse on 4 July 1895,[3] and tried to extend his appeal for Egypt's freedom into other countries by travelling to Vienna later that month.[4] In August he published a pamphlet, addressed to Europeans in general and the French in particular, the thesis of which was that the prompt evacuation of British troops from Egypt was necessary to assure the peace of Europe.[5]

Now that Deloncle could no longer be relied on to provide him with political contacts, Muṣṭafā had to seek a new supporter. Early in September he wrote to Mme Juliette Adam (1836–1936), the famous writer who founded and for many years edited the influential fortnightly, *La Nouvelle Revue*, asking for help in his campaign for Egypt's freedom.[6] She invited him to her office, and he asked her to use her influence to open to him the pages of one of France's leading newspapers. She persuaded him instead to submit a short article to her review.[7] Muṣṭafā's personal and political association with Mme Adam, which lasted without interruption until his death, enabled him to meet such leading French writers as Pierre Loti, Edouard Drumont (the famous anti-Semite who edited *La Libre Parole* and wrote *La France Juive*), Ernest Judet (editor of *Le Petit Journal* and *L'Éclair*), and Henri Rochefort (founder and editor of *L'Intransigeant*).[8] Except for the Turcophile Loti,[9] most

Anīs, *Ṣafaḥāt maṭwīyya min ta'rīkh al-za'īm Muṣṭafā Kāmil* (Cairo, 1962), pp. 21–29. Shaykh Aḥmad had been the private tutor of Princes 'Abbās and Muḥammad 'Alī in Europe, and was made an adviser to 'Abbās when he became khedive. The origin and nature of his connexion with Muṣṭafā Kāmil are unclear.

[1] Shaykh Aḥmad to Muṣṭafā Kāmil, Alexandria, 17 June 1895, Anīs, pp. 30–33; Muṣṭafā Kāmil to Shaykh Aḥmad, Paris, 27 June 1895, ibid., pp. 34–37; Muṣṭafā Kāmil to Aḥmad Shafīq, Paris, 27 June 1895, Shafīq, vol. II. i, p. 203.

[2] But he did have some Egyptian friends in Paris, such as Maḥmūd Abū al-Naṣr, Yūsuf Ṣiddīq, Ismā'īl Shīmī, Ibrāhīm al-Hilbāwī and Muḥammad Farīd. Apparently they were planning to establish a political party, with its own newspaper, in Paris in 1895. See n. 2, p. 315 below.

[3] M. Kamel, *Conférence sur l'Égypte faite à Toulouse le jeudi 4 juillet à l'Amphithéâtre de la faculté des lettres* (Toulouse, 1895). Also see Moustapha Kamel, *Égyptiens et Anglais* (Paris, 1906), pp. 21–43.

[4] Muṣṭafā Kāmil to Shaykh Aḥmad, 8 June 1895.

[5] In his letter to Shaykh Aḥmad, Paris, 15 Aug. 1895, Muṣṭafā explained that he believed that this approach would be the most effective in reaching French public opinion. See Anīs, pp. 56 f.

[6] Muṣṭafā Kāmil to Juliette Adam, Toulouse, 12 Sept. 1895, from *Egyptian-French letters*, p. 4. This collection of letters was edited by Mme Adam and must be used with caution. It would be interesting to know why he chose to write to Mme Adam in particular. Could it be that he wrote letters of this sort to many editors, and that she was the only one to send an encouraging reply?

[7] Ibid., p. 12. Articles by Muṣṭafā appeared in the 15 Oct., 15 Nov., and 15 Dec. 1895 issues of *La Nouvelle Revue*.

[8] *Egyptian-French letters*, p. 16; Rashād, pp. 23 f.

[9] One of whose numerous books on the East was *La Turquie agonisante*, in which he defended the Ottoman Empire against European criticism during the Balkan Wars. He dedicated a book about Egypt, *La mort de Philae*, to Muṣṭafā Kāmil.

of these politically conservative literati supported Muṣṭafā more because they disliked England than out of love for Egyptian nationalism. Yet their support did eventually open to Muṣṭafā the pages of some of the leading Paris newspapers.

In September 1895, however, Muṣṭafā lacked any such entrée into French journalism, and increasingly felt that he was being stymied by Palace intrigues against him, which he believed were being directed by Deloncle, with the object of cutting off his funds and forcing him to return to Egypt.[1] Such delusions of persecution seem to have been an occupational disease of Egyptian nationalists. On 19 September he sent a long report to the khedive, recommending that he be allowed to stay in Europe and use his journalistic contacts (and the Palace's funds) to win some influential French, Russian, and German newspapers to the Egyptian cause. He hoped this would have a greater effect on European public opinion than his earlier idea of forming an Egyptian party in Paris with its own newspaper.[2] He believed that Germany might be persuaded to join France and Russia in pressing Britain to withdraw her forces from Egypt, and predicted that the evacuation would be accomplished within the next sixteen months.[3] The Palace seems not to have provided Muṣṭafā with sufficient aid to stay in Europe, however, and he returned to Egypt in January 1896.

No longer content to be merely one of the khedive's secret agitators among susceptible Europeans, Muṣṭafā now sought to exercise the function hitherto performed by Shaykh 'Alī Yūsuf in *al-Mu'ayyad*, that of winning domestic support for the nationalist programme. Early in 1896 he addressed two public meetings in Alexandria, the first entirely Egyptian, the second composed mainly of European residents. At both he called for the evacuation of British troops from Egypt.[4] Like many more recent nationalists, Muṣṭafā denied any hostility toward foreigners as such. However, his attacks on the *dukhalā'* (intruders), in the speech delivered for domestic consumption, caused some non-Egyptian observers, especially the Syrian editors of *al-Muqaṭṭam*, to question his sincerity. Too little time had passed for the foreign residents of Egypt to have forgotten the Alexandria riots of 1882, generally thought to have been instigated by the leaders of the earlier nationalist movement. Muṣṭafā thereafter took great pains to show that his animosity was directed only at those foreigners who supported the British occupation.[5]

The British in Egypt were very much aware of the growing effervescence

[1] Muṣṭafā Kāmil to Shaykh Aḥmad, Paris, 4 Aug. 1895, from Anīs, pp. 46–51.

[2] As suggested in his letter to Shaykh Aḥmad on 8 June 1895 and approved in the shaykh's reply on the 17th, presumably with the authorization of the khedive.

[3] Muṣṭafā Kāmil to Khedive 'Abbās, Paris, 19 Sept. 1895, from Anīs, pp. 77–85.

[4] A.F.K., vol. iv, pp. 132–50, for text of Arabic speech; ibid., pp. 42–75 for translation of French speech; *Égyptiens et Anglais*, 119–56, 157–84.

[5] This must have seemed a fine distinction. See *al-Mu'ayyad* (7 Mar. 1896). Muṣṭafā's reply is given by A.F.K., vol. iv, pp. 169–74.

of the opposition, encouraged by the clandestine support of Khedive ʿAbbās. Muṣṭafā Kāmil was only one of many troublesome Egyptians, but nationalist sources claim that the British became so disturbed by his activities that they proceeded to demote and intern his brother, ʿAlī, an officer in the Egyptian army, on the grounds that he was spreading dissension among his fellow-officers.[1] Muṣṭafā persuaded the khedive to pardon ʿAlī, which annoyed Kitchener and greatly raised the morale of the nationalists. Muṣṭafā prudently left Egypt before his brother was restored to rank, and resumed his propaganda campaign in Europe.

Although it was Cromer's policy not to interfere with the freedom of the Egyptian press, the British decided to teach the nationalists a lesson when *al-Muʾayyad* published a secret telegram from Kitchener to the minister of War disclosing the number of casualties suffered in the Dongola campaign. The British ordered a criminal investigation of the telegraph-office employee suspected of having divulged the telegram's contents, and of Shaykh ʿAlī Yūsuf as his accomplice. The deputy public prosecutor, Muḥammad Farīd, reported that he could find no proof of the shaykh's complicity, but the British adviser to the minister of Justice insisted that the case must be tried. The final acquittal of the accused men on the grounds of insufficient evidence was regarded as a great victory for the nationalists, although evidence of British efforts to secure their conviction caused much dismay. As a consequence of this judgement, the presiding magistrate and Muḥammad Farīd were transferred from Cairo to the provinces. Farīd's refusal to accept his transfer and consequent resignation from the Parquet helped to launch him on his nationalist career, culminating in his election in 1908 to the presidency of the Nationalist Party, after Muṣṭafā's untimely death.[2]

The history of the nationalist movement during the following decade can be summarized briefly. For reasons soon to be made clear, the nationalist momentum slowed down, and the British did not leave Egypt. Muṣṭafā continued periodically to tour the main European capitals, where he would give interviews to the correspondents of leading newspapers, in which he would exhort the people of the relevant country to press their government to demand the evacuation of the British troops from Egypt and to restore to the khedive

[1] It must be remembered that this occurred at a time when the British were planning the reconquest of the Sudan, and probably some feared the existence of a tie between the nationalists and the Khalīfa. The most complete account of ʿAlī's demotion is his own. See A.F.K., vol. iii, pp. 217–23, and vol. iv, pp. 85–89 and 185–213. For another version, see Wood, pp. 161 f.

[2] On the Telegram Case, which was something of a *cause célèbre* in Nov. 1896, see the following: ʿAbd Allāh ʿInān, 'Baʿḍ al-qaḍāyā al-ṣuḥufiyya al-Miṣriyya: muḥākamat *al-Muʾayyad* fī qaḍiyyat al-tilighrāf,' *al-Kātib al-Miṣrī*, vol. xv (Dec. 1946), pp. 488–96; ʿAbd al-Raḥmān al-Rāfiʿī, *Muḥammad Farīd: ramz al-ikhlāṣ wa al-taḍḥiyya* (2nd edn.; Cairo, 1948), pp. 27–30; el-Hakkani [pseud. ?], 'La vie politique et parlementaire à l'étranger: l'Égypte', *Revue politique et parlementaire*, vol. x. 3 (Dec. 1896), pp. 682–6; Jehan d'Ivray, 'La littérature néo-égyptienne', *Revue des Revues*, vol. xxxi. 19 (1 Oct. 1899), p. 60; Shafīq, vol. II. i, pp. 230 f.

his rights guaranteed to him by the powers themselves. In his interviews and speeches he assured his European audience that the Egyptians were eager to absorb the fundamentals of Western civilization. He disclaimed any xenophobic or anti-Christian feeling, and tried to prove that Egypt was ready for self-government.[1] Muṣṭafā was understandably disappointed when France abandoned her claims to the upper Nile after the Fashoda incident of 1898, but his European campaigns did not cease.

As French interest in the Egyptian Question declined, the Egyptian nationalists looked increasingly to Turkey for support.[2] Although Khedive ʿAbbās had earlier received little encouragement from his Ottoman suzerain, Turkey's defeat of Greece in 1897 seems to have given Sultan Abdülhamid new confidence. Muṣṭafā began to make frequent visits to Istanbul, and sometimes defended Ottoman territorial integrity and Islamic solidarity. The sultan rewarded him with the rank of *Mütemayiz* (Excellency) in 1899 and made him a pasha in 1904, when he was barely thirty. Although sometimes he found the intrigue-ridden atmosphere of the Yıldız Palace oppressive, and once wrote to his brother that he was glad to have left Istanbul 'which has no sweetness except as the citadel of the Muslims and the seat of the Caliph of the believers',[3] he never publicly expressed any disloyalty to the Ottoman Empire. His Ottoman ties, understandable as a tactic in his struggle against Britain's effective control of the Nile valley, rendered him suspect in the eyes of the Syrians (some of whom were beginning to become Arab nationalists) and the Egyptian Copts.

The movement continued for some time to be centred around the Palace, but as Muṣṭafā's personal following grew, his ties with the khedive weakened. The change occurred very gradually. Aḥmad Luṭfī al-Sayyid (1872–1963) recalled in his memoirs that in 1896 Muṣṭafā invited him to join the Society for the Revival of the Nation, of which the khedive was the leader, and that he participated in the decision of the members to reconstitute it as the Nationalist Party, but it remained a secret society headed by ʿAbbās.[4] The nationalists sent Luṭfī to Geneva to acquire Swiss nationality, hence immunity from the native Penal Code, so that he could publish a party newspaper. His association with Muḥammad ʿAbduh, who was *persona ingratissima* at the Palace, caused Luṭfī to break with the nationalists, only to emerge a decade later as the ideologist for a rival party.

Until the end of the century, party activity appears to have been

[1] See, for example, Muṣṭafā's speech at Mme Adam's Paris salon on 18 June 1899, reprinted in *Égyptiens et Anglais*, pp. 209–28. Arabic translation in A.F.K., vol. ix, pp. 143–58.

[2] It is now frequently forgotten that Egyptian nationalists in those days were not Arab nationalists. To a representative of the latter group, like Najīb ʿAzūrī, Turkey was the oppressor, while the Egyptian nationalists courted Ottoman support against the British occupation.

[3] Muṣṭafā Kāmil to ʿAlī Fahmī Kāmil, Vienna, 10 June 1899, from A.F.K., vol. ix, pp. 140 f.

[4] Aḥmad Luṭfī al-Sayyid, *Qiṣṣat ḥayātī* (Cairo, 1962), p. 36. Salāma Mūsā, *The Education of Salāma Mūsā* (tr. by L. O. Schuman; Leiden, 1961), p. 29, lists the founding members as Muṣṭafā Kāmil, Muḥammad Farīd, Muḥammad ʿUthmān, [Maḥmūd] Labīb Muḥarram, Aḥmad Luṭfī al-Sayyid, and Saʿīd al-Shīmī.

Palace-centred, with its views articulated by *al-Mu'ayyad*. While Muṣṭafā used his political and journalistic connexions in Europe and Turkey to win foreign support for Egypt's independence, Shaykh 'Ali Yūsuf used his popular journal to win Egyptians to the cause.[1] As it became increasingly evident that no amount of campaigning would induce the European powers to risk war with Britain over Egypt, Muṣṭafā intensified his appeal to Egyptian public opinion. His growing popularity as a writer and orator gave him a base of support potentially independent of the khedive and 'Alī Yūsuf. The shaykh seems to have realized this, and began to restrict Muṣṭafā's access to the columns of *al-Mu'ayyad*.[2] Muṣṭafā finally decided to publish his own newspaper, *al-Liwā'*, which first appeared on 2 January 1900. The new journal, probably financed in large measure by wealthy nationalists like Farīd, struck out on a bold course almost at once. It attacked the Egyptian ministers for placing restrictions on the Pilgrimage to Mecca and their subservience to their British advisers.[3] Muṣṭafā penned his first appeal for a parliamentary system of government in October 1900, and proceeded to develop his demand for a constitution until it became one of the main points in the party programme.[4] Not surprisingly, *al-Liwā'* soon replaced *al-Mu'ayyad* as the main vehicle for the expression of nationalist opinion.[5] Muṣṭafā and 'Alī Fahmī Kāmil also took control of a new but foundering private school in 1899 and developed it into a flourishing institution.[6] The school, together with *al-Liwā'*, played an important role in disseminating nationalist ideas among Egypt's growing urban middle class.

After the Fashoda Affair, Khedive 'Abbās abandoned hope of using the French to help disembarrass himself of the British, or at least of Cromer.[7] His nationalist fellow-conspirators were increasingly a political liability. Muṣṭafā embarrassed him by sending a letter to Sultan Abdülhamid in

[1] The estimated circulation of *al-Mu'ayyad*, taken by G. Baer, *al-Ṣiḥāfa al-'Arabiyya* (Jerusalem, 1959), from Ilyās Zākhūra, *Mir'at al-'aṣr fī ta'rīkh wa-rusūm akābir al-rijāl bi-Miṣr* (Cairo, 1897), rose from 800 in Dec. 1889 to 2,800 in 1894, 4,000 in 1895, and 6,000 in Aug. 1896.

[2] A.F.K., vol. ix, pp. 126–9; Farīd memoirs, p. 57. References to the Farīd memoirs are to the pagination of the unpublished manuscript, and not to the published version edited by Muḥammad Ṣubayḥ (Cairo, 1964).

[3] Muṣṭafā Kāmil, 'The Government's Aggression against the Nation in Egypt', *al-Liwā'* (13 Jan. 1900), from A.F.K., vol. ix, pp. 236–40.

[4] Muṣṭafā Kāmil, 'The Government and the Nation in Egypt', *al-Liwā'* (5 Oct. 1900). See al-Rāfi'ī, *Muṣṭafā Kāmil, bā'ith al-ḥaraka al-waṭaniyya* (3rd edn.; Cairo, 1950), pp. 164 f.

[5] But its circulation in 1903 was estimated at only 1,500–2,000, as compared with 3,500–4,000 for *al-Muqaṭṭam* and 6,000–7,000 for *al-Mu'ayyad*. Germany, Auswärtiges Amt, Ägyptische Presse, Jenisch to von Bülow, 18 June 1903 (German Foreign Ministry Documents, Microfilm reel no. 38, University of Michigan).

[6] Louis Bertrand, generally critical of oriental pretensions, visited the school in 1906, and praised it highly in *Le Mirage oriental* (Paris, 1909), pp. 364–70.

[7] Muṣṭafā Kāmil wrote to Mme Adam on 21 June 1900 that the khedive could hardly be blamed for not resisting Britain, in view of the Fashoda Affair and Europe's indifference to what the British were doing in the Transvaal. *Egyptian-French Letters*, p. 66.

June 1901 complaining about the unchecked growth of Young Turk activity in Egypt.[1] 'Abbās visited England for the first time in 1900, and began to make his peace with the occupation. Although he may have subsidized *al-Liwā'* for a time, probably to annoy Cromer, it is doubtful that he was prepared to exchange his overbearing but astute mentor for a parliamentary government manipulated by a juvenile demagogue. Meanwhile Shaykh 'Alī Yūsuf continued his rise to prominence by moderating the policy of *al-Mu'ayyad* in tune with the views of the khedive. In 1904 he married, against her father's wishes, the daughter of the *shaykh al-Sādāt*, who vied with the *naqīb al-Ashrāf* for the leadership of the descendants of the Prophet. The khedive supported the marriage, although it scandalized Egyptian Muslim public opinion. When Muṣṭafā chided the khedive for this, 'Abbās retorted that public opinion meant nothing to him: 'If I were to put on a hat and walk around the streets of Cairo, no one would say anything.' Muṣṭafā, to whom public opinion meant everything, became so angry that he announced his break with the khedive in a letter to *al-Ahrām*.[2] It should also be remembered, however, that the Anglo-French *Entente Cordiale*, signed the same year, which ended all hope of French intervention against the British occupation, rendered the nationalists virtually useless to the khedive.

Now Muṣṭafā's writings assumed an increasingly militant Islamic tone.[3] He supported the Ottoman sultan against the British in the Ṭābā Incident in 1906, although his stand opened him to attack for being anti-Egyptian and may have stimulated the formation in Egypt of the initially pro-British, anti-Turkish Umma Party.[4] Japan's unexpected defeat of Russia in 1905 inspired him to write a book praising Japan as a model for Egyptian youth of the virtues of patriotism. Japan's victory was a powerful stimulus, in Egypt as in other countries under European political domination, to the hope of eventual freedom. Muṣṭafā's popularity among Egypt's educated youth grew to the point that he was able to organize a law students' strike in 1906, the first of many in Egypt's recent history. He helped form the Higher Schools Club (*Nādī'l-Madāris al-'Ulyā*),[5] which brought together the students and graduates of Egypt's several professional schools in a distinctly nationalist milieu. He is also credited with having been the first to call for the creation of the Egyptian university.[6]

[1] Shafīq, vol. II. i, p. 348.

[2] Farīd memoirs, p. 1; Shafīq, vol. II. ii, p. 59. Wearing a hat (Ar. *burnayṭa*) would presumably have signified apostasy from Islam, as it is impossible to perform the Muslim prayers while wearing a European-style hat with a brim.

[3] Muṣṭafā commenced a monthly magazine called *al-'Ālam al-Islāmī* (The Islamic World) in 1905.

[4] Jamal Mohammed Ahmed, *The intellectual origins of Egyptian nationalism* (London, 1960), p. 58. It is also true, however, that the party owed much of its impetus to British support and its opposition to the Khedive's autocratic pretensions.

[5] al-Rāfi'ī, *Muṣṭafā Kāmil*, p. 188.

[6] *al-Liwā'* (26 Oct. 1904 and 8 Jan. 1905), cited by al-Rāfi'ī, p. 234. See also *Egyptian-French Letters*, pp. 170, 178, 196, 206.

The Dinshawāy Incident of June 1906 greatly enhanced his political strength both at home and abroad. The propaganda attacks he and his Muslim fellow-journalists had made on the Egyptian government's policy in the Ṭābā Incident seem to have stirred up native Muslims and alarmed the British, who, for the first time since 1882 became aware of the insecurity of their position in Egypt. The hanging of four illiterate peasants and the flogging and imprisonment of many others, in retribution for the death of a British officer following a fracas between the Dinshawāy villagers and a group of officers on a pigeon-shooting expedition, accomplished more for the Egyptian nationalist movement than Muṣṭafā had been able to gain in twelve years of travelling and haranguing. The severe sentences, intended by the British to frighten the 'pan-Islamic agitators' into submissiveness, instead outraged European liberals and gave many hitherto apolitical Egyptians second thoughts about the benefits of the British occupation. Copts as well as Muslims flocked to Muṣṭafā's standard, and even the khedive saw fit to make tentative gestures toward a reconciliation through the Palace physician, Dr. Muḥammad Ṣādiq Ramaḍān (1868–1941), a close friend of the leading nationalists.[1] In October 1906 the khedive met secretly with Muṣṭafā Kāmil, Muḥammad Farīd, Laṭīf Salīm, and Dr. Ramaḍān, and agreed to make the Nationalist Party an open movement and to create a corporation, capitalized at £E20,000, to finance the publication of English and French versions of *al-Liwā'*.[2] The two papers, *The Egyptian Standard* and *L'Étendard Égyptien*, began publication in March 1907, and, although they never gained the influence over their intended public that *al-Liwā'* had on Egyptian opinion, the fact that they lasted for two years, despite heavy losses for their stockholders (and their European staffs, which frequently went unpaid), is indicative of the strength of nationalist feeling at this time.

The uproar caused by the Dinshawāy executions finally led the Liberal government in Britain to announce a new policy designed to prepare the Egyptians for self-government as quickly as possible, to be implemented by a new consul-general. In May 1907 Cromer retired because of ill-health, and Sir Eldon Gorst, the former financial adviser and a close friend of the khedive, replaced him. Cromer's exodus was hailed as a triumph by the nationalists and their supporters;[3] ironically, his successor's policies ultimately led them to ruin.

Muṣṭafā's success as a popular leader stimulated the efforts of other would-be leaders to counter his influence. Possibly his own vanity, which led him to consider himself the sole spokesman for the nation, alienated articulate Egyptians who might otherwise have co-operated with him.[4] But it is also true that the

[1] Farīd memoirs, p. 1.
[2] Ibid., Shafīq, vol. II. ii, p. 103.
[3] Notably Wilfrid Scawen Blunt, *My diaries* (1-vol. edn.; London, 1932), p. 581.
[4] Ibid., p. 592. Blunt is giving the opinion of Muṣṭafā Kāmil expressed by Ḥāfiẓ 'Awaḍ.

interests of the various classes of Egyptian society were much too diverse for Muṣṭafā to represent all of them. In March 1907 a group of wealthy landowners, probably backed by Cromer, founded a daily newspaper called *al-Jarīda* and named the ex-nationalist Luṭfī al-Sayyid as editor.

Muṣṭafā regarded *al-Jarīda* with considerable suspicion because of what seemed to him to be its Anglophile tendencies. He also realized that his own health was failing and that he would have to put his party on a firm organizational footing in case of his own death. He resumed his efforts to gain European support in the summer of 1907, but found himself stymied by political developments in Egypt. No sooner had Gorst reached Cairo than he began to woo the khedive away from the nationalists. ʿAbbās, who had never entirely trusted Muṣṭafā, sent a mission to London headed by a journalist named Ḥāfiẓ ʿAwaḍ (1877–1950). ʿAwaḍ made a speech at a political banquet urging the British to meet the more moderate demands of the nationalists, but soft-pedalling the question of the evacuation of the British troops. Muṣṭafā was outraged at what he took to be the duplicity of the khedive,[1] and the lines of political division began to form.

In September 1907 the Umma Party was founded by a group of wealthy notables, prominent government officials, and young intellectuals, and *al-Jarīda* became its official mouthpiece. Its programme was essentially moderate, calling for co-operation with the British, rejection of pan-Islamic appeals and discreet opposition to the khedive. Ḥasan ʿAbd al-Rāziq was its first president, and Maḥmūd Sulaymān replaced him after his death. Among the members or supporters of the Umma Party were Aḥmad Fatḥī Zaghlūl (and, unofficially at least, his brother Saʿd), ʿAbd al-ʿAzīz Fahmī, Ṭalʿat Ḥarb, ʿAlī Shaʿrāwī, and Ḥamad al-Bāsil. Many later became members of the Wafd.

Muṣṭafā Kāmil returned from Europe in October, and delivered a stirring address at Alexandria, proclaiming the existence of the Nationalist Party with the objectives of the immediate evacuation of British troops from Egyptian soil and the grant of a constitution by the khedive. He invited the Copts to join Egypt's Muslims under the nationalist banner,[2] pledged his party to respect Egypt's financial and treaty obligations (and the rights of foreign residents as guaranteed by the Capitulations) and to seek friendly relations with all the European powers and with the Ottoman Empire.[3]

The first general assembly of the Nationalist Party met at the headquarters of *al-Liwāʾ* on 27 December, debated and approved the draft of the party by-laws, elected officers and a thirty-member administrative committee,

[1] Muṣṭafā Kāmil to Dr. Ṣādiq Ramaḍān, Neuhausen, Switzerland, 23 Aug. 1907, from the private collection of Captain Jaʿfar Ṣādiq Ramaḍān, Heliopolis, U.A.R.

[2] Two of his leading disciples, Wīṣā Wāṣif and Murqus Ḥanna, were Copts, but their influence on the formation of Nationalist policy seems to have been negligible.

[3] The Nationalist Party's ten-point programme can be found in J. Alexander, *The truth about Egypt* (London, 1911), pp. 121–3; Fritz Steppat, *Nationalismus und Islam bei Muṣṭafā Kāmil* (Leiden, 1956), pp. 338 f.; Juliette Adam, *Angleterre en Égypte* (Paris, 1922), pp. 195–7.

which was to meet once a month. Conditions for party membership were laid down, and provision was made for an annual general assembly, open to all members. It was resolved that a Nationalist Party Club be established in Cairo, and that the party set up branch committees in the various districts of the capital, in Alexandria, and in the provinces. The party made *al-Liwā'* its official organ on matters concerning its activities.[1]

In December a third party, usually called the Constitutional Reform Party (*Ḥizb al-Iṣlāḥ 'ala'l-Mabādi' al-Dustūriyya*), was formed as a Palace body. Shaykh 'Alī Yūsuf was its president and *al-Mu'ayyad* its newspaper. Although many members of the khedivial family joined,[2] Khedive 'Abbās did not publicly commit himself to its support as long as Muṣṭafā Kāmil was alive.[3] Like its president, 'destitute of fixed principles',[4] the Reform Party strove neither to formulate an ideology nor to win a mass following.

So small was the following of the Umma and Reform Parties, and so talented was Muṣṭafā in articulating popular feelings (albeit without a concrete programme of social reform) and in organizing a mass movement, that his party might possibly have become the vehicle whereby Egypt attained her independence, had it not been for his untimely death on 10 February 1908, at a time when the Nationalists[5] were barely organized centrally and certainly not locally, and when the change in British policy had begun to rearrange the constellation of Egypt's political forces. The enormous number of Egyptians who followed Muṣṭafā's coffin through the streets of Cairo to his final resting-place certainly testified to the popularity of the leader, but could this be transformed into devotion to his principles?

At a special meeting on 14 February the members of the Nationalist Party unanimously elected Muḥammad Farīd, Muṣṭafā's most devoted follower, as his successor. While Farīd was a man of unquestioned sincerity and came from a family having a long tradition of service to Egypt,[6] he lacked the intelligence, decisiveness, and personal magnetism of his predecessor. Clouds of distrust, almost paranoiac in character, darkened the onset of his presidency. He suspected 'Alī Fahmī Kāmil of intriguing to get himself elected as his

[1] This distinction proved noteworthy later when Shaykh Shāwīsh attacked the Copts on its pages, whereupon the corporation of *al-Liwā'* held an extraordinary meeting, at which it resolved that everything published in *al-Liwā'*, unless attributed to the party, was to be considered the opinion of the paper; *al-Liwā'* (1 July 1908).

[2] Alexander, p. 128.

[3] The khedive met regularly with Muṣṭafā Kāmil until the latter's death. Farīd memoirs, p. 3. Ḥasan Ḥusnī Kāmil, Muṣṭafā's youngest brother, claims that 'Abbās visited Muṣṭafā during his final illness. The important point is that the khedive was reluctant to commit himself to a party opposed to the Nationalists until he was certain that he had nothing to lose by doing so.

[4] Alexander, p. 127.

[5] From this point, 'Nationalist' (with a capital initial) refers to the Nationalist Party.

[6] Aḥmad Farīd (1836–1901), Muḥammad's father, served three khedives in various capacities, finally becoming the director of the khedivial estates (*al-Dā'ira al-Saniyya*). The family was originally Turkish, but had come to Egypt shortly after the Ottoman conquest, and had held a hereditary post in the Egyptian mint.

brother's successor, aided by the khedive, who believed that Farīd (who was independently wealthy) could not be bought.[1] Farīd soon refused to accept any financial aid from the khedive, and announced in his first speech that the party would present a petition to His Highness demanding a constitution.[2] In response to attacks by *al-Mu'ayyad*, Farīd decided to increase the mass appeal of *al-Liwā'* (and also weaken the position of 'Alī Fahmī Kāmil, who had inherited the administration of the paper) by appointing Shaykh 'Abd al-'Azīz Shāwīsh (Jāwīsh) (1876–1929), an inspector of religious instruction in the Ministry of Education, as its new editor.[3] The son of a Tunisian immigrant to Alexandria, trained at al-Azhar and Borough Road Teachers' Training College, Shaykh Shāwīsh was more a pan-Islamist than an Egyptian nationalist. His critics, notably the late 'Abbās Maḥmūd al-'Aqqād, believed that he accepted the editorship of *al-Liwā'* to attack the minister of Education, Sa'd Zaghlūl, who had passed him over in favour of a relative when he appointed a director to the new Sharī'a Judges' School.[4]

When Farīd left for Europe to resume Muṣṭafā's campaign, Shāwīsh promptly got the newspaper into trouble, first with the Egyptian government by printing a rumour, which proved untrue, about the summary execution of seventy Sudanese rebels, and then with the party moderates by answering some editorials in *al-Waṭan* with a violent diatribe that offended the Copts. Shāwīsh was brought to trial for the first offence, but acquitted on the ground that he had printed the news about the executions in good faith. His acquittal was hailed as a Nationalist triumph, but it set in motion the successful campaign of Gorst and the Egyptian moderates to reimpose limitations on Egyptian press freedom.

That summer Ismā'īl Abāẓa headed a delegation of members of the General Assembly (Egypt's quasi-representative, consultative body) to London to ask the Foreign Office to institute some constitutional reforms. Although two of the members were Nationalists, Farīd criticized the mission, and suspected the khedive of sending it to undermine his party leadership.[5] He proceeded to ask the khedive, in the columns of *al-Liwā'*, to put an end to rumours that he was trying to destroy the Nationalist movement, an act that angered some of his more moderate supporters.[6]

The Nationalists suffered another setback when the Committee of Union and Progress, which they had long opposed, forced Sultan Abdülhamid to restore the suspended Ottoman Constitution. The Nationalists quickly

[1] Farīd memoirs, p. 4.

[2] al-Rāfi'ī, *Muḥammad Farīd*, p. 54.

[3] Farīd had met Shaykh Shāwīsh at the 1905 Congress of Orientalists, and had introduced him to Muṣṭafā Kāmil. They offered Shāwīsh the editorship of *al-Liwā'*, but he insisted on a five-year contract, which Muṣṭafā would not give. After Muṣṭafā's death, however, Farīd offered him the desired contract at £E40 per month. Farīd memoirs, pp. 45 f.

[4] al-'Aqqād, *Sa'd Zaghlūl*, pp. 133–5. The reader should be warned, however, that 'Aqqād never had any love for Shāwīsh.

[5] Farīd memoirs, p. 5.

[6] Muḥammad Farīd, 'Mādhā yaqūlūn', *al-Liwā'* (30 Sept. 1908).

veered around to support Turkish constitutionalism, even to the point of claiming that Egypt was entitled to representation in the Ottoman Parliament, but the Young Turks responded by disclaiming any ties with the Nationalists and praising Britain's work in Egypt.[1]

Even some party members opposed Farīd, mainly for criticizing the khedive, but also for tolerating Shāwīsh, whose articles were thought to appeal to a lower class of reader. ʿUmar Sulṭān, who had contributed large sums to the *Standard* and *L'Étendard*, and had been elected party treasurer as a reward, resigned his post and, under the influence of his attorney, Ṭalʿat Ḥarb, cut off all aid to the Nationalists.[2] The European newspapers soon went bankrupt and had to be discontinued. In November the editorial staff and printers of *al-Liwā'* went out on strike. Farīd suspected that they had the khedive's financial support.[3] The khedive's appointment of Buṭrus Ghālī as prime minister, although he was reputedly the main advocate of a *rapprochement* between the Palace and the British, was another bitter pill for the Nationalists.

On the more positive side, however, the Nationalist Party continued to gain new supporters,[4] organized its branch committees,[5] drew up a reply to the first Gorst report, obtained the endorsement of the Legislative Council for its constitutional demands, collected funds for the Ḥijāz Railway, the statue of Muṣṭafā Kāmil and a memorial *kuttāb* for Dinshawāy,[6] and began to set up night-schools for workers. Several new Nationalist newspapers were founded: *Wādī'l-Nīl* (Alexandria, daily), *Miṣr al-Fatāt* (Cairo, daily) and *al-Quṭr al-Miṣrī* (Cairo, weekly).

The growing strength and vehemence of the Nationalist press led the Buṭrus Ghālī ministry, backed by the British, to restore the 1881 Press Law, which Cromer had allowed to fall into desuetude. The Nationalists responded with press attacks and mass protest demonstrations, but to no avail. *Miṣr al-Fatāt* tried to gain immunity by placing itself under a German owner, while *al-Liwā'* named Dr. Manṣūr Rifʿat, who claimed American citizenship, as its political director. Although many of the Capitulatory Powers refused to admit the application of the Press Law to their own nationals in Egypt (thus one can see why the Nationalists supported the Capitulations, seem-

[1] Great Britain, F.O., Series 371, vol. 449, Lowther to Grey, Therapia, 28 Aug. 1908, no. 522 (30958/08); and vol. 541, Graham to Grey, Cairo, 27 Sept. 1908, no. 95 (34152/08).

[2] Farīd memoirs, p. 12.

[3] Ibid., p. 10.

[4] *al-Liwā'* (10 Oct. 1908). The administrative board announced that it had accepted 364 new members into the party in Sept. 1908, as against only one resignation.

[5] *al-Liwā'* (21 Dec. 1908).

[6] Muḥammad Farīd's speech before the Nationalists' general assembly, printed in *al-Liwā'* (25 Dec. 1908). The Dinshawāy *kuttāb*, largely paid for by British Liberals and especially Blunt, was never built. The statue, however, was carved by Leopold Savine, brought to Egypt in 1914, erected at the Muṣṭafā Kāmil School in 1921, and moved in 1940 to its present site in the middle of Cairo.

ingly a paradoxical position for them to take), neither the German nor the American consul did anything to help the Nationalists.[1] The Egyptian authorities reacted to the Nationalists' uprisings and subterfuges by suspending *al-Quṭr al-Miṣrī* and imprisoning its editor, Aḥmad Ḥilmī, for libelling the khedive. In August they warned *al-Liwā'* for printing an encomium on the Indian assassin of Sir Curzon Wyllie, and imprisoned Shāwīsh for an article attacking Buṭrus Ghālī and Aḥmad Fatḥī Zaghlūl for their role in the Dinshawāy trials three years before. The Nationalist Party seemed to be headed away from respectability toward revolution, but with neither a competent leader nor a revolutionary ideology.

Farīd travelled twice to Turkey in 1909 to express his party's support of the Ottoman Constitution and to cement political ties with the C.U.P., but with indifferent success.[2] The Egyptian students in Europe convoked a Young Egyptian Congress in Geneva in September. They invited representatives of the three principal Egyptian parties, and also some European sympathizers. One of these was Keir Hardie, whose speech contained an implied criticism of extremist tactics and angered many of the Nationalists, who concluded that the Congress was in the hands of their enemies.[3]

At home the party continued to grow in size (although not in social respectability), and generated more branch committees, night-schools, and significantly, secret societies.[4] After a period of calm, due to Shāwīsh's imprisonment and to the façade of unity presented by the three parties at the Geneva Congress, the Nationalist press resumed its vehement agitation, directed in particular against the scheme, introduced by the Suez Canal Company and supported by the Egyptian government and its British advisers, to extend the expiration date of the company's concession from 1968 to 2008. On 20 February 1910 Buṭrus Ghālī, who had been attacked in the Nationalist press for supporting the concession's extension, was shot by a Muslim druggist named al-Wardānī. The assassin, who appeared perfectly sane and made no attempt to hide his guilt, turned out to belong to a secret society which advocated the use of violent tactics to achieve Nationalist goals. The Nationalists quickly denied any knowledge of the society, but in fact al-Wardānī was a member of the party, and the reasons he gave for killing Buṭrus corresponded with

[1] Alexander, pp. 256–8.

[2] In Oct. 1909, for example, the Ottoman grand vezir gave an interview to the correspondent of *Le Temps*, saying that the Ottoman government had no relations with the Egyptian Nationalists and did not wish to have any. Alexander, p. 282.

[3] One of the student participants in the Congress, Luṭfī Jum'a, wrote in his diary that he managed to gain the floor after Keir Hardie's speech and answer it point by point, after which the students demonstrated in Jum'a's favour. Farīd later told Blunt that the khedive had used Muḥammad Fahmī, the president of the Congress, to weaken the Nationalists. Blunt, *My diaries*, p. 693.

[4] Great Britain, F.O. 371, vol. 890, Gorst to Grey, Cairo, 17 Apr. 1910 (13882/10), contains the attorney-general's report on one of these secret societies, *al-Taḍāmun al-Akhawī*, describing its evolution from an association for mutual exhortation with respect to scholastic duties into a conspiratorial organization.

those for which the late premier had been attacked in the Nationalist press. The British accordingly ignored Farīd's protestations and proceeded to investigate the party and its activities. They found that the Nationalist movement had become riddled with conspiratorial societies, plotting far more direct action against the British occupation (and especially the Egyptians supporting it) than anything ever publicly preached by Muṣṭafā Kāmil.[1]

Although the Nationalists scored a triumph when Muḥammad Sa'īd, supposedly sympathetic to the movement, succeeded Buṭrus Ghālī, and another when the General Assembly voted overwhelmingly to reject the extension of the Suez concession, the party's fortunes began to decline rapidly in 1910. A split developed when several of Muṣṭafā's heirs sued the corporation of *al-Liwā'* and obtained a favourable judgement (only eight days after the assassination) putting the newspaper under judicial sequestration. Farīd refused to submit to the orders of the sequestrator, severed the party's connexion with *al-Liwā'*, and founded a new party organ, *al-'Alam*.[2] The resulting journalistic confusion, enhanced by the suspension of *al-'Alam* after a fortnight and the subsequent adoption of *al-Sha'b* as its mouthpiece during the suspension period, reduced the party's influence by dividing it into two warring camps. Sooner or later, however, the majority crossed over from *al-Liwā'* to the faction of *al-'Alam*.[3]

Farīd went to Europe again in 1910, and spent most of the summer writing articles, making speeches, and preparing for the Egyptian Nationalist Congress, which was to be held in Paris (free from the influence of the Young Egyptian Congress Committee in Geneva) in September. The French, apparently on the advice of their consul-general in Cairo,[4] banned the Congress. The participants, including a number of Europeans, had to move to Brussels, where their proceedings had far less impact.[5]

Meanwhile in Cairo a proof-reader for *al-'Alam*, Shaykh 'Alī al-Ghāyātī, published a *dīwān* of patriotic verse with laudatory prefaces by both Farīd and Shāwīsh. When he discovered that the Egyptian government regarded his verse as outrageously seditious, he fled the country in disguise. The British in Egypt, determined not to allow a recrudescence of Nationalist agitation to cause another assassination, and embarrassed by attacks that summer by ex-President Theodore Roosevelt and by Conservative M.P.s against the Liberal policies which Gorst had been administering for the last

[1] See also the report submitted on the secret societies in Egypt by the Secret Service Bureau of the Ministry of the Interior, in Great Britain, F.O. 371, vol. 1114, Cheetham to Grey, Ramleh, 30 June 1911, secret and confidential (26809/11).

[2] Farīd memoirs, p. 13.

[3] The vacillation of 'Ali Fahmī Kāmil and even of Shaykh Shāwīsh is best described by *The Egyptian Gazette* (3 and 4 Mar. 1910).

[4] France, Ministère des Affaires Etrangères, Egypte: Politique Intérieure, Dossier Général, vol. iv (May–Dec. 1910), pp. 91 f. Ribot to Pichon, Cairo, 30 Aug. 1910, no. 368.

[5] Its proceedings were printed in a volume entitled *Œuvres du Congrès National Égyptien tenu à Bruxelles du 22 au 24 septembre 1910* (Brussels, 1910).

three years, decided to teach the Nationalists a lesson by putting Farīd and Shāwīsh on trial. Shāwīsh was given a three-month sentence, which he served. Farīd's trial was postponed until his return from Europe, which he delayed until the year's end. He was then tried and, despite his objection that he had never read the book, was found guilty and given a six-month sentence.

The assassination of Buṭrus Ghālī, a Copt, by al-Wardānī, a Muslim, had reopened the confessional press polemics. Gorst, by opposing such extreme demands as the institution of Sunday as the public day of rest instead of Friday, soon found himself hounded even more by the Copts than he already was being attacked by the Muslims. Both groups held Congresses early in 1911, and although the Nationalists did not join either *en bloc*, their two best-known Copts (now disaffected) attended the one at Asyūṭ, while the 'Egyptian' Congress at Heliopolis included such Nationalists as Shaykh Shāwīsh, Maḥmūd Abu'l-Naṣr, Ḥāfiẓ Ramaḍān and ʿAlī al-Shamsī as featured speakers. It was clear, however, that control of the Muslim Congress was in the hands of the moderates.[1]

Sir Eldon Gorst, who had served as British consul for four turbulent years, became ill and died in July 1911. Often accused of spinelessness by his contemporaries, he successfully weakened the Nationalist Party by detaching the khedive from it, whereupon the growing extremism of Muṣṭafā Kāmil's successors deprived the party of many of its most prosperous supporters. Gorst's *entente* with the khedive proved in the end to be a mixed blessing for the British, however, as it drove the Umma Party, which might conceivably have become a progressive but moderate movement, into a coalition with the Nationalists.

The appointment of Kitchener, whom the khedive had disliked since the 1894 Frontier Incident, as Gorst's successor had little immediate effect on the demoralized Nationalists. There is no evidence that they tried to resume their old Palace ties. The country's attention was diverted (just as Kitchener arrived in Cairo) by the Italian attack on Tripoli, and the Nationalists began a public subscription to aid the Ottoman defence effort. After *al-ʿAlam* was again suspended in December 1911, Shaykh Shāwīsh left Egypt, first to help smuggle arms into Tripoli, later to become editor of the C.U.P.'s Arabic newspapers.

Farīd also fled Egypt, after having been summoned before the Parquet to answer questions about the speech he had made at the party's general assembly in March 1912, criticizing the Egyptian government on the inadequacies of its economic and social policies.[2] Sentenced *in absentia* to a year's hard labour, Farīd chose not to return to Egypt. He spent five months in

[1] The Congress had the blessing of the British, and Riyāḍ Pasha served as its president. Its proceedings were also printed, as *Majmūʿat aʿmāl al-muʾtamar al-Miṣrī al-awwal al-munʿaqad bi-Hilyubulis* (Cairo, 1911).

[2] Complete text given in al-Rāfiʿī, *Muḥammad Farīd*, pp. 262–9.

Istanbul, where he quarrelled with Shāwīsh for not printing in the C.U.P. papers some of his articles attacking the khedive,[1] and tried to deny rumours that he was secretly taking money from His Highness.[2] After the Anglophile Kâmil Pasha became grand vezir, Farīd left Istanbul for Paris, where he published an article in *Le Siècle* accusing ʿAbbās of conspiring with the British to establish himself as an Arab caliph independent of the sultan.[3] The subsequent arrest at the Alexandria Customs of Aḥmad Mukhtār, an Egyptian student at the Istanbul Medical School, with a suitcase full of violently anti-khedivial leaflets (written, he alleged, by Shāwīsh or Farīd) seemed to portend new repression for the Nationalist Party. Its administrative board met and decided under the pressure of some of its more moderate members to ask Farīd to resign. Farīd, who had fled by this time to Switzerland to avoid extradition to Egypt in connexion with the Mukhtār affair, submitted his resignation, but it was never acted upon.[4]

The activities of the Nationalists in Egypt after 1912 are very obscure. After a brief recrudescence under the direction of ʿAlī Fahmī Kāmil, *al-Liwā'* was suppressed in September 1912, and was found to be practically bankrupt.[5] *al-ʿAlam* was banned two months later for printing an article by Farīd (mailed from Brussels) attacking Kâmil Pasha. *Wādī'l-Nīl* and *Miṣr al-Fatāt* had already been suppressed, which left the Nationalists only *al-Shaʿb*, edited by Amīn and ʿAbd al-Raḥmān al-Rāfiʿī, who had to write with great caution to avert the fate of the other newspapers.

The focus of Nationalist activity moved to Europe, where Farīd made his headquarters in Geneva, edited a pan-Islamic magazine, and travelled in genteel poverty from one group of Egyptian students to another, helping them to organize chapters of the crypto-Nationalist Sphinx Society. Several assassination plots, one directed against the khedive in 1911,[6] one against Muḥammad Saʿīd in 1912,[7] and one against Kitchener in 1913,[8] were attributed to Egyptian students in Europe, and finally the Egyptian government appointed supervisors to watch their activities.

Meanwhile the khedive, increasingly annoyed by Kitchener's restrictions on his freedom of action, began working through his agents in Europe to re-establish contact with Farīd.[9] He even paid Farīd's mistress, Aziza de Roche-

[1] Farīd memoirs, p. 17.
[2] Ibid., pp. 23–26.
[3] Mohamed Farid, 'La lutte du Khédive contre le Sultan pour le Khalifa [sic]', *Le Siècle* (14 Aug. 1912).
[4] ʿAlī Fahmī Kāmil to Farīd, Cairo, 13 Sept. 1912; Ibid., 8 Jan. 1913; ʿAbd al-Malik Ḥamza to Farīd, Cairo, 20 Jan. 1913.
[5] ʿAlī Fahmī Kāmil, to Farīd, Cairo, 11 Aug. 1912; Great Britain, F.O. 371, vol. 1364, Cheetham to Grey, Cairo, 9 Sept. 1912, no. 96 (38794/12).
[6] France. Ministère des Affaires Étrangères, Égypte: Politique Intérieure, Dossier Général, vol. v, pp. 2–15.
[7] Great Britain, F.O. 371, vol. 1363, Kitchener to Grey, Cairo, 3 July 1912, teleg. no. 38 (28284/12).
[8] Farīd memoirs, pp. 26 f., 48.
[9] Ibid., p. 54.

brune, whom Farīd suspected (probably unjustly) of spying for the khedive against him, to come to Cairo in December 1913, but he never saw her.[1] After the death of ʿAlī Yūsuf in October 1913, the khedive began to look for a new Palace journalist. He tried to win the support of Amīn al-Rāfiʿī with a £E1,000 contribution to *al-Shaʿb*, which did revive somewhat in 1914 and also began backing the khedive.[2] There are even signs that the Nationalist Party itself, riven by factional strife since the attempted dismissal of Farīd in 1912, was coming to life.[3] After the First World War broke out, however, it was forced underground by the declaration of martial law in Egypt.

The outbreak of the war was a windfall for Farīd, as it enabled him to put himself in the service of Turkey against the British. Khedive ʿAbbās, recuperating in Istanbul after an unsuccessful attempt on his life by a demented Nationalist (allegedly an agent of Shāwīsh or even the C.U.P.), was informed by the British ambassador that he would not be allowed to return to Egypt. Farīd hastened to Istanbul to effect a reconciliation with ʿAbbās, whom he tried to bring into Turkey's plans for an assault on the British in Egypt. He found himself opposed by the grand vezir, Mehmed Said Halim Pasha, who wanted to use the Egyptian campaign to promote his own claim to the khedivate,[4] and by Cemal Pasha, the commander of the campaign. The khedive was not allowed to accompany Cemal to the Egyptian front. Just as the British were announcing his deposition for collaborating with their enemies, Khedive ʿAbbās left Turkey for Vienna and then Switzerland, where he spent the next two years trying not to commit himself to either side, and embezzling large sums provided by the Germans to purchase controlling shares in the leading Paris newspapers through his financial agent, Bolo Pasha.[5]

Farīd followed the khedive to Switzerland, where he tried to prevent him from making a complete break with Turkey. Because of his loyalty to ʿAbbās, Farīd was attacked by Halim Pasha, who tried to turn the other Nationalists in Europe against him, notably Shaykh Shāwīsh, who was now in Berlin, and Fu'ād Salīm, who was appointed Ottoman ambassador in Berne.[6] Farīd went to Istanbul in February 1916 to try to counter rumours that he had turned against the C.U.P., but failed to overcome the suspicions of the increasingly influential minister of the Interior, Talât Bey.[7] Upon returning to Geneva, he began to consider retiring from politics, and even going to Vichy for his health until the war ended.[8] Instead, however, he went to

[1] Ibid., pp. 62 f., 79 f.

[2] Ibid., pp. 77 f.

[3] Aḥmad Wafīq to Farīd, Fāqūs (Egypt), 17 June 1914.

[4] Farīd memoirs, *passim*. Muḥammad Saʿīd Ḥalīm (Mehmed Said Halim) (1865–1921) was the son of Prince Muḥammad ʿAbd al-Ḥalīm and the grandson of Muḥammad ʿAlī. His father had lost his place in the khedivial succession when Ismāʿīl made the position hereditary on the basis of primogeniture.

[5] Farīd memoirs, pp. 155 f.; Shafīq, vol. iii, pp. 38–46.

[6] Farīd memoirs, p. 182.

[7] Ibid., pp. 182–98.

[8] Farīd to Aziza de Rochebrune, Rheinfelden (Switzerland), 25 Sept. 1916; Farīd memoirs, p. 213.

Berlin in 1917. He eventually persuaded Enver Pasha, the member of the C.U.P. triumvirate most sympathetic to the Egyptian Nationalists, to finance a committee in Stockholm to co-ordinate the party's activities, and Farīd went there to attend the Socialist Congress and to issue a monthly bulletin.[1] He ended his quarrel with Shakykh Shāwīsh, who was living in Berlin and publishing *Die islamische Welt* for the C.U.P., and admitted him to membership in the Nationalist Party.[2] Together with other exiled Nationalists, they were even able to hold rump sessions of the administrative board.[3]

The khedive, deserted by most of the Nationalists because of his vacillating policy, despaired of reaching an agreement with the British and returned late in 1917 to Istanbul, where he put himself in the service of the Ottoman propaganda effort.[4] When he came to Berlin in July 1918, an agreement was finally reached by all the groups opposed to the British occupation of Egypt, but by this time the German war effort was crumbling, and Turkey was practically out of the war.[5]

Although Farīd made efforts to communicate during the war with Nationalist secret societies in Egypt and to send in propaganda, it is doubtful that the emigré Nationalists had any significant bearing on the formation of the Wafd or the outbreak of the 1919 revolution. Farīd was suspicious of the fact that most of its leaders had been members of the Umma Party, and was sceptical of their devotion to the cause of Egypt's liberation.[6] Although he wired Sa'd Zaghlūl and offered his assistance, Farīd was not admitted to the Wafd, because Sa'd felt that he had been discredited by his Turco-German connexions and his association with the ex-khedive, whose reputation in Europe had suffered from his role in the Bolo affair.[7]

The *Waṭanī* Nationalists in Egypt were divided as to what policy they should follow concerning the Wafd, even though they tended to support the March 1919 revolution. Amīn al-Rāfi'ī became secretary of the Wafd's central committee and supported the Wafdist line in *al-Akhbār*. Others, however, tried to form their own delegation to the Paris Peace Conference. They desisted when the Wafd agreed to accept two Nationalist Party members. The *Waṭanī* Nationalists proceeded to delegate Aḥmad Luṭfī and Muṣṭafā al-Shūrbajī, two of their most uncompromising leaders, but the Wafd refused to accept them.[8] The Nationalists who did join the Wafd, such as Muṣṭafā

[1] Farīd memoirs, pp. 247 f. [2] Ibid., p. 265. [3] Ibid.

[4] Ibid., pp. 263 f.; Aḥmad Farīd to Muḥammad Farīd, Geneva, 3 Oct. 1917; Muḥammad Farīd to Ismā'īl Labīb, Berlin, 15 Sept. 1917; Shafīq, vol. iii, pp. 154–88; Elie Kedourie, *England and the Middle East* (London, 1956), p. 107.

[5] Shafīq, vol. iii, pp. 208–14, describes the khedive's *rapprochement* with the Nationalists in Istanbul in Jan. 1918. For the khedive's Berlin visit in July–Aug. 1918, it is necessary to see the Farīd memoirs, p. 284.

[6] Farīd memoirs, p. 304.

[7] Sa'd Zaghlūl to 'Abd al-Raḥmān Fahmī, Paris, 7 Nov. 1919, from Muḥammad Anīs, *Dirāsāt fī wathā'iq thawrat 1919* (Cairo, 1963), vol. i, p. 238.

[8] Maḥmūd Abu'l-Fatḥ, *al-Mas'ala al-Miṣriyya wa'l-Wafd* (Cairo, n.d.), p. 48.

al-Naḥḥās, had not been important in the party's inner councils. The *Waṭanī* leaders, some of whom had spent the war years in Egyptian prisons, reiterated their party's traditional refusal to countenance negotiations with the British until their troops had left Egyptian soil. Farīd himself had practically given up hope of co-operating with the Wafd by the time he died in Berlin in November 1919.

Although the *Waṭanī* Nationalists remained active as individuals in Europe and as a party in Egypt until all political parties were abolished after the 1952 revolution, they ceased to constitute an important bloc in Egyptian politics after the rise of the Wafd and the death of Farīd, which makes 1919 the most convenient terminal date for this study.

Why did the Nationalist Party of Muṣṭafā Kāmil and Muḥammad Farīd not become the movement by which Egypt actually gained her political independence from Britain? Would the Nationalists have succeeded if Muṣṭafā had lived longer, or if Farīd had been a more charismatic leader? Egyptians, like most other Mediterranean peoples, admire gifted orators, but they also seek leaders with a political programme couched in acceptable terms and promising solutions to their grievances. Was the programme formulated by Muṣṭafā Kāmil one that could inspire the Egyptian people once he had departed from the scene? His first point, the political independence of Egypt from Britain, was one on which most articulate Egyptians probably could agree in 1908, although they did not all agree with the Nationalists on how quickly or by what means their national sovereignty should be attained. As the preceding narrative makes clear, most Nationalists most of the time hoped that Britain could be persuaded to leave Egypt. No one (except perhaps Farīd in his March 1912 speech, and by then it was too late) stopped to consider what political independence might mean when Egypt depended on Britain as the chief buyer of her main cash-crop, cotton. Nor did the predominantly civilian Nationalists ever ask how Egypt, given her geographical position, controlling a strategic maritime passage between Europe and south Asia, would have defended herself against a foreign power determined to seize the Suez Canal.

Did the Nationalists want complete independence, even from the Ottoman Empire, still Egypt's nominal suzerain, or were their pan-Islamic views too strong for them to contemplate a break with the sultan-caliph? This question was of great significance to the Nationalists, who tended to defend their position on tactical grounds. Britain was their enemy; by supporting whatever group, the Hamidians or the C.U.P., had control of the Ottoman government, the Nationalists hoped that the Turks would persuade or force the British to leave Egypt. What then? For Muṣṭafā Kāmil, more than for Farīd or Shāwīsh, the Nile valley constituted a nation, most of whose inhabitants happened to be Muslims. But Muṣṭafa (and Farīd) used to stress their liberal nationalism whenever Europeans were listening, and resort to Islamic appeals for native consumption. As we have seen, they often reiterated their loyalty to the Ottoman sultan. Muṣṭafā exulted in Turkey's defeat of Greece in 1897, even though Egypt had no share in the victory. Farīd opposed the Arabs who favoured separation from the Ottoman Empire. He and Shāwīsh both laboured on behalf of Turkey both before and during the First World War.

What else could the Nationalists offer? For a Westerner, the idea of a parliamentary government with a responsible ministry is appealing, until one pauses to consider the economic and social condition of Egypt before 1914. Despite great advances in the standard of living and in Egypt's network of transport and communications (not paralleled, unfortunately, by an adequate expansion of the system of public instruction), most Egyptians were still very poor and ignorant. Less than ten per cent. of the adult population was literate. Most Egyptians probably did not know what a constitution was.[1] Even in Cairo, most Egyptians eligible to vote in the 1908 General Assembly elections refused to go to the polls.[2] Even if we omit consideration of Egypt's experience under parliamentary government from 1924 to 1952, could a European constitution have functioned effectively in Egypt despite inter-party wrangling of the sort experienced from 1907 to 1909, to say nothing of the endless struggles within the Nationalist Party?

Indeed, the party organization itself had serious weaknesses. Patterned in theory after the parliamentary parties of Europe, in fact the Nationalist Party's major decisions were not made by a majority vote of the general assembly in the glare of the public eye, or even by its elected representatives on the administrative board, but by the president and a small clique of advisers meeting in secret session. Their authority was frequently weakened by the intrigues of other Nationalists. One need only consider the origins of the Nationalist Party as a secret, Palace-based conspiracy against the British, a fact which the khedive and party historians later ignored or denied,[3] or note Farīd's belief that Muṣṭafā made some of his most important decisions without consulting him, the vice-president,[4] and that ʿAlī Fahmī Kāmil intrigued with the khedive to wrest control of the party from Farīd,[5] to which Farīd responded by secretly admitting his supporters to the administrative board of the European newspapers in order to outvote ʿAlī.[6] These examples, and others in the preceding narrative, make clear the real dynamics of the move-

[1] Following the Nationalist demonstrations protesting the 1909 Press Law, a story went around the British community in Cairo that one of the proletarian participants turned to a fellow-demonstrator and asked: 'Who is this Shaykh al-Dustūr whose *mūlid* we are celebrating?'

[2] Alexander, p. 137, based on Gorst's 1907 report.

[3] See Anīs, *Ṣafaḥāt maṭwiyya*, p. 15, for a reference to the khedive's denial in his memoirs, published in *al-Miṣrī* (18 May 1951). Neither al-Rāfiʿī nor ʿAlī Fahmī Kāmil discuss the khedive's role in the nationalist movement.

[4] Farīd memoirs, pp. 1 f. Specifically on matters of relations with the khedive and accepting money from the sultan.

[5] Ibid., p. 4.

[6] Ibid., p. 10.

ment. It can easily be understood why the party frequently had to work underground, given the preponderant power of the British in Egypt, but it was a disaster for its internal cohesion that this reliance upon secrecy and intrigue extended to activity within the party itself, especially after Muṣṭafā's death.[1]

The Nationalist Party was not truly a national party. Its membership represented mainly the small, Muslim, urban middle class. The Nationalists tried to attract their poorer compatriots by sponsoring night-schools, consumer co-operatives, and even trade unions, but these organizations quickly foundered for lack of funds. The formal leadership of the party came mainly from wealthy beys and pashas at first, but a number of younger members prominent in the Nationalist press and other activities were elected to the 1911 administrative board.[2] The over-all picture invites a comparison with the Wafd, or with some of the nationalist and constitutionalist groups which were arising at this time in other Muslim countries.

While the Nationalists did not succeed in carrying out their programme, they cannot simply be dismissed as a failure. The lives, and in particular the speeches and writings, of Muṣṭafā Kāmil and Muḥammad Farīd have continued to inspire Egyptians with patriotic ideals. Their courage in the face of the power of their enemies, so soon after the ʿUrabist débâcle, helped to restore the self-confidence of the Egyptian people and inspire the native cultural renascence of the twentieth century. Finally, they began the task of disseminating among the masses the idea that Egypt constituted a nation, and helped pave the way for the truly popular revolution of 1919 and the ultimate attainment of complete independence.

[1] It is conceivable that some of these intrigues were fomented by Palace agents within the Nationalist Party, as was suggested, after the publication in Cairo of the Farīd memoirs, by an Egyptian writer in *al-Akhbār* (8 June 1964). Egyptian historians might investigate this possibility at the Abdin Palace Archives.

[2] Such as ʿAbd al-Raḥmān al-Rāfiʿī and Muṣṭafā al-Shūrbajī, both in their early twenties, and also Muḥammad Zakī ʿAlī and Muḥammad Tawfīq al-ʿAṭṭār, who were editors on the staff of *al-ʿAlam*. For the complete list, see al-Rāfiʿī, *Muḥammad Farīd*, pp. 226 f.

The Origins of the Liberal Constitutionalist Party in Egypt

MAHMUD ZAYID

THE emergence of political parties in Egypt during the nineteenth century was made possible by the Egyptian awakening which followed at the heels of the French expedition in 1798 and received great impetus under Muḥammad Saʿīd Pasha (1854–63) and Ismāʿīl Pasha (1863–79). In the process of this awakening, Egyptian society saw the rise to positions of power and influence of a number of the hitherto suppressed Egyptians, who came to constitute the backbone of the political parties.

These Egyptians fall into three main categories: the educated, including the professional groups and government officials, the landowners, and the military officers. The educated were largely the product of the educational missions to Europe and the new schools founded in Egypt. A large number of these must have joined the government service. It has been stated that under Ismāʿīl, 50 per cent. of the civil servants were Egyptians.[1] The landowners emerged following the promulgation of Saʿīd's *Lāʾiḥa* on 5 August 1858, which conferred the right of landownership upon Egyptians.[2] The advance of military officers resulted from Saʿīd's military reforms and the promotion of Egyptians to high rank in the army.[3] By the seventh decade of the nineteenth century the socially advanced Egyptians had developed a sharper awareness of their identity, a genuine concern for their country and a strong desire to be their own masters. In 1877, McCoan noted that 'Egypt for the Egyptians' was unmistakably the 'national' aspiration.[4] The extravagance of Ismāʿīl Pasha, leading to bankruptcy and to foreign interference and control, greatly stimulated the patriotic feelings of the Egyptians.

The first political party in Egypt, which came into being on 2 April 1879,[5] and to which the name 'National Party' was applied,[6] grew out of a secret society which had been founded by the military officers in about 1876.[7] This

[1] Muḥammad Saʿīd Luṭfī, 'al-Nuhūḍ al-Ijtimāʿī', in *Ismāʿīl* (Cairo, 1945), p. 62.

[2] Ibid., and ʿAbd al-Raḥmān al-Rāfiʿī, *ʿAṣr Ismāʿīl* (2nd edn., Cairo 1948), vol. i, pp. 24–26.

[3] Al-Rāfiʿī, *ʿAṣr Ismāʿīl*, vol. i, pp. 28–31.

[4] J. C. McCoan, *Egypt as it is* (London, 1877), p. 83.

[5] On this political party read: John Ninet, 'Origin of the National Party in Egypt', *Nineteenth Century*, vol. xiii (Jan.–June 1883), pp. 128 ff.; al-Rāfiʿī, *ʿAṣr Ismāʿīl*, vol. ii, pp. 180–4; Jacob M. Landau, *Parliaments and parties in Egypt* (Tel Aviv, 1953), pp. 84–90.

[6] Al-Rāfiʿī, *ʿAṣr Ismāʿīl*, vol. ii, p. 181, n. 3, which states that the name was applied by the press.

[7] On the secret society read: Ninet, op. cit., p. 126; Najīb Makhlūf, *Nūbār Pāshā wa-mā tamma ʿalā yadihi* (Cairo, n.d.), pp. 140–1; also Landau, op. cit., pp. 76–77.

party was re-established on 4 November 1879, under the same name and came to be led by the fellah officer, Aḥmad 'Urābī Pasha.[1] The core of both parties was the military officers and the landowners. Both of them, however, were not political parties in the modern sense of the word. Neither made provision for membership nor for continuity. Yet they can be said to have expressed the aspirations of the Egyptians at the time. The military officers were opposed to the dominant position of the Turks in the army; the educated and the landowners wanted a constitutional government which would put an end to the personal rule of the khedive and allow them a share in ruling the country; and all of them resented foreign control and the humiliation involved in declaring Egypt bankrupt.

Though 'Urābī might have been mainly motivated by his anti-Turkish bias, the huge popular movement into which his party grew was the fruit of the combination of military and civilian elements, particularly the landowners,[2] who all recognized his leadership. To the Egyptians, 'Urābī became a symbol of freedom and justice.

His defeat and the British occupation of Egypt in 1882 not only stunned the Egyptians and weakened their morale, but also broke up the combination of forces which had produced his revolt. The khedive, who was not opposed to the occupation to which he owed the maintenance of his position, was able, prior to 'Urābī's defeat, to draw to himself a few influential landowners and government officials who had been among 'Urābī's supporters. The military, who had since the late 1870s been playing a central role in politics, disappeared from the scene following the disbandment of the army and the exile of its leaders. A good number of years was to pass before the Egyptians could again use force against the British authorities. The bulk of the non-urban Egyptians lost contact with the bewildered patriots in the cities.

It took those patriots several years before they recovered their composure and began to organize themselves. Reasons for dissatisfaction were not lacking. Although the British had not yet secured a legal title to their occupation and, therefore, Egypt's legal status continued to be the same (namely that of a tributary vassal state under the suzerainty of the Porte by the sanction of powers), the British authorities in Egypt actually ruled the country. Thus Egypt was *de facto* deprived of the great degree of autonomy she had enjoyed prior to the occupation. Furthermore, British declarations of intent to withdraw from Egypt had, since 1887, become less and less frequent. The preparation of Egyptians for self-rule seemed to be very slow. These, among other factors, led enlightened Egyptians to unite their efforts and seek means of articulation.

In 1889 some of those Egyptians, including Sa'd Zaghlūl, encouraged and

[1] Read about the formation of this party: Landau, op. cit., pp. 90 ff.; al-Rāfi'ī, *al-Thawra al-'Urābiyya wa'l-iḥtilāl al-Injilīzī* (2nd edn., Cairo 1949), pp. 70–73.

[2] For the role of the landowners in 'Urābī's revolt, see Ninet, op. cit., pp. 132–3.

helped Shaykh ʿAlī Yūsuf to found the daily newspaper *al-Muʾayyad* in order to combat the pro-British *al-Muqaṭṭam* and to provide a forum which would enlighten their countrymen on Egyptian affairs.[1] Through the energy of the self-made shaykh, *al-Muʾayyad* spread widely not only in Egypt but also in other Muslim countries. It was probably on the pages of this daily that the question of British withdrawal from Egypt was first publicly discussed by the Egyptians in the press.[2]

The opposition to the occupation was greatly stimulated by the succession of the young and ambitious ʿAbbās II in 1892. His attempt to exercise actual power soon brought him into conflict with Lord Cromer who twice humiliated him in less than two years.[3] Hence the khedive sought allies among the ambitious patriots and foreigners for assistance in his struggle against the British authorities. In the meantime, he became a popular figure and succeeded in rousing feeling against the occupation.

> Hostility to the foreign element in the administration and sullen opposition to its men and measures, showed themselves everywhere after the coming of Khedive Abbas. Public servants of all grades reflected the heat emanating from the Palace. ... So keen was the feeling of unrest that the British garrison was reinforced.[4]

Among the khedive's allies were Shaykh ʿAlī Yūsuf, Muṣṭafā Kāmil, and Aḥmad Luṭfī al-Sayyid. Until his death in 1913, Shaykh ʿAlī remained the staunch supporter of the khedive. With the other two, the khedive formed in 1897 a 'national party' to resist the British occupation.[5] On behalf of the party, Luṭfī al-Sayyid was sent in the same year to Switzerland to obtain Swiss nationality, and, consequently, capitulatory protection before returning to take over the editorship of an anti-occupation newspaper.[6] While there, Luṭfī al-Sayyid established contacts with Saʿd Zaghlūl, Qāsim Amīn, and Shaykh Muḥammad ʿAbduh. There, also, he came to the conviction that Egypt could not be liberated except by the Egyptians themselves. On his return, however, he found the khedive alienated on account of these contacts, while in Switzerland, with ʿAbduh.[7] Thus his alliance with the khedive came to an end.

The khedive had greater success with Muṣṭafā Kāmil who was more qualified than Luṭfī al-Sayyid for popular leadership. His magnetic personality, his vigorous patriotism and his abilities as a writer and orator enabled him, with the assistance of the khedive, to create a national movement in Egypt. His

[1] Qusṭākī Ilyās ʿAṭṭāra, *Taʾrīkh al-ṣuḥuf al-Miṣriyya* (Alexandria, 1928), pp. 127–8; ʿAbd al-Laṭīf Ḥamza, *Adab al-maqāla al-ṣuḥufiyya fī Miṣr*, part iv (2nd edn., Cairo, 1951), pp. 44, 78–79.

[2] Muḥammad Ḥusayn, *al-Ittijāhāt al-waṭaniyya fi'l-adab al-muʿāṣir* (Cairo, 1954), vol. i, pp. 143–4.

[3] For details see Cromer, *Abbas II* (London, 1915), pp. 7 ff.

[4] Auckland Colvin, *The making of modern Egypt* (London, 1906), p. 249.

[5] Luṭfī al-Sayyid's series of memoirs published in the weekly *al-Muṣawwar*, 1950, nos. 1351–64; see Ḥamza, op. cit., part vi (1954), pp. 49–50.

[6] Ibid.

[7] Ibid.

main theme was love for Egypt and opposition to the British occupation. He hoped that by rousing patriotic feelings in the Egyptians, and maintaining unity with the khedive, and through French and Turkish help, the British would be compelled to withdraw from his country. His desire to manipulate Turkey in Egypt's interest may explain his emphasis on Egypt's status as a Turkish dependency.

Though he won an enormous following in less than a decade after his return from Toulouse with a degree in law, most of this following were drawn from the younger elements of the urban population. In the meantime, some of the enlightened Egyptians came to believe that he was to a great extent unrealistic. The khedive, who had been one of the pillars of the national movement began, after the Fashoda crisis of 1898, to lean towards the occupation.[1] Kāmil tried hard to avoid a rupture with him, but finally could not. In 1904, he sent the khedive a letter in which he stated his intention to be 'away from your Excellency'.[2] Kāmil's great expectations of Turkey and France proved to be misplaced. The former, it had become evident, was in no position to get the British out. As for France, the Anglo-French Entente in 1904 destroyed whatever hopes the Egyptian nationalists had of her.

In 1906, there appeared on the political stage in Egypt a group of moderate nationalists who were not in full agreement with Kāmil's programme. The immediate reason for their emergence was the 'Aqaba Incident 'which shook the nation's nerves and re-opened the question of the occupation and the withdrawal [of the British] for discussion'.[3] The dispute which arose between Turkey and the British authorities in Egypt over a site to the west of 'Aqaba divided the Egyptians. Kāmil supported Turkey while this moderate group took the other side. To gain public hearing and support for their views on Egyptian affairs, they felt that they should establish a newspaper.[4]

Encouraged by Cromer, this moderate group met on July, 1906, in Maḥmūd Sulaymān Pasha's house where they decided to establish the newspaper. They subscribed an amount of £E15,000, and chose Luṭfī al-Sayyid as general editor. The members regarded themselves as a general assembly for which they formulated statutes. They also elected a board of twenty-four directors whose meetings would be attended by the general editor of the newspaper[5] which was issued in March, 1907, with the name *al-Jarīda*. On September 21, 1907, the group established *Ḥizb al-Umma* or the Party of the Nation. In less than four months the party had 720 members.[6]

Though this moderate party had a comparatively small following and though it was possibly true 'that its actions were scarcely noticeable',[7] it was destined to play a major role in the political thinking and development in Egypt during

1 Al-Rāfi'ī, *Muṣṭafā Kāmil* (3rd edn., Cairo, 1950), p. 123.
2 The text of the letter is in ibid., pp. 339–40.
3 Al-Rāfi'ī, ibid., p. 195.
4 Ḥamza, op. cit., part vi, p. 70.
5 *Al-Muqaṭṭam*, 24 July 1906.
6 *Al-Jarīda*, 7 Jan. 1908.
7 Quotation from J. Alexander, *The truth about Egypt* (London, 1911), p. 128.

the following three decades. It is in this group that we should look not only for the origins of the Liberal Constitutionalists but also of the Wafd. Among its members and supporters were Saʿd Zaghlūl, whom the khedive believed to be the mind behind the party,[1] Luṭfī al-Sayyid, ʿAbd al-ʿAzīz Fahmī, ʿAlī Shaʿrāwī, Muḥammad Maḥmūd, Ṭalʿat Ḥarb and Ḥamad al-Bāsil, all of whom with the exception of Ḥarb, came a few years later to be associated with the leadership of the national movement in Egypt.[2]

The political programme of the party was very much influenced by ʿAbduh's teaching in the post-revolutionary period of his thinking. Like ʿAbduh, the party, though in principle opposed to the occupation, advocated co-operation with the British in the gradual implementation of reform, particularly in education. The party was opposed to the militancy of Kāmil and his dependence on the khedive and outside powers for liberating Egypt. Egypt could not be liberated except by the Egyptians themselves and through reform. The khedive's powers, the party believed, should be assumed by the representatives of the people. Turkey was regarded as helpless, and actual Turkish rule was out of the question, not only because of present weakness, but also because of Turkey's previous record. Foreigners in the service of the government should be gradually replaced by native Egyptians.[3]

In the meantime and following the Dinshawāy incident (June 1906), Muṣṭafā Kāmil re-established contact with the khedive.[4] It is not unlikely that the meeting of the moderate group of July and their decision to establish a newspaper induced Kāmil to take a similar move. In the latter part of October 1906, the khedive and Kāmil held a meeting in which they decided to form a political party and a company with a capital of £E20,000, to issue, in addition to *al-Liwā'* which Kāmil had founded in 1900, the joint dailies: the *Egyptian Standard* and *L'Étendard Egyptien*.[5] Also the formation of the Umma Party in September, 1907, might have been the immediate cause which led Kāmil, a month later, to form *al-Ḥizb al-Waṭanī* or the National Party.

On 22 October 1907, Kāmil announced the formation of his party. Its programme covered his previous platform but in a moderate form and with more emphasis on internal reform.[6] Both this party and *Ḥizb al-Umma* aspired to achieve autonomy for Egypt as a step towards independence. But

[1] Ḥamza, op. cit., part iv, p. 150; Aḥmad Shafīq, *Mudhakkarātī fī niṣf qarn*, vol. ii, part 2 (Cairo, 1936), p. 129, found that Saʿd Zaghlūl joined in forming the *Umma* Party.

[2] The names of forty members are given in *al-Muqaṭṭam*, 24 July 1906, and *al-Jarīda*, 26 Jan. 1908.

[3] The programme of the Umma Party does not contain all their views. One has to refer to an important statement of the party's views written by Ḥasan ʿAbd al-Rāziq, the party's leader, and published in *al-Muqaṭṭam*, 17 Dec. 1907; and to Luṭfī al-Sayyid's articles in *al-Jarīda*. Long citations of a number of his articles are in Ḥamza, op. cit., part vi, pp. 99 ff.

[4] Muḥammad Farīd's memoirs quoted at length in Muḥammad Ṣubayḥ, *Mawāqif ḥāsima fī ta'rīkh al-qawmiyya al-ʿarabiyya: al-yaqẓa fi'l-qarnayn al-tasiʿ ʿashar wa'l-ishrīn*, vol. ii (Cairo, 1964), pp. 230–1; also Shafīq, *Mudhakkarātī*, pp. 101–3.

[5] Ibid.

[6] For the programme see Alexander, op. cit., pp. 121–3; for comments see Landau, op. cit., pp. 114 ff.

whereas *Ḥizb al-Umma* frequently made mention of independence as a final goal, the National Party, desiring to keep on good terms with Turkey, rarely made a point of that goal. The tenth point in the National Party's programme made the 'strengthening of the ties between Egypt and the Ottoman Empire' one of their aims, an attachment about which the leaders of the other party were not very enthusiastic.

During the following three years five other moderate political parties were formed in Egypt: the Constitutional Reformers (1907), the National Free Party, the Party of Independent Egyptians, the Young Egyptian Party, and the Party of Nobles.[1] The Constitutional Reform Party was formed by Shaykh 'Alī Yūsuf. Encouraged by the khedive, who must have felt that he could not get along well with the National Party, a number of older notables joined his party. However, all of those five parties were minor ones, and hardly influenced the course of events.

Muṣṭafā Kāmil's death in 1908 proved to be a great loss to his party. His successor Muḥammad Farīd, though sincere and able, lacked Kāmil's forcefulness and fiery oratory. The party also suffered from rivalry over leadership between 'Alī Fahmī, Kāmil's brother, who had wanted to be the party's leader, and Farīd.[2] The financial difficulties of the party and the re-enforcement of the Press Law of 26 November 1881, by Cromer's successor, Sir Eldon Gorst (1907–11), resulted in the disappearance of the party's three dailies after March 1910.[3] The Copts were alienated by the party as a result of the assassination of Buṭrus Ghālī, the Egyptian Coptic premier, in the same year by Ibrāhīm al-Wardānī. The latter was at the time a member of both the National Party and an underground society the activities of which included the assassination of the supporters of the occupation.[4]

An important shift in the alignment of the major political forces occurred under Sir Eldon Gorst. The khedive who had failed, following Kāmil's death, to win his successor, Farīd, to his side and to influence the National Party's platform, turned against this party.[5] Finding now no reason to compromise their platform, the National Party drew nearer to the Umma by emphasizing the demand for the constitution. This development resulted from the Umma Party's criticism of the British occupation as a result of Gorst's policy. Gorst conciliated the khedive and his ministers by relaxing British control, but made no substantial concessions to meet the nationalists' demand for constitutional rule. To silence the opposition, the Press Law of 26 November 1881, was

[1] On these parties see Alexander, op. cit., pp. 124–33; and Landau, op. cit., pp. 136–47.

[2] For further details, see Ṣubayḥ, op. cit., p. 238 ff.

[3] Ibid. and al-Rāfi'ī, *Muḥammad Farīd* (2nd edn., Cairo, 1948), pp. 100, 156–7.

[4] On the underground society see al-Rāfi'ī, ibid., pp. 154–6; a detailed description is in Muṣṭafā Amīn, 'Man alladhī amara bi-qatl ra'īs al-wuzarā'', *al-Akhbār*, 21 June 1964. This article is based on Farīd's memoirs and Shafīq Manṣūr's testimony to the court in 1924. Shafīq Manṣūr had been a member of the society.

[5] For more information on the khedive's attempt see Ṣubayḥ, op. cit., pp. 233–5.

re-enforced. But instead of diminishing the opposition, as Gorst must have hoped, the anti-British campaign grew stronger. The situation grew much more difficult with the breakdown of security, particularly in the provinces.

Gorst's successor, Lord Kitchener (1911–14), was appointed 'to use his strength and prestige to restore a deteriorating situation, while continuing a policy of cautious liberalization'.[1] He won some moderate nationalists by taking every opportunity to humiliate the 'wicked little Khedive' and to force his abdication, by his 'five feddan' law which prohibited the seizure of any peasant's land under five acres, and by conferring more power on the Legislative Assembly which he created to replace the two consultative councils established in 1883. He succeeded to a great extent in suppressing public agitation, but not opposition.

In the meantime, important developments took place in Egypt. Saʿd Zaghlūl, who had been a member of the Cabinet since 1906, had to resign in 1912 because, among other things, he had not been consulted on the question of Muḥammad Farīd's trial.[2] The latter was accused of urging the people to oppose the government. In order to avoid one year in prison, Farīd escaped to Europe. Free now of the fetters of office, Zaghlūl joined the opposition.

In the elections to the Legislative Assembly in December 1913, both the Umma and the National Party supported Zaghlūl.[3] After the elections both recognized him as leader of the opposition in the Assembly. Fully aware that Zaghlūl was much more qualified for leadership than any of his followers, Farīd wrote on 31 January 1914, urging the administrative committee of his party to get Zaghlūl to join it and even to succeed Aḥmad Luṭfī as under-secretary of the National Party. In the deliberations of the Assembly, Zaghlūl was able to attract to his group other members of the Assembly.

When the First World War broke out both the khedive and Kitchener had left Egypt, the former for Constantinople and the latter for England. Neither of them returned. Ḥusayn Rushdī Pasha, the Egyptian premier, became acting khedive, while Sir Milne Cheetham was appointed acting British agent. In August, the khedive wanted to go back but was prevented by the British government.[4] On 19 December 1914, the British government deposed the khedive, offered the throne to Prince Ḥusayn Kāmil with the title of 'sultan' and established a protectorate over Egypt. In its declaration of the protectorate, Great Britain assumed three functions: to replace Turkey as suzerain over Egypt, to assume the latter's defence, and to conduct her foreign relations.

That these developments did not provoke serious reactions and protests from the Egyptians should be explained not only by the war measures—

[1] Philip Magnus, *Kitchener* (London, 1958), p. 262.

[2] According to Kitchener, the resignation resulted from Zaghlūl's clash with the khedive—F.O. 371/1362, dispatch no. 15, Apr. 1912; see also, Shafīq, *Mudhakkarātī*, vol. ii, part 2, pp. 271–3.

[3] Farīd's memoirs in Ṣubayḥ, op. cit., pp. 281–2; al-Rāfiʿī, *Muḥammad Farīd*, pp. 317–18.

[4] Shafīq, *Mudhakkarātī*, vol. ii, part 2, pp. 332 ff.

martial law, censorship over the press, prohibition of public meetings and others—but also by the fact that Rushdī Pasha and the ministers, after consulting with Zaghlūl and his group, decided to continue in office pending the results of the great conflict.[1] They had recognized that the protectorate was a lesser evil than the incorporation of Egypt in the British Empire, a course which the Foreign Office had seriously considered early in September 1914.[2]

The story of the war, the grievances of the Egyptians against the British authorities and their great hopes in realizing their aspirations through Wilson's fourteen points and the Anglo-French declaration of November 1918, has been given extensive scholarly treatment. What is noteworthy for the purpose of this article is the fact that at the end of the war the leadership of the national movement in Egypt rested in Zaghlūl, ʿAbd al-ʿAzīz Fahmī, Luṭfī al-Sayyid, ʿAlī Shaʿrāwī, Muḥammad Maḥmūd and other nationalists whose outlook continued to be dominated by the idea of gradualism in the attainment of their goals at least until 1936. Furthermore, these leaders were able to win the co-operation of the National Party which, by this time, had lost much of its influence.

In its initial stages, the post-war Egyptian nationalist movement was a joint effort of both official and popular elements. Sultan Aḥmad Fu'ād (who had succeeded Sultan Ḥusayn Kāmil on his death in 1917) was supporting the nationalists, though from different motives deriving from his autocratic tendencies. The Delegation (Wafd) of Saʿd Zaghlūl, ʿAlī Shaʿrāwī and ʿAbd al-Azīz Fahmī, who on 13 November 1918, expressed their demand for independence to Sir Reginald Wingate, did so in full agreement with Rushdī Pasha, the prime minister.[3]

Although the Delegation demanded 'independence', they were willing to accept internal independence for Egypt under the protectorate.[4] However, the British government was then unwilling to concede so much, and refused to allow either Zaghlūl or Rushdī to proceed to London to discuss the Egyptian question with the Foreign Office. In the meantime, Zaghlūl, in order to prove the representative character of the Delegation, added other members, particularly from the National Party,[5] thus making the Delegation a completely representative body under his recognized leadership. His mandate as leader, drafted by himself, was signed by people from all walks of Egyptian life.

The first split in this alliance of forces which constituted the Egyptian national movement took place in March 1919. Zaghlūl had, on 6 December,

[1] For the attitude of Rushdī and Zaghlūl, see: *al-Siyāsa*, leading article of 19 Feb. 1923; Ronald Storrs, *Orientations* (definitive edn., London, 1943), pp. 132, 135, 140, 142–3; 'Miskīn Rushdī Bāshā', *Rouz el-Yousef*, no. 74, 31 Mar. 1927, p. 3.

[2] *al-Siyāsa, supra.*

[3] Mahmud Zayid, 'Nasha't Ḥizb al-Wafd al-Miṣri, 1918–24', *al-Abḥāth* (Beirut, June 1962), p. 248.

[4] Ibid., pp. 248–9.

[5] For the additions from the National Party see: al-Rāfiʿī, *Thawrat sanat 1919* (2nd edn., Cairo 1955), vol. i, pp. 125–6.

addressed a memorandum to the representatives of the powers in Egypt informing them of the formation of the Wafd and its aims; and on 26 December sent an appeal to President Wilson asking that the Wafd be allowed to attend the Peace Conference.[1] On 13 January, Zaghlūl declared that the protectorate had no legal validity and that Egypt's independence needed only recognition by the Peace Conference.[2] These revolutionary measures of Zaghlūl and his increasing power must have induced the sultan to reconsider his position. Hence he accepted Rushdī Pasha's resignation, which he had earlier twice refused. To the nationalists this meant a retreat by the sultan and withdrawal of his support to their cause.

The second split which ultimately led to the rise of the Liberal Constitutionalists occurred in Paris. Zaghlūl and his three colleagues who had been arrested and deported to Malta on the eve of the revolt of 1919, were released and allowed with the other members of the Wafd to proceed to Paris to present their case to the Peace Conference. In Paris, the Wafd were not only denied a hearing but also shocked at the recognition of the protectorate by President Wilson and several powers. This shock was so severe that Zaghlūl himself stated in his telegram of 13 May 1919 (to the Wafd's central committee, which had been established early in April) that 'all their [the Wafd's] efforts and endeavours have been lost'.[3] This shock and the differences within the Wafd soon led to the resignation from it by two members, the return to Cairo of another two, and the dismissal of three others.[4] Most of these members objected to what they considered to be Zaghlūl's conceit, obstinacy, and tendency to act alone.

At first Zaghlūl was worried about these developments in the Wafd, but in the meantime the news he was receiving from Cairo inspired him with further confidence and so strengthened his position that he believed no other Egyptian could challenge his leadership. The Wafd's central committee and its sub-committees, kept the public under control and informed of the Wafd's fortunes.[5] In this great task these committees were supported by the secret organization which Zaghlūl had founded early in 1919 and entrusted to ʿAbd al-Raḥmān Fahmī.[6] This organization was active in reporting the activi-

[1] Aḥmad Shafīq, *Ḥawliyyāt Miṣr al-siyāsiyya, Tamhīd*, vol. i (Cairo, 1926), pp. 166–70, 182–5.

[2] Al-Rāfiʿī, *Thawrat*, vol. i, pp. 144–7.

[3] The full text of the telegram is in Muḥammad Anīs, 'Aḍwā' jadīda ʿala'l-ḥaraka al-waṭaniyya al-Miṣriyya—al-murāsala al-sirriyya bayn Saʿd Zaghlūl wa ʿAbd al-Raḥmān Fahmī', *al-Ahrām*, 2 Feb. 1963.

[4] These members were respectively: ʿAzīz Mansī, ʿAlī Ramaḍān, Wīṣā Wāṣif, ʿAli Shaʿrāwī, Ṣidqī, Abu'l-Naṣr, and Ḥusayn Wāṣif. See Zayid, 'Nash'at Ḥizb al-Wafd', p. 257.

[5] On the Wafd's Central Committee and the subcommittees see Shafiq, *Ḥawliyyāt*, vol. i, pp. 329, 337; 'al-Gharāblī wa-kayfa dakhala al-Wafd al-Miṣrī', *al-Muṣawwar*, no. 422, 11 Nov. 1932, p. 9; Zayid, op. cit., pp. 256–7.

[6] For a short biography of Fahmī see: Muḥammad Anīs, *Dirāsāt fī wathā'iq thawrat sanat 1919*, vol. i (Cairo, 1963), pp. 7 ff. For information on the secret organisation see the long series of articles by Muṣṭafā Amīn, in *al-Akhbār*, Aug.–Oct. 1963.

ties of the British Residency and government officials, in obtaining weapons, and in threatening enemies and carrying out assassinations. The labourers were controlled through the trade unions Fahmī established.[1] By 5 September 1919, almost all newspapers in Egypt had become pro-Wafdist.[2] On 14 January 1920 a Wafdist women's committee was founded. On 17 March 1920, the Wafd's executive committee, according to Fahmī, could have its orders and instructions communicated to all parties of the country in 24 hours.[3] The Wafd's firm hold on the people became clear when the Egyptians boycotted the Milner Mission which had arrived in Egypt in December 1919, to investigate the causes of 'the late disorders in Egypt'.

Although the Milner-Zaghlūl informal conversations of 1920 in London further strengthened Zaghlūl's position through the implied recognition of his leadership by the British government, they also led to the second and more serious split in the Wafd. Like his colleagues, Zaghlūl was moderate in his aspirations, and sincerely wanted to reach a compromise with Milner. However, as the conversations progressed, he realized that the agreement to be reached would grant Egypt neither the internal independence he had hoped to get nor the 'complete independence' stipulated by the people's mandate to him. Moreover, Zaghlūl found that most of his colleagues were in favour of a compromise, and more inclined to follow the lead of ʿAdlī,[4] a respected and moderate politician whom Zaghlūl had invited to participate in the conversations. In order not to have the differences in the Wafd assume serious proportions, Zaghlūl continued the conversations. But he kept asking for modifications in the resulting agreement until Lord Milner made it clear that the agreement was the limit of what the Mission could recommend to the British government. Realizing that he could not reject the agreement without disrupting the Wafd's seeming unity, Zaghlūl accepted a suspension of the talks until Egyptian opinion regarding it was explored. Although the Egyptians suggested no serious changes, the British government did not accept the agreement. On 9 November 1920, Milner explained to the Wafd that a final settlement would follow formal negotiations between Egypt and Britain. Thus the conversations were suspended on 11 November 1920, and the Wafd left London for Paris.

Before ʿAdlī left for Cairo, two telegrams, inspired (according to Māhir) by Zaghlūl, were published in the Cairo daily *al-Akhbār*, accusing ʿAdlī of obstructing the Wafd, and describing him as a 'catastrophe for the Wafd'.[5]

[1] Fahmī's letter of 18 Oct. 1919, to Zaghlūl in Anīs, *Dirāsāt*, pp. 151–4.

[2] Fahmī's letter of 5 Sept. 1919 to Zaghlūl in ibid., pp. 141–4.

[3] Fahmī's letter of 17 Mar. 1920 to Zaghlūl in ibid., pp. 199–205.

[4] ʿAbbās Maḥmūd al-ʿAqqād, *Saʿd Zaghlūl* (Cairo, 1936), p. 318; *Majmūʿat khuṭab wa-aḥādīth ṣāḥib al-maʿālī Zaghlūl Bāshā* (Cairo, 1924), p. 77.

[5] For details Shafīq, *Ḥawliyyāt*, vol. i, pp. 847–52; Maḥmūd Abu'l-Fatḥ, *al-Mas'ala al-Miṣriyya wa'l-Wafd* (Cairo n.d.), pp. 288–90; Ḥamza, op. cit., part vii (1959), pp. 163–4; ʿAbd al-ʿAziz Fahmī, *Khuṭbat al-ra'īs al-ustadh ʿAbd al-ʿAzīz Fahmī* (Cairo, n.d.), p. 15.

Early in January, the pro-ʿAdlists suggested that ʿAdlī should form a Cabinet in Egypt and lead an official delegation for negotiating with the British government.[1] As Zaghlūl considered their suggestion to be suicide for himself and the Wafd, ʿAdlī's supporters—Luṭfī al-Sayyid, ʿAbd al-ʿAzīz Fahmī, Muḥammad Maḥmud, Muḥammad ʿAlī, and ʿAbd al-Laṭīf al-Makabbātī left for Cairo.[2] The cleavage, though undeclared, was a fact.

On 25 February 1921, the British government declared that 'the status of the Protectorate was not a satisfactory relation' and that it wanted to negotiate regarding Milner's recommendations with a delegation nominated by the sultan. On 16 March 1921, the sultan charged ʿAdlī with the formation of a Cabinet which would conduct the negotiations. ʿAdlī informed Zaghlūl, who was in Paris, of these developments and invited the Wafd to participate in the coming negotiations. On 4 April, Zaghlūl returned to Egypt, probably with the intention of destroying ʿAdlī and his supporters.

A struggle ensued between ʿAdlī and the Wafd's leader, apparently over the leadership of the delegation. Each claimed supreme command. On 14 May 1921, the pro-ʿAdlī Wafdist members declared themselves against Zaghlūl and with ʿAdlī.[3] By the end of the same month, ʿAlī Shaʿrāwī, Ḥāfiẓ ʿAfīfī, George Khayyāṭ, and ʿAbd al-Khāliq Madkūr had resigned from the Wafd.[4] As from 1 July 1921, ʿAlī Māhir ceased to attend the Wafd's meetings.[5]

While ʿAdlī was in London, following the failure of his negotiations with Lord Curzon, Tharwat informed him that his supporters in Egypt, were suggesting the formation of a political party under ʿAdlī's leadership. ʿAdlī then told Yūsuf Naḥḥās that he could not accept his supporters' offer on account of his need for a few months of rest, because of the great difficulty involved in organizing and administering such a party, and because the proposed party would perpetuate the conflict between the ʿAdlists and the Zaghlulists.[6] Naḥḥās remarked that the ʿAdlists were in need of a prominent personality to assist in forming a party and suggested that ʿAdlī should not refuse to help a group who wanted to follow a wise and rational policy.[7] ʿAdlī then explained that he did not refuse but would take a decision regarding the offer after he had returned to Egypt.[8]

One, however, would expect ʿAdlī to hesitate in accepting the leadership of the proposed party. ʿAdlī had led an easy and pleasant life, and developed a quiet and reserved personality shrinking from involvement in a tough political struggle. Although he had occupied several government posts, he had no contacts outside his immediate circle of well-to-do and influential people. It was most difficult, Bishrī writes, to visit him at home.[9] Moreover, it seems

[1] ʿAbd al-ʿAziz Fahmī, *Khuṭbat al-raʾīs al-ustadh ʿAbd al-ʿAzīz Fahmī* (Cairo, n.d.), p. 15.
[2] Ibid. [3] Shafīq, *Ḥawliyyāt*, vol. ii, p. 3.
[4] Ibid., pp. 79, 103–5. [5] Ibid., p. 293.
[6] Yūsuf Naḥḥās, *Ṣafḥa min taʾrīkh Miṣr al-ḥadīth—Mufāwaḍāt ʿAdlī-Curzon* (Cairo, 1951), pp. 115–16. [7] Ibid. [8] Ibid.
[9] ʿAbd al-ʿAzīz al-Bishrī, *Fiʾl-mirʾat* (Cairo, 1927), p. 19.

that ʿAdlī, following the failure of the negotiations, hoped that the Wafdists and the ʿAdlists would be reunited.

No sooner, however, had ʿAdlī returned to Egypt, than he began to realize that the unity of the nationalists was a thing of the past. On his return to Egypt from London, he was very badly received by the people because of a hostile Wafdist campaign.[1] On about 8 December 1921, Zaghlūl told Shafīq Pasha that he could co-operate with all the nationalists with the exception of ʿAbd al-ʿAzīz Fahmī, Muḥammad Maḥmūd, Muḥammad ʿAli, ʿAbd al-Laṭīf al-Makabbātī, Tharwat, Ismāʿīl Ṣidqī, and ʿAdlī.[2] Though the first four of these rejoined the Wafd following the second exile of Zaghlūl on 23 December 1921, they were soon alienated, and consequently they abandoned that party.

In the meantime, the leading ʿAdlists succeeded, with Lord Allenby's support, in obtaining the issue by the British government, on 28 February 1922, of the unilateral Declaration which announced the termination of the protectorate, the independence of Egypt, and the reservation of four points to the discretion of the British government: the security of British communications in Egypt, defence, the protection of foreigners, and the Sudan. ʿAdlī and his supporters now felt the need for forming a political party to support the new policy and Tharwat's cabinet, which was formed to carry it out, and to defend themselves against Wafdist and other accusations.

While the ʿAdlists were discussing the formation of a political party, the Wafdists and the National Party began to accuse them in their dailies of being inclined to sacrifice their country's interests for the sake of reaching agreement with the British.[3] The government of Egypt was very much criticized for assisting the ʿAdlists in inducing people to subscribe to the daily, *al-Siyāsa*, which was to be the ʿAdlists' organ.

On 30 October 1922 ʿAdlī announced the formation of the Liberal Constitutionalist Party in a speech to 300 supporters.[4] In this speech he defended the unilateral declaration. He said:

> Whatever the causes that induce some of our countrymen to show indifference regarding this result may be, it is true that the legal abolition of the protectorate over Egypt, the international recognition of her as a sovereign state, and the willingness [of both Egypt and Britain] to solve their problems through negotiations, the result of which would be decided upon by a chamber—all these have to be considered as political success.[5]

[1] For an account of his reception, see: Shafīq, *Ḥawliyyāt*, vol. ii, pp. 488–90.

[2] Ibid., pp. 492–3.

[3] Muḥammad Ḥusayn Haykal, *Mudhakkarāt fi'l-siyāsa al-Miṣriyya* (2 vols., Cairo 1951–3), vol. i, p. 147; *al-Liwā' al-Miṣrī*, Aug. 1922, pp. 26 ff.

[4] On the formation of the party and the text of the speech see: *al-Muqaṭṭam*, 1 Nov. 1922; Shafīq, *Ḥawliyyāt*, vol. iii, pp. 325–37; Aḥmad Baylī, *ʿAdlī Pāshā* (Cairo, 1922), pp. 251–74; Haykal, *Mudhakkarāt*, vol. i, pp. 14 ff.; Zayid, 'Nash'at Ḥizb al-Aḥrār al-Dustūriyyīn fī Miṣr, 1922–24', *al-Abḥāth*, Mar. 1963; Landau, op. cit., pp. 169–74.

[5] *al-Muqaṭṭam, supra.*

'Adlī then emphasized his party's aspiration to achieve independence by conciliatory means.

'Adlī was elected leader of the party, Muḥammad Maḥmūd its vice-president, and Muḥammad 'Alī, secretary. The 300 supporters, who were considered a general assembly, elected an administrative board of twenty-six persons to whom others were added later. A company was founded to finance the party's daily, *al-Siyāsa.*

While preparations had been made to form this party, *al-Liwā al-Miṣrī*'s correspondent in Alexandria was justified in reporting that the new party would be a faithful copy of the Umma.[1] In organization, the two parties were almost identical. A good portion of the new party's membership had been members of the Umma and the Legislative Assembly of 1913–14. Some of the members were drawn from the Democratic Party which had been formed in 1918 by young educated people who wanted to participate in political life.[2] A few members were drawn from 'the Group of Independent Egypt' which had been supporting 'Adlī.[3] The party's main elements were the wealthy, particularly the landowners, and the well-educated.

The differences between the Liberal Constitutionalists and the Wafdists did not lie so much in their programmes, which were similar, as in the degree of internal independence sought and the means to achieve it. Both believed in negotiation and compromise. But whereas the Wafdists would insist on a greater degree of internal independence and did not shrink from violence to achieve it, the Liberals, like the Umma, favoured gradualism and shunned violence.

In order to continue to exist as a party, the Liberals had to fight their way. In less than fifteen months they were confronted with a number of major crises. Their courage and the faith, at least of many of the educated members, in their principles, and the uneasy relations between the Wafd and the king helped them to overcome the crises and to live.[4]

[1] *Al-Liwā' al-Miṣrī*, 26 Aug. 1922.

[2] Haykal, *Mudhakkarāt*, vol. i, pp. 80–81; 'Alī 'Abd al-Rāziq, (ed.), *Min āthār Muṣṭafā 'Abd al-Rāziq* (Cairo, 1957), p. 62.

[3] On this group read: *Rouz el-Yousef*, 24 Apr. 1928, p. 4; Haykal, *Mudhakkarāt*, vol. i, p. 144; Shafīq, *Ḥawliyyāt*, vol. ii, pp. 337–441.

[4] For information on their difficulties see: Zayid, 'Nash'at Ḥizb al-Aḥrār al-Dustūriyyīn', pp. 44–49.

The Genesis of the Egyptian Constitution of 1923[1]

ELIE KEDOURIE

DURING the last year or so of Fu'ād's life, Sir David Kelly recounts in his memoirs, the king of Egypt, old and sick, would amuse himself by giving audiences to the British diplomat who was then acting high commissioner at Cairo, in which he expressed himself with great frankness. The king, according to Kelly, showed great contempt for the intellectual qualities of the British:

He said [as Sir David reported him] he understood the Italian, French and German characters thoroughly, but had given up trying to make any sense out of the actions of the British. He was especially bitter against the British for having 'imposed a constitution on the Belgian model' on the Egyptians, who were completely unsuited for parliamentary government on those lines. Our interest in Egypt, he said, was purely strategic; why had we not been content to leave him to run the country, as he well knew how to do, if we would only cease interfering, providing that as his part of the bargain he played up on all matters affecting our strategic interest and Empire communications?[2]

Some seven years before these audiences, the U.S. minister gave an account of Fu'ād's opinions which also reflected his bitterness towards the British, and in particular towards Allenby during whose time as high commissioner the Egyptian constitution which the king, according to Kelly, so disliked, had been promulgated. Fu'ād, so the American minister reported, found himself beset with difficulties. They were due 'first, to the passion of the small minority of politically-minded Egyptians for party-politics; second, the desire of his Ministers to get rich too [sic!] quickly; and third the difficulty of having always to placate and consider the British'. The king then went on to discuss Allenby. 'Lord Allenby', he said, 'had the true soldier-mind and was lacking in comprehension.' He complained, the American minister went on, 'that even though Lord Allenby knew very little French he would never have an interpreter, the result being that he frequently left the King, who does not speak English, seeming to have understood what His Majesty had said, and only later would it transpire that he had not understood at all'.[3] Allenby, in fact, knew French quite well,[4] and Fu'ād's remarks must therefore be considered

[1] I am greatly obliged to the Warden and Fellows of St. Antony's College, Oxford for making possible research in the U.S. National Archives, on which this paper draws.

[2] Sir David Kelly, *The ruling few* (London, 1952), p. 226.

[3] U.S. National Archives, Dept. of State records, 741.83/10, undated dispatch no. 43 from Alexandria (received 10 Oct. 1928).

[4] Brian Gardner, *Allenby* (London, 1965), p. 16.

all the more significant in disclosing the king's reaction to Allenby's mind and character, rather than to his linguistic attainments.

Fu'ād, then, seemed to think that those British with whom he had to deal did not understand Egypt, and that Allenby in particular excelled in blundering obtuseness; it is also clear that the king's resentment was due to his belief that without British insistence there would have been no constitution to give their opportunity to piddling and interested politicians, and make his own life a misery. Fu'ād's lamentations should not move us overmuch, for if the constitution had been pressed on him by Allenby, it was because Allenby was high commissioner; Allenby became high commissioner because Sir Reginald Wingate had lost the confidence of his superiors in London; the loss of confidence was the consequence of agitation in Egypt; and the hidden instigator of that agitation had been Fu'ād himself.[1]

But whatever sympathy Fu'ād's predicament arouses, it is interesting to notice that his judgement was exactly identical to that of Allenby's successor in Egypt, for it was Lord Lloyd's view that the British had 'forced' the parliamentary régime upon the country 'in the face of the King's wishes'.[2] To elucidate how this came about will throw some light on the subsequent vicissitudes of constitutional and representative government as it was attempted in Egypt between 1924 and 1952.

When Lord Allenby compelled Lloyd George and his colleagues in February 1922 to agree to his solution of the Egyptian problem, he promised them that his proposals 'if immediately accepted, will prove the basis of a lasting settlement in Egypt'.[3] They proved to be nothing of the kind, and even Allenby's three remaining years as high commissioner were full of unsettlement, agitation, and unrest, culminating in the sirdar's murder and the high-handed treatment to which the high commissioner subjected the Egyptian government; a course of conduct which lost him the confidence of the foreign secretary and led to his resignation. Thus, it may be said that Allenby's solution was really no solution. We may go further and say that it was this particular solution which was the breeding-ground of later difficulties; that these later difficulties were part of the high price with which Allenby purchased the illusion of 'a lasting settlement'. The Declaration of 28 February 1922, purported to give Egypt her independence, with four reservations which generally concerned the interests of Great Britain and the British Empire. The line of policy behind the Declaration is intelligible and superficially attractive. Britain, so the reasoning went, had certain interests in Egypt which were the real cause of her presence in the country. From 1882 to 1918 these interests

[1] See E. Kedourie, 'Sa'ad Zaghul and the British', *St. Antony's papers*, No. xi (Middle Eastern Affairs, No. 2) ed. Albert Hourani (London, 1961), pp. 139–60.

[2] C. F. Adam, *Life of Lord Lloyd* (London, 1948), p. 197, quoting a letter from Lloyd to a friend, written in 1927.

[3] Dispatch from Allenby to Curzon, 20 Jan. 1922, quoted in Lord Lloyd, *Egypt since Cromer*, vol. ii (London, 1934), p. 57.

were protected by Great Britain actually occupying Egypt and closely supervising its administration. But the events of 1919 and of the following years had shown that the Egyptian official classes at any rate had ceased to acquiesce in British control, and without their acquiescence Egypt was ungovernable. The good government of Egypt, however, was not a direct British interest; if the Egyptian official classes wished to resume the government of their country, the British could have no objection, provided Egypt was compelled to recognize and secure British interests. Hence the Declaration and its four reservations. But if this was the reasoning behind the Declaration—and only some such reasoning justified Allenby's claim that it provided the basis of a 'lasting settlement'—why then, as Fu'ād asked in his conversations with Kelly, not leave well alone and be content to see Egypt governed by a king in the same manner as it had been governed by the khedives? Or, if it be argued that Egypt under British control had irrevocably changed from what it used to be under Saʿīd and Ismāʿīl, why not leave Egyptians themselves to deal with this change as best they could? Why should Allenby take it upon himself, by sponsoring a constitution, officiously to pose as the midwife of history?

The answer is that in seeking to persuade London that his policy was the only feasible one, he had had to make sure of some Egyptian support, and that this committed him in turn to support a constitution. For the Egypt which Allenby had to govern was not a crown colony, it was a protectorate with its own indigenous government, and the high commissioner could not govern unless he could find Egyptians willing to take office as ministers. By the beginning of 1922 things had come to such a pass—the consequence of combined mismanagement by Allenby, Milner, and Lloyd George's government—that in order to escape from an impasse Allenby had to strike a bargain with some Egyptian politicians. He confesses as much when he writes to Curzon that his proposals are 'a result of exhaustive negotiations with Sarwat Pasha and his immediate adherents. They, on their part, have been in contact with wider circle, and Adly Pasha has been in close touch, and has lent valuable and disinterested assistance'.[1] The support of these politicians was indispensable to Allenby, but he had to pay for it by supporting them in his turn with all the prestige and influence of the high commissioner. Thus he found himself compelled to identify the Residency with a particular Egyptian faction, and consequently to alienate the rivals and enemies of this faction, namely Zaghlūl and the king. Allenby found himself compelled to do this in order to get his Declaration. The Declaration was a voluntary unilateral abrogation of the British position in Egypt; being unilateral, it secured no concession in return; being obtained at the price of supporting one faction and alienating its enemies, it made British interests in Egypt the perpetual sport of Egyptian factions; and having forsworn control over Egyptian politics, the Declaration made it difficult and at times quite impracticable for

[1] Allenby to Curzon, 12 Jan. 1922, quoted in Lloyd, op. cit., p. 56.

Great Britain to neutralize the factional disputes in which her interests became a pawn. This was the ruinous cost of Allenby's policy which led his successor to write in 1927: 'We have magnitude without position: power without authority; responsibility without control.'[1] This was very true at the time it was written, and became even truer as the years went by.

The Declaration of 28 February, then, committed Allenby to 'Sarwat Pasha and his immediate adherents'. What this commitment entailed may be gathered from a paragraph in the draft Declaration which Allenby sent to London. This paragraph would have had the British government 'view with favour the creation of a parliament with right to control the policy and administration of a constitutional, responsible government'. This paragraph was amended in London, and the Declaration, as finally published, did not commit the British government to the promotion of constitutionalism in a kingdom on which, by that very instrument, they were bestowing independence.[2] But the absence of constitutionalist manifestos from the Declaration of 28 February did not alter the fact that Tharwat and his friends were now in power, supported by the great prestige and influence of the high commissioner. They would naturally try to preserve and extend their power. In this enterprise they had to guard against two enemies: Zaghlūl with his Wafdist organization and his power over the mob, and the king who, imbued with the autocratic traditions of his house and coming late in life and unexpectedly to the throne, was all the more rapacious for power and impatient of any who might claim to share it with him. In arguing that Tharwat and his friends were primarily concerned to enjoy the power which their collaboration with Allenby had brought them, we do not mean to imply that they had no other purpose in politics. Tharwat and his associates did, after all, stand for constitutionalism, the rule of law and limited government; among them were to be found the representatives and heirs of the pre-war Umma Party from which Cromer had hoped and expected so much. A sentence in the speech which ʿAdlī Yakan delivered on 30 October 1922, at the first general meeting of the Liberal Constitutionalist Party—which Tharwat founded with his friends—may be taken to express their political hopes and ideals. 'The constitutional régime', he said, 'is the only form of government worthy of a nation such as ours which is steeped in civilisation.'[3] If, however, we remember the extremely cavalier manner in which the Liberal Constitutionalists later treated the constitution, we may fairly say that they insisted on a constitution in 1922 because it was then a convenient and useful instrument for limiting Fu'ād's power, and consolidating their own.

Their co-operation with Allenby seemed at first to have all the desirable results. Allenby had taken care to exile Zaghlūl and his supporters from Cairo before coercing his own government into issuing the Declaration of 28

[1] Adam, op. cit., p. 197.
[2] Kedourie, op. cit., pp. 158–9.
[3] Quoted in Aḥmad Baylī, *ʿAdlī Pāshā* (Cairo, 1922), p. 256.

February; and if the Declaration did not contain the constitutional manifesto which Allenby had designed, yet the very fact that Allenby was supporting Tharwat and his friends was enough, in the circumstances, to compel the king to give in to their desire for a constitution. The fact is that the king, in appointing Tharwat chief minister on 1 March 1922, requested him to prepare a draft constitution, and Tharwat accepted office on the specific understanding that the constitution would ensure the responsibility of ministers to parliament. On 3 April, the Council of Ministers approved a memorandum by the prime minister setting up a Constitutional Commission composed of thirty members. The first paragraph embodies the terms on which Tharwat took office and deserves quotation:

> The Royal Command to form a ministry which was addressed to me, [the memorandum declares] alluded to His Majesty's wish to bring about cooperation between the nation and the Government by means of a constitutional régime, and charged the ministry with the preparation of a draft project. The answer of the ministry to the Royal Command was to the effect that it would immediately put in hand the preparation of a draft constitution in conformity with the principles of modern public law, and that such a constitution would lay down the principle of ministerial responsibility, thus affording to the representative assembly the right to supervise future political activity.[1]

The Commission of Thirty which Tharwat appointed was presided over by Ḥusayn Rushdī Pasha. It included four ex-ministers, nine members of the Legislative Assembly which was prorogued in 1914, never to meet again, Shaykh ʿAbd al-Ḥamīd al-Bakrī, head of the Ṣūfī orders, Shaykh Muḥammad Bakhīt, an ex-*muftī* of Egypt, five Copts including the Coptic bishop of Alexandria, one Jew, representatives of the law, of commerce and of the bedouins, the governors of Cairo and Alexandria, the secretary-general of the Council of Ministers, and the permanent secretary of the Ministry of Finance. Of those who had played a part in recent political events, ʿAbd al-Laṭīf al-Makabbātī presumably represented the Nationalist Party; Muḥammad ʿAlī ʿAllūba and ʿAbd ad-ʿAzīz Fahmī had first co-operated with Zaghlūl in 1919–20, had broken with him over his devious methods and dictatorial habits, and were now associated with ʿAdlī and Tharwat; whilst ʿAlī Māhir who had also been associated with the Wafd, organizing a civil servants' strike in 1919, did not now seem to be identified with any group, but pursued in the Commission an individual and most interesting line of argument. As for the Wafd, they flatly refused to have anything to do with the Constitutional Commission which Zaghlūl denounced as 'the Malefactors' Commission' (*lajnat al-ashqiyā*'), alleging that a constitution was properly the business not of a commission but of a constituent assembly. Zaghlūl's tactics are easily appreciated: he was on the one hand boycotting and blackening a body

[1] Document, reproduced in Muḥammad Khalīl Ṣubḥī, *Ta'rīkh al-ḥayāh al-niyābiyya fī Miṣr*, vol. v (Cairo, 1939), p. 459.

created by his political rivals; while on the other, the demagogical powers, which he had successfully tested on the Egyptian masses, made him confident of controlling an elected constituent assembly.

The Commission, then, seemed to be well-balanced in affording representation to different interests and sections. It was ably assisted by a secretariat of legal experts and draughtsmen.[1] Its members collectively possessed a respectable body of political wisdom and legal expertise, and most of them were traditional and conservative in their views; their attitude to constitution-making may perhaps be summed up by the remark of a member who, the U.S. chargé d'affaires reported, 'said to me anent the difficult scholarly Arabic employed that incidentally it had the advantage that 'des petits gens [sic] . . . would not be able to understand it'.[2] But if this may be said to reflect the attitude of the majority, it certainly does not represent that of the few members who took an active and prominent part in the discussions. These members included ʿAbd al-Laṭif al-Makabbātī, ʿAbd al-ʿAzīz Fahmī, ʿAlī Māhir, and ʿAbd al-Ḥamīd Badawī, the secretary-general of the Council of Ministers. ʿAlī Māhir, in particular, took an extreme democratic line, in which he was occasionally seconded—it is interesting to note—by Shaykh Muḥammad Bakhīt, the ex-*muftī*, and which was quite remarkable in its contrast to his future career as a king's man. Discussions extending over many sittings ranged over the most fundamental principles of government, and different views and opinions were defended with spirit, learning, and not a little ingenuity: thus there were long debates over the right of the king to veto legislation, to dissolve the parliament and to preside over the Cabinet; debates over the status of the Royal Household officials, over the proportion of elected and appointed senators, and whether the president of the Senate should be elected by his peers or appointed by the king. There were other debates on matters equally fundamental, but the topics just mentioned proved in retrospect to be the most significant and to have given rise to the many vicissitudes which Egyptian constitutionalism suffered in its short but chequered history.[3]

Acute controversy occurred at the very first meeting of the Commission. ʿAbd al-Laṭīf al-Makabbātī and ʿAbd al-ʿAzīz Fahmī stood for a franchise embracing all Egyptians over twenty-one; Ismāʿīl Abāẓa, a notable who had been a member of the Legislative Assembly, opposed this suggestion saying

[1] The list of members is printed in Ṣubḥī, op. cit., pp. 493–4; Muḥammad Ḥusayn Haykal was a member of the secretariat and his memoirs give valuable glimpses of the working of the Commission; see *Mudhakkirāt fi'l-siyāsa al-Miṣriyya*, vol. i (Cairo, 1951), ch. iii.

[2] 883.00/436, Telegram from Cairo, 2 Oct 1922.

[3] The debates of the Commission and of a subcommittee of eighteen members drawn from the full Commission in order to consider first principles have been published: *Maḥādir al-lajna al-ʿāmma li-waḍʿ al-dustūr* and *Maḥāḍir lajnat waḍʿ al-mabādi' al-ʿāmma li'l-dustūr*; they have been substantially reproduced in a valuable commentary on the constitution: Muḥammad al-Sharīf,ʿ *Alā hāmish al-dustūr* (Cairo, 1938), 2 vols., in which the debates have been rearranged to follow the order of the articles as they appear in the constitution of 1923.

that he could not imagine how a peasant who merely tilled the earth and did not know how to read and write could be considered the equal of, say, ʿAbd al-ʿAzīz Fahmī or of himself. Those in favour of universal suffrage buttressed their contention by the argument that equality of burdens entailed equality of rights, and that since the peasant was subject to conscription, his right to vote was beyond dispute. Their opponents, however, argued that the vote was, as Haykal puts it, part of the process of government (*ʿamaliyya min ʿamaliyyāt al-ḥukm*), on which depended the choice of representatives who, by the expression of their confidence in the cabinet, made its continuance in power possible; it followed therefore, according to this view, that some acquaintance with political issues and some informed interest in the operation of government was required from the voter.[1] The debate, as may be appreciated, raised issues of principle which, if not speedily resolved in some fashion, threatened to prolong deliberations intolerably. The chairman, Ḥusayn Rushdī, acted quickly. At the second meeting, after prolonged debate, he succeeded in having appointed a subcommittee of eighteen members who were charged with formulating the basis on which the constitution ought to rest. The smaller numbers made the subcommittee more manageable, but here too issues of principle continued to be raised and defended with skill and pertinacity. The main dispute within the subcommittee lay between those who wanted to give the monarch some real powers and those who wanted his function to be merely ceremonial. According to Haykal, Ḥusayn Rushdī played a crucial part in these debates; Rushdī Pasha, he writes, was 'the real motive force behind its activity'; he got up in advance the subjects to be debated, he intervened frequently in the debates, trying to persuade the members to his point of view, and used the authority of the chair to adjourn the debate whenever it threatened to produce undesirable decisions. Haykal describes Rushdī's attitude with some precision:

> Notwithstanding his acceptance of public liberties and indeed his warm defence of them, [writes Haykal] Rushdī Pasha inclined to concede certain rights to the monarch. . . . Some people have expressed surprise at such an attitude in a man who had studied in France and had been particularly known for his courage and his preference for liberty. It seems to me that in these discussions the man was not defending a view in which he believed, but rather a policy which, he was convinced, was the only one to ensure the realisation of the greatest part of the Commission's aims. The policy depended on the fact that whatever was produced by the Commission was no more than a draft constitution which in order to take effect, had to be ratified by the monarch. If, therefore, such a draft deprived the monarch of all power, then it would be subject to radical revision: but if, on the other hand, satisfaction were given to the monarch on some issues, while basic rights were secured to the nation and its representatives, then it was most probable that nothing would prevent the draft constitution being promulgated.[2]

[1] Haykal, op. cit., p. 134.

[2] Haykal, op. cit., p. 137.

Haykal goes on to say that these considerations were also very much in the minds of those members of the Commission who were most in contact with Tharwat and his ministry. Two other motives, Haykal thought, further explain Rushdī's policy; the first, that with the constitutional issue out of the way, Egypt could begin to tackle Great Britain on the four reserved points of the Declaration of 28 February; the second, that if it came to a contest beween 'moderates' and 'extremists', as happened when 'Adlī and Zaghlūl clashed in the spring of 1921, a monarch with some effective constitutional power would exert his influence in favour of the 'moderates'. If this was really in Rushdī's mind the events which followed the promulgation of the constitution must have soon undeceived him.

The draft constitution produced by the Commission was, then, a compromise between Fu'ād's desire for unfettered power and the views of those on the Commission who stood for unfettered popular sovereignty. It was in form largely a codification and abridgement of constitutional practices and traditions which had grown up in Europe since the Middle Ages; which had been digested, summarized, and transformed into 'principles of public law' by the academic lawyers, mainly French, from whom members of the Commission derived much of their constitutional learning. The draft began by asserting (article 23) that 'All authority derives from the nation',[1] went on to divide governmental powers into a legislative (to be exercised by a parliament in conjunction with the king), an executive (of which the king was the head), and a judiciary. Executive power was to be exercised, under the king, by a Council of Ministers who were to resign from office on forfeiting the legislature's confidence. The king had a limited right of veto over legislation (articles 33 and 34), the power to dissolve a parliament (article 36) and the power to appoint and dismiss ministers (article 45). The Commission published a commentary to accompany the draft,[2] in which they explained that the right of dissolution was essential as a means of effecting a balance between the executive and the legislature, enabling the nation to be consulted whenever there was deadlock between the different powers in the state. The commentary also supplied a gloss on article 45 which gave the king power to appoint and dismiss the ministers, saying that the current convention was that the king chose the prime minister and on his advice appointed and dismissed ministers.

This, then, was a model, a textbook constitution, *sage comme une image*, full of checks and of balances, an ordered and intricate toyland in which everything was calm and beauty. Its radical failing in the actual conditions of Egyptian politics was that it assumed and took for granted that elections in Egypt could possibly elicit, as they did elsewhere, the will of the electorate. As the sequel, from 1923 to 1952, showed, they did nothing of the kind;

[1] The draft constitution is printed in Ṣubḥī, op. cit., pp. 495 ff.

[2] Printed in Ṣubḥī, op. cit., pp. 466–92.

Egyptian elections, rather proved to be ratifications by the masses of decisions taken by the king, or else by the Cairo politicians, depending on which side had, for the time being, the upper hand. Dissolutions, therefore, could not remotely help, as the Commission expected, in preserving the balance of the constitution, and their judicious and elaborate considerations merely manage to look ineffective and academic. This is also the case with their gloss on article 45 dealing with the appointment and dismissal of ministers; the Commission took for granted that a prime minister would be appointed only if he had a majority in the parliament, and fastened on the insignificant issue of the appointment and dismissal of other ministers. They did not consider the possibility that the king might make a literal use of his powers and appoint and dismiss his chief ministers as he liked. But this is what in fact repeatedly happened under the parliamentary régime in Egypt.

Given these conditions, the parliamentary régime which Tharwat and his friends desired and which Allenby was inclined to press on the king could not but justify Cromer's foreboding when at the end of his long rule in Egypt he affirmed that 'under the specious title of free institutions, the worst evils of personal government would reappear'.[1] Rushdī's judicious policies, and his tenacious attempts at compromise, availed nothing, for even if by some miracle he had succeeded in reconciling royal ambitions with constitutional government, he would yet have been powerless to endow with representativeness an Egyptian parliament, or to make possible limited government in a country where unlimited power was, and continued to be, a standing temptation, easy to fall into and safe to indulge. Therefore we may say that by supporting parliamentarianism in Egypt, Allenby was engaging his credit and the credit of his government in support of a farce.

For him, it was not even a profitable farce. One of the points which the Declaration of 28 February 'absolutely' reserved to the discretion of the British government was the Sudan, then administered as an Anglo-Egyptian condominium. The Constitutional Commission decided that the forthcoming constitution should indicate unmistakably that Fu'ād was king of Egypt and the Sudan. Such a proposal was defended alike by those who were the king's partisans and by those who wished to challenge British power in the Nile valley. When Allenby came to hear of this proposal, he objected strenuously, but in spite of the fact that Tharwat and his friends were in office owing to British support, his protests availed him nothing and the draft constitution when it was completed and handed to Tharwat stated, in article 29, that 'The king shall be called king of Egypt and the Sudan'.[2] The fact is that however much Rushdī, Tharwat, and their friends may have disliked this provision, they had no means of opposing it without giving the king and Zaghlūl a powerful pretext for attacking them as creatures of the British

[1] In his Report for 1906, Cmd. 3394 (1907), p. 7.

[2] A. P. Wavell, *Allenby, soldier and statesman* (London, 1946), p. 316; Ṣubḥī, op. cit., p. 498.

government. Haykal[1] tells us that Tharwat consulted ʿAdlī and his other political friends who advised him that the provision had to stand. Allenby used to complain that ʿAdlī was a broken reed, and that he much preferred to deal with Tharwat.[2] And it is true that ʿAdlī was not a fighter, but in this particular case it was Tharwat who let Allenby down, and could not do otherwise if he wanted to stay in power. The episode merely shows that the policy which Allenby thought worth coercing his government into following was of little use in the defence of British interests, and that, as hitherto, British interests had to be defended by constant British intervention, which after the Declaration of 28 February, could be (and was) legitimately denounced as interference.

Ḥusayn Rushdī could be as statesmanlike and moderate as he liked, but there was no disguising the fact that the draft constitution, however solicitous of the king's prerogative, represented a serious limitation of his powers. Fu'ād did not mean to be reduced to a constitutional monarch so that Tharwat and his friends might enjoy greater patronage and power. The Palace was traditionally a power in the land, and so long as a constitution was not promulgated the king retained vast power of initiative, intervention, and patronage which Fu'ād proceeded to wield for the undoing of his chief minister. During the summer of 1922 Fu'ād made clear his disapproval of Tharwat and his policies; and the ministry's supporters within the Constitutional Commission tried to make haste and complete their labours; a subcommittee was appointed to produce the final draft of the constitution, and another subcommittee to produce the final draft electoral law.[3] The texts were finally agreed and six months after beginning its work the Commission presented them to Tharwat on 21 October.

By then the prime minister's position was gravely weakened both by his disagreement with Allenby over the Sudan, and by the king's manifest disapproval. One of Fu'ād's tactics now was to adopt a popular stance and insist that Tharwat should obtain from the British the recall of Zaghlūl, the people's tribune, and of his friends from exile—to which they had been sent in December 1921, precisely in order that Tharwat might assume office unhindered! 'There is again a coolness between Sarwat, the Prime Minister, and the King', reported the U.S. chargé d'affaires on 2 October, 'due to a difference of opinion relative to the policy pursued with the Zaghlūl leaders. The King is afraid of their enmity and is for leniency. This Sarwat regards as weakness and opposes.'[4] The language of this telegram indicates not so much the king's actual motives as the impression which he desired outsiders to gather. The architect of this policy would seem to have been Tawfīq Nasīm, a former prime minister who since April 1922 was chief of the Royal Cabinet. It appears that he managed to achieve an understanding between the

[1] Haykal, op. cit., pp. 155–6.
[2] Wavell, op. cit., p. 309.
[3] Haykal, op. cit., pp. 141–2.
[4] 883.00/436 previously cited.

king and Zaghlūl's party which was presumably directed against the existing ministry.[1]

The upshot of these manœuvres was that the Wafd began to attack Tharwat's administration even more strongly, and to abound in fervent declarations of loyalty to the throne. In the telegram of 2 October previously cited, the U.S. chargé d'affaires reported that Tharwat was then unpopular and that his administration could not last for long; 'it is in effect', he added, 'imposed upon the country by measures taken or supported under martial law'. The observation is correct and applies not only to the last days of Tharwat's administration, but in fact to the whole of it; it had been brought in and supported by British power, but that the truth should now be openly said about it indicated that its days were numbered. In the event, Tharwat lasted until the end of November. The *coup de grâce* was delivered with the help of another Household official, Ḥasan Nash'at, whose role in Egyptian politics had hitherto been obscure, but who was to play a part of some importance in the following years. The king, attended by Tharwat and his other Ministers, was to go to al-Azhar for Friday prayers on 1 December. Nash'at distributed money among the Azhar students and incited them to demonstrate against Tharwat on the occasion of the royal visit. Tharwat heard of this plot, and rather than be subjected to the indignity of such a contrived attack, preferred to send in his resignation the day before. Nash'at brought Fu'ād's acceptance within the hour; Allenby told the American minister how sorry he was at Tharwat's fall, and heavily remonstrated with the king for his actions, 'informing him of the displeasure of the British Government at his treatment of a Minister who had been appointed to implement the policy of the Declaration'![2]

Tawfīq Nasīm, the new prime minister, had two assignments: to try and make the constitution as innocuous as possible, while maintaining the provision of article 29 which assured to Fu'ād the dual monarchy of Egypt and the Sudan. This latter object was, of course, impossible to achieve in the face of British objections. Allenby had protested against the offending article when Tharwat was in power, but may have found his style cramped by his desire to support him. Such considerations now no longer inhibited Allenby, and he coerced the king into signing a declaration giving up these pretensions.[3] We do not know the exact tenor of this declaration, but Allenby's threat seems to have been to the effect that if Fu'ād persisted in his claim he would have to give up the Egyptian throne not only for himself but for his heir as well. Fu'ād signed this declaration[4] at the beginning of February 1923, and, according to Allenby, Tawfīq Nasīm felt, as a result, that he could not

[1] 883.00/438, dispatch from U.S. minister, Cairo, 1 Dec. 1922.

[2] Wavell, op. cit., p. 318. For the events leading to Tharwat's resignation see Haykal, op. cit., pp. 155–6 and *al-Kashkūl*, 8 Jan. 1926, p. 4; also dispatch from U.S. minister, 1 Dec., 883.00/438.

[3] Wavell, op. cit., p. 320.

[4] So the U.S. minister reported in a dispatch from Cairo of 21 Oct. 1929; 741.8311/53.

continue in office. He resigned on 9 February, the king denouncing him as a coward.[1]

During his period of office, rumours became rife that the Palace and the ministry had amended the constitution drastically, that the clause stating that the nation was the source of authority was to be omitted, that the king was to be given wide prerogatives in the distribution of honours, the dissolution of parliament (and not merely of the Chamber of Deputies as the draft proposed), and in the control of religious endowments, that he was to have the power of issuing decree-laws even when the parliament was sitting, and that the proportion of senators appointed by the king was to be greatly increased. The Liberal Constitutionalists and ʿAbd al-ʿAzīz Fahmī in particular were loud in their protests.[2] Tawfīq Nasīm resigned before any amendments were officially published, but that drastic changes had been made to conform to Fu'ād's wishes is not in doubt.

It did not prove easy to appoint a successor to Tawfīq Nasīm. ʿAdlī Yakan was approached to form an administration, it would seem at Allenby's instance,[3] but the political situation which he confronted was complicated and treacherous in the extreme. Under Tawfīq Nasīm's inspiration, the king's policy had been from the summer of 1922 onwards, to encourage Zaghlūl's Wafd to maintain popular effervescence against Tharwat and his British patrons, by means of demonstrations and terrorist outrages. These outrages continued unchecked under Tawfīq Nasīm's administration. These tactics are clearly exhibited in a letter from Tawfīq Nasīm in answer to a protest by Allenby against the murder of Mr. Robson, a lecturer at the Law College. Tawfīq Nasīm asserted that such outrages indicated that British policy did not take into account 'the sentiments of the majority', which had been further exacerbated by the understanding reached between the British and 'a minority which had no real influence over the nation'.[4] Thus Allenby—'the Bull'—was baited and ridiculed for the ill-success of his famous Declaration. When ʿAdlī was asked to form a cabinet, he realized that if he succeeded, it would be in the teeth of determined and concerted opposition from the king and the Zaghlulists. He had had experience, when prime minister in 1921, of the lengths to which the Zaghlulists would go in demagogy and incitement,[5] and had no stomach for another such experience—this is what Allenby meant when he said that ʿAdlī was a broken reed. ʿAdlī thought to escape his difficulties by a compromise: he would take office only on condition that the Wafd supported him; let Zaghlūl and his friends be recalled from exile and in return, let the constitution as drafted by the Commission be promulgated.

[1] Wavell, op. cit., p. 320.

[2] Baylī, op. cit., p. 316; Aḥmad Shafīq, *Ḥawliyyāt Miṣr al-siyāsiyya, Tamhīd*, vol. iii Cairo, 1926), pp. 468 ff.

[3] 883.00/460, dispatch from U.S. minister, Cairo, 22 Feb. 1923.

[4] Text of letter dated 27 Dec. 1922, in Aḥmad Shafīq, op. cit., pp. 378–80.

[5] See Kedourie, op. cit., pp. 155–6.

Since Fu'ād's object was precisely to prevent this, and since the Wafdists had no desire to see their rival in power, much less support him, this compromise plan was quite useless. To help 'Adlī see things as they really were, Wafdist incitement and terrorist outrages were stepped up. In these activities it seems that Ḥasan Nash'at was so implicated that the British required his departure from Egypt and refused to let him return until the constitution was finally promulgated.[1] 'Adlī was told that he could have office with the king's approval if he agreed to issue the amended draft as a constitution. He preferred to give up the attempt.

A cabinet was not formed until 15 March. The prime minister was Yaḥyā Ibrāhīm, who was not a political personality, and was presumably acceptable both to Allenby and to the king. He was not of a calibre to stand up to either; but was merely the intermediary whose function was to prevent a direct clash between them. The king, we understand from Allenby's biography, had not abandoned his opposition to the draft constitution, and the high commissioner 'thought it judicious' to use his influence with him and 'accordingly advised him to allow himself to be guided by his Prime Minister'. Allenby's constitutional tuition lasted for a month before the king allowed himself to be converted and to promulgate the constitution on 19 April. In a report quoted by his biographer Allenby stated that Fu'ād's behaviour was running counter to 'unanimous and clearly expressed public opinion' and that he intervened because it was not in accord with 'the policy of the Declaration' that the king should arrogate 'undue' powers to himself, and because he wished to avoid a constitutional struggle between king and people.[2] As regards public opinion and the possibility of a struggle between king and people, there is no evidence to support Allenby's contentions. It is true that the king's ambitions were attacked—but only by the handful of politicians and academics who dreamed of a constitutional representative government for their country. As late as 15 April, four days before the promulgation of the constitution, 'Abd al-'Azīz Fahmī was addressing an open letter to the prime minister protesting against certain Egyptians offering the results of the anti-British struggle as a free gift to the royal house (*yahibūnahā ghanīma bārida li-umarā' al-bayt al-mālik*).[3] But such protests, noble and courageous as they may have been, were

[1] Nash'at, as is well known, was mentioned in the assassination trials which followed Sir Lee Stack's murder as having had a connexion in 1922–3 with the Wafd's apparatus; see the deposition before the *juge d'instruction* of Sulaymān Fawzī, editor of *al-Kashkūl* (who knew Nash'at) printed in this periodical in its issue of 12 Feb. 1926; see also a most interesting article on Nash'at in *al-Kashkūl*, 18 Dec. 1925, where it is stated that during the period when 'Adlī was considering the formation of a cabinet, the authorities seized the manuscripts of Wafdist manifestos translated into Arabic by the [publicist] Manfalūṭī who had been dismissed from his government post by the Tharwat administration and been employed subsequently by Nash'at in the Palace; these translations were further stated to have been corrected by Nash'at, and to have been originally drafted in French by another Palace official, [Achille?] Ṣayqalī [Sékaly?].

[2] Wavell, op. cit., p. 321.

[3] Text in Aḥmad Shafīq, op. cit., p. 518.

not the voice of 'unanimous and clearly-expressed public opinion'. They were on the contrary the voice of a minority of politicians who—'Abd al-'Azīz Fahmī excepted—by their later actions showed that their regard for constitutionalism speedily disappeared at the prospect of power. Again, Allenby was mistaken in thinking that an autocratic constitution would have precipitated a struggle between king and people—it might have precipitated a struggle between the king and Allenby's clients, but this is another story. As for Allenby's remaining motive, i.e. that the king's behaviour was contrary to 'the policy of the Declaration', it is most revealing. Allenby does not—and of course cannot—say that such behaviour was contrary to the Declaration, for there was nothing in the Declaration to show that Fu'ād had to be a constitutional figurehead, scrupulous in observing the proprieties, content merely to be consulted, to advise and to warn; 'the policy of the Declaration' is another matter altogether, and really signifies the assumptions on which Allenby had built his policy. Fu'ād was under no obligation to make these assumptions come true. Allenby as a constitutional mentor calls to mind the observation of a witty orientalist on the behaviour of al-Ma'mūn trying to force theological dogmas down the throats of his unwilling divines: '*C'était un libéral*', wrote Darmsteter of this caliph, '*c'est-à-dire qu'il envoyait les orthodoxes à la potence*'. *Mutatis mutandis*, the description fits the methods of Allenby the constitutionalist to perfection.

The constitution promulgated on 19 April differed in many ways from the draft completed the previous October. The extent of the king's original demands may be imagined from the wide prerogatives which this document still secured to him even after a month of powerful pressure from Allenby. Article 23, which asserted that the nation was the source of authority, remained in the constitution in spite of the fears of the Liberal Constitutionalists, but it was glossed with a curious commentary from the minister of Justice, Aḥmad Dhu'l-Faqār. 'The principle that the nation is the origin of all authority', stated his explanatory memorandum issued with the constitution, 'is not in contradiction with the origin of the Islamic monarchical and absolutist governments, because these monarchies used initially to depend on the explicit or implicit consent of the people represented by its elders and notables'.[1] The theory is not really tenable; but its effect is to substitute an autocratic interpretation for the democratic one intended by the original authors of article 23. The modifications introduced in the constitution itself were of greater importance, however, than the merely academic dispute about the proper meaning of article 23. The constitution[2] gave the king power to confer civil and military rank, decorations and titles at his own discretion,[3] it gave him power to appoint and dismiss military officers[4] and diplomats.[5]

[1] Ṣubḥī, op. cit., p. 542.
[2] Text in Ṣubḥi, op. cit., pp. 517–32.
[3] Art. 43, compared with Art. 41 of the draft.
[4] Art. 46, compared with Art. 42 of the draft.
[5] Art. 49, compared with Art. 45 of the draft.

The constitution also increased significantly the proportion of appointed senators and made the presidency of the Senate an office within the sole discretion of the monarch to bestow.[1] Again, it left religious endowments and the control of the Muslim religious institution solely within the power of the king, until the parliament should legislate otherwise.[2] The draft also specifically entrenched eight articles against amendment or abrogation, while the constitution was much more vague in stating that no proposal could be entertained which would change 'the provisions guaranteed by this constitution concerning the representative form of government, the order of succession to the throne and the principles of liberty and equality'.[3]

The king, then, got what he wanted, in part at least. But in order to get it, he had to enlist the help of Zaghlūl and his Wafdists, for which, of course, they exacted a price. The price was the king's support in gaining power. The extent to which Fu'ād was involved with Zaghlūl at that time may be gathered from the fact that at his first interview as prime minister with the high commissioner, Yaḥyā Ibrāhīm—who himself had no Wafdist connexions—asked Allenby to allow Zaghlūl and his companions to come back from their exile.[4] Egypt was at last endowed with a constitution and an electoral law.[5] Elections had therefore to be held, and when they were, at the end of 1923, the weight of administrative influence was exerted against the Liberal Constitutionalists,[6] and therefore in favour of Wafdists. Zaghlūl enjoyed a crushing majority and was appointed prime minister; later on, Fu'ād justified his behaviour in supporting Zaghlūl at this juncture by claiming that it was a far-sighted scheme for breaking the 'popular idol' by burdening him with responsibility.[7] But when he held this conversation, Fu'ād was surely sighing with relief that Zaghlūl's ineptitude and his failure to control the terrorist apparatus[8] had accidentally rid him of a prime minister whom his own machinations had brought to power, and who, when he unexpectedly fell, was bidding fair to overwhelm with a populist dictatorship Fu'ād's own autocracy.

[1] Arts. 74 and 80, compared with Arts. 71 and 75.

[2] Art. 153, without a counterpart in the draft.

[3] Art. 156, compared with Art. 146 of the draft.

[4] 'Abd al-'Azīz Fahmī, *Hādhihi ḥayātī* (Cairo, 1963), p. 143.

[5] Text of the Law of 30 Apr. 1923, in Ṣubḥī, op. cit., pp. 621 ff.

[6] Haykal, op. cit., p. 171.

[7] Conversation towards the end of 1924 with the managing director of the Suez Canal Co., *Austen Chamberlain Papers*.

[8] Directed successively by 'Abd al-Raḥmān Fahmī and Shafīq Manṣūr, two prominent Wafdists.

Some Political Consequences of the 1952 Revolution in Egypt[1]

P. J. VATIKIOTIS

Introduction

ONE necessarily approaches the task of describing the political consequences of the revolution of 1952 with trepidation. Thirteen years is too short a period of time for an accurate assessment of these consequences. Mere observation by the student suggests trends in the political orientation of the rulers of Egypt, perhaps traces the barest outline of their policy aims and the ways in which they try to achieve them. Yet vital information about the detailed political transactions and the motives of rulers for making them is not available to the student of politics in the short period of time since the leaders of a military conspiracy seized power on 23 July 1952. Compared to the historian who studies the less recent past, the student of politics is at a disadvantage.

In addition to the difficulty of time and information, there is the more complex problem of determining the extent to which far-reaching revolutionary change has in fact occurred in Egypt since 1952. Without necessarily subscribing to Pareto's theory of 'the circulation of elites', one still needs to ask the question: Did the displacement of one ruling group by another—even though the latter may be different in social composition, professional identity, and political outlook—constitute a revolution? To deal with this question adequately one must be able to study and analyse changes in the structure and functions of social, economic, and political institutions. The latter, after all, reflect in great measure the arrangements of authority for the maintenance of a political system and order.[2] The change that has

[1] The more general remarks about revolution and ideology derive from work I am pursuing on the intellectuals and radical revolution in the Arab states, and I wish to acknowledge the assistance of the Carnegie Seminar in Comparative Politics and the International Development Center, Indiana University, in the early stages of this work. A general examination of Arab politics upon which some of these remarks are based was partly supported by the Programme in Legal and Political Philosophy of the Rockefeller Foundation 1959–60.

[2] At this stage, one can only assume that new institutions are in the making. Until they can be clearly identified as such and their functions observed, one must avoid their premature assessment. This essay was written in April–October 1965.

In a recent article, 'Political development and political decay', *World Politics*, vol. xvii. 3 (Apr. 1965), pp. 386–430, Samuel P. Huntington distinguishes between 'political development' and modernization. The latter, especially in the new states of Africa and Asia, he finds, rests upon mass mobilization. He argues, however, that it is dangerously misleading to assume that modernization of this sort also constitutes political development. The latter he forcefully suggests rests primarily and fundamentally upon the institutionalization of political organizations and procedures. He further questions 'some tendencies frequently encompassed in the

occurred in these institutions reflects in part the desire of man for exceptionally new conditions of social life and organization, in short, for a new order. It also indicates action taken to fulfil this desire. Despite the progress being made, for example, by students of economic development in describing and analysing the economic policy of the Egyptian government since July 1952, they find it is still too early to assess its total impact upon, and consequences for, the country.[1]

Revolution, commonly understood, implies the overthrow of an existing order, a *status quo*, by a new group of leaders (or by a single activist) purporting to establish a new order. The modern Greek term for revolution, *epanástasis*, is instructive in this connexion, for it denotes simultaneous action in two directions: an *insurrection* against a ruler or a régime, and the resurrection of a society towards new achievement.[2] The Free Officers, led by Jamāl ʿAbd al-Nāṣir, embraced both these goals. The first was attained fairly quickly after their successful coup. The second, namely, to effect a revolution in Egyptian society of economic advancement, of political modernization and development, is the current major task of the régime. Meantime, a new dimension has been added to the revolution in Egypt since 1955 which extends to all the Arab states in the Middle East.

Recent studies of the régime in Egypt headed by President Jamāl ʿAbd al-Nāṣir fall into two distinct categories. First, there are those who, employing

concept of political development as characteristic of the "developing areas"', and with this the 'underlying commitment to the theory of progress'. He finds that there is a tendency towards simple political systems which depend on one individual and which are therefore neither stable nor capable of producing peaceful change. He suggests emphatically that 'Institutional decay has become a common phenomenon of the modernising countries'. The decline of institutions is reflected in the rise of charismatic leaders, or what I call here the modernizing leader, who personalize power and weaken institutions which might limit their power. 'Institutionalisation of power means the limitation of power which might otherwise be wielded personally and arbitrarily.'

[1] See C. Issawi, *Egypt in revolution, an economic analysis* (London, 1963); P. K. O'Brien, 'An economic appraisal of the Egyptian revolution', *The Journal of Development Studies*, vol. i. 1 (Oct. 1964), pp. 93–113. See also P. K. O'Brien, *The revolution in Egypt's economic system* (London, 1966) for the first systematic assessment of the régime's economic policy.

[2] There is in the Egyptian revolution led by the Free Officers just as potent a myth in terms of a faith in a future that is resplendent with modernity and power as in all other revolutionary movements. Its ideology may not be couched in the articulate and uncompromising terms of a dogma. Yet, its leader and *élite* contend that they reflect a popular will oriented towards such a future. It is in the name of, and for the sake of, this future that revolutionary leadership can exercise immense power to suppress all adversaries in order to act for the fulfilment of its aims. A near-Mazzinian conception of the people and the nation surrounded by political messianism tends to produce an autocracy (the Bonapartist parallel is tempting but dangerous) that is not in serious conflict with local and cultural tradition.

Talmon, *The origins of totalitarian democracy* (New York, 1960) and *Political messianism* (London, 1960) and Raymond Aron, *The opium of the intellectuals* (New York, 1962) are instructive in this connexion but not quite freely applicable to an Islamic-Arab or Egyptian setting. On the question of ideology and culture, see the article by Clifford Geertz, 'Ideology as a cultural system', in David E. Apter (ed.), *Ideology and discontent* (New York, 1964), pp. 47–76. See also the suggestive monograph by Chalmers Johnson, *Revolution and the social system* (Stanford, 1964).

a socio-economic analysis of Egyptian society, argue that there is no evidence that the traditional relationship between ruler and subject has changed. They support their contention by documenting the fact that the social and economic condition of 80 per cent. of the rural population comprising some 15 million out of a total 27 million inhabitants in Egypt has not improved materially, whether one measures this condition in terms of land-ownership, *per capita* income and share in total national wealth, or in terms of wage-earning employment in agriculture. They try to show moreover that the swelling of population in the urban centres of Egypt—the result of emigration from country to town and city—has produced a mass of abjectly poor and disinherited young Egyptians, amounting to 50 per cent. of the total 8–9 million urban population of the country.[1] Given such conditions, these observers conclude, among other things, that the revolution of 1952 has meant nothing more than the replacement of a monarchy (which was assisted in governing by a propertied group of landowners, financiers, and administrators, as well as by a foreign power) with a new state bureaucratic *élite* of soldiers, technocrats, and petty officials.[2]

There are those, on the other hand, who by an emphasis upon ideological trends in the Afro-Asian world, especially the movement against imperialism and colonialism, view the Egyptian Free Officers coup of July 1952 as the fountainhead of a profound revolution against a decadent order on behalf of a popular demand for social, economic and political emancipation. They discount the absence of a popular, or mass, uprising in July 1952, or of the involvement of any organized civilian groups associated with the Free Officer conspirators, in the overthrow of the monarchy and the *ancien régime* politicians.[3] In a sense, one may consider the holocaust of 26 January 1952, in Cairo as a desperate, and therefore futile, protest of the downtrodden against all opulence, European veneer civilization, and authority associated with the

[1] The United Nations, for instance, has recently reported that the U.A.R. has the smallest number of working inhabitants anywhere in the world—barely 30 per cent. of the total population of the country.

[2] These are essentially the conclusions of two recent studies by Egyptian Marxists in exile in Paris. See Anouar Abdel Malek, *Égypte, société militaire* (Paris, 1962), and Hasan Riad (pseudonym) *L'Égypte nassérienne* (Paris, 1964). See also 'Nasserism and socialism', *The Socialist Register 1964*, edited by Ralph Miliband and John Saville (London, 1964), pp. 38–55.

[3] A few examples of such studies are Wilton Wynn, *Nasser of Egypt* (Cambridge, Mass., 1959), Tom Little, *Egypt* (London, 1958), Jean and Simone Lacouture, *Egypt in transition* (New York, 1958), Charles Cremeans, *The Arabs and the world* (New York, 1963). A recent book by Leonard Binder, *The ideological revolution in the Middle East* (New York, 1964), attempts rather unsuccessfully to link such 'movements' as Arabism and socialism to earlier systems of Muslim philosophy. More cautious are the two articles by Malcolm Kerr, 'The emergence of a socialist ideology in Egypt', *The Middle East Journal*, vol. xvi. 2 (1962), pp. 127–44, and 'Arab radical notions of democracy', *St. Antony's Papers, No.* xvi (Middle Eastern Affairs, No. 3) ed. Albert Hourani (London, 1963), pp. 9–40. In my book *The Egyptian army in politics* (Bloomington, Ind., 1961), I primarily emphasized the way the military junta consolidated its power and rule: see especially chaps. 3–4.

status quo. The fact remains that a new rule and order were imposed six months later by a military junta, and consolidated over a period of ten years with the aid of an autocratic policy. This, however, is no departure from the behaviour of revolutionary groups that have come to power elsewhere. The Free Officers who overthrew the monarchy swiftly were anxious to stabilize their position by creating a new and unchallenged power structure.

Having suggested that it is premature to discuss revolutionary consequences for the Egyptian *nation*, I should like to confine my discussion of these consequences to the Egyptian *state* in terms of the concentration of power and personal rule.[1] Moreover, having to deal with such a short time-span in historical terms my discussion is perforce suggestive of propositions which cannot be historically documented until much later. I may justify a departure from a closely documented historical treatment by the simple observation that the rise of executive power is almost a universal phenomenon today. In many of the states of Asia and Africa, the emergence of supreme national leader–rulers, often in the form of Knights on Horseback, indicates even greater concentration of power in the hands of one man.[2]

I am not interested, for the purposes of this paper, in arguing the virtues or shortcomings of military rule. Studies of the involvement of the military in politics, the relationship of the military to society, and especially to civilian authority, abound.[3] Like Ibn al-Ṭiqṭaqa, who wrote in the fourteenth century, one may postpone judgement in this matter for the moment:

> The realm is guarded by the Sword and administered by the Pen. There has been disagreement of opinion as to which is more important among them, and which

[1] Besides the observable developments in new states, I have been led to this approach by a few more classic discussions of revolutions and their consequences for state power. Among these, Ortega y Gasset, *Revolt of the masses* (London, 1930), is still relevant. Bertrand de Jouvenel's work since 1945 has been concerned with this question. See his *On power* (London, 1945), and his more recent essay 'The Principate', *Political Quarterly*, Jan.–Mar. 1965. See also a similar suggestion in my 'The military in politics: A review', *The Journal of Conflict Resolution*, vol. ix. 1 (Mar. 1965), pp. 139–46.

[2] See Edward Shils, 'The military in the political development of new states', in John J. Johnson (ed.), *The role of the military in underdeveloped countries* (Princeton, 1962), pp. 7–68. See also his *Political development in the new states* (The Hague, 1962).

[3] For general discussions, see Alfred Vagts, *The history of militarism* (New York, 1937), Katherine Chorley, *Armies and the art of revolution* (London, 1934), John J. Johnson (ed.), op. cit., William Gutteridge, *The armed forces in new states* (London, 1962), S. E. Finer, *Man on horseback* (London, 1962), Samuel P. Huntington (ed.), *Changing patterns of military politics* (New York, 1961), Morris Janowitz, *The military in the political development of new nations* (Chicago, 1964). For the Middle East, see Morroe Berger, *Military elites and social change: Egypt since Napoleon* (Center for International Studies, Princeton: Research Monograph, No. 6), Majid Khadduri, 'The role of the military in Middle East politics', *American Political Science Review*, vol. xlvii. 2 (June 1953), pp. 511–24, Dankwart A. Rustow, 'The army and the founding of the Turkish republic', *World Politics*, vol. xi. 4 (July, 1959), pp. 513–52, Daniel Lerner and Richard D. Robinson, 'Swords and plowshares: The Turkish army as a modernising force', ibid., vol. xiii. 1 (Oct. 1960), pp. 19–44, Sydney N. Fisher (ed.), *The military in Middle Eastern society and politics* (Columbus, Ohio, 1963), Gordon H. Torrey *Syrian politics and the military* (Columbus, Ohio, 1964).

one should dominate the other. Some think the Pen should dominate the Sword because the latter upholds the former as a guardian and servant. Others have argued the contrary relationship between Sword and Pen on the grounds that the Men of the Pen provide those who wield the Sword with their wealth and livelihood and must be servile to them. Yet a third view upholds that Sword and Pen are equal in importance, and neither can do without the other.[1]

Nor do I intend here to describe in detail why and how the Free Officers came to power in Egypt in July 1952.[2] Suffice it to remark briefly that the impasse reached in the relations between King Fārūq on the one hand, and party politicians, especially the Wafd, on the other, produced deadlock in the processes of government, and rendered the political *élite* unable to rule. Internal political chaos, accompanied naturally by frequent breakdowns of public order, reflected the disarray of the ruling classes. When the latter augmented their difficulties by a breakdown in their relations with Britain in October 1951, they undermined their position even further. A combination of disorderly conditions at home and propitious circumstances abroad gave the military—the only organized institution remaining in the state with access to the use of force and, therefore, to the exercise of power—their first political victory: the overthrow of a dynasty which had reigned in Egypt since 1805.

Whereas in 1801–11 Muḥammad ʿAlī the Great established his authority and imposed his rule over an Egypt, which the factious Mamluk princes could not agree to govern, by a similar access to force, it nonetheless took him at least four years of negotiation and manœuvre to secure the necessary support of notables, religious leaders, and others who mattered politically in the country for his plans. The ruling *élite* he ousted from power did not relinquish it without fierce opposition. Only a cold-blooded and carefully planned massacre of Mamluk leaders in the Citadel in 1811 assured Muḥammad ʿAlī of his undisputed domination over the country. In the case of the Free Officers, their coup was swift, the resistance of the political *élite* itself divided, overconfident, and therefore, ineffective. There was no need for a massacre, because the monopoly of the means of violence rested with the military establishment of a modern state.

1. *The modernizing leader and the new* élite

It is difficult to assert a cause and effect relationship between the achievement of real political independence since 1954 and the revolution led by the Free Officers. Political independence, undiluted by the special relationship with Britain, might have come about without revolution. For Egyptians, however, there is a causal relationship between political independence and the revolution. They consider it, that is, a major consequence of the 1952 revolu-

[1] *Al-Fakhrī* (Cairo, 1899), pp. 45–46.

[2] Two such descriptions by Egyptians in English are Rashed al-Barawy, *The military coup in Egypt* (Cairo, 1952), and Anwar El Sadat, *Revolt on the Nile* (London, 1957). See also Keith Wheelock, *Nasser's new Egypt* (New York, 1960), and my book cited above, chaps. 3–5.

tion. They add to this a series of other consequences which they view as real achievements of the new *élite*: a radical and inspired programme of economic and social reform and development which has infused a sense of hope and purpose in the society. They see their new leaders as the first group of native Egyptians to govern their country in many centuries. Moreover, they believe that the new leadership is sincerely concerned with their welfare. Generally, Egyptians have experienced in the last ten years a psychological uplift (sometimes to the degree of dangerous euphoria) directly related to the inter-Arab and international prestige of their leader.

While these, and many other developments, have been consequences of the 1952 revolution, they do not explain the transformation of the structure of power in the state, its use and purposes as exercised by the new leadership. And I have assumed that the question of authority is central to the study of politics—in this instance, to the study of a revolution. What arrangements, then, appear to have been made so far for authority, and for the use and exercise of public power by the new revolutionary leadership? Despite the oft-repeated generalization that this is the era of 'mass participation' in politics (and participation is not synonymous with active involvement in the making and implementation of policy), one must still cope with the problem of leadership and *élites* who lead ever greater masses. The ideal revolutionary polity in which the masses truly govern has yet to appear anywhere in the world. It remains not only a myth, but also an unfulfilled prophecy. The leadership element, however, is very much with us, and especially in societies where:

1. the adequacy of previous institutional arrangements and procedures—actually political orders—has been seriously challenged and, in the case of Egypt, overthrown;
2. there is a rapid transformation of governmental functions to embrace a wide spectrum of public affairs;
3. a radical revolutionary ideology regards individual and group political freedoms as obstacles to political and economic modernization and development—in short, to progress; and suggests that the new leadership, supported by a carefully selected political cadre and related to the masses via a single state organization, is the only one that can bring about progress.

The question, then, is how this power structure in the state has been transformed? How is it limited and controlled? Is there an effective check against its rather narrow organization?

To deal with these questions one must consider two major consequences of the 1952 coup which lay at the heart of the revolution. One was the abolition of the monarchy within less than a year after the coup, and its replacement by a republic. The other was the suspension of political life by the suppression of all organized political groups. This process, initiated almost immediately after the coup and carried out throughout 1953 and 1954, was not merely directed at the known political parties and their leaders of the *ancien régime*, but also at all other groups and associations whose leadership had never participated in the formation of a government, and at many which were never represented in parliament.

Neither of these consequences is significant in itself. They must be viewed within the context of the struggle for power among the Free Officers group which went on between July 1952 and March 1954. The abolition of an unpopular monarchy was a relatively simple matter, accomplished by decree in July 1953. More difficult was the replacement, for purposes of governing, of the ousted cadres provided by the old political groups. Although many members of the old political organizations found no difficulty in switching their allegiance to the new rulers, the military junta was anxious to mobilize public support for its new rule. A Liberation Rally was launched to associate the masses with the new régime which now proclaimed a sweeping revolution in Egypt. The destruction of the old order was to be followed by a revolution in the social, economic, and political life of the country, aiming at greater material well-being, justice, and freedom within a democratic polity. Economically, the emphasis was placed on the redistribution of land through agrarian reform, together with intensive industrialization which would raise the standard of living for every Egyptian by the more equitable distribution of national wealth. Socially, the revolution implied a levelling process which would bridge gaping disparities between the very few 'haves' and the masses of 'have nots'. Politically, the revolution promised an elevated status for Egypt of sovereign independence, prestige in terms of a modern industrialized economy and modern military force, and power both at home and abroad.

While it is easy for soldiers to seize power, it is not easy for them to govern effectively under conditions of induced massive change. The centralization of power in Egypt is not a surprising phenomenon; it has a long history that needs no elaboration here. The accession to power of a radical officer group, which aimed at the establishment of a new revolutionary order, tended to increase the centralization of both political and economic power. The formulation of an all-embracing revolutionary policy for the modernization of Egyptian society was thus incompatible with notions of diffused power. Yet the persistent inability of the military régime to organize the masses in an effective political force is reflected in, and documented by, the consecutive failure of the Liberation Rally (abolished in 1956), and its successor the National Union (dissolved in 1961 upon the secession of Syria from the United Arab Republic). The Arab Socialist Union organization formulated and announced in President 'Abd al-Nāṣir's Charter (May 1962) represents the latest attempt in the continuous, but frustrating, search by the régime for a formula of organized mass support, and a basis for a permanent institutionalized political structure. Its prospects cannot be fairly assessed at the present time. The general outline of its organization is discussed briefly in the next section of this paper.

If the efforts of the military régime to organize popular support for their revolution proved difficult, the question of a new political apparatus for the control of government was more crucial once the old *élite* had been destroyed. It is in this essential feature of any rule that the revolution has been most successful. In the absence of wide participation by the citizens in the conduct of public affairs, at the local, provincial, or national level, a new state apparatus became necessary. Unwilling to risk their newly acquired power, the Free Officers had to consolidate their gains. Anxious to impose a new order of revolutionary achievement as outlined in their proclamations between 1952 and 1956, the military junta sought at first to recruit the cadres of their new power structure from their most obvious ally: the armed forces.

President ʿAbd al-Nāṣir has consistently reminded the armed forces that they constitute the vanguard and base of the revolution in Egypt. They have been in effect the major source of his active support, as well as his hungriest clients for power. Quickly army officers were first given watch-dog duties over civilian administrative organizations. Soon thereafter they acquired permanent bureaucratic functions. When in 1957 the nationalization of foreign commercial interests and capital began seriously, culminating in the July 1961 'socialist' measures, military personnel found themselves in key positions, responsible for the planning of economic and social policy. Diplomatic posts, provincial governorships, and all conceivable appointments in the higher echelons of state administrative services were opened to them.

Just as rapid development of agriculture, irrigation, and other public works related to the Egyptian economy in the nineteenth century led to the concentration of great power in the hands of Muḥammad ʿAlī, so also the desire for the rapid development of an industrial economy today leads to a similar, though greater, concentration of power in the hands of the revolutionary leader. The political power which economics affords the state and the ruler today as a result of the extension of governmental functions and services, including an enlarged bureaucracy, is far greater than any in the past. The resulting prestige of the executive, who is associated with radical and prompt action, enhances the chances for personal rule. The state in Egypt today is the greatest industrialist, economic and financial *entrepreneur*, and the biggest employer. The expanded power of the state over society is immense. Whereas in nineteenth-century Egypt, state power over society was frequently mitigated by the organized political and financial intercession of such groups as the *ʿulamā*', the merchants, the guilds of artisans and craftsmen, and the notables, today the prohibition on existence, let alone independent activity of intermediate groups has practically eliminated similar mitigating intercession.

In declaring itself against 'politics', i.e., against the existence of political groups in society which at least purport an alternative to power, the military régime had, by 1956, pre-empted all political activity in Egypt. But as political activity is never usefully confined to crass demagoguery and ideological excursions which lack any substantial intellectual and programmatic content, the military junta had to man an administration which would not only permit them to govern, but which would also enable them to maintain effective political power over society. It is in meeting this requirement by recruiting their cadres from the armed forces that the junta gradually transformed their régime for the first five years into what I shall call here a *stratiotocracy*.

By *stratiotocracy*[1] I mean a régime which, in contrast to a 'military oligarchy' involves the total military institution as a new political *élite*. It would be erroneous to refer to this *élite* as a new ruling class. Before the 1952 revolution, there was a ruling class in Egypt to the extent that its members were recruited from (*a*) members of the royal house (*b*) the rich landowners, high-ranking state administrators, liberal professions, the few industrialists and financiers most of whom were related either by blood, marriage, or common economic interests to the rich landowning families. The *stratiotocracy*, however, can only be designated an *élite*, because its members have varied social and economic backgrounds, or origins, even though one assumes that in terms of training, perhaps even education, its members share a common, if not uniform, experience. In the Egyptian army, perhaps more than in the armies of other Arab states, expertise in the disciplined use of violence is more developed, permitting a greater sense of professionalism among officers. It is doubtful at the moment, pending further study, if members of the *stratiotocracy* also share a strong sense of corporateness. To refer to them merely as New Men, as some Western observers have, without more precise information about them, is to suggest a misleading typology.

The modernizing leader can recruit widely from the ranks of this institution for the various services of the state. This *élite*, therefore, is not only the privileged group of the revolutionary régime, but should by definition be able to check as well as to assist the leader (the *strategós*) at its head in governing. Moreover the body politic is vested in this *élite* as the best representative of its revolutionary aims. It cannot derive its authority from any constitutional provision or arrangement, for it already possesses it as the maker of the revolution. The modernizing leader at the head of this *élite*, in turn embodies the vitality and goals of the revolutionary body politic and expresses its will. In this capacity he consolidates his power in the first instance via the *stratiotocracy*. But the basis of his legitimate authority too is the revolution, not any intricate legal or other formula for sovereign power. Later, as we shall see, he moves from the position of a *strategós* (leader of the *stratiotocracy*) to that

[1] I have used the term *stratiotocracy*, the rule of soldiers, in preference to others in order to express a more inclusive use of the military institution. It is borrowed from the Greek word for soldier, *stratiotes*. The term *strategós* commonly used for *general*, also denotes *commander*.

of a popular modernizing leader.[1] His leadership becomes temporarily a plebiscitary one when the myth of power reposing exclusively upon the masses, instead of a legislative body and its attending associational groups, is articulated. Soon this popular sovereignty permits the modernizing leader greater personalized power in accordance with new constitutional rules, and his personal rule becomes the supreme organ of popular sovereignty. He embodies the general will to lead the struggle against economic exploitation at home, imperialism abroad and, along with the *élite*, is entrusted with the task of achieving the goals of the revolution.

In the tenth and eleventh centuries, sultans and princes who had established powerful realms in various parts of the Islamic empire, legitimated their authority and dominion by resorting to a nice agreement with the almost powerless caliph: recognition of supreme, though nominal, caliphal authority by a mention of his name in the Friday prayers in exchange for his recognition of a sultanate or principality. Today, however, resort to such a convenient arrangement is not possible. How, then, does the popular innovator and modernizer at the head of a revolution justify the immense concentration of power in his hands and the personalization of his rule?

One can argue that action on any level of human activity is more readily associated with executive power. And the latter, in turn, is usually associated with a single person, not with deliberative bodies. Action was the strength of Muḥammad ʿAlī as the 'founder' of a modern state in Egypt. Action presumably impressed the Egyptians when they accepted Saʿd Zaghlūl as the 'father' of an independent Egyptian nation–state. Similarly, revolutionary action in the economic, social, and political development of the country renders the head of a *stratiotocracy* a modernizer. It is not unfair to suggest that long before the coup of July 1952, the military in Egypt were popularly associated with efficient action, whether in quelling disturbances when all other measures available to civilian authority had failed, or in accelerating the execution of large public works. Moreover, reform in Egypt has been traditionally associated with personal power.

But there is a more significant reason for the political success of the new *élite* and the concentration of power in the personal rule of its leader. The suppression of religious and other communal social units, the proscription of associations and other organized groups from urban Egyptian society—except as part of a state-decreed national organization—have contributed to this power concentration. Such units and organizations which, in addition to their local community functions and services, performed political functions

[1] The term 'modernizing leader' as it is used here comes closest in connotation to the Roman *princeps*. But it is also akin to the Machiavellian concept of *il principe* in the sense of a dynamic leader who seeks to rescusitate and strengthen his nation and state. The modernizing leader in this context is the supreme patriot. He moreover possesses a vision of a national future. His leadership is both demanding of his followers and protective of them. He plays the role of both an *eghétis* and *prostátes*.

recognized by the ruler are no longer officially permitted to do so.[1] The disbanding of both secular and religious political associations since 1953, accelerated the total control of the new *élite* over society, and increased the personal power of its leader. Traditional social units and modern political groups could conceivably have defended society from the excesses of personal rule. The 'people' (*al-shaʿb*) are never able to do this for themselves. The 'sovereignty of the people' divorced from any intermediate institutional devices and mechanisms to check ultimate power, has always presented the best chance for the concentration of that power in a single ruler or ruling *élite*.[2]

To argue that the old political *élite* of pre-1952 Egypt, which also represented a ruling class, has been eliminated is to state the obvious. It began to collapse sometime before the coup of July 1952. Although it was generally able for a period of thirty years to check the concentration of power in the hands of any single leader—king, Wafdist Naḥḥās, or other—it soon ceased to respond to, or even represent, public needs. Nor was it able to promote policies that would have met these needs. In these circumstances, not only did this *élite* dissipate its power, but it also lost its legitimacy. The latter condition was inevitable because the *élite* had anchored its authority in a constitutional formula which it ceased to respect. The crisis in the relations of the *élite* with an alienated, but articulate, minority of politically conscious young Egyptians produced, as in other instances in the history of revolutions, a liberator, who was easily and, in many respects justifiably, considered a saviour.

One must therefore examine the new political *élite* that has arisen with the revolution, if one assumes that *élites* are best equipped to check personal rule.

The consolidation of power by the new *élite* was determined by the outcome of the ʿAbd al-Nāṣir–Nagīb struggle for power in 1952–4. A strong leader emerged from that struggle. In 1954 this leader was still the recognized head of a functional *élite*, consisting of military officers, whose task it was to lead the revolution and 'to mobilise the masses' for the achievement of its goals. Strangely enough, only with the expansion of the composition of this *élite* since 1955 did the concentration of power in the hands of the modernizing leader occur. It is worthwhile to observe this development.

The mass exodus of foreigners, long resident in Egypt, from 1956 to date

[1] Even the activities of the Ṣūfī *ṭarīqas* with a reported membership at one time of 3,000,000, have, since 1960, come under strict state control. Thus one of the traditional checks on power in any Islamic society has been effectively removed, or at least neutralized. The bureaucratic control of the state is now complete over the religious teachers, upholders of tradition, and the Sacred Law. Their mobilization in the service of the socialist revolution became complete with the promulgation of the Law for the Reorganization of al-Azhar in June 1961. See my 'Islam and the foreign policy of Egypt', *Islam and international relations*, ed. J. Harris Proctor, (New York and London, 1965), pp. 120–57.

[2] This is when, as William Kornhauser has argued, a mass becomes available for mobilization by an *élite*. See his *The politics of mass society* (Glencoe, Ill., 1959).

represented a minor drain of human resources trained in certain tasks essential to the maintenance of a modern state, especially in the fields of trade, commerce, industry, and ancillary services ranging from insurance and the liberal professions to skilled crafts. The military could not provide adequate replacements for all these categories. The need to recruit native civilians from a variety of social strata into top technical and administrative state posts became urgent. Economic planners, development engineers, statisticians, and experts in a wide range of technical fields were brought into the various national organizations, many of which were directly controlled by the government, while others enjoyed quasi-independent status, to cope with the emergence of the state as the largest single *entrepreneur* and social services agency in Egypt.

The expansion of the public sector economy—its almost total control of the national economy—was organized into such bodies as planning commissions, economic councils, various boards dealing with trade and public services. Both military officers and civilian technologists were appointed to head many of these agencies. The expropriation of foreign and native capitalists, the nationalization of commercial enterprises, public utilities, the Suez Canal, and the socialist laws of 1961–2 made it impossible for the new *élite* to remain confined to the military institution. Its expansion to embrace an ever-wider civilian element became necessary.

A new state technocracy came into existence which was not a consulting one, but an integral part of the state bureaucracy. It did not belong to a fully formed professional community; it had no corporate ethos with all the independent attributes that this implies. Its members simply became state employees: a state technocracy, that is, which, when bureaucratized because the state required its skills and services, did not constitute a separate *élite* with serious political potential. Even though the economic and social interests of this new technocracy seem to converge with those of the ruling military *élite*, it cannot, so far, act as a check upon the power of the modernizing leader, because it has no alternative to state employment. Moreover, it cannot find refuge, or room to manœuvre, in a civilian political force.

One must note that the revolution has emphasized action in the economic and technological fields of national development. The premium placed on the old liberal professions which were closely allied with the *ancien régime* ruling *élite* is therefore at a minimum today. It is partly for this reason that the intellectuals have been denied their essential role of critics of the régime and of society. One may argue, of course, that, like many intellectuals the world over, those in Egypt too are attracted by a radical notion of a resplendent future. The appeal of a revolutionary ideology which promises a 'democratic socialist' society is indeed great.[1] Even though during the struggle for national independence the traditional ruling *élite* partly recruited its cadres from a

[1] A feature of radical revolution in both Egypt and Algeria has been the rejection of 'intellectualism' as an alien Western conception and activity. As such, it is associated with the

class of intellectuals, or from an intelligentsia which they produced, the latter unfortunately never acquired a proper political function in society. Today all intellectuals and members of the liberal professions are 'integrated' within a state-decreed Arab Socialist Union organization. Whereas in the inter-War period a privileged *élite* ruled with the help of these liberal professions, today an alliance (perhaps no more than an association) between politically (for the moment at least) unequal partners—soldiers and technocrats—governs. The soldiers are often loath to permit the political ascendancy of the civilian professional man. Together they constitute the *khāṣṣa*, or élitist group, of Islamic terminology; while the masses, or *al-sha'b*, retain their qualification as the *'āmma, hoi polloi.*

Because the chief executive can, as he needs, recruit scientists and experts (soldiers presumably being lacking in similar qualifications), his prestige and power are enhanced. He can retain his powerful position by maintaining a delicate balance between those two groups in the new composite *élite*. He is thus not just a bureaucratic lord, assisted in his task of governing and in his plan for national modernization by committees of technocrats, but he remains a commander at the head of a military institution. So long as no real civilian political force is organized on a mass scale, the soldiers can influence his authority and check his power. The technocrats in the *élite*, just as the intellectuals at large in society, cannot claim the same privileged role. As members of a bureaucratized technocracy, they find that their rights and privileges derive from the state. In this sense, it is difficult for them to curb the power of the modernizing leader so long as his *stratiotocracy* sustains him.

An important consequence of the revolution which is not, however, peculiar to Egypt, is the question of the control and limitation of public power. The capitalists have been eliminated between 1957 and 1962. Divested of their economic wealth they are without power or influence. Legislatures, whatever their virtues or vices, have no place in a radical autocracy. The beneficiary of these purges has been public authority, wielded by the new *élite* headed by the modernizing leader, the chief. Theoretically, the new limitors of public power are the technocrat–bureaucrats, alongside the military, since the modernizing leader as a *civilian chief* depends on them for the attainment of

previous rather moderate—in many instances superficially—liberal nationalist leadership in these states. It is, therefore, considered anti-populist (anti-*sha'bi*) and pro-imperialist. Not only are men of action and popular ruler–leaders (*zu'amā'*) preferred in these circumstances, but intellectuals are reduced to purveyors of the policies, pronouncements, and programmes initiated and decreed by the leader. The terminology and dialectic of the revolutionary ideology, including such movements as Arabism (*al-qawmiyya al-'arabiyya*), is most interesting and deserves separate study. See the interesting discussion 'The Language of Politics' in Hisham B. Sharabi, *Nationalism and revolution in the Arab world* (Princeton, N.J., 1966). Generally, on the role of the intellectuals in the Arab radical revolution as illustrated by the case of Egypt, see Majdī Wahba, 'Fī qalaq al-muthaqqafīn al-'arab', *Ḥiwār* (Beirut), vol. i. 4 (May 1963) pp. 29–40, and P. J. Vatikiotis, 'Al-muthaqqaf al-'arabī wa'l-mujtama' al-ḥadīth', ibid., pp. 41–51. See a discussion and rebuttal of the latter article in *al-Jumhuriyya* (Cairo), 13 and 19 June 1963.

his economic and technological goals, and must delegate some authority to them for the fulfilment of their tasks. In these circumstances, again theoretically, the technocrats acquire interests they must defend. But the *civilian chief* is also a *military chief* who so far depends for his coercive power upon his soldiers. Consequently, he is well-placed between these two heterogeneous groups in the *élite* to maintain the continued personal authority of his *zaʿāma*, or popular leadership, *vis-à-vis* the masses.

2. *The leader and the masses: The search for political organization and institutions*

If one considers the Charter of National Action presented to the Congress of Popular Forces in May 1962 as the official ideological handbook of the Egyptian revolution, it is clear that the régime has sought to achieve social and economic reform by revolutionary means. Ever since 1956–7, at least, the régime assumed that the sharp economic and social divisions in Egyptian society derived mainly from the exploitation of the many by the privileged few. Forceful state action was therefore necessary to end this exploitation by the economic and political liquidation of the privileged class and the improvement of the condition of the masses. The state in this revolutionary ideology acts as the dynamic liberating force of the masses. The containment, if not destruction, of the privileged classes would in turn lead to the eradication of social conflict. As their power was derived in great measure from their control over the economy, a programme of nationalization was begun in 1957 which lasted until the spring of 1964.

Land reform instituted in August 1952 and extended in 1961 abolished extensive landholdings, and distributed land to peasant farmers. Egyptianization of foreign companies in 1957 (a policy the beginnings of which can be traced back to the Companies Law of 1947), following the nationalization of the Suez Canal, put in national hands certain enterprises owned and operated by foreigners. The nationalization of banks and the press in 1960 placed financial and banking transactions as well as mass media and the publishing industry under state control. The nationalization of commercial and industrial enterprises in July 1961 (completed in August 1963) was soon followed by the sequestration order against certain local capitalists in November 1961. The latter measure was, to some extent, a political act during the crisis engendered by the secession of Syria from the United Arab Republic in September. A 50 per cent. nationalization of shipping companies followed a year later in October 1962. Cotton-exporting and flour mills came next in April–May 1963; petroleum in March 1964; and contracting companies in April 1964.

The programme of agrarian reform and nationalization of all sorts of enterprises was accompanied by the institution of planning for the state-controlled economy with a view to increasing both agricultural and industrial production, the doubling of national income within a period of ten years, the achievement of full employment, and the institution and implementation of successful social legislation for the benefit of the masses.

While forceful state action under a revolutionary régime finally eliminated the old privileged class and *élite* from the economic and political arenas of national activity, it also widened the periphery of the new *élite* of soldiers and technocrats with an expanded bureaucracy. So that lately two major political problems have confronted the Egyptian leadership, namely: (1) the improvement of bureaucratic performance in coping with a state-controlled and run economy, and (2) the mobilization of the masses into a state-devised single political organization to assist by its support the leadership in the achievement of its revolutionary goals.

A revolution in the ownership, management, and developmental planning of the economy has indeed occurred in Egypt. What has proved to be a more difficult task so far has been the organization of a mass political structure whose members will accept the responsibilities and the price of the ideological requirements of the revolution as these are identified and formulated by the modernizing leader and his *élite*.

The persistent search by the régime for a civilian formula of legitimate authority betrays its awareness of the danger inherent in an indefinite dependence upon a *stratiotocracy*, and the new *élite* of technocrats. The relentless efforts of the régime since 1953 to mobilize and integrate the masses into a single state organization have been expensive and unsatisfactory.

The secession of Syria from the U.A.R. in September 1961 constituted a watershed in the short history of the régime in Egypt. While it hardly elicited regret on the part of the general public, it moved the rulers to seek measures to safeguard themselves against all eventualities. Public self-criticism of Egyptian policy in Syria under the union was led off by the president himself especially in his famous speech of 16 October. Further isolation of elements in the country presumed to be inimical to the régime was effected by the expropriation measures in November. Now that the U.A.R. comprised only Egypt, the old National Union organization became obsolete. President ʿAbd al-Nāṣir declared that reactionaries had infiltrated the old National Union. He insisted that the most important task facing Egypt in the autumn of 1961 was the reorganization of the National Union in such a way as to make it 'a revolutionary instrument for the masses'. On a different level, the régime now recognized the urgent need to devise a scheme by which the leaders could associate selected sections of the public with the policies of the government. Towards the end of 1961, the government were exploring the possibility of launching a new mass state organization into which would be recruited the so-called popular forces in the country. This organization was formally announced in 1962 as the Arab Socialist Union. (A.S.U.)[1]

[1] *Al-ittiḥād al-ʿarabī al-ishtirākī.*

After the announcement of a new government on 18 October, a Preparatory Committee of Popular Forces met in Cairo in November. It was charged by the President to prepare for a National Congress which would produce a Charter of National Action. Consisting of 1,750 members elected by labour, professional syndicates, farmers, and other groups, the National Congress met in May 1962 to hear the president present his draft National Charter. A nation-wide debate followed and the Charter was quickly approved unamended. The National Congress, it turned out, did not lay down the Charter; they discussed and approved the draft submitted by the president.

The A.S.U. was declared in the National Charter to be the nation's single political organization. It did not differ drastically from its predecessor, the National Union, in so far as its pyramidal structure and organization, from the village and the basic units to those on the district, provincial, or governorate levels, were concerned. There were however two innovations. One consists of a provision that 50 per cent. of the seats in all selected A.S.U. structures at all levels shall be filled by farmers and workers as these two categories are defined in the National Charter. The other is a provision for elected A.S.U. basic units in factories, business firms, ministries, and state-controlled industrial enterprises. The latter extension is a logical outcome of the vast nationalization policy and industrialization programme since 1957.

Elections from the basic to the higher level units culminating in a National Conference began in May 1963. It is difficult to discuss them here for, at the time of writing, they were not yet completed.

The A.S.U. is designed to meet the ideological premise that there must be popular participation and representation on both the local and national levels of the revolution. The A.S.U. must represent the interests of all popular forces. These have been identified in the Charter as consisting of farmers (*fallāḥīn*), workers (not just labourers, but anyone who works for his living), intellectuals, 'national capitalists' (independent shopkeepers, etc.), members of organized professions (lawyers, doctors, teachers, journalists, engineers, and others), and soldiers. Participation by these forces in revolutionary activity must be in a single mass organization of the state in order to avoid social conflict. The latter was, according to the ideology of the revolution, the result of political party activity, when parties represented social classes. The revolution must prevent the emergence of political groups by mobilizing the popular forces in the A.S.U.

It is estimated that there are 5,000,000 members in the A.S.U. Theoretically, these are the militants of the revolution. Their task, as well as that of the government, is to spread and inculcate in the masses a sense of participation in the leader's implementation of the revolutionary programme.

Although not designated a party, the A.S.U. so far is organized in a hierarchical framework. It was noted that there are to be elected local committees, regional and provincial councils, a general conference or Congress, an organizational Secretariat, and an elected Higher Executive Committee. For the moment, the president of the A.S.U. is President ʿAbd al-Nāṣir. He has appointed the members of the present Higher Executive Committee consisting of the vice-presidents of the Republic, some of his old Free Officer colleagues. The eighteen to twenty members of the General Secretariat represent army officers, technicians, intellectuals, Marxists, and experts.

From the deliberations between the president, his Executive Committee and the General Secretariat it is clear that the political mobilization of the popular forces under a single state mass organization remains a difficult undertaking. It involves a series of crucial questions: What is the best means of committing the public to an enthusiastic participation in the régime's revolutionary programmes and policies, ranging from socialism to Arabism? How can an organization devised, and controlled, by the state elicit the active support of the public for planned industrialization and other policies at home and abroad? Most difficult, however, is the problem of a mass state organization in which the public can participate actively by criticizing technical matters of state administration, planning, and efficiency, but cannot oppose the established régime or its structure of power.

As there are also other so-called popular democratic organizations, such as farmers' co-operatives, trade unions, and professional syndicates, the problem has arisen of linking these to the A.S.U. The president has complained about the organization of the A.S.U. in that it has not so far been able to allocate responsibility in the various committees and on different levels of its structure; in short, that it has not been able to create a political cadre of leadership on any level. Another difficulty that has faced the A.S.U. organizers has been one of communication between local, provincial, and national leaders. This apparently has been a major obstacle in the formation of an initial political cadre.

The official view of the A.S.U. as expressed by the president reflects his desire for a public commitment to his programme. He considers the basic objective of the A.S.U. to be twofold: first, as a popular organization, it must explain to the public the aims and policies of the régime, and second, it must establish within its organization a political cadre structure. What this implies is that a core political party, consisting of militant elements unreservedly loyal to the régime, should exist within the A.S.U. in order to give the mass organization direction and control. It would also ensure that organized groups within the A.S.U. structures—especially in trade unions, co-operatives, syndicates—will not permit the rise of politically unfaithful leaders and cliques. Thus, what is envisaged is a mass organization, supervised by an organization of select militants approaching a party within it, both of which would be ultimately controlled by the régime.

Some confusion has arisen because of the existence of organized trade unions, professional syndicates, and other groups alongside the wider A.S.U. organization. Presumably members of these groups and their leaders are also members of the A.S.U. President 'Abd al-Nāṣir has suggested that this duplication be avoided by posing the question of whether to retain these secondary and parallel groups, or to amalgamate them into one A.S.U. structure. While certain members of the General Secretariat representing various interests—labour, agriculture, the professions—have expressed scepticism over the amalgamation of all organized groups into the A.S.U., the president appears anxious to do exactly that.[1]

On 10 March 1964 a general election was held for a 350-member National Assembly. About 1,750 candidates stood in the election, all of whom had to be literate, over thirty years old, and members of the A.S.U. One hundred and seventy-five constituencies were to be represented by two deputies at least one of whom had to be a worker or a farmer as defined in the National Charter. About 1,000 of these candidates were workers or farmers and some twenty-eight or thirty were women. Voting was compulsory with a fine of £E.1 for failure to do so. The absence of party affiliation for candidates led many electors to vote for their traditional local leaders.

A day before the Assembly convened on 26 March 1964, the president reorganized the government. A new Cabinet headed by 'Alī Ṣabrī replaced the old Executive Council of Ministers, operating since September 1962. The Presidential Council which was also formed in September 1962 was abolished. Instead, the president appointed his most trusted Free Officer colleagues to vice-presidencies. One, Marshal 'Abd al-Ḥakīm 'Āmir was appointed to the new office of first vice-president, the other three to plain vice-presidencies. At the same time a provisional constitution was proclaimed. Although it describes the National Assembly as the executive power of the state which controls the acts of the president and the Cabinet, the provisional constitution also states in Article 113 that the president 'in collaboration with the government lays down the general policy of the state in all political, economic, social and administrative fields, and supervises its execution'.

Charged with the task of drafting a permanent constitution, the present National Assembly is theoretically a constituent assembly. Also, theoretically, the Assembly is an organ of the A.S.U., that is, of the popular forces. When the A.S.U. meets as a National Congress it will have the primary responsibility of laying down the broad principles of the country's policies, and will be expected to supervise their implementation by the National Assembly, the president, and his Cabinet.

There is confusion and difficulty in these relationships between, on the one hand, the framework of which is still in the making, and the National Assembly, the president and the Cabinet on the other. It should be noted, moreover, that the 1963 and 1964 elections were only two in a series of periodical elections, constitutional and administrative organizations under the régime of the revolution since its inception. Despite the transformation of

[1] See *al-Ṭalī'a* (Cairo), vol. i. 2 (Feb. 1965), pp. 9–26.

the structure of power by the Free Officers, the stability and popularity of the leader, there were, between 1956 and March 1965, nine elections and referendums and three constitutions. Over the same period, President ʿAbd al-Nāṣir has effected eight major administrative reshufflings and changes at cabinet level. While retaining most of his early colleagues of 1952, he has continuously co-opted new aides from the military and from professional civilian groups. To some extent, changes in administrative and executive personnel were essential to the economic revolution the president was instituting. What is politically significant is that these changes reflect the unequal progress in the evolution of stable institutions.

For the first time in the recent history of Egypt, representation in the National Assembly extends to workers and small farmers. It is also no longer confined to urban professionals, lawyers, landowners, and men of affairs. In the sessions of the Assembly, moreover, there have been lively and dexterous deliberations of government policies, as well as uncomfortably close questioning of ministers. What has been signally lacking in both the Assembly and the A.S.U. so far has been initiative in legislative and other policy matters. The latter are still the exclusive function, if not prerogative, of the president, assisted by a Cabinet and a Higher Executive Committee of the A.S.U., both of which bodies he heads.

The attempts at decentralization initiated by the 1960 local government legislation continue to be hampered by the pyramidal structure envisaged in both the old National Union and the new A.S.U., and its ultimate control from the top. Events also play a part in this situation. Involvement in inter-Arab affairs, especially in south-west Arabia, with dubious results for Egypt, has diverted the attention and energies of the president and his government from sustained action in this direction at home. Moreover, like other measures of the revolutionary leadership in the past, the currently attempted political structure is blatantly a creation from the top. It is not the result of a gradual grass-roots development in the country at large. It is not too reckless to assert that the National Charter which declared the A.S.U. as the kingpin in the proposed new political system is the president's own idea. He must therefore depend upon his loyal and trusted aides for its implementation.

The major difficulty the president faces in this whole matter of a new political structure for Egypt arises partly from the nature of his rule and authority. He came to power at the head of a military conspiracy which effected a coup that has been phenomenally successful in the post-war world. He was not the theoretician, or leader, of a revolutionary party. With the exception of a few extremists on the Right and even fewer on the Left, neither were any of his junta colleagues in this category. In the country at large, such revolutionary militants as were to be found in the small and fragmented Communist Party were immediately rejected and incarcerated by the régime. Recently most of them have been rehabilitated in the A.S.U. organization, the nationalized press, and other state services. Judging from the recent mass arrests of fanatical Muslim brethren in July–August 1965, it is unlikely that the régime will readily delegate real powers to any of the institutions envisaged in the proclaimed political system.

3. *The quest for leadership in the Arab Middle East and Africa*

The most significant consequence of the Anglo-Egyptian Agreement in June 1954 for the evacuation of British troops from the country was the fact that the Egyptians had to shoulder alone the difficult task of governing themselves. The Agreement was moreover, concluded by the new leadership of native Egyptian officers. The contemporaneous withdrawal of effective British influence from other states in the Middle East had further consequences for the new régime in Egypt. It ushered into inter-Arab state relations an era of conflict and instability. Within this area of conflict, Egypt, under the military régime, became the foremost contender for power.

Although one can carefully document the past infrequent involvement of Egypt in the affairs of the traditional Arab political struggles in the Fertile Crescent and the Arabian peninsula until the Second World War, one cannot claim the total dissociation of Egyptian society from an Arab-Islamic orientation since the ninth century. But this orientation was religiously based and not often free of a political power conflict with other Arabs. The newly acquired and widely articulated Arabism of revolutionary Egypt since 1955 was not strictly a consequence of a revolution in the attitude or the cultural-political identity of Egyptians. It represents rather a response to power political realities. Without commenting on the Arab-Israeli issue, one may practically associate the intensity of Arabism as an adopted Egyptian policy in the last ten years with the new realities of inter-Arab politics in an area practically shorn of direct great power influence.

The revolution proclaimed by the Free Officers in 1952 for the benefit of the Egyptian people soon moved from its platform of Egyptian independence achieved in 1954–6 to that of independence from foreign control for all Arab states. By Arab independence, Egyptian leaders meant the severance of even those treaty relations between Arab states and foreign powers which were based on mutual sovereign status. To be sure, success in imposing total control at home through a state dirigistic system produced a basis for active policy abroad.

This new Arab orientation of Egypt was buttressed by encouragement from the East, whether this came from the Soviet bloc in Europe or from the new Afro-Asian bloc founded in Bandung in 1955. Egypt soon came to lead the Arab states in the ability to escape once and for all the political captivity of Western influence. The great power rivalry of the 1950s further aided this orientation and development of Egyptian Arab policy.

By May 1962, President ʿAbd al-Nāṣir was ready to inscribe the wider ramifications of his revolution in Egypt for the rest of the Arab world in his

Charter to the Egyptian nation. Radical revolution, based on scientific socialism and pragmatic endeavour for the creation of a powerful realm, was linked to the renascence of an essentially strong but for long submerged cultural entity: the Arab-Islamic dominion.

In this form, not only did the Egyptian revolutionary model carry great appeal for other Arabs, but in some cases led to the taking of active steps for its realization. Attempted coups in Jordan (1956–7), the bloody communal conflict in Lebanon (1958), the Iraqi rebellion of July 1958, and the civil war in the Yemen which began in September 1962 are all responsive echoes to the Egyptian cry of revolution.[1]

To a great extent the revolution in Egypt did not simply produce a confrontation with foreign powers in the area; such confrontation preceded the revolution. It accelerated an inter-Arab confrontation which some have described as a struggle between the new forces of radical revolution led by Egypt on one side and the old forces of conservatism and reaction on the other.

Egypt's attempts to extend her revolutionary leadership in Syria (1958–61), in Iraq in 1959 and again in 1964–5, in the Yemen since 1962 have so far proved expensive and not quite satisfactory. Failure in certain instances was due to lack of the necessary power and resources. But more significantly it was due to the late adoption by Egypt of an Arab policy which was, to a great extent, dictated by the requirements of national interest. Radical revolutionary nationalism, however, is integrative. Given the Free Officers coup in 1952 and the revolution it inaugurated, there was no reason why its nationalism —whether one calls it Egyptian or Arab—should not be just as integrative. In short, Egypt has, since 1955 at least, been anxious to fill a power vacuum in the Arab world.

The serious confrontations between leaders of the Egyptian revolution on the one hand, and the Baʿathists in Syria,[2] King Ḥusayn in Jordan, ʿAbd al-Karīm Qāsim as well as ʿAbd al-Salām ʿĀrif in Iraq, the *imām* in the Yemen, and King Fayṣal in Saudi Arabia proved to be serious obstacles in the realization of their aspirations in the Arab Middle East. Organic union schemes were abandoned in 1961–2 in favour of a policy of socialist revolution within each Arab state to precede closer unity. The latter, in turn, was diluted in the spring of 1963 by a new policy of co-operation between Egypt and the other Arab states in what was recognized as a politically pluralistic Arab world.[3]

[1] On the foreign and Arab policy of Egypt see my 'The foreign policy of Egypt', *Foreign policy in world politics*, ed. Roy C. Macridis, 2nd rev. edn. (Englewood Cliffs, N.J. 1962), pp. 335–50, and 'Islam and the foreign policy of Egypt', op. cit. See also Charles Cremeans, op. cit., and Leonard Binder, 'Nasserism: The protest movement in the Middle East', *The revolution in world politics*, Morton A. Kaplan, ed. (New York, 1962), pp. 152–74, and 'Egypt's positive neutrality', ibid., 175–91.

[2] See a most recent assessment by Patrick Seale, *The struggle for Syria* (London, 1965); see also Malcolm H. Kerr, *The Arab cold war*, Chatham House Essays (London, 1965).

[3] See Riyāḍ Ṭāhā, *Maḥāḍir muḥādathāt al-wiḥda* (Cairo, 1963), for the proceedings of the Summit Conferences in Mar.–Apr. 1963 between Iraq, Syria, and the U.A.R.

Direct Egyptian military involvement in the Yemen is also about to be abandoned. It appears that sovereignty and the interests of various ruling *élites* in the Arab states are too solid and tenacious realities to permit, for the moment at least, voluntary state liquidations in the name of wider Arab unions. The problem of leadership here too appears to be at the heart of the matter.

Similar difficulties and obstacles have faced the active African policy of the régime since 1958. An intensive Islamic and anti-imperialist (mostly anti-Western) Egyptian campaign in Africa from 1958 to 1962 sought to extend Egypt's revolutionary influence and leadership over the newly independent black African states. At the same time, it sought to undermine and, hoped to end the increasing relations between many of these new states and Israel. The latter entered the African scene as a supplier of technical assistance with fair success.

Active Egyptian interest in Africa was shown by members of the Muḥammad ʿAlī dynasty in the last century. Both Muḥammad ʿAlī the Great and his grandson, Khedive Ismāʿīl, conquered African territories south of the First Cataract. The Sudan, itself, has been a constant policy preoccupation of Egyptian rulers for an obvious and vital reason; namely, the control and distribution of Nile waters. With the revolution, however, and the active espousal of the anti-colonial cause of national independence in Africa and Asia, Egyptian leadership has sought to make Cairo the political, intellectual, and cultural capital of emancipated Africa. A series of African and Afro-Asian conferences to discuss all sorts of matters (non-alignment, youth, writers and intellectuals, neo-colonialism, the combating of the European Common Market) have been held in Cairo since the end of 1957. Also, since that time, Cairo Radio has been broadcasting a daily twelve- to fifteen-hour programme under the general title 'Cairo Speaks to Africa' in Swahili, Hausa, Somali, Amharic, Arabic, English, French, and Portuguese. The broadcasts presumably reach over 100 million Africans.

Financial and military assistance to rebel groups and organizations as in the Congo have been another facet of the régime's African policy. Support for the territorial claims of independent African states, such as Somalia, against lingering European enclaves and other older African states has been given liberally and readily. Denunciation of white supremacist policies as appear in South Africa and more recently in Southern Rhodesia has been vociferous.

Alongside these aspects of Egypt's African policy, an extensive Islamic campaign of religious education and cultural infiltration (executed primarily by the Islamic Congress founded in 1954, and the institutions of al-Azhar) has been especially marked in northern Nigeria and certain parts of Muslim west and east Africa. Cultural counsellors, who are Azhar-trained, have been attached to embassies and legations in Africa as missionaries. In 1964, a religious institute for the training of Muslim missionaries from Africa was opened in Cairo. Moreover, some seven to eight hundred Azhar teachers have been sent to African countries.

A combined political-religious campaign has sought since 1958 to extend Egyptian influence in Africa by identifying the leaders of the Egyptian revolution as the international spokesman for independent Africa. The régime has been anxious to elevate Egypt, astride the Arab Middle East and the African continent, to the position of the leader of an Africa in the process of political emancipation. It has also suggested that Egypt would be the country best qualified to act as its liaison with the Mediterranean and European world.

The difficulties Egypt faced with her policy of Arab unity and of a socialist revolution for all Arabs since that time, as well as the independent tendencies of new African leaders, have proved serious obstacles to the success of her African policy. More specifically, Negro Africans do not feel close to Muslim Arabs. The memory of Arab slave-traders in their continent is only too fresh in their minds. What has been even more shattering has been the harbouring and support by Egypt of rebel groups living in exile in Cairo, such as those grouped in the African Association, who work to subvert existing African régimes. Africans suspect that Egypt appears over-anxious in its desire for domination, and are naturally reluctant, now that they have escaped European colonial rule, to accept another hegemony. Even though Muslim black Africans may readily accept instruction and cultural training in Arabic—the sacred language of their faith—they have so far resisted the advances of political Arabism as professed by Cairo.

Considering the limited financial and technical resources Egypt can offer Africans, a number of African states have resisted Egyptian pressure upon them to sever their relations with Israel. By 1963, at the Addis Ababa Conference, President ʿAbd al-Nāṣir had recognized the limited impact that his African policy was having upon leaders of independent African states. His campaign of African unity was consequently diluted with the same alacrity which accompanied Egypt's reconsideration of Arab unity after the Arab Summit Conference in March–April 1963.

The conflict of economic and political interests between black Africa and the Arab Middle East, particularly Arab North Africa (Egypt, Libya, and the Maghrib) cannot be underestimated. An overpopulated Egypt, anxious to industrialize rapidly, would naturally seek to establish markets for its products in Africa through political influence which could succeed in keeping others out.[1]

For the Egyptian perhaps the sharpest consequence of the July 1952 revolution has been his projection very quickly into the wider Arab world and certain parts of Africa in the service of his state. His age-old, proverbial isolation has been at least outwardly shattered for some time in search of

[1] See a recent assessment by Jean-Claude Froelich, 'L'Égypte et les peuples noirs', *Orient*, vol. ix. 32–33 (1964–5), pp. 13–28.

national prestige and power. Yet, historians must note that the rulers of Egypt—whoever they are—respect the precedent set by the traditional policy of their predecessors of avoiding isolation, especially from the Arab East, at all costs.

Concluding remarks

Despite the basically Western continuing influence of technology, industry, and science, the 'Egyptianity' of the U.A.R. in terms of a rural community whose life is still greatly affected by the flow of the Nile and threatened by demographic profusion has hardly been shaken. The massive public works project begun in 1960 with Soviet aid to construct a dam at Aswān, desert reclamation projects, and active campaigns to introduce effective birth control are only some of the measures which currently occupy the authorities in Egypt in dealing with this permanent feature of their country. Attempts to erode this 'Egyptianity' began with Bonaparte; Muḥammad 'Alī and his successors tried to undermine it further. The first nationalists of this century thought they could modernize their political life by the adoption of European liberal ideas and institutions. Having had to do this in collaboration with a foreign power, and in a relationship of tutelage to it, these liberal nationalists were swept away as soon as this collaboration ended. Now, the radical revolution continues to adopt, emulate, and seek ways and means devised mostly by Europe for the attainment of modernity and power; but it insists upon the rejection of Europe's intellectual, cultural, and political legacy. Instead, the momentum of the attempted radical revolutionary change derives from a new combination: the political revival of the Islamic-Arab legacy and culture on the one hand, and a state socialism devised and applied in an autocratic political scheme on the other. The modernizing leader, embodies the force and spirit of the former, and plans the latter. In doing so, he remains the sole nexus of political loyalty and allegiance, aided both by modern techniques of control available to him for the concentration of power, and by the more traditional meaning of Islam with its implications for personalized rule.

There is no doubt that the modernizing leader and his new *élite* have succeeded in projecting an independent Egypt into the prominence of Arab and international affairs. They have successfully and without bloodshed dismantled an old privileged class that dragged its feet over social and economic reform. Significantly though, and in a characteristically Egyptian way, they have replaced it with a new establishment of soldiers, technocrats, and bureaucrats constituting a new and relatively prosperous group which make up the state apparatus. They may be the new political cadre of the Egyptian revolution. They are recruited mainly from a variety of social strata and are no longer confined to the old landed and administrative aristocracy. Among them are some 1,500 to 2,000 ex-military officers, lawyers, journalists, and technical experts (professors, engineers, economists, and administrators).

To this extent revolution has widened the participation of certain categories of Egyptians in the conduct of the affairs of the state. Nonetheless they function as part of the state apparatus, the revolutionary decisions of which continue to be largely the responsibility of the modernizing leader, assisted by aides who are personally loyal to him.

The revolutionary desire of Egyptians, as articulated by their modernizing leader and his *élite*, to attain respectable membership in the industrial civilization must be predicated upon political activism. It is this activism on a wider public scale that so far has eluded the leaders of the revolution and now constitutes a fundamental and urgent problem. Only institutionalized political activity can adequately provide for permanent and effective change. The leader with the immense concentration of power in his hands, and its use for the achievement of both social-economic and political aims, has shown the way. His invitation to a public that has traditionally been politically apathetic to become actively engaged in the revolution has so far been qualified by his reluctance to relinquish any real power from the centre in favour of other levels in society. He has repeatedly invited criticism, disagreement, and debate. But his invitations have always been prefaced with the warning that the system will not countenance rivals. The political activism of the dynamic modernizing leader is thus only faintly buttressed by an accompanying public political activity.

Perhaps accelerating the rate of economic growth and attaining a more equitable social system in Egypt do not require organized popular support: the state apparatus alone may be capable of bringing it about. The question however remains: how effective and lasting a change would this constitute without the active commitment of at least the majority of the population to the state scheme? The fact that the world has come to refer to Nasserism as a political phenomenon of the 1950s and 1960s attests to the central importance of the modernizing leader, and to the relative success of his political activism. His insistence upon a radical programme of social and economic reform and his uncompromising nationalism are indications of ʿAbd al-Nāṣir's achievement beyond the average Asian, African, or Latin American personal ruler, or ephemeral dictator.

Yet even Nasserism, committed as its leader has consistently been to the realization of a strong and prosperous socialist Egypt, and to an Arab world free of all outside influence and united under Egyptian leadership, has not so far been able to escape an autocratic political form in which to attain its revolutionary aims. The revolution of 1952 seems unable to escape this rather Egyptian legacy. Until it can successfully do so, one is left with historical contrasts and comparisons. An ambitious autocrat, Muḥammad ʿAlī the Great, succeeded, in the true Islamic-Ottoman style of the nineteenth century, in transforming Egypt into a modern state. In doing so, he permitted some of his subjects to acquaint themselves with the civilization and culture of Europe. The intellectual, cultural, and political descendants of those subjects later overthrew Muḥammad ʿAlī's dynasty. Today, an autocrat of the technological age—some have called him a Muḥammad ʿAlī of the twentieth century—nurtures wider revolutionary ambitions for his country, with power at his disposal far greater than any of his predecessors ever dreamt of possessing. He is moreover, using the immense power concentrated in his hands for the realization of revolutionary goals which will produce a modern society and polity in Egypt. What is even more significant is that Egyptians have responded with both loyalty and acquiescence, and deferred to this modernizing leader. They consider him both an efficient administrator, and a protector who has provided them so far with a way of overcoming their anxieties.[1] This essentially may be the major consequence of the revolution of 1952. What it portends for the long-range evolution of Egyptian society cannot be speculated upon at this early date.[2]

[1] It should be noted that in his speeches, President ʿAbd al-Nāṣir often encourages and sustains this public image of himself as a protector. For example, in his address to the opening of the second session of the National Assembly in Cairo on 12 Nov. 1964, he made it clear that Egypt considered the continued presence of British bases in Cyprus, south Arabia, and Libya a threat to Egyptian security and to the Arab nationalist cause. In his annual victory speech at Port Said on 23 Dec. 1964, he reiterated his leadership of the Arab nationalist struggle against imperialism.

[2] See my essay, 'Egypt 1966: the assessment of a revolution', *The World Today*, (June, 1966), pp. 241–252.

Index

PRINTED IN GREAT BRITAIN
AT THE UNIVERSITY PRESS, OXFORD
BY VIVIAN RIDLER
PRINTER TO THE UNIVERSITY